# M&E PROFESSIONAL STUDIES



Written by a team of practising lecturers and prepared und[illegible] a leading partnership of London accountancy tutors, the *M*[illegible] has been specially designed to meet the course needs [illegible] virtually all the examined subjects at appropriate professional, degree and diploma levels. The titles cover many of the subjects offered by the ACCA, ICA, ICMA, AIA, AAT, SCCA, ACEA, LCCI, RSA and numerous other bodies.

With carefully structured and thoroughly up-to-date contents, most titles include end-of-chapter progress tests based on the text, a large number of practice examination questions and suggested answers, a glossary of the more difficult key terms, and a very comprehensive index. An extensive programme of classroom testing, student surveys and independent assessment has been completed in relation to this series prior to publication.

With twenty substantial texts in the series, *M&E Professional Studies* constitutes a major contribution to business education, and will enable students throughout the English-speaking world gain the syllabus-related depth of knowledge and practice necessary to ensure a successful examination result.

## GENERAL EDITORS

### Emile Woolf

Emile Woolf first qualified in 1961 and joined the London Office of Deloitte Haskins & Sells. Since 1964 he has played a major part in pioneering accountancy education, first at Foulks Lynch and the London School of Accountancy, and then as founder and Chairman of the Emile Woolf Colleges in London and overseas. In 1984 he became a partner in Kingston Smith & Co. with special responsibility for technical standards and training. He is an established author, and a regular contributor to numerous professional and student journals and magazines in the UK and overseas. In 1980 he received the Distinguished Services Award for Authorship at Hartford University, Connecticut, USA. Recently he was commissioned by the ACCA to produce a series of audio cassettes and workbooks for students throughout the world. Between 1973 and 1979 he was also an Examiner for the ACCA in Advanced Auditing and Investigations. Emile Woolf lectures regularly on accountancy, financial and economic matters in Ireland, the UK, USA, Trinidad, Jamaica, Singapore, Hong Kong, Malaysia, Nigeria, Ghana and elsewhere. He also conducts seminars on financial management topics for industrial and commercial clients as well as for professional accountancy firms.

### Suresh Tanna

Suresh Tanna graduated in 1971 in chemical engineering from Edinburgh University. Following a career in business management he qualified as a chartered accountant in 1978. In 1981 he joined Karam Singh in setting up the City Accountancy Centre, which merged with the Emile Woolf Schools in March 1983, and is now Director of Studies on ACCA courses, and Financial Director of the enlarged FACT Group. He specialises in accounting, advanced accounting practice and advanced financial accounting.

### Karam Singh

After a period of project planning with Burmah Oil as a graduate chemical engineer, Karam Singh obtained his MBA from the Liverpool Business School whilst also engaged in part-time consultancy work for clothing manufacturers and retailers and research at a P & O subsidiary. In 1971 he joined the London accountancy firm of Harmood Banner and Company which later merged with Deloittes. He qualified as a chartered accountant in 1974, and lectured for several years at the London School of Accountancy and the North East London Polytechnic. In 1981 he joined Suresh Tanna in the formation of the City Accountancy Centre, where he began to develop study material geared for in-school and home studies students. At present he is Principal Lecturer for the FACT schools for Level 2 ACCA courses, specialising in quantitative analysis. He has contributed numerous articles to the various professional and students' journals.

### Contributing authors

The titles in this series have been prepared under the General Editorship of Emile Woolf, Suresh Tanna and Karam Singh in conjunction with the staff and tutors of the FACT Organisation, 23 Hand Court, High Holborn, London WC1V 6JF. All contributors and authors are practising lecturers with many years' experience of teaching accountancy at all levels.

M&E PROFESSIONAL STUDIES

# ADVANCED ACCOUNTING PRACTICE

General Editors

Emile Woolf FCA FCCA FBIM
Suresh Tanna BSc(Hons) FCA
Karam Singh BTech MBA FCA

MACDONALD & EVANS

*M&E Professional Studies series*

Advanced Accounting Practice
Advanced Auditing and Investigations
Advanced Financial Accounting
Advanced Taxation
Auditing
Company Law
Costing
Economics
Executorship and Trust Law and Accounts
Financial Management
Foundation Accounting
Law
Management Accounting
Managerial Economics
Numerical Analysis and Data Processing
Organisation and Management
Quantitative Analysis
The Regulatory Framework of Accounting
Systems Analysis and Design
Taxation

Macdonald & Evans Ltd.
Estover, Plymouth PL6 7PZ

First published 1985



British Library Cataloguing in Publication Data

Advanced accounting practice.—(M & E
professional studies, ISSN 0266–8475)
1. Accounting—Great Britain
657'.48'0941 HF5635

ISBN 0–7121–0497–6



Phototypeset by Wyvern Typesetting Limited, Bristol
Printed in Great Britain by
Redwood Burn Ltd, Trowbridge

# Preface

This book has been particularly designed for use in studying for the Chartered Association of Certified Accountants' Level 2 paper Advanced Accounting Practice. It will also be of use in studies for many of the accounting based subjects of the other professional bodies. Advanced Accounting Practice is a double paper with a very wide-ranging syllabus, and so the subject requires about twice the amount of study-time given to other Level 2 papers. This book assumes that you have already mastered the basics of accounting in Level 1 studies.

The first chapter is concerned with the presentation of published accounts for limited companies. This is an essential area to master but the student is advised not to underestimate the time needed to learn the disclosure requirements of the Companies Acts 1948 to 1981.

Chapter 2 deals with Statements of Standard Accounting Practice (SSAPs). This is a vital area of the syllabus and overlaps with the auditing paper and also with material in the Regulatory Framework of Accounting course leading to the ACCA qualification. Total familiarity with the SSAPs is required for the AAP examination because without it you will not be able to cope with the numerous computational and narrative questions testing the standards which always occur.

The preparation of statements of source and application of funds often presents difficulties. The methodological approach to this subject is explained in Chapter 3.

Chapter 4 on shares and debentures deals with the issue and forfeiture of shares and the redemption of debentures. The important matters of redemption of shares and a company's power to purchase its own shares are also covered in Chapter 1 as part of the discussion of the Companies Acts.

Chapter 5 on acquisitions and mergers plus Chapter 6 on capital reductions and reconstructions complete the section of the syllabus on the accounts of limited companies. These are areas which often appear in the ACCA Level 2 paper and many other AAP related subjects examined by other professional bodies.

The next section of the syllabus covers the accounts of groups of companies. Chapter 7 provides all the information you should need to answer questions on this area.

Students' attention is drawn to the generous number of questions provided on this topic at the end of the book.

The chapter on partnership accounting, Chapter 8, is designed to help you consolidate your knowledge of this subject gained at Level 1. At Level 2 it is more likely, when it comes to the examination, that this topic will be combined with the preparation of accounts from incomplete records (Chapter 9) or one of the miscellaneous accounts dealt with in Chapter 10. In addition to incomplete records, Chapter 9 includes detailed discussion of the preparation of the accounts of clubs and societies. This constitutes the necessary coverage of accounts for non-trading undertakings.

The accounting practice for specialised transactions is given a 15 per cent weighting in the ACCA 2.9 syllabus and has a similar importance in other accounting courses. This subject is covered in Chapter 10. It is likely that some area of this will be tested in every examination. Branch accounts and hire purchase accounts are probably the two most important areas, but to be safe the student is recommended not to ignore any part of the syllabus.

Interpretation of accounts, dealt with in Chapter 11, has a 20 per cent weighting in the ACCA syllabus and is yet another vital area of study. The latest version of the ACCA syllabus confirms that questions in this area may require the preparation of formal reports, and to cover this the chapter concludes with some hints on this subject.

Accounting for inflation, Chapter 12, is a subject around which controversy rages. The Accounting Standards Committee confirmed in their declaration on the subject (Statement of Intent), published in March 1984, that they thought the SSAP 16 approach had resulted in the production of useful information at relatively little cost. The coverage for the purposes of the AAP therefore continues to be based on SSAP 16. The paper on the Regulatory Framework of Accounting and, of course, the ACCA Level 3 Advanced Financial Accounting paper are more likely to call for the discussion of alternatives.

Each chapter of this book concludes with various progress questions to test your comprehension of the matter you will cover at each stage. At the end of the book in a set of appendices there are a sequence of examination-style questions and answers. It is absolutely essential that you make use of these as a central part of your revision.

*Note*

During the course of preparation of this book the consolidating legislation of the Companies Acts 1948–1983 came into force. The official Destination Table relating the components of the old legislation to the new Companies Act 1985, the Company Securities (Insider Dealing) Act 1985, the Business Names Act 1985 and the Companies Consolidation (Consequential Provisions) Act 1985 is reproduced in this text for the student's information. Permission to use this material is gratefully acknowledged from HMSO.

# Contents

# List of Illustrations

# List of Tables

# Table of Statutes

# Table of Statements of Standard Accounting Practice and Exposure Drafts

## Statements of Standard Accounting Practice

## Exposure Drafts



## IASC Exposure Drafts

# Table of Destinations

# Consolidation of the Companies Acts 1948–1983

The Companies Acts 1948–1983 were consolidated into four separate Acts namely—

The Companies Act 1985 (c. 6),
The Company Securities (Insider Dealing) Act 1985 (c. 8),
The Business Names Act 1985 (c. 7), and
The Companies Consolidation (Consequential Provisions) Act 1985 (c. 9).

The Table of Destinations relates the components of the Acts consolidated to the Acts, Parts of Acts, sections and Schedules which make up the entirety of the consolidation.

The following abbreviations are used in the Table—

| | |
|---|---|
| "1948" | = Companies Act 1948 (c. 38). |
| "1967" | = Companies Act 1967 (c. 81). |
| "1972 Sc." | = Companies (Floating Charges and Receivers) (Scotland) Act 1972 (c. 67). |
| "ECA 1972" | = European Communities Act 1972 (c. 68). |
| "SECOBA" | = Stock Exchange (Completion of Bargains) Act 1976 (c. 47). |
| "INS 1976" | = Insolvency Act 1976 (c. 60). |
| "1976" | = Companies Act 1976 (c. 69). |
| "1980" | = Companies Act 1980 (c. 22). |
| "1981" | = Companies Act 1981 (c. 62). |
| "STA 1982" | = Stock Transfer Act 1982 (c. 41). |
| "1983 (BI)" | = Companies (Beneficial Interests) Act 1983 (c. 50). |
| "OinC-1" | = Companies Acts (Pre-Consolidation Amendments) Order 1984 (S.I. 1984/134). |
| "OinC-2" | = Companies Acts (Pre-Consolidation Amendments) (No. 2) Order 1984 (S.I. 1984/1169). |

In the third column of the Table, specifying the provision of the consolidation in which a particular provision of the former Acts is to be found, each figure relates to a section or Schedule of the Companies Act 1985, unless otherwise stated. The letters ID indicate a section of the Company Securities (Insider Dealing) Act 1985; BN indicates a section of the Business Names Act 1985; and CP indicates a section of the Companies Consolidation (Consequential Provisions) Act 1985.

In the fourth column of the Table, settling out the statutory history of each section or Schedule of the Acts consolidated, the following additional abbreiviations are used—

"AM" indicates an amendment of the original provision by or under a subsequent Act;

"R" indicates repeal by a subsequent Act;

"PR" indicates the partial repeal of a section, subsection or Schedule;

"FA" indicates the Finance Act of a given year.

| Section of Act. | Subject matter. | Provision in consolidation. | Remarks. |
|---|---|---|---|
| | COMPANIES ACT 1948 (c. 38) | | |
| 1 | Mode of forming incorporated company. | 1 | Subs. (1) PR 1980, AM 1980 s. 2 (1), Sch. 3 para. 2. |
| 2 | Requirements as to memorandum. | 2, 25 | Subs. (1) AM 1980 Sch. 3 para. 3. See 1976 s. 30 as to Wales. Subs. (4) AM OinC-1 No. 1. |
| 3 | Stamp and signature. | 2 | PR FA 1970. |
| 4 | Restrictions on alteration of memorandum. | 2 | AM 1981 Sch. 3 para. 2. |
| 5 | Alteration of company's objects. | 4, 5, 6 | Subs. (4A), (4B), (4C) added, 1980 Sch. 3 para. 4. AM 1976 Sch. 1. Subs. (4B), (4C) AM 1981 Sch. 3 para. 2. Subs. (6) R 1981. Subs. (10) spent. |
| 6 | Articles of association. | 7 | |
| 7 | Regulations for unlimited company. | 7 | Subs. (1) AM OinC-1 No. 2. Subs. (3) AM 1976 Sch. 1. |
| 8 | Table A. | 8(1), (2) | |
| 9 | Printing, stamp and signature of articles. | 7(3) | PR FA 1970. |
| 10 | Alteration of articles. | 9 | PR 1980. AM 1981 Sch. 3 para 2. |
| 11 | Statutory forms of memorandum and articles. | 3, 8 | |
| 12 | Registration of memorandum and articles. | 10, 12 | AM 1976 Sch. 2. |
| 13 | Effect of registration. | 13 | Subs. (1) AM 1976 s. 38 (2), Sch. 2. Subs. (2) PR 1980. |
| 14 | Power of company to hold land. | — | R Charities Act 1960 (c. 58). |
| 15 | Conclusiveness of certificate of incorporation. | — | R 1980. |
| 16 | Registration of unlimited company as limited. | — | Inoperative from 27.10.67, being replaced by 1967 s. 44. See 1967 s. 45. |
| 17 | Companies not to be registered with undesirable name. | — | R 1981. |
| 18 | Change of name. | — | R 1981. |
| 19 | Power to dispense with "limited". | — | R 1981. |

| Section of Act. | Subject matter. | Provision in consolidation. | Remarks. |
|---|---|---|---|
| | COMPANIES ACT 1948 (c. 38) (cont.) | | |
| 20 | Effect of memorandum and articles. | 14 | |
| 21 | Memorandum and articles of company limited by guarantee. | 15, CP 10 | Subs. (2) applied, 1980 s. 1(3). |
| 22 | Alteration affecting liability of members. | 16 | |
| 23 | Power to alter conditions of memorandum which could have been in articles. | 17 | Subs. (1), (3) AM 1980 Sch. 3 para 6. |
| 24 | Copies of memorandum and articles to be given to members. | 19 | |
| 25 | Issued copy of memorandum to embody alterations. | 20 | |
| 26 | Definition of "member". | 22 | |
| 27 | Membership of holding company. | 23 | Modified, 1983 (BI). |
| 28 | Meaning of "private company". | — | R 1980. |
| 29 | Consequences of failure to comply with conditions for being private company. | — | R 1980. |
| 30 | Statement in lieu of prospectus, on company ceasing to be private. | — | R 1980. |
| 31 | At least 2 members required for company to carry on business. | 24 | Section substituted, 1980 Sch. 3 para. 7. |
| 32 | Form of contracts. | 36 | |
| 33 | Bills of exchange and promissory notes. | 37 | |
| 34 | Execution of deeds abroad. | 38 | |
| 35 | Official seal for use abroad. | 39 | |
| 36 | Authentication of documents. | 41 | |
| 37 | Dating of prospectus. | 62 | |
| 38 | Matters to be stated, and reports to be set out, in prospectus. | 56, 57, 66 | AM 1976 Sch. 2. Subs. (1), (3) PR S.I. 1984/716. |
| 39 | Exclusion of s.38 in certain cases. | — | R S.I. 1984/716. |
| 40 | Expert's consent to issue of prospectus with report by him. | 61 | |
| 41 | Registration of prospectus. | 64, 65 | Subs. (1) (b) PR S.I. 1984/716. |
| 42 | Restriction on alteration of prospectus. | — | R 1980. |
| 43 | Civil liability for mis-statement in prospectus. | 67, 68, 69 | |
| 44 | Criminal liability for mis-statement. | 70 | |
| 45 | Document containing offer of shares or debentures deemed a prospectus. | 58, 64 | |
| 46 | Interpretation of provisions relating to prospectus. | 71 | |
| 47 | No allotment unless minimum subscription received. | 83 | Subs. (3) R 1980. Subs. (6) PR 1980. Subs. (4), (5) applied, 1980 s. 16 (2). |
| 48 | In certain cases, no allotment without statement in lieu of prospectus. | — | R 1980. |
| 49 | Effect of irregular allotment. | 85 | Subs. (1), (2) AM 1980 Sch. 3 para. 8. |
| 50 | Application for, and allotment of, shares and debentures. | 82, 86 | Subs. (7) R S.I. 1984/716. |
| 51 | Allotment of shares etc. to be dealt with on stock exchange. | 86, 87 | AM 1976 Sch. 2 AM OinC-I No.3 |
| 52 | Return as to allotments. | 88 | AM 1976 Sch.1, 2 AM OinC-I No.4 |
| 53 | Commissions and discounts. | 97, 98 | Subs. (1) AM 1980 Sch. 3 para. 9. Subs. (6) R 1967. |
| 54 | No financial assistance by company for purchase of own shares. | — | R 1981. |
| 55 | Construction of references to offering shares to the public. | 59, 60 | Subs. (1) PR 1980. Subs. (3), (4) added 1980 Sch. 3 para. 11. |
| 56 | Application of share premiums. | 130 | Subs. (2) AM 1980 Sch. 3 para. 12. Subs. (2) PR 1981. |

COMPANIES ACT 1948 (c. 38) (cont.)

| Section of Act. | Subject matter. | Provision in consolidation. | Remarks. |
|---|---|---|---|
| 57 | Power to issue shares at a discount. | — | R 1980. |
| 58 | Power to issue redeemable preference shares. | — | R 1981. |
| 59 | Power to arrange for different amounts to be paid on shares. | 119 | |
| 60 | Reserve liability of limited company. | 120 | |
| 61 | Power of limited company to alter share capital. | 121 | |
| 62 | Notice to registrar of change in capital structure. | 122 | Subs. (1) AM 1976 Sch. 1 PR 1981. |
| 63 | Notice of increase of share capital. | 123 | Modified, 1967 s. 51 (1). |
| 64 | Unlimited company reserve share capital on registration. | 124 | AM 1967 s. 44 (6). See also 1980 s. 7 (4). |
| 65 | Power of company to pay interest out of capital. | — | R 1980. |
| 66 | Special resolution for reduction of share capital. | 135 | |
| 67 | Application to court for confirmation of share capital reduction. | 136 | |
| 68 | Court order confirming reduction. | 137 | |
| 69 | Registration of order and minute of confirmation. | 138 | Subs. (4) AM 1976 s. 38 (2), Sch. 2. |
| 70 | Liability of members after reduction of capital. | 140 | |
| 71 | Penalty for concealing creditor, etc. | 141 | |
| 72 | Rights of holders of special classes of shares. | 127 | |
| 73 | Nature of shares. | 182 (1) | |
| 74 | Numbering of shares. | 182 (2) | |

COMPANIES ACT 1948 (c. 38) (cont.)

| Section of Act. | Subject matter. | Provision in consolidation. | Remarks. |
|---|---|---|---|
| 75 | Production of instrument of transfer on registration. | 183 (1), (2) | AM STA 1982 Sch. 2. |
| 76 | Transfer by personal representative. | 183 (3) | |
| 77 | Registration of transfer at request of transferor. | 183 (4) | |
| 78 | Notice of refusal to register transfer. | 183 (5), (6) | |
| 79 | Certification of transfers. | 184 | |
| 80 | Duties of company with respect to share certificates. | 185 | AM SECOBA s. 1. AM STA 1982 Sch. 2. |
| 81 | Certificate to be evidence of title. | 186 | AM SECOBA s. 2 (3). |
| 82 | Evidence of grant of probate. | 187 | |
| 83 | Issue and effect of share warrant to bearer. | 188 | |
| 84 | Penalty for personation of shareholder. | — | R Theft Act 1968. |
| 85 | Offences in connection with share warrants (Scotland). | 189 | |
| 86 | Register of debenture holders. | 190 | AM 1976 Sch. 1. |
| 87 | Rights of inspection. | 191 | Subs. (2), (3) AM 1967 s. 52(1). |
| 88 | Liability of trustee. | 192 | |
| 89 | Perpetual debentures. | 193 | |
| 90 | Power to re-issue redeemed debentures. | 194 | |
| 91 | Saving for rights of certain mortgagees. | CP 13 | |
| 92 | Specific performance of contract to subscribe for debentures. | 195 | |
| 93 | Validity of debentures to bearer. | 197 | |

| Section of Act. | Subject matter. | Provision in consolidation. | Remarks. |
|---|---|---|---|
| | COMPANIES ACT 1948 (c. 38) (cont.) | | |
| 94 | Payment of debts out of assets subject to floating charge. | 196 | |
| 95 | Registration of charges created by companies. | 395, 396, 397, 398 | Subs. (2) AM S.I. 1972/1268. Subs. (8) AM 1976 Sch. 1. Subs. (8) proviso substituted, 1980 Sch 3 para. 5. |
| 96 | Duty of registration. | 399 | |
| 97 | Charge on property acquired. | 400 | |
| 98 | Register of charges to be kept by registrar of companies. | 401 | Subs. (2) AM 1976 Sch. 2. Subs. (1), (3), (4) PR 1976. |
| 99 | Endorsement of certificate of registration of debentures. | 402 | |
| 100 | Entries of satisfaction and release from charge. | 403 | AM 1976 Sch. 1. |
| 101 | Rectification of register of charges. | 404 | |
| 102 | Registration of enforcement of security. | 405 | Subs. (1), (4) PR 1976. Subs. (3A) added, 1976 Sch. 1. |
| 103 | Company to keep copies of instruments creating charges. | 406 | |
| 104 | Company register of charges. | 407 | |
| 105 | Right to inspect copies of charging instruments. | 408 | |
| 106 | Application of Part III. | 409 | AM 1981 Sch. 3 para 3. AM OinC-1 No. 5. |
| 106A | Registration of charges (Scotland). | 410, 411, 412, 413, 414 | Sections 106A-106K inserted as Part IIIA by 1972 Sc. s. 6. In s. 106A, subs. (2) AM SI 1972/1268; subs. (7) AM 1976 Sch. 1, 1980 Sch. 3 para. 15. |
| 106B | Duty of company to register charges. | 415 | |
| 106C | Charges on property acquired. | 416 | |
| 106D | Register to be kept by registrar of companies. | 417 | Subs (1), (2) PR 1976. |
| | COMPANIES ACT 1948 (c. 38) (cont.) | | |
| 106E | Certificate of registration to be issued. | 418 | AM 1976 Sch.2. |
| 106F | Entries of satisfaction and release. | 419 | Subs. (1) AM 1976 Sch 1. |
| 106G | Rectification of register. | 420 | |
| 106H | Companies to keep copies of instruments creating charges. | 421 | |
| 106I | Company register of charges. | 422 | |
| 106J | Right to inspect charging instruments and company register. | 423 | |
| 106K | Application of Part IIIA. | 424 | AM OinC-1 No. 6. |
| 107 | Registered office. | — | R 1976. |
| 108 | Publication of company name. | 348, 349, 350 | Modified for "old public companies" by 1980 s.76(3). |
| 109 | Restriction on commencement of business. | — | R 1980. |
| 110 | Register of members. | 191(7), 352, 353 | Subs. (1) AM 1981 s. 101(1). Subs. (3) AM 1976 Sch. 1. Subs (5), (6) added, 1981 s. 101(2). |
| 111 | Index of names. | 354 | |
| 112 | Entries in register in relation to share warrants. | 355 | |
| 113 | Inspection of register and index. | 356 | AM 1967 s. 52 (2). |
| 114 | Agent's failure to comply with requirements as to register. | 357 | |
| 115 | Power to close register. | 358 | |
| 116 | Power of court to rectify register. | 359 | |
| 117 | Trusts not to be entered on register. | 360 | |

| Section of Act. | Subject matter. | Provision in consolidation. | Remarks. |
|---|---|---|---|
| | COMPANIES ACT 1948 (c. 38) (cont.) | | |
| 118 | Register to be evidence. | 361 | |
| 119 | Power for company to keep dominion register. | 362; Sch. 14 Pt. I, Pt. II para. 1 | AM 1976 Sch. 1. |
| 120 | Regulations as to dominion register. | Sch. 14 Pt. II, paras. 2–7 | |
| 121 | Stamp duty in case of shares registered in dominion register. | Sch. 14 Pt. II, para. 8 | |
| 122 | Power to extend dominion register provisions to other countries. | 362(4), (5) | |
| 123 | Branch registers of oversea companies in United Kingdom. | Sch. 14 Pt. III | |
| 124 | Annual return of company with share capital. | 363 | Subs. (1) PR 1967, AM OinC–1 No. 7. Subs. (3) substituted, 1981 Sch. 3 para. 4. |
| 125 | Annual return of company without share capital. | 364 | Subs. (1) AM 1976 Sch. 1. Subs. (2) AM OinC-1 Nos. 8, 9. Subs. (3) substituted, 1981 Sch. 3 para. 4. |
| 126 | Time for completion of annual return. | 365 | Subs. (2) AM OinC-1 No. 10. |
| 127 | Documents to be annexed to annual return. | — | R 1976. |
| 128 | Annual return of private company. | — | R 1980. |
| 129 | Exemptions from s. 127. | — | R 1967. |
| 130 | Statutory meeting and statutory report. | — | R 1980. |
| 131 | Annual general meeting. | 366, 367 | |
| 132 | Convening of annual meeting on requisition. | 368 | |
| 133 | Length of notice for calling meetings. | 369 | |
| 134 | General provisions as to meetings and votes. | 370 | AM 1980 Sch. 3 para. 16. |
| 135 | Power of court to order meeting. | 371 | |
| 136 | Proxies. | 372 | |

| Section of Act. | Subject matter. | Provision in consolidation. | Remarks. |
|---|---|---|---|
| | COMPANIES ACT 1948 (c. 38) (cont.) | | |
| 137 | Right to demand a poll. | 373 | |
| 138 | Voting on a poll. | 374 | |
| 139 | Representation of corporations at company meetings. | 375 | |
| 140 | Circulation of members' resolutions. | 376, 377 | |
| 141 | Extraordinary and special resolutions. | 378 | |
| 142 | Resolutions requiring special notice. | 379 | |
| 143 | Registration of certain resolutions and agreements. | 380, 572 | Modified, 1967 s. 51(2). Applied, 1981 s. 49 (10). Subs. (4) AM 1980 Sch. 3 para. 17; AM OinC-1 No. 11. |
| 144 | Resolutions passed at adjourned meeting. | 381 | |
| 145 | Minutes of meetings. | 382 | Modified, 1980 s. 63(3). |
| 146 | Inspection of minute books. | 383 | |
| 147 | Keeping of books of account. | — | R 1976. |
| 148 | Profit and loss account and balance sheet. | — | R 1976. |
| 149 | Content and form of company accounts. | 227, 228, 245, 742 | Section inserted, 1981 s. 1 (1). |
| 149A | Content and form of company accounts. | 258, 742 | Originally numbered 149, re-numbered by 1981 s. 1 (1). AM 1976 Sch. 2, 1980 Sch. 3 paras. 18, 19. Modified, 1981 Sch. 2 para. 4 (1) |
| 150 | Group accounts of holding company. | 229, 239, 245, 736 | Subs. (1) substituted, 1976 s. 8 (1). Subs. (3) AM 1980 Sch. 3 para. 20, 1981 Sch. 3 para. 5 |
| 151 | Form of group accounts. | 229 | Subs. (1) AM 1976 Sch. 2. |
| 152 | Content of group accounts. | 230 | Section inserted, 1981 s. 2. AM OinC-1 No. 12. |

COMPANIES ACT 1948 (c. 38) (cont.)

| Section of Act. | Subject matter. | Provision in consolidation. | Remarks. |
|---|---|---|---|
| 152A | Content of group accounts. | 259 | Originally numbered 152, re-numbered by 1981 s. 2. Subs. (1) AM 1976 Sch. 2. Subs. (2) AM OinC-2 No. 1 Subs. (3) AM 1981 Sch. 2 para 4. |
| 153 | Financial year of holding company and subsidiary. | 227 | Subs (2) R 1976. |
| 154 | Meaning of "holding company" and "subsidiary". | 736, 744 | |
| 155 | Signing of balance sheet. | 238 (1), (2) | Subs (1), (3) AM 1976 Sch. 2. Subs (2) R Banking Act 1979 (c. 37) |
| 156 | Accounts and auditors' report to be annexed to balance sheet. | 238 (3), (4) | Subs. (1) AM 1976 Sch. 2. Subs. (3) R 1981. |
| 157 | Directors' report. | 235, 261 (2) | Subs. (1) AM 1976 Sch. 2, 198 s. 13(1). Subs.(1) PR 1981, AM 1981 Sch. 3 para. 6. Subs.(2), (3) R 1967. |
| 158 | Right to receive copy of accounts. | 240, 246 | AM 1967 s 24, 1976 Sch. 2. |
| 159 | Appointment and remuneration of auditors. | — | R 1976. |
| 160 | Resolution for appointment of auditors; their removal. | — | R 1976. |
| 161 | Qualification for appointment as auditor. | 389 | PR 1967, 1976. Replaced by 976 s. 13. |
| 162 | Auditors' right of access to company's books. | — | R 1967. |
| 163 | Documents to be attached to balance sheet. | 261 (3) | Proviso R 1981 (except for "special category companies"). |
| 164 | Investigation of company's affairs on application of members. | 431 | AM 1981 s. 86 (1), (2). |
| 165 | Investigation in other cases. | 432 | PR 1981 s. 86 (3). AM 1980 Sch. 3 para. 21. |
| 166 | Power of inspectors to investigate affairs of other bodies. | 433 | |

COMPANIES ACT 1948 (c. 38) (cont.)

| Section of Act. | Subject matter. | Provision in consolidation. | Remarks. |
|---|---|---|---|
| 167 | Production of documents etc. to inspectors. | 434, 435, 436 | Subs. (1), (3) AM 1967 s. 39. Subs. (1A), (1B) added, subs. (2), (3) AM, subs. (4) R 1981 s. 87. Subs. (2) AM OinC-l No. 13 |
| 168 | Inspectors' Report | 437 | Subs. (2) substituted, 1981 s. 88(1). |
| 169 | Proceedings on inspectors' report. | — | R 1967. |
| 170 | Expenses of investigation. | 439 | Subs. (1), (3) partially spent. AM 1967 ss. 37 (3), 40(2), (3). PR 1967. AM 1981 s.88 (2). Subs. (5) R 1970 c. 8. |
| 171 | Inspectors' report to be evidence. | 441 | AM 1981 s. 88 (2). |
| 172 | Investigation of company ownership. | 442, 443 | Subs. (2) AM 1981 Sch. 3 para. 8. Subs. (5) AM 1981 s.89. |
| 173 | Enforced disclosure of interest in shares etc. | 444 | Subs. (1) AM 1981 s. 90. |
| 174 | Power to impose restrictions on shares and debentures. | 445, 454, 455 456, 457, 732 | Heavily amended and supplemented by 1981 s.91. Subs. (1) PR ibid. |
| 175 | Saving for solicitors and bankers. | 452 | AM 1981 s. 103 (1). |
| 176 | Directors. | 282 | |
| 177 | Secretary. | 283 (1)–(3) | |
| 178 | Prohibition on certain persons being sole director or secretary. | 283 (4) | |
| 179 | Avoidance of acts done in dual capacity. | 284 | |
| 180 | Validity of acts of directors. | 285 | |
| 181 | Restrictions on appointment or advertisement of director. | — | R 1980. |
| 182 | Director's share qualification. | 291 | PR 1980. |
| 183 | Appointment of directors to be voted on individually. | 285, 292 | AM 1980 Sch. 3 para. 22. |
| 184 | Removal of directors. | 303, 304, CP 14 | |
| 185 | Retirement of directors under age limit. | 293 | Subs. (4) R 1976. Subs. (8) AM 1980 Sch. 3 para. 23. |
| 186 | Duty of directors to disclose their age. | 294 | |

| Section of Act. | Subject matter. | Provision in consolidation. | Remarks. |
|---|---|---|---|
| | COMPANIES ACT 1948 (c. 38) (cont.) | | |
| 187 | Undischarged bankrupt acting as director. | 302 | AM 1981 Sch. 3 para. 9. Subs. (5) added, OinC–2 No. 2. |
| 188 | Disqualification of persons from acting as director, etc. | 295–299; Sch. 12 | Heavily amended and supplemented, 1981 s. 93. Subs. (7) added, ibid. but unnecessary to be reproduced. |
| 189 | Prohition on tax-free payments to directors. | 311, CP 15 | Subs. (3) spent. |
| 190 | Prohibition of loans to directors. | — | R 1980. |
| 191 | Company approval required for payment for loss of office. | 312 | |
| 192 | Similarly, on payment in connection with transfer. | 313 | |
| 193 | Duty of director to disclose payment for loss of office. | 314, 315 | |
| 194 | Provisions supplementing ss. 191–3. | 316 | |
| 195 | Register of directors' shareholdings etc. | — | R 1967. |
| 196 | Particulars in accounts of directors' salaries. | 231, Sch. 5 Part V. | AM 1980 Sch. 3 para. 24, 1981 Sch. 3 para. 10. Subs. (6) PR 1981. |
| 197 | Particulars in accounts of loans to officers. | — | R 1980. |
| 198 | Duty of disclosure under ss. 195–197. | 231 (4) | PR 1967, 1980. |
| 199 | Directors to disclose interests in contracts. | 317 | Subs. (3) AM 1980 s. 60 (1), (2), Sch. 3 para. 25. |
| 200 | Register of directors and secretaries. | 288, 289, 290, Sch. 1. | AM 1976 s. 22 (1). Heavily amended, 1981 s. 95. |
| 201 | Particulars of directors in trade catalogues, etc. | 305 | AM 1981 Sch. 3 para. 11. Subs. (3), (4) PR 1981. Subs. (2) (c) R 1974 c. 39. |
| 202 | Limited company may have directors with unlimited liability. | 306 | |
| 203 | Special resolution making directors' liability unlimited. | 307 | |
| 204 | Assignment of office by directors. | 308 | |

| Section of Act. | Subject matter. | Provision in consolidation. | Remarks. |
|---|---|---|---|
| | COMPANIES ACT 1948 (c.38) (cont.) | | |
| 205 | Liability of officers and auditors. | 310 | AM 1980 Sch. 3 para. 26. Proviso (a) spent. |
| 206 | Power to compromise with creditors and members. | 425 | |
| 207 | Information as to compromise. | 426 | |
| 208 | Reconstruction and amalgamation of companies. | 427 | |
| 209 | Power to acquire shares of dissenting shareholder. | 428-430 | Subs. (2) (b) AM 1976 Sch.1. Subs. (6) spent. |
| 210 | Alternative remedy to winding up in cases of oppression. | — | R 1980. |
| 211 | Modes of winding up. | 501 | |
| 212 | Liability of contributories. | 502, 503 | As to consequences of re-registration, see 1967 ss.43 (6), 44 (7). |
| 213 | Definition of "contributory". | 507 | |
| 214 | Nature of contributory's liability. | 508 | |
| 215 | Contributories in case of member's death. | 509 | |
| 216 | Contributories in case of bankruptcy. | 510 | |
| 217 | Married women. | — | R Statute Law (Repeals) Act 1969. |
| 218 | Winding-up jurisdiction (England and Wales). | 512, 513 | Subs. (2) R Courts Act 1971. Money sum altered, 1976 c.60 s.l. PR by CP Act (Law Commission recommendation). |
| 219 | Transfer of proceedings. | 513, 514 | PR Supreme Court Act 1981. |
| 220 | Jurisdiction in Scotland. | 515 | Money sum altered, 1976 c.60 s.l. |
| 221 | Power in Scotland to remit to Lord Ordinary. | 516 | |
| 222 | Circumstances in which company may be wound up by the court. | 517 | See 1972 Sc. s.4 (1). AM 1980 Sch. 3 para. 27. PR 1980. |
| 223 | Definition of inability to pay debts. | 518 | Money sum altered, 1976 c.60 s.l, S.I. 1984/1199. |
| 224 | Petition for winding up. | 519 | Power of Secretary of State to present petition: see 1967 s.35(1). Subs. (1) AM 1980 Sch. 3 para. 28. PR 1980 |

| Section of Act. | Subject matter. | Provision in consolidation. | Remarks. |
|---|---|---|---|
| | COMPANIES ACT 1948 (c.38) (contd.) | | |
| 225 | Powers of court on hearing of petition. | 520 | Subs. (3) R 1980. |
| 226 | Power to stay or restrain proceedings against company. | 521 | |
| 227 | Avoidance of dispositions. | 522 | |
| 228 | Avoidance of executions. | 523 | |
| 229 | Commencement of winding up by the court. | 524 | |
| 230 | Copy of winding-up order to be registered. | 525 | |
| 231 | Actions stayed on winding-up order. | 525 | |
| 232 | Effect of winding-up order. | 525 | |
| 233 | The official receiver. | 526 | |
| 234 | Appointment of official receiver. | 527 | |
| 235 | Statement of company's affairs. | 528, 529 | As to statement as evidence, see 1967 s.50. |
| 236 | Report by official receiver. | 530 | |
| 237 | Power of court to appoint liquidators. | 531 | |
| 238 | Appointment and powers of provisional liquidator. | 532 | |
| 239 | Appointment of liquidators (England and Wales). | 533 | |
| 240 | Provisions where other than official receiver appointed. | 534 | |
| 241 | Liquidators in Scotland. | 535 | |
| 242 | General provisions as to liquidators. | 536 | |
| 243 | Custody of company property. | 537 | |
| 244 | Vesting of property in liquidator. | 538 | |
| 245 | Powers of liquidator | 539 | |
| 246 | Exercise and control of liquidator's powers. | 540 | |
| 247 | Books to be kept by liquidator. | 541 | |
| | COMPANIES ACT 1948 (c.38) (cont.) | | |
| 248 | Payments by liquidator into bank. | 542 | Subs. (1) AM 1976 c.60. Money sum altered ibid. |
| 249 | Audit of liquidator's accounts. | 543 | See 1976 c.60 s.2. Subs. (3) PR ibid. AM OinC-l No. 14. |
| 250 | Control of Secretary of State over liquidators (England and Wales). | 544 | |
| 251 | Release of liquidators. | 545 | |
| 252 | Meetings of creditors and contributories. | 546 | |
| 253 | Committee of inspection. | 547, Sch.17. | |
| 254 | Powers of Secretary of State where no committee appointed. | 548 | |
| 255 | Additional powers of committee in Scotland. | 547(2) | |
| 256 | Court's power to stay winding up. | 549 | |
| 257 | Settlement of list of contributories. | 550 | |
| 258 | Delivery of property to liquidator. | 551 | |
| 259 | Payment of debts due by contributory; set-off. | 552 | |
| 260 | Power of court to make calls. | 553 | |
| 261 | Payment into bank of money due to company. | 554 | |
| 262 | Order on contributory to be conclusive. | 555 | |
| 263 | Appointment of special manager (England and Wales). | 556 | |
| 264 | Power to exclude creditors not proving in time. | 557 | |
| 265 | Adjustment of rights of contributories. | 558 | |
| 266 | Inspection of company's books by creditors, etc. | 559 | |
| 267 | Costs of winding up payable out of assets. | 560 | |
| 268 | Power to summon persons suspected of having company property, etc. | 561 | |

| Section of Act. | Subject matter. | Provision in consolidation. | Remarks. |
|---|---|---|---|
| | COMPANIES ACT 1948 (c.38) (cont.) | | |
| 269 | Attendance of company officers at creditors' meetings. | 562 | |
| 270 | Public examination of promoters and officers. | 563, 564 | Subs. (9) PR Courts Act 1971. |
| 271 | Power to arrest absconding contributory. | 565 | |
| 272 | Powers of court cumulative. | 566 | |
| 273 | Delegation to liquidator of court's powers. | 567 | |
| 274 | Dissolution of company. | 568 | |
| 275 | Calls on contributories (Scotland). | 569 | |
| 276 | Enforcement throughout United Kingdom of court orders. | 570 | |
| 277 | Appeals from orders in Scotland. | 571 | |
| 278 | Circumstances in which company may be wound up voluntarily. | 572 | |
| 279 | Notice of voluntary winding up. | 573 | |
| 280 | Commencement of voluntary winding up. | 574 | |
| 281 | Effect on company's business and status. | 575 | |
| 282 | Avoidance of dispositions. | 576 | |
| 283 | Statutory declaration of solvency. | 577, 578 | AM and PR 1981 s.105. Subs. (2A), (4A) added, ibid. And see 1981 s.107. |
| 284 | Provisions applicable to members' winding up. | 579 | |
| 285 | Appointment and remuneration of liquidator. | 580 | |
| 286 | Power to fill vacancy in office of liquidator. | 581 | |
| 287 | Power of liquidator to accept shares, etc., as consideration for sale of company property. | 582 | |
| 288 | Duty of liquidator to call creditors' meeting, if company insolvent. | 583 | |
| | COMPANIES ACT 1948 (c.38) (cont.) | | |
| 289 | Duty to call company meeting at year's end. | 584 | |
| 290 | Final meeting and dissolution. | 585 | |
| 291 | Alternative provision as to annual meeting in case of insolvency. | 586 | |
| 292 | Provisions applicable to creditors' winding up. | 587 | |
| 293 | Meeting of creditors. | 588 | Subs. (1) substituted, 1981 s.106 (1). Subs. (7) added, 1981 s.106 (2). |
| 294 | Appointment of liquidator. | 589 | |
| 295 | Appointment of committee of inspection. | 590 | |
| 296 | Liquidator's remuneration; cesser of directors' powers. | 591 | |
| 297 | Power to fill vacancy in office of liquidator. | 592 | |
| 298 | Application of s.287. | 593 | |
| 299 | Duty of liquidator to call meetings. | 594 | |
| 300 | Final meeting and dissolution. | 595 | |
| 301 | Provisions applicable to every voluntary winding up. | 596 | |
| 302 | Distribution of company's property. | 597 | Section is subject to 1980 s.74(8) (distribution to employees). |
| 303 | Powers and duties of liquidator. | 598 | |
| 304 | Power of court to appoint and remove liquidator. | 599 | |
| 305 | Notice by liquidator of his appointment. | 600 | |
| 306 | Arrangements binding on creditors. | 601 | |
| 307 | Application to court for determination of questions. | 602 | |
| 308 | Power to control proceedings (Scotland). | 603, CP 17 | |
| 309 | Costs of voluntary winding up. | 604 | |
| 310 | Saving for rights of creditors and contributories. | 605 | |
| 311 | Power to order winding up subject to court supervision. | 606 | |
| 312 | Effect of petition for winding up under supervision. | 607 | |
| 313 | Application of ss.227, 228. | 608 | |
| 314 | Power of court to appoint and remove liquidator. | 609 | |

| Section of Act. | Subject matter. | Provision in consolidation. | Remarks. |
|---|---|---|---|
| | COMPANIES ACT 1948 (c. 38) (cont.) | | |
| 315 | Effect of supervision order. | 610 | |
| 316 | Proof of debts. | 611 | |
| 317 | Application of bankruptcy rules. | 612 | |
| 318 | Ranking of claims (Scotland). | 613 | |
| 319 | Preferential payments in winding up. | 614, Sch.19. | Various other debts made preferential by post-1948 legislation, under enactments relating to tax, excise duties, VAT employment protection, social security. Subs. (1) PR Statute Law (Repeals) Acts 1975 and 1981 and FA 1972. Subs. (1) (c)-(g) wholly or partially inoperative due to repeal of Acts referred to. AM Social Security Act 1973, Social Security Pensions Act 1975. In subs. (2), money sum altered, 1976 c.60 s.1. Subs. (5) extended to Scottish companies by Companies (Floating Charges) (Scotland) Act 1961. Subs. (8) (c) AM Social Security (Consequential Provisions) Act 1975. |
| 320 | Fraudulent preference. | 615 | Proviso to subs. (1) spent. Subs. (3) partially spent, AM OirC-1 No.15. |
| 321 | Liabilities and rights of those fraudulently preferred. | 616 | |
| 322 | Effect of floating charge. | 617, CP 18 | Subs. (3) added, 1972 Sc. s. 8; AM OinC-1 No 16. |
| 323 | Disclaimer of onerous property. | 618, 619, Sch. 20 Part I | |
| 324 | Liability for rentcharge on company's land. | 620 | |
| 325 | Restriction on creditor's right to levy execution. | 621 | Subs. (2) substituted, Charging Orders Act 1979. |
| 326 | Duties of sheriff. | 622 | Money sum altered, 1976 c. 60 s.l. |
| 327 | Effect of diligence (Scotland). | 623 | |
| 328 | Offences by officers of companies in liquidation. | 624, 626, 628, 629 | Money sums altered, 1976 c. 60 s.l. Subs. (1) PR Theft Act 1968. Subs. (2) PR Criminal Law Act 1967. Subs. (4) added, OinC-2 No. 3. |
| 329 | Penalty for falsification of books. | 627 | PR 1967. |
| 330 | Frauds by company officers. | 625 | Para. (a) R Theft Act 1968. |
| 331 | Liability where proper accounts not kept. | — | R 1976; replaced by ibid. s. 12. |
| 332 | Responsibility for fraudulent trading. | 458, 630 | Subs. (3) extended, 1981 s. 96. |
| 333 | Assessment of damages against delinquent directors. | 631 | |
| 334 | Prosecution of delinquent directors. | 632, 633 | Subs. (3), (5), (6) AM 1981 s. 92. Subs (3A) added, ibid. |
| 335 | Disqualification for appointment as liquidator. | 634 | |
| 336 | Corrupt inducement affecting appointment as liquidator. | 635 | |
| 337 | Enforcement of liquidator's duty to make returns. | 636 | |
| 338 | Notification that company is in liquidation. | 637 | |
| 339 | Exemption of certain documents from stamp duty. | 638 | PR FA's 1949, 1971. |
| 340 | Company's books to be evidence | 639 | |
| 341 | Disposal of company's books and papers. | 640 | |
| 342 | Information as to pending liquidations. | 641 | |
| 343 | Unclaimed assets (England and Wales). | 642 | See 1976 c. 60 s. 3. AM ibid. Sch. 2. |
| 344 | Unclaimed dividends (Scotland). | 643 | |
| 345 | Resolutions passed at adjourned creditors' meeting. | 644 | |
| 346 | Meeting to ascertain creditors' wishes. | 645 | |
| 347 | Judicial notice of officers' signatures. | 646 | |

| Section of Act. | Subject matter. | Provision in consolidation. | Remarks. |
|---|---|---|---|
| | COMPANIES ACT 1948 (c. 38) (cont.) | | |
| 348 | Special commission for receiving evidence. | 647 | Section substituted, OinC-l No. 17. |
| 349 | Examination of persons in Scotland. | 648 | |
| 350 | Costs of application for leave to proceed. | 649, CP 19 | |
| 351 | Affidavits, etc. in United Kingdom and overseas. | 650 | |
| 352 | Power of court to declare dissolution void. | 651 | |
| 353 | Registrar may strike defunct company off register. | 652, 653 | |
| 354 | Property of defunct company to be bona vacantia. | 654 | See 1981 s. 108 for amendment and partial repeal. |
| 355 | Crown's power to disclaim. | 656, 657, Sch. 20 Part II | Subs. (7) spent. |
| 356 | Liability for rentcharge after company's dissolution. | 658 | |
| 357–359 | Provisions as to stannaries. | — | R Consequential Provisions Act (s. 28) (Law Commission recommendation). |
| 360 | Companies Liquidation Account. | — | R 1976 c. 60; superseded by ibid. s. 3. |
| 361 | Investment of surplus funds on general account. | — | R 1976 c. 60. |
| 362 | Separate accounts of particular estates. | 660 | See Insolvency Services (Accounting and Investment) Act 1970. |
| 363 | Officers and remuneration. | 661 | |
| 364 | Returns by officers in winding up. | 662 | |
| 365 | General rules and fees in winding up. | 663 | Subs. (1) AM 1981 Sch. 3 para. 12.<br>PR 1970 c.8, Courts Act 1971, Law Reform (Misc. Prov.) (Scotland) Act 1966. |
| 366 | Disqualification of body corporate as receiver. | 489 | |
| 367 | Disqualification of undischarged bankrupt. | 490 | |
| 368 | Appointment of official receiver. | 491 | |
| 369 | Receivers and managers appointed out of court. | 492 | |
| 370 | Notification of appointment. | 493 | |
| 371 | Court's power to fix remuneration. | 494 | |

| Section of Act. | Subject matter. | Provision in consolidation. | Remarks. |
|---|---|---|---|
| | COMPANIES ACT 1948 (c.38) (cont.) | | |
| 372 | Information where receiver or manager appointed. | 495, 497 | Subs. (1) (a) AM 1976 Sch. 1.<br>AM OinC-l No. 18. |
| 373 | Statement submitted to receiver. | 496 | |
| 374 | Filing accounts of receivership. | 498 | Subs. (1) AM OinC-l No. 19. |
| 375 | Enforcement of duty to make returns. | 499 | |
| 376 | Construction of references to receivers and managers. | 500 | |
| 377 | Companies registered under former Companies Acts. | 675 | |
| 378 | Companies registered, but not formed, under former Acts. | 676 | |
| 379 | Unlimited companies formerly registered. | 677 | AM 1967 s. 53 (2). |
| 380 | Companies registered under Joint Stock Companies Acts. | 678 | |
| 381 | Exclusion of Irish and Northern Ireland companies. | 679 | |
| 382 | Companies cabable of being registered. | 680, 681 | AM 1976 Sch, 1, 1980 Sch. 3 para. 29.<br>Subs (3) added, ibid.; AM 1981 Sch. 3 para. 13.<br>Subs. (4) added, 1981 ibid.<br>PR by Consequential Provisions Act (s. 28) (Law Commission recommendation). |
| 383 | Definition of "joint stock company". | 683 | |
| 384 | Requirements for registration by joint stock company. | 684, 687 | AM 1976 Sch. 1<br>AM 1980 Sch. 3 para. 30; 1981 Sch. 3 para. 14; OinC-l Nos. 20, 21, 24.<br>Reference to "cost-book regulations" R Consequential Provisions Act (s. 28) (Law Commission recommendation). |

| Section of Act. | Subject matter. | Provision in consolidation. | Remarks. |
|---|---|---|---|
| | COMPANIES ACT 1948 (c.38) (cont.) | | |
| 385 | Other requirements for registration. | 686 (1) | AM OinC-I No. 22. Reference to "cost-book regulations" R Consequential Provisions Act (s. 28) (Law Commission recommendation). |
| 386 | Authentication of statements of existing companies. | 686 (2) | AM 1976 Sch. 1. |
| 387 | Registrar may require evidence as to nature of company. | 686 (3) | |
| 387A | Requirements as to name of company registering. | 687 | Section added, OinC-I No. 23. |
| 388 | Change of name for purpose of registration. | — | R 1981. |
| 389 | Addition of "limited" to name. | — | R 1981. |
| 390 | Certificates of registration of existing companies. | 688 | Subs. (1) AM 1976 Sch. 2; PR 1976. Subs. (2) added, 1980 Sch. 3 para. 31. |
| 391 | Vesting of property on registration. | 689, Sch. 21. | |
| 392 | Saving for existing liabilities. | | |
| 393 | Continuation of existing actions. | | |
| 394 | Effect of registration under Part VIII. | 511, 689, Sch. 21 | Subs. (2), (6) AM 1980 Sch. 3 para. 32. Applied, 1967 s. 53 (1). PR Consequential Provisions Act (s. 28) (Law Commission recommendation). |
| 395 | Power to substitute memorandum and articles for deed of settlement, etc. | 690 | |
| 396 | Power of court to stay or restrain proceedings. | 521 | |
| 397 | Actions stayed on winding-up order. | 525 | |
| 398 | Meaning of "unregistered company" in this Part. | 665 | AM Trustee Savings Banks Acts 1969, 1981. AM Transport Act 1962. |
| | COMPANIES ACT 1948 (c. 38) (cont.) | | |
| 399 | Winding up of unregistered companies. | 666 – 669 | Money sum altered, 1976 c. 60 s. 1, S.I. 1984/1199. Subs. (7) R Transport Act 1962. AM Trustee Savings Bank 1969. |
| 400 | Oversea company may be wound up, though dissolved. | 670 | |
| 401 | Contributories in winding up. | 671 | Subs. (2) PR Statute Law (Repeals) Act 1969. |
| 402 | Power of court to stay or restrain proceedings. | 672 | |
| 403 | Actions stayed on winding-up order. | 673 | |
| 404 | Provisions of Part IX to be cumulative. | 674 | |
| 405 | Enactments providing for winding up under former Companies Acts. | CP 31 (8) (c) | |
| 406 | Application of ss. 407–414. | 744 | |
| 407 | Documents to be delivered to registrar. | 691 | AM 1976 Sch. 1. Subs. (2A) added, 1981 Sch. 3 para. 15. AM OinC-I No. 25. |
| 408 | Power of oversea company to hold land. | — | R Charities Act 1960. |
| 409 | Return to registrar of documentary alterations. | 692 | Subs. (2) added, 1976 Sch. 2. AM OinC-I No. 26. |
| 410 | Accounts of oversea company. | — | R 1976. |
| 411 | Obligation to state name, whether limited, where incorporated. | 693 | |
| 412 | Service on oversea company. | 695 | |
| 413 | Office where documents to be filed. | 696 | |
| 414 | Penalties. | 697 | |
| 415 | Interpretation of ss. 407–414. | 698 | AM 1976 Sch. 2. |
| 416 | Companies incorporated in Channel Islands. | 699 | Section replaced, 1981 s. 109. |
| 417 | Dating of prospectus and matters to be contained in it. | 72, 73, 78 (3), (4) | Subs. (5) AM 1976 Sch. 2. |
| 418 | Exclusion of s. 417; relaxation of Sch. 4. | 76 | AM 1976 Sch. 2. |
| 419 | Experts' consents; allotment. | 74, 75 | |
| 420 | Registration of prospectus. | 77 | |

| Section of Act. | Subject matter. | Provision in consolidation. | Remarks. |
|---|---|---|---|
| | COMPANIES ACT 1948 (c. 38) (cont.) | | |
| 421 | Penalty for contravention of ss. 417–420. | 78 (1) | |
| 422 | Civil liability for false statement in prospectus. | 78 (2) | |
| 423 | Interpretation of provisions as to prospectus. | 79 | |
| 424 | Registration offices in Great Britain. | 704 | PR 1976. AM 1981 Sch. 3 para. 16. Subs. (4) R Consequential Provisions Act (s. 28) (Law commission recommendation). |
| 425 | Fees. | 708 | Subs. (1) R 1976. |
| 426 | Inspection, production, etc. of documents kept by registrar. | 709, 710 | AM 1976 Sch. 2, 1981 s. 98. Disapplied, 1981 s. 31 (5). |
| 427 | Removal of documents to Public Record Office. | 712 | |
| 428 | Enforcement of company's duty to make returns. | 713 | |
| 429–432 | Provisions about banking companies, etc. | — | R Banking Act 1979. |
| 433 | Banking and other companies to make periodical statement. | 720 | AM Insurance Companies Act 1974 s. 88 (1), Insurance Companies Act 1982 Sch. 5. PR Banking Act 1979. |
| 434 | Large partnerships. | 716 | Modified, 1967 s. 120. PR Banking Act 1979. Subs. (2) refers to Marine and Aviation (War Risks) Act 1952. PR Consequential Provisions Act (s. 28) (Law Commission recommendation). |
| 435 | Application of Act to unregistered companies. | 718, Sch. 22 | Extended variously, by 1967, ECA 1972 s. 9, 1976, 1980, 1981. |
| 436 | Form of registers, etc. | 722 | Extended, 1967 s. 56 (6), Sch. 4. AM 1976 Sch. 2. See SECOBA s. 3. |
| 437 | Service of documents on company. | 725 | |
| 438 | Penalty for false statements. | — | R 1980. |
| 439 | Penalty for improper use of word "limited". | 34 | AM 1976 Sch. 2. |
| | COMPANIES ACT 1948 (c.38) (cont.) | | |
| 440 | Default fines; meaning of "officer in default". | 730 (5) | Subs. (1) R 1980. See now 1980 s. 80 (2). Applied, 1980 s. 84 (1) (b). |
| 441 | Production and inspection of books, where offence suspected. | 721 | |
| 442 | Summary proceedings. | — | R 1967. |
| 443 | Indictment of bodies corporate in Scotland. | — | R Criminal Justice (Scotland) Act 1949. |
| 444 | Application of fines. | — | Spent. |
| 445 | Saving as to private prosecutors. | — | No longer operative. |
| 446 | Saving for privileged communications. | 732(3) | AM 1981 s.103 (2). |
| 447 | Costs in actions by certain limited companies. | 726 | |
| 448 | Power of court to grant relief. | 727 | |
| 449 | Power to enforce court orders. | 728 | |
| 450 | Jurisdiction of stannaries court. | — | R Consequential Provisions Act (s.28) (Law Commission recommendation). |
| 451 | Annual report by Secretary of State. | 729 | Extended, 1976 s.38 (1). AM 1980 Sch. 3 para. 33. AM 1981 Sch. 3 para. 18. |
| 452 | Authentication of documents issued by Secretary of State. | — | R 1967. |
| 453 | Orders and certificates of Secretary of State to be evidence. | — | R 1976. |
| 454 | Power to alter Tables and forms by statutory instrument. | 3, 8, 256, 720 | Amended variously, 1976, 1980, 1981. |
| 455 | Interpretation. | Part XXVI (passim) | Amended variously by post-1948 Acts. AM OinC-l No. 27. PR Consequential Provisions Act (s.28) (Law Commission recommendation). |
| 456 | Amendment of other Acts. | — | Mainly R or superseded. |
| 457 | Construction of references to other Acts. | — | Unnecessary. |
| 458 | Effect of provisions of former Acts as to registration of charges on land, etc. | — | Unnecessary. |
| 459 | Repeal and savings. | CP 31(9) | Unnecessary, except for subs. (14) in part. |

COMPANIES ACT 1948 (c.38) (cont.)

| Section of Act. | Subject matter. | Provision in consolidation. | Remarks. |
|---|---|---|---|
| 460 | Winding-up proceedings commenced before 1.11.29. | CP 22 | |
| 461 | Application to Northern Ireland. | 745 | |
| 462 | Short title; commencement. | — | |
| Sch. 1 | Tables A, B, C, D, E. | — | Tables not reproduced in consolidation, but now in statutory instruments under ss. 3 and 8 of the Companies Act 1985. |
| Sch. 2 | Form of licence to hold land. | — | R Charities Act 1960. |
| Sch. 3 | Form of statement in lieu of prospectus. | — | R 1980. |
| Sch. 4 | Matters to be stated in prospectus; reports to be set out. | Sch. 3 | AM 1976 s.33<br>PR 1967. |
| Sch. 5 | Form of statement in lieu of prospectus. | — | R 1980. |
| Sch. 6 | Contents and form of annual return. | Sch. 15 | PR 1967, 1980<br>See now S.I. 1977/1368, as amended by S.I. 1979/54 and 1980 Sch 3 para. 38.<br>AM CinC-I No. 28. |
| Sch. 7 | Interests in shares and debentures of private company. | — | R 1967. |
| Sch. 8 | Accounts. | Sch. 4 | Added by 1981 s.1 (2), Sch 1.<br>Part VA inserted by S.I. 1982/1092; AM S.I. 1984/1859.<br>Para. 38 (2) AM OinC-I No. 29.<br>Para. 60 modified, 1983 (BI). |
| Sch. 8A | Accounts of banking, shipping and insurance companies. | Sch. 9 | Originally numbered 8. Heavily amended, 1967 ss. 9, 10.<br>Re-numbered as 8A by 1981 s. 1 (2)<br>See 1981 s. 17, Sch. 2 for application of Schedule immediately prior to consolidation.<br>Para. 2 AM OinC-I No 30.<br>Para. 15 (3) modified, 1983 (BI).<br>Part III A inserted by S.I. 1982/1092;<br>AM S.I. 1984/1859. |

COMPANIES ACT 1948 (c.38) (cont.)

| Section of Act. | Subject matter. | Provision in consolidation. | Remarks. |
|---|---|---|---|
| Sch. 9 | Auditors' report. | — | R 1967. |
| Sch. 10 | Orders in winding-up proceedings pronounced in vacation (Scotland). | Sch. 16 | |
| Sch. 11 | Provisions not applying to winding up under supervision of court. | Sch. 18 | |
| Sch. 12 | Fees payable to registrar of companies. | — | R 1967. |
| Sch. 13 | Form of statement to be published under s. 433. | Sch. 23 | |
| Sch. 14 | Provisions of Act applying to unregistered companies. | Sch. 22 | Variously extended by post-1948 Acts. |
| Sch. 15 | Provisions referred to in s. 438. | — | R 1980. |
| Sch. 16 | Amendments of other Acts. | — | Unnecessary. |
| Sch. 17 | Repeals. | — | Spent. |
| Sch. 18 | Enactments saved. | — | R 1967. |

| Section of Act. | Subject matter. | Provision in consolidation. | Remarks. |
|---|---|---|---|
| | COMPANIES ACT 1967 (c. 81) | | |
| 1 | Meaning of "principal Act". | — | Unnecessary. |
| 2 | Abolition of exempt private company. | — | Spent. |
| 3 | Company accounts to identify subsidiaries. | 231, Sch. 5 Part I | AM 1980 Sch. 3 para. 41; 1981 Sch. 3 paras. 23, 24. |
| 4 | Disclosure of shareholdings in companies not subsidiaries. | 231, Sch. 5 Part II | AM 1980 Sch. 3 para. 41; 1981 s. 3, Sch. 2 para. 5, Sch. 3 paras. 23, 24. |
| 5 | Accounts to identify ultimate holding company. | 231, Sch. 5 Part IV | AM 1980 Sch. 3 para. 41; 1981 Sch. 3 para. 23. |
| 6 | Disclosure of directors' emoluments. | 231, 237, Sch. 5 Part V | AM S.I. 1979/1618; 1980 Sch. 3 para. 41; 1981 Sch. 3 para. 25. |
| 7 | Directors' emoluments waived. | 231, 237, Sch. 5 Part V | AM 1980 Sch. 3 para. 41; 1981 Sch. 3 para. 26. |
| 8 | Salaries of higher-paid employees. | 231, 237, Sch. 5 Part VI | AM S.I. 1979/1618; 1980 Sch. 3 para. 41; 1981 Sch. 3 para. 26. |
| 9 | Miscellaneous amendments as to accounts. | — | R 1981. |
| 10 | Limitation of operation of new provisions about accounts. | — | Unnecessary. |
| 11 | Certain entries to show figures for previous year. | 260 | AM 1981 Sch. 2. |
| 12 | Power to revoke certain Schedule 8 provisions. | — | R 1981. |
| 13 | Qualification for appointment as auditor. | 389 | PR 1976. |
| 14 | Auditors' report and right of access to company's books. | 236, 237, 241, 262, 387 (1) | AM 1976 Sch. 2; 1980 Sch. 3 para. 41; 1981 Sch. 2, 3. PR 1976, 1980. |
| 15 | Meaning of "directors' report" in ss. 16–24. | — | Unnecessary. |
| | COMPANIES ACT 1967 (c. 81) (cont.) | | |
| 16 | Additional matters of general nature to be stated in report. | 235, 261 (5), Sch. 7 Parts I, IV, V; Sch. 10 | Subs. (1) (b), (d), (2) R (with savings) 1981 s. 16 (2). Subs. (1)(c) R (with savings) 1980 s. 66 (2). Subs. (1)(g), (5)-(7) added, Health and Safety at Work Act 1974 s. 79. Subs. (1) (f) substituted by 1981 s. 13 (3), with saving in Sch. 2 para. 5 (4). Subs. (1) (h), (1A), (8) added, Employment Act 1982 s. 1. Subs. (4A) added, 1981 s. 13 (4), with saving in Sch. 2 para. 5 (4). Subs. (3) R 1981, subject to saving in 1980 s. 66 (2). |
| 16A | Directors' report to give particulars of acquisition by company of its own shares. | 235, Sch. 7 Part II | Section added, 1981 s. 14, with saving in Sch. 2 para. 5 (5). |
| 17 | Particulars of company's business. | 261 (6), Sch 10 | Applies to "special category accounts" only: see 1981 s. 16, Sch. 2 para. 5 (4). |
| 18 | Average number of employees and their wages. | 261 (6), Sch. 10 | Applies to "special category accounts" only: see 1981 s. 16. |
| 19 | Contributions for political and charitable purposes. | 235, Sch. 7 Part I | AM S.I. 1980/1055. |
| 20 | Particulars of exports. | — | R 1981. |
| 21 | Limitation of operation of ss. 16–20. | — | Spent. |
| 22 | Report to show corresponding amounts for previous year. | 261 (4) | R 1981, with saving in s. 16 (2) for "special category companies". |
| 23 | Penalty for directors' failure to comply with disclosure requirements. | 235 | Section substituted by 1976 Sch. 2. AM 1980 Sch. 3 para. 42. |
| 23A | Auditors' duties. | 237 | Section added, 1981 s. 15; saving in Sch. 2 para. 5 for "special category companies". |

| Section of Act. | Subject matter. | Provision in consolidation. | Remarks. |
|---|---|---|---|
| | COMPANIES ACT 1967 (c. 81) (cont.) | | |
| 24 | Right to receive copy of directors' report. | 240, 246 | |
| 25 | Directors' dealings in share options. | 323 | Subs. (2) (a) (b) AM 1976 Sch. 2. AM 1981 Sch. 3 para. 28. |
| 26 | Directors' service contracts. | 318 | AM 1976 Sch. 1, 1980 ss. 61, 63 (4). PR 1980. |
| 27 | Director to notify interests in company and subsidiaries. | 324, 732, Sch. 13 Parts II, III | AM 1976 s. 24, Sch. 2. AM 1981 Sch. 3 para. 28. |
| 28 | Rules for giving effect to s. 27. | Sch. 13 Part I | Subs. (1) – (4F) substituted, 1981 Sch. 3 para. 29. |
| 29 | Means of securing availability of information given under s. 27. | 325, 326, Sch. 13 Part IV | AM 1976 Sch. 1; 1981 Sch. 3 para 28. |
| 30 | Extension of s. 25 to spouses and children. | 327 | PR Children Act 1975. |
| 31 | Extension of s. 27 to spouses and children. | 328 | AM 1976 s. 24. |
| 32 | Investigation of share dealings. | 446, 452 | |
| 33 | Obligation to notify share dealings. | — | R 1981. |
| 34 | Provision for obtaining information under s. 33. | — | R 1981. |
| 35 | Power of Secretary of State to present winding-up petition. | 440 | PR 1976. Subs. (2) R 1980. |
| 36 | Repeal of 1948 s. 169 (1), (2). | — | Spent. |

| Section of Act. | Subject matter. | Provision in consolidation. | Remarks. |
|---|---|---|---|
| | COMPANIES ACT 1967 (c. 81) (cont.) | | |
| 37 | Power for Secretary of State to bring proceedings. | 438, 439 | |
| 38 | Extension of power of official investigation. | — | R 1980. |
| 39 | Power of inspectors to secure attendance of witnesses. | 434, 436 | |
| 40 | Expenses of investigation. | 439 | |
| 41 | Inspector to report malpractice to Secretary of State. | 433 (2) | |
| 42 | Extension of power to investigate foreign companies. | 453 | |
| 43 | Limited companies may be re-registered as unlimited. | 49, 50, 506 | Subs. (2)(b) PR FA 1970. Subs. (2)-(4) PR 1980. AM 1980 Sch. 3 para. 43. Subs. (1A) inserted, OinC-l No. 31. |
| 44 | Unlimited companies may be re-registered as limited. | 51, 52, 124, 505 | Subs. (1A) inserted, inserted, OinC-l No. 32. Subs. (2) substituted, 1980 Sch. 3 para. 44, AM 1981 Sch. 3 para. 30. Subs. (8) R FA 1973. |
| 45 | Cesser of 1948 s. 16. | — | Spent. |
| 46 | Power to require company to abandon misleading name. | 32 | AM 1981 Sch. 3 para. 31. AM Oinc-l No. 33. |
| 47 | Exception of certain companies from 1948 s. 127. | — | R 1976. |
| 48 | Fees. | — | R 1976. |
| 49 | Summary proceedings. | 731 | PR 1980. |
| 50 | Evidence. | 434 | AM 1981 Sch. 3 para. 32. |
| 51 | Exemption from obligation to print documents. | 123, 380 | |
| 52 | Increase of maximum charges for extracts from registers, etc. | 191, 356 | |
| 53 | Application of Part I to companies not formed under Companies Acts. | 677 | |
| 54 | Unregistered companies. | 718, Sch. 22 | PR 1976, 1981. |
| 55 | Construction of references. | — | Unnecessary. |

| Section of Act. | Subject matter. | Provision in consolidation. | Remarks. |
|---|---|---|---|
| | COMPANIES ACT 1967 (c. 81) (cont.) | | |
| 56 | Interpretation for Part I. | 722, 742 | AM 1981 Sch. 2 para. 5, Sch. 3 para. 33. PR 1976, 1980. |
| 57 | Commencement; power to make regulations. | — | Unnecessary. |
| 58–108 | Amendments of law about insurance companies. | — | Not part of the Companies Acts consolidation. |
| 109 | Power of Secretary of State to call for documents. | 447 | Subs. (1) (f) R Insurance Companies (Amendment) Act 1973. |
| 110 | Entry and search of premises. | 448 | AM Insurance Companies Act 1974. |
| 111 | Provision for security of information. | 449, CP 25 | Extended, 1976 s. 39 (2), 1980 s. 84 (3). AM 1973 c. 58 Sch. 1 para. 16. AM 1974 c. 49 Sch. 1. AM 1981 s. 104. AM Insurance Companies Act 1982. AM OinC-I No. 34. |
| 112 | Consequential cesser of certain statutory powers. | — | R 1976. |
| 113 | Destruction, mutilation of company documents. | 450 | Subs. (1) AM Insurance Companies Act 1974 Sch. 1, Insurance Companies Act 1982. |
| 114 | Penalty for furnishing false information. | 451 | |
| 115 | Application, for purposes of Part III, of certain provisions of Parts I and II. | 731, 732, 733, 734 | |
| 116 | Saving for solicitors and bankers. | 452 | Subs. (1) AM 1981 s. 103 (3), Insurance Companies Acts 1974, 1982. |
| 117 | Interpretation (Part III). | — | Unnecessary. |
| 118 | Extent of Part III. | — | Unnecessary. |
| 119 | Large banking partnerships. | — | R Banking Act 1979. |
| 120 | Other large partnerships. | 716, 744 | PR Banking Act 1979. |

| Section of Act. | Subject matter. | Provision in consolidation. | Remarks. |
|---|---|---|---|
| | COMPANIES ACT 1967, (c. 81) (cont.) | | |
| 121 | Limited partnerships. | 717, 744 | PR Banking Act 1979. |
| 122 | Extent of Part IV. | — | Unnecessary. |
| 123–125 | Moneylenders. | — | R Consumer Credit Act 1974. |
| 126 | Functions of Board of Trade. | — | R Industrial Expansion Act 1968. |
| 127 | Amendment of 1963 c. 16. | — | R Banking Act 1979. |
| 128 | Repeal of provision in 1949 c. 67. | — | Spent. |
| 129 | Cesser of spent or obsolete enactments. | — | Spent. |
| 130 | Short title, etc. | — | Unnecessary. |
| Sch. 1 | Amendments of 1948 Sch. 8. | Passim in Sch. 9 | |
| Sch. 2 | 1948 Sch. 8 as amended. | Sch. 9 | |
| Sch. 3 | Fees payable to registrar of companies. | — | R 1976. |
| Sch. 4 | Enactments in 1948 Act applied by s. 56 (6). | See under sections applied. | See under sections applied. |
| Sch. 5 | Amendments of Insurance Companies Act 1958. | — | Not material. |
| Sch. 6 | Other amendments relating to insurance companies. | — | Not material. |
| Sch. 7 | Spent or obsolete enactments ceasing to have effect. | — | Spent. |
| Sch. 8 | Enactments repealed. | — | Spent. |

| Section of Act. | Subject matter. | Provision in consolidation. | Remarks. |
|---|---|---|---|
| COMPANIES (FLOATING CHARGES AND RECEIVERS) (SCOTLAND) ACT 1972 (c. 67) | | | |
| 1 | Power of companies to create floating charge. | 462, 463 | |
| 2 | Creation of floating charges. | 462 | |
| 3 | Floating charge in relation to heritable property. | 462 | |
| 4 | Extension of court's power to wind up companies. | 517 | |
| 5 | Ranking of charges. | 464, 466 | |
| 6 | Registration of charges. | See Part IIIA (ss. 106A–106K) of 1948 Act. | |
| 7 | Alteration of floating charges. | 466 | |
| 8 | Floating charge not a fraudulent preference. | See 1948 s. 322 | |
| 9 | Amendment of 1948 s. 455 (1). | 744 | |
| 10 | Amendment of Industrial and Provident Societies Act 1967. | CP 26 | Effect of 1972 Sc. s. 10 consolidated as substituted section of 1967 c. 48. |
| 11 | Power to appoint receiver. | 467 | Subs. (7) added, OinC–2 No. 4. |
| 12 | Circumstances justifying appointment. | 468 | |
| 13 | Mode of appointment by holder of charge. | 469 | |
| 14 | Mode of appointment by court. | 470 | |
| 15 | Powers of receiver. | 471 | |
| 16 | Precedence among receivers. | 472 | |
| COMPANIES (FLOATING CHARGES AND RECEIVERS) (SCOTLAND) ACT 1972 (c. 67) (cont.) | | | |
| 17 | Agency and liability of receiver for contracts. | 473 | |
| 18 | Remuneration of receiver. | 474 | |
| 19 | Payment of debts subject to floating charge. | 475 | |
| 20 | Distribution of moneys. | 476 | |
| 21 | Disposal of interest in property. | 477 | |
| 22 | Cessation of appointment of receiver. | 478 | |
| 23 | Powers of court. | 479 | |
| 24 | Notification that receiver appointed. | 480 | |
| 25 | Information where receiver appointed. | 481 | AM OinC–1 No. 35. |
| 26 | Statement submitted to receiver. | 482 | |
| 27 | Enforcement of receiver's duty to make returns, etc. | 483 | |
| 28 | Interpretation of Part II. | 484 | |
| 29 | Prescription of forms, etc; regulations. | 485 | |
| 30 | Repeals; transitionals. | 465 | |
| 31 | Interpretation. | 468, 488 | |
| 32 | Citation, extent, etc. | 487 | Subs. (2) AM OinC–2 No. 5. |
| Sch. | Part IIIA inserted in Act of 1948. | Part XII, Chapter II | |

| Section of Act. | Subject matter. | Provision in consolidation. | Remarks. |
|---|---|---|---|
| | EUROPEAN COMMUNITIES ACT 1972 (c. 68) | | |
| 9 (1) | Power of directors to bind company. | 35 | |
| (2) | Contracts entered into on company's behalf, before formation. | 36 | |
| (3) | Registrar of companies to publish certain documents concerning company's affairs. | 42, 711 | AM 1976 ss. 1 (10), 7 (5), 22 (3), 23 (6), (7). AM 1980 Sch. 3 para. 45 (1), 1981 Sch. 3 para. 34. |
| (4) | Inability of company to rely on happening of certain events, when not officially notified. | 42 | |
| (5) | Alteration of memorandum or articles to be registered. | 18 | |
| (6) | Alterations made before ECA 1972. | — | Spent. |
| (7) | Information to be furnished on company correspondence, etc. | 351 | AM 1980 Sch. 3 para. 45 (2). |
| (8) | Construction of ECA 1972 with Companies Acts; unregistered companies. | Sch. 22 | AM OinC-l No. 36. |
| (9) | Entry into force of s. 9. | — | Unnecessary. |

| Section of Act. | Subject matter. | Provision in consolidation. | Remarks. |
|---|---|---|---|
| | STOCK EXCHANGE (COMPLETION OF BARGAINS) ACT 1976 (c. 47) | | |
| 1 | Exemption from obligation to prepare share certificate, etc. | 185 | |
| 2 | Official seals. | 40, 186, CP 11 | |
| 3 | Use of computers for company records. | 723 | AM 1976 Sch. 2; 1980 Sch. 3 para. 48. |
| 4 | Application of ss. 1–3 to unregistered companies. | 718, Sch. 22 | |
| 5 | Acquisition and disposal of securities by trustees. | — | Not material. |
| 6 | Forms of transfer for securities. | — | Not material. |
| 7 | Short title and interpretation. | 185, CP Sch. 2 | SECOBA s. 7 amended consequentially on consolidation. |

| Section of Act. | Subject matter. | Provision in consolidation. | Remarks. |
|---|---|---|---|
| | INSOLVENCY ACT 1976 (c. 60) | | |
| 1 | Increase in monetary limits in bankruptcy and winding up. | 512, 515, 518, 542, 622, 624, 664, 667(2), Sch. 19 para. 13. | This section repealed and replaced only in relation to winding up of companies. |
| 2 | Audit of accounts of trustees and liquidators. | 543 | This section not consolidated; amended and replaced by Consequential Provisions Act Sch. 2. |
| 3 | Insolvency Services Account. | 542 | Consequentially amended, Consequential Provisions Act Sch. 2. |
| 4–8 | Various bankruptcy matters. | — | Not material. |
| 9 | Disqualification of directors of insolvent companies. | 300 | Section heavily amended and supplemented, 1981 s 94. |
| 10–13 | Various matters. | — | Not material |
| 14 | Short title, etc. | — | Unnecessary |
| Sch. 1 | Monetary limits in bankruptcy and winding up. | see s. 1 (supra) | Part II of Schedule consolidated only so far as material. |
| Sch. 2 | Consequential amendments relating to Insolvency Services Account. | see 1948 ss. 248, 343 | Not material except in relation to 1948 Act. |
| Sch. 3 | Repeals. | — | Spent. |

| Section of Act. | Subject matter. | Provision in consolidation. | Remarks. |
|---|---|---|---|
| | COMPANIES ACT 1976 (c. 69) | | |
| 1 | Company's duty to prepare, lay and deliver accounts. | 227, 239, 241, 711, 742, 744 | |
| 2 | Accounting reference periods. | 224 | Subs. (3) spent. Subs. (6) unnecessary. |
| 3 | Alteration of accounting reference period. | 225, 226 | |
| 4 | Penalty for not complying with s. 1 in due time. | 243 | |
| 5 | Default order in case of continuing failure. | 244 | |
| 6 | Period allowed for laying and delivering accounts. | 242 | |
| 7 | Transitional provisions and savings. | — | Spent. |
| 8 | Group accounts. | 229, 245 | |
| 9 | Oversea company accounts. | 700 | AM 1980 Sch. 3. para. 49, 1981 s. 19. AM OinC–1 No. 37. |
| 10 | Accounting reference period of oversea company. | 701 | |
| 11 | Penalty for not complying with s. 9. | 702, 703 | |
| 12 | Accounting records. | 221, 222, 223 | |
| 13 | Qualification of auditors. | 389 | |
| 14 | Appointment and removal of auditors. | 384, 385, 386 | |
| 15 | Provisions supplementing s. 14. | 387 (2), 388 | |
| 16 | Resignation of auditors. | 390, 713 | |
| 17 | Right of resigning auditor to requisition company meeting. | 391 | |
| 18 | Powers of auditors in relation to subsidiaries. | 392 | |
| 19 | False statements, etc. to auditors. | 393 | |
| 20 | Auditors of body which is a trade union and also a company. | 394 | Subs. (2) spent. |
| 21 | On registration of company, statement as to first directors and secretary to be filed. | 10, 13, Sch. 1 | PR 1980. |
| 22 | Notification of changes in directors, etc. | 288, 711 | Subs. (2) unnecessary. |

| Section of Act. | Subject matter. | Provision in consolidation. | Remarks. |
|---|---|---|---|
| | COMPANIES ACT 1976 (cont.) | | |
| 23 | Registered office. | 10, 287, 711 | PR 1980. |
| 24 | Duty of director to notify acquisition of company's securities. | 328, Sch. 13 Part II | |
| 25 | Duty of company to notify stock exchange. | 329, 732 | |
| 26 | Duty to notify acquisition of voting shares. | — | R 1981. |
| 27 | Power of company to compel disclosure of shareholdings. | — | R 1981. |
| 28 | Persistent default in delivering documents to be grounds for disqualification. | — | R 1981. |
| 29 | Register of disqualification orders. | 301 | Section substituted, OinC–1 No. 38. |
| 30 | Companies with registered office in Wales. | 2, 21, 25, 351 | Subs. (2) PR 1980. Subs. (4) R 1981. |
| 31 | Name of oversea company trading in Great Britain. | 694, 697 | Heavily amended, 1981 s. 27. |
| 32 | Amendment of Business Names Act 1916. | — | R 1981. |
| 33 | Contents of prospectus (amendment of 1948 Sch. 4). | — | See 1948 Sch. 4. |
| 34 | Use of prescribed forms for notices. | Passim | Subs. (1) attracts Sch. 1, which consists of amendments. Subs. (2) R 1981. |
| 35 | Size and durability of documents to be deliverd to registrar. | 706 | |
| 36 | Power for registrar to accept information on microfilm, etc. | 707 | Subs. (3) R 1981. |
| 37 | Fees to registrar. | 708 | AM 1981 Sch. 3 para. 37. |
| 38 | Functions of Secretary of State and registrar. | 13, 138, 401, 688, 710, 729 | AM 1981 s. 99. PR 1981. |
| 39 | Criminal proceedings and enforcement. | 449 | |
| 40 | Application of Act to companies not formed under Companies Acts. | — | Spent. |
| 41 | Application to unregistered companies. | 718, Sch. 22 | |
| 42 – 44 | Various matters. | — | Spent or unnecessary. |
| 45 | Citation, commencement, etc. | 243 (6) | Power retained for 1976 s. 4 (3) and (4) to be brought into force by statutory instrument. |
| Sch. 1 | Prescribed forms for Acts of 1948 and 1967. | Passim | |
| Sch. 2 | Minor and consequential amendments. | Passim | |
| Sch. 3 | Repeals. | — | Spent. |

| Section of Act. | Subject matter. | Provision in consolidation. | Remarks. |
|---|---|---|---|
| | COMPANIES ACT 1980 (c. 22) | | |
| 1 | Classification of companies. | 1, 15 | |
| 2 | Membership and name of public company. | 1, 3, 25, 43, 685 | |
| 3 | Registration of companies. | 11, 12, 13 | |
| 4 | Public company share capital; minimum requirements. | 117 | |
| 5 | Re-registration of private companies as public. | 43, 44, 46, 47 | Subs. (1A) inserted, OinC-l No. 39. Subs. (5) AM OinC-l No. 40. Subs. (10) modified, 1981 Sch. 2 para. 6 (1). |
| 6 | Private company re-registering; requirements as to capital. | 45 | |
| 7 | Re-registration of unlimited company as public. | 48, 51, 124, 505 | Subs. (4) extends 1967 s. 44 (6), (7). |
| 8 | Old public companies. | CP 1–4 | |
| 9 | Failure of old public company to obtain new classification. | CP 5 | |
| 10 | Re-registration of public company as private. | 53, 55 | Subs. (2A) inserted, OinC-l No. 41. |
| 11 | Special resolution resulting in public company becoming private. | 54 | |
| 12 | Public company reducing capital below authorised minimum. | 139 | |
| 13 | Registration of joint stock companies as public companies. | 685, 688 | |
| 14 | Certain allotments requiring company approval. | 80, 380 | Subs. (10) AM OinC-l No. 42. |
| 15 | Shares and debentures of private company not to be offered to the public. | 81, CP 7 | Subs. (2) unnecessary. |
| 16 | Prospectus to state if shares are to be allotted, if not fully subscribed. | 84, 85 | |
| 17 | Pre-emption rights. | 89, 90, 91, 92, 93, 94. | Subs. (11) AM 1981 Sch. 3 para. 40. Subs. (13) added, ibid; AM OinC-l No. 43. |

| Section of Act. | Subject matter. | Provision in consolidation. | Remarks. |
|---|---|---|---|
| | COMPANIES ACT 1980 (c. 22) (cont.) | | |
| 18 | Disapplication of pre-emption rights. | 95 | |
| 19 | Pre-emption rights: transitional provisions. | 96 | |
| 20 | Subscription of share capital. | 99, 112 | |
| 21 | Prohibition of shares offered at discount. | 100, 112 | Subs. (2) substituted, 1981 Sch. 3 para. 41. |
| 22 | Payment for allotted shares. | 101, 112 | |
| 23 | Payment of non-cash consideration. | 102, 112 | |
| 24 | Expert's report on value of non-cash consideration. | 103, 108, 112 | Heavily amended, 1981 Sch. 3 para 42. Subs. (2A) AM OinC-1 No. 44. |
| 25 | Expert's report: supplementary. | 110, 111 | |
| 26 | Expert's report on non-cash asset acquired from subscriber. | 104, 105, 109, 112 | |
| 27 | Provisions supplementary to s. 26. | 109, 110, 111 | |
| 28 | Relief. | 113 | |
| 29 | Shares issued to subscriber of memorandum of public company. | 106 | |
| 30 | Contraventions of ss. 20–29. | 114, 115 | |
| 31 | Application of ss. 20–30 in special cases. | 116, CP 9 | |
| 32 | Variation of class rights. | 125, 126, 127 | |
| 33 | Registration of particulars of special rights. | 128 | Subs. (5) unnecessary. |
| 34 | Obligation to convene company meeting on serious loss of capital. | 142 | Subs. (4) spent. |
| 35 | Acquisition by company of its own shares. | 143 | Subs. (1), (2), (4) AM 1981 Sch. 3 para. 43. |
| 36 | Acquisition of company's shares by nominee. | 144, 145 | Subs. (6) modified, 1983 (BI). |
| 37 | Treatment of shares held by or on behalf of public company. | 146, 147, 148, 149, CP 6 | Subs. (1) AM 1981 Sch. 3 para. 44; modified, 1983 (BI). Subs. (9) AM OinC-1 No. 45. |
| 38 | Charge taken by public company on its own shares. | 150, CP 6 | |
| | COMPANIES ACT 1980 (c. 22) (cont.) | | |
| 39 | Profits available for distribution. | 263, 275 | Subs. (4) AM, (4A) added, 1981 Sch. 3 para. 45. PR 1981. |
| 40 | Restriction on distribution of assets. | 264, 275 | PR 1981. |
| 41 | Other distributions by investment companies. | 265, 266, 267 | Subs. (2) AM 1981 Sch. 3 para. 46 (but for "special category companies" only). PR 1981. |
| 42 | Realised profit of insurance company with long-term business. | 268 | |
| 42A | Treatment of development costs. | 269 | Section added, 1981, s. 84. |
| 43 | The relevant accounts. | 270, 271, 272, 273, 274, 275 | AM 1981 Sch. 3 para. 47. PR 1981. |
| 43A | Distributions in kind. | 276 | Section added, 1981, s. 85. |
| 44 | Consequences of making unlawful distribution. | 277 | See 1981 s. 60 (2). |
| 45 | Ancillary provisions. | 263, 278, 280, 281 | AM 1981 Sch. 3 para. 48. PR 1981. |
| 46 | Directors to have regard to interests of employees. | 309 | |
| 47 | Directors' contracts of employment. | 319 | |
| 48 | Substantial property transaction involving director. | 320, 321, 322 | Subs. (1) AM 1981 s.110 (2), (3). Subs. (1)(a) AM OinC-1 No. 46. Subs. (3) AM OinC–1 No. 47. Subs. (7), (8) added 1981 s. 110. |
| 49 | Prohibition of loans, etc. to directors and connected persons. | 330 | |
| 50 | Exceptions from s. 49. | 332, 333, 334, 335, 336, 337, 338 | Subs. (1) AM 1981 Sch. 3 para. 49. Subs. (2A) added, 1981 s. 111 (1). |
| 51 | Relevant amounts. | 339 | Subs. (1) AM 1981 s. 111 (2). Subs. (1) AM, and (2A) added, 1981. Sch. 3 para. 50. |
| 52 | Civil remedies for breach of s. 49. | 341 | |
| 53 | Criminal penalties for breach. | 342 | Subs. (4) AM OinC-2 No. 6. |

| Section of Act. | Subject matter. | Provision in consolidation. | Remarks. |
|---|---|---|---|
| | COMPANIES ACT 1980 (c. 22). (cont.) | | |
| 54 | Disclosure of directors' transactions in accounts. | 232, Sch. 6 Part I | Subs. (1), (6) AM, (2A) added, 1981 Sch. 3 para. 51. Subs. (8), (9) added S.I. 1984/1860. |
| 55 | Particulars to be disclosed under s. 54. | Sch. 6 Part II | AM OinC-l No. 48. Subs. (2) added S.I. 1984/1860. |
| 56 | Particulars of amounts outstanding to be given in accounts. | 233, 234, Sch. 6 Parts II, III | Subs. (2A), (4A) added, 1981 Sch. 3 para. 52. |
| 57 | Further provisions relating to recognised banks. | 343, 344 | Subs. (1) AM OinC-l No. 49. |
| 58 | Transactions excluded from ss. 54, 57. | 344, Sch. 6 Part I | Subs. (3) substituted, 1981 Sch. 3 para. 53. |
| 59 | Duty of company's auditors in case of breach of these requirements. | 237 | |
| 60 | Disclosure by directors of interests in contracts. | 317 | |
| 61 | Extension of 1967 s. 26. | 318 | |
| 62 | Power to increase financial limits under Part III. | 345 | |
| 63 | Shadow directors. | 232, 309, 317, 318, 319, 320, 330, 343, 382, 741 | Subs. (3) AM OinC-l No. 50. |
| 64 | Connected persons. | 346, Sch. 13 Part I | Subs. (3), (4) AM 1981 Sch. 3 paras. 54, 55. Subs. (1) AM OinC-2 No. 7 |
| 65 | Interpretation for Part III. | 331, 338, 340, 347 | Subs. (1) AM 1981 Sch. 3 Para. 56. |
| 66 | Consequential repeals and savings. | — | AM 1981 Sch. 3 para. 57. |
| 67 | Unregistered companies. | 718, Sch. 22 | AM 1981 Sch. 3 para. 58. |
| 68 | Prohibition of insider dealing. | ID 1, 3, 7, 16 | |
| 69 | Abuse of information obtained in official capacity. | ID2, 3, 7 | |
| 70 | Off-market deals. | ID 4, 5, 7, 12, 13 | |
| 71 | International bonds. | ID 6, 15 | AM 1981 s. 112. |
| 72 | Contraventions of ss. 68, 69. | ID 8 | AM 1981 Sch. 3 para. 59. |
| 73 | Interpretation for Part V. | ID 9, 10, 11, 12, 13, 14, 16 | |
| 74 | Power for company to provide for employees on cessation or transfer of business. | 659,719 | |
| 75 | Power of court to grant relief against company for members unfairly prejudiced. | 459-461 | |

| Section of Act. | Subject matter. | Provision in consolidation. | Remarks. |
|---|---|---|---|
| | COMPANIES ACT 1980 (c. 22) (cont.) | | |
| 76 | Trading under misleading name. | 33, CP 8 | Subs. (3) spent. |
| 77 | Companies with registered office in Wales. | 351 (3) | |
| 78 | Alternatives and Welsh equivalents of statutory designations. | 25, 26, 27 | Subs. (4) AM 1981 Sch. 3 para. 60. |
| 79 | Qualifications of company secretaries. | 286 | |
| 80 | Penalties and mode of trial. | 730 (4) Sch. 24 passim, BN 7 | |
| 81 | Amendment of 1948 s. 454. | — | R 1981 |
| 82 | Repeals in 1948 Act. | — | Spent. |
| 83 | Continued application of Protection of Depositors Act 1963. | CP 20 | |
| 84 | Enforcement of Companies Acts. | 713, 731 | |
| 85 | The authorised minimum. | 118 | |
| 86 | Companies not formed under 1948 Act. | — | Spent. |
| 87 | Interpretation. | 44, 107, 264, 331, 737, 738, 739, 743, 744 | AM 1981 Sch. 3 paras. 61, 62. |
| 88 | Minor and consequential amendments; repeals. | — | Spent or unnecessary. |
| 89 | Northern Ireland. | — | Not reproduced. |
| 90 | Short title, etc. | — | |
| Sch. 1 | Forms of memorandum of association for public company. | — | Forms now prescribed by statutory instrument under ss. 3 and 8 of the Companies Act 1985. |
| Sch. 2 | Increase of penalties, etc. | Passim | AM OinC–1 No. 51. |
| Sch. 3 | Minor and consequential amendments. | Passim | Unnecessary. |
| Sch. 4 | Repeals. | — | Spent. |

| Section of Act. | Subject matter. | Provision in consolidation. | Remarks. |
|---|---|---|---|
| | COMPANIES ACT 1981 (c. 62) | | |
| 1 | Form and content of company accounts. | See 1948 s. 149 | |
| 2 | Group accounts. | See 1948 s. 152 | |
| 3 | Extension of requirements of 1967 s. 4. | Sch. 5 paras. 8, 10, 11 | |
| 4 | Financial information about subsidiaries, etc. | 231, Sch. 5 Part III | Subs. (3), (6) AM OinC–2 Nos. 8, 9. |
| 5 | Companies entitled to accounting exemptions. | 247, 251 | |
| 6 | Exemptions for individual accounts. | Sch. 8 Part I | |
| 7 | Provisions supplementing s. 6. | | |
| 8 | Small and medium-sized companies. | 248, 249 | |
| 9 | Exclusion of exemption by reference to group size. | 250 | Subs. (6) AM (7) added, OinC–2 No. 10. |
| 10 | Group exemption. | 250, Sch. 8 Parts II, III | |
| 11 | Publication of accounts. | 254, 255 | |
| 12 | Dormant companies. | 247, 252, 253 | Subs. (5) AM OinC–1 No. 52. |
| 13 | Directors' report. | 235, Sch. 7 Part I | |
| 14 | Directors' report to give particulars of acquisition by company of own shares. | See 1967 s. 16A | |
| 15 | Auditors to check directors' report against accounts. | See 1967 s. 23A | |
| 16 | Certain provisions of Companies Acts to cease to be in force. | See 1967 ss. 17, 18 and other provisions amended | |
| 17 | Schedule 8A to 1948 Act given continued application to certain companies. | 257–262, Schs. 9–11 | |
| | COMPANIES ACT 1981 (c. 62) (cont.) | | |
| 18 | Alterations of requirements as to accounts. | See 1948 s. 454 | |
| 19 | Accounts of oversea companies. | See 1976 s. 9 | |
| 20 | Unregistered companies. | 718, Sch. 22 | |
| 21 | Interpretation of accounting and disclosure provisions. | 742, (5), (6) | |
| 22 | Prohibition on registration of certain names. | 26 | |
| 23 | Index of company names. | 714 | AM S.I. 1982/1654. |
| 24 | Change of name. | 28 | Subs. (3) substituted, OinC–1 No. 53. |
| 25 | Companies exempt from requirement to have "limited" as part of the name. | 30, 31, 380 | |
| 26 | Companies registering under 1948 Part VIII. | 682, 687 | Subs. (3) AM OinC–1 No. 54. |
| 27 | Name of oversea company. | 694 | |
| 28 | Control of business names. | BN 1, 2, 7, 8 | |
| 29 | Disclosure of names used in business. | BN 4, 7 | |
| 30 | Civil remedy for breach of s. 29. | BN 5 | |
| 31 | Words and expressions requiring approval of Secretary of State. | 29, BN 3 | Subs. (2) Am OinC–1 No. 55. Subs. (3) AM OinC–1 No. 56. |
| 32 | Regulations about names. | 29, BN 6 | |
| 33 | Temporary extension of power to require change of name. | — | Spent |
| 34 | Interpretation for Part II. | 26, BN 8 | |
| 35 | Transitory provisions. | — | Unnecessary. |
| 36 | Reliefs from 1948 s. 56 (share premium account). | 130, CP 12 | |
| 37 | Merger relief. | 131 | |
| 38 | Group reconstructions. | 132 | Section substituted, S.I. 1984/2007. |
| 39 | Retrospective reliefs. | CP 12 | |
| 40 | Provisions supplementing ss. 37–39. | 133, CP 12 | Subs. (2) unnecessary. For Subs. (3) see 1948 Sch. 8A para. 15 (5). |

| Section of Act. | Subject matter. | Provision in consolidation. | Remarks. |
|---|---|---|---|
| | COMPANIES ACT 1981 (c.62) (cont.) | | |
| 41 | Power to extend and restrict reliefs. | 134, CP 12 | |
| 42 | Financial assistance by company for purchase of own shares; general prohibition. | 151, 152, 153, 154 | |
| 43 | Relaxation of s. 42 for private companies. | 155, 156, 158 | Subs. (3) AM OinC–1 No. 57. |
| 44 | Provisions supplementing s. 43. | 155, 156, 157 | |
| 45 | Power of company to issue redeemable shares. | 159, 160, 161 | |
| 46 | Power of company to purchase own shares. | 162 | |
| 47 | Authority for off-market purchase. | 163, 164 | |
| 48 | Contingent purchase contracts. | 165 | |
| 49 | Authority for market purchase. | 163, 166, 380 | |
| 50 | Assignment or release of company's right to purchase own shares. | 167 | |
| 51 | Certain payments to be made out of distributable profits. | 168 | |
| 52 | Disclosure of contracts, etc. | 169 | |
| 53 | The capital redemption reserve. | 170 | |
| 54 | Power for private companies to redeem or purchase shares out of capital. | 170, 171, 172 | |
| 55 | Special resolution required under s. 54. | 173, 174 | |
| 56 | Publicity for proposed purchase out of capital. | 175 | |
| 57 | Objections by members or creditors. | 176, 177 | |
| 58 | Liability of past shareholders and directors. | 503, 504, 507, 519 | |
| 59 | Effect of company's failure to redeem or purchase own shares. | 178 | |
| 60 | Part III supplementary provisions. | 274, 277 | |
| 61 | Power to alter Part III. | 179, 274, 277(3), 504(6), 507(2) | |
| 62 | Interpretation, repeal, etc. | 155, 180, 181 | |
| | COMPANIES ACT 1981 (c.62) (cont.) | | |
| 63 | Obligation to notify interest in voting shares. | 198, 199, 200, 201, 202(1), (2) | |
| 64 | The prescribed percentage. | 201 | |
| 65 | Obligation to notify registered ownership of shares. | 202 | |
| 66 | Notification of family and corporate interests. | 203 | |
| 67 | Notification of group interests, where people act together. | 204, 205 | |
| 68 | Obligation of those acting together to keep each other informed. | 206 | |
| 69 | Application of s. 63 to cases within s. 66 or 67. | 207 | |
| 70 | Interests to be notified. | 208 | |
| 71 | Interests to be disregarded. | 209 | |
| 72 | Supplementary provisions. | 210, 455, 456, 457, 732 | |
| 73 | Register of interests. | 211 | |
| 74 | Power of company to require disclosure. | 212 | |
| 75 | Registration of interests disclosed under s. 74. | 213 | |
| 76 | Investigation and report on requisition of members. | 214, 215 | |
| 77 | Penalties for failure to provide information. | 216, 455, 456, 457 | Subs. (7) AM OinC–1 No. 58. |
| 78 | Removal of entries in register. | 217 | |
| 79 | Prohibition on removal otherwise. | 218 | |
| 80 | Inspection of register and reports. | 219 | |
| 81 | Offences by bodies corporate. | 210, 216, 733 | |
| 82 | Interpretation for Part IV. | 198, 220 | |
| 83 | Repeals, transitional provisions, savings. | 213 | |
| 84 | Development costs to be shown as asset. | See 1980 s. 42A. | |
| 85 | Distributions in kind. | See 1980 s. 43A. | |

| Section of Act. | Subject matter. | Provision in consolidation. | Remarks. |
|---|---|---|---|
| | COMPANIES ACT 1981 (c. 62) (cont.) | | |
| 86 | Investigation on application of company. | 431, 432 | |
| 87 | Duty of directors and others to assist inspectors. | 434, 435, 436 | |
| 88 | Disclosure and authentication of inspectors' reports. | 437, 441 | |
| 89 | Duty of directors and others to assist in investigation under 1948 s. 172. | 443 | |
| 90 | Extension of power to require information under 1948 s. 173. | 444 | |
| 91 | Amendment of 1948 s. 174. | 445, 454, 455, 456, 457, CP 23 | |
| 92 | Powers of Secretary of State under 1948 s. 334. | See 1948 s. 334 | |
| 93 | Disqualification orders. | See 1948 s. 188 | |
| 94 | Disqualification of directors of insolvent companies. | See 1976 c. 60 s. 9 | |
| 95 | Register of past directorships. | See 1948 s. 200 | |
| 96 | Criminal liability for fraudulent trading. | See 1948 s. 332 | |
| 97 | Companies' registered numbers. | 705 | |
| 98 | Inspection of copies of company records. | See 1948 s. 426 | |
| 99 | Sealing of documents. | See 1976 s. 38 | |
| 100 | Destruction of old records. | 715 | |
| 101 | Identification in register of different classes of shares. | See 1948 s. 110 | |
| 102 | Members' class rights. | 129 | |
| 103 | Privileged information. | See 1948 s. 446, 1967 s. 116; CP 25 | |
| 104 | Disclosure of information. | See 1967 s. 111 | |
| 105 | Amendment of 1948 s. 283. | See 1948 s. 283; CP 16 | |
| 106 | Minimum notice for meeting for voluntary winding up. | See 1948 s. 293 | |
| 107 | Conversion of creditors' winding up. | CP 24 | |

| Section of Act. | Subject matter. | Provision in consolidation. | Remarks. |
|---|---|---|---|
| | COMPANIES ACT 1981 (c. 62) (cont.) | | |
| 108 | Revival of dissolved companies. | 654 (2), 655 | |
| 109 | Channel Islands and Isle of Man companies. | See 1948 s. 416 | |
| 110 | Exclusion of certain inter-company arrangements from 1980 s. 48. | See 1980 s. 48 | |
| 111 | Additional exemption from 1980 s. 49. | See 1980 ss. 50, 51 | |
| 112 | International bonds. | See 1980 s. 71 | |
| 113 | Old public companies. | CP 1 | |
| 114 | Application of Act to certain companies not formed under Companies Acts. | — | |
| 115 | Enforcement. | 713, 731 | |
| 116 | Pre-consolidation amendment of Companies Acts. | — | Power exercised, S.I. 1984/134; S.I. 1984/1169. |
| 117 | Corresponding provisions for Northern Ireland | — | Not reproduced. |
| 118 | Interpretation. | Passim | |
| 119 | Citation and commencement. | — | Unnecessary. |
| Sch. 1 | Accounts (provisions replacing 1948 Sch. 8). | See 1948 Sch. 8 | |
| Sch. 2 | Preparation of accounts under 1948 Sch. 8A ("special category companies"). | 257–262, 279, Schs. 9–11 | |
| Sch. 3 | Minor and consequential amendments. | Passim | |
| Sch. 4 | Repeals. | — | |

| Section of Act. | Subject matter. | Provision in consolidation. | Remarks. |
|---|---|---|---|
| | COMPANIES (BENEFICIAL INTERESTS) ACT 1983 (c. 50) | | |
| 1–5 | Residual interests under pension and employee share schemes; trustees' and employers' rights; interpretation and supplementary provisions. | 23, 145, 146, 148, Sch. 2, Sch. 4 para. 60, Sch. 9 para. 19 (3). | 1983 (BI) s.i. AM OinC-l No. 59. |
| 6 | Northern Ireland. | — | |
| 7 | Short title, etc. | — | |
| Sch. | Vesting of residual interests. | Sch. 2 | |

CHAPTER ONE

# The Legal Framework—Companies

## 1.0 LEGAL BACKGROUND

### 1.1 Introduction

This brief synopsis gives the necessary legal background to the study of company accounting.

(a) *Definition of a company.* A company is a legal person (or entity) separate and distinct from its members. The capital of the company is divided into shares which are allotted to the members for cash or other assets transferred by them to the company.

(b) *Classification of companies* (*see* Fig. 1). Companies may be:

(i) incorporated under Royal Charter, e.g. Hudson Bay Company;

(ii) incorporated under special Act of Parliament, e.g. waterworks companies;

(iii) incorporated and registered under the provisions of the Companies Acts 1948 to 1981.

(c) *Registered companies.* The three kinds of registered companies are:

(i) Companies limited by shares—the most usual form; capital is divided into shares. The liability of each member is limited to the amount unpaid on his shares.

(ii) Companies limited by guarantee—each member undertakes to contribute a certain sum in the event of its winding up.

(iii) Unlimited companies—an unlimited company is one in which the liability of the members to contribute to the debts of the company is unlimited. A public company cannot be unlimited—Companies Act 1980.

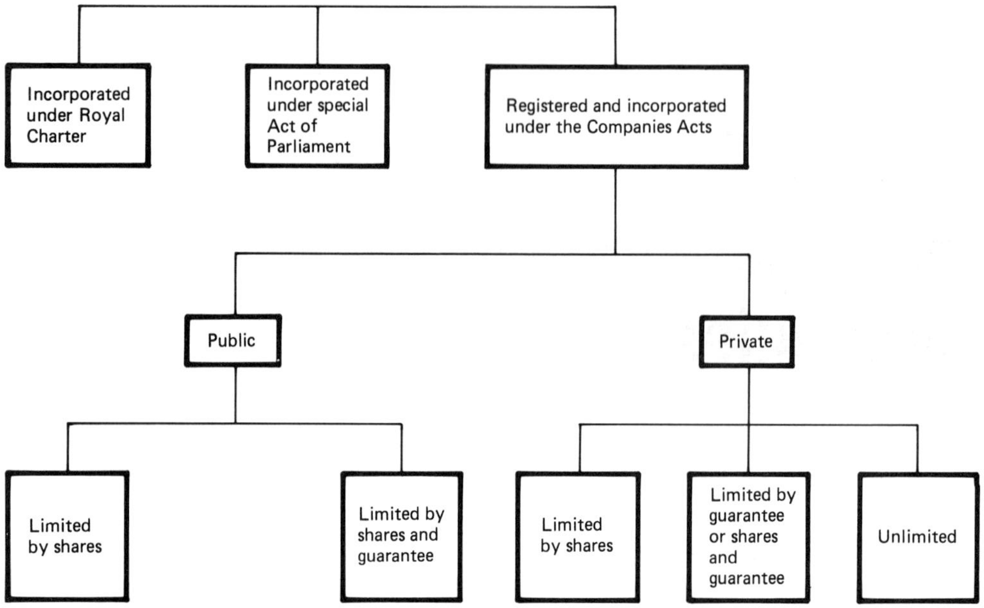


Fig. 1. *Types of companies.*

## 1.2 Companies contrasted with partnerships

Table 1 lists all the major differences between companies and partnerships as legal entities.

Table 1. COMPANIES AND PARTNERSHIPS CONTRASTED

| | *Partnership* | *Company limited by shares* |
|---|---|---|
| Liability | Unlimited except for a limited partner in a limited partnership | Limited to amount unpaid on shares |
| Constitution | Verbal agreement which may later be reduced to writing in form of deed or agreement and can be altered at any time by mutual consent | Filing of memorandum which can only be altered in accordance with provisions of the Act. Articles governing internal management can only be altered by requisite majority of shareholders |
| Legal status | No legal status as a body—each partner maintains his separate legal identity | Legal entity entire and separate from the shareholders |

Table 1. *cont.*

| | *Partnership* | *Company limited by shares* |
|---|---|---|
| Numbers | Number of partners limited to twenty with a number of exceptions, e.g. firms of accountants | No maximum, minimum of two members (CA 1980) |
| Regulation | Regulated by Partnership Act 1890 and Limited Partnership Act 1907 | Regulated by Companies Acts 1948 to 1981 |
| Capital | Contributed by partners in agreed proportions | Amount limited to authorised amount; can be altered only in special statutory manner |
| Profits | Distributed according to terms of agreement, if no agreement then equally | Distributed by way of dividend |
| Books and accounts | No legal obligation to keep books or prepare accounts | Proper accounting records must be kept and annual accounts lodged with the registrar |
| Audit | No legal obligation to have an audit | Annual audit by qualified auditor is compulsory |

## 1.3 Public and private companies

(a) *Public companies.* A public company is defined by s. 1 Companies Act 1980 as a company limited by shares or limited by guarantee and having a share capital where:

(i) the memorandum states that the company is to be a public company; and

(ii) it has been properly registered as a public company, or is an old public company or private company which has been properly re-registered as a public company.

The main characteristics are:

(i) the last words of its name must be "public limited company" (plc, or for Welsh companies ccc);

(ii) the authorised (and allotted) share capital must not be less than the statutory minimum of £50,000;

(iii) shares and debentures can be offered to the public for subscription and can be freely transferred—thus enabling a Stock Exchange quotation;

(iv) the CA 1980 imposes many stringent requirements with regard to share capital, e.g. it must be paid up as to at least one-quarter of the nominal value and the whole of any premium; and if shares are issued for non-cash consideration an audited independent valuation is necessary.

A large industrial or trading company requiring large amounts of capital would prefer public company status.

(b) *Private companies.* A private company is defined as any company which is not a public company. The main characteristics are:

(i) it cannot offer shares or debentures to the public;

(ii) many of the stringent CA 1980 provisions do not apply.

The private limited status is largely applicable to small or medium-sized companies.

(c) *Advantages.* The advantages of a public company over a private one, and vice versa, are set out in Table 2.

Table 2. COMPARATIVE ADVANTAGES OF PUBLIC AND PRIVATE COMPANIES

| *Public company* | *Private company* |
|---|---|
| (i) Capital can be raised by subscription from the public | (a) No prospectus required prior to first allotment of shares or debentures |
| (ii) Stock exchange permission for shares to be dealt in can be acquired, thus providing a market for the shares | (b) May be unlimited and therefore no need to file accounts |
| (iii) Shares are freely transferable | (c) Less expensive to form |
| | (d) Does not require certificate before commencing business |

## 1.4 Company officials

(a) *Directors.* The articles of association may fix the minimum and maximum number of directors. A private company must have at least one director and a public company at least two. Directors are appointed to direct the affairs of the company, and as a body are known as the board of directors. They act in two capacities:

(i) as quasi-trustees of the company money and property;

(ii) as agents acting on behalf of the company.

Directors need not hold shares, but if a share qualification is required they must comply with this within two months of appointment.

In relation to directors the articles may contain references to:

(i) powers and duties;

(ii) appointment and removal;

(iii) remuneration.

(b) *Secretary*. Every company must have a secretary, but a *sole* director of the company may not also be secretary. The secretary takes part in the authentication of documents issued on behalf of the company. The qualification of a secretary of a public company is governed by the CA 1980.

(c) *Auditors*. A company is required to have auditors whose duty it is to examine and report on the company's accounts. The appointment, qualification, remuneration and removal of auditors is governed by the Companies Acts.

## 1.5 Annual return

A company must make an annual return to the registrar of companies once in every calendar year within forty-two days after the annual general meeting.

(a) *First annual return*. The first annual return must be made after the first annual general meeting which must be held within eighteen months of incorporation.

(b) *Documents to be annexed to the annual return*. The following documents are required to be annexed to the annual return in the case of a limited company:

(i) accounts for the period to which the return relates;

(ii) auditors' report;

(iii) directors' report (not required for "small" companies).

(c) *Contents of the annual return*. Briefly these are:

(i) address of the registered office;

(ii) location of registers of members and debenture holders;

(iii) particulars of shares and debentures;

(iv) list of present and past members with number of shares held at the date of the return and transferred by them since the last return—full details need only be given once every three years provided changes in membership are recorded on an annual basis;

(v) particulars of directors and secretary.

## 1.6 Annual general meeting

Every company is required to hold an annual general meeting in each year and not more than fifteen months must elapse between one annual general meeting and the next. A company must hold its first annual general meeting within eighteen months of incorporation.

## 1.7 Classes of share capital

The share capital of a company may be divided into different classes, as follows.

(a) *Ordinary shares*. Ordinary shares are commonly referred to as equities. The ordinary shareholders are the real owners of the company and are ultimately entitled to share the capital and revenue profit after any preferential rights have been satisfied. Dividends paid to the ordinary shareholders are normally determined by the directors. On a winding-up of the company the ordinary shareholders will receive any surplus after all prior claims by creditors or preference shareholders have been met.

(b) *Preference shares*. Preference shares carry preferential rights to dividend, usually at a fixed rate. They will carry preferential rights to repayment of capital in the event of a winding-up, provided the articles or the terms of issue so provide.

Types of preference shares are as follows:

(i) *Cumulative* preference shares—these carry the right to receive arrears of preference dividend for earlier years before any dividend is paid to ordinary shareholders. Preference shares are deemed to be cumulative unless otherwise provided in the articles or terms of issue.

(ii) *Participating* preference shares—these entitle the holder to receive a further dividend in addition to the fixed rate, usually pro rata to the ordinary dividend—e.g. a further 1 per cent for each 10 per cent of ordinary dividend.

(c) *Deferred shares*. These may be issued to vendors as part of the purchase consideration on acquisition of a business. They are sometimes referred to as founders or management shares. For the purpose of dividends, deferred shares rank after all other classes.

(d) *Redeemable shares*. The Companies Act 1981 allows companies to issue redeemable shares, equity or preference. The procedure for redemption varies according to whether the company is public or private.

## 1.8 Classes of capital

(a) *Authorised capital*. This is sometimes referred to as nominal capital. It is the amount up to which the company may issue shares. The minimum for a public company is £50,000.

(b) *Issued and unissued capital*. Issued capital is the portion of authorised capital which has been issued. If the whole of the authorised capital has not been issued the balance is referred to as unissued capital. The CA 1980 refers to issued capital as allotted share capital.

(c) *Subscribed capital.* This is the amount of issued capital which has been taken up or subscribed for by shareholders.

(d) *Called-up and paid-up capital.* The distinction here is:

(i) called-up capital is the portion of subscribed capital which has been called up for payment, whereas

(ii) paid-up capital is the part of called-up capital actually paid. The called-up capital not paid is referred to as "calls in arrear".

(e) *Working capital.* This is an accounting term. A company's working capital is the excess of current assets over current liabilities. It is a guide to the solvency of the company.

(f) *Other capital terms.* The word capital is frequently used for accountancy purposes in the following ways:

(i) *capital expenditure*, meaning the purchase of fixed assets;

(ii) *capital receipts*, meaning cash received on the issue of shares and debentures or on the sale of capital assets;

(iii) *capital profits and capital losses*, meaning the profits and losses on the sale of fixed assets.

## 1.9 Publication of accounts

The directors must lay accounts before the company in general meeting within the following time limits after the end of the accounting reference period, as follows:

| | *No overseas interests* | *With overseas interest* |
|---|---|---|
| (a) Private companies | ten months | thirteen months |
| (b) Other companies | seven months | ten months |

These limits apply to the first accounting reference period of a company, except that where the first accounts are made up for a period exceeding twelve months, the limits are reduced by one month for each month in excess of twelve months, subject to leaving a minimum period of three months. (s. 6 CA 1976).

The balance sheet must be signed by two directors or by the sole director (s. 155 CA 1948).

## 1.10 Filing of accounts with Registrar

A copy of the accounts and reports for the relevant year must be submitted with the annual return to the Registrar of Companies in the case of *all limited companies* (s. 127 CA 1948; s. 2 CA 1967). An *unlimited* company does not normally need to file accounts.

## 1.11 Group accounts

Where, at the end of its financial year, a company has subsidiaries, group accounts dealing with the state of affairs and profit and loss of the company and its subsidiaries must be presented to the company at the meeting at which its own accounts are presented (s. 150(1) CA 1948).

The relationship of holding company (H) and subsidiary company (S) exists where:

(a) H is a member of S and controls the composition of its board of directors;

(b) S is a subsidiary of a company which is itself a subsidiary of H;

(c) H holds more than half of the equity share capital of S (s. 154 CA 1948).

*Note: Equity share capital* is the issued share capital of a company *excluding* any part thereof which, *neither* as respects dividends *nor* as respects capital, carries any right to participation beyond a specified amount in a distribution (s. 154(5) CA 1948) (i.e. it does *not include* most issues of *preference shares*).

The financial year of each subsidiary must coincide with that of the holding company unless there are, in the opinion of the directors of the holding company, good reasons against it (s. 153(1) CA 1948). If they do not coincide in the case of a particular subsidiary, the group accounts must deal with the position as at the end of the subsidiary's last complete financial year ending before that of the holding company, unless the DTI otherwise direct (s. 152(2) CA 1948). Where the DTI considers it desirable to extend the financial year of the holding company or a subsidiary to bring them into line, and for that purpose to postpone the production of accounts from one year to the next, the Department may exempt that company from the obligation to produce accounts, to hold an AGM, or to make an annual return for an earlier year (s. 153(2) CA 1948).

## 1.12 Distributable profits

(a) *Introduction.* The Companies Act 1980 made important changes to the definition of distributable profits. Some previous case law, and in particular the unsatisfactory case of *Dimbula Valley Tea Company* v. *Laurie* (1961), has now become obsolete.

Before proceeding to the detailed rules, it is worth noting that s. 43 CA 1980 prohibits the payment of a dividend if a company has a qualified audit report, unless the auditor states in writing that the subject matter of the qualification is not, in his opinion, material for determining whether the dividend is in contravention of the restrictions in ss. 39 to 41.

The auditor's statement to this effect must be laid before the members and filed with the Registrar.

(b) *Distribution limits placed on all companies (s. 39).* Section 39 provides that no company may make a distribution except out of *accumulated realised profits* less *accumulated realised losses.*

There is one exception to this. If a company has revalued a fixed asset, and subsequently calculates depreciation on the higher revalued figure, the depreciation attributable to the excess may be counted as a realised profit.

Section 84 CA 1981 provides that development costs capitalised must be treated as a realised loss in computing distributable profits in accordance with s. 39 CA 1980.

***Illustration (s. 39)***

A Ltd: Balance Sheet Year 1

| | £000 | | £000 |
|---|---|---|---|
| Share capital | 4,000 | Freehold building at cost | 4,000 |
| Reserves | 4,000 | *less:* Depreciation (2% p.a.) | 1,000 |
| | | | 3,000 |
| | | Sundry assets | 5,000 |
| | 8,000 | | 8,000 |

The distributable profits of this company are obviously £4,000,000.

Let us assume that at the beginning of Year 2 the building is revalued to £8,000,000, and that it is agreed that depreciation should continue at 2 per cent on this figure, and let us further assume that A Ltd made a profit of £1,000,000 in Year 2.

The balance sheet at the end of Year 2 will be:

A Ltd: Balance Sheet Year 2

| | £000 | | £000 |
|---|---|---|---|
| Share capital | 4,000 | Freehold building at valuation | 8,000 |
| Revaluation reserve | 5,000 | *less:* Depreciation (2% p.a.) | 160 |
| Reserves | 5,000 | | 7,840 |
| | | Sundry assets | 6,160 |
| | 14,000 | | 14,000 |

Clearly, if the revaluation had not taken place, depreciation on the building would have been 2 per cent of £4,000,000 or £80,000, not £160,000, and the profit for the year would have been £1,080,000, not £1,000,000.

Applying the rule laid down in s. 39(5), the distributable profit is:

| | £ |
|---|---|
| Reserves (£4,000,000+£1,000,000) | 5,000,000 |
| Depreciation attributable to revaluation excess | 80,000 |
| | £5,080,000 |

(c) *Further restrictions placed on public companies (s. 40).* Section 40 allows a *public* company to make a distribution only to the extent that its net assets exceed its share capital plus "undistributable reserves".

"Undistributable reserves" are defined as:

(i) share premium account;

(ii) capital redemption reserve;

(iii) accumulated unrealised profits, less accumulated unrealised losses;

(iv) any other reserve which the company is prohibited from distributing by statute or by its memorandum or articles.

In most cases, the application of this formula will give exactly the same answer as that laid down for all companies in s. 39.

*Illustration (s. 40)*

The balance sheet of B Ltd is as follows:

| | £000 | | £000 |
|---|---|---|---|
| Share capital | 1,000 | Sundry assets | 1,100 |
| General reserve | 500 | Trade investments | |
| | | (market value 200) | 400 |
| | 1,500 | | 1,500 |

Under s. 39 the distributable profit is £500,000, but under s. 40 the distributable profit is:

| | £ |
|---|---|
| Sundry assets (allowing for unrealised loss on investments) | 1,300,000 |
| *less:* Share capital | 1,000,000 |
| S. 40 distributable profit | £300,000 |

(d) *Special provisions for investment companies and certain insurance companies (s. 41 and s. 42).* Sections 41 and 42 CA 1980 lay down special rules governing the distributable profits of investment companies and insurance companies conducting long-term business (e.g. life assurance). It is thought that these provisions lie outside the present syllabus.

## 1.13 Dividend payments

(a) *Introduction.* A company normally takes power in its articles to pay dividends, giving the directors power to pay interim dividends, and the company in general meeting power to pay final dividends. It is usual to give the members the right to reduce a final dividend recommended by the directors, but not to increase it.

To pay a dividend a company needs:

(i) power in its articles to do so;

(ii) available profit as defined in ss. 39–42 CA 1980, as applicable;

(iii) a clean audit report, or a statement from the auditors that any qualification is not material in determining available profit (s. 43).

In addition, as a practical consideration it needs:

(iv) the cash to pay it without impairing the company's ability to meet other necessary expenditure.

(b) *Interim dividends.* In considering whether to pay an interim dividend the directors need to consider the four basic points mentioned in (a) above and in addition:

(i) results shown by interim accounts;

(ii) projected results for remainder of year;

(iii) effects of any seasonal influences on the company's affairs;

(iv) the need to pursue a responsible dividend policy in the best long-term interests of the members generally.

(c) *Final dividends.* Before the amount of the final dividend is decided upon, the audited trading result for the year will be known, and points (i), (ii) and (iii) in (b) above will not be relevant. Point (iv), however, assumes even greater importance and the directors must also try to allow for the likely future trend of profits.

Although it is, of course, possible for a dividend to be paid when the company has made a loss for the year, this should only be done after careful consideration of the prospects for future recovery by the company.

## 2.0 PROVISIONS RELATING TO FORM AND CONTENT OF ACCOUNTS

### 2.1 Introduction

Part I of the Companies Act 1981 (ss. 1 to 21 and Scheds. 1 and 2) effected major changes into the form and content of company accounts, including the creation of standard formats for the profit and loss account and balance sheet. This part of the Act was the introduction into UK law of the EEC Fourth Directive.

It is necessary to consider these provisions in three stages:

(a) the manner in which they are introduced (2.2 below);

(b) the new rules relating to small and medium-sized companies (2.3 below);

(c) the detailed disclosure requirements and the standard formats (2.4 to 2.7 below).

These paragraphs also include the provisions of the other Companies Acts concerning disclosure in the balance sheet and profit and loss account, in so far as they remain in operation.

### 2.2 Manner of introducing the 1981 requirements

The manner in which the changes were made is rather unusual, and this section (2.2) needs careful study to ensure that you understand it before proceeding further.

Section 1 CA 1981 introduced a new s. 149 into CA 1948. The existing s. 149 was renumbered 149A. The new s. 149 introduced a new 8th Schedule into CA 1948, and the existing 8th Schedule was renumbered as Schedule 8A. It is this new 8th Schedule which contains most of the new accounting provisions. The text of the new 8th Schedule appeared as Schedule 1 to the 1981 Act.

Section 2 CA 1981 introduced a new s. 152 into CA 1948. The existing s. 152 was renumbered 152A.

The main purpose of the *original* s. 149 was to impose the *original* 8th Schedule, and the main purpose of the *original* s. 152 was to extend the requirements of the *original* 8th Schedule to group accounts.

The 1981 replacing sections had as their main purpose the imposition of the new requirements.

If that is the case you may well wonder why the original provisions were retained as ss. 149A and 152A and Sched. 8A. The reason is that they *remain in force* for banking, insurance and shipping companies, and for all companies until the new provisions apply as from the appointed day.

The new position may be summarised as follows:

<table>
<tr><th colspan="3">Banking, insurance and shipping companies, and all companies for accounts until the appointed day</th><th colspan="3">All companies except banking, insurance and shipping companies, for accounts after the appointed day</th></tr>
<tr><td colspan="3">Accounts must comply with:</td><td colspan="3">Accounts must comply with:</td></tr>
<tr><td>(a)</td><td>s. 149A</td><td rowspan="3">Original provisions of CA 1948</td><td>(a)</td><td>s. 149</td><td rowspan="3">Added to CA 1948 by CA 1981</td></tr>
<tr><td>(b)</td><td>s. 152A</td><td>(b)</td><td>s. 152</td></tr>
<tr><td>(c)</td><td>Sched. 8A</td><td>(c)</td><td>Sched. 8</td></tr>
<tr><td>(d)</td><td colspan="2">Most other accounting provisions of CA 1981.</td><td>(d)</td><td colspan="2">Other accounting provisions of CA 1981.</td></tr>
</table>

The other changes are mainly introduced in the orthodox manner by new sections or schedules, but note how certain extra sections are also added to CA 1967 concerning the directors' report (*see* 3.0 below).

## 2.3 Exemptions for certain small and medium-sized companies (ss. 5 to 10)

(a) *Companies entitled to the exemptions.* In accordance with the flexibility allowed in the Fourth Directive, accounts *lodged with the Registrar* for "small" or "medium-sized" companies need not disclose the full details required for other companies. Note that these exemptions do not relate to accounts sent to shareholders, only to those lodged with the Registrar and hence available for public inspection.

A company is "small" or "medium-sized" for this purpose if in the year under review *and the preceding year* it meets any two of the following three requirements (s. 8):

| | *Small* | *Medium-sized* |
|---|---|---|
| Turnover | Not over £1.4m. | Not over £5.75m. |
| Balance sheet total | Not over £0.7m. | Not over £2.8m. |
| Average number of employees | Not over 50 | Not over 250 |

As a result of the preceding year rule, a company has to meet the requirements for a category for two consecutive years before it changes to that category.

A holding company is only eligible to be treated as small or medium-sized if the aggregate figures for the group are within the limits (s. 9). If the holding company qualifies as small or medium-sized in this way the group accounts lodged with the Registrar may take advantage of the exemptions (s. 10).

Certain companies cannot qualify for the exemptions:

(i) public companies;

(ii) banking, insurance or shipping companies (remember that they remain subject to the old disclosure requirements and are entitled to the exemptions given to them by those requirements);

(iii) members of an "ineligible group". (A group is ineligible if any of its members is within categories (i) or (ii) above, or if the group includes a body corporate (other than a company) which may issue shares or debentures to the public or operate as a banking or insurance company.)

(b) *Exemptions for small companies (s. 6)*. The exemptions for small companies are pretty extensive—they need to submit to the Registrar:

(i) A modified balance sheet (consisting of total figures for headings with Roman numerals I, II, III, etc. in pro formas as in 2.5 below).

(ii) No profit and loss account.

(iii) Notes to the balance sheet on the following matters only:

accounting policies;

share capital;

allotments of shares;

analysis of creditors showing amount due if any repayable more than five years after the balance sheet date and indication as to whether secured;

analysis of debtors falling due after more than one year;

basis of translating foreign currency;

comparative figures.

(iv) No details of directors'/employees' remuneration under s. 196 CA 1948 and ss. 6, 7 and 8 CA 1967.

(v) No director's report.

(c) *Exemptions for medium-sized companies (s. 6).* The exemptions for medium-sized companies are rather modest:

(i) No turnover figure need be given.

(ii) Certain items in the profit and loss account can be merged:

| | | |
|---|---|---|
| in Format 1: | items 1, 2, 3, 6 | *see* 2.6 below |
| in Format 2: | items 1 to 5 | |
| in Format 3: | items A1, B1, B2 | |
| in Format 4: | items A1, A2, B1 to B4 | |

(d) *Further action by the directors (s. 7).* If the company takes advantage of the exemptions, the directors must state the fact on the face of the balance sheet immediately above their signatures.

(e) *Action by the auditors (s. 7).*

(i) The auditors must provide a report *to the directors* stating whether in their opinion the accounts qualify for the exemptions (s. 7(6)).

(ii) The auditors' report sent to the members remains in the existing form required by s. 14 CA 1967, but the modified accounts sent to the Registrar must be accompanied by a special auditors' report stating that in their opinion the exemption requirements are satisfied, and reproducing the full text of the report sent to members (s. 7(4) and (5)).

## 2.4 Detailed disclosure requirements of the new 8th Schedule and other sections of the Companies Acts 1948 to 1981

| | Statutory reference (references are to the new 8th Schedule unless otherwise stated) |
|---|---|
| ***(a) General requirements*** | |
| Section 149 CA 1948 (inserted by s. 1 CA 1981) provides that all accounts must give a true and fair view of the state of the company's affairs and of its profit or loss for the year. The accounts must also comply with the detailed disclosure requirements listed in (b) below, *subject to the overriding need to show a true and fair view*. Any departure from the detailed disclosure requirements for this reason must be explained by note. | s. 149 CA 1948 (inserted by s. 1 CA 1981) |
| It remains possible under the new s. 149 CA 1948 for a holding company to omit its own profit and loss account if it prepares a consolidated profit and loss account disclosing the amount of the consolidated profit or loss dealt with in the accounts of the holding company. (A note to the group accounts must state that this has been done.) | s. 149(5) and (6) CA 1948 |
| Group accounts should, where practicable, comply with the | paras. 61, 62 |

requirements of the Companies Acts as if they were actual companies, and should combine the information given in the separate accounts of group companies.

### *(b) Detailed disclosure requirements*

#### (I) STANDARD FORMATS

The 8th Schedule contains two alternative balance sheet formats and four alternative profit and loss account formats. A company must consistently adopt one of each of these for its accounts, subject to its rights to modify them if small or medium-sized. — paras. 1 and 2

These formats are reproduced in 2.5 and 2.6 below exactly as they appear in the Companies Act 1981.

#### (II) ITEMS NOT TO BE TREATED AS ASSETS

The following items are not to be treated as assets:

preliminary expenses; — para. 3(2)

expenses or commission on any issue of shares or debentures;

research expenditure (*see* (x)(1) below for development expenditure).

#### (III) MATERIALITY

If there is no item under a particular heading or subheading for the period under review or the previous period the heading is not to be shown. — para. 3(5)

If items for subheadings (Arabic numerals in the formats) are not material they may be merged with other items under the same main headings. — para. 3(4)

There is a general provision that no amount that is not material needs to be disclosed at all. — para. 85

#### (IV) PROFIT FIGURE

Every profit and loss account must show the profit or loss on ordinary activities before taxation. — para. 3(6)

#### (V) MOVEMENTS OF RESERVES

All movements of reserves must be disclosed. — para. 3(7)(a)

#### (VI) DIVIDENDS PAID AND PROPOSED

The aggregate amount of dividends paid and proposed must be disclosed. — para. 3(7)(b)

#### (VII) CORRESPONDING FIGURES

Corresponding figures for the previous period must be disclosed. If any adjustments to corresponding figures are made, details of the adjustments and the reasons for them must be disclosed. — para. 4

#### (VIII) SET-OFF OF ITEMS

Assets and liabilities may not be set off against each other, nor may items of income and expenditure. — para. 5

### (IX) ACCOUNTING PRINCIPLES

Accounting principles to be adopted by companies are laid down. These are broadly as SSAP 2 with one interesting addition.

Unless there are special features justifying departure from them, the following accounting principles are to be followed:

The company is to be presumed to be a going concern.

Accounting policies are to be consistently applied from one year to the next.

The concept of prudence is to be applied, and in particular only *realised* profits are to be included in the profit and loss account, and all liabilities and losses relating to the period under review of which the directors are aware *up to the date they signed the balance sheet* must be included (for this purpose the term "realised profit" is defined in para. 90 to mean realised profit according to generally accepted accounting principles). paras. 9 to 14

The accruals concept is to be applied.

In determining the aggregate amount of any item the amount of each individual asset or liability that falls to be taken into account is to be determined separately.

(This last requirement would seem to impose on directors and auditors a potentially onerous duty which would need to be interpreted flexibly in the light of materiality and practicality.)

### (X) HISTORICAL COST ACCOUNTING RULES

*Introductory note*

Detailed rules for valuing assets are laid down. The starting point is the "historical cost accounting rules", which require fixed assets generally to be valued at cost less depreciation and current assets at the lower of cost and net realisable value. The historical cost accounting rules are followed by the "alternative accounting rules", which allow assets to be revalued, or shown at their current cost. If the alternative accounting rules are followed, depreciation is to be taken on the revised figure rather than on original cost, but there are detailed provisions to ensure that particulars of historical cost, and of depreciation based on historical cost, remain available. Note that the alternative accounting rules do not relate solely to current cost accounts. They also cover asset revaluations incorporated into the historical cost accounts.

#### *The historical cost accounting rules in detail*

(1) *Fixed assets*

Fixed assets are to be included in accounts at cost. *Note:* This does not apply to goodwill arising on consolidation. para. 17 and para. 66

| | |
|---|---|
| Depreciation, based on purchase price or production cost less estimated residual value if any, is to be provided for on all assets with a limited useful economic life. (No method of depreciation is stated, but it must be provided for "systematically".) | para. 18 |
| If a fixed asset (including shares in related companies* treated as fixed assets) suffers a diminution in value expected to be permanent, that diminution of value should be provided for and disclosed in the profit and loss account or by note. *Note:* This does not apply to goodwill arising on consolidation. | para. 19(1) and (2) and para. 66 |
| If, after a provision for diminution in value has been made, the circumstances requiring it later cease to apply in whole or part, the provision may be written back to the extent that it is no longer necessary, with disclosure in the profit and loss account or by note. | para. 19(3) |
| If development costs are capitalised, the reason for capitalising them and the period over which they are to be written off must be stated. | para. 20 |
| Goodwill must be depreciated over its useful economic life and the period chosen for its life together with the reasons for choosing that period must be stated. *Note:* (This does not apply to goodwill arising on consolidation (para. 66).) | para. 21 and para. 66 |
| (2) *Current assets generally* | |
| Current assets are to be valued at cost or net realisable value if lower. | paras. 22 and 23 |
| (3) *Treatment when an amount due to be repaid on a debt exceeds the value received* | |
| The excess to be repaid may be treated as an asset and must be completely written off before the date of repayment of the debt, with disclosure of the current balance in the accounts or by note. | para. 24 |
| (4) *Assets included at a fixed amount* | |
| Tangible fixed assets, raw materials or consumable items may be included at a fixed amount if the value is not material and not subject to material variation. | para. 25 |
| (5) *Determining purchase price or production cost* | |
| Purchase price means actual price paid plus incidental costs of acquisition. | |
| Production cost is permitted to include: | |
| raw materials and consumables; | |
| other direct costs attributable to the item; | para. 26 |

*A related company is defined in para. 91 as one in which 20 per cent or more of the equity share capital is held on a long-term basis and with a view to influencing its activities. Subsidiaries are excluded from the definition.

a reasonable proportion of indirect costs, excluding distribution costs;

interest on capital borrowed to finance production.

(If interest is included as above, the amount of it so included must be shown by note.)

(6) *Stock*
In valuing stock the general principles outlined in (5) above must be observed but the following methods of arriving at stock value are acceptable:

unit cost (actual cost of actual items); para. 27

first in first out (FIFO);

last in first out (LIFO);

weighted average price;

any other method similar to the above.

(7) *Investments* (and other assets made up of fungible* units)
The methods outlined in (6) above may be used for these also. para. 27

If the figure arrived at by applying the methods listed in (6) above differs to a material extent from replacement cost the difference must be disclosed by note.

(8) *Difficulty in arriving at original purchase price or production cost*
If the original purchase price or production cost of an asset cannot be obtained without unreasonable expense or delay, the earliest available record of value may be taken instead. para. 28

(XI) ALTERNATIVE ACCOUNTING RULES
*Introductory note*
Refer back to the introductory note at the beginning of item (x) above before continuing.

*The alternative accounting rules in detail*

(1) Intangible fixed assets other than goodwill may be valued at current cost (*see also* (6) to (8) below). para. 31

(2) Tangible fixed assets may be included at a valuation or at current cost (*see also* (6) to (8) below). para. 31

(3) Any investments held as fixed assets may be included at market value at the date of their last valuation or at directors' valuation. If the directors' valuation is used the para. 31

*"Fungible" means that individual items comprising an asset are identical and interchangeable. Examples of fungible assets are shares or a stock of identical components.

method of valuation and the reasons for adopting it must be disclosed (*see also* (6) to (8) below).

(4) Investments of any kind held as current assets may be valued at current cost (*see also* (6) to (8) below). para. 31

(5) Stocks may be included at current cost (*see also* (6) and (8) below). para. 31

(6) In all cases (1) to (5) above the basis of valuation must be disclosed by note and for all balance sheet items other than stocks the comparable amounts according to the historical cost accounting rules must be disclosed (including what depreciation based on historical cost would have been). para. 33

*Note:*
If these alternative accounting rules are followed two problems are created:

> How are surpluses and deficits arising on revaluation to be accounted for?
>
> How is depreciation to be dealt with?

The alternative accounting rules provide answers to these two problems as indicated in (7) and (8) below.

(7) *Depreciation*
Depreciation, where necessary, will normally be provided for on the value as determined under the alternative accounting rules, but para. 32 allows depreciation based on *historical cost* to be charged in the profit and loss account, provided the additional depreciation based on the revalued amount is disclosed separately in the profit and loss account or by note. para. 32

(8) *Revaluation adjustments*
Any surplus or deficit on revaluations must be credited or debited to a separate reserve described as "revaluation reserve". The revaluation reserve must appear separately in the balance sheet as indicated in the two formats (item K III of Format 1 or item A III of the liabilities in Format 2). para. 34

The directors may at their discretion transfer amounts out of the revaluation reserve if they consider that the amount standing to the credit of the reserve is no longer necessary for the purpose of the company's accounting policies.

An amount may only be transferred from the revaluation reserve to the credit of profit and loss account if it represents realised profit or if the amount in question was previously charged to profit and loss account.

### (XII) ITEMS TO BE DISCLOSED BY NOTE TO THE ACCOUNTS

*Introductory note*

A large number of matters are required to be disclosed by note to the accounts. The detailed provisions are reproduced below as they are in the Schedule. References in the text to paragraphs are to the paragraphs in the Schedule. These may be found in the right-hand margin of para. 2.4 throughout.

### *Accounting policies*

(1) *Disclosure of accounting policies*

The accounting policies adopted by the company in determining the amounts to be included in respect of items shown in the balance sheet and in determining the profit or loss of the company shall be stated (including such policies with respect to the depreciation and diminution in value of assets). para. 36

### *Information supplementing the balance sheet*

(2) *Share capital authorised and issued*

(A) The following information shall be given with respect to the company's share capital:

(a) the authorised share capital; and

(b) where shares of more than one class have been allotted, the number and aggregate nominal value of shares of each class allotted. para. 38

(B) In the case of any part of the allotted share capital that consists of redeemable shares, the following information shall be given:

(a) the earliest and latest dates on which the company has power to redeem those shares;

(b) whether those shares must be redeemed in any event or are liable to be redeemed at the option of the company; and

(c) whether any (and, if so, what) premium is payable on redemption.

(3) *Allotment of shares during the year*

If the company has allotted any shares during the financial year, the following information shall be given:

(A) the reason for making the allotment;

(B) the classes of shares allotted; and para. 39

(C) as respects each class of shares, the number allotted, their aggregate nominal value, and the consideration received by the company for the allotment.

(4) *Contingent rights to allotment*

(A) With respect to any contingent right to the allotment of shares in the company the following particulars shall be given:

(a) the number, description and amount of the shares in relation to which the right is exercisable;

(b) the period during which it is exercisable; and para. 40

(c) the price to be paid for the shares allotted.

(B) In sub-paragraph (A) above, "contingent right to the allotment of shares" means any option to subscribe for shares and any other right to require the allotment of shares to any person whether arising on the conversion into shares or securities of any other description or otherwise.

(5) *Issue of debentures during the year*

(A) If the company has issued any debentures during the financial year to which the accounts relate, the following information shall be given:

(a) the reason for making the issue;

(b) the classes of debentures issued; and

(c) as respects each class of debentures, the amount issued and the consideration received by the company for the issue.

(B) Particulars of any redeemed debentures which the company has power to reissue shall also be given. para. 41

(C) Where any of the company's debentures are held by a nominee of or trustee for the company, the nominal amount of the debentures and the amount at which they are stated in the accounting records kept by the company in accordance with s. 12 Companies Act 1976 shall be stated.

(6) *Fixed assets*

(A) In respect of each item shown under the general item "fixed assets" in the company's balance sheet the following information shall be given: para. 42

(a) the appropriate amounts in respect of that item as at the date of the beginning of the financial year and as at the balance sheet date respectively;

(b) the effect on any amount shown in the balance sheet in respect of that item of:

(i) any revision of the amount in respect of any assets

included under that item made during that year on any basis mentioned in paragraph 31 above;

(ii) acquisitions during that year of any assets;

(iii) disposals during that year of any assets; and

(iv) any transfers of assets of the company to and from that item during that year.

(B) The reference in sub-paragraph (A)(a) above to the appropriate amounts in respect of any item as at any date there mentioned is a reference to amounts representing the aggregate amounts determined, as at that date, in respect of assets falling to be included under that item either:

(a) on the basis of purchase price or production cost (determined in accordance with paragraphs 26 and 27 above); or

(b) on any basis mentioned in paragraph 31 above; (leaving out of account in either case any provision for depreciation or diminution in value).

(C) In respect of each item with sub-paragraph (A) above the following should be stated:

(a) the cumulative amount of provisions for depreciation or diminution in value of assets included under that item as at each date mentioned in sub-paragraph (A)(a);

(b) the amount of any such provisions made in respect of the financial year;

(c) the amount of any adjustments made in respect of any such provisions during that year in consequence of the disposal of any assets; and

(d) the amount of any other adjustments made in respect of any such provisions during that year.

(D) Where any fixed assets of the company (other than listed investments) are included under any item shown in the company's balance sheet at an amount determined on any basis mentioned in paragraph 31 above, the following information shall be given: para. 43

(a) the years (so far as they are known to the directors) in which the assets were severally valued and the several values; and

(b) in the case of assets that have been valued during the financial year, the names of the persons who valued them or particulars of their qualifications for doing so and (whichever is stated) the bases of valuation used by them.

(E) In relation to any amount which is or would but for paragraph 3(4)(b) above be shown in respect of the item "land and buildings" in the company's balance sheet there shall be stated:

(a) how much of that amount is ascribable to land of freehold tenure and how much to land of leasehold tenure; and

(b) how much of the amount ascribable to land of leasehold tenure is ascribable to land held on long lease and how much to land held on short lease.

(7) *Investments*

(A) In respect of the amount of each item which is or would but for paragraph 3(4)(b) above be shown in the company's balance sheet under the general item "investments" (whether as fixed assets or as current assets) there shall be stated: para. 45

(a) how much of that amount is ascribable to listed investments; and

(b) how much of any amount so ascribable is ascribable to investments as respects which there has been granted a listing on a recognised stock exchange and how much to other listed investments.

(B) Where the amount of any listed investments is stated for any item in accordance with sub-paragraph (A)(a) above, the following amounts shall also be stated:

(a) the aggregate market value of those investments where it differs from the amount so stated; and

(b) both the market value and the stock exchange value of any investments of which the former value is, for the purposes of the accounts, taken as being higher than the latter.

(8) *Reserves and provisions*

(A) Where any amount is transferred: para. 46

(a) to or from any reserves; or

(b) to any provisions for liabilities and charges; or

(c) from any provision for liabilities and charges otherwise than for the purpose for which the provision was established;

and the reserves or provisions are or would but for paragraph 3(4)(b) above be shown as separate items in the company's balance sheet, the information mentioned in sub-paragraph (B) below shall be given in respect of the aggregate of reserves or provisions included in the same item.

(B) That information is:

(a) the amount of the reserves or provisions as at the date of the beginning of the financial year and as at the balance sheet date respectively;

(b) any amounts transferred to or from the reserves or provisions during that year; and

(c) the source and application respectively of any amounts so transferred.

(C) Particulars shall be given of each provision included in the item "other provisions" in the company's balance sheet in any case where the amount of that provision is material.

(9) *Provision for taxation*
The amount of any provision for taxation other than deferred taxation shall be stated. para. 47

(10) *Details of indebtedness*

(A) In respect of each item shown under "creditors" in the company's balance sheet there shall be stated: para. 48

(a) the aggregate amount of any debts included under that item which are payable or repayable otherwise than by instalments and fall due for payment or repayment after the end of the period of five years beginning with the day next following the end of the financial year; and

(b) the aggregate amount of any debts so included which are payable or repayable by instalments any of which fall due for payment after the end of that period;

and in the case of debts within paragraph (b) above the aggregate amount of instalments falling due after the end of that period shall also be disclosed for each such item.

(B) Subject to sub-paragraph (C) below, in relation to each debt falling to be taken into account under sub-paragraph (A) above, the terms of payment or repayment and the rate of any interest payable on the debt shall be stated.

(C) If the number of debts is such that, in the opinion of the directors, compliance with sub-paragraph (B) above would result in a statement of excessive length, it shall be sufficient to give a general indication of the terms of payment or repayment and the rates of any interest payable on the debts.

(D) In respect of each item shown under "creditors" in the company's balance sheet there shall be stated:

(a) the aggregate amount of any debts included under that item in respect of which any security has been given; and

(b) an indication of the nature of the securities so given.

(E) Reference above in this paragraph to an item shown under "creditors" in the company's balance sheet include references where amounts falling due to creditors within one year and after more than one year are distinguished in the balance sheet:

(a) in a case within sub-paragraph (A) above, to an item shown under the latter of those categories; and

(b) in a case within sub-paragraph (D) above, to an item shown under either of those categories;

and references to items shown under "creditors" include references to items which would but for paragraph 3(4)(b) above be shown under that heading.

(11) *Arrears of cumulative dividends*

If any fixed cumulative dividends on the company's shares are in arrear, there shall be stated: para. 49

(a) the amount of the arrears; and

(b) the period for which the dividends or, if there is more than one class, each class of them are in arrear.

(12) *Guarantees and other financial commitments*

(A) Particulars shall be given of any charge on the assets of the company to secure the liabilities of any other person, including, where practicable, the amount secured. para. 50

(B) The following information shall be given with respect to any other contingent liability not provided for:

(a) the amount or estimated amount of that liability;

(b) its legal nature; and

(c) whether any valuable security has been provided by the company in connection with that liability and if so, what.

(C) There shall be stated, where practicable:

(a) the aggregate amount or estimated amount of contracts for capital expenditure, so far as not provided for; and

(b) the aggregate amount or estimated amount of capital expenditure authorised by the directors which has not been contracted for.

(D) Particulars shall be given of:

(a) any pension commitments included under any provision shown in the company's balance sheet; and

(b) any such commitments for which no provision has been made;

and where any such commitment relates wholly or partly to pensions payable to past directors of the company separate particulars shall be given of that commitment so far as it relates to such pensions.

(E) Particulars shall also be given of any other financial commitments which:

(a) have not been provided for; and

(b) are relevant to assessing the company's state of affairs.

(F) Commitments within any of the preceding sub-paragraphs undertaken on behalf of or for the benefit of:

(a) any holding company or fellow subsidiary of the company; or

(b) any subsidiary of the company;

shall be stated separately from the other commitments within that sub-paragraph (and commitments within paragraph (a) above shall also be stated separately from those within paragraph (b) above).

(13) *Use of earliest value of asset rather than actual purchase price or production cost*
Particulars shall be given of any case where the purchase price or production cost of any asset is for the first time determined under paragraph 28 above. para. 51(1)

(14) *Loans to permit the acquisition of shares in the company*
Where any outstanding loans made under the authority of s. 42(6)(b) or (c) or 43 Companies Act 1981 are included under any item shown in the company's balance sheet, the aggregate amount of those loans shall be disclosed for each item in question. para. 51(2)

(15) *Proposed dividend*
The aggregate amount which is recommended for distribution by way of dividend shall be stated. para. 51(3)

***Information supplementing the profit and loss account***

(16) *Separate statement of certain items of income and expenditure*

(A) Subject to the following provisions of this paragraph, each of the amounts mentioned below shall be stated. para. 53

(B) The amount of the interest on or any similar charges in respect of:

(a) bank loans and overdrafts, and loans made to the company (other than bank loans and overdrafts) which:

(i) are repayable otherwise than by instalments and fall due for repayment before the end of the period of five years beginning with the day next following the end of the financial year; or

(ii) are repayable by instalments the last of which falls due for payment before the end of that period; and

(b) loans of any other kind made to the company.

This sub-paragraph does not apply to interest or charges on loans to the company from group companies, but, with that exception, it applies to interest or charges on all loans, whether made on the security of debentures or not.

(C) The amounts respectively set aside for redemption of share capital and for redemption of loans.

(D) The amount of income from listed investments.

(E) The amount of rents from land (after deduction of ground rents, rates and other outgoings).

This amount need only be stated if a substantial part of the company's revenue for the financial year consists of rents from land.

(F) The amount charged to revenue in respect of sums payable in respect of the hire of plant and machinery.

(G) The amount of the remuneration of the auditors (taking "remuneration", for the purposes of this sub-paragraph, as including any sums paid by the company in respect of the auditors' expenses).

(17) *Particulars of tax*

(A) The basis on which the charge for United Kingdom corporation tax and United Kingdom income tax is computed shall be stated. para. 54

(B) Particulars shall be given of any special circumstances

which affect liability in respect of taxation of profits, income or capital gains for the financial year or liability in respect of taxation of profits, income or capital gains for succeeding financial years.

(C) The following amounts shall be stated:

(a) the amount of the charge for United Kingdom corporation tax;

(b) if that amount would have been greater but for relief from double taxation, the amount which it would have been but for such relief;

(c) the amount of the charge for United Kingdom income tax; and

(d) the amount of the charge for taxation imposed outside the United Kingdom of profits, income and (so far as charged to revenue) capital gains.

These amounts shall be stated separately in respect of each of the amounts which is or would but for paragraph 3(4)(b) above be shown under the following items in the profit and loss account, that is to say "tax on profit or loss on ordinary activities" and "tax on extraordinary profit or loss".

(18) *Particulars of turnover*

(A) If in the course of the financial year the company has carried on business of two or more classes that, in the opinion of the directors, differ substantially from each other, there shall be stated in respect of each class (describing it): para. 55

(a) the amount of the turnover attributable to that class; and

(b) the amount of the profit or loss of the company before taxation which is in the opinion of the directors attributable to that class.

(B) If in the course of the financial year the company has supplied markets that, in the opinion of the directors, differ substantially from each other, the amount of the turnover attributable to each such market shall also be stated.

In this paragraph "market" means a market delimited by geographical bounds.

(C) In analysing for the purposes of this paragraph the source (in terms of business or in terms of market) of turnover or (as the case may be) of profit or loss, the directors of the company shall have regard to the manner in which the company's activities are organised.

(D) For the purposes of this paragraph:

(a) classes of business which, in the opinion of the directors, do not differ substantially from each other shall be treated as one class, and

(b) markets which, in the opinion of the directors, do not differ substantially from each other shall be treated as one market;

and any amounts properly attributable to one class of business or (as the case may be) to one market which are not material may be included in the amount stated in respect of another.

(E) Where in the opinion of the directors the disclosure of any information required by this paragraph would be seriously prejudicial to the interests of the company, that information need not be disclosed, but the fact that any such information has not been disclosed must be stated.

(19) *Particulars of staff*

(A) The following information shall be given with respect to the employees of the company: para. 56

(a) the average number of persons employed by the company in the financial year; and

(b) the average number of persons so employed within each category of persons employed by the company.

(B) The average number required by sub-paragraph (A)(a) or (b) above shall be determined by dividing the relevant annual number by the number of weeks in the financial year.

(C) The relevant annual number shall be determined by ascertaining for each week in the financial year:

(a) for the purposes of sub-paragraph (A)(a) above, the number of persons employed under contracts of service by the company in that week (whether throughout the week or not);

(b) for the purposes of sub-paragraph (A)(b) above, the number of persons in the category in question of persons so employed;

and, in either case, adding together all the weekly numbers.

(D) In respect of all persons employed by the company during the financial year who are taken into account in determining the relevant annual number for the purposes of sub-paragraph (A)(a) above there shall also be stated the aggregate amounts respectively of:

(a) wages and salaries paid or payable in respect of that year to those persons;

(b) social security costs incurred by the company on their behalf; and

(c) other pension costs so incurred;

save in so far as those amounts or any of them are stated in the profit and loss account.

(E) The categories of persons employed by the company by reference to which the number required to be disclosed by sub-paragraph (A)(b) above is to be determined shall be such as the directors may select, having regard to the manner in which the company's activities are organised.

(20) *Prior year items and extraordinary or exceptional items*

(A) Where any amount relating to any preceding financial year is included in any item in the profit and loss account, the effect shall be stated. para. 57

(B) Particulars shall be given of any extraordinary income or charges arising in the financial year.

(C) The effect shall be stated of any transactions that are exceptional by virtue of size or incidence though they fall within the ordinary activities of the company.

### General matters

(21) *Translation of foreign currency amounts*
Where sums originally denominated in foreign currencies have been brought into account under any items shown in the balance sheet or profit and loss account, the basis on which those sums have been translated into sterling shall be stated. para. 58(1)

(22) *Provision for comparative figures for matters dealt with by note*
Subject to the exceptions listed below, for every item stated in a note to the accounts the corresponding amount for the previous year is also to be given. If the corresponding amount is not comparable, it must be adjusted and details of the adjustment and the reasons for it given. para. 58(2)

The only items required to be stated by note for which comparative figures are not required are:

(a) details of shareholdings in subsidiaries and other companies as required by ss. 3 and 4 CA 1967;

(b) particulars of loans to and contracts with directors and others under ss. 54 and 56 CA 1980;

(c) movements of fixed assets;

(d) movements of reserves and provisions.

### *Further disclosure required by provisions of Companies Acts 1948 to 1980 not superseded by CA 1981*

(23) *Details of directors' and employees' remuneration*

Directors' emoluments—show aggregate emoluments under the following headings: s. 196 CA 1948

fees ss. 6 to 8 CA 1967

salaries (including benefits in kind)

pensions to former directors and their dependants

compensation for loss of office.

In addition, if total fees and salaries (excluding pension contributions) exceed £40,000 *or* the company is a member of a group, also show:

chairman's emoluments (excluding pension contribution)

highest paid director's emoluments (if paid more than the chairman) (excluding pension contribution)

*number* of directors in each "£5,000 band" of remuneration paid by the company (excluding pension contribution)

*number* of directors waiving remuneration and *amount* of emoluments waived

(may be given in a statement annexed to the accounts).

*Employees* paid more than £20,000—show number whose emoluments (excluding pension contributions) fall in each "£5,000 band"

(may be given in a statement annexed to the accounts).

(24) *Contracts and loans involving directors*

Full details of substantial contracts with directors and persons connected with them are required. For each loan or agreement the accounts must disclose: ss. 54 and 55 CA 1980

name of director or other person concerned

amount of loan at beginning and end of period including interest maximum loan during period

amount of interest due but not paid

amount of any provision against failure of the borrower to repay

amount of any guarantee or security

details of any agreement to enter into a loan or similar transaction.

(25) *Loans to officers other than directors*
The aggregate amount of loans etc. outstanding at the end of the period must be disclosed plus the number of officers concerned. s. 56 CA 1980

(26) *Name of ultimate holding company*
A subsidiary must state the name and country of incorporation of its ultimate holding company, unless it has overseas business and obtains Department of Trade and Industry agreement that to disclose the name would harm the interests of a group company. s. 5 CA 1967

(27) *Details of companies in which substantial shareholdings are held*
If a company has:

(a) subsidiaries

(b) investment in non-subsidiaries exceeding:

10 per cent of that company's equity capital

10 per cent of that company's total allotted capital

10 per cent of the investing company's total assets,

ss. 3 and 4 CA 1967 as amended by s. 4 CA 1981

it must disclose:

name

country of incorporation

number and type of shares held

proportion of each class of capital held

Department of Trade and Industry may authorise non-disclosure as in (26) above.

If the company's holding of the allotted share capital of the other company exceeds 20 per cent, it must also disclose, if material, the capital, reserves and results of that company as shown in its latest published accounts. (This information is *not* required for a consolidated subsidiary or for an associated company included in the group accounts using the equity basis of valuation.) s. 4 CA 1981

### *Provisions regarding group accounts—holding company's own accounts*

(*See also* 2.4(a) and 2.4(b) (xii) (27) above, also Chapter 7.)

(28) For any relevant balance sheet item, a note must disclose separately:

the amount attributable to dealings with or interests in any holding company or fellow subsidiary — para. 59

the amount attributable to dealings with or interests in any subsidiary.

(29) Number, description and amount of shares or debentures in the company beneficially held *by* subsidiaries must be disclosed. — para. 60

(30) *Non-consolidation*
If a holding company does not prepare group accounts, or omits one or more subsidiaries from consolidation, it must show by note:

the reason for non-consolidation;

a statement of any qualifications in the auditors' report of any subsidiary not consolidated which are material for the group, if not referred to in the holding company's accounts; — para. 69

if the holding company is a wholly owned subsidiary of another UK company, the directors' opinion as to the value of the subsidiary as shown in the balance sheet;

if the holding company is *not* a wholly owned subsidiary of another UK company, the aggregate value on the equity basis of the unconsolidated subsidiaries.

The Department of Trade and Industry may grant exemption from para. 69.

(31) *Non-coterminous financial years*
If any subsidiaries have financial years differing from that of the holding company the notes must state:

the reasons — para. 70

the actual dates of the subsidiaries' financial years (or the earliest and latest dates).

### *Provisions regarding group accounts—consolidated accounts*

(*See also* 2.4(a) and 2.4(b) (xii) 27 to 30 above.)

(32) *Information not required*
The information about directors' and employees' remuneration, directors' and officers' transactions, and shares in — para. 63

*non*-subsidiaries, as listed in paras. (23), (24), (25) and (27) above, is *not* required on a group basis but need be given for the holding company only.

## 2.5 Standard formats for the balance sheet

As indicated in 2.1 above, the CA 1981 introduces standard formats for the balance sheet and profit and loss account.

There are two almost identical formats for the balance sheet. The only difference between them is the treatment of creditors. In Format 1, creditors falling due within one year are shown as a deduction from current assets, while in Format 2 assets appear "gross" and all creditors are shown with share capital and reserves. Note 13 requires the split between long-term and short-term creditors to be shown by note to the balance sheet.

*Balance Sheet Format 1*

A. Called-up share capital not paid (1)

B. Fixed assets:

I Intangible assets:

1. Development costs
2. Concessions, patents, licences, trade marks and similar rights and assets (2)
3. Goodwill (3)
4. Payments on account

II Tangible assets:

1. Land and buildings
2. Plant and machinery
3. Fixtures, fittings, tools and equipment
4. Payments on account and assets in course of construction

III Investments:

1. Shares in group companies
2. Loans to group companies
3. Shares in related companies
4. Loans to related companies
5. Other investments other than loans
6. Other loans
7. Own shares (4)

C. Current assets:

I Stocks:

1. Raw materials and consumables
2. Work in progress

3. Finished goods and goods for resale
4. Payments on account

II Debtors (5):

1. Trade debtors
2. Amounts owed by group companies
3. Amounts owed by related companies
4. Other debtors
5. Called-up share capital not paid (1)
6. Prepayments and accrued income (6)

III Investments:

1. Shares in group companies
2. Own shares (4)
3. Other investments

IV Cash at bank and in hand

D. Prepayments and accrued income (6)

E. Creditors: amounts falling due within one year:

1. Debenture loans (7)
2. Bank loans and overdrafts
3. Payments received on account (8)
4. Trade creditors
5. Bills of exchange payable
6. Amounts owed to group companies
7. Amounts owed to related companies
8. Other creditors including taxation and social security (9)
9. Accruals and deferred income (10)

F. Net current assets (liabilities) (11)

G. Total assets less current liabilities

H. Creditors: amounts falling due after more than one year:

1. Debenture loans (7)
2. Bank loans and overdrafts
3. Payments received on account (8)
4. Trade creditors
5. Bills of exchange payable
6. Amounts owed to group companies
7. Amounts owed to related companies
8. Other creditors including taxation and social security (9)
9. Accruals and deferred income (10)

I. Provisions for liabilities and charges:

1. Pensions and similar obligations
2. Taxation, including deferred taxation
3. Other provisions

J. Accruals and deferred income (10)

K. Capital and reserves:

- I Called-up share capital (12)
- II Share premium account
- III Revaluation reserve
- IV Other reserves:
  1. Capital redemption reserve
  2. Reserve for own shares
  3. Reserves provided for by the articles of association
  4. Other reserves
- V Profit and loss account

### *Balance Sheet Format 2*

*Assets*

A. Called-up share capital not paid (1)

B. Fixed assets:

- I Intangible assets:
  1. Development costs
  2. Concessions, patents, licences, trade marks and similar rights and assets (2)
  3. Goodwill (3)
  4. Payments on account
- II Tangible assets:
  1. Land and buildings
  2. Plant and machinery
  3. Fixtures, fittings, tools and equipment
  4. Payments on account and assets in course of construction
- III Investments:
  1. Shares in group companies
  2. Loans to group companies
  3. Shares in related companies
  4. Loans to related companies
  5. Other investments other than loans
  6. Other loans
  7. Own shares (4)

C. Current assets:

I Stocks:

1. Raw materials and consumables
2. Work in progress
3. Finished goods and goods for resale
4. Payments on account

II Debtors (5):

1. Trade debtors
2. Amounts owed by group companies
3. Amounts owed by related companies
4. Other debtors
5. Called-up share capital not paid (1)
6. Prepayments and accrued income (6)

III Investments:

1. Shares in group companies
2. Own shares (4)
3. Other investments

IV Cash at bank and in hand

D. Prepayments and accrued income (6)

*Liabilities*

A. Capital and reserves:

I Called-up share capital (12)

II Share premium account

III Revaluation reserve

IV Other reserves:

1. Capital redemption reserve
2. Reserve for own shares
3. Reserves provided for by the articles of association
4. Other reserves

V Profit and loss account

B. Provisions for liabilities and charges:

1. Pensions and similar obligations
2. Taxation including deferred taxation
3. Other provisions

C. Creditors (13):

1. Debenture loans (7)
2. Bank loans and overdrafts

3. Payments received on account (8)
4. Trade creditors
5. Bills of exchange payable
6. Amounts owed to group companies
7. Amounts owed to related companies
8. Other creditors including taxation and social security (9)
9. Accruals and deferred income (10)

D. Accruals and deferred income (10)

### *Notes on the balance sheet formats*

(1) *Called-up share capital not paid*
(Formats 1 and 2, items A and C II 5.)
This item may be shown in either of the two positions given in Formats 1 and 2.

(2) *Concessions, patents, licences, trade marks and similar rights and assets*
(Formats 1 and 2, item B I 2)
Amounts in respect of assets shall only be included in a company's balance sheet under this item if either:
(a) the assets were acquired for valuable consideration and are not required to be shown under goodwill; or
(b) the assets in question were created by the company itself.

(3) *Goodwill*
(Formats 1 and 2, item B I 3)
Amounts representing goodwill shall only be included to the extent that the goodwill was acquired for valuable consideration.

(4) *Own shares*
(Formats 1 and 2, items B III 7 and C III 2)
The nominal value of the shares held shall be shown separately.

(5) *Debtors*
(Formats 1 and 2, items C II 1 to 6)
The amount falling due after more than one year shall be shown separately for each item included under debtors.

(6) *Prepayments and accrued income*
(Formats 1 and 2, items C II 6 and D)
This item may be shown in either of the two positions given in Formats 1 and 2.

(7) *Debenture loans*
(Format 1, items E 1 and H 1 and Format 2, item C 1)
The amount of any convertible loans shall be shown separately.

(8) *Payments received on account*
(Format 1, items E 3 and H 3 and Format 2, item C 3)
Payments received on account of orders shall be shown for each of these items in so far as they are not shown as deductions from stocks.

(9) *Other creditors including taxation and social security*
(Format 1, items E 8 and H 8 and Format 2, item C 8
The amount for creditors in respect of taxation and social security shall be shown separately from the amount for other creditors.

(10) *Accruals and deferred income*
(Format 1, items E 9, H 9 and J and Format 2, items C 9 and D)
The two positions given for this item in Format 1 at E 9 and H 9 are an alternative to the position at J, but if the item is not shown in a position corresponding to that at J it may be shown in either or both of the other two positions (as the case may require).
The two positions given for this item in Format 2 are alternatives.

(11) *Net current assets (liabilities)*
(Format 1, item F)
In determining the amount to be shown for this item any amounts shown under "prepayments and accrued income" shall be taken into account wherever shown.

(12) *Called-up share capital*
(Format 1, item K I and Format 2, item A I)
The amount of allotted share capital and the amount of called-up share capital which has been paid up shall be shown separately.

(13) *Creditors*
(Format 2, items C 1 to 9)
Amounts falling due within one year and after one year shall be shown separately for each of these items and their aggregate shall be shown separately for all of these items.

## 2.6 The standard formats for the profit and loss account

For the profit and loss account there is a choice of four formats—two "vertical" (Formats 1 and 2) and two "horizontal" (Formats 3 and 4).

Format 1 most closely resembles the profit and loss account presented by most UK companies before the CA 1981—in fact there is very little difference apart from the disclosure of more information about the expenditure.

Format 2 classifies expenditure by type rather than operational function. For example, staff costs are shown as a heading in Format 2 whereas in Format 1 they are included where appropriate in cost of sales, distribution costs, and administrative expenses.

Formats 3 and 4 are merely the horizontal equivalents of Formats 1 and 2.

***Profit and Loss Account Format 1*** (*see* note (17) below)

1. Turnover
2. Cost of sales (14)
3. Gross profit or loss
4. Distribution costs (14)
5. Administrative expenses (14)

6. Other operating income
7. Income from shares in group companies
8. Income from shares in related companies
9. Income from other fixed-asset investments (15)
10. Other interest receivable and similar income (15)
11. Amounts written off investments
12. Interest payable and similar charges (16)
13. Tax on profit or loss on ordinary activities
14. Profit or loss on ordinary activities after taxation
15. Extraordinary income
16. Extraordinary charges
17. Extraordinary profit or loss
18. Tax on extraordinary profit or loss
19. Other taxes not shown under the above items
20. Profit or loss for the financial year

*Profit and Loss Account Format 2*

1. Turnover
2. Change in stocks of finished goods and in work in progress
3. Own work capitalised
4. Other operating income
5. (a) Raw materials and consumables
   (b) Other external charges
6. Staff costs:
   (a) wages and salaries
   (b) social security costs
   (c) other pension costs
7. (a) Depreciation and other amounts written off tangible and intangible fixed assets
   (b) Exceptional amounts written off current assets
8. Other operating charges
9. Income from shares in group companies
10. Income from shares in related companies
11. Income from other fixed-asset investments (15)
12. Other interest receivable and similar income (15)
13. Amounts written off investments
14. Interest payable and similar charges (16)
15. Tax on profit or loss on ordinary activities
16. Profit or loss on ordinary activities after taxation
17. Extraordinary income
18. Extraordinary charges
19. Extraordinary profit or loss
20. Tax on extraordinary profit or loss
21. Other taxes not shown under the above items
22. Profit or loss for the financial year

### *Profit and Loss Account Format 3* (*see* note (17) below)

*A. Charges*

1. Cost of sales (14)
2. Distribution costs (14)
3. Administrative expenses (14)
4. Amounts written off investments
5. Interest payable and similar charges (16)
6. Tax on profit or loss on ordinary activities
7. Profit or loss on ordinary activities after taxation
8. Extraordinary charges
9. Tax on extraordinary profit or loss
10. Other taxes not shown under the above items
11. Profit or loss for the financial year

*B. Income*

1. Turnover
2. Other operating income
3. Income from shares in group companies
4. Income from shares in related companies
5. Income from other fixed-asset investments (15)
6. Other interest receivable and similar income (15)
7. Profit or loss on ordinary activities after taxation
8. Extraordinary income
9. Profit or loss for the financial year

### *Profit and Loss Account Format 4*

*A. Charges*

1. Reduction in stocks of finished goods and in work in progress
2. (a) Raw materials and consumables
   (b) Other external charges
3. Staff costs:
   (a) wages and salaries
   (b) social security costs
   (c) other pension costs
4. (a) Depreciation and other amounts written off tangible and intangible fixed assets
   (b) Exceptional amounts written off current assets
5. Other operating charges
6. Amounts written off investments
7. Interest payable and similar charges (16)
8. Tax on profit or loss on ordinary activities
9. Profit or loss on ordinary activities after taxation
10. Extraordinary charges
11. Tax on extraordinary profit or loss
12. Other taxes not shown under the above items
13. Profit or loss for the financial year

*B. Income*

1. Turnover
2. Increase in stocks of finished goods and in work in progress
3. Own work capitalised
4. Other operating income
5. Income from shares in group companies
6. Income from shares in related companies
7. Income from other fixed-asset investments (15)
8. Other interest receivable and similar income (15)
9. Profit or loss on ordinary activities after taxation
10. Extraordinary income
11. Profit or loss for the financial year

### Notes on the profit and loss account formats

(14) *Cost of sales; distribution costs; administrative expenses*
(Format 1, items 2, 4 and 5; Format 3, items A 1, 2 and 3)
These items shall be stated after taking into account any necessary provisions for depreciation or diminution in value of assets.

(15) *Income from other fixed-asset investments; other interest receivable and similar income*
(Format 1, items 9 and 10; Format 2, items 11 and 12; Format 3, items B 5 and 6; Format 4, items B 7 and 8)
Income and interest derived from group companies shall be shown separately from income and interest derived from other sources.

(16) *Interest payable and similar charges*
(Format 1, item 12; Format 2, item 14; Format 3, item A 5; Format 4, item A 7)
The amount payable to group companies shall be shown separately.

(17) *Formats 1 and 3*
The amount of any provision for depreciation and diminution in value of tangible and intangible fixed assets falling to be shown under items 7(a) and A 4(a) respectively in Formats 2 and 4 shall be disclosed in a note to the accounts in any case where the profit and loss account is prepared by reference to Format 1 or Format 3.

## 2.7 Illustrations of accounts conforming to CA 1981 requirements

*Note:* Comparative figures have been omitted in the interests of clarity. They are rarely required in examination questions. The similarity to the previous format is more noticeable than would at first sight be thought from a study of the formats given in the previous paragraph. This is because the specimens below deal with the items likely to be found in practice and do not include some of the more exotic items. The use of notes to present much of the detail required in the balance sheet also helps to keep the format familiar, and this is good examination practice as well as being the normal method followed by companies.

Study these illustrations carefully in conjunction with the earlier coverage of the disclosure requirements and the standard formats.

### *(a) Profit and loss account following Format 1*

Profit and Loss Account for the year ended 31st December 19X3

| | Notes | £m. | £m. |
|---|---|---|---|
| Turnover | 2 | | 226.2 |
| Cost of sales | | | 144.8 |
| Gross profit: | | | 81.4 |
| Distribution costs | | 13.3 | |
| Administrative expenses | | 22.7 | |
| | | | (36.0) |
| | | | 45.4 |
| Other operating income | | | 1.1 |
| Income from shares in related companies (none listed) | | | 0.6 |
| Income from other fixed asset investments (all listed) | | | 0.2 |
| Other interest receivable and similar income: | | | 1.2 |
| Interest payable and similar charges | 5 | | (4.9) |
| Profit on ordinary activities before taxation: | 2, 3, 4 | | 43.6 |
| Tax on profit on ordinary activities | 6 | | (20.9) |
| Profit on ordinary activities after taxation: | | | 22.7 |
| Extraordinary loss | 7 | 5.8 | |
| Tax on extraordinary loss | 8 | 2.6 | |
| | | | (3.2) |
| Profit for the financial year: | | | 19.5 |
| Dividends paid and proposed | | | 8.8 |
| Amount set aside to reserves | | | 10.7 |

### *(b) Balance sheet following Format 1*

Balance Sheet as at 31st December 19X3

| | Notes | £m. | £m. |
|---|---|---|---|
| Fixed assets: | | | |
| Intangible assets | 9 | 10.0 | |
| Tangible assets | 10 | 78.3 | |
| Investments | 11 | 8.1 | |
| | | | 96.4 |
| Current assets: | | | |
| Stocks | 12 | 51.6 | |
| Debtors | 13 | 63.2 | |
| Investments | 14 | 11.9 | |
| Cash at bank and in hand | | 2.1 | |
| | | 128.8 | |
| Creditors: amounts falling due within one year | 15 | 81.2 | |
| Net current assets | | | 47.6 |
| Total assets *less* current liabilities | | | 144.0 |

| | Notes | £m. | £m. |
|---|---|---|---|
| Creditors: | | | |
| amounts falling due after more than one year | 16 | | 36.9 |
| Provisions for liabilities and charges | 17 | | 14.3 |
| Capital and reserves: | | | |
| Called-up share capital | 18 | 18.3 | |
| Share premium account | 19 | 12.1 | |
| Revaluation reserve | 19 | 10.4 | |
| Profit and loss account | 19 | 52.0 | |
| | | | 92.8 |
| | | | 144.0 |

### *(c) Notes to the accounts*

(1) Accounting policies (including basis of translating foreign currency) (not detailed)

(2) Analysis of turnover and profit:

| | Turnover | Profit before taxation |
|---|---|---|
| | £m. | £m. |
| Product A | 136.7 | 21.3 |
| Product B | 89.5 | 22.3 |
| | 226.2 | 43.6 |

Geographical analysis of turnover:

| | |
|---|---|
| UK | 141.4 |
| Europe other than UK | 39.1 |
| USA and Canada | 26.9 |
| Rest of world | 18.8 |
| | 226.2 |

(3) Profit on ordinary activities before taxation is calculated after charging the following:

| | £m. | £m. |
|---|---|---|
| Staff costs: | | |
| Wages and salaries | 56.3 | |
| Social security costs | 4.5 | |
| Other pension costs | 5.8 | |
| | | 66.6 |
| Depreciation (*see also* notes 9 and 10 below) | | 18.8 |
| Auditors' remuneration | | 0.1 |
| Directors' remuneration (*see also* note 4 below) | | 0.5 |

(4) Directors' and employees' remuneration
Directors' remuneration consisted of:

| | £ |
|---|---|
| Fees | 15,000 |
| Other remuneration (including pension contributions £71,000) | 488,000 |
| Pensions to past directors | 10,000 |
| | £513,000 |

The remuneration of the chairman was £56,208.

The highest paid director received £61,360.

| Particulars of other directors' remuneration: | Number |
|---|---|
| £0 to £5,000 | 2 |
| £5,001 to £10,000 | 2 |
| £20,001 to £25,000 | 4 |
| £30,001 to £35,000 | 7 |

The number of UK employees whose total remuneration exceeded £20,000 was as follows:

| | |
|---|---|
| £20,001 to £25,000 | 25 |
| £25,001 to £30,000 | 6 |
| £30,001 to £35,000 | 1 |

(5) Interest payable

| | £m. |
|---|---|
| Interest payable on bank and other borrowings repayable within five years | 2.3 |
| Interest payable on long-term borrowings | 2.6 |
| | 4.9 |

(6) Tax on profit on ordinary activities

| | |
|---|---|
| Taxation on profit for the year at 52 per cent | 7.4 |
| Relief for overseas tax | (6.3) |
| UK advance corporation tax | 3.7 |
| | 4.8 |
| Overseas tax | 16.1 |
| | 20.9 |

(7) Extraordinary loss
Cost of reorganisation and rationalisation of the company's activities and products 5.8

(8) Tax on extraordinary loss
UK corporation tax 2.6

| (9) Intangible assets | £m. | £m. |
|---|---|---|
| Goodwill: Cost | | 25.0 |
| Accumulated depreciation at 1st January 19X3 | 10.0 | |
| Provision for year to 31st December 19X3 | 5.0 | 15.0 |
| At 31st December 19X3 | | 10.0 |

The goodwill is being written off over a period of five years, which in the opinion of the directors is a reasonable approximation of its useful life.

(10) Tangible assets

| | Land and buildings £m. | Plant and machinery £m. | Total £m. |
|---|---|---|---|
| Cost: | | | |
| At 1st January 19X3 | 41.4 | 58.4 | 99.8 |
| Additions | 10.8 | 11.3 | 22.1 |
| Disposals | (4.4) | (7.1) | (11.5) |
| At 31st December 19X3 | 47.8 | 62.6 | 110.4 |
| Accumulated depreciation: | | | |
| At 1st January 19X3 | 8.4 | 17.1 | 25.5 |
| Provision for the year | 3.2 | 10.6 | 13.8 |
| Disposals | (2.3) | (4.9) | (7.2) |
| At 31st December 19X3 | 9.3 | 22.8 | 32.1 |
| Net book amount at 31st December 19X3 | 38.5 | 39.8 | 78.3 |
| Net book amount at 31st December 19X2 | 33.0 | 41.3 | 74.3 |

| The net book amount of land and buildings comprises: | £m. |
|---|---|
| Freeholds | 26.1 |
| Long leases | 9.3 |
| Short leases | 3.1 |
| | 38.5 |

(11) Investments

| | Shares in related companies (none listed) £m. | Other investments (all listed) £m. | Total £m. |
|---|---|---|---|
| Cost or amount under equity method of accounting: | | | |
| At 1st January 19X3: | 4.7 | 2.4 | 7.1 |
| Additions | 4.2 | — | 4.2 |
| Disposals | (3.6) | — | (3.6) |
| Increase in company's share of post-acquisition retained profits of related companies | 0.4 | — | 0.4 |
| At 31st December 19X3 | 5.7 | 2.4 | 8.1 |

Shares in related companies include £0.6m. in respect of the company's share of the post-acquisition retained profits of those companies.

Listed investments included in the balance sheet at £2.4m. had a market value at 31st December 19X3 of £3.4m.

| (12) Stocks | £m. |
|---|---|
| Raw materials and consumables | 21.4 |
| Work in progress | 3.6 |
| Finished goods and goods for resale | 26.6 |
| | 51.6 |

| (13) Debtors | £m. |
|---|---|
| Trade debtors | 53.6 |
| Amounts owed by related companies | 1.1 |
| Other debtors | 6.4 |
| Prepayments and accrued income | 2.1 |
| Total | 63.2 |

| (14) Investments | £m. |
|---|---|
| Short-term deposits | 11.9 |

| (15) Creditors: amounts falling due within one year | £m. |
|---|---|
| Bank loans and overdrafts | 15.1 |
| Trade creditors | 42.5 |
| Taxation and social security | 8.4 |
| Other creditors | 6.9 |
| Accruals and deferred income | 3.3 |
| Proposed dividend | 5.0 |
| | 81.2 |

| (16) Creditors: amounts falling due after more than one year | £m. |
|---|---|
| Debentures: | |
| 11 per cent debenture stock 2002, secured by a floating charge on the company's assets | 24.0 |
| Taxation and social security | 11.6 |
| Other creditors | 1.3 |
| | 36.9 |

| (17) Provisions for liabilities and charges | £m. |
|---|---|
| Pension and similar obligations | 6.4 |
| Taxation, including deferred taxation | 7.0 |
| Other provisions | 0.9 |
| | 14.3 |

| (18) Called-up share capital | £m. |
|---|---|
| Allotted, issued and fully paid: | |
| Ordinary shares of £1 each | 18.3 |
| Authorised 25m. ordinary shares of £1 each | 25.0 |

(19) Reserves

| | Share premium account £m. | Revaluation reserve £m. | Profit and loss account £m. |
|---|---|---|---|
| At 1st January 19X3 | 12.1 | 10.4 | 41.3 |
| Amount set aside from profit of year | — | — | 10.7 |
| At 31st December 19X3 | 12.1 | 10.4 | 52.0 |

(20) Particulars of employees

The average number of persons employed by the company during the year was:

| | |
|---|---|
| UK | 4,906 |
| Europe other than UK | 518 |
| USA and Canada | 490 |
| Rest of world | 593 |
| | 6,507 |

(21) Contingent liabilities

There is a legal action pending against the company in respect of a claim by a customer for late delivery of goods. The company has denied liability under the contract. The maximum amount which could arise as a liability is £1.2m.

*Note:* A directors' report would obviously be required but this is not reproduced. (*See* 3.0 below for directors' report disclosure requirements.)

### *(d) Modified accounts for a small company*

(*Note:* This balance sheet uses the figures as in (b) above divided by 1,000.)

Balance Sheet as at 31st December 19X3

| | Notes | £000 | £000 |
|---|---|---|---|
| Fixed assets: | | | |
| Intangible assets | | 10.0 | |
| Tangible assets | | 78.3 | |
| Investments | | 8.1 | |
| | | | 96.4 |
| Current assets: | | | |
| Stocks | | 51.6 | |
| Debtors | | 63.2 | |
| Investments | | 11.9 | |
| Cash at bank and in hand | | 2.1 | |
| | | 128.8 | |
| Creditors: amounts falling due within one year | | 81.2 | |
| Net current assets | | | 47.6 |
| Total assets *less* current liabilities | | | 144.0 |

| | Notes | £000 | £000 |
|---|---|---|---|
| Creditors: amounts falling due after more than one year | 2 | | 36.9 |
| Provisions for liabilities and charges | | | 14.3 |
| Capital and reserves: | | | |
| Called-up share capital | 3 | 18.3 | |
| Share premium account | | 12.1 | |
| Revaluation reserve | | 10.4 | |
| Profit and loss account | | 52.0 | |
| | | | 92.8 |
| | | | 144.0 |

The directors have relied on the exemption for individual accounts on the grounds that the company is entitled to the benefit of those exemptions as a small company.

A. Smith<br>
B. Jones } Directors

### *(e) Notes to modified accounts*

(1) *Accounting policies* (including basis of translating foreign currency) (not detailed)

(2) *Creditors: amounts falling due after more than one year*
The total of £36,900 includes £24,000 falling due more than five years after the balance sheet date. This loan is secured by a floating charge on the company's assets.

(3) *Called-up share capital*

| | £000 |
|---|---|
| Allotted, issued and fully paid ordinary shares of £1 each | 18.3 |
| Authorised: | |
| 25,000 ordinary shares of £1 each | 25.0 |

## 3.0 THE DIRECTORS' REPORT

### 3.1 Introduction

The contents of the directors' report were modified somewhat by CA 1981. The disclosure list in 3.3 below incorporates all the provisions of the Companies Acts 1948 to 1981 concerning the directors' report.

### 3.2 Changes introduced by the Companies Act 1981

The Companies Act 1981 introduced changes into the directors' report requirements by adding some new sections to CA 1967 and amending other provisions of that Act and CA 1948.

(a) *General nature of the directors' report*
Section 13(1) CA 1981 amended s. 157 CA 1948, which required the report to indicate "the state of the company's affairs". It is now necessary for the report to contain "a fair view of the development of the business of the company and its subsidiaries during the financial year ending with the balance sheet date and of their position at the end of it".

(b) *Additional disclosure in the directors' report*
Section 13(2 & 3) CA 1981 repealed s. 16(1)(f) CA 1967 (which required the disclosure of any material matter not specifically disclosable under other provisions of the Companies Acts) and replaced it with the requirement to disclose:

(i) particulars of any important events affecting the company or any of its subsidiaries which have occurred since the end of that year;

(ii) an indication of likely future developments in the business of the company and of its subsidiaries; and

(iii) an indication of the activities (if any) of the company and its subsidiaries in the field of research and development.

(c) *Disclosure if the company has acquired its own shares* (*see* 7.0 below)
Section 14 CA 1981 inserted a new s. 16A into CA 1967, requiring the directors' report to give full details if the company has purchased its own shares under the arrangements introduced by ss. 46 to 62 CA 1981. Acquisition as a result of forfeiture and nominee purchases are covered, as well as straightforward purchases by the company. (The detailed disclosure requirements are listed in 3.3(m) below and are therefore not repeated here.)

(d) *Auditors to consider the consistency of the directors' report and accounts*
Section 15 CA 1981 inserted a new s. 23A into CA 1967 requiring the auditors to consider whether the information given in the directors' report is consistent with the accounts, and if they consider that the accounts and the directors' report are not consistent with each other, to state that fact in their report.

(e) *Minor changes*
Section 16 CA 1981 made minor changes to the directors' report requirements, often because the provisions of CA 1967 requiring disclosure of some matters in directors' reports were superseded by sections of CAs 1980 and 1981 requiring disclosure of the information in some other way.
The detailed changes introduced by s. 16 are given in Table 3.

(f) *Flexibility in presentation*
It is no longer allowed for items required to be disclosed in the accounts to be included in the directors' report (s. 13(4) CA 1981).

Table 3. CHANGES IN DIRECTORS' REPORT MADE BY s. 16 COMPANIES ACT 1981

| *Item no longer required in directors' report* | *Superseded CA 1967 reference* | *New reference if any* |
|---|---|---|
| (i) Exports. | s. 20 | Disclosure not now required. |
| (ii) Turnover and profitability by class of business. | s. 17 | Segmental disclosure now required by note under para. 55, 8th Schedule. |
| (iii) Number of UK employees and their remuneration. | s. 18 | Details now required by note under para. 56, 8th Schedule. |
| (iv) Details of issue of shares or debentures during the year. | s. 16(1)(b) | Details now required by note under paras. 39 (shares) and 41 (debentures), 8th Schedule. |
| (v) Arrangements for directors to acquire shares or debentures. | s. 16(1)(d) | s. 54 CA 1980 |

## 3.3 The new directors' report contents

| | | Statutory references |
|---|---|---|
| (a) | A fair review of the development of the business of the company and its subsidiaries during the financial year ending with the balance sheet date and of their position at the end of it. | s. 13 CA 1981 |
| (b) | Proposed dividend. | s. 157 CA 1948 |
| (c) | Proposed transfers to reserves. | s. 157 CA 1948 |
| (d) | Names of directors who held office at any time in the period. | s. 16 CA 1967 |
| (e) | Principal activities of the company and its subsidiaries and any significant changes in those activities. | s. 16 CA 1967 |
| (f) | Details of significant changes in fixed assets of the company or its subsidiaries. | s. 16 CA 1967 |

| | | Statutory references |
|---|---|---|
| (g) | Indication of difference between book and market value of land and buildings of company (or any of its subsidiaries) if significant. | s. 16 CA 1967 |
| (h) | Details of significant contracts with the company in which director interested. | s. 16 CA 1967 |
| (i) | Directors' interests in shares or debentures of group companies at beginning of period (or later date of appointment) and at end of period. (This information may now be given by note to the accounts (s. 13(4) CA 1981).) | s. 16 CA 1967 |
| (j) | Particulars of any important events affecting the company or any of its subsidiaries which have occurred since the end of that year. | s. 13 CA 1981 |
| (k) | An indication of likely future developments in the business of the company and of its subsidiaries. | s. 13 CA 1981 |
| (l) | An indication of the activities (if any) of the company and its subsidiaries in the field of research and development. | s. 13 CA 1981 |
| (m) | Details of any acquisition by the company of its own shares, including acquisition by forfeiture and acquisition by nominees.<br>The full details required are: | s. 14 CA 1981 |
| | (i) number and nominal value of shares acquired in any way, the aggregate consideration paid and the reasons for purchase; | introducing s. 16A CA 1967 |
| | (ii) number and nominal value of shares charged, and the amount of the charge; | |
| | (iii) maximum number and nominal value of shares held during the year; | |
| | (iv) number and nominal value of shares held which were disposed of during the year, and the amount of consideration for the sale in each case; | |
| | (v) for all disclosures (i) to (iv) above, the percentage of called-up share capital involved. | |
| (n) | Totals of UK political and charitable contributions of the company (or, if any made by subsidiaries, of the group), unless together not more than £200. The amount and name of political party or person paid must be disclosed for each political contribution over £200. Wholly owned subsidiaries of UK companies are exempt. | s. 19 CA 1967 |

(o) Report on employment policy. Companies with 250 or more employees must include a statement as to the company's policy for the employment, training, career development and promotion of disabled people.

# 4.0 TAXATION IN COMPANY ACCOUNTS

## 4.1 Statutory disclosure requirements summarised

The 8th Schedule CA 1948 (as revised by CA 1981) requires companies to disclose full details of taxation charges, provisions and liabilities in their accounts.

(a) *Profit and loss account*
The standard formats call for separate disclosure of:

(i) tax on profit or loss from ordinary activities

(ii) tax on extraordinary profit or loss.

(b) *Balance sheet*
The standard formats require disclosure of the creditors for taxation and social security.

(c) *Notes to accounts*
The notes must show:

(i) the basis of charge for UK corporation tax and income tax,

(ii) details of any special circumstances affecting the tax charge for the current year or succeeding years,

(iii) the tax charge on profit or loss on ordinary activities, separating
UK corporation tax
UK corporation tax before double taxation relief
UK income tax
foreign taxes,

(iv) information as in (iii) relating to extraordinary profit or loss,

(v) the separation of amounts provided for taxation and amounts for deferred taxation. (Note that deferred taxation is now to be grouped under the heading "Provisions for liabilities and charges").

## 4.2 Basic taxation background

Corporation tax is charged on company profits and is due for payment some time after the end of each accounting period. The interval between the end of an accounting period and the due date for payment may be anything from nine months to nearly twenty-one months.

Whenever the interval exceeds twelve months there will normally be a liability to tax for two outstanding years in the balance sheet: that for the present year and that for the previous year.

## 4.3 Deferred taxation account

The profit for tax purposes may be considerably different from that for accounting purposes. The main reason for this is usually that most fixed assets are written off for tax purposes at a faster rate than for accounting purposes.

*Illustration*

In its first year of operation A Ltd has profits of £100,000 after charging depreciation of £20,000 on plant costing £80,000. The plant attracts capital allowances at 100 per cent.

The profit for tax purposes will be £40,000 (£100,000 plus £20,000 and minus £80,000).

The profit and loss account for year 1 might show:

| | £ |
|---|---|
| Trading profit | 100,000 |
| *deduct:* Corporation tax at 50% (on £40,000) | 20,000 |
| Profit after taxation | £80,000 |

If the profit and depreciation are the same for year 2, with no fresh capital expenditure, the profit and loss account for that year might show:

| | £ |
|---|---|
| Trading profit | 100,000 |
| *deduct:* Corporation tax at 50% (on £120,000) | 60,000 |
| Profit after taxation | £40,000 |

Shareholders and others looking at the accounts might reasonably be puzzled by the mysterious arithmetic applied by the company in deducting the tax charge. While the profit before taxation remains exactly the same, that available for dividend is apparently halved.

An unusually low tax charge in one year (as in year 1 for A Ltd above) is likely to be followed by unusually high charges in later years (as in year 2).

A *deferred taxation account* is opened to adjust for material differences in the timing of charges against profit. (Straight-line depreciation for accounting purposes; 100 per cent write-off in year of expenditure for tax purposes.) When the tax charge is low in relation to profits, deferred taxation account is *credited*, and when the tax charge is high in relation to profits, the deferred taxation account is *debited*.

*Illustration*

Facts as in the previous illustration but with a deferred taxation account.

Profit and Loss Account year 1:

| | £ | £ |
|---|---|---|
| Trading profit | | 100,000 |
| *deduct:* Corporation tax at 50% | 20,000 | |
| Transfer to deferred taxation account | 30,000 | |
| | | 50,000 |
| Profit after taxation | | £50,000 |

Profit and Loss Account year 2:

| | £ | £ |
|---|---|---|
| Trading profit | | 100,000 |
| *deduct:* Corporation tax at 50% | 60,000 | |
| Transfer from deferred taxation account | 10,000 | |
| | | 50,000 |
| Profit after taxation | | £50,000 |

Entries in deferred taxation account:

| | | | |
|---|---|---|---|
| Year 1 Balance carried forward | 30,000 | Year 1 Profit and loss account | 30,000 |
| Year 2 Profit and loss account | 10,000 | Year 2 Balance brought forward | |
| Balance carried forward | 20,000 | | 30,000 |
| | | Year 3 Balance brought forward | 20,000 |

If a debit balance arises on deferred taxation account it should be carried forward only if there is reasonable certainty of its recovery, normally within the next accounting period.

## 4.4 Accounting for advance corporation tax (ACT)

(a) *Introduction and taxation background*

With the introduction of the imputation system of company taxation with effect from April 1973, there are changes in the method of dealing with tax relating to distributions made by companies. These changes and their effect on a company's published accounts and the underlying bookkeeping entries now have to be considered.

When a company pays a dividend on or after 6th April 1973 the members receive a "net" amount. The member includes the gross equivalent of the dividend in his total income for tax purposes and is entitled to a credit against his tax liability for the amount by which the "net" dividend is grossed up.

*Illustration*

| | £ | £ |
|---|---|---|
| Dividend paid by C Ltd | | 28,000 |
| Dividend received by member Q | | 280 |
| Amount included in Q's total income dividend received | 280 | |
| tax credit (deducted from tax liability) | 120 | |
| | | 400 |

The tax credit amounts to $\frac{3}{7}$ of the dividend paid. This grosses up the dividend for basic rate tax at 30 per cent. (Where the basic rate of tax is 33 per cent, the tax credit amounts to $\frac{33}{67}$; where the basic rate is 34 per cent, the tax credit is $\frac{34}{66}$ and so on.)

The member is receiving a benefit (the right to offset tax credit against his tax liability) and it is not immediately obvious how the Revenue is recouping this tax from the company. In fact, *the credit allowed to the taxpayer comes out of the corporation tax payable by the company*. A portion of the corporation tax is said to be "imputed" to or allocated to the dividend and it is this which permits the member to receive his credit. To protect the Revenue against the possibility of allowing credit to members in cases where no corporation tax on profits is due a special system has been devised.

For the examples which follow, it is assumed that the basic rate of tax is 30 per cent.

Whenever a company makes a distribution it is required to make a payment on account of corporation tax equal to $\frac{3}{7}$ of the distribution. Thus the Revenue is assured of having received an amount of corporation tax at least equal to its obligation to give tax credit to the company's member.

The company's payment on account of corporation tax is termed "advance corporation tax", and is normally offset against the company's eventual corporation tax liability.

The rules for offsetting advance corporation tax are:

(i) offset against corporation tax for the accounting period *in which the dividend is paid*;

(ii) carry *back* against corporation tax liabilities of earlier periods commencing up to two years previously;

(iii) carried *forward* without time limit against profits of later periods.

In any year the maximum offset allowable is 30 per cent of taxable profits, *excluding* chargeable capital gains.

If a company receives dividends from other UK companies it will be receiving a "net" sum to which a tax credit attaches.

The paying company has already paid the ACT to the Revenue.

The receiving company will deduct the tax attaching to the dividends received (franked investment income) from ACT due to the Revenue on its own dividends (franked payments).

### *Illustration*

D Ltd makes up its accounts to 30th September. For the year ended 30th September 19X4 it has trading profits of £40,000 (corporation tax £20,000) and received dividends from F Ltd, another UK company, amounting to £2,800 in May 19X4.

D Ltd paid a dividend of £14,000 in August 19X4.

D Ltd will be required to pay ACT on its dividend on 14th October 19X4 (fourteen days after the end of the quarter in which the dividend was paid).

It will pay $\frac{3}{7} \times$ (£14,000 − £2,800) = £4,800.

The accounting consequences of the introduction of the imputation system and the concept of advance corporation tax are considered in (b), (c), (d) and (e) below.

(b) *Dividends paid in an accounting period*
The ACT paid by a company for dividends paid *in* an accounting period will normally be deducted from its corporation tax liability for that period. The dividend will appear "net" in the profit and loss account.

Any ACT paid will therefore normally reduce the liability in the balance sheet for corporation tax on the profits of the current period, leaving the profit and loss account tax charge unaffected. In other words, ACT is treated as a payment on account of corporation tax.

(c) *Preference shares and preference dividends*
The removal of the requirement to deduct income tax at source for dividends applies to preference dividends as well as ordinary dividends.

It is therefore necessary to change the description of preference shares in the accounts. For example, a preference share previously carrying a gross dividend of 10 per cent (after tax at 30 per cent equals 7 per cent) is now to be described as 7 per cent (the actual percentage to be paid).

*Specimen balance sheet description:*
100,000 7 per cent (formerly 10 per cent gross) preference shares of £1 each £100,000.

(d) *Proposed dividends*
Proposed dividends are included in the balance sheet as creditors, without the addition of the attributable ACT.

The ACT on a proposed dividend will be offset against the corporation tax liability of the following period, when the dividend is paid. There is therefore a current *liability*, the obligation to pay the ACT when the dividend is paid, and a deferred *asset*, the right to offset the ACT in due course.

ACT on proposed dividends will therefore appear as a current tax liability on one side of the balance sheet *and* as a deferred asset on the other.

If the company maintains a deferred taxation account (*see* 4.3) with a sufficient credit balance on it, the recoverable ACT will be debited to this account instead of appearing as a deferred asset.

### *Illustration of bookkeeping entries*

E Ltd makes up its accounts annually to 31st March.

In the year ended 31st March 19X5 it had a trading profit of £100,000 on which corporation tax at 50 per cent is £50,000. Corresponding figures for the year ended 31st March 19X4 were £80,000 (tax £40,000). E Ltd had no deferred taxation account.

It paid the following dividends:

| | | £ |
|---|---|---|
| Year ended 31st March 19X4: | | |
| 1st December 19X3: | Interim | 7,000 |
| 1st June 19X4: | Final | 28,000 |
| Year ended 31st March 19X5: | | |
| 1st December 19X4: | Interim | 14,000 |
| 1st June 19X5: | Final | 35,000 |

Show the bookkeeping entries in the books of E Ltd.

## Bookkeeping Entries (year ended 31st March 19X5 items only)

### Dividend Account

| | | £ | | | £ |
|---|---|---|---|---|---|
| 19X4 | | | 19X4 | | |
| 1 June | Cash account: *Last year's dividend paid* | 28,000 | 1 Apr | Balance brought forward: *Proposed dividend 31st March 19X4* | 28,000 |
| 1 Dec | Cash account: *Interim dividend paid* | 14,000 | | | |
| 19X5 | | | 19X5 | | |
| 31 Mar | Balance carried forward: *Proposed dividend 31st March 19X5* | 35,000 | 31 Mar | Profit and loss account: *Provision for year to 31st March 19X5* | 49,000 |
| | | £77,000 | | | £77,000 |
| | | | 19X5 | | |
| | | | 1 Apr | Balance brought forward: *Proposed dividend 31st March 19X5* | 35,000 |

### Corporation Tax Account

| | | £ | | | £ |
|---|---|---|---|---|---|
| 19X5 | | | 19X5 | | |
| 31 Mar | ACT account: *ACT offset* | 18,000 | 31 Mar | Profit and loss account: *Provision for year to 31st March 19X5* | 50,000 |
| | Balance carried forward: *Tax payable* | 32,000 | | | |
| | | £50,000 | | | £50,000 |
| | | | 19X5 | | |
| | | | 1 Apr | Balance brought forward: *Tax payable* | 32,000 |

Advance Corporation Tax Account

| | | £ | | | £ |
|---|---|---|---|---|---|
| 19X4 | | | 19X4 | | |
| 1 Apr | Balance brought forward: *Deferred asset* | 12,000 | 1 Apr | Balance brought forward: *ACT on proposed dividend £28,000* | 12,000 |
| 14 Jul | Cash account: *ACT paid on due date* | 12,000 | | | |
| 19X5 | | | 19X5 | | |
| 14 Jan | Cash account: *ACT paid on due date* | 6,000 | 31 Mar | Corporation tax account: *Offset of ACT on dividends paid in year to date* | 18,000 |
| 31 Mar | Balance carried forward: *ACT payable on proposed final dividend* | 15,000 | | Balance carried forward: *Deferred asset: ACT recoverable* | 15,000 |
| | | £45,000 | | | £45,000 |
| 19X5 | | | 19X5 | | |
| 1 Apr | Balance brought forward: *Deferred asset: ACT recoverable* | 15,000 | 1 Apr | Balance brought forward: *ACT on proposed final dividend* | 15,000 |

(e) *Irrecoverable ACT*
As explained in paragraph (a) above, advance corporation tax paid can only be offset against available corporation tax charged on company profits. If set-off is not available in the current period or by carrying back against the two previous years, ACT paid may be carried forward without time limit for offset against corporation tax relating to future profits.

Although the tax legislation allows carry-forward without time limit, it may be imprudent from an accounting point of view for the ACT to remain in the balance sheet as a deferred asset, since there may never be sufficient future tax liability to permit set-off.

Unless it can be seen with reasonable confidence that the ACT will be recoverable against corporation tax *relating to the next accounting period*, it should be written off as an additional tax charge of the period in which it arose. Such ACT written off is termed *irrecoverable ACT*. It remains available indefinitely for offset under the taxation legislation but is written off in the accounts as a matter of prudence. It may be reinstated in any later year in which set-off in fact becomes available.

## 5.0 LIMITATIONS IN COMPANY PUBLISHED ACCOUNTS

### 5.1 Introduction

*The Corporate Report*, published by the Accounting Standards Committee in July 1975, indicated that there were a number of areas in which current reporting practice was inadequate to meet the needs of users.

The traditional statements provided by companies in their published accounts are:

(a) balance sheet;

(b) profit and loss account;

(c) directors' report;

(d) auditors' report;

(e) chairman's statement;

(f) statement of source and application of funds;

(g) table showing summarised details of the accounts of the previous five or ten years;

(h) inflation-adjusted accounts (by some companies).

*The Corporate Report* identified a number of areas in which information was deficient, and the Government Green Paper, *The Future of Company Reports*, published two years later in July 1977, was in broad agreement with its proposals.

## 5.2 The additional statements

*The Corporate Report* proposed the following additional statements:

(a) value added statement;

(b) employment report;

(c) statement of money exchanges with government;

(d) statement of transactions in foreign currency;

(e) statement of future prospects;

(f) statement of corporate objectives;

(g) analysis of activities (disaggregation).

*The Future of Company Reports* recommended all but (c) of those listed above, and added a proposal for a statement of energy usage.

The only one of these statements likely to be the subject of a computational examination question is (a), the value added statement, but a basic knowledge of the existence and objectives of the others is necessary to deal with written questions on ways of improving current company published accounts. A short explanation of each one is given in the paragraphs which follow.

## 5.3 The value added statement

"Value added" in the context of a value added statement means the wealth created by the activities of an enterprise. It is the difference between gross revenue and the cost of goods and services purchased. At first sight this seems similar to the traditional trading and profit and loss account of a business, but the difference lies in the manner in which the information is laid out. The most important conceptual difference is that money paid to employees (wages, salaries and other benefits) is regarded as a share of the value added which the employees have helped to create, rather than as a cost. Also, depreciation is not classified as a cost, but as a retention of value intended to provide for the maintenance and expansion of the business.

The technique for preparing a statement of value added is simply a matter of rearranging the items in the trading and profit and loss account into the format shown in the following simple illustration (taken from *The Corporate Report*):

***Illustration***

A Manufacturing Company: Statement of Value Added

| | | Year to 31st December 1974 | | Preceding year |
|---|---|---|---|---|
| | | £m. | | £m. |
| Turnover | | 103.9 | | 102.3 |
| Bought-in materials and services | | 67.6 | | 72.1 |
| *Value added* | | £36.3 | | £30.2 |
| Applied the following way | | | | |
| *To pay employees* | | | | |
| Wages, pensions and fringe benefits | | 25.9 | | 17.3 |
| *To pay providers of capital* | | | | |
| Interest on loans | 0.8 | | 0.6 | |
| Dividend to shareholders | 0.9 | 1.7 | 0.9 | 1.5 |
| *To pay government* | | | | |
| Corporation tax payable | | 3.9 | | 3.1 |
| *To provide for maintenance and expansion of assets* | | | | |
| Depreciation | 2.0 | | 1.8 | |
| Retained profits | 2.8 | 4.8 | 6.5 | 8.3 |
| *Value added* | | £36.3 | | £30.2 |

Ratios of value added per employee, or per £000 of capital employed, are useful indicators of a company's performance.

The form of the statement emphasises that gross value added is created from the joint contributions of employees, the providers of capital and the government. After providing for necessary retentions, the balance is the value added. (If you have trouble thinking what the government contribution is, the answer is the provision of a stable working environment in which the activities of the business can take place. That is the theory, at any rate.)

## 5.4 The employment report

The employment report is intended to provide statistics relating to employees. A very long and detailed list of suggested items for inclusion appears in *The Corporate Report* and is broadly agreed by *The Future of Company Reports*.

The main items suggested are:

(a) Numbers employed, average for the financial year and actual on the first and last days.

(b) Broad reasons for changes in the numbers employed.

(c) The age distribution and sex of employees.

(d) The functions of employees.

(e) The geographical location of major employment centres.

(f) Major plant and site closures, disposals and acquisitions during the past year.

(g) The hours scheduled and worked by employees giving as much detail as possible concerning differences between groups of employees.

(h) Employment costs including fringe benefits.

(i) The costs and benefits associated with pension schemes and the ability of such schemes to meet future commitments.

(j) The cost and time spent on training.

(k) The names of unions recognised by the entity for the purpose of collective bargaining and membership figures where available or the fact that this information has not been made available by the unions concerned.

(l) Information concerning safety and health including the frequency and severity of accidents and occupational diseases.

(m) Selected ratios relating to employment.

## 5.5 Statement of money exchanges with government

The intention is that the statement of money exchanges with government should deal with local government as well as home and overseas national governments. Also, PAYE collected from employees would be regarded as a contribution to government by the enterprise.

Proposed headings for the statement are:

(a) PAYE collected and paid over.

(b) VAT collected and paid over.

(c) Corporation tax and similar taxes paid over and borne by the entity.

(d) Rates and similar levies paid over to local authorities and borne by the entity.

(e) Other sums paid to government departments and agencies including social security, training levies and duties.

(f) Money receipts from government including grants and subsidies.

## 5.6 Statement of transactions in foreign currency

The recommendation is that this statement should show:

(a) UK cash receipts for direct exports of goods and services.

(b) Cash payments from the UK to overseas concerns for direct imports distinguishing between imports of a capital nature (e.g. plant and machinery for use rather than resale) and those of a revenue nature (e.g. raw materials and services).

(c) Overseas borrowings remitted to or repaid from the UK.

(d) Overseas investments and loans made from or repaid to the UK.

(e) Overseas dividends, interest or similar payments received in the UK or UK dividends, interest or similar payments remitted overseas.

## 5.7 Statement of future prospects

The proposal that information should be given about a company's future prospects is a controversial one, and obviously it could not be required that companies give details of projects they wish to keep concealed from competitors.

However, *The Corporate Report* proposes that information should be given of:

(a) Future profit levels.

(b) Future employment levels and prospects.

(c) Future investment levels.

## 5.8 Statement of corporate objectives

It is proposed that general information as to corporate objectives should be provided in the following areas:

(a) Sales.

(b) Added value.

(c) Profitability.

(d) Investment and finance.

(e) Dividends.

(f) Employment.

(g) Consumer issues.

(h) Environmental matters.

(i) Other relevant social issues.

## 5.9 Analysis of activities (disaggregation)

The 8th Schedule CA 1948 (as amended by CA 1981) requires a company carrying on two or more classes of business to disclose by note to its accounts an analysis of turnover and profit by class of business and an analysis of turnover by geographical market if the directors consider that the company has supplied substantially different markets.

*The Corporate Report* proposes additions to these requirements so that geographical and product analysis is available for:

(a) Turnover.

(b) Value added.

(c) Profits or losses before tax.

(d) Capital employed.

(e) Employment information.

### 5.10 Statement of energy usage

As noted in 5.2 above, *The Corporate Report* does not recommend this statement but *The Future of Company Reports* does do so. The declared object is to assist government energy-saving measures.

### 5.11 Conclusions

In the years since these proposals were made, many larger companies have voluntarily added many of these new statements to their published accounts. Some of them will probably be embodied in future company disclosure legislation.

## 6.0 REDEEMABLE SHARES (ss. 45 AND 53 TO 62)

### 6.1 Issue of redeemable shares

Section 58 of the Companies Act 1948 gave a company power to issue redeemable *preference* shares and laid down the procedure for redemption. Section 58 is repealed by CA 1981 and replaced by new provisions as explained below.

Section 45 gives a limited company with a share capital power to issue redeemable shares of any kind, preference or equity, provided its articles allow, and provided the company has some share capital which is not redeemable.

### 6.2 Redemption of redeemable shares—public companies

The procedure for redemption under s. 45 and s. 53 is very similar to that under s. 58 CA 1948. The redemption arrangements are:

(a) Shares must be fully paid on redemption.

(b) Redemption must be out of distributable profits or from the proceeds of a fresh issue of shares.

(c) Any premium on redemption must be paid out of distributable profits, except that where the shares were originally *issued* at a premium, the premium on redemption may be covered by the proceeds of a fresh issue of shares up to a limit which is the *lower* of:

(i) the premium received on issue;

(ii) the balance on the company's share premium account after the fresh issue.

*Note:*
If the shares were issued before CA 1981 came into force, any premium on redemption may be paid out of share premium account in accordance with s. 56(2) CA 1948.

(d) If the premium on redemption is paid out of the proceeds of a fresh issue, under the provisions explained in (c) above, the amount so paid must be debited to share premium account.

(e) If the redemption is wholly out of profit, the amount by which the share capital is diminished must be transferred to "the capital redemption reserve" (any capital redemption reserve fund established under s. 58 CA 1948 is to be renamed "capital redemption reserve"—s. 62 CA 1981).

(f) If the redemption is wholly or partly out of the proceeds of a fresh issue, the amount by which the *proceeds* of the fresh issue falls short of the *nominal value* of the shares redeemed must be transferred to capital redemption reserve.

(g) The capital redemption reserve can only be used to issue fully paid bonus shares to the members.

## 6.3 Redemption of redeemable shares—private companies

Section 54 allows a *private* company to redeem shares *out of capital*, subject to careful safeguards imposed by ss. 55 to 58.

A capital redemption reserve may still be required. The rules are:

if the amount redeemed out of capital plus the *proceeds* of any fresh issue is *less than* the *nominal value* of the shares redeemed, the difference must be transferred to capital redemption reserve.

if the amount redeemed out of capital plus the *proceeds* of any fresh issue *exceeds* the *nominal value* of the shares redeemed, the excess may be debited to capital redemption reserve, share premium, fully paid share capital or a credit balance on a revaluation reserve. (*See* 6.4(b) below for the accounting entries.)

The safeguards are:

(a) The members must approve the payment by special resolution, and voting rights attaching to the shares to be redeemed cannot be exercised (s. 55).

(b) The directors must make a statutory declaration that having made a full enquiry into the affairs and prospects of the company the payment out of capital does not in their opinion jeopardise the company's ability to pay its debts at the date of the payment out of capital or to continue in business and pay its debts as they fall due in the year following the payment. The amount to be paid out of capital is referred to in the Act as the "permissible capital amount".

(c) The statutory declaration by the directors (b) above must be accompanied by a report addressed to the directors by the auditors stating that they have inquired into the company's state of affairs, that the amount to be paid out of capital has been properly determined and that the opinion expressed by the directors is reasonable. The statutory declaration by the directors and the auditors' report on it must be open for inspection by the members at the meeting to pass the special resolution approving the payment.

(d) The resolution for payment out of capital ((a) above) must be passed within one week of the directors' declaration, and the payment must be made not earlier than *five* weeks after the date of the resolution and not later than *seven* weeks after it.

(e) Within one week of the passing of the special resolution authorising the payment, the company must give publicity to the proposed payment by:

(i) inserting a notice giving details of the proposal in the London Gazette;

(ii) either putting a similar notice in a national newspaper or giving notice to each of its creditors individually.

Any notices given under (i) or (ii) above must state that any creditor has the right to apply to the court for an order prohibiting the payment (s. 56).

(f) Within five weeks of the passing of the resolution any member who did not vote in favour of the resolution, or any creditor, may apply to the court for the cancellation of the resolution (s. 57).

(g) If a company is wound up within one year of the payment out of capital and the assets are insufficient to pay the liabilities, the person from whom the shares were redeemed is liable to repay an amount not exceeding the amount received for the shares.

The directors who signed the statutory declaration ((b) above) are jointly and severally liable with the person from whom the shares were redeemed unless they can show that they had reasonable grounds for forming their opinion.

## 6.4 Accounting entries on redemption or purchase

(a) *Public companies*

ILLUSTRATION 1

Redemptor plc has 1,000 £1 redeemable shares in issue. They were originally issued at par after the CA 1981 came into force and are now redeemable at £1.10. Show the accounting entries if:

(i) the shares were redeemed out of distributable profits;

(ii) the shares are redeemed partly out of the proceeds of a fresh issue of 500 £1 shares issued at £1.50 each.

| | | £ | £ |
|---|---|---|---|
| (i) Share capital | Dr. | 1,000 | |
| Profit and loss account (premium)* | Dr. | 100 | |
| Redemption of shares account | Cr. | | 1,100 |
| Redemption of shares account | Dr. | 1,100 | |
| Cash | Cr. | | 1,100 |
| Profit and loss account | Dr. | 1,000 | |
| Capital redemption reserve | Cr. | | 1,000 |

| (ii) | | £ | £ |
|---|---|---|---|
| Cash | Dr. | 750 | |
| Share capital | Cr. | | 500 |
| Share premium | Cr. | | 250 |
| Share capital | Dr. | 1,000 | |
| Profit and loss account (premium)* | Dr. | 100 | |
| Redemption of shares account | Cr. | | 1,100 |
| Redemption of shares account | Dr. | 1,100 | |
| Cash | Cr. | | 1,100 |
| Profit and loss account | Dr. | 250 | |
| Capital redemption reserve | Cr. | | 250 |

**Note:* If the shares had been issued before CA 1981 came into force, the premium on redemption could have been debited to share premium account.

(b) *Private companies*

ILLUSTRATION 2

Redeemer Ltd has 1,000 £1 redeemable shares in issue. They were originally issued at par after the CA 1981 came into force and are now redeemable at £1.10. Show the accounting entries if the shares are redeemed:

(i) wholly out of distributable profits;

(ii) £500 covered by distributable profits
£600 out of the proceeds of a fresh issue of shares at par;

(iii) £700 out of capital
£250 out of the proceeds of a fresh issue of shares at par
£150 out of distributable profits;

(iv) wholly out of capital.

| | | £ | £ |
|---|---|---|---|
| (i) Share capital | Dr. | 1,000 | |
| Profit and loss account* | Dr. | 100 | |
| Redemption of shares account | Cr. | | 1,100 |
| Redemption of shares account | Dr. | 1,100 | |
| Cash | Cr. | | 1,100 |
| Profit and loss account | Dr. | 1,000 | |
| Capital redemption reserve (full nominal value) | Cr. | | 1,000 |

| | | | £ | £ |
|---|---|---|---|---|
| (ii) | Cash | Dr. | 600 | |
| | Share capital | Cr. | | 600 |
| | Share capital | Dr. | 1,000 | |
| | Profit and loss account* | Dr. | 100 | |
| | Redemption of shares account | Cr. | | 1,100 |
| | Redemption of shares account | Dr. | 1,100 | |
| | Cash | Cr. | | 1,100 |
| | Profit and loss account | Dr. | 400 | |
| | Capital redemption reserve (£1,000 – £600) | Cr. | | 400 |
| (iii) | Cash | Dr. | 200 | |
| | Share capital | Cr. | | 200 |
| | Share capital | Dr. | 1,000 | |
| | Profit and loss account* | Dr. | 100 | |
| | Redemption of shares account | Cr. | | 1,100 |
| | Redemption of shares account | Dr. | 1,100 | |
| | Cash | Cr. | | 1,100 |
| | Profit and loss account | Dr. | 50 | |
| | Capital redemption reserve (£1,000 *less* (£700 + £250)) | Cr. | | 50 |
| (iv) | Cash | Dr. | 1,100 | |
| | Share capital | Cr. | | 1,100 |
| | Share capital | Dr. | 1,000 | |
| | CRR (if any) otherwise share premium account | Dr. | 100 | |
| | Redemption of shares account | Cr. | | 1,100 |
| | Redemption of shares account | Dr. | 1,100 | |
| | Cash | Cr. | | 1,100 |

**Note:* If the shares had been issued before CA 1981 came into force, the premium on redemption could have been debited to share premium account in these cases.

## 7.0 COMPANY'S POWER TO PURCHASE ITS OWN SHARES (ss. 46 TO 62)

### 7.1 Introduction

Section 46 of the Companies Act 1981 gives any limited company with a share capital the right to purchase its own shares, if authorised to do so by its articles, and as long as the purchase leaves an outsider holding some shares which are not redeemable.

The purchase is subject to the same restrictions as the redemption of shares.

A purchase requires the prior approval of the members, by ordinary resolution if the purchase is a "market purchase" (i.e. through a recognised stock exchange) and by special resolution if it is an "off-market purchase" (i.e. not through a recognised stock exchange).

## 7.2 Purchase of a company's own shares—public companies

Public companies may purchase their own shares, subject to the general restrictions explained in 7.1 above and the following further conditions:

(a) The shares must be fully paid (*cf.* 6.2 (a) above).

(b) The purchase must be out of distributable profit or from the proceeds of a fresh issue of shares (*cf.* 6.2 (b) above).

(c) If the purchase is wholly out of profit, the amount by which the share capital is diminished must be transferred to the "capital redemption reserve" (*cf.* 6.2 (e) above).

(d) If the purchase is wholly or partly out of the proceeds of a fresh issue, the amount by which the proceeds of the fresh issue exceed the *nominal value* of the shares purchased must be transferred to capital redemption reserve (*cf.* 6.2 (f) above).

## 7.3 Purchase of a company's own shares—private companies

A private company can purchase its own shares *out of capital* subject to exactly the same conditions as those relating to a redemption of shares by a company.

The provisions of s. 54, and the safeguards imposed by ss. 55 to 58 as outlined in 6.3 above, apply to a company purchasing its own shares exactly as they apply to a company redeeming its shares.

# 8.0 RELIEF FROM s. 56 CA 1948 (SHARE PREMIUM ACCOUNT) (ss. 36 TO 41)

## 8.1 Introduction

The purpose of s. 56 Companies Act 1948 is to limit the purposes for which a share premium can be used, and in particular to prohibit its distribution.

In general, s. 56 achieves a reasonable purpose quite smoothly, but there is one situation in which it has caused difficulties when two or more companies merge and wish to preserve the distributability of their pre-merger profits by adopting the "merger accounting"* method of recording the transaction.

Several major mergers adopted this method in the late 1960s and 1970s, in spite of the dubious legality of the fact that no share premium account was created. In 1980 the matter was tested in the courts (*Shearer* v. *Bercain* (1980)) and it was held that it was not acceptable to fail to account for the premium on the issue of shares. Sections 36 to 41 give a measure of relief from s. 56 CA 1948 in cases within the definition of a merger contained in s. 37.

## 8.2 Transactions qualifying for relief

(a) *Acquisitions using the merger basis on or after 4th February 1981.*
Section 37 allows the merger accounting method to be adopted (i.e. no share

*A brief explanation of merger accounting as opposed to acquisition accounting appears in 8.3.

premium account) if a company acquires 90 per cent or more of the equity share capital of another company under any arrangement involving the allotment of its own equity shares.

(b) *Intra-group reconstructions on or after 4th February 1981.*
Section 38 extends relief to cases in which a wholly-owned subsidiary issues shares to its holding company or to a fellow wholly-owned subsidiary in exchange for shares in another subsidiary (whether wholly-owned or not).

(c) *Transactions before 4th February 1981.*
Retrospective relief is given by s. 39 for transactions before 4th February 1981 in which a company issued shares at a premium in exchange for shares in another company which thereby became its subsidiary.

## 8.3 Distinction between acquisition accounting and merger accounting

The distinction between acquisition accounting and merger accounting is shown in the following illustration.

*Illustration*

The balance sheets of X plc and Y plc at 31st December are:

X plc

| | £ | | £ |
|---|---|---|---|
| Share capital | 10,000 | Sundry assets | 15,000 |
| Reserves | 5,000 | | |
| | £15,000 | | £15,000 |

Y plc

| | £ | | £ |
|---|---|---|---|
| Share capital | 8,000 | Sundry assets | 16,000 |
| Reserves | 8,000 | | |
| | £16,000 | | £16,000 |

X plc is to acquire all the share capital of Y plc in exchange for shares in X plc which will be allotted to the shareholders in Y plc. It is agreed that the value of Y plc is £16,000 and that the consideration will be discharged by issuing 8,000 £1 shares in X plc.

You are required to show the balance sheet of X plc after the acquisition if it is accounted for:

(a) using the acquisition method

(b) using the merger method

(A) ACQUISITION METHOD

X plc

| | £ | | £ |
|---|---|---|---|
| Share capital | 18,000 | Sundry assets | |
| Share premium | 8,000 | (£15,000 + £16,000) | 31,000 |
| Distributable reserves | 5,000 | | |
| | £31,000 | | £31,000 |

(B) MERGER METHOD

X plc

| | £ | | £ |
|---|---|---|---|
| Share capital | 18,000 | Sundry assets | 31,000 |
| Distributable reserves | 13,000 | | |
| | £31,000 | | £31,000 |

*Notes:*
In (a) the new shares issued are taken as being issued for £16,000, giving rise to the creation of a share premium account.

In (b) the new shares are included at the nominal value, with the result that the pre-acquisition distributable reserves of Y plc remain available for distribution in X plc.

## PROGRESS TEST 1

1. Contrast companies and partnerships. (1.2)
2. Contrast private and public companies. (1.3)
3. Outline the various classes of share capital. (1.7)
4. Outline the various classes of capital. (1.8)
5. What are distributable profits and what restrictions govern their distribution? (1.12)
6. Briefly discuss dividend payments and final dividends. (1.13)
7. What new provisions governing the form and the content of accounts were introduced by CA 1981? (2.1)
8. What exemptions from the above (2.1) exist for small companies? (2.3)
9. What are the detailed disclosure requirements of the new 8th Schedule? (2.4)
10. What are the historical accounting rules in detail? (2.4(b)(x))
11. What affects does CA 1981 have on the directors' report? (3.2)
12. Write out the *new* directors' report contents. (3.3)
13. What form should the deferred taxation account adopt? (4.3)
14. How may one account for advance corporation taxation? (4.4)
15. What are the traditional statements provided in a company's published accounts? (5.1)
16. What is the value added statement? (5.3)

17. Give details of what may be contained in the employment report. (5.4)
18. What statements must be given of transactions in a foreign currency? (5.6)
19. What statements must be given of the following:
    (a) corporate objectives, (5.8)
    (b) analysis of activities? (5.9)
20. What are redeemable shares and how does their redemption differ between public and private companies? (6.2, 6.3)
21. What powers does a company have to purchase its own shares? (7.0)
22. What relief may be available for a company from s. 56 CA 1948 (share premium account)? (8.0)

CHAPTER TWO

# Statements of Standard Accounting Practice

## 1.0 INTRODUCTION

The 1970s will be remembered in accounting circles as the decade in which first attempts were made, in a serious and co-ordinated way, to standardise the permissible accounting treatments in given circumstances.

The major professional bodies in the United Kingdom have appointed representatives to sit on the Accounting Standards Committee (ASC). The task of this committee is to select specific accounting problems whose treatment often varies to an unacceptable degree, thus resulting in inconsistency, loss of comparability, and consequent difficulty in interpreting the data thus presented. The problems selected are considered by the ASC, which then issues its recommendations on accounting treatment and disclosure in the form of Exposure Drafts (EDs) for the purpose of general public comment and debate.

After a suitable "exposure" period a definitive version is published which takes into account all responsible comments received, and which it is expected will be observed in practice by the members of all the contributing professional bodies. The definitive version is as a Statement of Standard Accounting Practice (SSAP).

## 2.0 ACCOUNTING FOR RESULTS OF ASSOCIATED COMPANIES—SSAP 1

### 2.1 Introduction

Accounting for the results of associated companies in accordance with SSAP 1 is shown in diagrammatic form in Fig. 2.

(a) *Current legal requirements*
It is accepted accounting practice for a company not to take credit in its own profit and loss account and balance sheet for its share of the profits of other

companies (subsidiary or otherwise) which have not been distributed. The inclusion of undistributed profits would ignore the separate legal entities of the companies concerned and, as regards the investing company, be in breach of the principle that credit should not be taken for investment income until it is received or receivable.

Where a company conducts an important part of its business through the medium of other companies, whether more or less than 50 per cent owned, the mere disclosure of dividend income is unlikely to be sufficient to give

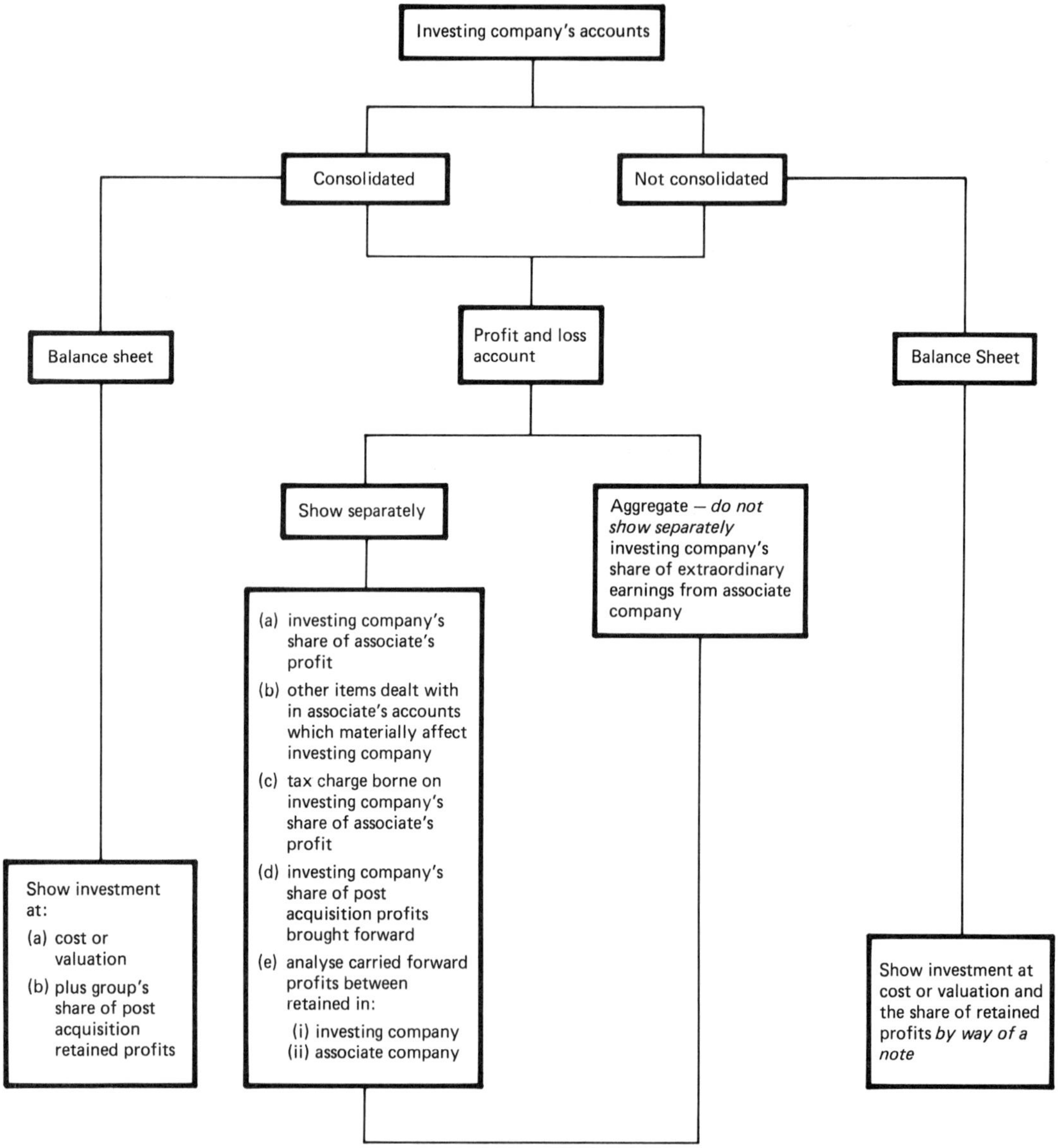


Fig. 2. *Accounting for the results of associated companies.*

shareholders adequate information regarding the sources of their income and of the manner in which their funds are being employed.

(b) *Recent developments*
Two important developments have taken place in recent years:

(i) the growing practice of conducting part of a company's business through other companies, *either*:
on a consortium basis, *or*
by way of a joint venture
where the interest of the investing company is substantial but not controlling.

(ii) the importance which investors now attach to earnings (as distinct from dividends).

In the light of these developments it is considered necessary to extend *consolidation* to include associated company interests. The investing company's accounts should include the share of earnings or losses of companies which are by definition associated companies.

(c) *Nature of investments*
This approach recognises a difference in principle between the nature of investments in associated companies (as defined in the Statement) and other forms of trade investment. The investing company actively participates in the commercial and policy decisions of its associated companies; it thus has a measure of direct responsibility for the return on its investment, whereas it will normally seek to exert direct management influence over the operating policy of other companies in which it invests.

## 2.2 Definition of "associated company"

A company, other than a subsidiary, is an associate of an investing company if *either*:

(a) the interest is effectively that of a partner in a joint-venture or consortium, *or*

(b) the interest is both substantial and can exercise significant influence. Substantial normally means not less than 20 per cent of the equity voting rights.

In both cases the investing company should be represented on the board of the associated company.

## 2.3 Bases of accounting for profits of associated companies—companies with subsidiaries

(a) *Holding company's profit and loss account should include:*

dividends received and

dividends receivable in respect of accounting periods ending on or before the accounting date

(b) *Consolidated profit and loss account:*

*exclude dividends received and receivable from associated companies.*

*profits before tax:* show separately the investing company's share of the aggregate of the before-tax profits less losses of the associate

*taxation:* show separately the tax charge borne on the investing company's share of the associate company's profit

*extraordinary items:* include with similar items already in the group's accounts. Separate disclosure is only necessary if the amount involved is material

*other items:* the group's share of other items, such as turnover and depreciation, in the associate's accounts should not be shown unless significant

*profits brought forward:* show separately the group's proportion of retained profits of the associate at the beginning of the year

*profits carried forward:* show the retained profits carried forward split between the group and the share of associate's undistributed post-acquisition profits.

(c) *Consolidated balance sheet:* add to the cost (or valuation) of investments in associated companies, the proportion of post-acquisition profits retained by associates.

## 2.4 Bases of accounting for profits of associated companies—companies without subsidiaries

(a) *Profit and loss account:* all the adjustments necessary to show interests in associated companies in the consolidated profit and loss account also apply to the normal profit and loss account. In practice one further adjustment is necessary—the company's share of post-acquisition profits retained in the associated company at the year end is deducted so that the carry-forward figure represents the retained profits of the investing company.

(b) *Balance sheet:* in the investing company's own balance sheet the share of post-acquisition retained profits is shown by way of a note (with a consolidated balance sheet it is shown as a separate item under reserves and added to the cost of shares in associated companies).

## 2.5 Sundry matters

(a) *Associated companies' accounts:* accounts used for the purpose of including associated companies' results should be audited accounts which are either coterminous with the investing companies' accounts or made up to a date not more than six months before, or shortly after the date of the investing company's accounts. In the absence of audited accounts, the investing company must satisfy itself as to the reliability of the unaudited figures.

Where accounts are not coterminous, dates of year-ends should be disclosed. Where unaudited accounts are used, the fact should be disclosed. Where an associated company is itself listed on the Stock Exchange, only publicly available financial information should be used for incorporation in the accounts of the investing company.

(b) *Accounting adjustments:* where the effect is material on the results of the investing company, adjustments should be made to remove such items as unrealised profits on stocks transferred from or to associates.

(c) *Particulars of associated companies:* the investing group or company should give particulars of the names of interests in companies treated as associated companies, and of any other companies in which it holds not less than 20 per cent of the equity voting rights but which are not treated as associated companies in its accounts.

(d) *Corresponding figures:* corresponding amounts for the preceding period should be stated.

(e) *Effective date:* accounting periods which started on or after 1st January 1971.

## 2.6 Companies Act 1967

The requirements of the Companies Act 1967, Sched. 2, para. 5A, must be followed and where these requirements do not provide the full information necessary then the additional information must be appropriately disclosed.

## 2.7 Pro-forma consolidated profit and loss account

| | £ | £ |
|---|---|---|
| Turnover (of the investing company and subsidiaries) | | 1,800,000 |
| Operating profit (after charging depreciation and all other trading expenses of the investing company and subsidiaries) | | 120,000 |
| Share of profits *less* losses of associated companies | | 3,000 |
| Profit before taxation | | 123,000 |
| *deduct:* UK taxation based on profits for the year: | | |
| Corporation tax: | | |
| Investing company and subsidiaries | 48,000 | |
| Associated companies | 1,000 | |
| | | 49,000 |
| | | 74,000 |
| *deduct:* Minority interests | | 9,000 |
| Profit after taxation and before extraordinary items | | 65,000 |
| *add:* Extraordinary profits (group proportion after taxation after deducting minority interests and including share of associated companies' items) | | 23,000 |
| Carried forward | | 88,000 |

| | £ | £ |
|---|---|---|
| Brought forward | | 88,000 |
| *add:* Balance brought forward from previous years: | | |
| Group | 90,000 | |
| Associated companies | 4,500 | 94,500 |
| | | 182,500 |
| *deduct:* Dividends | | 15,000 |
| Retained profits carried forward | | £167,500 |

| | £ |
|---|---|
| *Note:* Net profit retained is made up as follows: | |
| Investing company | 137,000 |
| Subsidiaries | 22,000 |
| Associated companies | 8,500 |
| | £167,500 |

## 2.8 Pro-forma consolidated balance sheet

| | £<br>Cost | £<br>Aggregate depreciation | £ |
|---|---|---|---|
| *Employment of capital* | | | |
| Fixed assets: | | | |
| Short leases | 200,000 | 80,000 | 120,000 |
| Plant and machinery | 90,000 | 42,000 | 48,000 |
| | £290,000 | £122,000 | 168,000 |
| Investments: | | | |
| Shares in associated companies at cost | | 50,000 | |
| Post-acquisition profit attributable thereto | | 8,500 | 58,500 |
| Current assets: | | | |
| Stocks | | 160,000 | |
| Debtors (including dividends receivable from associated companies) | | 180,000 | |
| Bank balance | | 68,000 | |
| | | 408,000 | |
| *deduct:* Current liabilities: | | | |
| Creditors | 170,000 | | |
| Corporation tax | 48,000 | | |
| Proposed dividend | 15,000 | 233,000 | 175,000 |
| | | | £401,500 |

| *Capital employed* | Authorised £ | Issued and fully paid £ |
|---|---|---|
| Share capital: | | |
| Ordinary shares of £1 each | 250,000 | 200,000 |
| Reserve on consolidation | | 15,000 |
| Revenue reserves: | | |
| Profit and loss account: | | |
| Retained by group | 159,000 | |
| Retained by associated companies | 8,500 | |
| | | 167,500 |
| | | 382,500 |
| Minority interest | | 19,000 |
| | | £401,500 |

*Note:* The group holds 25 per cent and 30 per cent respectively of the equity share capital of X Ltd and Y Ltd, associated companies.

## 2.9 Pro-forma profit and loss account for a company without subsidiaries

| | £ | £ |
|---|---|---|
| Turnover (of the investing company) | | 1,450,000 |
| Operating profit (after charging depreciation and all other trading expenses of the investing company) | | 70,000 |
| Share of profits *less* losses of associated companies | | 1,750 |
| Profit before taxation | | 71,750 |
| *deduct:* UK taxation based on profits for the year: | | |
| Corporation tax: | | |
| Investing company | 31,000 | |
| Associated companies | 750 | |
| | | 31,750 |
| Profit after taxation and before extraordinary items | | 40,000 |
| *add:* Extraordinary profits (investing company and share of associated companies' items) after taxation | | 13,000 |
| | | 53,000 |
| *add:* Balance brought forward from previous years: | | |
| Investing company | 55,000 | |
| Associated companies | 2,000 | |
| | | 57,000 |
| | | 110,000 |
| *deduct:* Dividends | | 8,000 |
| | | 102,000 |
| *deduct:* Investing company's share of post-acquisition profits retained by associated companies | | 3,250 |
| Retained profits carried forward | | £98,750 |

## 2.10 Pro-forma balance sheet for a company without subsidiaries

| | £ Cost | £ Aggregate depreciation | £ |
|---|---|---|---|
| *Employment of capital* | | | |
| Fixed assets: | | | |
| Freehold property | 43,750 | — | 43,750 |
| Plant and machinery | 34,000 | 16,000 | 18,000 |
| Motor vehicles | 4,200 | 1,800 | 2,400 |
| | 81,950 | 17,800 | 64,150 |
| Investments: | | | |
| Shares in associated companies at cost | | | 40,000 |
| Current assets: | | | |
| Stocks at cost | | 42,800 | |
| Debtors (including dividends receivable from associated companies) | | 28,000 | |
| Cash balances | | 200 | |
| | | 71,000 | |
| *deduct:* Current liabilities: | | | |
| Creditors | 12,000 | | |
| Bank overdraft (secured) | 5,400 | | |
| Corporation tax | 31,000 | | |
| Proposed dividend | 8,000 | 56,400 | |
| | | | 14,600 |
| | | | £118,750 |

| *Capital employed* | Authorised £ | Issued and fully paid £ |
|---|---|---|
| Share capital: | | |
| Ordinary shares of £1 each | 20,000 | 20,000 |
| Reserves: | | |
| Profit and loss account | | 98,750 |
| | | £118,750 |

*Note:* The company holds 25 per cent of the issued ordinary share capital of A Ltd and Z Ltd. The members' share of the associated companies' post-acquisition retained profits is £3,250.

# 3.0 DISCLOSURE OF ACCOUNTING POLICIES—SSAP 2

## 3.1 Fundamental accounting concepts

(a) *Definition.* These are the basic assumptions normally applied by accountants in producing periodic financial accounts. The following four concepts are those most widely adopted:

(i) the "going concern" concept—that a business will continue for the foreseeable future;

(ii) the "accruals" concept—that revenue and costs are earned and incurred *not* as cash is received or paid but as they are recognised as being applicable to a particular period;

(iii) the "consistency" concept—that similar treatment must be given to similar items within an accounting period and from one period to the next;

(iv) the "prudence" concept—that revenue and profits are only earned when represented either by cash or by some other asset with a reasonably certain future cash value;

Where there is a conflict the "prudence" concept prevails.

(b) *Application.* Problems arise in the application of fundamental concepts, since business transactions have financial effects spreading over a number of years. Decisions have to be made with regard to:

(i) carrying forward expenditure incurred in one year which can reasonably be expected to produce revenue in future years;

(ii) carrying forward revenue received for goods or services, which will involve some later expenditure.

There is a presumption that the four fundamental concepts have been observed. Where this is not the case, the facts should be fully explained.

## 3.2 Accounting bases

These are the methods used for applying fundamental accounting concepts. In particular, they are used in defining the limits within which the "accruals" concept is applicable, both as regards revenue and profit, and the amount at which balance sheet items should be shown.

They provide a consistent framework for financial statements. Common examples include bases for calculating:

(a) depreciation;

(b) stocks and work in progress;

(c) deferred taxation.

Judgement has to be exercised as to the choice of those bases which are most appropriate to the circumstances of the business. Generalised rules cannot be formulated, and limitations for the regulating of accounting bases must be accepted.

## 3.3 Accounting policies

These are the accounting bases chosen by management as being best suited for use by a particular business in the preparation of financial accounts.

When management can reasonably choose from a number of accounting bases the accounting policy followed can have a material effect on the periodic results of the business. It is therefore essential that the policy followed be made explicit. Matters for which different accounting bases are recognised as having a material effect on financial statements include:

(a) depreciation of fixed assets;

(b) treatment and amortisation of intangibles such as research and development expenditure, patents and trademarks;

(c) stocks and work in progress;

(d) long-term contracts;

(e) deferred taxation;

(f) hire-purchase or instalment transactions;

(g) leasing and rental transactions;

(h) conversion of foreign currencies;

(i) repairs and renewals;

(j) consolidation policies;

(k) property development transactions;

(l) warranties for products or services.

Accounting policies followed for dealing with items materially affecting the profit or loss for the year and the financial position of the business, should be disclosed by way of note to the accounts.

## 4.0 EARNINGS PER SHARE—SSAP 3

### 4.1 Introduction

A fundamental requirement of financial reporting is the disclosure of the salient features of the accounts in the clearest possible form. Outstanding among the matters of interest to shareholders in quoted companies are earnings per share, dividends per share and the trend of these two figures over a number of years.

As new shares are issued, either for the purpose of acquisition or by way of rights issues, a company may well show rising profits without reflecting a corresponding growth in earnings per share.

Earnings per share forms the basis for calculating the "price–earnings ratio" which is a standard stock-market indicator. Price–earnings ratios relating to both past and prospective profits are widely used by investors in judging the relative worth of a share.

The annual accounts of a quoted company should therefore disclose earnings per share calculated in accordance with accepted standards. The record of adjusted earnings per share will assist in the assessment of the past performance of a company so far as concerns its equity shareholders.

## 4.2 Determination of earnings per share

(a) *Earnings for equity*. Earnings per share means the profit in pence attributable to each equity share based on the consolidated profit of the period (including the earnings of associated companies)

(i) after tax,

(ii) after deducting minority interests,

(iii) after preference dividends,

(iv) before extraordinary items,

divided by the number of equity shares in issue and *ranking for dividend* in respect of the period.

(b) *Taxation*. Where no provision is made for deferred taxation and there exist material taxation liabilities which may crystallise at some future date, reference to this fact should be made against the earnings per share figures.

(c) *Preference dividends*.

(i) cumulative preference shares—the full dividend for the period should be taken into account whether or not it has been earned or declared.

(ii) non-cumulative—the deduction should be the amount of preferential dividend paid or proposed.

(d) *Losses*.

(i) where a loss is incurred, earnings per share should be determined in the normal manner and the result shown as a loss per share.

(ii) where the tax charge is distorted by losses brought forward:

earnings per share should be calculated with reference to the tax charge for the year shown in the profit and loss account

explanation of the effects of the incidence of tax relief on earnings per share for that year and the preceding year should be given.

(e) *Sinking fund*. Transfers to a loan redemption reserve or to a sinking fund should not be deducted in calculating the earnings of the period. They merely divide the profits between those available for immediate distribution and those distributable later.

(f) *Equity share capital*. Earnings should be apportioned over different classes of shares in accordance with their dividend rights or other rights to participate in profits.

(g) *Example using simple capital structure*

Capital structure

Issued share capital:

£500,000 in 10 per cent cumulative preference shares of £1

£1,000,000 in ordinary shares of 25p = 4,000,000 shares

| Trading results | Year ended 31st December | |
|---|---|---|
| | 19X4 | 19X3 |
| | £ | £ |
| Profit after tax | 550,000 | 450,000 |

Assumptions

No change in the issued share capital during the two years

| | Year ended 31st December | |
|---|---|---|
| Calculation of earnings per share | 19X4 | 19X3 |
| | £ | £ |
| Profit after tax | 550,000 | 450,000 |
| *less:* Preference dividend | 50,000 | 50,000 |
| Earnings | £500,000 | £400,000 |
| Number of ordinary shares | 4,000,000 | 4,000,000 |

| Illustration of presentation in the profit and loss account | Year ended 31st December | |
|---|---|---|
| | 19X4 | 19X3 |
| Earnings per ordinary share of 25p | 12½p | 10p |

*Note:* The calculation of earnings per share is based on earnings of £500,000 (19X3 £400,000) and four million ordinary shares in issue throughout the two years ended 31st December 19X4.

## 4.3 Standard accounting practice

(a) *Application.* Earnings per share should be shown on the face of the profit and loss account, with a figure for the corresponding previous period. This applies to companies having a stock exchange quotation.

Details:

(i) amount of earnings

(ii) number of equity shares

used in the calculation should be disclosed in the profit and loss account, or by way of note.

(b) *Dilution of earnings.* In addition to the basic earnings per share, fully diluted earnings per share should be shown where the company has:

(i) issued a separate class of equity shares which do not rank for any dividend in the period under review, but which will in the future;

(ii) issued debentures, loan stock or preference shares convertible into equity shares of the company;

(iii) granted options or issued warrants to subscribe for equity shares of the company.

(c) *Disclosure of diluted earnings.* In the circumstances outlined in (b) above:

(i) the basis of calculation of fully diluted earnings per share should be disclosed;

(ii) fully diluted earnings per share need not be given unless the dilution amounts to 5 per cent or more of the basic earnings per share;

(iii) the fully diluted earnings per share for the corresponding previous period should not be shown unless the assumptions on which it was based still apply;

(iv) where both basic and fully diluted earnings per share are disclosed, each should receive equal prominence.

(d) *Effective date.* These accounting practices have been regarded as applicable in respect of accounts relating to periods which started on or after 1st January 1972.

## 4.4 Effect of changes in equity share capital on calculation of earnings per share

In cases where further equity shares have been issued during the financial year it will be necessary to take into account the circumstances of the issue in determining the earnings per share. The following are the methods by which a company may increase its share capital:

(a) issue of new shares at full market price;

(b) bonus issue by capitalisation of profits and reserves;

(c) share exchange;

(d) rights issue (at less than full market price).

Where shares are issued part way through a year it would not be "true and fair" to apportion the year's earnings against the larger year-end capital. To achieve a fair figure earnings should be apportioned over the average equity share capital and some form of "weighted average" calculation is necessary.

Treatments in each of the circumstances mentioned above are summarised below.

## 4.5 Issue of new shares at full market price

It is not normal for new shares to be issued for cash at full market price. However, where equity shares have been issued for the acquisition of an asset or cancellation of a liability, the earnings should be apportioned over the weighted average number of shares ranking for dividend during the period.

*Illustration*

The year end of a company was 31st December 19X3 and its equity share capital to 30th September 19X3 was one million £1 shares. On 1st October the company acquired freehold premises by the issue of a further one million £1 shares at full market price.

Weighted average calculation, 31st December 19X3:

| | |
|---|---|
| Shares in issue at 1st January 19X3 | 1,000,000 |
| Issued 1st October 19X3 1,000,000 × $\frac{3}{12}$ = | 250,000 |
| Weighted average number of shares for calculating earnings per share | 1,250,000 |

No adjustment is required for the corresponding year's figures, i.e. 1,000,000 shares.

## 4.6 Bonus issue by capitalisation of profits or reserves

Where new equity shares have been issued by way of capitalisation of reserves during the period, the earnings should be apportioned over the number of shares ranking for dividend after the capitalisation.

*Illustration*

The year end of a company is 31st December 19X3 and its share capital to 30th June 19X3 is one million £1 shares. On 1st July 19X3 the company issued a further one million £1 shares by way of capitalising reserves on a one-for-one basis.

The full amount of the bonus issue will be added to the share capital to arrive at the number of shares issued when calculating the earnings per share. The previous years' earnings per share will also have to be adjusted to the revised capital issued figure for comparative purposes.

*Note:* In this instance no weighted average calculation is required because there is *no consideration* for the issue of the shares.

## 4.7 Share exchange

Where equity shares are issued in exchange for the majority interest in another company the consolidated results will include the profits of the newly acquired subsidiary. Inconsistencies exist in accounting methods for dealing with pre-acquisition profits of such subsidiaries and the alteration of accounting year ends; also, frequently, the actual issue is made at a later date than the period for which earnings are included in consolidated profits.

For the purposes of the earnings per share calculation it should be assumed that the relevant shares were issued on the first day of the period for which profits of the new subsidiary are included.

*Illustration*

A company whose year end is 31st December 19X3 acquires a subsidiary by the issue of ordinary shares on 31st March 19X3.

The company acquired also has a year-end date of 31st December 19X3.

The acquiring company decides to consolidate the whole of the acquired company's profits without any adjustment for pre-acquisition profits on the grounds that substantial agreement had been reached with the acquired company by 1st January 19X3.

In such circumstances the new shares are assumed to have been issued for the full period for which earnings are taken into account—i.e. from 1st January 19X3.

## 4.8 Rights issue

(a) *Bonus element in a rights issue*
Where equity shares ranking *pari passu* with an existing class are issued during the financial year in the form of a rights issue, they will be offered at a price which is below the current market price. A rights issue is therefore equivalent to a cash issue at full market price, combined with a subsequent capitalisation issue. This notional capitalisation issue reflects the bonus element inherent in the rights issue, and may be measured by comparing the market price of the shares cum rights with the equivalent price ex-rights. An illustration of the choices of action before a shareholder demonstrating the calculation of the theoretical ex-rights price is set out below.

*Illustration*

Consider a shareholder who holds 360 shares, market price £1 each, in a company which makes a rights issue of 1 for 4 at 50p each. He has, in theory, four choices before him:

| | |
|---|---|
| (a) Take up the rights. If he subscribes for his whole entitlement this will cost him £45. He will then hold | 450 shares worth £405 or 90p per share. |
| (b) Sell shares cum rights and use the proceeds to subscribe for new shares. If he does not wish to put up any new money, he may sell one-ninth of his existing shares at the cum rights price of £1 each for £40. The proceeds may be used to subscribe for 80 new shares at 50p = £40. He will then hold | 400 shares worth £360 or 90p per share. |
| (c) Sell sufficient rights to enable him to take up the remaining rights. If he does not wish to put up any new money, he may sell five-ninths of his rights at the theoretical price of 40p each, i.e. 50 rights for £20, and use the proceeds to subscribe for 40 new shares. He will then hold | 400 shares worth £360 or 90p per share. |

(d) Sell the renounceable allotment letter. If he does not wish to put up any new money, he may sell the whole of his entitlement to 90 new shares at the theoretical premium of 40p per share for £36. He will then hold — 360 shares worth £324 or 90p per share.

Thus the theoretical ex-rights price is 90p per share.

It will be evident from the illustration above that so far as the shareholder is concerned, a similar result would have been achieved if, instead of the rights issue of 1 for 4 at 50p per share, the company had made a cash issue of 1 for 8 for the full consideration of £1 per share, and a subsequent capitalisation issue of 1 for 9. In the case of the rights issue all earnings per share thereto would be adjusted by $\frac{90p}{100p}$; in the case of the issue for full consideration and subsequent capitalisation issue, the factor would be $\frac{9}{10}$.

(b) *Computation of the factor for adjusting past earnings per share*
It is recommended that the factor for adjustment of past earnings per share after a rights issue be based on the closing price* on the last day of quotation of the shares cum rights. The factor is therefore:

$$\frac{\text{theoretical } \textit{ex rights} \text{ price}}{\text{actual } \textit{cum rights} \text{ price on the last day of quotation cum rights}}$$

Where a rights issue is made during the year under review, the earnings per share for the previous year, and for all earlier years, will need to be adjusted by the factor, calculated as above, to correct for the bonus element in the rights issue.

*i.e. the official middle market quotation published on the following day.

(c) *Computation of earnings per share for the year in which a rights issue is made*
For the current year, it would be undesirable to split the earnings into two periods, one before the rights issue and one after this event. It is necessary to adjust the weighted average share capital by taking the proportion of the capital in issue before the rights issue, applying to this figure the reciprocal of the factor set out above, i.e. $\frac{\text{actual cum rights price}}{\text{theoretical ex-rights price}}$, and adding the proportion in issue after the rights issue.

(d) *Summary*
Where equity shares are issued by way of rights during the period, all past earnings per share should be adjusted by the factor, $\frac{\text{theoretical ex rights price}}{\text{actual cum rights price}}$, in order to allow for the bonus element in the rights issue.

In calculating the earnings per share for the year under review, the weighted average share capital should be computed after adjusting the proportion of the capital in issue before the rights issue by the reciprocal of the factor shown above.

### *Illustration*

The year end of a company is 31st December 19X3 and its issued equity share capital up to 30th June 19X3 is £1,000,000 in ordinary shares of 25p each (i.e. 4,000,000 shares).

On 1st July the company made a rights issue of 1 for 4 at 50p per share (i.e. 1,000,000 shares for £500,000).

The market price of the shares on the last day of quotation on a cum rights basis was 100p.

Calculation of earnings per share:

(a) *Factor:*
The holder of 100 shares could take up 25 new shares for £12.50. He would then hold 125 shares worth (100 at £1 each + 25 at 50p each) £112.50, which give an average price of 90p per share.

The factor for adjustment of past earnings is:

$$\frac{\text{theoretical ex-rights price}}{\text{actual cum rights price}} = \frac{90}{100}.$$

(b) *Past earnings:*
Assume actual earnings per share in 19X2 is reported as 10p per share. This would be adjusted for 19X3 as a result of the rights issue, as follows:

$$10\text{p} \times \frac{90\ (\text{ex})}{100\ (\text{cum})} = 9\text{p}.$$

(c) *Current earnings:*
Assume earnings for 19X3 amount to £425,000.
Number of shares to 30th June 19X3:

| | Shares |
|---|---|
| $4{,}000{,}000 \times \frac{6}{12} \times \frac{(\text{rights})\ 100\ (\text{cum})}{(\text{factor})\ 90\ (\text{ex})} =$ | 2,222,222 |
| $5{,}000{,}000 \times \frac{6}{12} =$ | 2,500,000 |
| Weighted average numbers of shares adjusted for rights factor | 4,722,222 |
| Earnings | £425,000 |
| Earnings per share | 9p |

## 4.9 Dilution of future earnings

A company may have entered into obligations to *dilute* the earnings per share in the future. The following are circumstances in which this could occur:

(a) a separate class of equity shares that do not rank for a current dividend but will in future periods.

(b) debentures, loan stock or preference shares convertible into equity shares.

(c) options or warrants to subscribe for shares of the company.

Where such a situation arises, in addition to the basic earnings per share (calculated on the equity shares ranking for dividends in respect of the period) the *fully diluted* earnings should also be calculated.

In this calculation assume that this class of shares did in fact rank for dividends from the beginning of the period (or appropriate later date).

# 5.0 THE ACCOUNTING TREATMENT OF GOVERNMENT GRANTS—SSAP 4

## 5.1 Introduction

The accounting treatment of government grants has varied as different grant schemes have been produced by successive governments. With the advent of regional development grants under the Industry Act 1972 it is desirable to standardise the accounting treatment of these new grants.

## 5.2 Types of grant

(a) *Revenue-based grants*—the Industry Act 1972 makes provision for grants to be made by reference to specified categories of revenue expenditure. Such grants do not produce accounting problems, as they clearly should be credited to revenue in the same period in which the revenue expenditure to which they relate is charged.

(b) *Capital-based grants*—the Industry Act 1972 also makes provision for grants to be made by reference to certain types of capital expenditure. In the past, where expenditure on the acquisition of a fixed asset was eligible for a government grant, there have been different views about the choice of accounting treatments.

The most appropriate treatment favours treating the amount of the grant as a deferred credit, a portion of which is transferred annually to revenue.

## 5.3 Standard accounting practice

Grants relating to fixed assets under the Industry Act 1972 should initially be treated as deferred credits pending transfer to profit and loss account on a basis which fairly reflects the benefit over the expected useful life of the asset. If material, it should be shown separately in the balance sheet. It should not be included under current liabilities or shown as part of shareholders' funds.

## 6.0 ACCOUNTING FOR VALUE ADDED TAX—SSAP 5

### 6.1 General

VAT is a tax on the supply of goods and services eventually borne by the final consumer but collected at each stage of the production and distribution chain. As a general principle therefore the treatment of VAT in the accounts of a trader should reflect his role as a collector of the tax and VAT should not be included in income or in expenditure whether of a capital or revenue nature. There will however be circumstances, as noted below, in which a trader will himself bear VAT and in such circumstances the accounting treatment should accordingly reflect that fact.

### 6.2 Persons not accountable for VAT

Persons not accountable for VAT will suffer VAT on inputs. For them, VAT will increase the cost of all goods and services to which it applies and should be included in such costs.

### 6.3 Accountable persons who also carry on exempted activities

In the case of accountable persons who also carry on exempted activities there will be a residue of VAT, which will fall directly on the trader, normally arrived at by division of his output as between taxable outputs (including zero-rated) and those which are exempt. Such VAT will be part of the trader's costs and should be so treated in his accounts; in particular, the appropriate portion of VAT allocable to fixed assets should, if irrecoverable, be added to the cost of the fixed assets concerned. In some cases, e.g. where financial and VAT accounting periods do not coincide, an estimate may be necessary.

### 6.4 Amounts due to or from the revenue authorities

Amounts due to or from the revenue authorities in respect of VAT should be included as part of debtors or creditors and will not normally require separate disclosure.

### 6.5 Capital commitments

The estimated amount of capital commitments should include the appropriate amount, if any, of irrecoverable VAT.

### 6.6 Standard accounting practice

(a) *Turnover* shown in the profit and loss account should exclude VAT on taxable outputs.

(b) *Irrecoverable VAT* allocable to fixed assets should be treated as part of their cost. Other items disclosed separately in the accounts should be stated at amounts inclusive of irrecoverable VAT allocable to them where such inclusion is material.

## 7.0 EXTRAORDINARY ITEMS AND PRIOR YEAR ADJUSTMENTS—SSAP 6

## A. EXTRAORDINARY ITEMS

### 7.1 Introduction

Accounts are produced at regular intervals throughout the life of an entity to show:

(a) the result of the entity's activities since the last accounts were produced; and

(b) the state of the entity's affairs at the accounting date.

In order to provide a comprehensive picture of the entity's activities, it is necessary to include the results of *all* transactions in the profit and loss account, the only items transferred direct to reserves being *unrealised* gains and losses, e.g. profit on revaluation of assets; goodwill on consolidation written off, and so on.

Some transactions recorded in the profit and loss account may fall outside the scope of the entity's normal activities. These are termed *extraordinary* items. The ASC maintains that it is necessary to distinguish extraordinary from ordinary items in the accounts, so that users of the accounts can assess the entity's performance in the *normal* course of events. Under the provisions of SSAP 3, therefore, earnings per share are calculated *before* taking extraordinary items into account.

### 7.2 What makes an item "extraordinary"?

The ASC's definition, given below, is rather vague:

Extraordinary items

(a) derive from events and transactions outside of the ordinary activities of the business,

(b) are material, and

(c) are expected not to occur frequently or regularly.

It is the event or transaction measured in money terms which is extraordinary, not the size or incidence of the item in the accounts. Items of abnormal size (e.g. a specific bad debt provision) may require separate disclosure under the Companies Acts in order to give a true and fair view, but they are not extraordinary unless the above criteria are fulfilled.

### 7.3 Examples

An event which is extraordinary in the context of one business may not be so in another. The following events, taken in context, *could* be extraordinary:

(a) The discontinuance of a significant part of a business.

(b) The sale of an investment not originally acquired for resale (e.g. shares in associated companies and subsidiaries).

(c) The writing off of intangible assets (e.g. goodwill) because of developments during the period.

(d) The expropriation of assets (e.g. nationalisation of mines).

## 7.4 Exceptions

(a) *Share premium account*
The following revenue items may, under the Companies Acts, be written off against share premium account:

(i) Preliminary expenses of a company.

(ii) Expenses and commission paid, or discount allowed, on an issue of shares or debentures.

(iii) Premium payable on the redemption of redeemable preference shares or debentures.

(b) *Transfers to reserves*
The articles of association of some property and investment companies stipulate that profits/losses on the sale of property and investments should be carried direct to reserves. Under SSAP 6, the above items should be put through the profit and loss account and then transferred to reserves.

## 7.5 Problems

(a) *Theoretical problems*

(i) *Identification*
The classification of an event as extraordinary ultimately depends largely upon subjective judgement. There have been several instances of disagreement between directors and auditors as to whether items are extraordinary, particularly with regard to provisions for future losses, and losses due to the liquidation of companies in which investments were held.

(ii) *Effect of extraordinary items upon earnings per share*
Certain events in the entity's history may be extraordinary, but they remain actual fact. Since earnings per share and certain statistical information are computed on profits *before* accounting for extraordinary items, a review of the company's performance may be distorted by the omission. In particular, since extraordinary losses show a tendency to exceed extraordinary gains, shares valued on the basis of the price–earnings ratio are likely to be overvalued.

If it were accepted in principle that all of a company's activities contributed to its income, whether extraordinary or not, a valid figure for earnings per share could be calculated *after* taking account of extraordinary items. Any investor sophisticated enough to take heed of earnings per share will in any case analyse the factors contributing to earnings.

(b) *Practical problems*

(i) *Non-compliance with the Standard*
A number of companies appear to be acting entirely outside the spirit of the Standard, for example by crediting unrealised surpluses on revaluation of assets to the profit and loss account as extraordinary items.

(ii) *Foreign currency dealings*
No guide is provided by the Standard as to the accounting treatment of material profits and losses arising when the transactions of foreign branches, associates and subsidiaries are brought into the parent company accounts for a year in which there has been a material realignment of currency.

Although the accounting policy used should be disclosed by the company under the provisions of SSAP 2, a multiplicity of accounting policies are currently employed by companies.

## B. PRIOR YEAR ADJUSTMENTS

### 7.6 Introduction

"Prior year adjustments" are material adjustments applicable to prior accounting years, arising from:

(a) a change in accounting policy; or

(b) the correction of a fundamental error.

SSAP 6 recommends that:

(a) the effect of prior year adjustments on the opening balance of the profit and loss account should be disclosed; and

(b) if practical, accounts of the prior year should be restated in the light of the adjustment. Such adjustments are rare. Normal adjustments in respect of prior year items, e.g. correcting over and under provisions for corporation tax, are not prior year adjustments for this purpose, and should be taken direct to profit and loss account.

### 7.7 Advantages of restating prior year accounts

Restatement preserves consistency of accounting data from one year to the next and prevents misleading comparisons being made, particularly in the treatment of earnings.

## 7.8 Disadvantages of restating prior year accounts

(a) Restatement may destroy public confidence in the accounts;

(b) restatement is not always practicable, in which case some degree of inconsistency remains between the restated portion of the accounts and those areas in which restatement is not possible;

(c) even if the accounts are restated to reflect a change in policy, the facts of managerial decisions taken on the basis of the old policy cannot be changed. The adjusted accounts may not, therefore, reflect an accurate picture of the company's activities in the prior year.

## 7.9 Comment

The ASC has been criticised for basing SSAP 6 (often word for word) on Opinion 9 of the Accounting Principles Board of the American Institute of Certified Public Accountants, at a time when this was coming under heavy criticism and has since been modified by Opinion 30.

Some of the problems of SSAP 6 would be solved by:

(a) defining extraordinary items more precisely; and

(b) defining four aspects of profit:

  (i) prior year's items

  (ii) extraordinary items

  (iii) ordinary items

  (iv) effects of disposing of a segment of the business (not an unusual practice in a period of recession, but illustrated as a possible extraordinary item by SSAP 6).

*Illustration of layout*

(This appendix is illustrative only, and does not form part of the Statement of Standard Accounting Practice.)

Statement of Profit and Loss for the year ended 31st December 19X7

| | | 19X7 | | 19X6 |
|---|---|---|---|---|
| | | £000 | | £000 |
| Turnover | | 183,000 | | 158,000 |
| Operating profit after charging or including: | | 19,400 | | 18,100 |
| Depreciation | 4,100 | | 4,000 | |
| Exceptional loss on major contract (Note 2) | 1,000 | | — | |
| Other items | 325 | | 310 | |
| Carried forward | | 19,400 | | 18,100 |

| | 19X7 | 19X6 |
|---|---|---|
| | £000 | £000 |
| Brought forward | 19,400 | 18,100 |
| Other income: | | |
| Investment income | 300 | 500 |
| Profit before taxation and extraordinary items | 19,700 | 18,600 |
| Taxation | 9,850 | 8,835 |
| Profit before extraordinary items | 9,850 | 9,765 |
| Extraordinary items (less taxation) (Note 3) | 835 | 850 |
| Profit after extraordinary items | 9,015 | 8,915 |
| Dividends | 4,410 | 4,200 |
| Retained profit | 4,605 | 4,715 |

Statement of Retained Profits/Reserves

| | | 19X7 | | 19X6 |
|---|---|---|---|---|
| | | £000 | | £000 |
| Retained profit for the year | | 4,605 | | 4,715 |
| Retained profits/reserves at beginning of year: | | | | |
| As previously reported | 48,890 | | 44,000 | |
| Prior year adjustment (Note 1) | 450 | | 275 | |
| As restated | | 48,440 | | 43,725 |
| Retained profits/reserves at end of year | | 53,045 | | 48,440 |

*Notes:*

(1) The policy followed in accounting for research and development expenditure, which in prior years was written off over a period of four years, was changed during the year ended 31st December 19X7 and such expenditure is now written off in the year in which it is incurred. It is considered that the new policy will give a fairer presentation of the results and the financial position of the company. The prior year adjustment of £450,000 represents research and development expenditure carried forward at 31st December 19X6 (less attributable taxation £340,000). In restating the results for 19X6 on the basis of the new policy, the charge for research and development in that year has been increased by £175,000. The remainder, £275,000 relating to 19X5 and earlier years, has been charged against retained profits at the beginning of 19X6.

(2) Items within the normal activities of the company which require disclosure on account of their abnormal size and incidence.

(3) Description of actual items.

## 8.0 ACCOUNTING FOR CHANGES IN THE PURCHASING POWER OF MONEY—SSAP 7 (Provisional)

This standard suggests that companies should account for inflation by including in their published accounts a supplementary statement in which its results and financial position should be disclosed in terms of "current purchasing power" (CPP) based upon the Retail Prices Index. It was declared "provisional" pending the outcome of the parallel researches of the government committee on inflation accounting under Mr Francis Sandilands. The Sandilands Committee rejected CPP accounting and favoured instead a method of price level accounting, based largely on replacement costs, known as "current cost accounting" (CCA). It was intended by the Committee that CCA should eventually replace historical cost accounting (HCA) as the conventional method of accounting.

The ASC considered CCA and proposed its implementation as an accounting standard via Exposure Draft (ED) 18, a very complex document which was duly rejected by members of the ICAEW at a special meeting called to consider the matter in July 1977.

In March 1980, SSAP 16 introduced a somewhat simplified version of CCA. Full details are given in Chapter 6.

## 9.0 THE TREATMENT OF TAXATION UNDER THE IMPUTATION SYSTEM IN THE ACCOUNTS OF COMPANIES—SSAP 8

### 9.1 Introduction

The principal features of the imputation system of corporation tax, which started in April 1973, are broadly as follows:

(a) corporation tax is charged at a single rate on a company's income whether distributed or undistributed.

(b) in the absence of a dividend the whole of the tax is payable on the same dates as before.

(c) when in an accounting period a company makes a distribution to shareholders, it does not withhold income tax from the payment, but is required to make an advance payment of corporation tax (ACT). This ACT will normally be set off against the company's total liability for corporation tax on its income (but not on its chargeable gains) of the same accounting period.

(d) the resultant net liability is known as the *mainstream corporation tax*.

(e) the charge for corporation tax therefore comprises the total of the mainstream corporation tax and the ACT.

From the paying company's point of view, the concept of "gross" dividends and the deduction of income tax at source therefrom has disappeared. However, an individual shareholder receiving the dividend is chargeable to tax on an amount of income equivalent to the dividend plus the imputed tax credit. This tax credit (generally equivalent to the ACT paid by the company) will discharge the basic rate liability to income tax of a United Kingdom resident or would in certain circumstances be recoverable. For corporate shareholders the concept of franked investment income continues.

### 9.2 Definitions

(a) *Recoverable ACT*
That amount of the ACT paid or payable on outgoing dividends paid and proposed which can be:

(i) set off against the corporation tax liability on the profits of the period under review or of previous periods,

(ii) properly set off against a credit balance on deferred tax account or

(iii) expected to be recoverable taking into account expected profits and dividends—normally those of the next accounting period only.

(b) *Irrecoverable ACT*
ACT paid or payable on outgoing dividends paid and proposed other than recoverable ACT.

## 9.3 Standard accounting practice

(a) *Profit and loss account*
The following items should be included in the taxation charge in the profit and loss account, and where material should be separately disclosed:

(i) the amount of the United Kingdom corporation tax specifying:

the total corporation tax on the income of the year before setting off any recoverable ACT (where such corporation tax includes transfers between the deferred taxation account and the profit and loss account, these also should be separately disclosed where material);

tax attributable to franked investment income;

irrecoverable ACT;

the relief for overseas taxation.

(ii) the total overseas taxation relieved and unrelieved, specifying that part of the unrelieved overseas taxation which arises from the payment or proposed payment of dividends.

*Notes:*
If the rate of corporation tax is not known for the whole or part of the period covered by the accounts, the latest known rate should be used and disclosed.

Outgoing dividends should not include either the related ACT or the attributable tax credit.

Incoming dividends from United Kingdom resident companies should be included at the amount of cash received or receivable plus the tax credit.

(b) *Balance sheet*

(i) dividends proposed (or declared and not yet payable) should be included in current liabilities, without the addition of the attributable ACT. The ACT on proposed dividends (whether recoverable or irrecoverable) should be included as a current tax liability.

(ii) if the ACT on proposed dividends is regarded as recoverable, it should be deducted from the deferred tax account if available for this purpose. In the absence of a deferred taxation account ACT recoverable should be shown as a deferred asset.

(iii) where the title of a class of preference shares (or participating or preferred ordinary shares) issued before 6th April 1973 includes a fixed rate of dividend, the new rate of dividend should be incorporated in the description of the shares in the balance sheet.

### 9.4 Illustration of suggested layout for a note to the profit and loss account showing all the details required both by the Companies Act 1967 and by SSAP 8

| | £ |
|---|---|
| Corporation tax on income at 50% (including £4,500 transferred from deferred taxation account) | 9,850 |
| *deduct:* Relief for overseas taxation | 1,650 |
| | 8,200 |
| Overseas taxation (including £1,000 arising from the payment of dividends) (*see* tutorial note) | 1,550 |
| Tax credit on UK dividends received | 950 |
| Irrecoverable advance corporation tax | 800 |
| | 11,500 |

*Tutorial note:*
Disclosure of this amount is only required where it is material.

## 10.0 STOCK AND WORK IN PROGRESS—SSAP 9

### 10.1 Summary of SSAP 9

(a) *Stocks and short-term work in progress* should be valued at the *lower* of *cost* and *net realisable value* of the separate items of stock and work in progress, or of groups of similar items.

(b) *Long-term contract work in progress* should be valued at cost plus attributable profit less attributable losses, less progress payments received and receivable.

If anticipated losses exceed the result of the above valuation, the excess should be shown separately as a provision.

The following reasons for the above are given:

(i) Owing to the length of time taken to complete long-term contracts, if profit were not taken into account until the contract were completed, then the profit and loss account would not reflect a true and fair view of the *activities* of the company during the year, but only of the results relating to contracts completed by the year end.

(ii) Profit should therefore be taken in proportion to work carried out by the accounting date, taking into account inequalities in profitability of the various parts of the contract, and also all contingencies, such as increased costs, penalties etc., which may arise before completion.

Attributable profit should be included only when the contract is substantially complete and a profit may reasonably be forecast.

Many businesses, such as construction and building companies, carry out contracts whose outcome cannot reasonably be assessed before conclusion of the contract. In these cases, it is obviously prudent not to take any profit on uncompleted contracts, yet this point is overlooked in the standard. The practice of taking profit on uncompleted contracts has also been criticised as being inconsistent with the practice employed on "short-term" contracts.

(c) *Disclosure*

The following information should be disclosed in the published financial accounts or in notes to the accounts:

(i) Accounting policies used to calculate:
cost
net realisable value
attributable profit
foreseeable losses.

(ii) Classes of stock and work in progress, indicating the amount held in each category. This classification should be under headings appropriate to the business.

(iii) Long-term contracts. The following items should be stated:
Work in progress at cost plus attributable profits less foreseeable losses.
Cash received and receivable at accounting date as progress payments for contracts in progress.

(d) *Date from which effective*

The practices laid down in the standard have been regarded as applicable in respect of accounts relating to periods which started on or after 1st January 1976.

## 11.0 STATEMENTS OF SOURCE AND APPLICATION OF FUNDS—SSAP 10

### 11.1 Introduction

The profit and loss account of a company shows the amount of profit generated during the year: the balance sheet shows the position of the company's funds at the end of the year.

For a fuller understanding of the company's affairs, it is necessary to identify the movements in assets, liabilities and capital that have taken place during the year, and to ascertain the effect of these movements on the company's net liquid assets (i.e. cash at bank and in hand; investments held as current assets; bank overdrafts and other short-term borrowings repayable within one year).

The funds statement selects, reclassifies and summarises information disclosed in the profit and loss account and balance sheet, and shows how the operations of the company have been financed and how its financial resources have been deployed.

This is achieved by:

(a) showing how funds have flowed into the company and how they have been used;

(b) showing how the surplus of net liquid assets has been used, or how the deficit has been financed; and

(c) distinguishing short-term and long-term sources and applications of funds.

The following basic rules should be observed wherever possible:

(a) Figures making up the funds statement should not be netted off against one another, as this may mask the significance of individually important figures, e.g. the proceeds of sale of one set of premises, and the cost of purchasing another set of premises.

(b) It should be possible to locate figures used in the funds statement in the balance sheet and profit and loss account. If adjustments have been made to balance sheet and profit and loss account figures before including them in the funds statement, details of the adjustment should be provided in notes to the funds statement so that relevant balance sheet and profit and loss account figures may be identified.

(c) Funds statements of companies with subsidiaries should be based on the group accounts. They should reflect purchases and disposals of subsidiaries in terms of purchases and disposals of the holding company's share of the underlying assets and liabilities.

(d) It is also necessary to disclose how much of the purchase consideration for a subsidiary was paid in cash and how much was paid in shares.

(e) The funds statement should be included in the audited accounts of a company.

## 11.2 Scope of SSAP 10

Like SSAP 9, SSAP 10 became standard in respect of financial statements relating to accounting periods beginning on or after 1st January 1976.

The standard applies to all financial accounts *except* the accounts of enterprises with a turnover or gross income of less than £25,000 per annum.

## 11.3 Disclosure requirements

To comply with the standard, the statement should show:

(a) profit or loss for the period, together with adjustments for items which did not use or provide funds during the period;

(b) dividends paid;

(c) acquisitions and disposals of fixed and other non-current assets;

(d) funds raised by increasing (or expended by repaying or redeeming) medium- or long-term loans or the issued capital of the company;

(e) increase or decrease in working capital, subdivided into its components and movements in net liquid funds. Net liquid funds are:

| *Positive* | *Negative* |
|---|---|
| Cash at bank | Bank overdrafts |
| Cash in hand | Other borrowings repayable within one year of accounting date |
| Cash equivalents (e.g. investments held as current assets) | |

## 11.4 Notes on the examples given

The following examples are taken from the appendix to SSAP 10. They do not form part of the standard and, so long as the basic disclosure requirements are met, any other form may be used.

The following points should be noted:

(a) *Profit before tax*
The statement remains silent on whether to show profit before or after tax. The "before tax" figure is more logical since tax (apart from ACT) remains in the company for at least nine months after the accounting date, and is, during that period, a source of funds. The examples used in the appendix show profits *before* tax.

Correspondingly, tax actually paid during the year is treated as an application.

If the "before tax" figure is used, there is no need to adjust profit in respect of deferred taxation.

(b) *Minority interests*
Example 2 shows the funds statement for a *group*. The minority's share of the profits is deducted from the main pre-tax profit, but added back under the adjustments. This deduction and adding back serves only to emphasise that the minority's share of retained profits is a source for the group, and has little other impact on the statement as a whole.

(c) *Profits retained in associated companies*
Although SSAP 1 recommends consolidation of the associated company's profits, these are omitted from the source and application of funds statement. Since an associated company is not a member of the group, any part of its profit which is not remitted to the group is excluded from the statement. Group investment income from the associate's dividends would therefore be included in profits, but the group's share of the associate's profits would be excluded.

(d) *Working capital*

(i) Any item included in the main part of the statement (e.g. payment of tax and dividends) is *excluded* from working capital.

(ii) Whatever layout is adopted for the working capital section, net liquid funds should be grouped together.

(e) *General presentation*
It is not essential that all applications should be shown as negative figures, or that the statement should reconcile to the movement in working capital.

## 11.5 Examples

*Example 1*

Company Without Subsidiaries Ltd.
Statement of Source and Application of Funds

| | This year | | | Last year | | |
|---|---|---|---|---|---|---|
| | £000 | £000 | £000 | £000 | £000 | £000 |
| *Source of funds* | | | | | | |
| Profit before tax | | | 1,430 | | | 440 |
| Adjustments for items not involving the movement of funds: | | | | | | |
| Depreciation | | | 380 | | | 325 |
| Total generated from operations | | | 1,810 | | | 765 |
| Funds from other sources: | | | | | | |
| Issue of shares for cash | | | 100 | | | 80 |
| | | | 1,910 | | | 845 |
| *Application of funds* | | | | | | |
| Dividends paid | | (400) | | | (400) | |
| Tax paid | | (690) | | | (230) | |
| Purchase of fixed assets | | (460) | | | (236) | |
| | | | (1,550) | | | (866) |
| | | | 360 | | | (21) |
| *Increase/decrease in working capital* | | | | | | |
| Increase in stocks | | 80 | | | 114 | |
| Increase in debtors | | 120 | | | 22 | |
| (Increase) decrease in creditors, excluding taxation and proposed dividends | | 115 | | | (107) | |
| Movement in net liquid funds: | | | | | | |
| Increase (decrease) in | | | | | | |
| Cash balances | (5) | | | 35 | | |
| Short-term investments | 50 | | | (85) | | |
| | | 45 | | | (50) | |
| | | | 360 | | | (21) |

*Example 2*

Statement of Source and Application of Funds
(based on the accounts of the group and showing the effects of acquiring a subsidiary on the separate assets and liabilities of the group)

| | This year | | | Last year | | |
|---|---|---|---|---|---|---|
| | £000 | £000 | £000 | £000 | £000 | £000 |
| *Source of funds* | | | | | | |
| Profit before tax and extraordinary items, less minority interests | | | 2,025 | | | 2,610 |
| Extraordinary items | | | 450 | | | (170) |
| | | | 2,475 | | | 2,440 |
| Adjustments for items not involving the movement of funds: | | | | | | |
| Minority interests in the retained profits of the year | | | 25 | | | 30 |
| Depreciation | | | 345 | | | 295 |
| Profits retained in associated companies | | | (40) | | | — |
| Total generated from operations | | | 2,805 | | | 2,765 |
| Funds from other sources: | | | | | | |
| Shares issued in part consideration of the acquisition of subsidiary* | | | 290 | | | — |
| Capital raised under executive option scheme | | | 100 | | | 80 |
| | | | 3,195 | | | 2,845 |
| *Application of funds* | | | | | | |
| Dividends paid | | (650) | | | (650) | |
| Tax paid | | (770) | | | (970) | |
| Purchase of fixed assets* | | (660) | | | (736) | |
| Purchase of goodwill on acquisition of subsidiary* | | (30) | | | — | |
| Debentures redeemed | | (890) | | | — | |
| | | | (3,000) | | | (2,356) |
| | | | 195 | | | 489 |
| *Increase/decrease in working capital* | | | | | | |
| Increase in stocks* | | 120 | | | 155 | |
| Increase in debtors* | | 100 | | | 122 | |
| Decrease in creditors—excluding taxation and proposed dividends* | | 75 | | | 28 | |
| Movement in net liquid funds: | | | | | | |
| Increase (decrease) in cash balance* | (35) | | | 10 | | |
| Increase (decrease) in short-term investments | (65) | (100) | | 174 | 184 | |
| | | | 195 | | | 489 |

*Summary of the Effects of the Acquisition of Subsidiary Limited

| Net assets acquired | | Discharged by | |
|---|---|---|---|
| Fixed assets | 290 | Shares issued | 290 |
| Goodwill | 30 | Cash paid | 60 |
| Stocks | 40 | | |
| Debtors | 30 | | |
| Creditors | (40) | | |
| | 350 | | 350 |

The detailed procedure for preparing statements of source and application of funds is dealt with in the next chapter.

## 12.0 ACCOUNTING FOR DEFERRED TAXATION—SSAP 11

SSAP 11 was withdrawn in October 1978 and replaced by SSAP 15 (*see* below).

## 13.0 ACCOUNTING FOR DEPRECIATION—SSAP 12

### 13.1 Introduction

Exposure Draft 15, "Accounting for Depreciation", was published in January 1975. The basic context of the Exposure Draft remained largely unaltered when the standard was issued in January 1978. The purpose of the standard is to establish uniform practices regarding *what* is depreciated rather than *how* it is depreciated.

### 13.2 Definition

"Depreciation: the measure of the wearing out, consumption or other loss of value of a fixed asset whether arising from use, effluxion of time or obsolescence through technology and market changes."

It should be noted that the word "cost" is omitted from the definition. Presumably this is to avoid any changes in the standard as current cost accounting develops.

### 13.3 Standard accounting treatment

(a) All assets having a finite life should be depreciated including freehold buildings (but not freehold land).

(b) Where the life of an asset is predetermined (e.g. leases) the rate of depreciation will be governed by the number of years of life.

(c) Residual value should always be estimated but where it is very small, it should be regarded as nil when calculating the annual depreciation charge.

(d) Where circumstances necessitate a slower or faster write off of an asset, the standard states that one should take the present net book value and recalculate the annual depreciation charge for the remaining life of the asset. One does not make a retrospective adjustment in respect of previous years' charges.

(e) Where the method of depreciation is altered, this is achieved by applying the new method to the existing book value. Where there is a material difference in the year of change, this should be separately disclosed.

(f) Wherever the book value of an asset is regarded as excessive, then the value should be written down immediately.

### 13.4 Disclosure

The following should be disclosed in the financial statement for each major class of depreciable asset:

(a) the depreciation methods used;

(b) the useful lives assumed or depreciation rates used;

(c) the total depreciation charged for the period;

(d) the gross amount of depreciable assets and accumulated depreciation.

### 13.5 Effective date

The accounting and disclosure requirements set out in the standard should have been adopted as soon after its publication as possible, but had to be regarded as an essential feature for all financial statements starting on or after 1st January 1978.

### 13.6 Investment properties

*See* 20.0 below for details of SSAP 19 applying to investment properties.

## 14.0 ACCOUNTING FOR RESEARCH AND DEVELOPMENT—SSAP 13

### 14.1 Introduction

The first Exposure Draft on research and development (ED 14) suggested that all expenditure should be written off in the year it was incurred. However, the ASC had second thoughts after hearing the views of interested parties, and in April 1976 published Exposure Draft 17 and it is this which forms, without material alteration, the new standard.

The purpose of the standard is to standardise the treatment of research and development expenditure and rules are laid down for the treatment of any expenditure which may be carried forward.

## 14.2 Definitions

The following definitions are included in the standard:

(a) *Pure research*
This is the original investigation undertaken to gain new technical knowledge. It is not primarily directed to any specific practical application.

(b) *Applied research*
Defined as above, but directed to a specific practical application.

(c) *Development*
The use of technical knowledge to produce new products etc. prior to the commencement of commercial production.

## 14.3 Standard accounting treatment

(a) Fixed assets should always be capitalised as they may be used for another project even if they are bought for a specific one.

(b) The basic rule is that all expenditure on research and development should be written off. The reason for this is that to maintain a company's position in a chosen trade it is necessary to continue the investment in research and development. Another reason is that it is difficult to quantify future benefits from the expenditure and different parties may have different opinions as to how much has in fact derived from the research and development.

The exception to the basic rule is development expenditure and provided it follows a set of tests laid down by the standard, it can be deferred (in part at least) to later periods.

A summary of these circumstances is given below:

(i) There is a clearly defined project.

(ii) The development expenditure to be incurred is separately identifiable.

(iii) There is reasonable certainty that the project is technically feasible and environmentally and commercially viable.

(iv) Expected future revenue will exceed all costs.

(v) There will be sufficient resources to carry the project through and that if further finance is needed for development, it will be available.

(vi) The deferring of development expenditure will only continue where there is certainty as to its recovery.

(vii) Once development expenditure has been written off, it will not be written back.

## 14.4 Disclosure

(a) Movements of deferred development expenditure and the amount carried forward at the beginning and the end of the period should be disclosed.

(b) Deferred development expenditure should be separately disclosed and should not be valued in current assets.

(c) The accounting policy followed should be clearly explained.

### 14.5 Effective date

The accounting and disclosure requirements set out in this statement should have been adopted as soon after its publication as possible and regarded as standard in respect of financial statements relating to periods starting on or after 1st January 1978.

## 15.0 GROUP ACCOUNTS—SSAP 14

(*See also* Chapter 7)

### 15.1 Introduction and background

SSAP 14 has effect for accounting periods commencing on or after 1st January 1979. It does little more than codify good group accounting practice but it does clarify several matters as explained below. SSAP 14 and the notes which follow should be studied in conjunction with the details of statutory requirements and consolidation procedures dealt with in Chapter 7.

### 15.2 Exclusions from consolidation under the Companies Acts

Section 150 Companies Act 1948 does not require group accounts in the following cases:

(a) where the holding company concerned is itself a *wholly-owned* subsidiary of another company;

(b) where the directors believe that it would be:

(i) impracticable, or

(ii) of no real value to the members, or

(iii) unduly expensive or would cause delay out of proportion to the value to the members, or

(iv) misleading, or

(v) harmful, or

(vi) unreasonable to treat companies engaged in very different trades as a single undertaking.

The consent of the Department of Trade and Industry is necessary if it is desired to invoke reasons (v) or (vi).

## 15.3 SSAP 14 provisions as to exclusion from consolidation

SSAP 14 lays down the accounting treatment to be followed in three situations in which consolidation would probably be misleading:

(a) When control is imperfect, because the holding company, although owning more than 50 per cent of the equity share capital, either does not control more than 50 per cent of the voting power or does not have the right to appoint more than 50 per cent of the directors. In this case SSAP 14 requires the subsidiary to be treated as an associated company provided the conditions stipulated in SSAP 1 for such treatment are satisfied, as they normally will be.

(b) When control is temporary. The investment in the subsidiary should be included in the consolidated balance sheet as a current asset valued at the lower of cost and net realisable value.

(c) When control is restricted on a long-term basis. The investment in the subsidiary should be included in the consolidated balance sheet value on the equity basis as at the date the restrictions came into force. No further accruals of profits or losses since that date should be made.

## 15.4 Acquisitions and disposals of subsidiaries—effective date

The effective date for recording the acquisition or disposal of subsidiaries should be the earlier of:

(a) the date on which consideration passes, and

(b) the date on which the offer becomes unconditional.

## 15.5 Premium or discount arising on acquisitions

The purchase consideration on acquisition should be allocated to the tangible assets acquired on the basis of their fair value to the acquiring company. The difference between the sum of these values and the total consideration represents the premium (goodwill) or discount (capital reserve) arising on acquisition.

## 15.6 Disposals of subsidiaries

On the disposal of a subsidiary it is necessary to disclose:

(a) the profit or loss of the subsidiary *up to the date of the disposal*;

(b) the profit or loss arising *on the disposal*, normally as an extraordinary item.

## 15.7 Standardisation of accounting dates of group companies

Section 153 Companies Act 1948 requires group companies to have the same accounting date "unless in the opinion of the directors there are good reasons against it".

Schedule 1 Companies Act 1981 (para. 70) requires the disclosure of the directors' reasons for not bringing the subsidiaries' accounting dates into line with the holding company, and the dates on which the subsidiaries' financial years ending last before that of the holding company, or the earliest and latest dates.

### 15.8 Group accounting policies

SSAP 14 requires group companies to adopt uniform accounting policies and to disclose the reasons for and effect of any unavoidable divergences.

## 16.0 ACCOUNTING FOR DEFERRED TAXATION—SSAP 15

### 16.1 Introduction

The basic concept of deferred taxation was introduced in the Chapter (4.3). It is now necessary to study the subject in greater detail.

The amount of taxation payable on the profits of a particular period often bears little relationship to the amounts of income and expenditure appearing in the profit and loss account. This results from the different basis on which profits are arrived at for the purpose of computing taxation as opposed to the amounts at which profits are stated in accounts.

This different basis of arriving at profits for tax purposes derives from two main sources: first, the fact that certain types of income may be tax-free or that certain expenditure is disallowable, giving rise to "permanent differences" between taxable and book profits; and second, the existence of items which are included in the accounts in a period different from that in which they are dealt with for taxation, giving rise to "timing differences".

Clearly permanent differences do not give rise to a deferral of tax and they need not concern us further. The concept of deferred taxation arises when the effect of a transaction is reflected in one period for accounting purposes and in another for taxation purposes. The easiest example is capital expenditure on plant, which is normally depreciated over several years in accounts, while immediate relief is given by way of first-year allowances in the tax computation. The result is a reduction in tax payable by reference to the year in which the expenditure is incurred, followed by an increase in later years when the timing difference is "reversed" because depreciation is added back without a corresponding reduction for capital allowances. There is no permanent reduction in the amount of tax payable, only a deferment of payment.

Deferred taxation is the tax attributable to timing differences.

### 16.2 The SSAP 11 requirement to provide for deferred taxation in full

SSAP 11, issued in 1975 and withdrawn in October 1978 when SSAP 15 appeared, required that the taxation effect of all timing differences should be allowed for by the creation of a deferred taxation account. It was quickly realised that this could result in the accumulation of a very large credit balance on deferred taxation account, representing a deferred liability much of which was unlikely ever to crystallise as an actual liability but would be indefinitely deferred. The reason for this (taking the case of accelerated capital allowances) is that fresh capital expenditure in later years will give rise to further first year allowances, and so on. In other words, the reversal of the timing difference would be cancelled by a further "originating timing difference".

## 16.3 The revised requirement of SSAP 15

As a result of general dissatisfaction with SSAP 11, SSAP 15 provides, for accounting periods commencing on or after 1st January 1979, that a company *which is a going concern* need not provide for deferred taxation, other than on short-term timing differences, if:

(a) *it can be seen on reasonable evidence that the timing difference will not "reverse" for at least three years;*

(b) *there is no indication that after this period of three years the situation is likely to change so as to crystallise the liabilities.*

## 16.4 Types of timing differences

*Timing differences* are differences between profits as computed for taxation purposes and profits as stated in financial accounts which result from the inclusion of items of income and expenditure in taxation computations in periods different from those in which they are included in financial accounts. Timing differences *originate* in one period and are capable of *reversal* in one or more subsequent periods. The revaluation of an asset is regarded as creating a timing difference when it is incorporated in accounts.

Timing differences arise from *five* main sources:

(a) *Short term timing differences* from the use of the receipts and payments basis for tax purposes and the accruals basis in accounts: these differences normally reverse in the next accounting period.

(b) Availability of *capital allowances* in taxation computations which are in excess of the related depreciation charges in accounts.

(c) Availability of *stock appreciation relief* in taxation computations for which there is no equivalent charge in the accounts.

(d) *Revaluation surpluses* on fixed assets for which a taxation charge does not arise until the gain is realised on disposal.

(e) Surpluses on disposals of fixed assets which are subject to *rollover relief.*

## 16.5 Short-term timing differences

It is generally accepted that deferred taxation should be fully provided for on short-term timing differences.

Examples of short-term timing differences are:

(a) interest receivable accrued in the accounting period, but taxed when received;

(b) dividends from foreign subsidiaries accrued in a period prior to that in which they arise for tax purposes;

(c) intra-group profits on stock deferred upon consolidation until realisation to third parties;

(d) interest or royalties payable accrued in the accounting period, but allowed when paid;

(e) pension costs accrued in the accounts but allowed for tax purposes when paid or contributed or otherwise over an extended period;

(f) provisions for repairs and maintenance made in the accounts but not allowed for tax purposes until the expenditure is incurred;

(g) bad debts provision not allowed for tax purposes unless and until they become specific;

(h) provisions for revenue losses on closing down plants or for costs of reorganisation, upon which tax relief is not obtained until the costs are incurred or losses realised.

## 16.6 Accelerated capital allowances

As already explained in previous paragraphs, the timing differences attributable to accelerated capital allowances are a major cause of deferred taxation adjustments.

## 16.7 Stock appreciation relief

SSAP 15 calls for full provision for deferred taxation in respect of stock appreciation relief except to the *extent that it can be demonstrated with reasonable probability* that stock values will not be reduced in the future by reason of lower volumes or prices. The risk of a fall in stock values is of particular significance in the case of stocks which are seasonal in production or subject to sharp fluctuations in price. To the extent that the government announces that stock relief granted will not be reclaimed, the provision may be reduced from time to time.

## 16.8 Revaluation surpluses

When an asset is revalued, the asset account is debited and a non-distributable reserve account credited. No taxation liability arises until the asset is sold without a claim for rollover relief.

Accordingly, *no* transfer to deferred taxation account for tax attributable to the unrealised gain is required *until a decision is made in principle to sell the asset without claiming rollover relief.*

## 16.9 Surpluses on sale

When an asset is sold at a profit, a tax liability will normally arise and a normal provision for that tax be made.

Deferred taxation will need to be provided for when rollover relief is claimed, unless it is clear that no liability will arise for at least three years because the directors do not intend to sell the replacing asset.

## 16.10 Debit balances arising from timing differences

Debit balances on deferred taxation account arising from timing differences should be carried forward only if there is reasonable certainty of their recovery in future periods.

## 16.11 Trading losses

While trading losses by definition give rise to timing differences, prudence dictates that they should not be recognised through the deferred taxation account, since there can be no certainty that future profits will be earned of sufficient amount to absorb them.

One exception to this rule is recognised by SSAP 15. If there is a credit balance on deferred taxation account at the time the loss arises, and that credit balance is attributable to tax on income against which the loss could be offset, a credit may be released to profit and loss account to the extent of the tax relief obtainable when the loss is utilised.

When profits are subsequently earned and the loss relief obtained, the transfer from deferred taxation balance will need to be reinstated.

## 16.12 Advance corporation tax (ACT)

ACT is normally recovered by setting it off against the corporation tax liability of the period in which the related distribution is made. It may also be carried back for two years, and carried forward without time limit. Although the tax rules allow ACT to be carried forward without time limit, SSAP 8 normally requires it to be written off as irrecoverable if it cannot be seen with reasonable certainty that set-off will be possible within the next accounting period.

SSAP 8 recognises an exception to this one-year limit as follows: Where a deferred taxation account is maintained, unrelieved ACT may be deducted from deferred taxation account even if set-off is not reasonably certain within the next period. Note that a deferred taxation balance attributable to chargeable gains cannot be used for this purpose, as ACT cannot be offset against tax on such gains.

The illustration which follows shows the calculations necessary.

*Illustration*

X Limited has incurred capital expenditure as follows:

| | | Tax rate |
|---|---|---|
| Year 1 | £10,000 | 50% |
| Year 2 | £12,000 | 52% |
| Year 3 | £4,000 | 53% |
| Year 4 | £14,000 | 51% |

100 per cent first-year allowances are claimed in all years, while depreciation at 25 per cent per annum straight line is consistently provided for in full in the year of acquisition.

You are required to calculate the timing differences arising and show the deferred taxation accounts using:

(a) the liability method;

(b) the deferral method assuming that reversals are accounted for:

(i) on an average basis

(ii) on a FIFO basis. (*See* notes below.)

*Notes:*

(1) In the calculations for the liability method, all deferred tax will be computed at the rate ruling for the year in question, an adjustment being made to convert the balance at the beginning of the year when the rate changes.

(2) If the deferral method is used, the originating timing differences will be made at the rate ruling for the year in question, but no adjustment will be made to the opening balance. Reversals must be put through *at the rate ruling when the originating timing difference took place*. For this reason calculations using the deferral method may be made assuming either that reversals take place at the average tax rate or that they take place on a FIFO basis.

ANSWER

Transfers to (from) deferred taxation

| Timing differences | | | (a) Liability method £ | (b) (i) Deferral method Average £ | (b) (ii) Deferral method FIFO £ |
|---|---|---|---|---|---|
| Year 1 (50%): | | | | | |
| Capital allowances | 10,000 | | | | |
| Depreciation | 2,500 | 7,500 | 3,750 | 3,750 | 3,750 |
| Year 2 (52%): | | | | | |
| Tax rate adjustment (2% × £7,500) | | | 150 | | |
| Capital allowances | 12,000 | | | | |
| Depreciation | 5,500 | 6,500 | 3,380 | 3,380 | 3,380 |
| | | 14,000 | 7,280 | 7,130 | 7,130 |
| Year 3 (53%): | | | | | |
| Tax rate adjustment (1% × £14,000) | | | 140 | | |
| Capital allowances | 4,000 | | | | |
| Depreciation | 6,500 | (2,500) | (1,325)* | (1,273)* | (1,250)* |
| | | 11,500 | 6,095 | 5,857 | 5,880 |
| Year 4 (51%): | | | | | |
| Tax rate adjustment (2% × £11,500) | | | (230) | | |
| Capital allowances | 14,000 | | | | |
| Depreciation | 10,000 | 4,000 | 2,040 | 2,040 | 2,040 |
| | | 15,500 | 7,905 | 7,897 | 7,920 |

*See explanation below for calculation of reversal figures

Calculation of reversals in Year 3:

(a) *Liability method.* Under the liability method the opening balance for Year 3 (£14,000) is already expressed in terms of the rate ruling for that year (53 per cent). The reversal of £2,500 is accordingly £2,500 at 53 per cent or £1,325.

(b) (i) *Deferral method using average rate.* The reversal of £2,500 is assumed to come out of the opening balance of £14,000 according to the average rate at which deferred taxation has been provided.

The average rate is 50.92 per cent (£7,130 as a percentage of £14,000) and accordingly the calculation is £2,500 at 50.92 per cent or £1,273.

(ii) *Deferral method using FIFO.* The reversal of £2,500 is assumed to come from the *first* amount credited to the deferred taxation account. This was the deferred taxation created at 50 per cent on the £7,500 in Year 1.

The reversal is accordingly calculated at 50 per cent.

Note that the calculations for originating timing differences are *exactly the same* regardless of the method used. A difference only arises when reversing timing differences arise, when the rules are:

| | |
|---|---|
| (a) *Liability method* | Reverse at current rate. |
| (b) *Deferral method (average)* | Reverse at the average rate at which the opening balance has been created. |
| (c) *Deferral method (FIFO)* | Reverse at the rate attributable to the earliest item credited to the account. |

Entries in deferred taxation account are next shown, taking figures using the liability method. (The entries using the two deferral methods will obviously be very similar. The only real difference lies in the fact that the tax rate adjustment transfers are not required.)

Deferred Taxation

| Year | | £ | Year | | £ |
|---|---|---|---|---|---|
| 1 | Balance carried down | £3,750 | 1 | Profit and loss account | 3,750 |
| 2 | Balance carried down | 7,280 | 2 | Balance brought down | 3,750 |
| | | | | Profit and loss account: | |
| | | | | Tax rate adjustment | 150 |
| | | | | Profit and loss account | 3,380 |
| 3 | Profit and loss account | 1,325 | 3 | Balance brought down | 7,280 |
| | Balance carried down | 6,095 | | Profit and loss account: | |
| | | | | Tax rate adjustment | 140 |
| | | £7,420 | | | £7,420 |
| 4 | Profit and loss account: | | 4 | Balance brought down | 6,095 |
| | Tax rate adjustment | 230 | | | |
| | Balance carried down | 7,905 | | Profit and loss account | 2,040 |
| | | £8,135 | | | £8,135 |
| | | | 5 | Balance brought down | 7,905 |

### 16.13 The deferral method and the liability method of providing for deferred taxation

There are two ways of calculating deferred taxation: the "deferral" method and the "liability" method. SSAP 15 allows either to be used, though the method chosen must obviously be disclosed as an accounting policy to comply with SSAP 2.

Whether the deferral method or the liability method is used, the amounts taken to the deferred taxation account represent *tax on the originating timing differences at the rate in force for the year in which those differences arose.*

The *deferral method* requires that those amounts remain unchanged, despite subsequent changes in tax rate, and that reversals take place at the same, original rate. Thus, the balance at any time on the deferred taxation account will represent the sum of the tax savings which have been obtained on those originating timing differences which have not been reversed.

Under the *liability method* the tax effects of timing differences are regarded as amounts of taxation ultimately due by or to the company. The tax charge in the accounts is computed on the profit shown by those accounts (after adjusting for permanent differences) and the differences between that tax charge and the amount of tax assessable for the year is treated either as a future liability for, or prepayment of, tax, as the case may be. Thus deferred taxation balances on this approach are maintained at the current rate of tax, since the latest known rate is regarded as the best indication of the position which will exist when the liability falls due or the benefit or repayment is received.

The practical difficulty of estimating future tax rates compels the use of the current rate in making the estimate of the future "liability" and this leads to revisions of the estimate whenever the rate changes.

## 17.0 CURRENT COST ACCOUNTING—SSAP 16

SSAP 16, issued in March 1980, establishes the requirement for certain companies to supplement their published historical cost accounts with current cost accounts which attempt to adjust the profit or loss and the assets for the effects of inflation. SSAP 16 applies to accounting periods commencing on or after 1st January 1980. Full details and a worked example are to be found in Chapter 12.

## 18.0 ACCOUNTING FOR POST BALANCE SHEET EVENTS—SSAP 17

### 18.1 Introduction and definitions

SSAP 17, which came into effect for accounting periods beginning on or after 1st September 1980, standardised the treatment of post balance sheet events along the lines proposed in ED 22 on which it is based.

Post balance sheet events are defined as events, both favourable and unfavourable, which occur between the balance sheet date and the date on which the financial statements are approved by the board of directors.

Post balance sheet events may be:

(a) adjusting events

(b) non-adjusting events.

*Adjusting events* are post balance sheet events which provide additional evidence of conditions existing at the balance sheet date. They include events which because of statutory or conventional requirements are reflected in financial statements.

*Non-adjusting events* are post balance sheet events which concern conditions which did not exist at the balance sheet date.

The full text of the standard is reproduced below:

1. Financial statements should be prepared on the basis of conditions existing at the balance sheet date.

2. A material post balance sheet event requires changes in the amounts to be included in financial statements where:

(a) it is an adjusting event; or

(b) it indicates that application of the going concern concept to the whole or a material part of the company is not appropriate.

3. A material post balance sheet event should be disclosed where:

(a) it is a non-adjusting event of such materiality that its non-disclosure would affect the ability of the users of financial statements to reach a proper understanding of the financial position; or

(b) it is the reversal or maturity after the year end of a transaction entered into before the year end, the substance of which was primarily to alter the appearance of the company's balance sheet.

4. In respect of each post balance sheet event which is required to be disclosed under para. 3 above, the following information should be stated by way of notes in financial statements:

(a) the nature of the event; and

(b) an estimate of the financial effect, or a statement that it is not practicable to make such an estimate.

5. The estimate of the financial effect should be disclosed before taking account of taxation, and the taxation implications should be explained where necessary for a proper understanding of the financial position.

6. The date on which the financial statements are approved by the board of directors should be disclosed in the financial statements.

## 18.2 Examples of adjusting events

The following are examples of post balance sheet events which normally should be classified as adjusting events:

(a) Fixed assets. The subsequent determination of the purchase price or of the proceeds of sale of assets purchased or sold before the year end.

(b) Property. A valuation which provides evidence of a permanent diminution in value.

(c) Investments. The receipt of a copy of the financial statements or other information in respect of an unlisted company which provides evidence of a permanent diminution in the value of a long-term investment.

(d) Stocks and work in progress.

  (i) The receipt of proceeds of sales after the balance sheet date or other evidence concerning the net realisable value of stocks.

  (ii) The receipt of evidence that the previous estimate of accrued profit on a long-term contract was materially inaccurate.

(e) Debtors. The renegotiation of amounts owing by debtors, or the insolvency of a debtor.

(f) Dividends receivable. The declaration of dividends by subsidiaries and associated companies relating to periods prior to the balance sheet date of the holding company.

(g) Taxation. The receipt of information regarding rates of taxation.

(h) Claims. Amounts received or receivable in respect of insurance claims which were in the course of negotiation at the balance sheet date.

(i) Discoveries. The discovery of errors or frauds which show that the financial statements were incorrect.

## 18.3 Examples of non-adjusting events

The following are examples of post balance sheet events which normally should be classified as non-adjusting events:

(a) Mergers and acquisitions.

(b) Reconstructions and proposed reconstructions.

(c) Issues of shares and debentures.

(d) Purchases and sales of fixed assets and investments.

(e) Losses of fixed assets or stocks as a result of a catastrophe such as fire or flood.

(f) Opening new trading activities or extending existing trading activities.

(g) Closing a significant part of the trading activities if this was not anticipated at the year end.

(h) Decline in the value of property and investments held as fixed assets, if it can be demonstrated that the decline occurred after the year end.

(i) Changes in rates of foreign exchange.

(j) Government action, such as nationalisation.

(k) Strikes and other labour disputes.

(l) Augmentation of pension benefits.

## 19.0 ACCOUNTING FOR CONTINGENCIES—SSAP 18

SSAP 18, like SSAP 17, comes into effect for accounting periods beginning on or after 1st September 1980.

It has been a statutory requirement for many years that details of the "general nature" of contingent liabilities must be disclosed in published accounts. SSAP 18 extends this requirement by calling for details of contingent *assets* as well as contingent liabilities.

It also requires, for both assets and liabilities, a statement of the uncertainties which are expected to affect the ultimate outcome and a prudent estimate of the financial effect, if practicable.

Where there is disclosure of an estimate of the financial effect of a contingency, the amount disclosed should be the potential financial effect. In the case of a contingent loss, this should be reduced by:

(a) any amounts accrued; and

(b) the amounts of any components where the possibility of loss is remote.

The net amount only need be disclosed.

The estimate of the financial effect should be disclosed before taking account of taxation, and the taxation implications of a contingency crystallising should be explained where necessary for a proper understanding of the financial position.

Examples of contingencies which may arise are:

(a) contingent liabilities:

(i) product warranties or guarantees;

(ii) guarantees on behalf of subsidiary companies;

(iii) legal claims for faulty goods or other alleged breaches of contract;

(iv) pension liabilities, if unfunded and not provided for.

(b) contingent assets:

(i) insurance recovery expected in respect of a loss previously provided for;

(ii) legal claims initiated by the company, where damages are expected to be awarded;

(iii) compensation payable by a foreign government for assets nationalised and written off.

Table 4 sets out the different degrees of probability which may exist, and the resultant accounting treatment in financial statements based on the standard.

Table 4. DEGREES OF PROBABILITY AND ACCOUNTING TREATMENTS

| | *Accounting treatment* | |
|---|---|---|
| *Degree of probability* | *Contingent asset* | *Contingent liability* |
| Remote | No disclosure | No disclosure |
| Possible/probable | No disclosure | Disclosure |
| Highly probable | Disclosure | Provision |
| Virtually certain | Accrual | Provision |

## 20.0 ACCOUNTING FOR INVESTMENT PROPERTIES—SSAP 19

### 20.1 Introduction

Under the accounting requirements of SSAP 12, *Accounting for Depreciation*, fixed assets are generally subject to annual depreciation charges to reflect on a systematic basis the wearing out, consumption or other loss of value whether arising from use, effluxion of time or obsolescence through technology and market changes. Under those requirements it is also accepted that an increase in the value of such a fixed asset does not generally remove the necessity to charge depreciation to reflect on a systematic basis the consumption of the asset.

A different treatment is, however, required where a significant proportion of the fixed assets of an enterprise is held not for consumption in the business operations but as investments, the disposal of which would not materially affect any manufacturing or trading operations of the enterprise. In such a case the current value of these investments, and changes in that current value, are of prime importance rather than a calculation of systematic annual depreciation. Consequently, for the proper appreciation of the financial position, a different accounting treatment is considered appropriate for fixed assets held as investments (called in this standard "investment properties").

Investment properties may be held by a company which holds investments as part of its business, such as an investment trust or a property investment company.

Investment properties may also be held by a company whose main business is not the holding of investments.

Where an investment property is held on a lease with a relatively short unexpired term, it is necessary to recognise the annual depreciation in the financial statements to avoid the situation whereby a short lease is amortised against the investment revaluation reserve while the rentals are taken to the profit and loss account.

This standard requires investment properties to be included in the balance sheet at open-market value. The standard does not require the valuation to be made by qualified or independent valuers; but calls for disclosure of the names or qualifications of the valuers, the bases used by them and whether the person making the valuation is an employee or officer of the company. However, where investment properties represent a substantial proportion of the total assets of a major enterprise (e.g. a listed company) the valuation thereof would normally be carried out (a) annually by persons holding a recognised qualification and having recent post qualification experience in the location and category of the properties concerned; and (b) at least every five years by an external valuer.

## 20.2 Definition of investment property

SSAP 19 applies to properties held for their investment potential, any rental income being negotiated at arm's length. It follows that property occupied by a company for its own purposes, or a property let by one group company to another, is outside the scope of the standard.

Property owned by charities is also excluded.

## 20.3 The requirements of the standard

(a) This standard does not apply to investment properties owned by charities.

(b) Investment properties should not be subject to periodic charges for depreciation on the basis set out in SSAP 12, except for properties held on lease which should be depreciated on the basis set out in SSAP 12 at least over the period when the unexpired term is twenty years or less.

(c) Investment properties should be included in the balance sheet at their open-market value.

(d) The names of the persons making the valuation, or particulars of their qualifications, should be disclosed together with the bases of valuation used by them. If a person making a valuation is an employee or officer of the company or group which owns the property this fact should be disclosed.

(e) Subject to (f) below, changes in the value of investment properties should not be taken to the profit and loss account but should be disclosed as a movement on an investment revaluation reserve, unless the total of the investment revaluation reserve is insufficient to cover a deficit, in which case the amount by which the deficit exceeds the amount in the investment revaluation reserve should be charged in the profit and loss account. In the special circumstances of investment trust companies (as mentioned in para. 10 of SSAP 6) and of property unit trusts it may not be appropriate to deal with such deficits in the profit and loss account. In such cases they should be shown prominently in the financial statements.

(f) Paragraph (e) above does not apply to the financial statements of pension funds and the long-term business of insurance companies where changes in value are dealt with in the relevant fund account.

(g) The carrying value of investment properties and the investment revaluation reserve should be displayed prominently in the financial statements.

### 20.4 Effective date

The accounting and disclosure requirements in this standard should have been adopted as soon as possible after publication and had to be regarded as standard in respect of financial statements relating to accounting periods starting on or after 1st July 1981.

## 21.0 ACCOUNTING FOR FOREIGN CURRENCY TRANSLATIONS—SSAP 20

SSAP 20 was issued in April 1983, and is effective for accounting periods beginning on or after 1st April 1983.

It recognises two types of foreign currency operations:

(a) business transactions denominated in a foreign currency;

(b) foreign business transactions conducted through a foreign subsidiary which maintains its accounting records in its own local currency.

SSAP 20 also recognises that there are two stages to account for these foreign operations:

(a) the individual stage (i.e. preparing accounts of the holding company and/or subsidiary companies);

(b) the consolidated financial statements stage.

It contrasts the uses of two different methods of treatment of foreign currency transactions:

(a) the closing-rate/net-investment method;

(b) the temporal method.

Full details of SSAP 20 together with worked examples are to be found in section 8.0 of Chapter 7.

## 22.0 ACCOUNTING FOR LEASES AND HIRE PURCHASE CONTRACTS—SSAP 21

### 22.1 Introduction

SSAP 21 was issued in August 1984, and is applicable as follows:

(a) lessors and finance companies—accounting periods beginning on or after 1st July 1984 for leases and contracts:

(i) entered into on or after 1st July 1984, or

(ii) which have five years or more to run on 1st July 1984.

(b) lessees and hirers—accounting periods beginning on or after 1st July 1987.

SSAP 21 was based on the contents of ED 29 published in October 1981.

## 22.2 Types of leases

(a) Operating lease—short-term nature.

(b) Finance lease—longer-term.

## 22.3 Accounting treatment—operating lease

The charges in any accounting period should be written off to the profit and loss account.

## 22.4 Accounting treatment—finance lease

(a) Include as an asset the present value of the minimum lease payments.

(b) Depreciate the asset over the lower of

  (i) the lease term;

  (ii) the useful life of the asset.

(c) Include a liability for the net present value of the minimum lease payments.

(d) Analyse subsequent payments to the lessor between

  (i) finance charge;

  (ii) reduction of liability.

(e) Allocate the finance charge to each year's profit and loss account using one of the following methods:

  (i) actuarial method;

  (ii) sum of digits method;

  (iii) straight line method.

## 22.5 Accounting treatment—hire purchase contracts

These should be treated the same way as assets held by lessees under finance leases.

## 22.6 Disclosure of finance leases and hire purchase contracts

(a) For each major class of assets disclose:

  (i) gross cost and accumulated depreciation;

  (ii) depreciation for the year.

(b) State separately from other liabilities: net obligations under leases and hire purchase contracts analysed between:

  (i) amounts payable within one year;

(ii) amounts payable in two to five years;

(iii) amounts payable after five years, aggregated.

(c) Indicate the aggregate finance charges allocated to the period.

(d) Give the amount of any commitments at the balance sheet date for finance leases which have been entered into, but whose inception occurs after the year end.

(e) State the accounting policies adopted.

## 22.7 Disclosure of operating leases

(a) Indicate the total lease rentals in the profit and loss account, distinguishing between:

(i) amounts payable in respect of plant and machinery;

(ii) amounts payable in respect of other operating leases.

(b) State the payments the lessee is committed to pay in the next year, split between:

(i) commitments that expire within one year;

(ii) commitments lasting two to five years;

(iii) commitments lasting over five years.

(c) Indicate the accounting policies adopted.

## 22.8 Accounting treatments in the books of the lessor

(a) Operating leases:

(i) income recognised on a straight-line basis over the length of the lease;

(ii) asset depreciated over the lease.

(b) Finance leases—allocate the finance charge using one of the following:

(i) actuarial method before tax;

(ii) sum of digits method;

(iii) actuarial method after tax;

(iv) investment period method.

## 22.9 Disclosure by lessors

(a) For each finance lease or hire purchase agreement, disclose the net investment at each balance sheet date.

(b) For operating leases, disclose:

(i) the gross amounts of assets held for use, and

   (ii) the accumulated depreciation.

(c) Indicate the accounting policy adopted for operating and finance leases.

(d) Indicate the policy adopted for finance lease income.

(e) Show the aggregate rentals received in an accounting period with relation to:

   (i) finance leases;

   (ii) operating leases.

(f) Indicate the cost of assets acquired, whether by purchase or finance lease, for the purpose of letting under finance lease.

## 23.0 ACCOUNTING FOR GOODWILL—SSAP 22

### 23.1 Introduction

SSAP 22 was issued in December 1984, and is the standard for accounting periods starting on or after 1st January 1985; however, the principles should be adopted as soon as possible.

The subject of goodwill was first raised in a discussion paper published by the ASC in June 1980. This prompted the issue of ED 30 in October 1982, the main contents of which are included in SSAP 22, subject to some adjustments discussed later.

### 23.2 Types of goodwill

(a) *Purchased*—excess cost of an investment over the net assets acquired.

(b) *Non-purchased*—any goodwill that is not purchased (i.e. the difference between the value of the business as a going concern and the value of the net assets).

### 23.3 Treatment of purchased goodwill

(a) Write off immediately to reserves and not to profit and loss account.

(b) Negative goodwill should be credited to reserves.

(c) Although it is the best practice to write off goodwill, it may be carried as an asset and be amortised through the profit and loss account over its useful life. If this is done the following points apply:

   (i) The goodwill should not be revalued, but any permanent diminution in value should be written off to the profit and loss account immediately.

   (ii) The useful economic life should be estimated at the date of acquisition.

   (iii) The economic life may be subsequently shortened but not lengthened.

(d) The amount to be attributed to purchased goodwill should be the difference between the fair value of the consideration and the aggregate of the fair values of the separable net assets acquired (excluding intangible assets).

### 23.4 Treatment of non-purchased goodwill

(a) Write off immediately to reserves and not to profit and loss account.

(b) Never carry forward in the balance sheet.

### 23.5 Disclosure requirements

(a) Include a note of the accounting policy used.

(b) Quantify the goodwill relating to each acquisition in the year (if material).

(c) If the amortisation treatment is adopted treat the goodwill in the balance sheet as a separate item under intangible fixed assets. In addition the following should be disclosed:

 (i) movement on the account in the year, showing opening and closing net book values, cost and accumulated amortisation, and amortisation for the year, and

 (ii) the rate of amortisation used for each major acquisition.

### 23.6 Comparisons with ED 30

(a) ED 30 proposed that goodwill should be defined as the difference between the fair value of the business as a whole and the fair value of its net assets.

(b) ED 30 proposed either

 (i) a write-off to reserves, or

 (ii) amortisation to the profit and loss account.

(c) ED 30 proposed a maximum write-off period of 20 years.

## 24.0 SOME RECENT EXPOSURE DRAFTS—ED 33 AND ED 35

### 24.1 Accounting for deferred taxation—ED 33 and Finance Act 1984

(a) *Introduction*
The reasons why the ASC considered that SSAP 15 required revision included:

 (i) The implications of the Companies Act 1981.

 (ii) The treatment of stock relief as a permanent difference following the Finance Act 1981. (Stock relief is now to disappear—Finance Act 1984.)

 (iii) Comments made as a result of experience of SSAP 15.

ED 33 was issued in June 1983. It was intended that a standard based on ED 33 would eventually replace SSAP 15. A statement of intent was issued in April 1984.

(b) *Possible approaches to deferred taxation*
It would be useful to summarise the principal ways in which the tax effects of timing differences can be calculated:

(i) *Full provision or comprehensive allocation basis*
This method fails to distinguish between:

(1) timing differences which are likely to reverse without replacement; and

(2) timing differences which are more or less permanently deferred as a result of future originating timing differences (e.g. capital expenditure).

In previous years when SSAP 11 was in operation, the method often resulted in large and increasing deferred tax balances in company balance sheets, which were unlikely to become payable in the foreseeable future. This approach has been rejected by SSAP 15 and ED 33.

(ii) *Nil provision or flow-through basis*
Under this approach, deferred tax is ignored—no provision is ever made. This approach considers that only the tax payable in respect of the current period should be charged as a liability in the period.

The problem with this method is that the tax charge may bear no relation to reported profit. The reported tax rate (tax as a percentage of accounting profit) may fluctuate wildly from period to period.

This method has never been acceptable in the UK, although it has been advocated by some accountants.

(iii) *Partial provision basis*
This is the basis required by SSAP 15 and advocated by ED 33. This basis falls between the two extremes of (i) and (ii). Deferred tax is provided only where it is probable that tax will become payable as a result of reversal of timing differences.

The advantage of this approach is that it avoids the possibility of the "fictitious" liabilities of the full deferral approach, and the fluctuations which might result from the flow-through basis.

A disadvantage is that the method is more subjective than the other methods. Judgement is required in assessing likely future capital expenditures and disposals.

(c) *Main proposals of ED 33*

(i) Deferred tax should be provided in respect of the tax effects arising from all timing differences of material amount to the extent that it is probable that a liability will crystallise. (Note that short-term timing differences and other timing differences need to be considered together when attempting to assess whether a tax liability will crystallise. This is a difference compared with SSAP 15 which required deferred tax to be accounted for on all short-term timing differences irrespective of circumstances.)

(ii) Deferred tax should not be provided to the extent that it is probable that a liability will not crystallise. (Note the important change in emphasis as compared with SSAP 15.)

(iii) Reasonable assumptions need to be formulated in order to assess whether or not it is probable that tax liabilities will crystallise as a result of the reversal of timing differences and, accordingly, whether or not a deferred tax provision is necessary.

(iv) Reasonable assumptions will be based on all information available up to the date of approval of the financial statements, and on management intentions.

This will require consideration of financial plans and projections covering a sufficient period of time to assess the pattern of future tax liabilities.

For many businesses, the time period will cover, say, three to five years. For businesses with irregular expenditure patterns the period may need to be longer.

(v) The deferred tax provision should be reduced by any deferred tax debit balances arising from:

(1) timing differences;

(2) trading losses; or

(3) advance corporation tax,

and should be available for offset against these liabilities.

(vi) Deferred tax debit balances arising from:

(1) timing differences;

(2) trading losses; or

(3) ACT,

should *not* be carried forward as a deferred tax asset *except* to the extent that recovery *without replacement by equivalent debit balances* is assured beyond reasonable doubt.

(vii) *Profit and loss account*

(1) The deferred tax element of the tax on profit on ordinary activities should be separately disclosed, either on the face of the profit and loss account or in a separate note.

(2) Similar disclosure is required for the deferred tax element of extraordinary items.

(3) Adjustments to the deferred tax balance arising solely from changes in tax rates or in rates of relief should be separately disclosed wherever material.

An important point is that significant adjustments to the deferred tax balance arising from changes in the basis of taxation should be treated as extraordinary items. Note that this covers the implications for the deferred tax balance of the 1984 Budget.

(viii) *Balance sheet*

(1) The deferred tax account balance should be separately shown in the balance sheet. ED 33 also proposed that a note should indicate the period(s) of time within which it is likely to crystallise. This proposal will *not* appear in the future standard.

(2) Transfers to and from the deferred tax balance should be disclosed by way of note.

(3) Movements on deferred tax relating to reserve (as opposed to profit and loss account) items should be separately disclosed.

(4) The amount of any unprovided deferred tax should be disclosed by way of note, analysed into its major components.

(5) Where the value of an asset is shown by way of note, and that value differs from the book value, the note should also show (if material) the tax effects which would have resulted from the realisation of the asset on the balance sheet date at the stated value.

(d) *Finance Act 1984*

Although the Finance Act 1984 makes no difference to the principles of deferred tax (i.e. the basis to be used will continue to be the partial provision basis using the liability method), clearly it will have a major impact on the computations and size of balance.

The main changes are summarised briefly:

(i) *Capital allowances*

| Expenditure between: | FYA rate |
|---|---|
| 14th March 1984 and 31st March 1985 | 75% |
| 1st April 1985 to 31st March 1986 | 50% |
| 1st April 1986 onwards | nil |

The annual writing-down allowance will remain at 25 per cent.

(ii) *Corporation tax rates*

| Year ended: | General rate | Small companies rate |
|---|---|---|
| 31st March 1984 | 50% | 30% |
| 31st March 1985 | 45% | 30% |
| 31st March 1986 | 40% | 30% |
| 31st March 1987 onwards | 35% | 30% |

These changes taken together clearly form an overall package and will result in a significant adjustment to the deferred tax account arising from changes in the basis of tax. This will therefore give rise to an extraordinary item (*see* 24.3(e)).

(e) *Statement of intent*

ED 33, *Accounting for Deferred Tax—Statement of Intent,* was published at the end of April 1984. The main points aree referred to below:

(i) *General matters*

(1) The ASC has agreed that a revised standard should be prepared along the lines of ED 33.

(2) Following the 1984 Budget, the question of accounting for stock relief no longer arises.

(3) The revised standard will continue to require companies to account for deferred tax on the partial provision basis. This appears to be consistent with the Companies Act definition of provision ("amounts likely to be incurred . . .").

(ii) *Changes to SSAP 15*

(1) Short-term and other timing differences should be considered together when an assessment is made of whether a tax liability will crystallise.

Note that it will *not* be necessary to account for deferred tax on *all* short-term timing differences.

(2) Deferred tax debit balances should not be carried forward unless recovery without replacement is assured beyond reasonable doubt.

(3) Provisions and other items should *not* be stated net of tax, so that all deferred tax should be accounted for within the deferred tax account at the rates anticipated to be applicable when the timing differences are expected to reverse. (For illustration of the calculations, see the numerical example below.)

(4) Companies should assess the dates of crystallisation of deferred tax liabilities by reference to their own circumstances rather than by reference to a specified minimum period of three years.

A three-year period may be sufficient in some cases. However, if it is known that tax rates and the incidence of reliefs will change in future years (e.g., the situation in 1984 following the Budget), companies will need to look further ahead and carefully consider the timing of events.

(5) Substantiated calculations and assumptions made in assessing the amount of the partial provision (SSAP 15, para. 30) are no longer required to be disclosed.

(iii) *Changes compared with ED 33*

(1) Clarification will be given of the circumstances in which debit balances arising from ACT may be carried forward.

(2) There will be no requirement to indicate the period(s) of time within which the deferred tax account balance is likely to crystallise. Instead of this companies will continue (as under SSAP 15) to be required to disclose the principal categories of deferred tax both provided and unprovided.

(iv) *Additional clarification*

(1) A significant adjustment to the deferred tax account, following the Budget/Finance Act 1984 and regarded as arising from a change in the basis of tax, should be treated as an extraordinary item.

(2) Companies will generally be required to show the tax effects of realising assets which are stated in a note at a value other than book value.

(3) Wholly-owned subsidiaries will not be exempt from the standard.

(4) The full amount of any unprovided deferred tax will require to be disclosed. The calculation of this amount should be based on the expected long-term tax rate.

(*Note:* Again, a piece of important guidance following the 1984 Budget.)

(v) *Status of SSAP 15 and the implications of the 1984 Budget*

(1) SSAP 15 remains in force until a revised standard is issued.

(2) All accounts approved by a board of directors after 13th March 1984 should reflect the effects of the proposed legislation.

(3) For accounting periods ending prior to 13th March 1984, the Budget statement represents an adjusting post-balance sheet event.

(4) Where companies foresee deferred tax liabilities crystallising, they should provide immediately for those liabilities at the rates at which they are expected to crystallise.

(5) A significant adjustment to the deferred tax account following the budget changes should be treated as an extraordinary item.

(6) The unprovided element should be computed at the expected long-term tax rate and disclosed by note.

### *Example*

The purpose of this example is to illustrate the partial provision approach in the light of the budget changes. The figures below are meant only to be illustrative. However, the tax rates are those fixed in the Finance Act 1984. Assume that the small company rates are not applicable.

(i) *Position at 31st March 1983*

At 31st March 1983, the excess of accounts' written-down value over the tax written-down value of the plant and machinery of Expansive PLC was £400.

The company had prepared the following projections based on its capital expenditure plans for the three years ending 31st March 1986.

| Year | Excess of capital allowances over depreciation |
|---|---|
| | £ |
| 1984 | 130 |
| 1985 | 150 |
| 1986 | 160 |

Since no timing differences were expected to reverse within the foreseeable future, no deferred tax was required.

In the financial statements for 1983, there would be a nil deferred tax provision in the balance sheet. However, a memorandum note would disclose potential deferred tax of £208 (i.e. 52 per cent × £400).

(ii) *Position at 31st March 1984—ignoring effects of budget*
If no budget changes had taken place and assuming the company's capital expenditure plans remained the same as before, no deferred tax provision would have been required at 31st March 1984 since projections would have shown:

| Year | Excess of capital allowances over depreciation |
|---|---|
| | £ |
| 1985 | 150 |
| 1986 | 160 |
| 1987 and beyond | substantial excess |

However, a note indicating potential deferred tax of £275.6 [52 per cent × (400 + 130)] would have been required.

(iii) *Reassessing the position in the light of budget changes*
If the company recalculated the above projections at 31st March 1983 and 31st March 1984 taking effect of the capital allowances changes, assume the figures would appear as:

| Year | Excess of capital allowances over depreciation | Cumulative net reversals foreseen as at: 31st March 1983 | Cumulative net reversals foreseen as at: 31st March 1984 |
|---|---|---|---|
| | £ | £ | £ |
| 1984 | 130 | (90) (1984–1988) | |
| 1985 | (60) | | (220) (1985–1988) |
| 1986 | (70) | | |
| 1987 | (40) | | |
| 1988 | (50) | | |

1989 and thereafter: originating timing differences (i.e. capital allowances exceed depreciation).

(iv) *Adjustment to opening deferred tax balance as a result of a fundamental change in the basis of taxation*
The extraordinary item would be calculated as follows:

| | £ | £ |
|---|---|---|
| 1984 | 130 at 50% | 65 |
| 1985 | (60) at 45% | (27) |
| 1986 | (70) at 40% | (28) |
| 1987 | (40) at 35% | (14) |
| 1988 | (50) at 35% | (17.5) |
| Extraordinary item | | £(21.5) |

(v) *Provision required at 31st March 1984*

| | £ | £ |
|---|---|---|
| 1985 | (60) at 45% | (27) |
| 1986 | (70) at 40% | (28) |
| 1987 | (40) at 35% | (14) |
| 1988 | (50) at 35% | (17.5) |
| | | £(86.5) |

(vi) *Summary of deferred tax account*

| | £ |
|---|---|
| Balance at 1st April 1983 | Nil |
| Profit and loss account: | |
| Tax charge (50% × £130) | 65 |
| Extraordinary item | 21.5 |
| Balance at 31st March 1984 | £86.5 |

(vii) *Total potential deferred tax at 31st March 1984*
The memorandum note calculation would be:

| | Timing differences £ | Total potential deferred tax £ |
|---|---|---|
| Provided (as in (vi)) | 220 | 86.5 |
| Unprovided (at long-term tax rate of 35%) | 310 × 35% | 108.5 |
| Excess of accounts WDV over tax WDV at 31st March 1984 | £530 | £195.0 |

## 24.2 Background to ED 35—Accounting for the Effects of Changing Prices

(a) *ASC Statement, April 1983*
The ASC Statement, published in April 1983, incorporated the *Interim Report of the CCA Monitoring Working Party.*

The working party was originally set up to investigate the implementation of SSAP 16. The working party's major findings were as follows:

1. The debate on CCA has been confused by the misapprehension that SSAP 16, which is only applicable to companies' external financial reporting, was also intended to apply to their internal accounting.

2. Most people believe that pure historical cost (HC) accounts are unsatisfactory at a time of significant price changes, although there is considerable uncertainty as to the purpose of adjusting HC accounts for the effects of changing prices.

3. Only a small number of preparers and auditors believe that SSAP 16 should be left substantially unamended.

4. Many of those who were originally enthusiastic supporters of CCA have lost their enthusiasm in the light of their experience of SSAP 16, although there are some who remain convinced of its merits.

5. Although a majority of users (analysts and fund managers) would be content to let SSAP 16 stand for some years yet without major amendment, they in fact make little use of SSAP 16 information. A small minority of users make substantial use of CCA information.

6. There is no consensus among those who are unhappy with both SSAP 16 and pure HC accounts as to what should follow SSAP 16.

7. Many companies make allowances for the effects of changing prices in a variety of ways in managing their businesses. A number of companies make adjustments for management purposes for additional depreciation and cost of sales and, to a lesser extent, for monetary working capital, but very few companies do so in a manner which complies with all the requirements of SSAP 16.

8. The inclusion of two sets of accounts in the annual report is widely regarded as confusing and as bringing the accounting profession (in the widest sense) into discredit. On the other hand because SSAP 16 accounts do not command general acceptance and because there is no consensus as to what should replace HC accounts, many people regard the continued use of supplementary information (rather than adjusting the accounts to reflect changing prices) as unavoidable for the foreseeable future.

9. Of the SSAP 16 adjustments to the profit and loss account, those for depreciation and cost of sales are nearest to commanding general support in principle, although a large number of companies have serious difficulties with the calculation of the depreciation adjustment. The monetary working capital and gearing adjustments command less support than the others, with criticism of the gearing adjustment being directed at the method of calculation required by SSAP 16 rather than at the principle of the adjustment.

10. A CC balance sheet is widely regarded as misleading, since it may be

taken to show the current value of the company's assets, which it does not do.

11. Many of the non-compliers with SSAP 16 are from industries—such as shipping, contracting, commodity trading and plantation owners—which do not regard its provisions as appropriate to their particular requirements.

12. Small businesses appear to be almost unanimously opposed to any extension of SSAP 16 to them.

Its recommendations were as follows.

In the light of its findings, and of its view of the purpose of annual reports and accounts, the working party recommends that the Inflation Accounting Subcommittee should consider substantially amending SSAP 16 along the following lines:

1. The standard should require accounts to show the effects of changing prices, when these effects are material.
2. The standard, in common with other SSAPs, should apply to all entities whose accounts are intended to give a true and fair view.
3. The standard should permit different methods of calculating the effects of changing prices.
4. The standard should not require an adjusted balance sheet.
5. Where historical trend information is given, the standard should require it to be adjusted by the Retail Price Index.
6. The working party recommends that an auditing guideline should be issued at the same time as the accounting standard, clarifying the position of auditors.
7. It has been stated above that where a company's financial performance is materially affected by changing prices, the directors should ensure that the accounts provide adequate information accordingly. Indeed, there seems to be a consensus that pure HC information is insufficient in these circumstances. At the same time, preparing two sets of accounts is widely regarded as confusing and as discrediting the accountancy profession. The working party therefore recommends that information on the effects of changing prices should be incorporated in companies' main accounts.

Note that recommendations 2 and 3 have *not* been taken up by ED 35.

(b) *Work of the ASC*

Apart from the work referred to above, ASC took the following into account in its review of SSAP 16:

(i) the final report of the CCA Monitoring Working Party;

(ii) the proposals of the ASC Inflation Accounting Subcommittee;

(iii) a submission to ASC from the Council of the Institute of Cost and Management Accountants;

(iv) surveys by the Association of Certified Accountants and the Institute of Chartered Accountants in Ireland;

(v) research studies sponsored by the Institute of Chartered Accountants in England and Wales and the Institute of Chartered Accountants of Scotland.

(c) *Statement of intent*
The ASC's statement of intent on current cost accounting was published in March 1984. As ED 35 has now been published, details of the SOI are not given.

## 24.3 Preface to ED 35

(a) *Introduction*
The preface indicates that important changes to SSAP 16 are proposed as a result of the extensive consultations.

These changes relate to disclosures rather than the concepts associated with having to account for the effects of changing prices (which is still CCA-based).

(b) *Results of studies*
Some general points have emerged:

(i) during periods of significant price changes, historical cost accounts are unsatisfactory;

(ii) there is no consensus of how companies should reflect the effect of changing prices in their financial statements;

(iii) there was no general support for the inclusion of two separate sets of accounts—consequently ED 35 proposes a single set of accounts with additional notes;

(iv) some people took current cost balance sheets as showing the current value of the business, which is clearly not the case. ED 35 does not require a current cost balance sheet.

(c) *Uses in other countries*
CCA is one of the recognised methods in USA, Canada, South Africa, Australia and New Zealand.

(d) *Users of accounts*
Some users made use of current cost information, particularly with regard to dividend decisions.

ASC expect the simplification of current cost information to result in a greater understanding and use of current cost figures.

ASC point out that the costs of preparing CCA information should not exceed the benefits likely to be derived from it. ASC clearly considers that this test is satisfied for large companies. ASC considers it is particularly important to narrow the areas of difference and variety in accounting practice.

However, ASC is not yet satisfied that methods have been developed that provide useful information about the effects of changing prices on value-based and private companies at a cost that can be justified. Consequently, ED 35 is not mandatory for such companies.

(e) *Main features of ED 35*
These are:

(i) The standard applies to public limited companies that are neither value-based companies nor wholly-owned subsidiaries.

(ii) Current cost information is prescribed as the most appropriate method for such companies to use in accounting for the effects of changing prices.

(iii) The current cost information is to be given in the *main* accounts either in a note or as part of full current cost accounts and *not* in supplementary current cost accounts.

(iv) For companies within the scope of the standard, and where the information is material, compliance is essential to give a true and fair view.

A new standard embodying the features of ED 35 is likely to be adopted during 1985.

Non-mandatory guidance notes will also be published.

(f) *Gearing adjustment*
ED 35 refers to three different gearing adjustments. Further research on certain legal implications is to be carried out.

## 24.4 Explanatory note

(a) *Limitations of historical cost accounting*
This section summarises the well-rehearsed weaknesses of historical cost accounting, including:

(i) inflated reported profits;

(ii) failure to provide up-to-date measure of resources employed;

(iii) overstated return on capital employed;

(iv) failure to show extent to which a company is earning sufficient funds to maintain its capital in real terms, *or* the extent to which these funds can prudently be distributed.

Thus the overall picture is one of misleading impressions of growth and profitability, overdistribution of dividends and misallocation of resources both within and between companies.

ED 35 points out that these limitations of historical cost accounts are not confined to periods of high inflation.

(b) *Alternatives to historical cost*

(i) *Definition of profit*
Profit should be the amount which a company could distribute during the year without eroding its real capital.

Capital may be regarded in either of the following ways:

(1) in financial terms—whereby profit is arrived at after providing for the maintenance of the financial capital of the business (this approach includes current purchasing power, CPP);

(2) in operating terms—whereby profit is arrived at after maintaining the operating capability of the business (e.g. current cost accounting, CCA).

(ii) *ASC viewpoint*
ASC consider that for most businesses, an accounting standard based on the concept of maintenance of operating capability is appropriate.

Assets are measured at current cost, and profit is determined after providing for the maintenance of the operating capability of the business.

ASC acknowledge that current cost information is often more subjective than the equivalent historical cost information. However, any loss of precision will usually be compensated for by the greater relevance of the information.

(iii) *Usefulness of current cost (CC) information*

(1) Information required by ED 35 will enable users to calculate key indicators such as:

(A) earnings per share;

(B) dividend cover;

(C) return on capital employed; and

(D) asset cover,

all on a current cost basis.

(2) Evaluation of trends in current cost return on capital employed will help in assessing a company's future profitability and cash flows.

(3) Current cost gearing ratio and asset cover will provide a better indication of future borrowing capacity as compared with traditional historical cost measures.

(4) Information on the current cost of stocks assists in the evaluation of a company's liquidity.

(c) *Maintenance of operating capability*

(i) *Profit concept*
Profit is determined after allowing for the effects of specific price changes on the funds required to maintain the net operating assets (i.e. operating capability) of the business, after taking account of the way in which these assets are financed.

As with SSAP 16, adjustments required will include:

| | | |
|---|---|---|
| (1) | depreciation adjustment | for operating capability maintenance |
| (2) | cost of sales adjustment | |
| (3) | monetary working capital adjustment | |
| (4) | gearing adjustment | to take account of financing |

(1), (2) and (3) have the same meaning and measurement under SSAP 16.

The gearing adjustment concept has changed.

(ii) *Gearing adjustment*
ED 35 puts the view that a gearing adjustment is needed to recognise the effect of debt capital, and points out that various types of gearing adjustment have been suggested.

ED 35 states, "As there is less agreement on how the gearing adjustment should be calculated than on the other current cost adjustments, this statement gives a choice of three methods for calculating the gearing adjustment. The method selected must be explained and applied consistently."

The three methods are as follows.

(1) *Method 1 (the SSAP 16 method)*
This indicates the extent to which the additional cost of business maintenance recognised by the current cost adjustments above (i.e. DA, COSA, MWCA) is attributable to debt capital. It may be regarded as an abatement of the current cost adjustments for the year to the extent that they fall upon providers of loan capital rather than equity. It is calculated by applying the gearing ratio to the sum of the other current cost adjustments.

(2) *Method 2*
This gearing adjustment represents those parts of the other current cost adjustments and the unrealised revaluation surpluses arising in the year that may be regarded as being financed by borrowing. If operating capability is to be maintained, an amount equal to this gearing adjustment could be borrowed, and the gearing ratio would remain unchanged.

This method has been advocated by ICI.

(3) *Method 3*
This method attempts to reflect the effect of general price changes

on the net borrowing (or, in rare cases, on net monetary assets other than those included in monetary working capital).

If this gearing adjustment is combined with the net charge (or credit) for interest paid (or received) during the year in *money* terms, it shows the net interest charge (or credit) for the year in *real* terms.

The adjustment is calculated by applying the rate of increase in general prices to the average net borrowings (or net monetary assets other than those included in MWC) during the year.

(iii) *Other adjustments*

In appropriate circumstances, adjustments will also be required in respect of the following matters:

(1) net gains or losses on disposal of fixed assets (the fixed-asset disposal adjustment);

(2) share of profits or losses of associated companies;

(3) minority interests;

(4) extraordinary items.

These adjustments are required to be shown separately. However, for (3) and (4), instead of showing the amounts of the adjustments, the adjusted amounts may be shown.

(iv) *Balance sheet items*

Current costs of stocks and fixed assets are required to be shown. This will enable users to compare the "adjustments to profits" with the assets to which they relate.

(v) *Presentation*

The current cost information should be given in the company's statutory accounts either in a note or in main current cost accounts. The information will therefore be covered by the statutory true and fair opinion.

The information is not permitted to be shown in supplementary current costs accounts (in contrast to the position under SSAP 16).

(d) *Materiality*

The proposed standard need not be applied to immaterial items.

(e) *Scope*

Ideally, the accounts of *all* businesses should reflect the effect of changing input prices in order to give a true and fair view.

ED considers that the benefits arising from providing current cost information are most apparent for a public company where the following factors usually contribute to the benefits:

(i) separation of ownership and management;

(ii) a market for the capital of the company;

(iii) a large number and wide range of users of the accounts.

Public companies which are wholly-owned subsidiaries of other companies are specifically excluded from the scope of ED 35.

Companies outside the mandatory scope of ED 35 are encouraged to account for changing prices using an appropriate method.

## PROGRESS TEST 2

1. Draw a block diagram indicating the results that should be indicated concerning associated companies. (2.0)
2. What is an associated company? (2.3)
3. What are the fundamental accounting policies? (3.1)
4. What are accounting bases? (3.2)
5. What matters have a material effect on financial statements when different accounting bases are used? (3.3)
6. How may earnings per share be determined? (4.1)
7. What is the standard accounting practice governing earnings per share? (4.3)
8. How may a change in a company's equity share capital affect the earnings per share calculation? (4.4)
9. How can one calculate the factor for adjusting past earnings per share in a rights issue case? (4.8(b))
10. What sorts of grant can a company receive from the government? (5.2)
11. What persons are not accountable for VAT? (6.2)
12. What is the standard accounting practice governing VAT? (6.6)
13. What is an extraordinary item? (7.2)
14. List the problems associated with extraordinary items. (7.5)
15. What are prior year adjustments? (7.6)
16. What advantages and disadvantages exist when restating prior year accounts? (7.7, 7.8)
17. What provisions were set down in SSAP 7 concerning inflation accounting? (8.0)
18. What are the principal features of the imputation system of corporation tax? (9.1)
19. Define the following terms: (a) recoverable ACT; (b) irrecoverable ACT. (9.2)
20. How may one indicate the movement of assets, liabilities and capital within a company? (11.1)
21. What is the statement on source and application of funds required to cover? (11.3)
22. What is depreciation? (13.2)
23. What is the standard accounting treatment of depreciation? (13.3)
24. What is the standard accounting treatment of research and development? (14.3)
25. What accounting treatments does SSAP 14 lay down for group accounts in cases when consolidation would be misleading? (15.3)
26. What is the SSAP 11 requirement to account for deferred taxation in full? (16.2)
27. What are timing differences? (16.4)
28. What are short-term timing differences? (16.5)

29. Discuss revaluation surpluses in relation to SSAP 15. (16.8)
30. Give six examples of adjusting events. (18.0)
31. Outline the standard method of accounting for contingencies. (19.0)
32. Define and explain the accounting conventions governing investment property. (20.2, 20.3)
33. Name three possible approaches to the treatment of deferred taxation. (24.1(b))
34. Outline the main proposals of ED 33. (24.1(c))
35. What effect did FA 1984 have on SSAP 15? (24.1(e))
36. Describe the details contained in the ASC (April 1983) statement which forms the basis of ED 35. (24.2(a))
37. What are the main features of ED 35? (24.3(e))
38. How useful would you say is current cost information? (24.4(b)(iii))
39. Outline the three methods of gearing adjustment. (24.4(c)(ii))

CHAPTER THREE

# Statements of Source and Application of Funds

## 1.0 FORMAT AND PURPOSE OF STATEMENTS OF SOURCE AND APPLICATION OF FUNDS (FUNDS STATEMENTS)

### 1.1 Introduction

As we have already seen, a company must publish a profit and loss account for a period to an accounting date and a balance sheet as at that date. These show the amount of profit made during the year and how the resources of the company were employed at the end of that year.

Information which is not displayed in these accounts is the identification of changes in the balance sheet items over the year under consideration. A statement showing this information assists in determining whether the management of the company has used the resources coming into its control during the year to the greatest advantage. It is usually called a statement of source and application of funds, or a funds statement.

### 1.2 Sources and applications

Table 5 summarises the main sources and applications of funds that normally have to be dealt with in a funds statement.

Some of the items in the table are self-explanatory, but be clear on the following points:

(a) Profit is before tax and dividends because the tax and dividends shown in the profit and loss account will be *paid in a later year*. Dividends and tax actually *paid in the year under review* are shown separately as applications.

(b) A loss for the year should properly be treated as a negative source of funds rather than as an application of funds.

(c) When fixed assets are sold, the *proceeds of sale* are the funds flowing into the business, not the book value of the assets. In the financial accounts, the

Table 5. FUNDS STATEMENT—MAIN SOURCES AND APPLICATIONS OF FUNDS

| *Sources* | | *Applications* | |
|---|---|---|---|
| 1. | Profit for the year *before*:<br>taxation<br>dividends. | 1. | Dividends *paid* during the year.<br>Taxation *paid* during the year. |
| 2. | Depreciation and other non-cash expenses dealt with *before* arriving at profit for the year. | 2. | Profit on sale of fixed and non-current assets and other non-cash items dealt with *before* arriving at profit for the year. |
| 3. | Proceeds of issue of shares or debentures. | 3. | Payments for the redemption of shares or debentures. |
| 4. | Proceeds of sale of fixed and non-current assets. | 4. | Cost of fixed and non-current assets acquired. |
| 5. | Reduction in current assets. | 5. | Increase in current assets. |
| 6. | Increase in current liabilities. | 6. | Reduction in current liabilities. |

difference between book value and proceeds is the profit or loss shown in the profit and loss account. This profit or loss on sale should be included in the funds flow statement as an adjustment not involving the movement of funds.

(d) It may be difficult at first to appreciate that a reduction in current assets is a source of funds. The point is that a reduction in current assets is the liberation of resources to be deployed elsewhere. Similarly, an increase in current liabilities is a source of funds since the loan or extra credit obtained is available to be deployed in the business ("applied") in acquiring new assets.

(e) A funds flow statement is usually made up to include items 1–4 of sources and application reconciling to the movement in working capital which are items 5–6 of sources and applications. (*See* the specimen layout used in answering Illustration 1 below.)

## 1.3 Why does the funds statement "balance"?

When a funds statement is correctly prepared, the difference between sources and applications equals the net working capital movement. In other words, the statement "balances". A moment's thought should convince you that if two balance sheets balance, a summary of the differences between them should also balance.

In examination questions, every item given in each of the two balance sheets must be reflected *once* in the funds statement. This may be done by entering the difference between them straight to the funds statement or by entering the separate opening and closing items to a working account. If additional information is given in the question apart from the balance sheets, each of these items of additional information must be reflected *twice* in the answer to preserve the balance.

These rules are exactly the same in principle as the rules applied when preparing accounts from a trial balance with additional information requiring adjustment.

As with all accounting problems, practice is the only way to build up speed and accuracy in preparing funds statements.

## 2.0 PREPARING A FUNDS STATEMENT

### 2.1 The basics

A funds statement is produced by analysing and classifying the movements which have taken place between the balance sheet of a company at the beginning of the period under review and the balance sheet at the end of that period.

In examination questions, it will not always be possible to enter a movement straight into the funds statement: it will be necessary to open working ledger accounts for the item, entering the opening and closing balances given in the question, adding further entries to reflect details of transactions which have taken place during the year, and finally calculating as the balancing figure the cash movement which must have taken place.

This balancing figure is then entered onto the funds statement. (*See* Illustration 2 below for an example of the use of ledger account workings in preparing funds statements.)

Let us consider some illustrations, beginning with a very simple one.

*Illustration 1*

DG LTD: Balance Sheet as at 31st December 19X5

| | 31st December | |
|---|---|---|
| | 19X5 | 19X4 |
| | £ | £ |
| Issued share capital | 46,000 | 36,000 |
| Retained profits | 18,400 | 15,000 |
| 10% debentures | 15,000 | 12,000 |
| Trade creditors | 13,200 | 12,200 |
| Proposed dividends | 1,200 | 1,000 |
| | £93,800 | £76,200 |
| | £ | £ |
| Fixed assets | 37,600 | 40,000 |
| Stocks | 29,390 | 18,700 |
| Debtors | 8,300 | 8,400 |
| Balance at bank | 18,510 | 9,100 |
| | £93,800 | £76,200 |

There were no purchases or sales of fixed assets during the year.

You are required to prepare a funds flow statement of DG Ltd.

DISCUSSION

(a) Note that a profit and loss account is often not given in a question on funds statements. The profit, and hence the cash flow generated by the profit, must be calculated by adjusting the movement in the retained profit (here an increase of £3,400) for any items given in the question which must have been charged or credited in arriving at that final movement.

(b) The movements:

(i) Issued share capital has increased by £10,000. There is no share premium account and therefore we have a *source of funds* £10,000 to pick up.

(ii) Retained profits have increased by £3,400. This figure is the starting point for our working to arrive at the cash flow generated from trading operations.

(iii) 10 per cent debentures have increased by £3,000. Another *source of funds*.

(iv) Trade creditors have increased by £1,000. This increase is shown along with the movements in stock, debtors and cash (*see* (g) below) in the summary of movements in working capital.

(v) Proposed dividends. Be careful here. It is the practice to show dividends separately in the funds statement. The opening provision of £1,000 must have been paid during the year (an *application*), while the closing provision of £1,200 must be added back to the retained profits as part of the calculation of the profit for the year. (*See* (b) above and the ledger account in the working below.)

(vi) Fixed assets have gone down by £2,400. As there are no purchases or sales of fixed assets during the year this reduction must be attributable to depreciation.

(vii) Stock, debtors and cash. It is customary to show the overall movement on current assets and liabilities (working capital) as the balancing figure in the statement, separately analysing the individual movements.

(c) Technique for preparing the funds statement
The stages in preparing the funds statement are:

(i) Draw up the outline format (*see* below).

(ii) Proceed line by line through the question, calculating differences and transferring them either direct to the statement or to working ledger accounts if adjustments or further calculations are necessary. (In this simple question only one working is necessary—that for profit—as all other differences are straightforward and can go direct to the statement. The use of working ledger accounts is shown in later illustrations.)

SOLUTION

(a) *The outline format*

DG LTD: Statement of Source and Application of Funds for the year ended 31st December 19X5

| | | | £ |
|---|---|---|---|
| Sources of funds: | | | |
| Profit before tax | | | x |
| Adjustment for items not involving movement of funds: | | | x |
| Total generated from operations | | | x |
| Funds from other sources | | | x |
| | | | x |
| Application of funds | | | x |
| | | | x |
| Increase/decrease in working capital: | | | |
| | Increase | Decrease | |
| | £ | £ | |
| Stocks | x | | |
| Debtors | | x | |
| Creditors | x | | |
| Net liquid funds | | x | |
| | x | x | x |

(b) *The answer (the outline format with figures added)*

DG LTD: Statement of Source and Application of Funds for the year ended 31st December 19X5

| | £ | £ |
|---|---|---|
| Sources of funds: | | |
| Profit before tax (*see* working) | | 4,600 |
| Adjustment for items not involving the movement of funds: | | |
| Depreciation | | 2,400 |
| Total generated from operations | | 7,000 |
| Funds from other sources: | | |
| Issue of shares for cash | 10,000 | |
| Issue of debentures for cash | 3,000 | 13,000 |
| | | 20,000 |
| Application of funds: | | |
| Dividend paid | | 1,000 |
| Carried forward | | 19,000 |

| | | | £ |
|---|---|---|---|
| | | Brought forward | 19,000 |
| Increase/decrease in working capital: | | | |
| | Increase | Decrease | |
| | £ | £ | |
| Stocks | 10,690 | | |
| Debtors | | 100 | |
| Creditors | | 1,000 | |
| Net liquid funds | 9,410 | | |
| | £20,100 | £1,100 | £19,000 |

WORKINGS

Calculation of Profit Before Tax
Profit and Loss Account

| | £ | | £ |
|---|---|---|---|
| | | Profit before dividend (balancing figure) | 4,600 |
| Provision for dividend | 1,200 | | |
| Balance | 3,400 | | |
| | £4,600 | | £4,600 |

## 2.2 Some complications in preparing funds statements

(a) *Purchases and sales of fixed assets during the period*
When there are purchases and sales of fixed assets during the period it is necessary to open working ledger accounts for:

(i) fixed-asset cost;

(ii) fixed-asset depreciation;

(iii) fixed-asset disposal

The information given in the question is then entered to these accounts and the cash movements required for the funds statement obtained as balancing figures. The technique is exactly the same as that used in calculating missing figures in incomplete records exercises. Illustration 2 below shows the use of these accounts.

(b) *Taxation*
A taxation working account will be required to calculate the actual cash paid for taxation during the year. (*See* Illustration 2 below.)

(c) *Deferred taxation*
Transfers to or from deferred taxation account must be adjusted for in the reserve accounts from which they came. If the profit and loss account has been

debited with a figure for deferred taxation that debit must be entered in a working profit and loss account as part of our calculation of profit before taxation.

(d) *Dividends*
It may well be necessary to open a working dividend account to calculate the actual cash paid out as dividend during the year.

(e) *Revaluation of fixed assets*
When assets are revalued, *no funds move in or out of the company*. Therefore there is no record of revaluation in the funds statement. The difference between the opening and closing asset value is cancelled by the increase in the relevant reserve, leaving no net difference to be accounted for.

Now work methodically through Illustration 2 below, using the explanatory notes in the discussion which precedes the answer.

### *Illustration 2*

From the information provided you are required to prepare a "source and application of funds" statement explaining how the cash position of RS Limited has deteriorated during the year ended 31st December 19X4.

Workings should be shown.

The summarised balance sheets of RS Limited at 31st December 19X3 and 31st December 19X4 are given below:

| | 19X3 | 19X4 |
|---|---|---|
| | £ | £ |
| Issued ordinary share capital | 200,000 | 250,000 |
| Share premium | 30,000 | 40,000 |
| Retained profits | 82,000 | 90,000 |
| 8% redeemable debentures | 100,000 | 68,000 |
| Depreciation on: | | |
| Plant | 70,000 | 82,000 |
| Fixtures and fittings | 11,000 | 12,000 |
| Taxation | 45,000 | 43,000 |
| Bank overdraft | — | 42,000 |
| Creditors | 48,000 | 83,000 |
| Proposed dividends | 30,000 | 25,000 |
| | £616,000 | £735,000 |
| | £ | £ |
| Freehold property, at cost | 220,000 | 190,000 |
| Plant and machinery, at cost | 180,000 | 234,000 |
| Fixtures and fittings, at cost | 28,000 | 32,000 |
| Stocks | 72,000 | 159,000 |
| Debtors | 84,000 | 120,000 |
| Bank balance | 32,000 | — |
| | £616,000 | £735,000 |

The following information is relevant:

(a) Debentures of a nominal value of £32,000 were redeemed during the year.

(b) An interim dividend of £20,000 was paid during the year.

(c) The taxation account is summarised below:

| | | 19X3 | 19X4 |
|---|---|---|---|
| | | £ | £ |
| Provision on profits of: | 19X2 | 19,000 | — |
| | 19X3 | 26,000 | 23,000 |
| | 19X4 | — | 20,000 |
| | | £45,000 | £43,000 |

ACT is to be ignored.

(d) The following disposals of fixed assets took place during the year.

(i) Freehold property which had cost £30,000 was sold for £70,000.

(ii) A boring machine which had cost £20,000, the book value of which was £2,000, was sold for £4,000.

(iii) Fixtures which had cost £4,000, the book value of which was £1,000, were sold for £500.

The profits and losses on these transactions had been dealt with through the profit and loss account.

DISCUSSION

(a) *Proceed as in Illustration 1:*

(i) Draw up outline statement.

(ii) Proceed line by line through the question, entering differences either straight to the answer or to working ledger accounts.

(b) *The movements*

(i) Ordinary share capital has gone up by £50,000 and share premium account has gone up by £10,000. No further information is given, so we can take it that there has been an issue of shares realising £60,000.

Enter "Proceeds of issue of shares 60,000" inset under "Funds from other sources" in your outline statement.

(ii) Retained profits are up by £8,000. This cannot go straight to the statement, so open a profit and loss working account and enter the £8,000 as it would appear in the profit and loss account; i.e. on the debit side as "Closing balance".

(iii) Eight per cent redeemable debentures are down by £32,000. Show this as an application.

(iv) Next we have depreciation figures. Immediately open working accounts for plant and fixtures cost, plant and fixtures depreciation, plant and fixtures disposal. Enter the opening and closing depreciation figures to the depreciation accounts as they must be in the books. (Enter the opening figures as the top line on the credit side of the account, enter the closing balances three or four lines lower down on the debit side.)

(v) Taxation. Open a taxation working account incorporating the detail in Note 3 in the question.

(vi) Bank overdraft. You have already entered in your outline statement provision to record increases or decreases in working capital in inset columns. To get the movement on the bank balance it is necessary to refer to the assets side of the balance sheet for the opening balance in hand. The account has moved from £32,000 in hand at the beginning of the year to £42,000 overdrawn at the end, a total movement of £74,000. Is it an increase or a decrease in working capital? Clearly a decrease, so enter it in the "Decreases" column.

(vii) Creditors. Enter the increase in creditors £35,000 as a decrease in working capital. Note that it is the increase or decrease in working capital we are concerned with. When creditors *increase*, working capital *decreases*.

(viii) Dividends. Open a dividend account and enter opening and closing balances.

(ix) Freehold property. Open a working account and enter the opening and closing balance (we cannot put the difference between the two straight to the statement because we have details of a transaction to be recorded (Note 4 (a) in the question).

(x) Plant and machinery at cost.
Fixtures and fittings at cost.

Enter the opening and closing balances to the working cost accounts you have already opened (*see* (iv) above). *Don't* do any more to the figures yet!

(xi) Stocks
Debtors

Both have increased, thus increasing working capital. Enter the figures accordingly straight to your statement.

(xii) Note 1—debentures: already dealt with.

(xiii) Note 2. Debit the dividend account with £20,000 and show as an application (remember that every item given as an adjustment must be entered *twice* in your answer).

(xiv) Note 3—taxation: already dealt with.

(xv) Note 4 (a): enter the proceeds to the credit of the freehold property working account and also show as a source of funds on your statement (*thereby recording twice*).

(xvi) Note 4 (b): (i) Transfer the £20,000 from plant cost to plant disposal.

(ii) If book value is £2,000, depreciation must be £18,000, so transfer this figure from plant depreciation to plant disposal.

(iii) Enter the sale proceeds of £4,000 to the credit of plant disposal and show as a source of funds in your statement (*thereby recording twice again*).

(xvii) Note 4 (c): proceed as in 4 (b) above for the fixtures.

We have now transferred every item of information in the question to our answer or to workings. It is now necessary to go through the working accounts, calculating the balancing figures of cash paid or received and transferring them to the statement. It is also necessary to calculate balancing figures of profits on sales and depreciation. (In the working accounts, all figures produced as balancing figures are boxed.) Leave the profit working till last, as it will be necessary to calculate the dividend and taxation debited against profit in the appropriation account, and credit these to profit to obtain the profit *before* dividend and taxation.

SOLUTION

RS Limited: Statement of Source and Application of Funds
for the year ended 31st December 19X4

| | £ | £ | £ |
|---|---|---|---|
| Sources of funds: | | | |
| Profit before tax (working) | | | 70,000 |
| Adjustment for items not involving the movement of funds: | | | |
| Depreciation | | 34,000 | |
| Loss on sale of fixtures | | 500 | |
| Profit on sale of plant | | (2,000) | |
| Profit on sale of freehold property | | (40,000) | |
| | | | (7,500) |
| Total generated from operations | | | 62,500 |
| Funds from other sources: | | | |
| Proceeds of issue of shares | | 60,000 | |
| Proceeds of sale of freehold property | | 70,000 | |
| Proceeds of sale of plant and fixtures | | 4,500 | |
| | | | 134,500 |
| | | | 197,000 |
| Applications of funds: | | | |
| Capital expenditure | | 82,000 | |
| Redemption of debentures | | 32,000 | |
| Tax paid | | 19,000 | |
| Dividends paid: Final 19X3 | 30,000 | | |
| Interim 19X4 | 20,000 | | |
| | | 50,000 | |
| | | | 183,000 |
| | | Carried forward | 14,000 |

| | | | £ |
|---|---|---|---|
| | | Brought forward | 14,000 |
| Increase/decrease in working capital: | | | |
| | Increases | Decreases | |
| | £ | £ | |
| Stocks | 87,000 | | |
| Debtors | 36,000 | | |
| Creditors | | 35,000 | |
| Net liquid funds | | 74,000 | |
| | £123,000 | £109,000 | £14,000 |

Workings

Profit and loss account (for year)

| | £ | | £ |
|---|---|---|---|
| Dividends: Interim paid | 20,000 | Profit before tax etc. | 70,000 |
| Proposed | 25,000 | | |
| Tax | 17,000 | | |
| Closing balance | 8,000 | | |
| | £70,000 | | £70,000 |

Plant and Fixtures (cost)

| | Plant | Fixtures | | Plant | Fixtures |
|---|---|---|---|---|---|
| | £ | £ | | £ | £ |
| Opening balances | 180,000 | 28,000 | Disposal account | 20,000 | 4,000 |
| Cash: Additions | 74,000 | 8,000 | Closing balances | 234,000 | 32,000 |
| | £254,000 | 36,000 | | £254,000 | 36,000 |

Plant and Fixtures (depreciation)

| | Plant | Fixtures | | Plant | Fixtures |
|---|---|---|---|---|---|
| | £ | £ | | £ | £ |
| Disposal account | 18,000 | 3,000 | Opening balances | 70,000 | 11,000 |
| | | | Profit and loss | 30,000 | 4,000 |
| Closing balances | 82,000 | 12,000 | | | |
| | £100,000 | 15,000 | | £100,000 | 15,000 |

Plant and Fixtures (disposal)

| | Plant £ | Fixtures £ | | Plant £ | Fixtures £ |
|---|---|---|---|---|---|
| Asset account | 20,000 | 4,000 | Depreciation account | 18,000 | 3,000 |
| Profit and loss | 2,000 | | | | |
| | | | Cash: Sale proceeds | 4,000 | 500 |
| | | | Profit and loss | | 500 |
| | £22,000 | 4,000 | | £22,000 | 4,000 |

Taxation

| | £ | | £ |
|---|---|---|---|
| Cash | 19,000 | Opening balance 19X2 | 19,000 |
| | | 19X3 | 26,000 |
| Closing balance 19X3 | 23,000 | | |
| 19X4 | 20,000 | Profit and loss (£20,000 less over-provision £3,000) | 17,000 |
| | £62,000 | | £62,000 |

Dividends

| | £ | | £ |
|---|---|---|---|
| Cash: Final for previous year | 30,000 | Opening balance | 30,000 |
| Cash: Interim | 20,000 | | |
| Closing balance | 25,000 | Profit and loss | 45,000 |
| | £75,000 | | £75,000 |

Freehold Property

| | £ | | £ |
|---|---|---|---|
| Opening balance | 220,000 | Cash | 70,000 |
| Profit and loss | 40,000 | Closing balance | 190,000 |
| | £260,000 | | £260,000 |

The technique of preparing funds statements is a rather mechanical one which must be thoroughly learnt. This means:

(a) working through the above illustrations *several times*, until the pattern of the operation becomes clear, and the logic understood;

(b) tackling the relevant examples at the end of the manual, without looking at the answers first.

## 3.0 INTERPRETATION OF FUNDS STATEMENTS

No accounting document is worth preparing unless it conveys useful information, and the funds statement is no exception.

The analysis of the movements between two balance sheets enables the user to see how efficiently management has handled the funds coming under its control. The review of the funds statement needs to be considered as part of the general process of interpreting the accounts as a whole, as dealt with in the next chapter.

Specific points which will emerge from a study of the funds statement are:

(a) The manner in which the expenditure of the business has been financed. We shall be expecting that long-term investment is financed by long-term means, that expenditure on fixed assets has been undertaken without creating pressure on working capital items.

(b) The manner in which the funds entering the business have been used. This point is to a large extent the converse of (a) above. Even if specific capital is not being raised by a decision of the directors (as when a fresh issue of shares is made), funds will automatically become available if the business is profitable. The funds statement will show whether these resources are being deployed in income-producing fixed assets, or lying idle as unnecessarily large balances of stock or cash at bank.

## PROGRESS TEST 3

1. What is the purpose of statements of source and application of funds? (1.0)
2. What sources and applications of funds need to be dealt with in a funds statement? (1.2)
3. Why does a funds statement balance? (1.3)
4. Outline some of the complications which may arise when making up a funds statement. (2.2)
5. Discuss the interpretation of the funds statement. (4.0)

CHAPTER FOUR

# Company Accounting—Shares and Debentures

## 1.0 ISSUE AND FORFEITURE OF SHARES

The issue and forfeiture of shares is illustrated in Fig. 3.

### 1.1 Legal aspects

(a) There is no restriction on issuing at *par* or *premium*. Any premium is subject to restrictions of s. 56 Companies Act 1948. The share premium account may only be applied in:

(i) paying up unissued shares to be issued as fully paid bonus shares;

(ii) writing off preliminary expenses;

(iii) writing off:

expenses of issue of,
commission paid on, or
discount allowed on issue of shares or debentures;

(iv) providing premium on redemption of redeemable preference shares or debentures.

(b) To issue shares at a *discount*, Court permission must be obtained and other provisions of s. 57 CA 1948 complied with.

(c) Any application form for shares offered to the public must be accompanied by a prospectus (s. 38(3)).

(d) First allotment by a public company may not proceed until *minimum subscription* is achieved (s. 47).

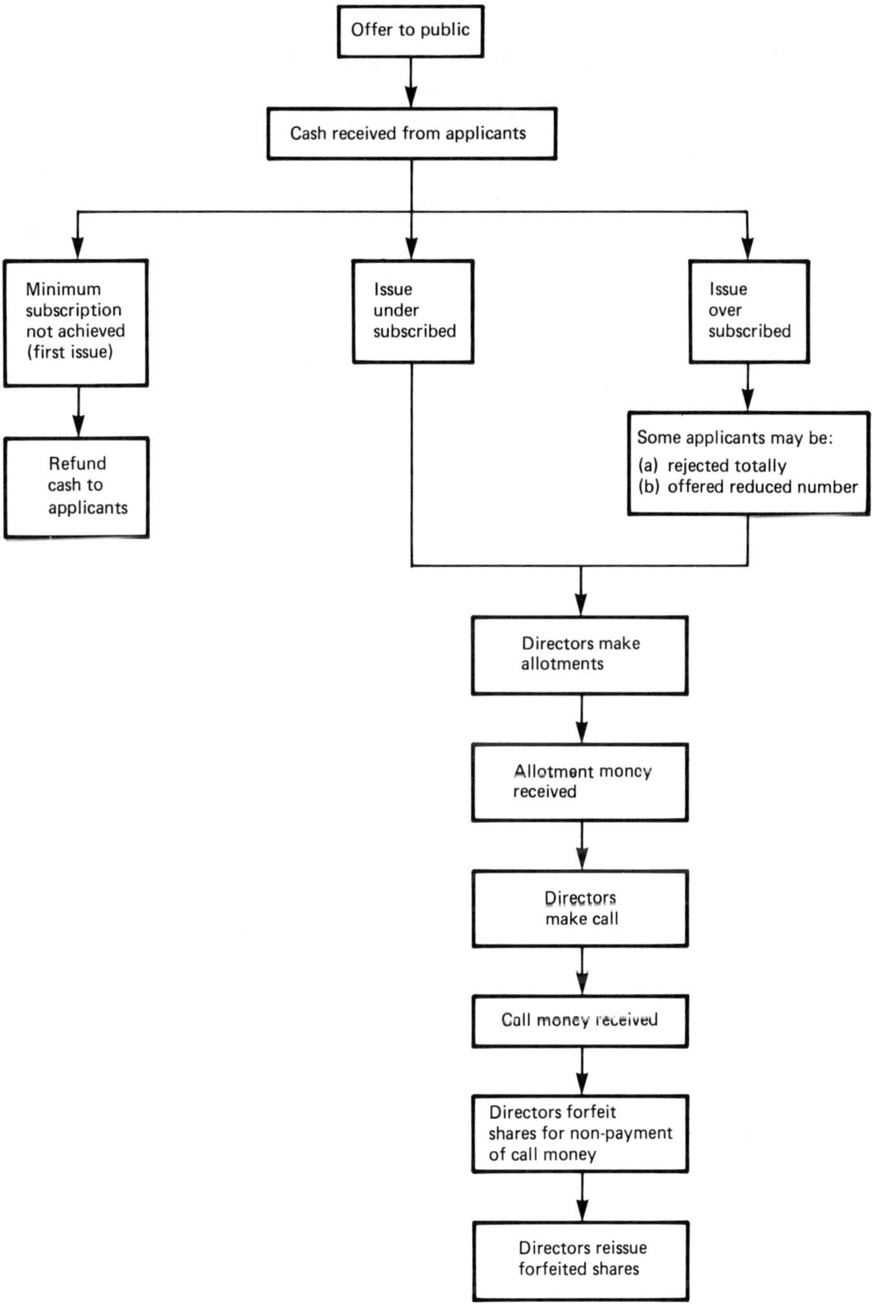


Fig. 3. *Issue and forfeiture of shares.*

(e) Application money may not be less than 5 per cent of nominal value of shares (s. 47).

(f) Calls on shares may be made in accordance with:

 (i) terms of share issue, or

 (ii) the company's articles, or

 (iii) table A, art. 15, which states that a call may not exceed 25 per cent of the share's nominal value and at least 14 days' notice must be given.

(g) If a company is to *forfeit shares*, the relevant authority must be contained in its articles. Forfeiture normally occurs after a *board resolution*, giving the shareholder *fourteen days* to pay an *unpaid call*.

(h) Reissue of forfeited shares may be at any price which is not below the amount of unpaid calls. Any premium paid is disregarded when arriving at the minimum price.

(i) Shares of *no par value* are not permitted under current company legislation.

## 1.2 Accounts required and their purposes

(a) *Application and allotment account*

 (i) Records cash received on application and allotment and refunds to applicants.

 (ii) Shows amounts due on application and allotment, both on *share capital account* and *share premium account* (if appropriate).

 (iii) The balance, if any, represents allotment money due.

(b) *Share capital account*
Records the amount of *called-up capital*.

(c) *Call account*

 (i) Records the amount of call when made.

 (ii) The balance, if any, represents:
  calls in arrears (debit);
  calls in advance (credit).

(d) *Forfeited shares account*

 (i) Credited with called-up value of shares at date of forfeiture, and

 (ii) Debited with calls in arrears.

 (iii) The balance represents amounts actually *received on share capital account*.

(e) *Forfeited shares reissued account*

 (i) Debited with called-up value of shares at date of reissue.

(ii) Credited with amounts received on reissue.

(iii) Credited with amounts already received on capital account for the shares prior to forfeiture.

(iv) Any balance, *which must be a credit balance*, represents the "share premium" on reissue.

## 1.3 Sundry matters

(a) *Under-subscription:* if shares applied for are fewer than those offered for sale, entries in the accounts will obviously be made only for those applied for.

(b) *Over-subscription:* if share applications exceed the number available for issue:

(i) some applications may be totally rejected and the application money returned, or

(ii) allotment may be made for a smaller number of shares than those applied for and the excess application money utilised for reducing amounts due on allotment.

(c) *Treatment of balance on forfeited shares account.* Until all forfeited shares have been reissued the balance on forfeited shares account cannot be regarded as a "premium" and must be carried forward.

(d) *Application and allotment account and call accounts.* Are in fact total or control accounts on share issues. The detailed entries will be made in the *memorandum accounts* of individual shareholders and total amounts only entered in the above-mentioned accounts.

## 1.4 Double entry

The double entry involved in the issue and forfeiture of shares is summarised in Table 6.

Table 6. DOUBLE ENTRY IN ISSUE AND FORFEITURE OF SHARES

| *Transaction* | *Debit* | *Credit* |
|---|---|---|
| (a) Application money received | Cash account | Application and allotment account |
| (b) Application money refunded | Application and allotment account | Cash account |
| (c) Allotment by directors when total due on application *and* allotment is due | Application and allotment account | Share capital account |
| (d) Share premium included in amounts due on application and allotment (if any) | Application and allotment account | Share premium account |

Table 6. DOUBLE ENTRY IN ISSUE AND FORFEITURE OF SHARES —cont.

| *Transaction* | *Debit* | *Credit* |
|---|---|---|
| (e) Allotment money received | Cash account | Application and allotment account |
| (f) Call made by directors | Call account | Share capital account |
| (g) Call money received | Cash account | Call account |
| (h) Called-up value of shares forfeited by directors | Share capital account | Forfeited shares account |
| (i) Calls in arrears on forfeited shares | Forfeited shares account | Call account |
| (j) Paid-up value of forfeited shares reissued | Forfeited shares reissued account | Share capital |
| (k) Cash received on reissued shares | Cash account | Forfeited shares reissued account |
| (l) Amounts received prior to forfeiture in respect of shares reissued | Forfeited shares account | Forfeited shares reissued account |
| (m) Share premium on reissue, being balance on forfeited shares reissued account | Forfeited shares reissued account | Share premium account |

## 1.5 Account outlines

Application and Allotment Account

| | £ | | £ |
|---|---|---|---|
| Cash account: *refunded in respect of applications not accepted* | 120 | Cash account: *amounts received from applicants for shares* | 6,120 |
| Share capital account: *capital amount due on application and allotment* | 12,000A | Cash account: *amounts received on allotment* | 8,000 |
| Share premium account: *premium due on application and allotment* | 2,000B | | |
| | £14,120 | | £14,120 |

Call Account

| | £ | | £ |
|---|---|---|---|
| Share capital account: *amount of call* | 8,000C | Cash account: *call money received* | 7,920 |
| | | Balance carried down: *calls in arrear* | 80 |
| | £8,000 | | £8,000 |
| Balance brought down | 80 | Forfeited shares account: *calls in arrear at date of forfeiture* | 80D |
| | £80 | | £80 |

Share Capital Account

| | £ | | £ |
|---|---|---|---|
| Forfeited shares account: *called-up value at date of forfeiture* | 200E | Application and allotment account: *capital amount due on application and allotment* | 12,000A |
| Balance carried down: *called-up value of issue of shares capital* | 19,960 | Call account: *amount of call* | 8,000C |
| | | Forfeited shares reissued account: *called-up value at date of reissue* | 160G |
| | £20,160 | | £20,160 |
| | | Balance brought down | 19,960 |

Share Premium Account

| | £ | | £ |
|---|---|---|---|
| | | Application and allotment account: *premium due on application and allotment* | 2,000B |
| | | Forfeited share reissued account: *premium on reissue of shares* | 40H |
| Balance carried down | 2,040 | | |
| | £2,040 | | £2,040 |
| | | Balance brought down | 2,040 |

Forfeited Shares Account

| | £ | | £ |
|---|---|---|---|
| Call account: *calls in arrear at date of forfeiture* | 80D | Share capital account: *called-up value at date of forfeiture* | 200E |
| Forfeited shares reissued account: *amount paid up as forfeited shares now reissued* | 96F | | |
| Balance carried down: *shares not yet reissued* | 24 | | |
| | £200 | | £200 |
| | | Balance brought down | 24 |

Forfeited Shares Reissued Account

| | £ | | £ |
|---|---|---|---|
| Share capital account: *called-up value at date of reissue* | 160G | Forfeited shares account: *amounts received on forfeited shares now reissued* | 96F |
| Share premium account: *premium if any, on reissue of shares* | 40H | Cash account: *cash received on shares reissued* | 104 |
| | £200 | | £200 |

## 2.0 REDEMPTION OF PREFERENCE SHARES

*See* Chapter 1, 6.0.

## 3.0 DEBENTURES

The main principles of debentures are illustrated in Fig. 4.

### 3.1 Legal aspects

(a) *Definition*
A debenture is a written acknowledgement of a debt by a company.

(b) *Security*
A debenture may be:

(i) naked (unsecured), giving no form of security;

(ii) fully or partly secured by:
a fixed charge, giving a mortgage of specific assets;
a floating charge, giving a charge over the general assets of the company, present and future.

(c) *Priority*
A company may issue several series of debentures which rank either in order of priority (1st debentures, 2nd debentures, etc.), usually by reference to the date of issue, or *pari passu* (equally).

(d) *Convertible debentures*
A debenture issue may carry the right to convert into equity share capital on or after a specific date, possibly at a specified price.

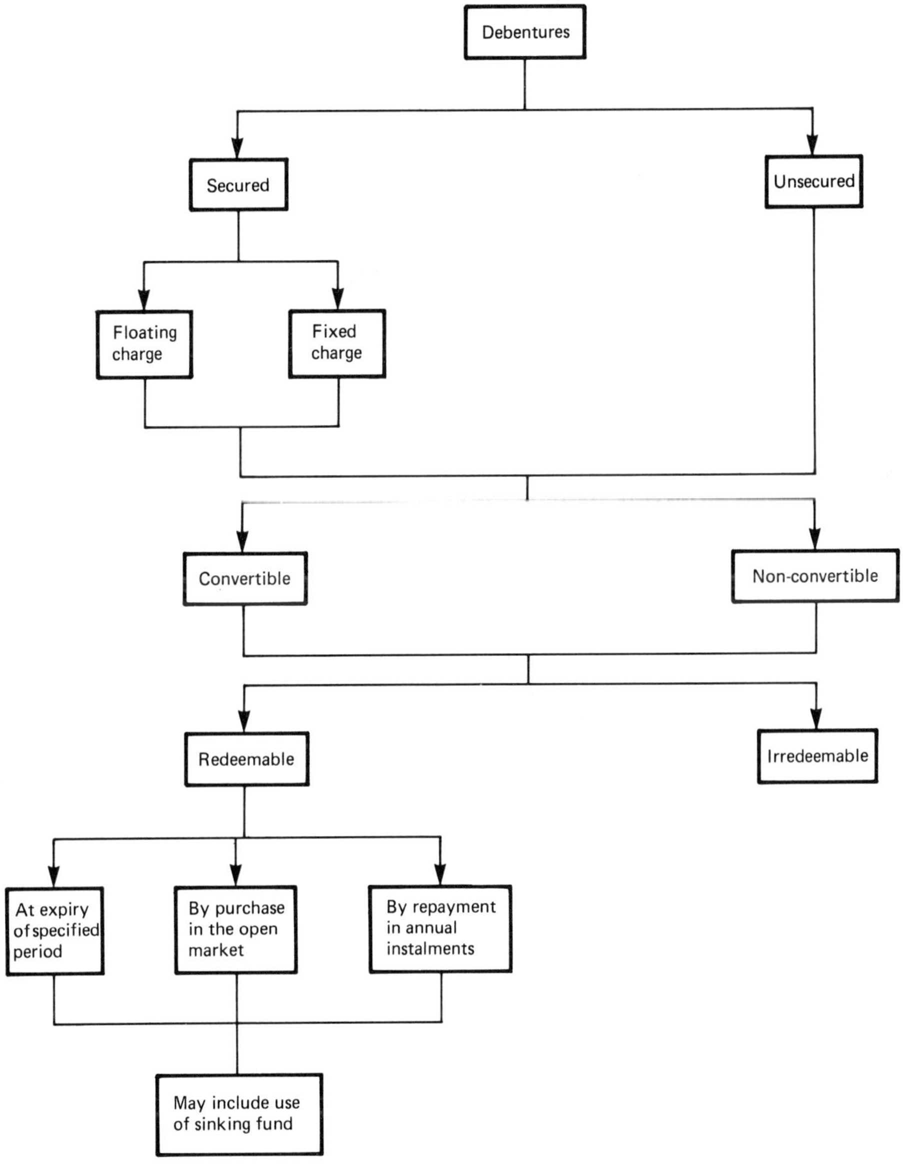


Fig. 4. *Principles of debentures.*

(e) *Permanence*
A debenture may be:

(i) irredeemable;

(ii) redeemable, either:
at expiry of specified period;
by purchase in the open market;
by repayment of part of the issue by annual drawings.

(f) *Trustees for debenture holders*
Where there are a number of debenture holders, it is usual for the security to be charged in favour of trustees who will act on behalf of all the debenture holders.

The debenture trust deed will specify the various terms as to payment of interest, repayment of capital, the establishment of a sinking fund to finance redemption and other provisions to safeguard the rights of the debenture holders.

## 3.2 Accounts required and their purpose

(a) *Debentures account.* Records the nominal value of debentures issued by a company.

(b) *Debenture premium account.* Records the premium (if any) on issue of debentures. *Note:* This is not transferred to the share premium account and while the Companies Acts do not prohibit the payment of a dividend out of a premium on issue of debentures this is not normally done.

(c) *Debenture discount account.* Records the discount (if any) on issue of debentures. This would generally be written off to share premium account or profit and loss account or alternatively carried forward as a separate item in the balance sheet and deducted from the aggregate of share capital and reserves.

(d) *Debenture redemption account.* Shows the nominal value of debentures to be redeemed, plus any premium on redemption, plus interest due to date of redemption.

(e) *Sinking fund account.* Credited with amounts available for investment to provide funds for redemption of debentures. Sources of credit are:

(i) annual transfer from profit and loss account;

(ii) profits on sale of sinking fund investments (losses debited);

(iii) income from sinking fund investments;

(iv) profits on purchase of own debentures in open market (losses debited).

The balance on the sinking fund account should equal the balance on the sinking fund investment account (*see* (f) below) plus any balance on sinking fund cash account (*see* (g) below).

(f) *Sinking fund investment account.* This shows the investments held to provide the funds for the debenture redemption.

(g) *Sinking fund cash account.* It may be convenient to maintain a separate cash account for funds pending investment.

## 3.3 Sundry matters

(a) It is absolutely vital to appreciate that debenture holders are merely *creditors* of the company, unlike preference shareholders who are *members*.

(b) While it is not mandatory, it is accepted as good financial practice to transfer to a general reserve an amount equivalent to the nominal value of the debentures redeemed, in order to preserve the company's capital structure.

(c) Where debentures are redeemable at a premium, and a sinking fund is to be employed, this should be sufficient to pay the premium as well as the nominal value of the debentures. Where there is no sinking fund, the premium may be debited to share premium account or, if there is none, must be written off to profit and loss account or against a reserve.

(d) The interest due on the debentures will be credited to the sinking fund account (debit debenture interest account) and included in the transfer to the profit and loss account.

## 3.4 Issue of debentures

(a) *Issue at par, premium or discount*
Debentures, like shares, may be issued at par or at a premium or at a discount. The Companies Acts are silent as to what may be done with a premium on issue, although normal commercial prudence would require it to be classified as a non-distributable reserve. A discount on issue may be written off to the share premium account.

(b) *Double entry*
The double entry involved in the issue of debentures is summarised in Table 7.

Table 7. DOUBLE ENTRY IN THE ISSUE OF DEBENTURES

| *Nature of issue* | *Transaction* | *Debit* | *Credit* |
|---|---|---|---|
| At par | Cash received on issue of debentures at par | Cash account | Debentures account |
| At premium | Par value of debentures issued | Cash account | Debentures account |
| | Premium on issue of debentures | Cash account | Debenture premium account |
| At discount | Cash received on issue of debentures at discount | Cash account | Debentures account |
| | Discount on issue of debentures | Debenture discount account | Debentures account |

## 3.5 Redemption without a sinking fund

(a) *Double entry*
The double entry involved in redemption is summarised in Table 8.

Table 8. DOUBLE ENTRY IN REDEMPTION WITHOUT A SINKING FUND

| *Transaction* | *Debit* | *Credit* |
|---|---|---|
| Nominal value of debentures to be redeemed | Debentures account | Debenture redemption account |
| Premium on redemption of debentures | Share premium account | Debenture redemption account |
| Interest accrued to date of redemption | Profit and loss account | Debenture redemption account |
| Total amount paid to debenture holders | Debenture redemption account | Cash account |

(b) *Account outline*

Debenture Redemption Account

| | £ | | £ |
|---|---|---|---|
| Cash account: *total amount due to debenture holders* | 12,300 | Debentures account: *nominal value of debentures redeemed* | 10,000 |
| | | Share premium account *or* profit and loss account: *premium payable on redemption* | 2,000 |
| | | Profit and loss account: *debenture interest due to date of redemption* | 300 |
| | £12,300 | | £12,300 |

## 3.6 Redemption with a sinking fund

(a) *Introduction*
It is easiest to consider the accounting entries for redemption with a sinking fund in the following four stages:

(i) annual entries for appropriation, receipt of income on investments and investment of available cash;

(ii) entries relating to a sale of investments;

(iii) entries for a partial redemption of debentures by purchase in the open market;

(iv) entries for a final redemption of all outstanding debentures.

(b) *Double entry*
The double entry involved in redemption is summarised in Tables 9 to 12.

Table 9. ANNUAL ENTRIES FOR APPROPRIATION, RECEIPT OF INCOME ON INVESTMENTS AND INVESTMENT OF AVAILABLE CASH

| *Transaction* | *Debit* | *Credit* |
|---|---|---|
| Annual appropriation out of profits | Profit and loss account | Sinking fund account |
| Transfer of cash to special bank account | Sinking fund cash account | General cash account |
| Receipt of interest on sinking fund investments (in all but the first year) | Sinking fund cash account | Sinking fund account |
| Investment of cash | Sinking fund investments account | Sinking fund cash account |

These entries are simply repeated every year.

Table 10. ENTRIES RELATING TO A SALE OF INVESTMENTS

| *Transaction* | *Debit* | *Credit* |
|---|---|---|
| Sale proceeds of investment of sinking fund | Sinking fund cash account | Sinking fund investments account |
| Profit on sale of investments (reverse entries for a loss) | Sinking fund investments account | Sinking fund account |

Table 11. ENTRIES FOR A PARTIAL REDEMPTION OF DEBENTURES BY PURCHASE IN THE OPEN MARKET

| *Transaction* | *Debit* | *Credit* |
|---|---|---|
| Cost of debentures purchased | Debenture redemption account | Sinking fund cash account |
| Accrued interest included in purchase price (assuming "cum div" price) | Debenture interest account | Debenture redemption account |
| Accrued interest re-imbursed out of general cash | Sinking fund cash account | General cash account |
| Nominal value of debentures redeemed | Debentures account | Debenture redemption account |
| Sinking fund no longer required being amount equivalent to nominal value of debentures redeemed | Sinking fund account | General reserve account |

Table 12. ENTRIES FOR A FIÑAL REDEMPTION OF ALL OUTSTANDING DEBENTURES

| *Transaction* | *Debit* | *Credit* |
|---|---|---|
| Nominal value of debentures to be redeemed | Debentures account | Debenture redemption account |
| Premium payable on redemption | Sinking fund account | Debenture redemption account |
| Cash payment to debenture holders | Debenture redemption account | Sinking fund cash account |
| Balance on sinking fund account no longer required | Sinking fund account | General reserve account |
| Any cash remaining in the sinking fund bank account | General cash account | Sinking fund cash account |

(c) *Account outlines*

On 1st January 19X3 a company had in issue £90,000 6 per cent debentures. The debenture trust deed provided that:

(i) interest was payable on 30th June and 31st December;

(ii) a sinking fund for redemption of debentures was to be built up by an annual appropriation of £1,500 which together with any interest received on the investments of the sinking fund were to be invested on 31st December in each year; and

(iii) sinking fund investments could be realised at any time to purchase debentures in the open market at or below par for immediate cancellation.

You ascertain that:

the sinking fund balance at 1st January 19X3 was £8,000;

sinking fund investments were realised on 1st March for £950 (cost £925) and the proceeds were used to purchase debentures of a nominal value of £1,000;

interest on sinking fund investments for the year ended 31st December amounted to £450 on which date the available funds were duly invested.

Write up the relevant ledger accounts for the year ended 31st December 19X3.

Assume taxation at 50p in the £.

### 6 per cent Debentures Account

| | £ | | £ |
|---|---|---|---|
| Debenture redemption account: | 1,000A | Balance brought down | 90,000 |
| Sinking fund account: *profit redeemed* | | | |
| Balance carried down | 89,000 | | |
| | £90,000 | | £90,000 |
| | | Balance brought down | 89,000 |

### Sinking Fund Account

| | £ | | £ |
|---|---|---|---|
| General reserve account: *nominal value of debentures redeemed* | 1,000 | Balance brought down: *amount of sinking fund at commencement of period—should equal balance on investment account* | 8,000 |
| Balance carried down | 9,035 | Sinking fund cash: *investment income* | 450G |
| | | Sinking fund investment account: *profit on realisation of investments* | 25C |
| | | Debenture redemption account: *profit on purchase of debentures* | 60F |
| | | Profit and loss appropriation account: *annual appropriation* | 1,500H |
| | £10,035 | | £10,035 |
| | | Balance brought down | 9,035 |

### Sinking Fund Investment Account

| | £ | | £ |
|---|---|---|---|
| Balance brought down: *amount of sinking fund investments at commencement of period* | 8,000 | Sinking fund cash account: *proceeds of realisation of investments* | 950C |
| Sinking fund account: *profit on realisation of investments* | 25E | Balance carried down | 9,035 |
| Carried forward | 8,025 | Carried forward | 9,985 |

| | | £ | | £ |
|---|---|---|---|---|
| Brought forward | | 8,025 | Brought forward | 9,985 |
| Sinking fund cash account: *purchase of investments made up of:* | £ | 1,960I | | |
| *Annual appropriation* | *1,500* | | | |
| *Interest received* | *450* | | | |
| *Accrued interest on redeemed debentures reimbursed from general cash* | *10* | | | |
| | *£1,960* | | | |
| | | £9,985 | | £9,985 |
| Balance brought down | | 9,035 | | |

Debenture Redemption Account

| | £ | | £ |
|---|---|---|---|
| Sinking fund cash account: *purchase of debentures on open market* | 950D | Debentures account: *nominal value of debentures redeemed* | 1,000A |
| Sinking fund account: *profit on debentures redeemed* | 60F | Debenture interest account: *accrued interest included in purchase price of debentures* | 10B |
| | £1,010 | | £1,010 |

Debenture Interest Account

| | £ | | £ |
|---|---|---|---|
| Debenture redemption account: *accrued interest included in purchase price of debentures* | 10B | Profit and loss account: *debenture interest charge for year* | 5,350 |
| Cash account: *interest on remaining debentures, less tax* | 2,670 | | |
| Taxation account: *tax deducted on debenture interest paid* | 2,670 | | |
| | £5,350 | | £5,350 |

Sinking Fund Cash Account

| | £ | | £ |
|---|---|---|---|
| Sinking fund investment account: *proceeds of realisation of investment* | 950C | Debenture redemption account: *purchase of debentures on open market* | 950D |
| Sinking fund account: *interest on investments* | 450G | Sinking fund investment account: *purchase of investments at end of period* | 1,960I |
| General cash account: *reimbursement of interest on debentures redeemed* | 10 | | |
| General cash account: *annual instalment* | 1,500H | | |
| | £2,910 | | £2,910 |

*Note:* It will very often be found in practice that a sinking fund cash account is not maintained and that payments and receipts are dealt with in the general cash account.

Examination questions do not normally require a debenture interest account which is shown in order to clarify the position.

## PROGRESS TEST 4

1. Draw a block diagram indicating the issue and forfeiture of shares. (1.0)
2. How does the law provide for under- and over-subscribed shares? (1.4)
3. Draw a block diagram illustrating the principles of debentures. (3.0)
4. What debenture accounts must be kept? (3.2)
5. Outline the procedures governing the issue of debentures (a) at par; (b) at premium; (c) at a discount. (3.4)
6. Discuss redemption with and without a sinking fund. (3.5, 3.6)

CHAPTER FIVE

# Acquisitions and Mergers

## 1.0 INTRODUCTION: DEFINITIONS AND REVISION OF BASIC PRINCIPLES

This is a topic already studied for an earlier examination but it is perhaps as well to begin by revising definitions and basic principles.

It is possible for companies to combine or for one company to take a financial interest in another in a variety of ways:

(a) *Acquisition or absorption*. One company sells all or most of its assets to another, receiving in exchange cash, debentures or shares.

The selling company is wound up and the assets and liabilities taken over are incorporated in the balance sheet of the purchasing company.

(b) *Amalgamation or merger*. Two or more companies sell their assets to a new company formed for the purpose.

The selling companies are wound up and the new company's balance sheet is constructed from the assets and liabilities taken over and the shares or debentures issued.

(c) *Purchase of shares*. One company acquires the whole or a controlling interest in the *shares* of another.

There is no winding up or company formation. (This topic is covered in Chapter 7.)

This chapter is concerned with the accounting consequences of (a) and (b) above. From an accounting point of view there is no difference between the two as regards the closing of the selling company's books. In the purchasing company's books there is no real difference in the accounting, apart from the fact that in an acquisition the purchasing company is usually already in existence and the additional assets and liabilities are incorporated into its balance sheet, whereas in an amalgamation a new company is formed with an opening balance sheet consisting solely of the assets and liabilities taken over and the shares or debentures issued in settlement of the agreed consideration.

There is, however, an important difference in end result between the two. In an acquisition the reserves of the acquiring company at the date of acquisition *remain available for distribution*, whereas in an amalgamation, since a new company is formed, they do not.

Consider the following simple example:

*Illustration 1*

The balance sheets of X Ltd and Y Ltd as at 31st December 19X8 are shown below:

X Ltd: Balance Sheet

| | £ | | £ |
|---|---|---|---|
| Share capital | 10,000 | Sundry assets | 22,000 |
| Reserves | 12,000 | | |
| | £22,000 | | £22,000 |

Y Ltd: Balance Sheet

| | £ | | £ |
|---|---|---|---|
| Share capital | 5,000 | Sundry assets | 15,000 |
| Reserves | 10,000 | | |
| | £15,000 | | £15,000 |

You are required to show the resultant balance sheets if:

(a) X Ltd takes over the net assets of Y Ltd for £15,000 in return for shares £15,000;

(b) A new company, Z Ltd, is formed to take over X Ltd for £22,000 and Y Ltd for £15,000, in return for shares £37,000.

*Solution*

(a) Balance sheet of X Ltd after the takeover:

| | £ | | £ |
|---|---|---|---|
| Share capital | 25,000 | Sundry assets | 37,000 |
| Reserves | 12,000 | | |
| | £37,000 | | £37,000 |

(b) Balance sheet of Z Ltd after the takeover:

| | £ | | £ |
|---|---|---|---|
| Share capital | 37,000 | Sundry assets | 37,000 |
| | £37,000 | | £37,000 |

In (a) the £12,000 reserves of X Ltd remain available for distribution while in (b) they do not.

## 2.0 PROBLEMS IN ANSWERING QUESTIONS ON ACQUISITIONS AND MERGERS

### 2.1 Calculation of purchase consideration

It is usually necessary to calculate purchase consideration before answering a question, or to use a given purchase consideration figure to calculate a balancing figure like goodwill.

Purchase consideration may be built up in two main ways:

(a) by adding the elements of the consideration:
shares
debentures
cash
liabilities taken over; or

(b) by adding together the values of the assets to be acquired.

It is frequently necessary to calculate both (a) and (b) in order to arrive at the goodwill figure as the difference between the purchase consideration (a) and the tangible assets acquired (b).

Alternatively, goodwill may be calculated by one of the methods described in 2.2 below, in which case one of the elements in the purchase consideration may need to be arrived at as a balancing figure.

If the purchasing company agrees to meet the realisation expenses of the seller, these expenses must also be added into the purchase consideration (*see* 3.7 below).

### 2.2 Calculation of goodwill

"Goodwill" may be defined as the additional value attributable to the ability of a business to earn profit in excess of a "normal" profit for the particular trade.

In examination questions it may be necessary to compute the value of goodwill from information given. The examiner may ask for the application of either of two methods:

(a) *Computation based on weighted average past profits*

*Illustration 2*

The profits of Q Ltd for the three years to 31st December 19X8 were:

| Year ended 31st December | Weights to be applied | £ |
|---|---|---|
| 19X6 | 1 | 9,000 |
| 19X7 | 2 | 12,000 |
| 19X8 | 3 | 15,000 |

You are required to compute the value to be placed on the goodwill of the company, taking two years' purchase of the average profits of the company, weighted as indicated.

You may assume that an adjustment to reflect the effect of inflation has already been made.

CALCULATION

| | | £ |
|---|---|---|
| 19X6 | 1 × £9,000 | 9,000 |
| 19X7 | 2 × £12,000 | 24,000 |
| 19X8 | 3 × £15,000 | 45,000 |
| | 6 | £78,000 |

$$\frac{£78{,}000}{6} = £13{,}000$$

Goodwill = two years' purchase: £26,000

This method has little to recommend it for practical application, since it implies the existence of some goodwill even when profits are very low.

(b) *Computation based on "super-profits"*

*Illustration 3*

R Ltd made a profit after tax of £35,000 in the year ended 31st December 19X9. The company's net tangible assets were valued at £150,000 as at that date.

It is agreed that 20 per cent post-tax would represent a reasonable rate of return on capital employed for R Ltd.

You are required to compute the value of the company's goodwill.

| | £ |
|---|---|
| Profit of R Ltd | 35,000 |
| "Normal" profit: | |
| 20% × £150,000 | 30,000 |
| Super-profit | £5,000 |
| | |
| Goodwill, capitalised at given 20% rate | |
| [(100 ÷ 20) × £5,000] | £25,000 |

## 2.3 Treatment of existing debentures replaced by others issued by the purchasing company on different terms

In examination questions and in practice the terms of issue of debentures may be changed as a result of an acquisition.

For example, the holders of £10,000 9 per cent debentures in the selling company may agree to accept £9,000 worth of 10 per cent debentures in the new company in full settlement.

(a) *Treatment in selling company's books*

The treatment of this in the selling company's books is simply:

| | | £ | £ |
|---|---|---|---|
| 9% debentures account | Dr. | 10,000 | |
| To purchasing company's account | Cr. | | 10,000 |

The point is that the selling company has been relieved of a £10,000 liability.

The fact that the purchasing company has agreed a higher or lower sum with the debenture holders is *irrelevant*. That is purely a matter between the debenture holders and the purchasing company.

(b) *Treatment in purchasing company's books*
In the purchasing company's books, the debentures should be brought in at the par value of the new debentures issued unless the question clearly states a premium or discount.

## 3.0 CLOSING THE BOOKS OF THE SELLING COMPANY

### 3.1 Accounts required

Three main accounts are needed to bring about the closure of the selling company's books:

(a) *the realisation account*, in which the profit or loss on the realisation is calculated by bringing together the book value of the assets disposed of and the agreed purchase consideration (*see* 3.2 below);

(b) *the purchasing company's account*, in which the total consideration and the manner in which the purchasing company discharges it are computed (*see* 3.3 below);

(c) *the sundry members account*, in which the amount finally due to the members is calculated (*see* 3.4 below).

### 3.2 The realisation account

The realisation account is *debited* with:

(a) the book value of the assets to be disposed of (credit asset accounts).

(b) the expenses of realisation paid by the seller (credit cash)—*see also* 3.6 below.

The realisation account is *credited* with:

(a) Provisions relating to assets (e.g. doubtful debts) (debit provision accounts).

(b) Purchase consideration (debit purchasing company's account)—*see* 3.3 below.

The balance on the realisation account is then the profit or loss on the realisation and is transferred to sundry members account (*see* 3.4 below).

### 3.3 Purchasing company's account

The purchasing company's account is *debited* with:

(a) Total purchase consideration (credit realisation account, as in 3.2 above).

The purchasing company's account is *credited* with all the elements of the purchase consideration:

(a) cash (debit cash);

(b) shares (debit shares in purchasing company account);

(c) debentures (debit debentures in purchasing company account);

(d) liabilities taken over (debit liabilities accounts) (*see also* 3.8 below).

## 3.4 Sundry members account

The sundry members account is *debited* with all distributions to the members:

(a) cash (credit cash);

(b) shares in purchasing company (credit shares in purchasing company account);

(c) debentures in purchasing company (credit debentures in purchasing company account);

(d) loss (if any) on realisation (credit realisation account).

The sundry members account is *credited* with all claims by the members of the company:

(a) share capital;

(b) share premium account;

(c) reserve accounts;

(d) profit (if any) on realisation (debit realisation account).

When there are several classes of shareholder, separate sundry members accounts for each class must be opened. It is usually convenient to open such accounts in columnar form. In the absence of special provisions in the articles of association, preference shareholders will be entitled to receive their capital back in priority to the ordinary shareholders, but will not participate in any surplus.

## 3.5 Assets and liabilities not taken over (*see* 3.6 below for cash not taken over)

Some assets are not taken over but are sold separately. The entry for this is to credit the proceeds to the asset account and transfer the resultant profit or loss to realisation account.

Liabilities not taken over must be paid by the selling company. Once again, any discount or premium arising is transferred to the realisation account.

## 3.6 Cash not taken over

If, as is frequently the case, the cash is not taken over, the cash account is kept open and the balance, after recording cash transactions during the realisation, forms part of the assets available to meet the final amount due to members as shown in the sundry members account.

## 3.7 Expenses of realisation paid by the purchaser

If the purchaser agrees to pay the expenses of realisation, they are debited to the purchasing company's account instead of to the realisation account. In calculating the purchase consideration, the amount of the expenses must be *added on*, since the purchasing company is effectively agreeing to meet a liability of the seller.

## 3.8 Alternative treatment of liabilities taken over

In the summary of entries given in previous paragraphs, the purchasing company's agreement to take over liabilities has been regarded as *part of the consideration given for the gross assets*, and has accordingly resulted in liabilities being credited to the purchasing company account. It *is* possible to deal with liabilities by crediting them to the realisation account instead, along with the assets, so arriving at a purchase price for the *net* assets in the purchasing company's account. Use of this method produces no difference at all to the final answer, but most authorities regard it as inferior to the "gross" method.

## 3.9 Sundry reserves and provisions

It is sometimes difficult to decide what to do with reserves and provisions when closing the books of the seller. Table 13 summarises the correct treatments.

Table 13. CORRECT TREATMENTS FOR RESERVES AND PROVISIONS IN CLOSING THE BOOKS OF A SELLING COMPANY

| *Item* | *Treatment* | *Reason* |
|---|---|---|
| Reserves of all kinds. | Credit to sundry members account. | Reserves by definition are not intended to meet any particular contingency and must therefore be part of shareholders' funds. |
| Provision for loss in value of assets being taken over. | Credit to realisation account alongside asset concerned. | Realisation account should show net book value of asset. |
| Provision for loss in value of asset *not* being taken over. | Credit to asset account in calculating profit or loss on ultimate disposal by selling company. | Net profit or loss on item must be calculated for transfer to realisation account. |
| Provision for liability being taken over. | Credit to purchasing company's account. | Provision is best estimate of liability being assumed by purchasing company. |
| Provision for liability *not* being taken over. | On settlement of liability by selling company, credit cash and debit provision account. Balance then transferred to realisation account. | Gain or loss on paying liability forms part of final profit or loss on realisation. |

# 4.0 OPENING THE BOOKS OF THE PURCHASING COMPANY

## 4.1 Accounts required

Entries in the purchasing company's books are straightforward. Only *one* account is required—a purchase of business account. This is *debited* with the elements of the purchase consideration (credit share capital, share premium account, debentures account, sundry liability accounts or cash as appropriate) and *credited* with the tangible assets taken over (debit asset accounts). The balancing figure will be goodwill or reserve arising (*see* 4.2 (a) below).

Because of the simplicity of the accounting in the books of the purchaser, the usual examination requirement is to show the *opening balance sheet* of the new company (or the expanded balance sheet of an existing company) instead.

## 4.2 Some points to note

(a) *Asset values*
The values at which the assets are brought into the new company are *not* necessarily the values in the books of the old company. Assets should be introduced at their fair value to the acquiring company, any balance being treated as goodwill or reserve arising on the acquisition.

(b) *Realisation expenses of the seller paid by the purchaser*
As explained in 3.7 above, realisation expenses paid by the seller will be added to the purchase consideration. In the purchasing company's books they will be treated as preliminary expenses (credit the purchase of business account and debit the preliminary expenses account). They will appear as such in the opening balance sheet unless the question tells you to write them off in some way.

## 4.3 Debtors and creditors not taken over by the purchaser but collected by him on behalf of the seller

On some occasions the debtors and creditors are not taken over by the purchasing company but are collected and paid by the company on behalf of the vendor. The net amount paid or received in respect of these creditors and debtors is settled by payment to or from the vendor.

Often the same debtors and creditors accounts are used by the company.

As the debtors at the date of purchase of the business are not the company's assets there will be included in the books a compensating account with an equal but opposite balance usually termed the *debtors suspense account.*

All transactions related to the vendor's debtors are passed through the account. Should the vendor's debtors not have paid in full at the company's balance sheet date, the balance on the *debtors suspense account* will be deducted from the debtors balances.

For debtors not taken over but collected by the purchasing company on behalf of the vendor the entries are as given in Table 14.

Table 14. ENTRIES FOR DEBTORS NOT TAKEN OVER BUT COLLECTED BY PURCHASER

| *Nature of entry* | *Account to debit* | *Account to credit* |
|---|---|---|
| Value of vendor's debtors at date of acquisition of business | Debtors | Debtors suspense |
| Cash received from debtors | Cash | Debtors |
| Discounts allowed | (a) Discount allowed<br>(b) Debtors suspense | Debtors<br>Discount allowed |
| Bad debts | (a) Bad debts<br>(b) Debtors suspense | Debtors<br>Bad debts |
| Cash payable to vendor in respect of cash received | Debtors suspense | Vendor |
| Cash paid to vendor | Vendor | Cash |

A similar principle is used in connection with the creditors not taken over by the purchasing company but paid on behalf of the vendor. Where creditors are paid by the purchasing company on behalf of the vendor the entries are as given in Table 15.

Table 15. ENTRIES FOR CREDITORS PAID BY PURCHASING COMPANY

| *Nature of entry* | *Account to debit* | *Account to credit* |
|---|---|---|
| Value of vendor's creditors at date of acquisition of business | Creditors suspense | Creditors |
| Cash paid to creditors | Creditors | Cash |
| Discount received from creditors | (a) Creditors<br>(b) Discount received | Discount received<br>Creditors suspense |
| Amount due from vendor in respect of cash paid to creditors | Vendor | Creditors suspense |
| Cash received from vendor | Cash | Vendor |

*Illustration 4*

The balance sheet of Andrew James at 31st December 19X7 was as follows:

| | £ | | £ |
|---|---|---|---|
| Share capital | 25,000 | Land and buildings | 12,000 |
| Profit and loss account | 5,400 | Plant and machinery | 8,500 |
| Creditors | 3,800 | Stock | 7,200 |
| | | Debtors | 4,500 |
| | | Balance at bank | 2,000 |
| | £34,200 | | £34,200 |

On 1st January 19X8 CD Ltd acquired the fixed assets and stock for a consideration of £30,000, payable in £1 ordinary shares at par. The company revalued the premises at

£13,000. CD Ltd agreed to collect the debts and pay the creditors on behalf of James. During the three months ended 31st March 19X8 the creditors of James were paid subject to a discount of £140. Cash of £4,320 was received from the debtors of James; discount allowed was £165 and it was agreed that a debt of £15 be written off as bad. The company continued to operate the old debtor and creditor accounts.

Show in CD Ltd books:

(a) the journal entries to record the acquisition of the business;

(b) the ledger entries to record the settlement of the amounts paid and received on behalf of James.

| 19X8 | | £ | £ |
|---|---|---|---|
| Jan 1 | Business purchase account | 30,000 | |
| | A James | | 30,000 |
| | Agreed purchase price | | |
| | Land and buildings | 13,000 | |
| | Plant and machinery | 8,500 | |
| | Stock | 7,200 | |
| | Goodwill | 1,300 | |
| | Business purchase account | | 30,000 |
| | Valuation of assets acquired | | |
| | A James | 30,000 | |
| | Ordinary share capital | | 30,000 |
| | Issue of 30,000 £1 ordinary shares in settlement | | |
| | Debtors | 4,500 | |
| | Debtors suspense account | | 4,500 |
| | Debtors balances to be collected on behalf of James | | |
| | Creditors suspense account | 3,800 | |
| | Creditors | | 3,800 |
| | Creditors balance to be paid on behalf of James | | |

Total Debtors Account

| 19X8 | | £ | 19X8 | | £ |
|---|---|---|---|---|---|
| Jan 1 | Balance | 4,500 | Mar 31 | Cash | 4,320 |
| | | | | Discounts allowed | 165 |
| | | | | Bad debts | 15 |
| | | £4,500 | | | £4,500 |

Cash Book

| 19X8 | | £ | 19X8 | | £ |
|---|---|---|---|---|---|
| Mar 31 | Debtors (James) | 4,320 | Mar 31 | Creditors (James) | 3,660 |
| | | | | James | 660 |
| | | £4,320 | | | £4,320 |

Debtors Suspense Account

| 19X8 | | £ | 19X8 | | £ |
|---|---|---|---|---|---|
| Mar 31 | Discounts allowed | 165 | Jan 1 | Balance: Debtors not taken over from James | 4,500 |
| | Bad debts | 15 | | | |
| | James (cash received on behalf) | 4,320 | | | |
| | | £4,500 | | | £4,500 |

Total Creditors Account

| 19X8 | | £ | 19X8 | | £ |
|---|---|---|---|---|---|
| Mar 31 | Discounts received | 140 | Jan 1 | Balance b/f | 3,800 |
| | Cash | 3,660 | | | |
| | | £3,800 | | | £3,800 |

Creditors Suspense Account

| 19X8 | | £ | 19X8 | | £ |
|---|---|---|---|---|---|
| Jan 1 | Balance: Creditors not taken over from James | 3,800 | Mar 31 | Discount received | 140 |
| | | | | James (cash paid on behalf) | 3,660 |
| | | £3,800 | | | £3,800 |

James

| 19X8 | | £ | 19X8 | | £ |
|---|---|---|---|---|---|
| Mar 31 | Creditors suspense account | 3,660 | Mar 31 | Debtors suspense account | 4,320 |
| | Cash | 660 | | | |
| | | £4,320 | | | £4,320 |

## 5.0 ILLUSTRATIONS

To facilitate understanding we now work through two illustrative questions, the first fairly straightforward and the second rather more difficult.

*Illustration 5*

Ebb Ltd and Flow Ltd decided to amalgamate their businesses through the medium of a new company, Tide Ltd, formed for that purpose to take over all their assets and liabilities.

Tide Ltd is incorporated with an authorised share capital of £250,000 divided into ordinary shares of £1 each.

Ordinary shares in Tide Ltd are to be issued, fully paid, at par to Ebb Ltd and Flow Ltd and these two companies are to be wound up.

The summarised balance sheets of the two companies, as on 31st December 19X0, showed the following:

| | Ebb Ltd | | Flow Ltd | |
|---|---|---|---|---|
| | £ | £ | £ | £ |
| Fixed assets: | | | | |
| Freehold property, at cost | | 25,000 | | 7,000 |
| Plant and machinery, at cost, less depreciation | | 42,000 | | 14,000 |
| Trade investment | | 15,000 | | — |
| | | 82,000 | | 21,000 |
| Current assets: | | | | |
| Debtors | 10,400 | | 5,700 | |
| Stock | 40,000 | | 16,000 | |
| Balance at bank | 4,900 | | 3,300 | |
| | | 55,300 | | 25,000 |
| | | 137,300 | | 46,000 |
| *less:* Current liabilities | | 35,200 | | 12,000 |
| | | £102,100 | | £34,000 |
| Representing: | | | | |
| Share capital: authorised and issued ordinary shares of £1 each | | 40,000 | | 16,000 |
| General reserve | | 50,000 | | 10,000 |
| Profit and loss account | | 12,100 | | 8,000 |
| | | £102,100 | | 34,000 |

You are also given the following information:

(a) It is agreed:

(i) that the fixed assets be revalued as follows:

| | Ebb Ltd | Flow Ltd |
|---|---|---|
| | £ | £ |
| Freehold property | 30,000 | 8,000 |
| Plant and machinery | 36,440 | 10,570 |
| Trade investment | 20,000 | — |

(ii) that a provision of 10 per cent be made on debtors for bad and doubtful debts,

(iii) that stocks be reduced by $12\frac{1}{2}$ per cent, and

(iv) that the goodwill of Ebb Ltd be valued at £59,500 and of Flow Ltd at £11,000.

(b) After the amalgamation Tide Ltd immediately issued for cash additional ordinary shares by means of a "rights" issue in the ratio of one new share for every four held. The issue was made at £1.25 per share payable in full upon application. At the same time the company also issued £100,000 10 per cent debentures at 99 payable in full upon application. Both issues were fully subscribed and all moneys received.

You are required to:

(a) calculate the number of shares in Tide Ltd to be issued to the shareholders of Ebb Ltd and Flow Ltd respectively, indicating the ratio thereof to their former holdings,

(b) show the ledger accounts in the books of Ebb Ltd and Flow Ltd to record their winding up,

(c) show the balance sheet of Tide Ltd immediately after the above transactions.

DISCUSSION

The purchase consideration is not given and it is necessary to calculate it in this case by adding the given revised values of the assets:

| | Ebb Ltd | Flow Ltd |
|---|---|---|
| | £ | £ |
| Freehold property | 30,000 | 8,000 |
| Plant and machinery | 36,440 | 10,570 |
| Trade investment | 20,000 | — |
| Debtors | 9,360 | 5,130 |
| Stock | 35,000 | 14,000 |
| Cash | 4,900 | 3,300 |
| Goodwill | 59,500 | 11,000 |
| | £195,200 | 52,000 |

This will be discharged by:

| | Ebb Ltd | Flow Ltd |
|---|---|---|
| | £ | £ |
| Taking over creditors | 35,200 | 12,000 |
| Issue of ordinary shares at par (balancing figure) | 160,000 | 40,000 |
| | £195,200 | £52,000 |

Each Ebb Ltd shareholder will receive four shares in Tide Ltd for each Ebb Ltd share held.

Each Flow Ltd shareholder will receive five shares in Tide Ltd for each two Flow Ltd shares held.

We now proceed logically through the answer:

(a) Covered by calculation in discussion above. Of course, the working for the purchase consideration will need to be shown as part of your answer.

(b) Logical stages for (b) are:

(i) Open necessary ledger accounts:
realisation account;
Tide Ltd (purchasing company);
shares in Tide Ltd;
sundry members account.

(ii) Clear items in order:
assets to realisation account at book values;
liabilities taken over to Tide Ltd account;
share capital and reserves to sundry members account.

(iii) Insert the calculated purchase consideration (credit realisation account and debit Tide Ltd), and transfer the resultant profit to sundry members account.

(iv) Show the discharge of the remainder of the purchase consideration (credit Tide Ltd and debit sundry members account). In theory, this entry should pass through a "shares in Tide Ltd" account, but for examination purposes a short cut is permissible.

(c) The opening balance sheet for the new company is done quite independently from the closure of the books of the old companies. The values to be used for the assets are the agreed values for the purpose of the amalgamation, *not* the book values.

Show your workings for the cash figure.

Work carefully through the answer which follows.

ANSWER

(a) Shares in Tide Ltd issued:

(i) to Ebb Ltd shareholders: four for each Ebb Ltd share;

(ii) to Flow Ltd shareholders: five for each two Flow Ltd shares.

(See workings in discussion above.)

(b) Realisation Account

| | Ebb Ltd | Flow Ltd | | Ebb Ltd | Flow Ltd |
|---|---|---|---|---|---|
| | £ | £ | | £ | £ |
| Sundry assets | 137,300 | 46,000 | Tide Ltd: purchase consideration | 195,200 | 52,000 |
| Profit transferred to sundry members account | 57,900 | 6,000 | | | |

Tide Ltd

| | Ebb Ltd | Flow Ltd | | Ebb Ltd | Flow Ltd |
|---|---|---|---|---|---|
| | £ | £ | | £ | £ |
| Realisation account: purchase consideration | 195,200 | 52,000 | Sundry liabilities taken over | 35,200 | 12,000 |
| | | | Shares in Tide Ltd a/c | 160,000 | 40,000 |

Shares in Tide Ltd

| | Ebb Ltd | Flow Ltd | | Ebb Ltd | Flow Ltd |
|---|---|---|---|---|---|
| | £ | £ | | £ | £ |
| Tide Ltd | 160,000 | 40,000 | Sundry members account | 160,000 | 40,000 |

Sundry Members Account

| | Ebb Ltd | Flow Ltd | | Ebb Ltd | Flow Ltd |
|---|---|---|---|---|---|
| | £ | £ | | £ | £ |
| Shares in Tide Ltd | 160,000 | 40,000 | Share capital | 40,000 | 16,000 |
| | | | General reserve | 50,000 | 10,000 |
| | | | Profit and loss account | 12,100 | 8,000 |
| | | | Realisation account: profit | 57,900 | 6,000 |

(c)

Tide Ltd
Balance Sheet as at 1st January 19X1

| | | £ |
|---|---|---|
| Share capital authorised and issued | | |
| 250,000 ordinary shares of £1 each, fully paid | | 250,000 |
| Share premium account (*see* working 1) | | 11,500 |
| | | 261,500 |
| 10 per cent debentures | | 100,000 |
| | | £361,500 |
| | £ | £ |
| Represented by: | | |
| Fixed assets: | | |
| Freehold property | | 38,000 |
| Plant and machinery | | 47,010 |
| | | 85,010 |
| Goodwill | | 70,500 |
| Trade investment | | 20,000 |
| Carried forward | | 175,510 |

| | £ | £ |
|---|---|---|
| Brought forward | | 175,510 |
| Current assets: | | |
| Stock | 49,000 | |
| Debtors | 14,490 | |
| Cash at bank (*see* working 2 below) | 169,700 | |
| | 233,190 | |
| *less:* Current liabilities | 47,200 | |
| | | 185,990 |
| | | £361,500 |

WORKINGS

| | £ |
|---|---|
| (a) Share premium arising on rights issue | 12,500 |
| *less:* Discount on debentures written off | 1,000 |
| | £11,500 |
| (b) Cash | |
| From Ebb Ltd and Flow Ltd | 8,200 |
| Proceeds of issue of shares | 62,500 |
| Proceeds of issue of debentures | 99,000 |
| | £169,700 |

*Notes:*
(1) Don't expect anything quite as easy as this in the examination. This was just a starter to establish basic principles.
(2) The discount on debentures has been written off against share premium account as allowed by s. 56 Companies Act 1948. Always do this if possible in examination questions rather than show such items as debit balances in the balance sheet.

We now turn to a rather more difficult question. It is in fact based on the one set for the Certified Accounting 4 examination in June 1979. It shows another way in which the examiner can approach the topic. When you have worked this through, turn to the questions in Appendix 2 and work carefully through the relevant ones. Remember that this is very nearly a "banker" topic for the examination. You must prepare for it by working and *reworking* questions until you thoroughly understand the subject. In particular, Blough (question 25) and Kris Ltd (question 26) are difficult ones which will repay study.

### *Illustration 6*

Following negotiations, A Ltd and B Ltd, who had commenced similar businesses on the same day some years previously, decided to amalgamate.

It was agreed that a holding company would be formed on 1st April 19X9 to be called AB Ltd, which would acquire all the shares in both companies.

The basis of the agreement was as follows:

(1) It was agreed that the accounts of B Ltd for the two years ended 31st March 19X9 should be adjusted to conform with the accounting practices of A Ltd.

(2) B Ltd's stock would have to be revalued to accord with the valuation basis adopted by A Ltd. This would require a reduction in value of £1,500 at 31st March 19X8 and of £3,700 at 31st March 19X9.

(3) The twenty-one-year lease owned by B Ltd had a further twelve years to run from 31st March 19X9. The aggregate amortisation had been provided at £500 per annum. It was agreed that the valuation should be adjusted so as to reflect the effluxion of time.

(4) The plant and equipment depreciation of both companies had been provided on the straight line basis. The plant of both companies had been purchased on the same day.

(5) In both 19X8 and 19X9, B Ltd had made a general provision against doubtful debts of 2 per cent of debtors, whereas A Ltd had made no such provision.

(6) The deferred expenses in the balance sheet of B Ltd represented new product development costs incurred in the year ended 31st March 19X8, which were being written off over three years. A Ltd had written off similar expenditure as it had been incurred.

(7) The unrealised gain on the necessary revaluation of B's investments was not to be credited to its profit and loss account for the purpose of 9 (ii) below.

(8) The pretax profits of the two companies were:

| | Year ended 31st March | |
|---|---|---|
| | 19X8 | 19X9 |
| | £ | £ |
| A Ltd | 34,500 | 47,250 |
| B Ltd | 45,825 | 33,470 |

(9) The settlement of the purchase price of each company's shares was to be:

(i) £1 of 10 per cent convertible loan stock of AB Ltd for every £1 of net assets (as adjusted) owned by each company at 31st March 19X9.

(ii) £0.25 ordinary shares of AB Ltd based on a two-year purchase of the profits of each company before taxation, the profits to be the average profits of the two years, with the year ended 31st March 19X9 being weighted on a 2:1 basis.

The balance sheets of both companies as at 31st March 19X8 and 19X9 are as follows:

| | A Ltd | | B Ltd | |
|---|---|---|---|---|
| | 19X8 | 19X9 | 19X8 | 19X9 |
| | £ | £ | £ | £ |
| Share capital: ordinary shares of £1 each fully paid | 60,000 | 60,000 | 80,000 | 80,000 |
| Reserves: Capital | | 8,000 | | |
| Retained | 12,820 | 26,200 | 26,900 | 40,180 |
| Capital employed | £72,820 | £94,200 | £106,900 | £120,180 |

| | A Ltd | | B Ltd | |
|---|---|---|---|---|
| | 19X8 | 19X9 | 19X8 | 19X9 |
| | £ | £ | £ | £ |
| Freeholds, at cost | 25,000 | 25,000 | | |
| Leaseholds, at cost | | | 21,000 | 21,000 |
| *less:* Amortisation | | | 4,000 | 4,500 |
| | £25,000 | £25,000 | £17,000 | £16,500 |
| Plant and equipment, at cost | 28,000 | 28,000 | 40,500 | 40,500 |
| *less:* Depreciation | 7,000 | 8,400 | 8,100 | 9,720 |
| | £21,000 | £19,600 | £32,400 | £30,780 |
| *Total fixed assets* | 46,000 | 44,600 | 49,400 | 47,280 |
| Quoted investments: | | | | |
| At market price | | 32,000 | | |
| At cost (market price £45,000) | | | | 43,500 |
| *Current assets* | | | | |
| Stocks, at cost | 14,850 | 15,780 | 28,400 | 36,300 |
| Trade debtors | 28,620 | 22,310 | 24,500 | 36,750 |
| Deferred expenses | | | 9,000 | 6,000 |
| Bank balance | 8,550 | 3,600 | 27,600 | |
| | 52,020 | 41,690 | 89,500 | 79,050 |
| *Current liabilities:* | | | | |
| Sundry current liabilities | 25,200 | 24,090 | 32,000 | 49,650 |
| Working capital | 26,820 | 17,600 | 57,500 | 29,400 |
| Capital employed | £72,820 | £94,200 | £106,900 | £120,180 |

You are required:

(a) to set out the calculations of:

(i) the adjusted profits and adjusted net assets of B Ltd, and

(ii) the weighted profits of both companies,

leading to the determination of the purchase price for the shares of both companies, and state the detail of the debentures and shares of AB Ltd issued in settlement,

and

(b) to prepare the balance sheet of AB Ltd as at 1st April 19X9 after the transactions have been completed. (A consolidated balance sheet is *not* required.)

Ignore taxation and formation expenses.

DISCUSSION

This is a very long question but the answer, when we get it, is surprisingly brief.

Notice first of all that AB Ltd is to acquire the *shares* in A Ltd and B Ltd. Therefore these companies will not be wound up and the assets of AB Ltd will be shares in the two companies rather than their net assets. What the question is really about is the calculation of purchase price. This could, of course, lead on to a normal amalgamation involving liquidations, but as already pointed out in this case it does not.

First let us read the instruction paragraph at the end of the question. We are to produce adjusted profits and adjusted net assets for B Ltd only. What about A Ltd? Instruction 1 at the beginning of the question tells us that the accounts of B Ltd are to be adjusted so as to conform with the accounting practices of A Ltd. Presumably, therefore, A Ltd's figures are not to be adjusted at all. Next we have to calculate the weighted profits (weights are given in instruction 9 (ii), so that shouldn't be difficult). Finally, we have to prepare the balance sheet of AB Ltd after the completion of the acquisitions. It is clear that the tricky part of the question is (a) (i), the adjustment of B Ltd's profit and net assets. All we can do is set up a neat working (*see* part (a) (i) of answer) and proceed line by line through the question making necessary additions to or subtractions from the figures from the accounts of B Ltd. The opening entries will be the two profit figures (from Instruction 8) and the net assets (£120,180 from the balance sheet).

| | *Instruction* | *Action* |
|---|---|---|
| (2) | Adjust stock | Take care! It is easy to overlook when working against time that a stock adjustment can affect two years. The reduction in the opening stock £1,500 reduces the 19X8 profit but increases that for 19X9. |
| (3) | Adjust lease amortisation | Refer to balance sheet to pick up figures. The lease should have been amortised at the rate of £1,000 per annum and the closing figure should have been £12,000, not £16,500. |
| (4) | Adjust plant depreciation | Again refer to balance sheet to pick up figures. A Ltd's plant was depreciated by 25 per cent in the 19X8 accounts, while B's was only depreciated by 20 per cent. It is clear from the increase in the aggregate depreciation that A Ltd is depreciating at 5 per cent while B Ltd is using 4 per cent. Remedy? Adjust B Ltd. |
| (5) | Bad debts provision | As B Ltd's accounts are to be adjusted to conform with A Ltd's, the provision is to be written back. £490 and £735? No! We must remember that the debtor figures shown are after deducting the provision. The provisions are accordingly two ninety-eighths of the debtor figures shown. Another trick. The provision for 19X9 is to be £750. *But*, £500 was already provided in 19X8 so that only another £250 is required, not the full £750. |
| (6) | Deferred expenses | The £9,000 must be written off in 19X8. It is clear that nothing at all was in fact written off in 19X8 in B Ltd's accounts, because the £3,000 actually written off in 19X9 (£9,000 minus £6,000) is one third of £9,000. |

(7) Investments — At first sight this is a confusing instruction, suggesting that £1,500 has been credited to B Ltd's profit and loss account for the revaluation of the investments. Reference to the balance sheet, however, shows that no revaluation has been reflected in the accounts, and the instruction merely refers to the need to adjust the investments to market value in computing the net assets of B Ltd.

That completes requirement (a)(i). The next stage, (a)(ii), is self-explanatory, as is (b), the opening balance sheet of AB Ltd.

(a)(i) *Calculation of adjusted profits and net assets of B Ltd*

| | Profits 19X8 | | Profits 19X9 | | Net assets 19X9 | |
|---|---|---|---|---|---|---|
| | £ | £ | £ | £ | £ | £ |
| | + | − | + | − | + | − |
| Per accounts | 45,825 | | 33,470 | | 120,180 | |
| Stock | | 1,500 | 1,500 | 3,700 | | 3,700 |
| Lease amortisation | | 500 | | 500 | | 4,500 |
| Plant depreciation | | 405 | | 405 | | 2,430 |
| Bad debt provision | 500 | | 250 | | 750 | |
| Deferred expenses | | 9,000 | 3,000 | | | 6,000 |
| Investments | | | | | 1,500 | |
| | 46,325 | 11,405 | 38,220 | 4,605 | 122,430 | 16,630 |
| | 11,405 | | 4,605 | | 16,630 | |
| | £34,920 | | £33,615 | | £105,800 | |

(a)(ii) *Weighted profits*

| | | | £ |
|---|---|---|---|
| A Ltd | 19X8 | 1 × £34,500 | 34,500 |
| | 19X9 | 2 × £47,250 | 94,500 |
| | | 3 | 129,000 |
| Weighted average profits £129,000 ÷ 3 | | | 43,000 |
| Two years' purchase £43,000 × 2 | | | £86,000 |

| | | | £ |
|---|---|---|---|
| B Ltd | 19X8 | 1 × £34,920 | 34,920 |
| | | 2 × £33,615 | 67,230 |
| | | 3 | 102,150 |
| Weighted average profits £102,150 ÷ 3 | | | 34,050 |
| Two years' purchase £34,050 × 2 | | | £68,100 |

Purchase price of shares is accordingly:

| | A Ltd | B Ltd |
|---|---|---|
| | £ | £ |
| Two years' purchase of profits | 86,000 | 68,100 |
| Net assets | 94,200 | 105,800 |
| | £180,200 | £173,900 |
| Ordinary shares: | | |
| 344,000 at 25p | 86,000 | |
| 272,400 at 25p | | 68,100 |
| 616,400 | | |
| 10 per cent convertible loan stock | 94,200 | 105,800 |
| | £180,200 | £173,900 |

(b) AB Ltd:
Balance Sheet as at 1st April 19X9

| | £ |
|---|---|
| Issued share capital: | |
| 616,400 shares of 25p each, fully paid | 154,100 |
| 10 per cent convertible loan stock | 200,000 |
| | £354,100 |
| Represented by: | |
| Investment in subsidiary companies at cost | |
| A Ltd | 180,200 |
| B Ltd | 173,900 |
| | £354,100 |

Not a particularly difficult question. The main problem, as with so many accounting exercises, is completing the work accurately within the time limit of 45 minutes.

## 6.0 PRE-INCORPORATION PROFITS AND LOSSES

A company is sometimes formed to acquire a business from a date prior to its incorporation. According to the terms of the agreement made with the vendor, all profits and losses from the date of acquisition may belong to the company. But, as the company had no legal existence before incorporation, any profits earned before incorporation are not available for distribution.

It may be possible to prepare separate accounts up to the date of incorporation to obtain the exact profit and loss prior to incorporation. However, if there is no stocktaking at the date of incorporation it will *not* be possible to do this and accounts will be prepared for a period covering the period from the date of acquisition to a date after incorporation. It will then be necessary to apportion profit and loss account items for the period as in Table 16.

Table 16. APPORTIONMENT OF PRE-INCORPORATION PROFIT AND LOSS ACCOUNT ITEMS

| *Item* | *Basis* |
|---|---|
| Gross profit | Turnover |
| Rents received | Time |
| Fixed charges: rent, rates, etc. | Time |
| Expenses varying with sales: e.g. salesmen's commission | Turnover |
| Company expenses: e.g. debenture interest, directors' remuneration | Post-incorporation only |
| Formation expenses | Post-incorporation only |
| Depreciation | Time basis: according to period for which assets are owned |
| Bad debts | According to information given in the problem |
| Interest on purchase price | Time basis: covering the period for which the interest is paid |

*Profits prior to incorporation*—may be:

(a) credited to a non-distributable reserve, or

(b) credited to goodwill, thereby reducing it.

*Losses prior to incorporation*—may be:

(a) added to goodwill, or

(b) carried forward against post-incorporation profits, or

(c) debited to a "loss prior to incorporation account" and written off out of subsequent profits.

### *Illustration 7*

Rowlock Ltd was incorporated on 1st October 19X7 to acquire Rowlock's mail order business, with effect from 1st June 19X7.

The purchase consideration was agreed at £35,000 to be satisfied by the issue on 1st December 19X7 to Rowlock or his nominee of:

20,000 ordinary shares of £1 each, fully paid, and
£15,000 7 per cent debentures.

The entries relating to the transfer were not made in the books, which were carried on without a break until 31st May 19X8.

On 31st May 19X8 the trial balance extracted from the books showed the following:

| | £ | £ |
|---|---|---|
| Sales | | 52,185 |
| Purchases | 38,829 | |
| Wrapping | 840 | |
| Postage | 441 | |
| Warehouse rent and rates | 921 | |
| Packing expenses | 1,890 | |
| Office expenses | 627 | |
| Stock on 31st May 19X7 | 5,261 | |
| Director's salary | 1,000 | |
| Debenture interest | 525 | |
| Fixed assets | 25,000 | |
| Current assets (other than stock) | 9,745 | |
| Current liabilities | | 4,162 |
| Formation expenses | 218 | |
| Capital account: Rowlock, 31st May 19X7 | | 29,450 |
| Drawings account: Rowlock | 500 | |
| | £85,797 | £85,797 |

You should also ascertain the following:

(a) Stock on 31st May 19X8 amounted to £4,946.

(b) The average monthly sales for June, July and August were one-half those for the remaining months of the year. The gross profit margin was constant through the year.

(c) Wrapping, postage and packing expenses varied in direct proportion to sales, whilst office expenses were constant each month.

(d) Formation expenses are to be written off.

You are required to prepare the trading and profit and loss account for the year ended 31st May 19X8, apportioned between the periods before and after incorporation, and balance sheet as on that date. Ignore taxation.

Rowlock Ltd: Trading and Profit and Loss Account
for the year ended 31st May 19X8

| | £ | | £ |
|---|---|---|---|
| Stock at 1st June 19X7 | 5,261 | Sales | 52,185 |
| Purchases | 38,829 | | |
| | 44,090 | | |
| *less:* Stock at 31st May 19X8 | 4,946 | | |
| | 39,144 | | |
| Gross profit | 13,041 | | |
| | £52,185 | | £52,185 |

| | 1st June X7 to 30th Sept X7 | 1st Oct X7 to 31st May X8 | | 1st June X7 to 30th Sept X7 | 1st Oct X7 to 31st May X8 |
|---|---|---|---|---|---|
| | £ | £ | | £ | £ |
| Wrapping | 200 | 640 | Gross profit | 3,105 | 9,936 |
| Postages | 105 | 336 | | | |
| Rent and rates | 307 | 614 | | | |
| Packing expenses | 450 | 1,440 | | | |
| Office expenses | 209 | 418 | | | |
| Director's salary | | 1,000 | | | |
| Debenture interest | | 525 | | | |
| Net profit to reserve | 1,834 | | | | |
| Net profit | | 4,963 | | | |
| | £3,105 | £9,936 | | £3,105 | £9,936 |
| Formation expenses | | 218 | Net profit | | 4,963 |
| Balance carried forward | | 4,745 | | | |
| | | £4,963 | | | £4,963 |

WORKINGS

(a) Gross profit:

| | |
|---|---|
| June, July, August: | 1 unit of sales each |
| Other months: | 2 units of sales each |
| Annual units of sales: | 3 + 18 = 21 |
| 1st June to 30th September: | $\frac{5}{21} \times$ £13,041 = £3,105 |

(b) Goodwill

| | £ |
|---|---|
| Purchase consideration | 35,000 |
| *less:* Tangible assets acquired, represented by Rowlock's capital account £29,450, *less* drawings £500 | 28,950 |
| | £6,050 |

Rowlock Ltd:
Balance Sheet as at 31st May 19X8

| | £ | £ |
|---|---|---|
| Goodwill | | 6,050 |
| Tangible assets | | 25,000 |
| Current assets | 14,691 | |
| *less:* Current liabilities | 4,162 | 10,529 |
| | | £41,579 |
| Share capital: | | |
| 20,000 ordinary shares of £1 each, fully paid | | 20,000 |
| Reserves: | | |
| Pre-incorporation profits | 1,834 | |
| Profit and loss account | 4,745 | 6,579 |
| | | 26,579 |
| 7% debentures | | 15,000 |
| | | £41,579 |

## 7.0 CONCLUSION

This topic is one of the examiner's favourites. The key to skill at it is practice, practice, practice. Work methodically through the relevant examples in Appendix 2 *without* looking at the answers first! Aim to work over them *several times* until the method of attack to adopt is really clear in your mind.

## PROGRESS TEST 5

1. Outline the basic principles attached to acquisition and merger accounting. (1.0)
2. What method would you use for coping with the problem of calculating the purchase consideration attached to acquisition and merger accounting? (2.1)
3. How can one calculate goodwill in acquisition and merger problems? (2.2)
4. What are the three main accounts needed to bring about the closure of the selling company's books? (3.1, 3.2, 3.3, 3.4)
5. What accounts are required when opening the books of the purchasing company? (4.1)

CHAPTER SIX

# Capital Reductions and Reconstructions

## 1.0 INTRODUCTION: DEFINITIONS AND EXPLANATION OF TERMS

(a) *Capital reduction* (s. 66 Companies Act 1948)
For examination purposes, a capital reduction is almost always the writing down of the share capital of a company in an attempt to put it on a better footing to continue.

It may also be undertaken when a company has surplus capital which it wishes to repay to members or when it wishes to extinguish the liability on partly paid shares for similar reasons.

Before a company can reduce its capital it must:

(i) have power to do so in its articles of association;

(ii) pass a special resolution authorising the reduction;

(iii) obtain confirmation of the reduction from the Court.

(b) *Internal reconstruction* (often under s. 206 Companies Act 1948)
An internal reconstruction is an extension of the principle of capital reduction in which the creditors agree to a reduction or modification of their claims as well as the members.

(c) *External reconstruction* (s. 287 Companies Act 1948)
In an external reconstruction a new company is formed to take over part of the assets of a company in difficulties. The old company is then wound up. An external reconstruction may form part of a members' voluntary winding up or, with Court approval, a creditors' voluntary winding up.

# 2.0 CAPITAL REDUCTIONS

## 2.1 Objects and normal features of a scheme for capital reduction

As indicated in 1.0 above, the object of a scheme of capital reduction is to make it possible for a company which is in difficulties to continue to operate.

The normal features of a scheme of capital reduction are:

(a) substantial writing down of share capital and share premium account;

(b) the use of the credit liberated by (a) to write off a debit balance on profit and loss account and to write down overvalued assets;

(c) the issue of further shares as a rights issue to provide working capital.

## 2.2 Bookkeeping entries

The bookkeeping entries to give effect to an approved scheme of capital reduction are fairly simple. A capital reduction account is opened and credited with the amounts produced by 2.1(a) above. It is then debited with the amounts required to effect the write-offs called for in 2.1(b) above.

Study the following illustration.

*Illustration 1*

The summarised balance sheet of Tina Ltd at 28th February 19X8 was:

| | £ | £ |
|---|---|---|
| Authorised and issued capital: | | |
| 50,000 6% cumulative preference shares of £1 each | | 50,000 |
| 100,000 ordinary shares of £1 each | | 100,000 |
| 10% debenture (secured on land and buildings) | 25,000 | |
| *add:* Accrued interest | 1,250 | |
| | | 26,250 |
| Bank overdraft | | 30,000 |
| Creditors | | 42,500 |
| Directors' loans | | 11,500 |
| | | £260,250 |

*Notes*

(1) Dividends on the preference shares are three years in arrear.

(2) There is a contingent liability for damages of £5,000.

| | £ |
|---|---|
| Goodwill | 12,500 |
| Patent and trade marks | 5,000 |
| Land and buildings | 44,000 |
| Plant and machinery | 43,000 |
| Shares in subsidiary at cost | 15,000 |
| Stock | 36,500 |
| Debtors | 49,250 |
| Deferred revenue expenditure: advertising | 12,500 |
| Profit and loss account | 42,500 |
| | £260,250 |

A capital reduction scheme, duly approved, was set out as follows:

(a) The preference shares to be reduced to 80p each, and the ordinary shares to 25p each. The preference shareholders waive two-thirds of the dividend arrears, and are to receive ordinary shares for the balance. The authorised capital to be restored to £50,000 8 per cent cumulative preference stock, and £100,000 ordinary stock, after shares as reduced had been converted into preference and ordinary stock respectively, in units of £1.

(b) All intangible assets to be eliminated, and bad debts of £3,750 and obsolete stock of £5,000 to be written off.

(c) The shares in the subsidiary are sold to an outside interest for £30,000.

(d) The debenture holder agreed to take over one of the company's properties (book value £9,000) at a price of £12,500 in part satisfaction of the debentures and to provide further cash of £7,500 on a floating charge. The arrears of interest are paid.

(e) The contingent liability materialised in the sum stated but the company recovered £2,500 of these damages in an action against one of the directors. This was charged to his loan account of £4,000, the balance of which was repaid in cash on his subsequent resignation.

(f) The remaining directors agreed to take ordinary stock in satisfaction of their loans.

You are required to:

(a) Set out the ledger accounts to record the above.

(b) Prepare the balance sheet of Tina Ltd after the scheme had been completed.

(Ignore taxation.)

DISCUSSION

Several points emerge in this question:

(a) What are we going to do with the arrears of preference dividend (item a)? Every question on capital reduction includes this point.

First of all, the arrears waived for no consideration are ignored. (They are not a liability and are not recorded in the books.) If the preference shareholders receive any consideration for their waiver of arrears, that consideration must be regarded as a cost of the reduction scheme. This is effectively the position of the one-third arrears for which the preference shareholders are to receive ordinary shares.

The entry for the *consideration paid* in order to induce the preference shareholders to give up their claim is:

| | | £ | £ |
|---|---|---|---|
| Capital reduction account | Dr. | 3,000 | |
| To ordinary share capital account | Cr. | | 3,000 |

(b) What about the property surrendered to the debenture holder (item d)? This is equivalent to a sale of the property (book value £9,000) for £12,500.

The entries are therefore:

| | | £ | £ |
|---|---|---|---|
| Debentures | Dr. | 12,500 | |
| To land and buildings | Cr. | | 9,000 |
| capital reduction account | Cr. | | 3,500 |

(c) Finally, what about the contingent liability (item e)? The treatment of a contingent liability is exactly the same as that of arrears of preference dividend. The amount which crystallises as a liability must be debited to the capital reduction account. In this case a contribution is received from a director and the entry is accordingly:

| | | £ | £ |
|---|---|---|---|
| Director's loan account | Dr. | 2,500 | |
| Capital reduction account | Dr. | 2,500 | |
| To creditor | Cr. | | 5,000 |

ANSWER

(a) Ledger accounts

Capital Reduction Account

| | £ | | £ |
|---|---|---|---|
| Goodwill | 12,500 | Preference share capital | 10,000 |
| Patents and trade marks | 5,000 | Ordinary share capital | 75,000 |
| Stock | 5,000 | Profit on sale of shares | |
| Debtors | 3,750 | in subsidiary | 15,000 |
| Deferred revenue expenditure | 12,500 | Surplus on property taken | |
| Profit and loss account | 42,500 | over by debenture holder | 3,500 |
| Ordinary share capital | | | |
| (shares issued for arrears of | | | |
| preference dividend | 3,000 | | |
| Contingent liability | 2,500 | | |
| Surplus transferred to capital | | | |
| reserve | 16,750 | | |
| | £103,500 | | £103,500 |

Share Capital Accounts

| | Preference | Ordinary | | Preference | Ordinary |
|---|---|---|---|---|---|
| | £ | £ | | £ | £ |
| Capital reduction | 10,000 | 75,000 | Balance | 50,000 | 100,000 |
| Balance | 40,000 | 35,500 | Capital reduction account | | 3,000 |
| | | | Director's loans | | 7,500 |
| | £50,000 | £110,500 | | £50,000 | £110,500 |

(b) Balance Sheet (after completion of scheme)

| | £ | £ |
|---|---|---|
| Fixed assets: | | |
| Land and buildings | | 35,000 |
| Plant and machinery | | 43,000 |
| | | 78,000 |
| Current assets: | | |
| Stock | 31,500 | |
| Debtors | 45,500 | |
| Balance at bank | 4,750 | |
| | 81,750 | |
| *deduct:* Current liabilities: | | |
| Creditors | 47,500 | 34,250 |
| | | £112,250 |
| Share capital: | | |
| Authorised | | |
| 8% cumulative preference stock | | 50,000 |
| Ordinary stock | | 100,000 |
| | | 150,000 |
| Issued and fully paid: | | |
| 8% cumulative preference stock | | 40,000 |
| Ordinary stock | | 35,500 |
| | | 75,500 |
| Reserves: | | |
| Capital reserve | | 16,750 |
| Loans: | | |
| 10% debentures (secured) | 12,500 | |
| Loan stock | 7,500 | 20,000 |
| | | £112,250 |

### 2.3 Further problems with capital reductions

By the nature of the topic it is not really possible for the examiner to make a capital reduction question very difficult. Most of the complications were shown in the example immediately above. Those few which remain are dealt with below.

(a) *Expenses of reduction scheme*
As you would expect, these are debited to capital reduction account.

(b) *Disposal of a balance on the capital reduction account*
In most examination questions the examiner either contrives a situation in which there is no balance (if you get the right answer) or indicates an asset against which any remaining balance is to be written off.
A credit balance should be transferred to a non-distributable reserve account. The treatment of a debit balance is more awkward. Some textbooks recommend showing it as goodwill, but this must surely be wrong. It is most unlikely that a debit balance will be allowed to arise in practice, but if it does it is suggested that it should be shown as a deduction from the total of share capital and reserves and described as "adverse balance remaining after capital reduction scheme".
In examination questions the existence of a balance, especially a debit balance, probably indicates that you have made a mistake.

## 3.0 INTERNAL RECONSTRUCTIONS

### 3.1 Introduction

An internal reconstruction is really a capital reduction in which debenture holders and creditors also accept a reduction in their claims against the company, often in exchange for an issue of ordinary shares.

The bookkeeping is exactly the same as that for capital reduction described in 2.0 above, except that the working account will be entitled "reconstruction account" instead of "capital reduction account".

### 3.2 Devising a scheme of internal reconstruction

Factors for consideration in devising a scheme:

(a) Write down (up) tangible assets to a realistic valuation.

(b) Write off:

   (i) any debit balance on profit and loss account;

   (ii) any intangible assets (unless they can be shown to be of value, e.g. patents).

(c) Consider arrears of cumulative preference dividend:

   (i) A dividend is not a debt until approved, so, in the event of liquidation, preference shareholders will normally receive nothing in respect of arrears.

(ii) Arrears of cumulative preference dividend simply appear by way of note to the accounts and are not reflected in the accounts themselves.

(iii) The reduction scheme should normally take care of any arrears, and not leave them outstanding; otherwise ordinary shareholders will receive nothing until the preference dividend is up to date.

(iv) Normally, preference shareholders will receive shares (either preference or ordinary) and/or a slightly increased dividend rate—if they receive anything at all—for writing off arrears.

(d) Consider the interests of the various parties:

(i) Are any debentures secured? If so, on what?

(ii) To what are preference shareholders entitled in the event of liquidation? They will usually be entitled to repayment at par, but they may be entitled to a premium, or even to share rateably in shareholders' funds with equity shareholders. Consult the Memorandum and Articles to make sure.

(e) Consider what would happen in the event of liquidation:

(i) If there would be nothing left after repaying the debenture holders, there is probably no saving the business.

(ii) If the preference shareholders would probably be repaid in full, it is unrealistic to expect them to vote for a scheme which reduces their stake in the business, and the whole loss will have to be taken by the ordinary shareholders.

(f) Devise a scheme. Normally:

(i) Don't expect the debenture holders or loan stock holders to bear any part of the loss.

(ii) Write off substantially the whole of the loss against ordinary shareholders.

(iii) But do not write off ordinary share capital entirely: some ordinary shares must remain.

(iv) Any balance must be suffered by the preference shareholders.

(v) Give the preference shareholders an increased dividend rate or ordinary shares in compensation for (1) any reduction in capital; (2) writing off arrears of dividend.

Remember, that ordinary shares need not be £1 shares; they could be as little as 1p in nominal value.

(g) Test the effects of the scheme at various likely profit levels.

Points to remember:

(a) Any reduction in the nominal value of the preference shares hits preference shareholders two ways:

(i) It reduces their income.

(ii) It reduces their claim on the assets in the event of liquidation.

(b) Any reduction in the nominal value of the ordinary shares normally has no effect:

(i) They are still entitled to the whole income remaining after the preference dividends have been paid.

(ii) They are still entitled to the whole of the assets remaining on a liquidation after the preference shares have been repaid.

(c) If the preference shareholders give up part of their capital stake or agree to the writing off of arrears, it is not unreasonable for them to receive a stake in the equity in exchange—in which case control of the company will pass partly to former preference shareholders.

## 4.0 EXTERNAL RECONSTRUCTIONS

### 4.1 Introduction

We now turn to a more difficult topic—the external reconstruction in which a new company is formed to take over part of the assets and liabilities of a company in difficulties. The consideration is normally shares in the new company and the result is usually a loss on the realisation. The purpose of the exercise is to work out how that loss is to be borne by the members, sometimes with a contribution also from debenture holders or creditors.

### 4.2 The entries in the books of the new company

The entries in the books of the new company are exactly the same as those on any acquisition (*see* Chapter 5, 4.0).

### 4.3 The bookkeeping entries in the books of the old company

The entries in the books of the old company are basically similar to those explained in Chapter 5, 3.0, with one exception—we replace the realisation account with a realisation and reconstruction account. The realisation and reconstruction account is built up in two stages. Stage 1 is to debit the account with the book value of the assets being disposed of and credit it with the agreed purchase consideration. The resultant balance (probably a loss) is carried down to Stage 2 of the account. The purpose of Stage 2 of the account is to arrive at the final allocation of the loss arising. All reserve accounts which would be transferred to the sundry members account in a normal realisation are transferred here. The resultant loss is then distributed between ordinary and preference shareholders as they have agreed by crediting the realisation and reconstruction account and debiting the sundry members account.

Study these account outlines carefully:

The following is the summarised balance sheet as at 31st December 19X3 of AB Ltd:

| | £ | | £ |
|---|---|---|---|
| *Share capital: authorised, issued and fully paid* | | | |
| Ordinary £1 shares | 30,000 | Sundry assets | 60,000 |
| 6% preference shares of £1 each | 10,000 | | |
| | 40,000 | | |
| *Deduct:* Profit and loss account | 20,000 | | |
| | 20,000 | | |
| 8% debentures | 10,000 | | |
| Creditors | 30,000 | | |
| | £60,000 | | £60,000 |

The following scheme of reconstruction was agreed by all parties and the necessary sanctions obtained.

A new company, AB (19X4) Ltd, was to be registered with a capital of 35,000 shares of £1 each to acquire as from 1st January 19X4, the undertaking and assets of the old company for a consideration to be satisfied partly in cash and partly in the new company's shares and debentures sufficient to implement the following agreed terms:

(a) the new company to assume the old company's debenture liability by issuing to the holders corresponding debentures in the new company, together with one fully paid share in the new company for every £10 of debenture stock held;

(b) the creditors of the old company to accept £10,000 in cash and the balance to be satisfied by an issue of £20,000 shares in the new company;

(c) the preference shareholders in the old company to receive one fully paid share in the new company for every five shares held in the old company;

(d) the ordinary shareholders in the old company to receive one fully paid share in the new company for every thirty shares held;

(e) costs of £1,000 to be borne by the new company and regarded as part of the purchase consideration.

Realisation and Reconstruction Account

| | | £ | | £ |
|---|---|---|---|---|
| Above the line | Asset accounts: *assets at book value* | 60,000B/S | Purchaser's account: *amount of purchase consideration* | 45,000E |
| | | | Balance carried down | 15,000F |
| | | £60,000 | | £60,000 |

| | | £ | | £ |
|---|---|---|---|---|
| Below the line | Balance brought down | 15,000F | Sundry members account: *preference shareholders' amount of reduction of preference shareholders' capital* | 8,000H |
| | Profit and loss account: *debit balance* | 20,000B/S | | |
| | Debenture account: *premium paid to debenture holders* | 1,000 | Sundry members account: *ordinary shareholders' amount of reduction of ordinary shareholders' capital* | 29,000 |
| | Purchaser's account: *costs paid by purchasing company* | 1,000 | | |
| | | £37,000 | | £37,000 |

## Purchaser's Account

| | £ | | £ | £ |
|---|---|---|---|---|
| Realisation and reconstruction account: *amount of purchase consideration* | 45,000E | Creditors account: *shares issued in part satisfaction of liabilities* | 20,000 | |
| | | *cash paid in part satisfaction of liabilities* | 10,000 | 30,000B/S |
| | | Debentures account: *satisfaction of liability to debenture holders by issue of share and debentures* | | 10,000B/S |
| | | Realisation and reconstruction account: *premium to debenture holders* | | 1,000A |
| | | Realisation and reconstruction account: *costs paid by purchasing company* | | 1,000D |
| | | Sundry members account (preference): *issue of shares in new company to shareholders of old company* | | 2,000C |
| | | Sundry members account (ordinary): *issue of shares in new company to shareholders of old company* | | 1,000B |
| | £45,000 | | | £45,000 |

## Sundry Members Account

| | Ordinary £ | Preference £ | | Ordinary £ | Preference £ |
|---|---|---|---|---|---|
| Purchaser's account: *shares in new company issued to shareholders* | 1,000B | 2,000C | Share capital | 30,000B/S | 10,000B/S |
| Realisation and reconstruction account: *amount of capital reduction* | 29,000G | 8,000H | | | |
| | £30,000 | £10,000 | | £30,000 | £10,000 |

## PROGRESS TEST 6

1. Explain the following terms:
   (a) capital reductions;
   (b) internal reconstructions;
   (c) external reconstructions. (1.1)
2. What are the objects of a normal capital reduction? (2.1)
3. List some of the common problems associated with capital reductions. (2.3)
4. List the points that should be observed when devising a scheme for capital reconstruction. (3.2)

CHAPTER SEVEN

# Group Accounts

## 1.0 INTRODUCTION AND DEFINITIONS

### 1.1 Introduction

In recent years there has been a growth in business merger activity. A company (the *holding* company) comes to exercise control over another company (the *subsidiary* company) or comes to exercise significant influence over another company (the *associated* company). Any unit of companies connected in these ways is collectively called a *group* of companies. (Fuller definitions are provided in 1.3 below.)

Prior to 1945 there was no statutory requirement imposed upon holding companies to prepare and present to its members anything more than its own balance sheet and profit and loss account. They were under no obligation to provide information about the group's balance sheet and profit and loss account and had no responsibility to their members to indicate the underlying net assets or earnings attributable to their investment in subsidiaries and associated companies.

The Companies Act 1948 recognised that this was an unsatisfactory state of affairs and required every holding company to present to its members, in addition to its own balance sheet and profit and loss account, the following:

(a) a consolidated balance sheet—to show instead of the cost of investment in a subsidiary company, the underlying net assets attributable to the holding company's investment; and

(b) a consolidated profit and loss account—to include instead of dividends receivable or received, the underlying earnings attributable to the holding company's investment.

Note that there was no requirement to incorporate results of the associated company. In fact this condition did not appear anywhere in companies legislation until the enactment of the Companies Act 1981 which introduced a new type of investment—the *related* company.

## 1.2 Associated companies

An associated company is a company which although not a subsidiary is, in substance, more than a mere investment producing a stream of dividend income. It is a company over which the investor has the ability to exercise direct influence. For an investment to be classed as an associated company such influence should, at least, extend to participation in the determination of the dividend policy of the investee company.

In *very general terms*, an associated company is one in which the investor has substantial (between 20 and 50 per cent) long-term interest.

The accounting treatment of an associated company is dealt with fully in 7.0 below.

## 1.3 Definitions

(a) *Holding company*. Section 154 Companies Act 1948, by inference, defines a holding company as one which exercises control over another company—the *subsidiary* company.

(b) *Subsidiary company*. This is a company over which control is exercised by a holding company by reason of the fact that the holding company either:

  (i) holds more than 50 per cent of the nominal value of the issued *equity* share capital; or

  (ii) controls the composition of the board of directors of the subsidiary.

(c) *Equity share capital*. This comprises any part of the issued share capital which carries the right to participate *beyond* a specified amount in either a capital or a revenue distribution. It thus normally includes all share capital other than non-participating preference shares. The precise rights given in the company's articles of association must be determined in each case.

(d) *Group of companies*. The holding company together with its subsidiary company or companies forms a group.

### *Examples*

(a) Under (b)(i) above, S is a subsidiary of H because H owns more than 50 per cent of the equity capital of S.

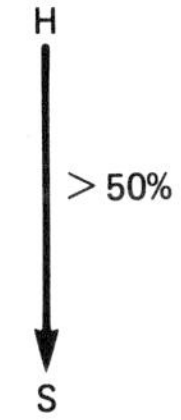

(b) Under (b)(ii) above

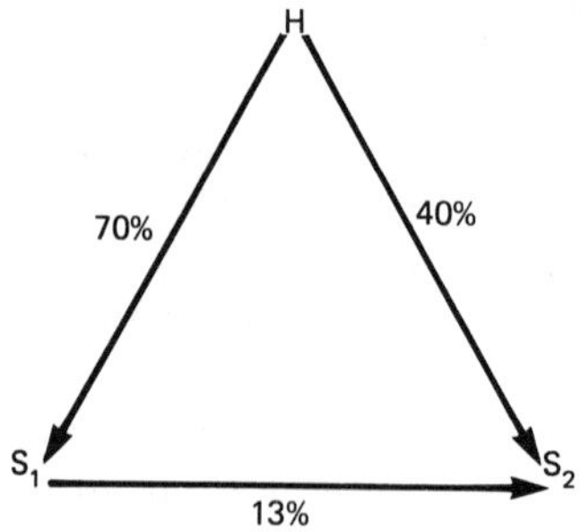


$S_1$ is a subsidiary of H (> 50% rule).

| | |
|---|---|
| H controls *directly* $S_2$ | 40% |
| H controls indirectly $S_2$ via $S_1$ | 13% |
| | 53% |

H is in a position to *control* 53 per cent of the equity capital of $S_2$ which is therefore H's subsidiary.

The test to determine whether a holding–subsidiary relationship exists is to establish whether *control* exists, not the degree of control which is only required for consolidation purposes. Therefore, for consolidation purposes, the group interest in $S_2$ is determined as follows:

| | |
|---|---|
| Directly by H | 40% |
| Indirectly via $S_1$ (70% × 13%) | 9.1% |
| | 49.1% |

*Note:* Although the group holding is less than 50 per cent, $S_2$ is nevertheless a *subsidiary* because *control* exists.

(c) If both conditions mentioned above are satisfied then $S_2$ is a subsidiary of H under the following circumstances:

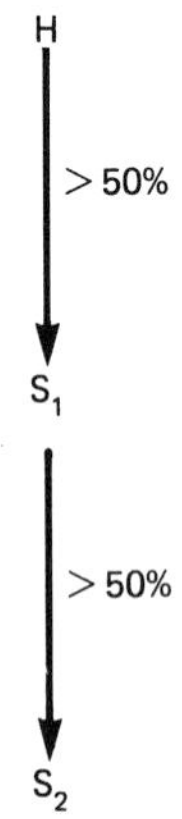


This is commonly known as being *a subsidiary of a subsidiary.*

$S_1$ is the *intermediate* holding company and H is the *ultimate* holding company of $S_2$.

## 1.4 Group accounts

(a) *Introduction*
It is important to appreciate at this stage the distinction between group accounts and consolidated financial statements:

(i) *Group accounts*
SSAP 14 defines these as the financial statement of a group.

(ii) *Consolidated financial statements*
SSAP 14 defines these as one form of group accounts which presents the information contained in the separate financial statements of a holding company and its subsidiaries as if they were the financial statements of a single entity.

(b) *Standard accounting practice*
A holding company is required to prepare group accounts in the form of a single set of consolidated financial statements covering the holding company and its subsidiaries, at home and overseas.

If a group prepares group accounts in a form other than consolidated financial statements, the onus is on the directors to justify and state the reasons for reaching the conclusion that the resulting group accounts give a fairer view of the financial position of the group as a whole.

# 2.0 CONSOLIDATED BALANCE SHEET

## 2.1 Object

The object of a consolidated balance sheet is to disclose similar information to that which would have been shown if the H Ltd of 1.3 above had acquired the net assets of S rather than its equity capital.

*Remember that:*

Share capital + reserves = net assets

Where H acquires 100 per cent of S Ltd, it has in effect acquired 100 per cent of its net assets.

(a) *Goodwill on consolidation*
This is also known as premium on acquisition and the amount can be negative as well as positive, i.e. a credit balance known as *reserve* on consolidation.

The premium (or reserve) is calculated by comparing the *cost* of investment in the subsidiary (i.e. the price paid for the shares of S) and the *NET assets* of S Ltd at the date of *acquisition.*

The same result is obtained by comparing the cost of investment with the *share capital* and *reserves* of S Ltd at the date of *acquisition.* These reserves are known as the *pre-acquisition* reserves.

The term used in SSAP 14 is "premium or discount on acquisition".

(b) *Pre-acquisition reserves of S Ltd*
As mentioned in (a), these represent the net assets of S Ltd at the date of acquisition and cannot, therefore, be distributed. In other words, these reserves are *capitalised.*

Payment of a dividend by S Ltd out of its pre-acquisition profits is tantamount to distribution of its net assets and must be regarded as a *capital* distribution, and as such it must be seen to reduce the cost of investment in S Ltd by H Ltd.

(c) *Post-acquisition reserves of S Ltd*
These represent profits earned by S Ltd since H Ltd acquired its interest. Any distribution out of these profits can properly be credited by H Ltd to its own separate profit and loss account and undistributed profits should be aggregated with those of the holding company's distributable reserves.

## 2.2 Preparation of consolidated balance sheet

(a) *Accounting records*
It is important to appreciate at the outset that all *individual* companies maintain their own separate accounting records and prepare their own legal accounts for presentation to their own members.

For group accounts purposes however, accounts of the holding company and all the subsidiaries are summarised and consolidated after making appropriate adjustments in the "books" of the *group* referred to as *workings*. *No* adjustments are made in the books of the individual companies.

(b) *Workings*
The following "T" accounts should be opened:

| *Account* | *Object* |
|---|---|
| (i) Adjustment (cost of control; goodwill) account | To determine the premium or discount on acquisition. |
| (ii) Reserves of the subsidiary | To analyse and allocate the *total* reserves at the year end between the group, and further analyse between pre- and post-acquisition and the minority shareholders' interest. |
| (iii) Consolidated reserves | To aggregate the total distributable reserves of the group (made up of *all* the reserves of H Ltd plus the *group share* of the *post-acquisition* reserves of S Ltd). |
| (iv) Minority shareholders account | To determine the minority shareholders' interest in the *net assets* at the year-end (made up of their share in the *share capital* and the *reserves* of the subsidiary). |

| *Account* | *Object* |
|---|---|
| (v) Outside debenture holders account | To contrast intra-group holdings and determine outsider interest in the debentures, loan stock or other loan capital issued by S Ltd. |
| (vi) Dividend elimination account | To contrast intra-group dividends (i.e. group share of dividends paid or proposed by S Ltd) so that only dividend payable to minority shareholders is disclosed. |

(c) *Technique*
Essentially, the preparation of a consolidated balance sheet involves the addition of all the assets and liabilities of the holding company and all its subsidiaries adjusting for intra-group items. The balance sheet should be prepared on *double entry* principles. Items on the individual balance sheets should either be incorporated on the consolidated balance sheet or transferred to one of the "T" accounts in the workings. All the "T" accounts should then be closed after the relevant adjustments have been made, and the balances transferred to the consolidated balance sheet.

(d) *Double entry*
Entries should be made in the "T" accounts in order as follows:

| *Debit* | *Credit* |
|---|---|
| (i) *Adjustment account* | |
| 1. Credit cost of investment in S Ltd in H Ltd's books. | 2. Debit S Ltd's share capital with group share of the nominal value<br>3. Debit S Ltd's reserves with group share of the pre-acquisition reserves of S Ltd. |
| Balance equals discount on acquisition. | Balance equals premium on acquisition. |
| (ii) *S Ltd's reserves* | |
| 3. Credit group share of the pre-acquisition reserves.<br>5. Credit consolidated reserves with group share of the post-acquisition reserves.<br>6. Credit minority interest with their share of the total reserves. | 4. Debit S Ltd's reserves. |

No balance should arise on this account provided the adjustments are reflected properly.

| Debit | Credit |
|---|---|
| (iii) *Consolidated reserves* | |
| Balance equals consolidated reserves. | 7. Debit H Ltd's reserves.<br>5. Debit S Ltd's reserves with group share of the post-acquisition reserves. |
| (iv) *Minority shareholders account* | |
| Balance equals minority interest in the net assets of the subsidiary. | 2. Debit S Ltd's share capital with minority share of the nominal value.<br>6. Debit S Ltd's reserves with minority share of the total reserves. |

Items (1) and (7) are notional entries in the books of H Ltd which eliminate respectively the cost of investment in S Ltd and the reserves.

Items (2) and (4) are notional entries in the books of S Ltd which eliminate respectively S Ltd's share capital and reserves.

All the other adjustments are actual adjustments made in the "workings".

## 2.3 Two comprehensive examples

*Example 1*

Balance Sheets

| | H Ltd | S Ltd | | H Ltd | S Ltd |
|---|---|---|---|---|---|
| | £ | £ | | £ | £ |
| Share capital (£1 shares) | 10,000 | 8,000 | Investment in S Ltd | 8,000 | — |
| Reserves | 5,000 | 2,000 | Net assets | 7,000 | 10,000 |
| | £15,000 | £10,000 | | £15,000 | £10,000 |

Assume that H Ltd acquired 8,000 shares in S Ltd at par on the formation of S Ltd. There would therefore be no premium on acquisition, no minority shareholder interest, and the whole of S Ltd reserves represent post-acquisition profits.

The *consolidated* balance sheet would appear as follows:

| | £ |
|---|---|
| Share capital (H Ltd only) | 10,000 |
| Consolidated reserves (5,000 + 2,000) | 7,000 |
| | £17,000 |
| Sundry net assets | £17,000 |

*Example 2*

Assume that H Ltd acquired 8,000 shares in S Ltd for £12,000 when S Ltd's reserves were £1,000.

| | H Ltd | S Ltd | | H Ltd | S Ltd |
|---|---|---|---|---|---|
| | £ | £ | | £ | £ |
| Share capital (£1 shares) | 10,000 | 8,000 | Investment in S Ltd | 12,000 | — |
| Reserves | 9,000 | 2,000 | Net assets | 7,000 | 10,000 |
| | £19,000 | £10,000 | | £19,000 | £10,000 |

Adjustment Account

| | £ | | £ |
|---|---|---|---|
| Cost of investment in S Ltd | 12,000 | Nominal value of shares in S Ltd | 8,000 |
| | | Pre-acquisition profits (100% × 1,000) | 1,000 |
| | | Premium on acquisition (balance) | 3,000 |
| | £12,000 | | £12,000 |

S Ltd Reserves

| | £ | | £ |
|---|---|---|---|
| Adjustment account: pre-acquisition profits (100% × 1,000) | 1,000 | Balance brought down | 2,000 |
| Consolidated reserves [100% × (2,000 − 1,000)] | 1,000 | | |
| | £2,000 | | £2,000 |

Consolidated Reserves

| | £ | | £ |
|---|---|---|---|
| Balance carried down | 10,000 | H Ltd brought down | 9,000 |
| | | S Ltd—post-acquisition | 1,000 |
| | £10,000 | | £10,000 |

Consolidated Balance Sheet

| | £ | | £ |
|---|---|---|---|
| Share capital | 10,000 | Premium on acquisition | 3,000 |
| Consolidated reserves | 10,000 | Net assets | 17,000 |
| | £20,000 | | £20,000 |

You will have observed in the above two examples that the share capital shown in the consolidated balance sheet must *always* be the share capital of H Ltd. The share capital of S Ltd is transferred to the adjustment account.

## 3.0 MINORITY INTERESTS

Where the investor acquires less than 100 per cent in the investee, the balance of shares held outside the group is known as the *minority shareholders' interest*. In preparing the consolidated balance sheet of the group, the minority interest should be reflected by showing the aggregate assets and liabilities of the group, and then separately disclosing the minority interest in the *net assets* of the subsidiary companies.

Situation 1

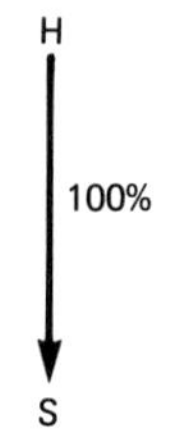


S is a *wholly-owned subsidiary* of H.

Situation 2

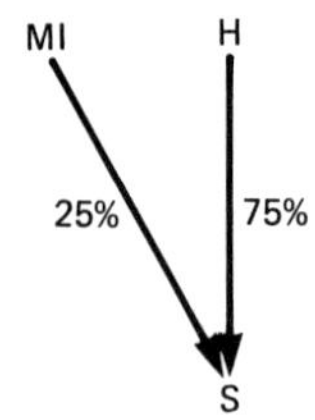


S is a partly-owned subsidiary of H and MI represents the *minority interest* in S.

Situation 3

There is a 30 per cent minority interest in $S_1$ and 40 per cent minority interest in $S_2$.

However, for consolidation purposes the minority interests in subsidiaries is calculated:

| | |
|---|---|
| $S_1$: Group holding equals | 70% |
| ∴ Minority interest equals | 30% |
| | 100% |
| $S_2$: Group holding equals 70% × 60% | 42% |
| ∴ Minority interest equals | 58% |
| | 100% |

In this situation, $S_2$ is a subsidiary of $S_1$ which is a subsidiary of H. Because H *controls* $S_2$, then $S_2$ is a subsidiary of H although the effective holding is 42 per cent. The minority interest effectively comes to be controlled by the "majority" interest holder.

*Example*

Balance Sheets

| | H Ltd | S Ltd | | H Ltd | S Ltd |
|---|---|---|---|---|---|
| | £ | £ | | £ | £ |
| Share capital (£1 shares) | 75,000 | 40,000 | Investment in S Ltd | 42,000 | — |
| Reserves | 25,000 | 12,000 | Net assets | 58,000 | 52,000 |
| | £100,000 | £52,000 | | £100,000 | £52,000 |

Assume H acquired 30,000 shares in S Ltd when S's reserves were £8,000.

Step 1
The first step is to compute the share holding:

| | |
|---|---|
| Group | 75% |
| Minority | 25% |
| | 100% |

Step 2
Determine the *pre-acquisition* reserves of S. They equal £8,000.

Step 3
Open the relevant "T" accounts and clear all the items on the individual balance sheet *line by line.*

Adjustment Account

| | £ | | £ |
|---|---|---|---|
| Cost of investment in S Ltd | 42,000 | Nominal value of shares in S Ltd | 30,000 |
| | | Pre-acquisition reserves | 6,000 |
| | | Balance = premium on consolidation | 6,000 |
| | £42,000 | | £42,000 |

S Ltd Reserves

| | £ | | £ |
|---|---|---|---|
| *Adjustment account* | | Brought down | 12,000 |
| Pre-acquisition reserves (75% × 8,000) | 6,000 | | |
| *Consolidated reserves* | | | |
| Post-acquisition reserves [75% × (12,000 − 8,000)] | 3,000 | | |
| *Minority interest* | | | |
| (25% × 12,000) | 3,000 | | |
| | £12,000 | | £12,000 |

Consolidated Reserves

| | £ | | £ |
|---|---|---|---|
| Transfer to consolidated balance sheet | 28,000 | Brought down | 25,000 |
| | | S Ltd post-acquisition reserves | 3,000 |
| | £28,000 | | £28,000 |

Minority Interest Account

| | £ | | £ |
|---|---|---|---|
| Transfer to consolidated balance sheet | 13,000 | Nominal value of shares in S Ltd | 10,000 |
| | | Reserves | 3,000 |
| | £13,000 | | £13,000 |

Consolidated Balance Sheet

| | £ | | £ |
|---|---|---|---|
| Share capital | 75,000 | Net assets | 110,000 |
| Consolidated reserves | 28,000 | Premium on consolidation | 6,000 |
| | 103,000 | | |
| Minority interest | 13,000 | | |
| | £116,000 | | £116,000 |

*Note:* The minority shareholders *always* have an interest in the *net assets* (represented by share capital and reserves) at the end of the year.

| *Check:* | net assets of S Ltd | = | £52,000 |
|---|---|---|---|
| | 25% thereof | = | £13,000 |

## 4.0 SUNDRY POINTS

### 4.1 Dividends from pre-acquisition profits, paid by a subsidiary

Two situations may occur:

(a) Where a proposed dividend at the date of acquisition is paid to the former shareholders (i.e. outside the group).

The balance sheet would show the proposed dividends as a liability and the profit and loss account would have been charged.

Consider:

Balance Sheet of S Ltd—30th June 19X6

| | £ | | £ |
|---|---|---|---|
| Share capital | 100,000 | Assets | 125,000 |
| Reserves | 20,000 | Proposed dividend | 5,000 |
| | £120,000 | | £120,000 |

H Ltd purchased all of the share capital of S Ltd on 30th June 19X6 for £150,000.

H is therefore acquiring £120,000 worth of net assets.

Cost of Control Account

| | £ | | £ |
|---|---|---|---|
| Cost of investment | 150,000 | Shares of subsidiary | 100,000 |
| | | Pre-acquisition profits | 20,000 |
| | | Premium on consolidation | 30,000 |
| | £150,000 | | £150,000 |

*Note:* The same principle would apply if a dividend, which had not been proposed at the date of acquisition, but was later paid to the former shareholders, i.e. the net assets, and, therefore, pre-acquisition reserves, are reduced by the dividends.

(b) Where a dividend is payable out of pre-acquisition profits by the subsidiary to the parent company.

Consider the balance sheet of S Ltd under (a). In the earlier example H Ltd was purchasing net assets worth £120,000 because the dividend (similar to other liabilities) was payable outside the group.

In this situation the dividend is payable inside the group to H Ltd and therefore the net assets purchased by the parent equals £125,000.

Cost of Control Account

| | £ | | £ |
|---|---|---|---|
| Cost of investment | 150,000 | Shares of subsidiary | 100,000 |
| | | Profit and loss account | 25,000 |
| | | Goodwill | 25,000 |
| | £150,000 | | £150,000 |

Let us now consider the situation when the dividend is paid by the subsidiary and received by the parent. This dividend is the distribution of pre-acquisition profits and *is not distributable*; the parent should *not* debit cash, while crediting the profit and loss account, as this would be treating it as distributable.

What should be done is:

Debit: Cash
Credit: Cost of investment in subsidiary

This has the effect of reducing the cost of the investment and ensuring that the dividend is not distributable. When we come to consolidate, we transfer the group's share of the pre-acquisition profits of the subsidiary, after deducting the pre-acquisition dividend.

Thus:

Cost of Control Account

| | £ | | £ |
|---|---|---|---|
| Cost of investment *less* pre-acquisition dividend (150,000 − 5,000) | 145,000 | Shares of subsidiary | 100,000 |
| | | Profit and loss account | 20,000 |
| | | Goodwill | 25,000 |
| | £145,000 | | £145,000 |

You will notice, in both cases, that goodwill was computed at £25,000. In the first case we transferred the full £25,000 profits, effectively reversing the proposed dividend. In the second case we transferred only £20,000 profits; the other £5,000 had been capitalised by crediting the capital cost of the investment account.

## 4.2 Dividends paid and proposed

We are dealing only with the dividends of the subsidiary; the dividend paid and proposed by H Ltd needs *no adjustment.*

Dividends paid by the subsidiary. Because the dividend is *paid* we cannot reverse the situation; what we can do, however, is to ensure that, from a *consolidation* point of view, the dividend is treated correctly with regard to the parent company and the minority.

(a) *Parent*
If the dividend has been paid from pre-acquisition profits the correct accounting treatment for the parent company is to:

Debit: Cash
Credit: Investment in subsidiary

If the parent has *wrongly* credited the pre-acquisition dividend to its profit and loss account then for consolidation purposes we must correct this mistake.

The procedure for instance can be:

Debit: Parent company's profit and loss account
(thus removing the pre-acquisition dividend from profits)
Credit: Investment in subsidiary

We capitalise the group's share of pre-acquisition profits of the subsidiary, after deduction of the dividend.

If the dividend of the subsidiary has been paid from post-acquisition profits then the parent can quite correctly:

Debit: Cash
Credit: Profit and loss account

i.e. treat the dividend as distributable.

(b) *Minority*
Pre- and post-acquisition profits have no relevance when one discusses the minority. The transfer of profits to the minority interest account shows the full proportion of net assets of the subsidiary financed by outsiders.

All that is necessary, when discussing minority, is to ensure that they have been charged with their share of any dividend paid to them. Normally, when consolidating, we start with profits after any dividend payment, therefore the minority has been charged with the dividend.

Thus:

Subsidiary Ltd: Profit and Loss Account

| | | | |
|---|---|---|---|
| Minority interest: share of A and B | C | Profits brought forward | A |
| | | Profits of year, *post*-dividend | B |

Of course, the full story is that the minority are entitled to their share of profits, before dividend; which is then reduced by any dividend paid to them.

(c) *Dividends proposed by the subsidiary*
A dividend proposed by a subsidiary is a good example of an *inter-group item*, i.e. the subsidiary will be showing a liability which will be payable, inter-group, to the parent company.

Again two situations may occur:

(i) Where the subsidiary has accounted for the proposed dividend, and the parent company has *not* accounted for its share of dividend receivable.

*Example*

Extract of Balance Sheet of S Ltd

| | £ |
|---|---|
| Profit and loss account | 40,000 |
| Current liabilities: | |
| Proposed dividend | 10,000 |

The subsidiary has accounted for the proposed dividend as follows:

Debit: Profit and loss account
Credit: Dividend payable

It is suggested that the proposed dividend is *reversed*, i.e.:

Debit: Dividend payable
Credit: Profit and loss account

Dividend Payable Account

| | £ | | £ |
|---|---|---|---|
| Reversing entry | £10,000 | Per balance sheet | £10,000 |

Profit and Loss Account

| | | | £ |
|---|---|---|---|
| | | Per balance sheet | 40,000 |
| | | Reversing entry | 10,000 |

The profit and loss account stands at £50,000. We will assume that the subsidiary is 75 per cent owned and therefore the minority is 25 per cent.

Minority Interest Account

| | | | £ |
|---|---|---|---|
| | | Shares (25% × 120,000) | 30,000 |
| | | Profit and loss account (25% × 50,000) | 12,500 |
| | | | £42,500 |

The minority have provided finance of £42,500 and this would normally be shown as long-term finance on the consolidated balance sheet. However, a refinement is to split the total (£42,500) between long-term finance and the proposed dividend element that would be paid to the minority.

What proportion of the subsidiary's proposed dividend of £10,000 would be paid to the minority? The answer is 25 per cent, i.e. £2,500.

It is suggested that of the total due to the minority, i.e. £42,500, £40,000 is shown as long-term finance and £2,500 as proposed dividend of the subsidiary payable to the minority.

Minority Interest Account

| | £ | | £ |
|---|---|---|---|
| Balances carried down | | Shares | 30,000 |
| Proposed dividend | 2,500 | Profit and loss | |
| Long-term finance | 40,000 | account | 12,500 |
| | £42,500 | | £42,500 |

Extract of Consolidated Balance Sheet

| | £ |
|---|---|
| Capital and reserves | |
| Called-up share capital | x |
| Consolidated reserves | x |
| Shareholders' funds | x |
| Minority interest | 40,000 |
| | x |

Creditors—amounts falling due within one year:

| | £ |
|---|---|
| Proposed dividend: | |
| Minority shareholders | 2,500 |
| Company shareholders | x |

(ii) Where the subsidiary has accounted for the proposed dividend, and the parent company has accounted for its share of the dividend receivable.

Extract of Balance Sheet of H Ltd

| | £ |
|---|---|
| Profit and loss account | 120,000 |
| Current assets: | |
| Dividend receivable | 7,500 |

Extract of Balance Sheet of S Ltd

| | |
|---|---|
| Profit and loss account | 40,000 |
| Current liabilities: | |
| Proposed dividend | 10,000 |

Here it is *not* absolutely necessary to reverse the dividend of the subsidiary. Instead it is possible to *cancel* the inter-group items by transferring the amounts to the dividend elimination account:

Dividend Elimination Account

| | £ | | £ |
|---|---|---|---|
| H Ltd dividend receivable brought down | 7,500 | S Ltd dividend payable brought down | 10,000 |
| Balance payable to minority interest | 2,500 | | |
| | £10,000 | | £10,000 |

The cancellation will leave £2,500 payable by the subsidiary; this can be shown as a current liability of the group.

Minority Interest Account

| | £ | | £ |
|---|---|---|---|
| | | Shares (as in previous example) | 30,000 |
| Balance: long-term finance | 40,000 | Profit and loss account ($\frac{1}{4}$ × 40,000) | 10,000 |
| | £40,000 | | £40,000 |

Extract of Consolidated Balance Sheet

| | £ |
|---|---|
| *Share capital and reserves* | |
| Shares and reserves | x |
| Minority interest | 40,000 |
| *Creditors—amounts falling due within one year* | |
| Proposed dividend of subsidiary, payable to outside shareholders | 2,500 |

## 4.3 Current accounts

(a) *Definition*
The expression "current account" suggests that companies within a group are trading together and it represents the debtor–creditor relationship between the companies.

(b) *Treatment of current accounts*

(i) Correct any mistakes that have been made in the accounting of any company.

(ii) Cancel "debtor" current accounts against "creditor" current accounts; the difference, if any, should be debit and will represent cash in transit, which is shown as a cash item on the consolidated balance sheet.

## 4.4 Preference dividends

Generally, preference dividends have a prior charge on the profits of a company, i.e.

| | £ |
|---|---|
| Profit for the financial year | x |
| *less:* Preference dividend | (x) |
| Available to ordinary shareholders | x |

This fact is important in relation to the minority interest. What function does the minority interest account fulfil?

To identify their ownership of the shares and reserves of a subsidiary.

It is necessary to ensure, when transferring shares of profit to the minority interest account, that the preference dividend is provided.

*Example*

Balance Sheets

| | H Ltd | S Ltd | | H Ltd | S Ltd |
|---|---|---|---|---|---|
| | £ | £ | | £ | £ |
| Share capital: | | | Investment in S: | | |
| Ordinary | 100,000 | 60,000 | Ordinary | 83,000 | — |
| 8% preference | — | 40,000 | Preference | 10,700 | — |
| Reserves | 75,000 | 25,000 | Net assets | 101,300 | 132,600 |
| | 175,000 | 125,000 | | | |
| Proposed dividends: | | | | | |
| Ordinary | 20,000 | 6,000 | | | |
| Preference | — | 1,600 | | | |
| | £195,000 | £132,600 | | £195,000 | £132,600 |

Assume that H acquired 80 per cent and 25 per cent of the ordinary and preference share capitals respectively when the reserves of S Ltd were £10,000. H Ltd's policy is to take credit for dividends from S Ltd on a receivable basis, but the above amounts have not yet been reflected in the accounts of H Ltd.

Step 1

| Holdings | Ordinary | Preference |
|---|---|---|
| Group | 80 | 25 |
| Minority | 20 | 75 |
| | 100 | 100 |

Step 2

Pre-acquisition reserves £10,000

Step 3

"T" accounts

Adjustment Account

| | £ | | £ |
|---|---|---|---|
| Cost of investment: | | Share capital: | |
| Ordinary | 83,000 | Ordinary (80% × 60,000) | 48,000 |
| Preference | 10,700 | Preference (25% × 40,000) | 10,000 |
| | | Reserves | 8,000 |
| | | Premium on consolidation | 27,700 |
| | £93,700 | | £93,700 |

### S Ltd Reserves

| | £ | | £ |
|---|---|---|---|
| Adjustment account: | | Brought down | 25,000 |
| Pre-acquisition profits | | | |
| (80% × 10,000) | 8,000 | | |
| Consolidated reserves | | | |
| [80% (25,000 − 10,000)] | 12,000 | | |
| Minority interest | | | |
| (20% × 25,000) | 5,000 | | |
| | £25,000 | | £25,000 |

### Consolidated Reserves

| | £ | | £ |
|---|---|---|---|
| Carried down | 92,200 | Brought down | 75,000 |
| | | S Ltd | 12,000 |
| | | Dividends receivable: | |
| | | Ordinary (80% × 6,000) | 4,800 |
| | | Preference (25% × 1,600) | 400 |
| | £92,200 | | £92,200 |

### Minority Shareholders

| | £ | | £ |
|---|---|---|---|
| Carried down | 47,000 | Share capital: | |
| | | Ordinary (20% × 60,000) | 12,000 |
| | | Preference (75% × 40,000) | 30,000 |
| | | Reserves | 5,000 |
| | £47,000 | | £47,000 |

### Dividend Elimination Account

| | £ | £ | | £ |
|---|---|---|---|---|
| Consolidated reserves | | | S Ltd—proposed dividends: | |
| Dividend receivable: | | | Ordinary | 6,000 |
| Ordinary | | 4,800 | Preference | 1,600 |
| Preference | | 400 | | |
| Carried down: | | | | |
| Ordinary | 1,200 | | | |
| Preference | 1,200 | | | |
| | | 2,400 | | |
| | | £7,600 | | £7,600 |

Step 4 Consolidated Balance Sheet

| | £ | | £ |
|---|---|---|---|
| Share capital | 100,000 | Intangible fixed asset: | |
| Consolidated reserves | 92,200 | Premium on consolidation | 27,700 |
| Shareholders' funds | 192,200 | Net assets | 233,900 |
| Minority interest | 47,000 | | |
| Creditors due within one year: | | | |
| Proposed dividends: | | | |
| H Ltd | 20,000 | | |
| Minority | 2,400 | | |
| | £261,600 | | £261,600 |

## 4.5 Inter-group transactions

(a) *Provision for unrealised profits (PUP)*

If a group trades internally, i.e. between themselves, then certain transactions may be made at a profit. If the goods are then "sold on" to outsiders no adjustments are required.

However, if the goods are held within the group at the balance sheet date the *unrealised* profit must be eliminated from the consolidated accounts.

For examination purposes, the *whole* of the provision should be charged *wholly against consolidated reserves* without any charge to the minority.

The accounting policy note to the consolidated accounts will state that "Provision has been made for the whole of the unrealised profit on intra-group transactions in the separate books of the holding company."

The adjustment to reflect any provision for unrealised profits will be:

Debit: Consolidated reserves
Credit: Asset (normally stock)

(i) *Stock*

*Example*

H Ltd sells to S Ltd stock at an invoice price of £1,100. H Ltd makes 10 per cent profit based on *cost*. The whole of the stock remains unsold at the balance sheet date.

Calculate the provision for unrealised profits (PUP).

SOLUTION

Say: cost = £100
Cost + gross profit = selling price
∴ 100 + 10 = £110
The profit or "mark-up" equals $\frac{1}{10}$ on cost.
The profit or "mark-up" also equals $\frac{1}{11}$ on selling price.
∴ PUP = $\frac{1}{11} \times$ £1,100 = £100
£100 is the amount of unrealised profit.

| | | £ | £ |
|---|---|---|---|
| Debit: | Consolidated reserves | 100 | |
| Credit: | Group stock | | 100 |

(ii) *Fixed assets*
Apart from adjusting the fixed asset to bring it back to pure cost, it may also be necessary to adjust the depreciation charge, based on that asset.

*Example*

S Ltd purchased a machine from H Ltd at a cost to S Ltd of £200,000. H Ltd made a profit on the sale of £50,000. The group provides for depreciation at 10 per cent on the straight-line method.

SOLUTION
*For consolidation purposes* the following adjustments must be made:

| | | | £ | £ |
|---|---|---|---|---|
| (A) | Debit: | Consolidated reserves | 50,000 | |
| | Credit: | Machine | | 50,000 |

This reduces the fixed asset to pure cost.

(B) Further, the depreciation should be based on true cost, i.e.:
10 per cent of £150,000 = £15,000
The depreciation provision which stands at £20,000 must be reduced to £15,000. Therefore:

| | | £ | £ |
|---|---|---|---|
| Debit: | Depreciation | 5,000 | |
| Credit: | Consolidated reserves | | 5,000 |

## 5.0 INDIRECT SUBSIDIARIES

### 5.1 Methods of consolidation

So far we have dealt with the case of only one subsidiary. Consider a situation where a group is made up of more than one subsidiary, some of which may be *direct* and others *indirect*.

Essentially, there are two methods which can be used to prepare consolidation accounts by H Ltd, the ultimate holding company.

### 5.2 Direct method

Under this method, the consolidation accounts of the intermediate holding company are prepared first, followed by the consolidation of these accounts with those of the ultimate holding company.

### 5.3 Indirect method

Under this method, the ultimate holding company's *direct* and *indirect* interests in subsidiaries are calculated and using the percentage computed, the share capital and reserves of the subsidiaries are allocated.

## 5.4 Method recommended for examination

It is strongly recommended that the indirect method be adopted for examination purposes since it is simpler and less time consuming.

The indirect method of consolidation has been used throughout in this text.

H Ltd is the ultimate holding company;
S Ltd is the *direct* subsidiary;
T Ltd is the *indirect* subsidiary.

## 5.5 Technique for indirect method

The following "T" accounts should be opened in order as follows:

| *Debit* | *Credit* |
|---|---|
| (a) *Adjustment account* | |
| 1. H's cost of investment in S. | 3. Group share of nominal share capital in S and T, using the percentages computed using direct and indirect interests. |
| 2. H's share of cost of investment by S in T. | 4. Group share of pre-acquisition reserves of S and T using percentages as above. |
| | Balance equals premium (discount) on consolidation. |
| (b) *Minority interests* | |
| 2. Minority's share of cost of investment by S in T. | 3. Minority's share of nominal share capital in S and T, using the percentages computed using direct and indirect interests. |
| | 5. Minority share of reserves in S and T, using percentages as above. |

*Notes*
(1) The total of (2) must equal the cost of investment in T by S.
(2) The total of (3) must equal the total share capitals of S and T.

### *Example*

| | H Ltd | S Ltd | T Ltd |
|---|---|---|---|
| | £ | £ | £ |
| Cost of investment: | | | |
| S Ltd (45,000 £1 shares) | 65,000 | — | — |
| T Ltd (30,000 £1 shares) | — | 55,000 | — |
| Net assets | 80,000 | 33,000 | 75,000 |
| | £145,000 | £88,000 | £75,000 |

| | H Ltd | S Ltd | T Ltd |
|---|---|---|---|
| | £ | £ | £ |
| Called-up share capital: | | | |
| £1 ordinary shares | 100,000 | 60,000 | 50,000 |
| Profit and loss account | 45,000 | 28,000 | 25,000 |
| | £145,000 | £88,000 | £75,000 |

The investments in S Ltd and T Ltd were acquired several years ago when the balance on their respective profit and loss accounts were £10,000 and £8,000.

You are required to prepare the consolidated balance sheet of the H Group.

Step 1
Compute the effective interest in S and T by H:

| | S Ltd | | T Ltd |
|---|---|---|---|
| Group (direct) | 75% | (75% × 60%) | 45% |
| Minority | 25% | | 55% |
| | 100% | | 100% |

Remember, T Ltd is a subsidiary of H Ltd because it is a subsidiary of a subsidiary. *Control* therefore exists, although for consolidation purposes the degree of control equals 45 per cent only.

Step 2

| | S Ltd | T Ltd |
|---|---|---|
| Pre-acquisition reserves | £10,000 | £8,000 |

Step 3
Open all the relevant "T" accounts.

Adjustment Account

| | £ | | £ |
|---|---|---|---|
| Cost of investment: | | Ordinary share capital: | |
| S Ltd | 65,000 | S Ltd (75% × 60,000) | 45,000 |
| T Ltd (75% × 55,000) | 41,250 | T Ltd (45% × 50,000) | 22,500 |
| | | Pre-acquisition reserves: | |
| | | S Ltd | 7,500 |
| | | T Ltd | 3,600 |
| | | Premium on acquisition | 27,650 |
| | £106,250 | | £106,250 |

Reserves of S Ltd and T Ltd

| | S Ltd £ | T Ltd £ | | S Ltd £ | T Ltd £ |
|---|---|---|---|---|---|
| Adjustment a/c: | | | Brought down | 28,000 | 25,000 |
| 75% × 10,000 | 7,500 | — | | | |
| 45% × 8,000 | — | 3,600 | | | |
| Consolidated reserves: | | | | | |
| 75% (28,000 − 10,000) | 13,500 | — | | | |
| 45% (25,000 − 8,000) | — | 7,650 | | | |
| Minority interest: | | | | | |
| 25% × 28,000 | 7,000 | — | | | |
| 55% × 25,000 | — | 13,750 | | | |
| | £28,000 | £25,000 | | £28,000 | £25,000 |

Consolidated Reserves

| | £ | | £ |
|---|---|---|---|
| Balance carried down | 66,150 | Brought down: H Ltd | 45,000 |
| | | S Ltd | 13,500 |
| | | T Ltd | 7,650 |
| | £66,150 | | £66,150 |

Minority Interest

| | £ | | £ |
|---|---|---|---|
| Cost of investment: | | Ordinary share capital: | |
| T Ltd (25% × 55,000) | 13,750 | S Ltd (25%) | 15,000 |
| | | T Ltd (55%) | 27,500 |
| Balance carried down | 49,500 | Profit and loss account: | |
| | | S Ltd | 7,000 |
| | | T Ltd | 13,750 |
| | £63,250 | | £63,250 |

Step 4

Consolidated Balance Sheet

| | £ |
|---|---|
| Intangible fixed assets: | |
| Premium on acquisition | 27,650 |
| Net assets | 188,000 |
| | £215,650 |

| Capital and reserves: | £ |
|---|---|
| Called-up share capital | 100,000 |
| Consolidated reserves | 66,150 |
| Shareholders' funds | 166,150 |
| Minority interest | 49,500 |
| | £215,650 |

## 6.0 CONSOLIDATED PROFIT AND LOSS ACCOUNT

### 6.1 Object

The object of a consolidated profit and loss account is to show a true and fair view of the earnings (or losses) of the group for the year, attributable to the members of the holding company. This is achieved by incorporating in the holding company's profit and loss account the group's share of the underlying profit (or losses) of all the subsidiaries and associated companies in substitution for any dividend for which the holding company may have taken credit in its *own* profit and loss account.

### 6.2 Intra-group transactions

Just as intra-group balances are eliminated on consolidation of the balance sheets, so are intra-group transactions eliminated upon the preparation of the consolidated profit and loss account.

Examples of intra-group transactions are dividends receivable and profit on unrealised transactions.

### 6.3 Minority interest

Since H Ltd *controls* S Ltd (as opposed to just being in a position to exert significant influence), then it is only appropriate that the *whole* of the results of the subsidiary are consolidated and the minority interest in the subsidiary is separately disclosed.

*Example*

| | H Ltd | S Ltd |
|---|---|---|
| | £ | £ |
| Operating profit | 100,000 | 50,000 |
| Taxation | 50,000 | 25,000 |
| Retained for the financial year | £50,000 | £25,000 |

Assume H Ltd acquired 80 per cent of S Ltd several years ago.

The consolidated profit and loss account is prepared as follows:

| | £ |
|---|---|
| Operating profit (100,000 + 50,000) | 150,000 |
| Taxation (50,000 + 25,000) | 75,000 |
| Profit on ordinary activities after taxation | 75,000 |
| Minority interest (20% × 25,000) | 5,000 |
| Retained for the financial year | £70,000 |

## 6.4 Preference shares

If the subsidiary has preference shares in issue, then the following adjustments must be made first, before working out the minority interest in the current year's profits of the subsidiary.

(a) Preference dividends must be allowed for before arriving at profits attributable to ordinary shareholders. This adjustment must be made irrespective of whether the preference dividend is paid, proposed, or even not proposed by the subsidiary.

(b) The preference dividend may be attributable either partly to the holding company and partly to the minority, or alternatively wholly to either the minority or the holding company.

*Example*

The facts are the same as in the above example, except that S Ltd has £50,000 10 per cent preference shares of which 50 per cent are issued to H Ltd.

The minority interest in S Ltd after taxation will be:

| | Total | % | Minority interest |
|---|---|---|---|
| | £ | | £ |
| Profit after taxation | 25,000 | | |
| *deduct:* Preference dividend (10% × 50,000) | 5,000 | 50 | 2,500 |
| Available for ordinary shareholders | 20,000 | 20 | 4,000 |
| | | | £6,500 |

The consolidated profit and loss account will be:

| | £ |
|---|---|
| Operating profit (as before) | 150,000 |
| Taxation (as before) | 75,000 |
| Profit on ordinary activities after taxation | 75,000 |
| Minority interest | 6,500 |
| Retained for the financial year | £68,500 |

Retained profit comprises:

| | £ | |
|---|---|---|
| H Ltd profit after tax | | 50,000 |
| S Ltd profit after tax | 25,000 | |
| *less:* Minority interest | 6,500 | 18,500 |
| | | £68,500 |

## 6.5 Pre-acquisition profits

This adjustment relates to the holding company's share of the pre-acquisition profits in the *current* year's profits of the subsidiary. Hence, this adjustment will occur only if the holding company acquired its shares in the subsidiary *during the year*. To calculate the pre-acquisition profit simply time-apportion the profits of the subsidiary.

*Example*

Facts as in the first example above, except that H Ltd acquired 80 per cent interest in S Ltd on 30th June and the accounts are prepared to 31st December.

The consolidated profit and loss account will be:

| | £ |
|---|---|
| Operating profit [100,000 + ($\frac{1}{2}$ × 50,000)] | 125,000 |
| Taxation [50,000 + ($\frac{1}{2}$ × 25,000)] | 62,500 |
| | 62,500 |
| Minority interest [20% × ($\frac{1}{2}$ × 25,000)] | 2,500 |
| Retained for the financial year | £60,000 |

## 6.6 Profits brought forward

Where the holding company acquires the shares in the subsidiary during the year, there will not be any post-acquisition profits brought forward in the subsidiary since all profits of the subsidiary prior to the acquisition of shares will be pre-acquisition.

Where the subsidiary is not acquired during the year, the retained profits brought forward should only include the group's share of S Ltd's *post-acquisition* profits.

*Example*

Facts as in the first example above.

| | H Ltd | S Ltd |
|---|---|---|
| | £ | £ |
| Retained profit for the financial year | 50,000 | 25,000 |
| Retained profits brought forward | 30,000 | 15,000 |
| Retained profits carried forward | £80,000 | £40,000 |

Assume that H Ltd acquired 80 per cent of S Ltd when the latter's reserves were £5,000.

The consolidated profit and loss account will be:

| | £ |
|---|---|
| Operating profit | 150,000 |
| Taxation | 75,000 |
| Profit on ordinary activities after taxation | 75,000 |
| Minority interest | 5,000 |
| Retained for the year | 70,000 |
| Retained profits brought forward [30,000 + 80% (15,000 − 5,000)] | 38,000 |
| Retained profits carried forward | £108,000 |

## 6.7 Extraordinary items

Under the provisions of SSAP 6, these items are disclosed in the separate accounts of H Ltd and S Ltd where applicable, net of tax, *after* the profit after taxation has been arrived at.

In the consolidated profit and loss account, the extraordinary item is dealt with *after* profit, *after taxation* and *minority interests*. It follows that the extraordinary item disclosed in the consolidated profit and loss account must comprise of:

(a) the *whole* of the extraordinary item of H Ltd; and

(b) the group share of the extraordinary item of S Ltd.

## 6.8 Appropriations

These comprise of dividends and transfers to reserves.

(a) *Dividends*
Intra-group dividends are eliminated for the purposes of consolidation. Thus only dividends paid and proposed by H Ltd are brought into the consolidated profit and loss account.

(b) *Transfers to reserves*
The transfers to consolidated reserves are always those of H Ltd and *group's share* of the transfers of S Ltd.

## 6.9 Miscellaneous points

(a) *"Framed as" profit and loss account*
The Companies Acts 1948–81 require the holding company to submit to its members both its own profit and loss account and the consolidated profit and loss account of the group. However, s. 149 of the 1948 Act has been amended by s. 1 of the 1981 Act, and permits a holding company to dispense with its *own* profit and loss account provided that the profit and loss account is framed as a consolidated profit and loss account, dealing with all or any of the company's subsidiaries as well as the company itself and:

(i) complies with the requirements of the Acts relating to consolidated profit and loss accounts; and

(ii) discloses how much of the group profit has been dealt with in the separate accounts of H Ltd; and

(iii) discloses the fact that the advantage of the s. 149 exemption has been taken, by way of note to the accounts.

(b) *Group profit dealt with in the separate accounts of H Ltd*
This normally comprises of:

(i) H Ltd's profit after tax,

*plus:*

(ii) dividends received from S Ltd out of the post-acquisition profits,

*less:*

(iii) any provision for unrealised profits resulting from intra-group activities.

## 6.10 Companies Act 1981 disclosure requirements

| *Item* | *Comments* | £ |
|---|---|---|
| Turnover | H and S excluding intra-group sales | x |
| Cost of sales | H and S excluding:<br>(i) intra-group purchases<br>(ii) provision for unrealised profits | (x) |
| Gross profit | | x |
| Distribution costs | H and S | (x) |
| Administrative expenses | H and S | (x) |
| Operating profit | | x |
| Investment income | H and S excluding intra-group and interest on intra-group debenture holdings | x |
| Interest payable | | (x) |
| Profit on ordinary activities before taxation | | x |
| Tax on profit on ordinary activities | H and S | (x) |
| Profit on ordinary activities after taxation | | x |
| Minority interest | In profit after tax of S Ltd | (x) |
| Profit before extraordinary items | | x |
| Extraordinary items | H and group's share of S | x |
| Profit attributable to the members of H Ltd | Section 149 requirements to disclose amount dealt with in the separate accounts of H Ltd | x |
| Appropriation: | | |
| Dividends | H only | (x) |
| Transfers to reserves | H and group's share of S | (x) |
| Retained for the year | | x |
| Retained profits brought forward | H Ltd and group's share of post-acquisition of S Ltd reserves | x |
| Retained profits carried forward | | £x |

# 7.0 ASSOCIATED COMPANIES

## 7.1 Methods of accounting for investments

There are a wide variety of methods for accounting for investments in the accounts of an investor.

(a) *Cost method*
Under this method, an investment is carried in the investing company's balance sheet at its original (or historical) cost to the investing company unless there has been a permanent diminution in the value of the investment.

In the profit and loss account of the investing company, the investment is accounted for on the basis of dividend received or receivable.

(b) *Valuation method*
Under this method, an investment is carried in the investor's balance sheet at a valuation which approximates to its fair market value.

(c) *Consolidation method*
Under this method, the investing company and each of the investments are consolidated as a single entity. Minority interests in investee companies are disclosed separately as a single figure.

(d) *Equity method*
Under this method, the balance-sheet carrying value of the investment is:

(i) the cost of the investment,

*plus:*

(ii) the investor's share of the post-acquisition reserves of the investee,

*less:*

(iii) any amounts written off in respect of (i) and (ii).

## 7.2 Variants of the equity method

The profit and loss account treatment is the same for each of the main variants of the equity method.

(a) *Cost plus*
The investment is carried forward at its original cost plus (or minus) the share of post-acquisition profits (or losses).

(b) *Underlying net asset value*
On the acquisition of the investment, the cost is written down to either the fair value or the book value of its underlying net assets. The share of the post-acquisition profits (losses) is added (deducted) from this amount, so that the carrying value is maintained at the investor's attributable share of the underlying net assets of the investment.

(c) *Adjustment for premium on acquisition*
The premium on acquisition is distinguished and treated according to the investor's policy for accounting for goodwill.

## 7.3 Partial consolidation

This method is a hybrid between the consolidation and the equity method. The investor's share of each asset, liability, or profit and loss account item is aggregated with the respective item in the investor's accounts.

## 7.4 SSAP 1 approach

The standard has specified equity accounting, which itself is a middle course between cost or valuation methods and consolidation, as the appropriate accounting method for accounting for investments in associated companies. Partial consolidation may be appropriate for application to certain forms of partnerships and non-corporate joint ventures.

## 7.5 Definition of associated companies (SSAP 1—Revised)

A company not being a subsidiary of the investing group or investing company is an associated company if:

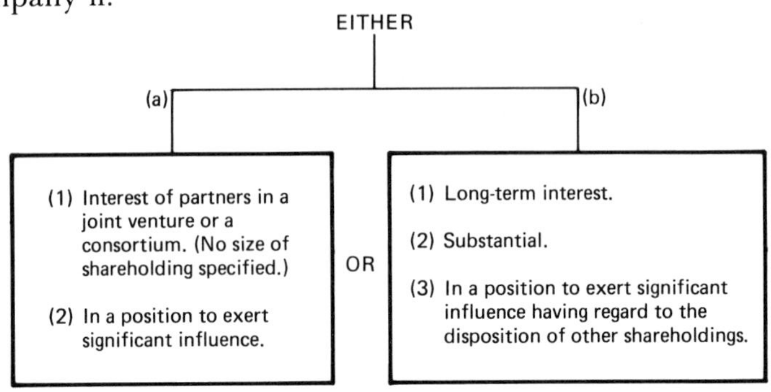


*Note:* The ability to exert significant influence must be present in both cases.

## 7.6 Companies Act 1981

The Companies Act 1981 makes specific provision for the equity method of accounting to be used in consolidated financial statements under appropriate circumstances.

In addition, the Act calls for certain separate disclosures in respect of what it terms "related companies". These are defined in para. 91 of Sched. 1 to the Act as follows:

(1) For the purposes of this Schedule, "related company", in relation to any company, means any body corporate (other than one which is a group company in relation to that company) in which that company holds on a long-term basis a qualifying capital interest for the purpose of securing a contribution to that company's own activities by the exercise of any control or influence arising from that interest.

(2) In this paragraph "qualifying capital interest" means, in relation to any body corporate, an interest in shares comprised in the equity share capital of that body corporate of a class carrying rights to vote in all circumstances at general meetings of that body corporate, and "equity share capital" has the meaning given by section 154(5) of this Act.

(3) Where:
   (a) a company holds a qualifying capital interest in a body corporate; and
   (b) the nominal value of any relevant shares in that body corporate held by that company is equal to twenty per cent or more of the nominal value of all relevant shares in that body corporate,

it shall be presumed to hold that interest on the basis and for the purpose mentioned in sub-paragraph (1) above, unless the contrary is shown.

In this sub-paragraph "relevant shares" means, in relation to any body corporate, any such shares in that body corporate as are mentioned in sub-paragraph (2) above.

This definition is very similar to that given in SSAP 1 for associated companies, but is not identical. In fact, the definition of a related company is wider than that of an associated company. The former does not specify the degree of influence required. Consequently, a body corporate may be a related company without being an associated company, but if it is an associated company it will almost always be a related company.

## 7.7 Comments on SSAP 1 (Revised)

(a) *Minimum holding*
Under part (a), a minimum holding of 20 per cent is *not* required. For example, an investment held equally by eight companies would give rise to an investor/associate relationship, provided, of course, that each of the investing companies is in a position to exert significant influence over the investee.

(b) *"Long-term interest"*
Whether an investment is held for a long term or not depends upon the reason for which that investment was acquired and the intentions of the investor. Generally speaking, an investment can be assumed to be for a long term where it is, in effect, an extension of the trade of the investor, unless there is an intention to dispose of it. Where an investment is made mainly for the purpose of achieving capital growth, it will not normally be appropriate to consider it as a long-term investment.

(c) *"Substantial, and having regard to disposition of other shareholdings"*
The original version of SSAP 1 linked the term "substantial" with a holding of at least 20 per cent of the equity capital of the company in which the investment is made.

The effect of the proviso, "having regard to disposition of other shareholdings", can be demonstrated in the following examples:

*Example*

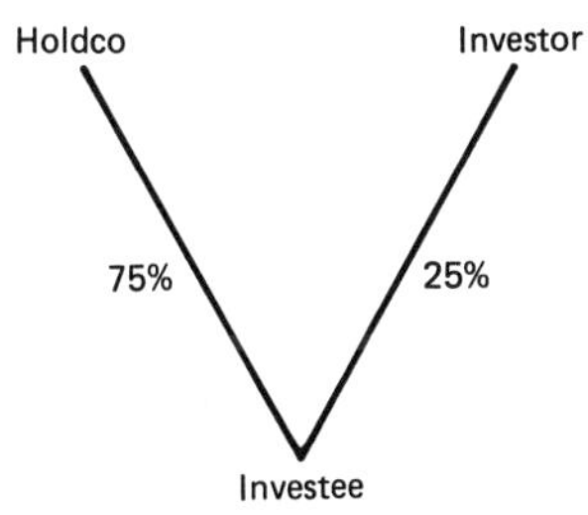


Since Investor has a substantial interest in Investee (more than 20 per cent), it is *prima facie* an associated company. However, since investee is already a *subsidiary* of Holdco, it is extremely unlikely that Investor could exercise a *significant* influence over Investee, which should not, therefore, be regarded as an associated company.

*Example*

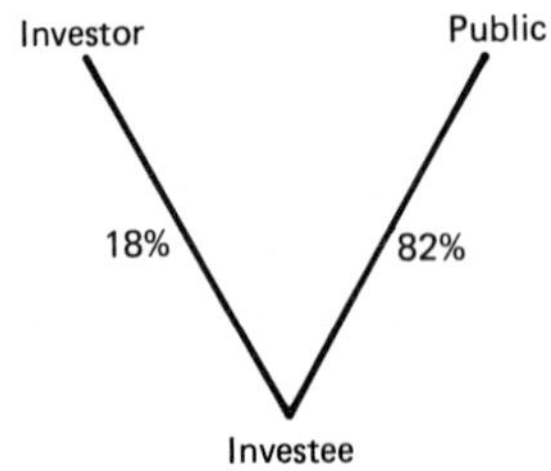


Assume that no single shareholder holds more than 1 per cent in Investee.

Since Investor's holding amounts to less than 20 per cent of the equity, it should be presumed that Investor does not have the ability to exercise significant influence unless it can be clearly demonstrated otherwise. In this example, the demonstration should include a statement from the Investee that it accepts that the Investor is in a position to exercise significant influence over it.

(d) *Significant influence*
Having a significant influence on a company is certainly not the same as having actual control of that company. However, it is essential that the investor participates in the financial and operating policy decisions of the company, including the company's dividend policy.

## 7.8 Investing group

(a) *Profit and loss account*
Since the investor participates in the financial and operating policy decisions of the associated company, it would normally take credit into its own profit and loss account, dividends received and *receivable* from the associated companies. This is consistent with the policy adopted for the treatment of dividends received and receivable from its subsidiary.

(b) *Consolidated profit and loss account*

| *Item* | *Comments* | £ |
|---|---|---|
| Turnover | H and S excluding intra-group sales. Turnover of the associates, if material, should be disclosed by way of a note to the accounts. | x |
| Cost of sales | H and S excluding intra-group purchases and provision for unrealised profits. Depreciation charges of the associates, if material, should be disclosed by way of note to the accounts. | (x) |
| Gross profit | | x |
| Distribution costs | H and S. | (x) |
| Administrative expenses | H and S. | (x) |
| Operating profit | Carried forward | x |

| *Item* | *Comments* | | £ |
|---|---|---|---|
| Operating profit | Brought forward | | x |
| Investment income | H and S excluding intra-group dividends. | | x |
| Share of profits (less losses) of associated companies | Group's share of the associated company's operating profit. | | x |
| Interest payable | H and S. | | (x) |
| Profit on ordinary activities before taxation | | | x |
| Taxation on profit on ordinary activities | | £ | |
| Group | H and S. | x | |
| Associated companies | Group's shares of the associated company's tax charge. | x | (x) |
| Profit on ordinary activities after taxation | | | x |
| Minority interest | In profit after tax of subsidiaries. | | (x) |
| Profit before extraordinary items | | | x |
| Extraordinary items | H and S's share of the extraordinary items of subsidiaries and associated companies (if material). | | x |
| Profit attributable to the members of the holding company | Section 149. | | x |
| Dividends paid and proposed | H only. | | (x) |
| Retained for the financial year | Divided between: (i) holding company (ii) subsidiaries (iii) associated companies. | | £x |

(c) *Consolidated balance sheet*
SSAP 1 (revised) requires that investment in associated companies be divided into three separate elements as follows:

(i) the investing group's share of the net assets other than goodwill of the associated companies stated, where possible, after attributing fair values to the net assets at the time of acquisition of the interest in an associated company; and

(ii) the investing group's share of the goodwill of the associated companies; together with

(iii) the premium paid (or discount) on the acquisition of the interests in the associated companies.

(d) *Inter-company balances*
There are two different forms of inter-company balances: loans between the

investor and an associated company; and those which represent normal trading balances.

(i) *Loans*. Separate disclosure is required in the consolidated balance sheet both of loans to, and loans from, associated companies.

(ii) *Trading balances*. Normal trading balances between an investing group and its associated companies should be included under current assets or liabilities as appropriate. Where material, they should be disclosed separately.

## 7.9 Investing company

(a) *The Companies Acts*
The Companies Acts 1948–81 only allow *realised profits* to be taken into the profit and loss account. If one included the share of profits of an associated company in the accounts of a company (not group) it would contravene the requirements of the Act. The Standard, therefore, requires such companies either to prepare a separate additional profit and loss account and balance sheet *or* to show the necessary information in a supplementary form.

(b) *Illustration of profit and loss account of a company without subsidiaries*

| | £000 | £000 |
|---|---|---|
| Turnover | | 2,000 |
| Cost of sales | | 1,400 |
| Gross profit | | 600 |
| Distribution costs | 175 | |
| Administrative expenses | 125 | |
| | | 300 |
| Profit on ordinary activities before taxation | | 300 |
| Tax on profit of ordinary activities | | 85 |
| Profit on ordinary activities after taxation | | 215 |
| Aggregate amount of dividends proposed | | 80 |
| Amount set aside to reserves | | £135 |

Supplementary statement incorporating results of associated companies:

| | £000 |
|---|---|
| Share of profits less losses of associated companies | 50 |
| *less:* Tax | 15 |
| Share of profits after tax of associated companies | 35 |
| Profit on ordinary activities after taxation (as above) | 215 |
| Profit attributable to members of the investing company | 250 |
| Aggregate amount of dividends proposed | 80 |
| Net profit retained (£35,000 by associated companies) | £170 |

*Note:* The earnings per share figure would be based on £250,000.

(c) *Illustration of balance sheet of a company without subsidiaries*

| | Note | £000 | £000 |
|---|---|---|---|
| Fixed assets | | | |
| Tangible assets | | | 1,500 |
| Investments | | | 400 |
| | | | 1,900 |
| Current assets: | | | |
| Stock | | 1,200 | |
| Debtors | 1 | 600 | |
| Cash at bank and in hand | 1 | 100 | |
| | | 1,900 | |
| Creditors: amounts falling due within one year | 2 | 1,200 | |
| | | | 700 |
| | | | £2,600 |
| Creditors: amounts falling due after more than one year: | | | |
| Bank loans and overdrafts | | 880 | |
| Amount owed to associated companies | | 120 | |
| | | | 1,000 |
| Provisions for liabilities and charges: | | | |
| Taxation, including deferred taxation | | | 200 |
| Capital and reserves: | | | |
| Called-up share capital | | 200 | |
| Profit and loss account | | 1,200 | |
| | | | 1,400 |
| | | | £2,600 |

Supplementary statement incorporating investing company's share of associated company reserves:

| | £000 |
|---|---|
| Shares in associated companies: | |
| Investing company's share of net assets of associated companies other than goodwill | 650 |
| Goodwill of associated companies | 150 |
| | 800 |
| Net assets of investing company other than shares in associated companies | 1,000 |
| | £1,800 |
| Capital and reserves: | |
| Called-up share capital | 200 |
| Profit and loss account (including £400,000 investing company's share of associated company reserves) | 1,600 |
| | £1,800 |

*Notes:*

| | | £000 |
|---|---|---|
| (1) | Debtors: | |
| | Trade debtors | 450 |
| | Amounts owed by related companies (all associated) | 90 |
| | Other debtors | 60 |
| | | £600 |

| | | |
|---|---|---|
| (2) | Creditors: amounts falling due within one year: | |
| | Bank loans and overdrafts | 650 |
| | Trade creditors | 340 |
| | Amounts owed to related companies (all associated) | 60 |
| | Other creditors, including taxation and social security | 70 |
| | Proposed dividend | 80 |
| | | £1,200 |

## 7.10 Consolidated financial statements of a group with associated companies

### *Problem*

Consider the following situation:

Profit and Loss Accounts

| | H Ltd | S Ltd | A Ltd |
|---|---|---|---|
| | £ | £ | £ |
| Turnover | 275,000 | 165,000 | 110,000 |
| Cost of sales | 125,000 | 70,000 | 45,000 |
| Gross profit | 150,000 | 95,000 | 65,000 |
| Distribution costs | (30,000) | (20,000) | (15,000) |
| Administrative expenses | (20,000) | (15,000) | (10,000) |
| Operating profit | 100,000 | 60,000 | 40,000 |
| Investment income: | | | |
| S Ltd | 9,600 | — | — |
| A Ltd | 2,400 | — | — |
| | 112,000 | 60,000 | 40,000 |
| Taxation | 50,000 | 30,000 | 20,000 |
| | 62,000 | 30,000 | 20,000 |
| Proposed dividend | (25,000) | (12,000) | (8,000) |
| Retained profit for the financial year | 37,000 | 18,000 | 12,000 |
| Retained profit brought forward | 117,000 | 77,000 | 48,000 |
| Retained profit carried forward | £154,000 | £95,000 | £60,000 |

Balance Sheets

| | H Ltd | | S Ltd | | A Ltd | |
|---|---|---|---|---|---|---|
| | £ | £ | £ | £ | £ | £ |
| Fixed assets: | | | | | | |
| Tangibles | | 125,000 | | 50,000 | | 30,000 |
| Investments: | | | | | | |
| S Ltd | | 92,000 | | | | |
| A Ltd | | 15,000 | | | | |
| | | 232,000 | | | | |
| Current assets: | | | | | | |
| Debtors | 160,000 | | 100,000 | | 70,000 | |
| Bank | 100,000 | | 87,000 | | 43,000 | |
| Dividends receivable | 12,000 | | — | | — | |
| | 272,000 | | 187,000 | | 113,000 | |
| Creditors: amounts falling due within one year: | | | | | | |
| Creditors | 75,000 | | 55,000 | | 40,000 | |
| Dividends proposed | 25,000 | | 12,000 | | 8,000 | |
| | 100,000 | | 67,000 | | 48,000 | |
| Net current assets | | 172,000 | | 120,000 | | 65,000 |
| Net assets | | £404,000 | | £170,000 | | £95,000 |
| Capital and reserves: | | | | | | |
| Called-up share capital | | 250,000 | | 75,000 | | 35,000 |
| Profit and loss account | | 154,000 | | 95,000 | | 60,000 |
| | | £404,000 | | £170,000 | | £95,000 |

Assume the following:

(a) H acquired 80 per cent of S and 30 per cent of A when their reserves were £15,000 and £10,000 respectively.

(b) There were no inter-company trading transactions.

(c) H has a representation on the board of directors of A.

Prepare consolidated financial statements.

SOLUTION

H Group
Consolidated Profit and Loss Account for the year ended X

| | £ | £ |
|---|---|---|
| Turnover | | 440,000 |
| Cost of sales | | 195,000 |
| Gross profit | | 245,000 |
| Distribution costs | | (50,000) |
| Administrative expenses | | (35,000) |
| Operating profit | | 160,000 |
| Share of profit of associated company | | 12,000 |
| Profit on ordinary activities before taxation | Carried forward | 172,000 |

| | £ | £ |
|---|---|---|
| Brought forward | | 172,000 |
| Taxation on profit on ordinary activities: | | |
| Group | 80,000 | |
| Associated company | 6,000 | |
| | | 86,000 |
| Profit on ordinary activities after taxation | | 86,000 |
| Minority interest | | (6,000) |
| Profit for the financial year | | 80,000 |
| Dividends—proposed | | (25,000) |
| Retained profit for financial year | | £55,000 |
| Retained profit for the year: | | |
| The company | | 37,000 |
| Subsidiary company | | 14,400 |
| Associated company | | 3,600 |
| | | £55,000 |

H Group
Consolidated Balance Sheet at X

| | £ | £ |
|---|---|---|
| Fixed assets: | | |
| Tangibles | | 175,000 |
| Intangible—premium on consolidation | | 20,000 |
| Investment in associated company: | | |
| Share of net assets | 28,500 | |
| Premium on acquisition | 1,500 | |
| | | 30,000 |
| | | 225,000 |
| Current assets: | | |
| Debtors | 260,000 | |
| Bank | 187,000 | |
| Dividend receivable from Associated Co. | 2,400 | |
| | £449,400 | |
| Creditors: amounts falling due within one year: | | |
| Creditors | 130,000 | |
| Proposed dividend | | |
| Company shareholders | 25,000 | |
| Minority shareholders | 2,400 | |
| | £157,400 | |
| Net current assets | | 292,000 |
| Net assets | | £517,000 |
| Capital and reserves: | | |
| Called-up share capital | | 250,000 |
| Profit and loss account | | 233,000 |
| Shareholders' funds | | 483,000 |
| Minority interest | | 34,000 |
| Total capital employed | | £517,000 |

Workings

(a) Shareholdings:

| | S | A |
|---|---|---|
| | % | |
| Group | 80 | 30% |
| Minority | 20 | |
| | 100 | |

(b) Pre-acquisition reserves £15,000 £10,000

(c) Consolidated profit and loss workings for relevant amounts to be included for the A Ltd

| | | | | £ |
|---|---|---|---|---|
| (i) Operating profit | 30% | × 40,000 | = | 12,000 |
| (ii) Taxation | 30% | × 20,000 | = | 6,000 |
| (iii) Retained profit for the year | 30% | × 12,000 | = | 3,600 |
| (iv) Post-acquisition profits brought forward | 30% | × (48,000 − 10,000) | = | 11,400 |
| (v) Post-acquisition profits carried forward | 30% | × (60,000 − 10,000) | = | 15,000 |

(d) Minority interest (20% × 30,000) 6,000

(e) Consolidated Balance Sheet Schedules

(i) Adjustment Account

| | £ | | £ |
|---|---|---|---|
| Cost of investment | 92,000 | OSC | 60,000 |
| | | Pre-acquisition reserves | 12,000 |
| | | Premium on consolidation | 20,000 |
| | £92,000 | | £92,000 |

(ii) S Ltd Reserves

| | £ | | £ |
|---|---|---|---|
| Adjustment a/c (80% × 15,000) | 12,000 | Balance brought down | 95,000 |
| Consolidated reserves [80% (95,000 − 15,000)] | 64,000 | | |
| Minority interest (20% × 95,000) | 19,000 | | |
| | £95,000 | | £95,000 |

(iii) Consolidated Reserves

| | £ | | £ |
|---|---|---|---|
| Consolidated balance sheet | 233,000 | Brought down | 154,000 |
| | | S Ltd—post-acquisition | 64,000 |
| | | A Ltd—post-acquisition (working 3(v)) | 15,000 |
| | £233,000 | | £233,000 |

(iv) Minority Interest

| | £ | | £ |
|---|---|---|---|
| Consolidated balance sheet | 34,000 | OSC | 15,000 |
| | | Reserves | 19,000 |
| | £34,000 | | £34,000 |

(v) Dividend Elimination

| | £ | | £ |
|---|---|---|---|
| Dividend receivable (H Ltd) | 9,600 | Dividend payable (S Ltd) | 12,000 |
| Minority interest (consolidated balance sheet) | 2,400 | | |
| | £12,000 | | £12,000 |

(f) Associated companies

(i) Share of net assets:
30% (share capital + reserves)
30% × (35,000 + 60,000) £28,500

(ii) Premium on acquisition

| | £ | | £ |
|---|---|---|---|
| Cost of investment | 15,000 | Share capital (30% × 35,000) | 10,500 |
| | | Pre-acquisition reserves (30% × 10,000) | 3,000 |
| | | Premium | 1,500 |
| | £15,000 | | £15,000 |

# 8.0 ACCOUNTING FOR FOREIGN CURRENCY TRANSLATIONS

## 8.1 Background

(a) *Introduction*
Accounting for foreign currency translations has for a long time been a controversial accounting topic. In the UK and Ireland, ASC have issued the following exposure drafts on the subject:

(i) ED 16 (September 1975), supplement to "extraordinary items and prior year adjustments";

(ii) ED 21 (September 1977) on accounting for foreign currency transactions;

(iii) ED 27 (October 1980) on accounting for foreign currency translations.
SSAP 20 (*Accounting for Foreign Currency Translation*) was published in April 1983.

IASC has also issued more than one exposure draft on the subject:

(i) E 11 (December 1977) on accounting for foreign transactions and translation of foreign financial statements;

(ii) E 23 (March 1982) on accounting for the effects of foreign exchange rates.

IAS 21 was published in July 1983.

Finally, the subject has been equally controversial in the United States! For many years, US companies (and some UK companies with US listings) had to follow FAS 8 (accounting for the translation of foreign currency transactions and foreign currency financial statements). Subsequently, the Financial Accounting Standards Board issued an exposure draft and standard on lines similar to ED 27 and SSAP 20.

For examination purposes, a thorough knowledge of SSAP 20 is essential, and these notes concentrate on the details of SSAP 20. However, a knowledge of the issues making the subject a controversy is required, and later parts of this section refer back to ED 21, FAS 8 etc.

(b) *Types of foreign currency operations*
SSAP 20 distinguishes between two types:

(i) First of all, a company may enter directly into business transactions which are denominated in foreign currencies. A UK company, for example, will need to translate the results of these transactions into pounds sterling so that they may be entered in the accounting records.

(ii) Secondly, foreign operations may be conducted through a foreign subsidiary company which maintains its accounting records in terms of its own local foreign currency. For a UK holding company, say, to prepare consolidated financial statements, it will be necessary to translate into pounds sterling the complete financial statements of the foreign subsidiary.

(c) *Accounting procedures*
SSAP 20, following on from the above, considers the accounting procedures for foreign operations in two stages:

(i) the individual company stage, i.e. the preparation of the individual financial statements of a company (this will include the accounts of the holding company, and possibly also the accounts of individual subsidiary companies).

(ii) the consolidated financial statements stage.

This distinction is followed in the sections below.

## 8.2 The individual company stage

(a) *Requirements of SSAP 20*

Para. 46 Subject to the provisions of paragraphs 48 and 51 each asset, liability, revenue or cost arising from a transaction denominated in a foreign currency should be translated into the local currency at the exchange rate in operation on the date on which the transaction occurred; if the rates do not fluctuate significantly, an average rate for a period may be used as an approximation. Where the transaction is to be settled at a contracted rate, that rate *should* be used. Where a trading transaction is covered by a related or matching forward contract, the rate of exchange specified in that contract *may* be used.

Para. 47 Subject to the special provisions of paragraph 51, which relate to the treatment of foreign equity investments financed by foreign currency borrowings, no subsequent translations should normally be made once non-monetary assets have been translated and recorded.

Para. 48 At each balance sheet date, monetary assets and liabilities denominated in a foreign currency should be translated by using the closing rate or, where appropriate, the rates of exchange fixed under the terms of the relevant transactions. Where there are related or matching forward contracts in respect of trading transactions, the rates of exchange specified in those contracts may be used.

Para. 49 All exchange gains or losses on settled transactions and unsettled short-term monetary items should be reported as part of the profit or loss for the year from ordinary activities (unless they result from transactions which themselves would fall to be treated as extraordinary items, in which case the exchange gains or losses should be included as part of such items).

Para. 50 Exchange gains and losses on long-term monetary items should also be recognised in the profit and loss account; however, it is necessary to consider on the grounds of prudence whether, in the exceptional cases outlined in paragraph 11, the amount of the gain, or the amount by which exchange gains exceed past exchange losses on the same items to be recognised in the profit and loss account, should be restricted.

*Notes*

(1) Paragraph 11 is referred to in Note 3 to the second table of (b)(iv) below.
(2) Paragraph 50 is further referred to in (b)(iv) below.
(3) Paragraph 51 is referred to in 8.6 below.

(b) *Examples (in each case the year-end of the UK company is 30th September 19X4)*

(i) *Purchase of fixed assets*

A UK company purchases plant and machinery for use in the UK from a German company for DM800,000 in July 19X4. At that date the exchange rate was £1 = DM3.95.

The UK company records the purchase price in its own accounting records as £202,532 (800,000 ÷ 3.95). The depreciation charge for the year will be based on this figure; the asset should not be translated again and no exchange differences will arise.

The only change to this amount, apart from writing-down as a result of depreciation, would be if it were necessary to write-down to estimated recoverable amount in accordance with para. 19 of SSAP 12.

Note that fixed assets and stock are sometimes classified as non-monetary assets, as opposed to debtors and creditors which are classified as monetary items.

(ii) *Debtors*

A UK company sells goods to a German company in May 19X4 for DM300,000. Payment is received in August 19X4.

Exchange rates were:

May 19X4 DM3.71 = £1,
August 19X4 DM4.02 = £1.

The UK company would make the following entries in the ledger account, the exchange difference (loss) of £6,235 being reflected in profit from ordinary operations.

Debtor Account

| 19X4 | £ | 19X4 | £ |
|---|---|---|---|
| May | | August | |
| Sales a/c | 80,862 | Cash a/c | 74,627 |
| (300,000 ÷ 3.71) | | (300,000 ÷ 4.02) | |
| | | September | |
| | | Profit and loss a/c | 6,235 |
| | £80,862 | | £80,862 |

Sales Account

| | £ | | £ |
|---|---|---|---|
| | | 19X4 | |
| | | May | |
| | | Debtor a/c | £80,862 |

Note that the above example assumes that the UK company invoices the German company in DM. If the invoicing were in sterling, accounting problems would be far simpler!

(iii) *Creditors*
A UK company purchases goods from a German company in July 19X4 for DM550,000. The company paid off DM200,000 in August 19X4 and the balance was outstanding at the end of the year.
Exchange rates were:

| | |
|---|---|
| July 19X4 | DM3.90 = £1, |
| August 19X4 | DM4.02 = £1, |
| 30th September 19X4 | DM4.21 = £1. |

Creditor Account

| | £ | | £ |
|---|---|---|---|
| 19X4 | | 19X4 | |
| August—cash a/c | | July—purchases a/c | |
| (200,000 ÷ 4.02) | 49,751 | (550,000 ÷ 3.90) | 141,026 |
| September | | | |
| Creditor carried down | | | |
| (350,000 ÷ 4.21) | 83,135 | | |
| Profit and loss a/c | | | |
| (balancing figure) | 8,140 | | |
| | £141,026 | | £141,026 |
| | | Balance brought down | £83,135 |

Purchases Account

| | £ | | £ |
|---|---|---|---|
| 19X4 | | 19X4 | |
| July—creditor a/c | £141,026 | | |

*Notes*

(1) The amount outstanding at the end of the year (DM350,000) is a monetary item and should be translated into pounds sterling at the year-end exchange rate.

(2) The exchange gain of £8,140 should be reported as part of the profit for the year from ordinary operations.

(3) If any of the goods purchased were in closing stock, they would be stated at cost based on £141,026 (assuming net realisable value exceeded this amount).

(iv) *Long-term loans*
A UK company takes out a 10-year loan from a German bank in July 19X4 for DM2,000,000. The proceeds of the loan are converted to pounds sterling and remitted to the UK when the exchange rate was DM3.90 = £1.

Assuming the exchange rates at the respective year-ends were:
30th September 19X4 DM4.21 = £1,
30th September 19X5 DM3.75 = £1,
then the loan account in the books of the UK company would appear as follows:

Loan Account

| | £ | | £ |
|---|---|---|---|
| 19X4 | | 19X4 | |
| September | | | |
| Balance carried down | 475,059 | July cash a/c | |
| (2,000,000 ÷ 4.21) | | (2,000,000 ÷ 3.90) | 512,820 |
| Profit and loss a/c | | | |
| (balancing figure) | 37,761 | | |
| | £512,820 | | £512,820 |
| 19X5 | | 19X4 | |
| | | 1st October | |
| September | | Balance brought down | 475,059 |
| Balance carried down | 533,333 | | |
| (2,000,000 ÷ 3.75) | | 19X5 | |
| | | September | |
| | | Profit and loss a/c | |
| | | (balancing figure) | 58,274 |
| | £533,333 | | £533,333 |
| | | 1st October | |
| | | Balance brought down | £533,333 |

*Notes*

(1) The amounts outstanding at the year-end (DM2,000,000) should be translated into pounds sterling at the exchange rate each year-end.

(2) Exchange differences (19X4 gain of £37,761, 19X5 loss of £58,274) should, according to the requirements of SSAP 20, be reported in the profit and loss account as part of the profit from ordinary operations.

(3) This has proved to be one of the more controversial aspects of SSAP 20. Much consideration was given to the implications of the Companies Act 1981.

The relevant extracts from SSAP 20 are reproduced below:

*Part 1 Explanatory note*

Para. 9: "When dealing with long-term monetary items, additional considerations apply. Although it is not easy to predict what the exchange rate will be when a long-term liability or asset matures, it is necessary, when stating the liability or the asset in terms of the reporting currency, to make the best estimate possible in the light of the information available at the time;

generally speaking translation at the year-end rate will provide the best estimate, particularly when the currency concerned is freely dealt in on the spot and forward exchange markets."

Para. 10: "In order to give a true and fair view of results, exchange gains and losses on long-term monetary items should normally be reported as part of the profit or loss for the period in accordance with the accruals concept of accounting; treatment of these items on a simple cash movements basis would be inconsistent with that concept. Exchange gains on unsettled transactions can be determined at the balance sheet date no less objectively than exchange losses; deferring the gains whilst recognising the losses would not only be illogical by denying in effect that any favourable movement in exchange rates had occurred but would also inhibit fair measurement of the performance of the enterprise in the year. In particular, this symmetry of treatment recognises that there will probably be some interaction between currency movements and interest rates and reflects more accurately in the profit and loss account the true results of currency involvement."

Para. 11: "For the special reasons outlined above, both exchange gains and losses on long-term monetary items should be recognised in the profit and loss account. However, it is necessary to consider on the grounds of prudence whether the amount of the gain, or the amount by which exchange gains exceed past exchange losses on the same items, to be recognised in the profit and loss account should be restricted in the exceptional cases where there are doubts as to the convertibility or marketability of the currency in question."

*Part 4 Legal requirements in UK and Ireland*

Para. 65: "For companies other than exempt companies, all exchange gains taken through the profit and loss account, other than those arising on unsettled long-term monetary items, are realised.

"For such companies, the application of paragraph 50 of this statement [see (a) above] may result in unrealised exchange gains on unsettled long-term monetary items being taken to the profit and loss account. In this statement the need to show a true and fair view of results, referred to in the note on paragraph 10 above, is considered to constitute a special reason for departure from the principle under paragraph 15 of the Schedule (this means a departure from the prudence concept which permits only profits realised at the balance sheet date to be included in the profit and loss account)."

(v) *Extraordinary items*

A UK company sold a property in Germany in April 19X4 for DM800,000 when the exchange rate was DM3.52 = £1. Payment was received in August 19X4 when the exchange rate was DM4.02 = £1.

The profit on sale of the property would be calculated as follows:

| | £ |
|---|---|
| Net book value at date of sale | x |
| Sale consideration (800,000 ÷ 3.52) | 227,273 |
| Profit (loss on sale) | x |

If the above profit (loss) was classified according to SSAP 6 as an extraordinary item, then the related exchange difference of £28,273 should be included as part of the gain or loss on sale of the property and included as an extraordinary item.

*Working*

| | £ |
|---|---|
| Sale consideration at exchange rate at date of sale (800,000 ÷ 3.52) | 227,273 |
| Proceeds (800,000 ÷ 4.02) | 199,000 |
| Exchange loss | £28,273 |

(c) *Explanations*

(i) Once non-monetary assets (e.g. plant and machinery, land and buildings, stock) have been translated and recorded, they will be carried in terms of the currency in which the company reports. No subsequent translations of these assets will need to be made in the company's accounting records.

(ii) Monetary assets and liabilities outstanding at the balance sheet date should be translated:

(1) using the rate of exchange at the year-end, or

(2) where appropriate, the exchange rate at which it is contracted to receive or pay the amount in question in the future.

This approach will produce the best available estimate of the amount which will be realised or paid when settlement is eventually made.

(iii) Exchange gains or losses in the context of an individual company's operations will ultimately be reflected in cash flows. For example, a change in the exchange rate will increase or decrease the amount which will be received in cash settlement of a debtor account. Such differences should therefore be recognised as part of the profit or loss for the year.

(d) *Transactions between group companies*

These include transactions between a holding company and its subsidiaries (e.g. a proposed dividend of a foreign subsidiary accrued at the year-end by the holding company) and transactions between fellow subsidiaries (e.g. inter-company trading and current accounts).

Exchange gains or losses arising from such transactions should be reported in the financial statements of the individual company concerned as part of the profit or loss for the year from ordinary operations. Such exchange differences are thus treated in the same way as differences arising from transactions with third parties (*see* examples above).

The main exception to this is the special case of proceeds of foreign loans used to finance certain foreign equity investments (*see* 8.6).

## 8.3 The consolidated financial statements stage

(a) *Introduction*

The object of the exercise is to express financial statements of foreign entities (subsidiaries, branches, associated companies) in pounds sterling so that they may be incorporated into the consolidated financial statements.

Two major problems are:

(i) What translation method should be used (e.g. closing rate method or temporal method)?

(ii) How should exchange differences be treated (e.g. included in the profit and loss account, or taken direct to reserves)?

Different accounting statements (*see* 8.1(a) above) have taken different views on this subject. This section is concerned solely with the requirements of SSAP 20. Other views will be considered later.

(b) *Which translation method?*

SSAP 20 says that the method to be used depends on the relationship between the holding company and the foreign entity (e.g. subsidiary) concerned.

(i) *The closing-rate method (net-investment approach)*

This approach recognises that the holding company's investment is in the net worth of a foreign business enterprise, rather than being a direct investment in its individual assets and liabilities. This investment will remain until the business is liquidated or the investment disposed of.

Note the following four characteristics which are typical of the situations where the closing-rate method should be used:

(1) The day-to-day business operations of a foreign subsidiary are not usually dependent on the holding company's reporting currency (e.g. pounds sterling);

(2) the foreign subsidiary may be wholly or partly financed by local currency borrowings;

(3) the holding company's investment will not be withdrawn in the short term;

(4) the holding company's investment is in a business operation taken as a whole and not in the individual assets and liabilities of the subsidiary.

SSAP 20 states that in almost all circumstances the closing-rate method should be used. The variant of the closing-rate method dealt with in SSAP 20 is referred to as the closing-rate/net-investment method. This distinguishes it from the version of the closing-rate method dealt with in an earlier exposure draft, ED 21.

(ii) *The temporal method*
SSAP 20 states that in certain specified circumstances the temporal method should be used instead of the closing-rate method.

The specified circumstances relate to cases where the affairs of a foreign subsidiary company are so closely interlinked with those of the holding company that the business of the foreign subsidiary should be regarded as a direct extension of the business of the holding company rather than as a separate or quasi-independent business.

SSAP 20 gives the following as examples of situations where the temporal method should be used:

(1) The subsidiary acts as a selling agency receiving stocks of goods from the holding company, selling them in local currency and remitting the proceeds back to the holding company.

(2) The subsidiary produces a raw material or manufactures parts or subassemblies which are then shipped to the holding company for inclusion in its own products.

(3) The subsidiary is located overseas for tax, exchange control or similar reasons to act as a means of raising finance for other companies in the group. In such cases the currency of the holding company may be the functional currency rather than the local currency in which the subsidiary maintains its records.

(iii) *Each subsidiary company must be considered separately*
The relationship between each subsidiary and the holding company must be considered separately. Once the appropriate translation method has been determined for each subsidiary, it should be used consistently from period to period unless the financial and other operational relationships change which exist between the holding company and the subsidiary.

## 8.4 The closing-rate/net-investment method

(a) *The net-investment concept*

(i) *Introduction*
The net-investment concept takes the view that the accounting treatment adopted for translation purposes should reflect the manner

in which a company operates. Where an overseas business operation is semi-independent and self-financing the exchange risk exposure of the holding company is its net investment in the overseas operation taken as a whole and is not a risk which can be identified with individual assets and liabilities.

(ii) *Treatment of exchange differences:*

| *Nature* | *Accounting treatment* |
|---|---|
| 1. Exchange differences which are measurements of cash flow differences (occurring immediately or in the future). | Part of operating profit. |
| 2. Other exchange differences which arise mainly from the need to translate foreign financial statements for consolidation purposes. | Movements on reserve. |

Note that type 2 arise on the restatement of local currency net assets that are not expected to be converted to the group currency in the foreseeable future. They do *not* represent a measure of cash flow effects in the currency of the holding company nor of economic effects on the individual subsidiary or in the group as a whole. They are regarded as a change in the book value of the subsidiary, and so are taken direct to reserve rather than to profit and loss account.

(b) *Accounting requirements*

(i) *Balance sheet of subsidiary*
All balance sheet items should be translated into sterling using the rate of exchange ruling at the balance sheet date. (This must be taken to refer to the various assets and liabilities which are combined with like items for other companies and included under respective consolidated headings.)

(ii) *Profit and loss account of subsidiary*
Amounts should be translated either at an average rate for the period, or at the closing rate. It is important to note the choice. (This includes depreciation, tax and extraordinary items, but not dividends. Inter-company dividends paid or proposed are eliminated on consolidation.)

(iii) *Exchange differences on consolidation*
These may arise for two reasons:

(1) The rate of exchange ruling at the balance sheet date is different from that ruling at the previous balance sheet date. For example,

land and buildings translated last year at one rate will be included in the consolidated balance sheet this year at a different rate.

(2) The average rate used to translate the profit and loss account differs from the closing rate.

SSAP 20 uses the term "net investment" which is defined as the effective equity stake of the subsidiary (or associated company) and comprises the holding company's proportion of share capital and reserves.

SSAP 20 specifies:

Para. 53 Exchange differences arising from the retranslation of the opening net investment in a foreign enterprise at the closing rate should be recorded as a movement on reserves [*see* (1) above].

Para. 54 . . . The difference between the profit and loss account translated at an average rate and at the closing rate should be recorded as a movement on reserves [*see* (2) above].

(c) *Example*

The above accounting requirements will be illustrated by the following example:

(i) London PLC acquired 80 per cent of the share capital of Ohio Inc. in 19X1 when the reserves of Ohio were \$2,500. The cost of the investment was £2,450.

(ii) Ohio Inc. raises its finance locally and the company is semi-independent as most decisions are made by its local board of directors.

(iii) The draft financial statements for the year ended 30th November 19X9 are shown below.

(iv) During the year, Ohio purchased fixed assets at a cost of \$2,800.

(v) Relevant exchange rates are:

| | |
|---|---|
| At acquisition | \$2.20 = £1 |
| At 30th November 19X8 | \$2.40 = £1 |
| At 30th November 19X9 | \$2.50 = £1 |
| Average for 19X9 | \$2.45 = £1 |
| At date of dividend payment | \$2.47 = £1 |

(vi) Operating profit is arrived at after charging depreciation of:

| | |
|---|---|
| London | £4,730 |
| Ohio | \$2,260 |

Profit and Loss Accounts
for the year ended 30th November 19X9

| | London £ | Ohio $ |
|---|---|---|
| Operating profit | 29,392 | 10,600 |
| Dividends received | 259 | — |
| Dividends receivable | 384 | — |
| Profit before tax | 30,035 | 10,600 |
| Taxation | 12,650 | 4,200 |
| Profit after tax | 17,385 | 6,400 |
| Extraordinary item (redundancy costs) | — | (2,500) |
| | 17,385 | 3,900 |
| Dividends: Paid | (4,000) | (800) |
| Proposed | (8,000) | (1,200) |
| Retained profit | 5,385 | 1,900 |
| Balance at 1st December 19X8 | 17,966 | 7,500 |
| Balance at 30th November 19X9 | £23,351 | $9,400 |

(Note: 80% × 800 ÷ 2.47 = 259 etc.)

Balance Sheets at 30th November 19X9

| | London £ | Ohio $ |
|---|---|---|
| Fixed assets: Cost | 47,300 | 22,600 |
| Depreciation | 11,400 | 6,600 |
| | 35,900 | 16,000 |
| Investment in Ohio Inc. | 2,450 | — |
| Stocks | 18,200 | 4,100 |
| Debtors | 5,960 | 2,350 |
| Dividends receivable | 384 | — |
| Cash at bank | 907 | 2,000 |
| | £63,801 | $24,450 |
| Long-term loans | 6,000 | 3,000 |
| Creditors | 16,450 | 6,850 |
| Dividends payable | 8,000 | 1,200 |
| Ordinary share capital | 10,000 | 4,000 |
| Profit and loss account | 23,351 | 9,400 |
| | £63,801 | $24,450 |

Required: Consolidated balance sheet, consolidated profit and loss account, and relevant extracts from the fixed-asset schedule as regards the fixed assets of Ohio. Profit and loss account is to be translated at average rate.

(d) *Workings and solution*

(i) Translation of Balance Sheet of Ohio Inc.

| | $ | Rate | £ |
|---|---|---|---|
| Fixed assets: Cost | 22,600 | 2.50 | 9,040 |
| Depreciation | (6,600) | 2.50 | (2,640) |
| | 16,000 | | 6,400 |
| Stocks | 4,100 | 2.50 | 1,640 |
| Debtors | 2,350 | 2.50 | 940 |
| Cash at bank | 2,000 | 2.50 | 800 |
| Long-term loans | (3,000) | 2.50 | (1,200) |
| Creditors | (6,850) | 2.50 | (2,740) |
| Dividends payable | (1,200) | 2.50 | (480) |
| | $13,400 | | £5,360 |
| Equity interest: | | | |
| Ordinary share capital | 4,000 | 2.20 | 1,818 |
| Profit and loss account | 9,400 | Balance | 3,542 |
| | $13,400 | | £5,360 |

*Note*
All assets and liabilities must be translated at the closing rate. However, the equity interest of $13,400 is eliminated on consolidation, so this rule does not have to be applied to the constituent parts of shareholders' funds.

For convenience of workings (particularly in calculating goodwill on consolidation) share capital is translated at the rate of exchange corresponding with when the shares were acquired, and the accumulated profit and loss account is a balancing figure.

(ii) Consolidation Workings

Adjustment (Goodwill) Account

| | £ | | £ |
|---|---|---|---|
| Cost of investment | 2,450 | Ordinary share capital (80%) | 1,454 |
| | | Reserves | 909 |
| | | | 2,363 |
| | | Goodwill | 87 |
| | £2,450 | | £2,450 |

Reserves (Profit and Loss Account) of Ohio

| | £ | | £ |
|---|---|---|---|
| Adjustment a/c (pre-acquisition) [80% × (2,500 ÷ 2.20)] | 909 | Balance | 3,542 |
| Minority interest (20% × 3,542) | 708 | | |
| Consolidated reserves (balance) | 1,925 | | |
| | £3,542 | | £3,542 |

Minority Interest

| | £ | | £ |
|---|---|---|---|
| Balance carried down | 1,072 | Ordinary share capital (20%) | 364 |
| | | Reserves | 708 |
| | £1,072 | | £1,072 |

Consolidated Reserves (Profit and Loss Account)

| | £ | | £ |
|---|---|---|---|
| Balance carried down | 25,276 | London | 23,351 |
| | | Ohio | 1,925 |
| | £25,276 | | £25,276 |

Dividend Payable (Ohio)

| | £ | | £ |
|---|---|---|---|
| Contra | 384 | Balance | 480 |
| Minority interest carried down (20%) | 96 | | |
| | £480 | | £480 |

Dividend Receivable (by London)

| | £ | | £ |
|---|---|---|---|
| Balance | 384 | Contra | 384 |

*Note: Calculation of goodwill on consolidation*

| | | £ |
|---|---|---|
| Cost of investment | | 2,450 |
| Equity interest = net assets at acquisition | $ | |
| Ordinary share capital | 4,000 | |
| Reserves | 2,500 | |
| | $6,500 | |
| Translated at 2.20 (exchange rate at acquisition) | £2,954 | |
| × group share (80%) | | 2,363 |
| Goodwill | | £87 |

(iii) Consolidated Balance Sheet at 30th November 19X9

| | £ | £ | £ |
|---|---|---|---|
| Fixed assets: | | | |
| Intangible assets—goodwill on consolidation | | | 87 |
| Tangible assets | | | 42,300 |
| | | | 42,387 |
| Current assets: | | | |
| Stocks | | 19,840 | |
| Debtors | | 6,900 | |
| Cash at bank | | 1,707 | |
| | | 28,447 | |
| Creditors: amounts falling due within one year: | | | |
| Creditors | 19,190 | | |
| Dividends payable: | | | |
| Holding company | 8,000 | | |
| Minority | 96 | 27,286 | |
| | | | 1,161 |
| | | | 43,548 |
| Debenture loans | | | (7,200) |
| | | | 36,348 |
| Minority shareholders' interest | | | (1,072) |
| | | | £35,276 |
| Capital and reserves: | | | |
| Called-up share capital | | | 10,000 |
| Profit and loss account | | | 25,276 |
| | | | £35,276 |

(iv) Fixed-asset note (items relating to Ohio only)

| *Cost* | £ | *Working* $ | Rate | £ |
|---|---|---|---|---|
| Balance at 1st December 19X8 | 8,250 | 19,800 | 2.40 | 8,250 |
| Exchange adjustment | (330) | — | Balance | (330) |
| Additions | 1,120 | 2,800 | 2.50 | 1,120 |
| Balance at 30th November 19X9 | £9,040 | $22,600 | 2.50 | £9,040 |

| *Depreciation provision* | £ | *Working* $ | Rate | £ |
|---|---|---|---|---|
| Balance at | | | | |
| 1st December 19X8 | 1,808 | 4,340 | 2.40 | 1,808 |
| Provided during year | 922 | 2,260 | 2.45 | 922 |
| Exchange adjustment | (90) | — | Balance | (90) |
| Balance at | | | | |
| 30th November 19X9 | £2,640 | $6,600 | 2.50 | £2,640 |
| *Net book values* | | | | |
| 30th November 19X9 | £6,400 | $16,000 | 2.50 | £6,400 |
| 30th November 19X8 | £6,442 | $15,460 | 2.40 | £6,442 |

(v) Translation of Profit and Loss Account of Ohio

| | $ | Rate | £ |
|---|---|---|---|
| Operating profit | 10,600 | 2.45 | 4,326 |
| Taxation | 4,200 | 2.45 | 1,714 |
| | 6,400 | | 2,612 |
| Extraordinary item | (2,500) | 2.45 | (1,020) |
| | 3,900 | | 1,592 |
| Dividends: Paid | (800) | 2.47 | (324) |
| Proposed | (1,200) | 2.50 | (480) |
| Retained profit | $1,900 | | £788 |

(vi) Calculation of Exchange Difference

(1) *Calculation of total exchange difference*

| | | £ |
|---|---|---|
| Equity interest at 30th November 19X9 at closing exchange rate (working in 8.4(d)(i)) | | 5,360 |
| Equity interest at 30th November 19X8 at last year's closing rate | | |
| OSC | $ 4,000 | |
| Reserves | $ 7,500 | |
| | $11,500 | |
| | ÷ 2.4 | 4,792 |
| Increase during year | | 568 |
| Retained profit per working in (v) above | | 788 |
| ∴ Total exchange loss | | (220) |
| Proportion charged direct to reserves [80% × (220)] = | | (176) |

(2) *Analysis of exchange difference*

| | Equity interest 100% $ | Rate | Equity interest 100% £ | Net invest-ment 80% £ |
|---|---|---|---|---|
| Balance at 1st December 19X8 | 11,500 | 2.40 | 4,792 | 3,834 |
| Loss on retranslation of opening net investment (balancing item) | — | — | (192) | (154) |
| Opening net investment retranslated at closing rate | 11,500 | 2.50 | 4,600 | 3,680 |
| Retained profit (working in (v) above) | 1,900 | various | 788 | 630 |
| Difference between profit and loss a/c translated at average and closing rates (balancing item) | — | — | (28) | (22) |
| Closing net investment at closing rate | $13,400 | 2.50 | £5,360 | £4,288 |

Note that exchange loss taken direct to reserves is still £176 (i.e. £154 + £22).

(vii) *Consolidated profit and loss account workings*

| | | £ |
|---|---|---|
| (1) | Profit on ordinary activities before tax (29,392 + 4,326) | 33,718 |
| (2) | Tax (12,650 + 1,714) | 14,364 |
| (3) | Minority interest (20% × 2,612) | 522 |
| (4) | Extraordinary items [80% × (1,020)] | (816) |
| (5) | Profit and loss account balance at 1st December 19X8: | |
| | Equity interest at acquisition $6,500 ÷ 2.20 | 2,954 |
| | Equity interest at 1st December 19X8 $11,500 ÷ 2.40 | 4,792 |
| | Increase (100%) | £1,838 |

| | £ |
|---|---|
| Ohio (80% × 1,838) | 1,470 |
| London | 17,966 |
| | £19,436 |

(viii) Consolidated Profit and Loss Account
for the year ended 30th November 19X9

| | £ | £ |
|---|---|---|
| Profit on ordinary activities before taxation | | 33,718 |
| Tax on profit on ordinary activities | | 14,364 |
| Profit on ordinary activities after taxation | | 19,354 |
| Minority shareholders' interest | | (522) |
| | | 18,832 |
| Extraordinary charges | | (816) |
| Profit for the financial year | | 18,016 |
| Dividends: Paid | 4,000 | |
| Proposed | 8,000 | 12,000 |
| Retained profit | | £6,016 |

*Note: reserves*

| | £ |
|---|---|
| Profit and loss account at 1st December 19X8 | 19,436 |
| Retained profit | 6,016 |
| Exchange loss | (176) |
| Profit and loss account at 30th November 19X9 | £25,276 |

(e) *Variants of the closing-rate method*
Two possible areas of difference are as follows:

(i) *The method of translating the profit and loss account*
ED 27 proposed that profit and loss account items should be translated at the average rate of exchange. The previous exposure draft, ED 21, permitted the profit for the year to be translated at the closing or average rate.

ED 27 preferred the average rate for three reasons:

(1) The average rate more fairly reflects the profits and cash flows which arise through an accounting period.

(2) The profits disclosed in quarterly statements (e.g. for stock exchange purposes) do not have to be restated if the exchange rate is different at the year-end from the rates prevailing during the year.

(3) The Financial Accounting Standards Board (in the US) makes the use of an average rate mandatory. In view of the extent of international harmonisation achieved in this whole area, the method of translation of the profit and loss account would not appear to be of such importance that it was necessary for there to be a difference between the standards.

SSAP 20 permits either average or closing rate. The justification for this option is stated in paragraph 17 of SSAP 20:

Para. 17: "Amounts in the profit and loss account of a foreign enterprise should be translated at the closing rate or at an average rate for the accounting period. The use of the closing rate is more likely to achieve the objective of translation, stated in paragraph 2, of reflecting the financial results and relationships as measured in the foreign currency financial statements prior to translation. However, it can be argued that an average rate reflects more fairly the profits or losses and cash flows as they arise to the group throughout an accounting period. The use of either method is therefore permitted provided that the one selected is applied consistently from period to period."

(ii) SSAP 20 and ED 27 require exchange differences arising on the consolidation of the financial statements to be taken direct to reserves.

ED 21, however, proposed that while exchange differences relating to fixed assets should be dealt with through reserves, all other exchange differences should be reported in the profit and loss account as a separate item after the profit for the year from ordinary operations. However, a special treatment was proposed for foreign currency net borrowings in that exchange deficits on foreign currency net borrowings could be wholly or partly dealt with through reserves (instead of the profit and loss account) by being offset against an equal or smaller gain arising on translating the net book amount of overseas fixed assets. (This was sometimes referred to as the "cover" concept.)

*Example*

Using the information from the previous example, what would have been the effect on the consolidated financial statements, assuming the proposals of ED 21 had been followed with profit and loss items being translated at the closing rate?

(1) *Consolidated balance sheet*
All workings would have been identical and the final balance sheet identical. The fixed asset schedule in (d)(iv) above would have shown depreciation as £904 (2,260 ÷ 2.50) and exchange adjustment £72.

(2) *Translation of profit and loss account of Ohio*

| | $ | Rate | £ |
|---|---|---|---|
| Operating profit | 10,600 | 2.50 | 4,240 |
| Taxation | 4,200 | 2.50 | 1,680 |
| | 6,400 | | 2,560 |
| Extraordinary item | (2,500) | 2.50 | (1,000) |
| | 3,900 | | 1,560 |
| Dividends: Paid | (800) | 2.47 | (324) |
| Proposed | (1,200) | 2.50 | (480) |
| Retained profit | $1,900 | | £756 |

(3) *Calculation of exchange difference*

(A) *Total exchange difference* (*see* workings in (d)(v))

| | £ |
|---|---|
| Equity interest at 30th November 19X9 | 5,360 |
| Equity interest at 30th November 19X8 | 4,792 |
| Increase during year | 568 |
| Retained profit (calculated above) | 756 |
| Total exchange loss | (188) |

(B) *Analysis*

| | £ |
|---|---|
| Loss on translation of opening net investment (previous working in (d)(v)(2)) | (192) |
| Gain on payment of interim dividend: | |
| 800 ÷ 2.47 = £324 | |
| 800 ÷ 2.50 = £320 | |
| | 4 |
| | £(188) |

However, for ED 21 purposes, it was necessary to analyse (£192) between its constituent parts. To do this it is first necessary to analyse opening equity interest:

| | $ |
|---|---|
| Opening equity interest (= net assets): | |
| Ordinary share capital | 4,000 |
| Reserves | 7,500 |
| | $11,500 |

| At 30th November 19X8 | $ |
|---|---|
| Fixed assets (per previous working in (d)(v)) | 15,460 |
| Loan (assume no change during year) | (3,000) |
| ∴ Net current liabilities (balancing figure) | (960) |
| | $11,500 |

So the exchange loss on retranslation of the opening net investment (£192) could be analysed as follows:

| | | At 2.40 | At 2.50 | Difference |
|---|---|---|---|---|
| | $ | £ | £ | £ |
| Fixed assets | 15,460 | 6,442 | 6,184 | (258) |
| Loan | (3,000) | (1,250) | (1,200) | 50 |
| Net current liabilities | (960) | (400) | (384) | 16 |
| | $11,500 | £4,792 | £4,600 | £(192) |

Under ED 21, the exchange difference would be dealt with as follows (remember group interest in subsidiary is 80 per cent):

| | | £ |
|---|---|---|
| Through profit and loss a/c: | 80% × (50 + 16) | 53 |
| Through reserves: | 80% × (258) | (207) |
| | | £(154) |

The final calculations are:

| | £ |
|---|---|
| Through profit and loss a/c: | |
| As above | 53 |
| Gain on payment of dividend 80% × 4, say | 4 |
| | £57 |
| Through reserves: | |
| As above | £(207) |

*Note on cover concept*
Note that the "cover" does not apply, since in this case there is a gain of £50 on foreign currency net borrowings and a *loss* on translating fixed assets.

The consolidated profit and loss account would appear:

| | £ | £ |
|---|---|---|
| Profit on ordinary activities before taxation | | 33,632 |
| Tax on profit on ordinary activities | | 14,330 |
| Profit on ordinary activities after taxation | | 19,302 |
| Minority shareholders' interest (20% × 2,560) | | (512) |
| | | 18,790 |
| Extraordinary items (80% × 1,000) | (800) | |
| Exchange gain | 57 | |
| | | (743) |
| Profit for the financial year | | 18,047 |
| Dividends: Paid | (4,000) | |
| Proposed | (8,000) | |
| | | (12,000) |
| Retained profit | | £6,047 |

*Note: Reserves*

| | £ |
|---|---|
| Profit and loss account at 1st December 19X8 | 19,436 |
| Retained profit | 6,047 |
| Exchange loss | (207) |
| Profit and loss account at 30th November 19X9 | £25,276 |

*Comment on ED 21 treatment of exchange differences*

The ED 21 proposals to analyse the exchange gain (or loss) between working-capital and fixed-asset elements were criticised by many commentators. For example, Unilever commented:

> ". . . We find a fundamental inconsistency between the concept of net investment at risk . . . and the attempt to allocate varying treatments to the individual parts of the net investment.
>
> "For example, in the circumstances of a permanent foreign-based operation in a country whose currency has hardened against sterling, we can see no difference of character between an increase in the sterling equivalent of fixed assets and an increase in the sterling equivalent of working capital, certainly none which should lead one to allocate the first to reserves and the second to income. . . . Our understanding of the closing rate method leads us to disagree with the proposals in the exposure draft for the treatment of differences arising on translation. We believe that such differences do not represent genuine changes in the income for the period, since no physical movement of assets or liabilities across currencies occurs or is contemplated. . . ."

This viewpoint was shared by many commentators and the ED 27 and SSAP 20 proposals to take all such exchange differences direct to reserves have achieved widespread support.

## 8.5 The temporal method

(a) *Introduction*

SSAP 20 requires that the temporal method should be used in cases where the affairs of a foreign subsidiary are so closely interlinked with that of the holding company that the business of the foreign subsidiary should be regarded as a direct extension of the business of the holding company.

SSAP 20 then goes on to say that the financial statements of the foreign subsidiary should be included in the consolidated financial statements as if all transactions had been entered into by the holding company itself in the currency of the holding company.

The temporal method should be used where the cash flows of the foreign subsidiary impact directly upon the cash flows of the holding company. The holding company is providing the principal source of finance for the subsidiary and the additions to and disposals of assets by the subsidiary are reflected in corresponding cash flows between the holding company and the subsidiary.

(b) *Accounting requirements of SSAP 20*

In those circumstances where the trade of the foreign enterprise is more dependent on the economic environment of the investing company's currency than that of its own reporting currency, the temporal method should be used.

Translation differences arising from the use of the temporal method should be reported either as part of the profit for the year from ordinary operations or as an extraordinary item, as the case may be.

(c) *Detailed rules*
Although not specified in SSAP 20, the following are the usual treatments of profit and loss account and balance sheet items:

(i) *Profit and loss items:*

| *Item* | *Rate* |
|---|---|
| Sales, cost of sales | Average |
| Depreciation charge | Historical (same as for FA) |
| Expenses | Average |
| Tax charge | Average |
| Dividend paid | Actual |
| Dividend proposed | Year-end (closing) |

(ii) *Balance sheet items:*

| *Item* | *Rate* |
|---|---|
| Fixed assets | (1) If acquired before subsidiary became part of group: exchange rate at date of acquisition of subsidiary.<br>(2) If acquired post-acquisition, exchange rate at date of purchase of fixed asset. |
| Stock | Rate at date of acquisition of stock (year-end rate is usually a reasonable, practical approximation). |
| Debtors, cash, creditors, loans | Year-end (closing). |

(d) *Example*
The same facts are used as for the London/Ohio example. The following additional information is required:

(i) Exchange rates at acquisition of fixed assets:

| | | | |
|---|---|---|---|
| Assets acquired prior to 19X9 | \$2.31 | = | £1 |
| Assets acquired in 19X9 | \$2.48 | = | £1 |

(ii) Depreciation charge

| | \$ |
|---|---|
| Pre-19X9 assets | 1,980 |
| 19X9 assets | 280 |
| | \$2,260 |

(iii) Extraordinary item
Assume this relates to charges incurred when the exchange rate was \$2.45 = £1.

(e) *Workings and solution*

(i) *Translation of balance sheet at 30th November 19X9:*

| | | $ | Rate | £ |
|---|---|---|---|---|
| Fixed assets: | Cost (pre-19X9) | 19,800 | 2.31 | 8,571 |
| | Cost (19X9) | 2,800 | 2.48 | 1,129 |
| | Depreciation (pre-19X9) | (6,320) | 2.31 | (2,736) |
| | Depreciation (19X9) | (280) | 2.48 | (113) |
| Stocks | | 4,100 | 2.50 | 1,640 |
| Debtors | | 2,350 | 2.50 | 940 |
| Cash at bank | | 2,000 | 2.50 | 800 |
| Long-term loans | | (3,000) | 2.50 | (1,200) |
| Creditors | | (6,850) | 2.50 | (2,740) |
| Dividends payable | | (1,200) | 2.50 | (480) |
| | | $13,400 | | £5,811 |

| *Equity interest* | $ | Rate | £ |
|---|---|---|---|
| Ordinary share capital | 4,000 | 2.20 | 1,818 |
| Reserves (profit and loss a/c) | 9,400 | Balance | 3,993 |
| | $13,400 | | £5,811 |

(ii) *Consolidation workings*

Adjustment account, dividends payable and dividends receivable—as per closing rate method.

Reserves (Profit and Loss Account) of Ohio

| | £ | | £ |
|---|---|---|---|
| Adjustment a/c (pre-acquisition) 80% × 52,500 ÷ 2.20 | 909 | Balance | 3,993 |
| Minority interest 20% × 3,993 | 799 | | |
| Consolidated reserves (balance) | 2,285 | | |
| | £3,993 | | £3,993 |

Minority Interest

| | £ | | £ |
|---|---|---|---|
| Balance carried down | 1,163 | Ordinary share capital | 364 |
| | | Reserves | 799 |
| | £1,163 | | £1,163 |

Consolidated Reserves (Profit and Loss Account)

| | £ | | £ |
|---|---|---|---|
| | | London | 23,351 |
| Balance carried down | 25,636 | Ohio | 2,285 |
| | £25,636 | | £25,636 |

| | £ |
|---|---|
| Tangible assets | |
| London | 35,900 |
| Ohio (9,700 − 2,849) | 6,851 |
| | £42,751 |

(iii) Consolidated Balance Sheet at 30th November 19X9

| | £ | £ | £ |
|---|---|---|---|
| Fixed assets: | | | |
| Intangible assets: goodwill on consolidation | | | 87 |
| Tangible assets | | | 42,751 |
| | | | 42,838 |
| Current assets: | | | |
| Stocks | | 19,840 | |
| Debtors | | 6,900 | |
| Cash at bank | | 1,707 | |
| | | 28,447 | |
| Creditors: Amounts falling due within one year: | | | |
| Creditors | 19,190 | | |
| Dividends payable: | | | |
| Holding company | 8,000 | | |
| Minority | 96 | 27,286 | 1,161 |
| | | | 43,999 |
| Debenture loans | | | (7,200) |
| | | | 36,799 |
| Minority shareholders' interest | | | (1,163) |
| | | | £35,636 |

| | £ |
|---|---|
| Capital and reserves: | |
| Called-up share capital | 10,000 |
| Profit and loss account | 25,636 |
| | £35,636 |

(iv) Translation of Profit and Loss Account of Ohio

| | $ | Rate | £ |
|---|---|---|---|
| Profit before depreciation (10,600 + 2,260) | 12,860 | 2.45 | 5,249 |
| Depreciation: Pre-19X9 assets | (1,980) | 2.31 | (857) |
| 19X9 additions | (280) | 2.48 | (113) |
| Operating profit | 10,600 | | 4,279 |
| Taxation | 4,200 | 2.45 | 1,714 |
| | 6,400 | | 2,565 |
| Extraordinary item | (2,500) | 2.45 | (1,020) |
| | 3,900 | | 1,545 |
| Dividends: Paid | (800) | 2.47 | (324) |
| Proposed | (1,200) | 2.50 | (480) |
| Retained profit | $1,900 | | £741 |

(v) *Calculation of total exchange difference*
This may be calculated from:

(1) Equity interest at 30th November 19X9 (£5,811, above)
(2) Equity interest at 30th November 19X8 (unknown in £)
(3) Retained profit (£741, above).

Equity interest at 30th November 19X8 in $ is:

| | $ |
|---|---|
| Ordinary share capital | 4,000 |
| Reserves | 7,500 |
| | $11,500 |

Under the temporal method, the different parts of this figure are translated at different exchange rates:

| Working backwards: | $ |
|---|---|
| Fixed assets | 15,460 |
| Loan (assume no changes during year) | (3,000) |
| Net current liabilities (balancing figure) | (960) |
| | $11,500 |

Translating at 30th November 19X8 or historical exchange rates as appropriate:

| | $ | Rate | £ |
|---|---|---|---|
| Fixed assets | 15,460 | 2.31 | 6,693 |
| Loan | (3,000) | 2.40 | (1,250) |
| Net current liabilities | (960) | 2.40 | (400) |
| ∴ Equity interest at 30th November 19X8 | $11,500 | | £5,043 |

Calculation of exchange difference:

| | £ |
|---|---|
| Equity interest at 30th November 19X9 | 5,811 |
| Equity interest at 30th November 19X8 | 5,043 |
| Increase during year | 768 |
| Retained profit | 741 |
| ∴ Exchange gain | £27 |

The whole of this exchange gain is treated as part of the profit for the year from ordinary operations.

(vi) *Consolidated profit and loss account workings*

| | | £ |
|---|---|---|
| (1) | Profit on ordinary activities before tax (29,392 + 4,279) | 33,671 |
| | Exchange gain | 27 |
| | | 33,698 |
| (2) | Tax (12,650 + 1,714) | 14,364 |
| (3) | Minority interest [20% × (2,565 + 27)] (Note treatment of exchange gain) | 519 |
| (4) | Extraordinary items [80% × (1,020)] | (816) |
| (5) | Profit and Loss Account Balance at 1st December 19X8 | |

| | £ |
|---|---|
| Equity interest at acquisition ($6,500 ÷ 2.20) | 2,954 |
| Equity interest at 1st December 19X8 (*see* (v) above) | 5,043 |
| Increase | 2,089 |

| | £ |
|---|---|
| Ohio (80% × £2,089) | 1,671 |
| London | 17,966 |
| | £19,637 |

(vii) Consolidated Profit and Loss Account for the year ended 30th November 19X9

| | £ | £ |
|---|---|---|
| Profit on ordinary activities before tax | | 33,698 |
| Tax on profit on ordinary activities | | 14,364 |
| Profit on ordinary activities after tax | | 19,334 |
| Minority shareholders' interest | | 519 |
| | | 18,815 |
| Extraordinary item | | 816 |
| Carried forward | | 17,999 |

| | | £ | £ |
|---|---|---|---|
| | | Brought forward | 17,999 |
| Dividends: | Paid | 4,000 | |
| | Proposed | 8,000 | 12,000 |
| Retained profit | | | £5,999 |

*Note: Reserves*

| | £ |
|---|---|
| Profit and loss account at 1st December 19X8 | 19,637 |
| Retained profit | 5,999 |
| Profit and loss account at 30th November 19X9 | £25,636 |

(f) *Comment on the temporal method*

A particular problem with the temporal method relates to the treatment of long-term loans denominated in a foreign currency.

In the above example, the foreign loan amounted to $3,000. This was included in the consolidated balance sheets at 30th November 19X8 and 30th November 19X9 as follows:

| | £ |
|---|---|
| At 30th November 19X8: $3,000 ÷ 2.40 | 1,250 |
| At 30th November 19X9: $3,000 ÷ 2.50 | 1,200 |
| Difference (exchange gain) | £50 |

Under the temporal method, this difference forms part of the profit from ordinary operations. This is consistent with the temporal principles outlined in (a) above.

This can cause difficulties, as was found with US statement FASB 8. American companies could be trading profitably but overseas loans in the accounts of subsidiaries could result in substantial exchange losses being reflected in the profit-before-tax figure. With independent or semi-independent subsidiaries this might not make a great deal of sense.

If the loan and the related assets (whether working capital or fixed assets) were located in the same country, related exchange differences should be considered together. This is, of course, the situation in SSAP 20 where exchange differences on both loans and fixed assets are taken direct to reserve.

It is hardly surprising that SSAP 20 requires the temporal method to be used only in restricted situations.

## 8.6 SSAP 20—Further considerations

(a) *Disclosure*

(i) The methods used in the translation of the financial statements of foreign enterprises and the treatment of exchange differences;

(ii) for all companies or groups other than exempt companies (special cases defined in SSAP 20), the net amount of exchange gains and losses on foreign currency borrowings less deposits, distinguishing separately:

(1) the amount offset in reserves under the provisions of paragraphs 51, 57 and 58 (this is explained in (c) below); and

(2) the net amount charged/credited to the profit and loss account;

(iii) for all companies or groups, the net movement on reserves arising from exchange differences.

(b) *Companies Act 1981 profit and loss formats*
For classification purposes, the nature of each foreign exchange gain or loss should be considered separately.

(i) Gains or losses arising from trading transactions should normally be included under "other operating income or expense".

(ii) Gains or losses which may be considered as financing should be disclosed separately as part of "other interest receivable/payable and similar income/expense".

(iii) Exchange gains or losses which arise from events which themselves fall to be treated as extraordinary items should be included as part of such items.

(c) *Equity investments financed by foreign borrowings*
Exchange gains or losses on foreign currency borrowings are normally included in the profit and loss account as part of the profit or loss on ordinary activities.

However, where borrowings have been used to finance foreign equity investments, or where the purpose of the borrowings is to provide a hedge against the exchange risk associated with existing (i.e., previously acquired) equity investments, the company or group may be covered in economic terms against any movement in exchange rates.

SSAP 20 provides an option for companies or groups. This is dealt with in two parts:

(i) the accounts of the investing company (this option was not available in ED 27).

(ii) the accounts of the group (although relief was available in ED 27, the provisions were subsequently redrafted).

(d) *Accounts of the investing company*

(i) *General considerations*
The situation is one where a company has used foreign currency borrowings either:

(1) to finance foreign equity investments; or

(2) to provide a hedge against its foreign equity investments.

(ii) *Relief available*

(1) The equity investments may be denominated in the appropriate foreign currency(ies) and the carrying amounts translated into pounds sterling at each balance sheet date at the closing rate. Thus the same investment could be included at different pound sterling amounts in successive balance sheets.

(2) Exchange differences resulting from (1) should be taken direct to reserve.

(3) Exchange gains/losses on foreign currency borrowings should then be offset as a reserve movement against these exchange differences.

Note that the above is an option. However, once it is chosen, the treatment in (1), (2) and (3) must be adopted consistently from one year to the next.

(iii) *Conditions to be satisfied*
Three conditions must be satisfied:

(1) in any accounting period, exchange gains or losses arising on the borrowings may be offset only to the extent of exchange differences arising on the equity investments;

(2) the foreign currency borrowings, whose exchange gains or losses are used in the offset process, should not exceed, in the aggregate, the total amount of cash that the investments are expected to be able to generate, whether from profits or otherwise; and

(3) the accounting treatment adopted should be applied consistently from period to period.

*Example*

Horace PLC acquired an 80 per cent shareholding in a French company, Gilbert SA, several years ago at a cost of 800,000 francs. At the date of acquisition, the exchange rate was 4 francs = £1.

A year after acquisition, Horace took out a loan of 600,000 francs to provide a hedge against the investment in Gilbert. The loan is repayable after 16 years.

The exchange rates at 31st December 19X2 and 31st December 19X3 were 3.20 and 2.90 respectively.

(1) Ignoring option:
The shares would be included in the balance sheet at a fixed amount of £200,000 (800,000 ÷ 4).

The loan would appear in successive balance sheets as follows:

| | | |
|---|---|---|
| 31st December 19X2: 600,000 ÷ 3.20 | = | £187,500 |
| 31st December 19X3: 600,000 ÷ 2.90 | = | £206,897 |

The loss on translation of £19,397 should be debited to profit and loss account.

(2) Taking advantage of option:
Equity investment is denominated in foreign currency, i.e. Fr.800,000.

The investment will appear as a fixed asset in successive balance sheets as follows:

| | | |
|---|---|---|
| 31st December 19X2: 800,000 ÷ 3.20 | = | £250,000 |
| 31st December 19X3: 800,000 ÷ 2.90 | = | £275,862 |

The loan will appear in successive balance sheets as:

| | | |
|---|---|---|
| 31st December 19X2: 600,000 ÷ 3.20 | = | £187,500 |
| 31st December 19X3: 600,000 ÷ 2.90 | = | £206,897 |
| The gain on the investment is | | £25,862 |
| The loss on the loan is | | £19,397 |
| Net gain | | £6,465 |

The net gain of £6,465 is taken direct to reserves. Note that since the loan is less than the investment, the limit on offset in condition (1) is not applicable.

For clarity, both investment and loan are in francs, although SSAP 20 does not insist that they are both in the same currency as long as there is a genuine hedge.

(e) *Accounts of the group*

(i) *General considerations*

Within a group, foreign borrowings may have been used to finance group investments in foreign enterprises or to provide a hedge against the exchange risk associated with similar existing investments.

Paragraph 30 of SSAP 20 states:

> "Any increase or decrease in the amount outstanding on the borrowings arising from exchange movements will probably be covered by corresponding changes in the carrying amount of the net assets underlying the net investments (which would be reflected in reserves). Since in this case the group will be covered in economic terms against any movement in exchange rates, it would be inappropriate to record an accounting profit or loss when exchange rates change."

(ii) *Relief available*

In the group accounts, the exchange gains or losses on such foreign currency borrowings (which would otherwise be taken to the group profit and loss account) may be offset as reserve movements against exchange differences on the retranslation of the net investments.

(iii) *Conditions to be satisfied*

Four conditions must be satisfied:

(1) the relationships between the investing company and the foreign

enterprises concerned justify the use of the closing-rate method for consolidation purposes;

(2) in any accounting period, the exchange gains and losses arising on foreign currency borrowings are offset only to the extent of the exchange differences arising on the net investments in foreign enterprises;

(3) the foreign currency borrowings, whose exchange gains or losses are used in the offset process, should not exceed, in the aggregate, the total amount of cash that the net investments are expected to be able to generate, whether from profits or otherwise; and

(4) the accounting treatment is applied consistently from period to period.

*Example*

Wilson PLC acquired 80 per cent of the equity share capital of a German company, Singer GmbH. The acquisition was partly financed by a German loan repayable in ten years' time.

The following extracts relate to the group working papers:

(1) Foreign loan:

| | | £ |
|---|---|---|
| 1st January 19X3: | DM8,600,000 ÷ 8.70 | 988,506 |
| Exchange translation loss | | 23,258 |
| 31st December 19X3: | DM8,600,000 ÷ 8.50 | £1,011,764 |

(2) Net investment in Singer:

| | 100% £ | 80% £ |
|---|---|---|
| Exchange gain on retranslation of opening net investment | 26,790 | 21,432 |
| Exchange gain: profit and loss account translated at average rate and at closing rate | 9,231 | 7,385 |

(A) *Without the option*
£23,258 would be debited to profit and loss account. Both £21,432 and £7,385 would be credited direct to reserves.

(B) *Taking advantage of option*
The exchange loss on the loan of £23,258 may be partially offset against the gain on opening net investment of £21,432. This would leave £1,826 to be debited to group profit and loss account. Note that £7,385 should be credited direct to reserve.

Again, note that this is an option but once taken up should be applied consistently from one period to the next.

(f) *Foreign branches*
Foreign branches should be accounted for according to the nature of the business operation concerned:

(i) Where the branch operates as a separate business entity with local finance, it should be accounted for in a way similar to that for a subsidiary, i.e. using the closing-rate method.

(ii) Where the branch operates as an extension of the trade of the holding company, and the branch's cash flows impact directly upon those of the holding company, the temporal method should be used.

(g) *Associated companies*
An interest in an associated company should be accounted for on a similar basis to an investment in a subsidiary using the closing-rate/net-investment method.

(h) *Permanent impairment situations*
There may be situations where translation of the net investment in a particular subsidiary gives rise to continuing adverse exchange differences, and where this trend is likely to continue, where appropriate, provision for permanent impairment in value should be made.

## 8.7 Foreign currency translation—Comments on UK Exposure Drafts

(a) *Comparison of ED 16, ED 21, ED 27—consolidated financial statements*
The three exposure documents are compared in Table 17.

(b) *Comments on ED 21*
ED 27 (Appendix 2) reported the following comments or reactions to ED 21:

(i) Lack of clarity in distinction between the treatment of exchange differences in individual companies and that of differences arising on consolidation.

(ii) Two methods of translation should not be allowed when the closing-rate method was so widely adopted in the UK and Ireland.

(iii) The occasions when the cover concept could be applied were not clear.

(iv) The different treatment given to current assets as opposed to fixed assets was not supported (see, for example, the comments of Unilever referred to above).

(v) Support for the use of the closing rate and for the use of the average rate for translating profit and loss items was evenly divided.

(vi) The net investment concept in the exposure draft was inadequately developed (see, for example, the Unilever comments, and subsequent ideas expressed in ED 27 itself).

Table 17. COMPARISON OF EXPOSURE DRAFTS ON FOREIGN CURRENCY TRANSLATION

| *Aspects* | *ED 16* | *ED 21* | *ED 27* |
|---|---|---|---|
| Translation method to be used. | Choice of closing-rate (C) or temporal (T). | C or T, but C preferred. | (1) Method to be used depends on relationship between HC and subsidiary. (2) In most cases, C would be used. |
| Translation of profit and loss a/c under closing-rate method. | No rules specified. | Items to be translated at either closing rate or average rate. | Items to be translated at average rate. |
| Treatment of exchange differences under closing-rate method. | (1) Differences relating to extraordinary items should be treated as extraordinary. (2) Differences arising on translation of fixed asset amounts should be treated as if unrealised surpluses or deficits on revaluation. (3) Other differences should be dealt with in profit and loss a/c as part of profit from ordinary activities of the business. | (1) As for (1) in ED 16. (2) As for (2) in ED 16 (except that deficits on translation of fixed asset not covered by previous surplus for the same asset, should be dealt with in profit and loss a/c, as for (3) below). (3) Other differences to be reported as separate item in profit and loss a/c after post-tax profits from ordinary operations. | (1) As for (1) in ED 16 and ED 21. (2) All other translation differences should be treated as movements on reserves. |
| "Cover" methods available. | Exchange losses on translation of foreign currency net borrowings may be wholly or partly offset (for profit and loss a/c purposes) against equal or smaller gains arising on translating overseas fixed assets at closing rate. | Translation deficits on net borrowings denominated in foreign currency may be wholly or partly offset against differences on the translation of fixed assets at closing rates. | (1) Cover as for ED 16 and ED 21 is unnecessary, as under ED 27 most exchange differences taken direct to reserve. (2) ED 27 proposals where proceeds of foreign loans used to finance equity investments. |

(vii) There was strong support for keeping exchange differences out of operating profit, but little support for displaying them as quasi-extraordinary items.

## PROGRESS TEST 7

1. What documents did the Companies Act 1948 require holding companies to prepare and present to their members concerning group accounts? (1.0)
2. What is an associated company? (1.2)
3. Define the following:
   (a) holding company; (1.3(a))
   (b) subsidiary company; (1.3(b))
   (c) equity share capital; (1.3(c))
   (d) group of companies. (1.3(d))
4. Distinguish between group accounts and consolidated financial statements. (1.4)
5. Describe the object of a consolidated balance sheet and define "goodwill on consolidation". (2.1)
6. Draw a diagram indicating the standard presentation of the "T" accounts opened when preparing consolidated balance sheets. (2.2(b))
7. What are minority interests? (Illustrate your answer with diagrams) (3.0)
8. What two situations may occur which demand details of dividends from pre-acquisition profits, paid by a subsidiary? (4.1)
9. Give an example of an inter-group item. (4.2(c), 4.5)
10. What are current accounts? Discuss their treatment. (4.3)
11. How would you establish the ownership of the reserves and shares of a subsidiary? (4.4)
12. Discuss the provisions laid down concerning the treatment of unrealised profits. (4.5(a))
13. Discuss two possible methods of consolidating information about indirect subsidiaries. (5.0)
14. Outline the indirect method. (5.5)
15. Describe the object of the consolidated profit and loss account. (6.1)
16. What effect would a subsidiary's holding of preference shares have on the presentation of a consolidated profit and loss account? (6.4)
17. According to SSAP 6 where and how should extraordinary items be recorded? (6.7)
18. What are appropriations? (6.8)
19. Draw up a table illustrating the Companies Act 1981 disclosure requirements concerning consolidated profit and loss accounts. (6.10)
20. What four methods are there for accounting for investments in the accounts of an investor? (7.1)
21. What variants exist concerning one of the methods referred to in Q. 20? (7.2)
22. Give the SSAP 1 (Revised) definition of an associated company. (7.5)
23. How does Schedule 1 of Companies Act 1981 define "related companies"? (7.6)
24. Draw a table illustrating the typical features of the consolidated profit and loss accounts of an investing group. (7.8)

25. In what circumstances might the temporal method be appropriate for group accounts? (8.5(a))
26. What are the principal disclosure requirements of SSAP 20? (8.6)
27. Under Companies Act 1981, where should exchange gains be presented in the profit and loss account? (8.6(b))
28. Outline the use of the cover method for individual companies. What conditions must be satisfied? (8.6(d))
29. Explain the logic of the cover method for groups, state the assumptions to be satisfied and outline possible accounting effects. (8.6(e))
30. What are the basic rules for translation of foreign currency items by an individual company? (8.1(b))
31. Why should unrealised exchange gains relating to the translation of long-term loans be included in the profit and loss account? (8.2(b)(iv))
32. For groups of companies, what are the two main approaches to currency translation? (8.3(a))
33. List four main characteristics which might indicate the appropriateness of the .closing-rate method (8.3(b))
34. Under the closing-rate method, how should the various possible exchange differences be treated? (8.4(b))
35. Under the closing-rate method, how should profit and loss account items be translated? (8.4(b)(ii))

CHAPTER EIGHT

# Partnership Accounting

## 1.0 INTRODUCTION

An outline of what is required for an understanding of partnership accounts is illustrated in Fig. 5.

## 2.0 PARTNERSHIP LAW AND PRACTICE

### 2.1 Partnership agreement

(a) *Types of agreement*
Whenever a number of people carry on a business together with a view to profit, it is desirable that there should be some agreement between them as to how they are to conduct the business. A partnership agreement may be created by:

(i) deed,

(ii) writing,

(iii) word of mouth,

(iv) course of dealing.

(b) *Subject matter of agreement*
A partnership agreement will contain a number of matters, the most important of which are as follows:

(i) partners' capital and current accounts;

(ii) profit and loss sharing ratio;

(iii) partners' drawing rights;

(iv) interest on capital, current and drawings accounts;

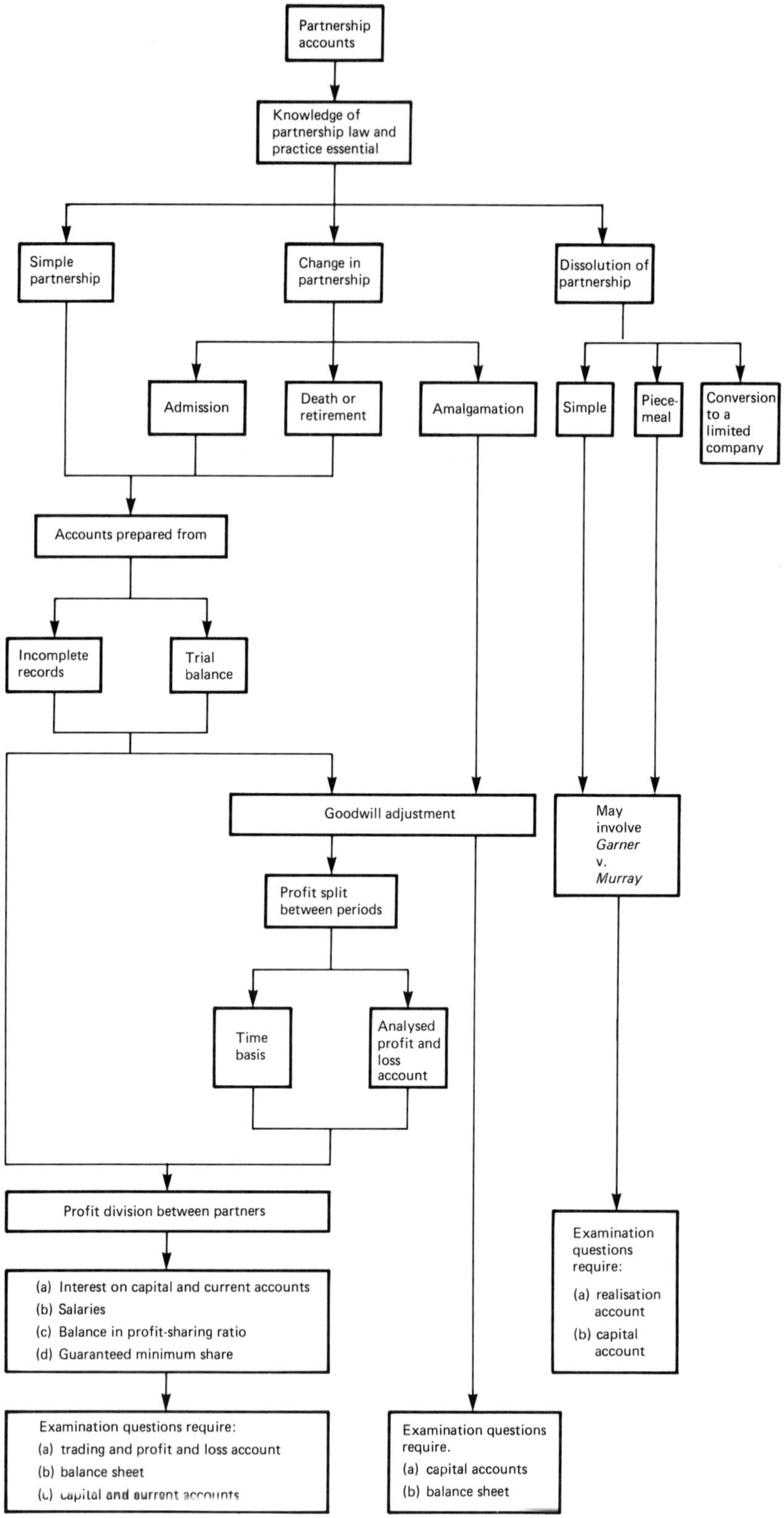


Fig. 5. *Partnership accounts.*

(v) partners' salaries;

(vi) valuation of goodwill;

(vii) provisions relating to death or retirement of partners.

## 2.2 Partnership Act 1890

(a) *Rights of partners IN ABSENCE OF AGREEMENT TO CONTRARY (s. 24)*

Accounting:

(i) All partners are entitled to share equally in capital and profits and must contribute equally to losses.

(ii) Partners are not entitled before ascertaining profits to interest on capital.

(iii) Partners are not entitled to salaries.

(iv) A partner is entitled to interest at 5 per cent per annum on advances beyond the amount of his agreed capital.

Administration:

(v) Partnership books to be kept at place of business (or principal place) and every partner may inspect and copy.

(vi) The firm must indemnify every partner in respect of payments made and personal liabilities incurred by him:

(1) in the ordinary and proper conduct of the business of the firm, or

(2) in or about anything necessarily done for the preservation of the business or property of the firm.

(vii) Every partner may take part in management.

(viii) No person may be introduced as a partner without the consent of all existing partners.

(ix) Ordinary differences may be decided by a majority, but no change may be made in the nature of the business without the consent of all.

(b) *Duties of partners (ss. 28–30)*

(i) Partners are bound to render true accounts and full information of all things affecting the partnership to any partner or his legal representative.

(ii) Every partner must account for all profits derived without the consent of the others from any partnership transaction or use of firm name or connection. This applies to transactions after the death of one partner and before the partnership affairs have been completely wound up.

(iii) No partner may carry on another business of the same nature or compete with another firm without consent, and, if he does, he must account for and pay over all profits made.

(c) *Rule for distribution of assets on final settlement of accounts (s. 44)*
Subject to agreement to the contrary, the following rules apply on dissolution:

(i) Losses, including losses and deficiencies of capital shall be paid first out of profits, next out of capital, and lastly, if necessary by the partners individually in the proportion in which they were entitled to share profits.

(ii) The assets, including sums, if any, contributed by partners to make up losses or deficiencies of capital shall be applied as follows:

(1) in paying debts and liabilities to persons not partners;

(2) in repaying loans by partners;

(3) in paying each partner rateably the amount of his capital;

(4) the residue, if any, to be divided among the partners in profit-sharing ratio.

(d) *Right of outgoing partner in certain cases to share profits made after dissolution (s. 42)*

(i) Where a partner dies or ceases to be a partner and the surviving partners continue the business without a settlement of accounts the outgoing partner is entitled (in the absence of contrary agreement) to either:

(1) such post-dissolution profits as the court may find attributable to the use of his share, *or*

(2) interest at 5 per cent p.a. on the amount of his share.

(ii) Where, by agreement, an option is given to surviving partners to purchase the interest of an outgoing or deceased partner and that option is exercised, the outgoing partner (or his estate) is not entitled to any further share in profits. If the option is not exercised then paragraph (i) applies.

(e) *Retiring or deceased partner's share to be a debt (s. 43)*
Subject to agreement to the contrary the amount due to an outgoing partner (or his estate) is a debt accruing from date of dissolution or death.

## 3.0 ACCOUNTS REQUIRED AND THEIR PURPOSE

As well as the normal trading, profit and loss account and balance sheet, a partnership requires a number of other accounts in order to meet its special accounting requirements.

### 3.1 Profit and loss appropriation account

The profit and loss appropriation account is used to divide the partnership profits among the partners. The partnership agreement will deal with:

(a) partners' salaries,

(b) interest on capital and current accounts,

(c) profit-sharing ratio (p.s.r.).

### 3.2 Capital accounts

Two situations must be distinguished with regard to capital accounts:

(a) *Capital is fixed and current accounts are maintained*
Many partnership agreements provide for a fixed amount of capital to be subscribed by the partners and thereafter to be maintained. In this case the balances on capital account remain fixed until the partners agree to a variation.

(b) *Current accounts are not maintained*
Where separate current accounts are not maintained, all partners' transactions are recorded in the capital accounts. They will therefore record capital introduced, profit divisions, drawings and goodwill adjustments. The balance on capital account at any time records the interest of a partner in the partnership.

### 3.3 Current accounts

Where current accounts are maintained, they show the share of profit due to a partner and the drawings he makes against such share. If a partner draws more than his eventual share of profit he may have a debit balance on his current account which will have to be rectified by paying in cash or by drawing less in the next period.

### 3.4 Loan accounts

Where a partner advances money to the partnership above his agreed capital or where a retiring partner leaves money in the partnership this must be clearly shown as a loan and *not* as partners' capital.

### 3.5 Goodwill account

Particular problems arise concerning the recording of, and adjustments for, goodwill. Attention must be paid to examination questions to determine whether or not goodwill is to be recorded in the partnership accounts.

## 4.0 APPROPRIATION OF PROFITS

### 4.1 Introduction

Profit appropriation involves the division of the partnership profits between the partners as specified in the partnership agreement.

Where there have been no changes in the partnership this is simply a matter of dividing the profits of the year among the partners.

Where there has been a change in the partnership during the year, it is first necessary to *split* the profits between the period before the change and the period after the change and, then, to *divide* the profits of each period between the partners who are entitled to them.

## 4.2 Profit split

There are two ways in which a profit split can be achieved.

(a) *Profit split on time basis*
This is the simpler of the two methods as the net profit shown by the profit and loss account is split between the various periods on a time basis.

(b) *Profit split by analysed profit and loss account*
This involves the use of separate columns in the profit and loss account for the various periods:

(i) Gross profit is split between the periods on the basis of turnover.

(ii) Fixed charges are split on the basis of time.

(iii) Variable charges are split on the basis of turnover.

(iv) Charges about which special information is given are split according to that information.

## 4.3 Profit division

Most examination questions will state the terms of the agreement and deal exhaustively with the division of profits. The agreement may provide the following:

(a) interest on current accounts;

(b) interest on capital accounts;

(c) salaries;

(d) interest on drawings;

(e) division of profits after dealing with (a)–(d);

(f) guaranteed minimum share for one or more partners.

Where there has been a change in the partnership and profits have been split between periods it is most important to remember that interest and salaries are *per annum*, and where a period is shorter than a year, they must be scaled down.

## 5.0 ACCOUNT OUTLINES

### 5.1 Profit and loss appropriation account

| | £ | £ | | £ | £ |
|---|---|---|---|---|---|
| Salaries: | | | Net profit: | | |
| Albert | 1,000 | | Brought down | | 15,420 |
| Boris | 800 | 1,800 | | | |
| Interest on capital: | | | Interest on drawings: | | |
| Albert 10% on £10,000 | 1,000 | | Albert | 50 | |
| Boris 10% on £5,000 | 500 | | Boris | 20 | |
| Cyril 10% on £2,000 | 200 | 1,700 | Cyril | 10 | 80 |
| Balance in profit-sharing ratio: | | | | | |
| Albert ($\frac{1}{2}$) | 6,000 | | | | |
| Boris ($\frac{1}{3}$) | 4,000 | | | | |
| Cyril ($\frac{1}{6}$) | 2,000 | 12,000 | | | |
| | | £15,500 | | | £15,500 |

### 5.2 Balance sheet

| | | £ | | £ |
|---|---|---|---|---|
| Fixed assets: | | | | |
| Freehold premises | | | | 8,000 |
| Plant and machinery | | | | 5,920 |
| | | | | 13,920 |
| Current assets: | | | | |
| Stock | | 5,000 | | |
| Debtors | | 11,000 | | |
| Bank balance | | 2,000 | | |
| | | 18,000 | | |
| *deduct:* Current liabilities: | | | | |
| Creditors | | 8,000 | | 10,000 |
| | | | | £23,920 |
| | Albert | Boris | Cyril | |
| | £ | £ | £ | £ |
| Capital accounts | 10,000 | 5,000 | 2,000 | 17,000 |
| Current accounts | 4,150 | 2,080 | 690 | 6,920 |
| | £14,150 | £7,080 | £2,690 | £23,920 |

### 5.3 Current accounts

| | Albert | Boris | Cyril | | Albert | Boris | Cyril |
|---|---|---|---|---|---|---|---|
| | £ | £ | £ | | £ | £ | £ |
| Drawings | 4,500 | 3,500 | 2,000 | Brought down | 700 | 300 | 500 |
| Interest on drawings | 50 | 20 | 10 | Salaries | 1,000 | 800 | — |
| Carried down | 4,150 | 2,080 | 690 | Interest on capital | 1,000 | 500 | 200 |
| | | | | Balance in profit-sharing ratio | 6,000 | 4,000 | 2,000 |
| | £8,700 | 5,600 | 2,700 | | £8,700 | 5,600 | 2,700 |

## 6.0 GOODWILL

### 6.1 Definition

Goodwill is an intangible asset, arising from a business's ability to earn a differential return of profit on the capital employed; that is a higher return than arises in a comparable business.

### 6.2 Sources of goodwill

Goodwill may arise from all or any of the following:

(a) reputation of owners;

(b) quality of goods dealt in;

(c) site monopoly or advantage;

(d) advantageous patents and trade marks;

(e) growth element.

### 6.3 Valuation

No exact formula can be laid down for accurate measurement of goodwill but the following methods are commonly used:

(a) figure arising from multiplication of average profits by agreed number of years (*see* 6.4(a) below);

(b) as for (a) above except the average profit is adjusted for:

(i) reasonable management remuneration;

(ii) interest on capital (which can be "pure" interest or risk interest) (*see* 6.4(b) below);

(c) as for (a) above but the figure used as the basis of return for an investment, less the net tangible assets (*see* 6.4(c) below).

## 6.4 Examples of goodwill valuations

(a) Goodwill valued on basis of, say:
"four years' purchase of average of last five years' profits"
Profits as follows:

| | £ |
|---|---|
| 19X1 | 12,000 |
| 19X2 | 14,000 |
| 19X3 | 18,000 |
| 19X4 | 20,000 |
| 19X5 | 21,000 |

*Answer:*

| | |
|---|---|
| Total profits | = £85,000 |
| Average profits | = £17,000 p.a. |
| Four years' purchase | = £68,000 |

(b) Goodwill valued on basis of, say:
"six years' purchase of average of last five years' profits after deducting reasonable salaries to partners, say £5,000 p.a. and reasonable interest on partners' capital, say £2,000 p.a."
Profits as in example (a).

*Answer:*

| | |
|---|---|
| Total profits | = £85,000 |
| Average profits | = £17,000 p.a. |
| Salaries and interest | = £ 7,000 p.a. |
| Profits after salaries and interest | = £10,000 p.a. |
| Six years' purchase | = £60,000 |

(c) Goodwill valued on basis of, say:
"excess of ten per cent capitalised value of average of last five years' profit over value of net tangible assets"
Profits as in (a) above.

Value of net tangible assets = £150,000

*Answer:*

| | |
|---|---|
| Total profits | = £85,000 |
| Average profits | = £17,000 p.a. |
| Ten per cent capitalised value | |
| of average profits | = £ |
| 100 ÷ 10 × £17,000 | = 170,000 |
| Value of net tangible assets | = 150,000 |
| Goodwill | = £20,000 |

## 6.5 Unrecorded goodwill

Goodwill may be wholly excluded from the accounts of a partnership or it may be included at a figure which is below its true value.

Whenever there is a change in the partnership, an adjustment must be made in respect of the *unrecorded amount*.

## 6.6 Adjustments for goodwill

Adjustments will have to be made in respect of the unrecorded goodwill in any of the following situations:

(a) admission of new partner;

(b) retirement of partner;

(c) death of partner;

(d) combination of (a), (b) and (c);

(e) dissolution;

(f) change in profit-sharing ratio;

(g) change in basis of accounting.

Various goodwill adjustments arising on changes in a partnership are illustrated in Fig. 6.

## 6.7 Adjustment for unrecorded goodwill

The adjustment to be made in respect of unrecorded goodwill is always the same:

Credit: old partners' capital account with unrecorded goodwill in the old profit-sharing ratio;
Debit: new partners' capital accounts with unrecorded goodwill in the new profit-sharing ratio.

This can always be remembered as "credit at old—debit at new".

In some cases, "short-cut" adjustments can be made but the "credit at old—debit at new" adjustment can be made in every case.

## 6.8 Cash paid for goodwill by incoming partner

Three situations can arise:

(a) Incoming partner introduces cash without any part being designated for goodwill—total cash introduced is credited to the incoming partner's capital account. The usual "credit at old—debit at new" adjustment is made.

(b) Incoming partner introduces cash as capital and a specified sum in respect of goodwill—total cash introduced by partner, including cash for capital and cash for goodwill is credited to the incoming partner's capital account. The usual "credit at old—debit at new" adjustment is made.

(c) Incoming partner introduces cash as capital and makes a payment to the partners privately in respect of goodwill—the private payment should be recorded in the capital accounts by crediting the incoming partner with the amount he has paid and debiting the old partners with the amounts they have received. The usual "credit at old—debit at new" adjustment is made.

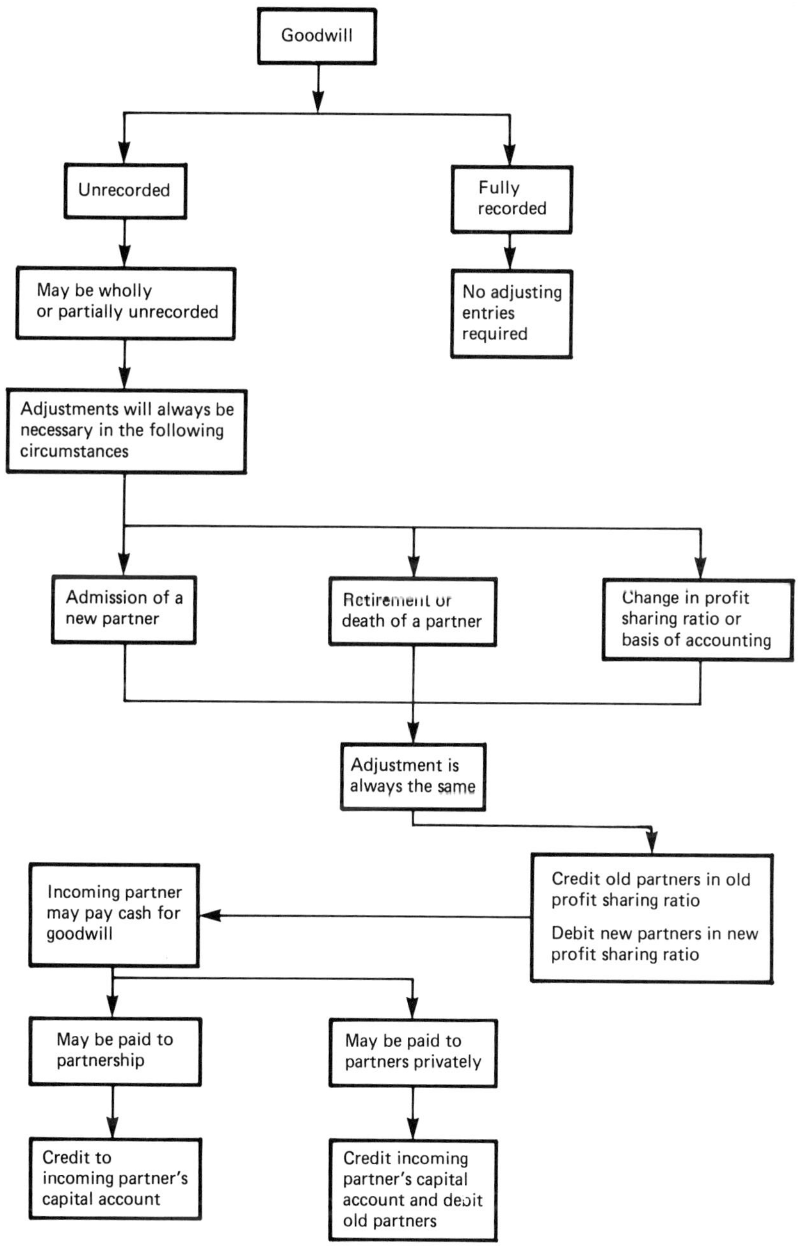


Fig. 6. *Goodwill adjustments arising on changes in a partnership.*

## 6.9 Premium

In some questions, the examiner does not give the new profit-sharing ratio but instead gives the premium paid by the incoming partner for his share of the unrecorded goodwill. This premium expressed as a fraction of the total unrecorded goodwill will give the incoming partner's share in profits and losses.

## 6.10 Goodwill and current accounts

In some questions, the examiner requires the adjustment for goodwill to be made in the current account and not the capital accounts. Always study the examiner's requirements before making the goodwill adjustment.

# 7.0 AMALGAMATIONS

## 7.1 Examination questions

Examination questions usually require:

(a) partners' capital accounts;

(b) balance sheet after amalgamation.

*Note:* There are three types of amalgamation possible:
two sole traders combine forming a partnership;
an existing partnership combines with a sole trader;
two existing partnerships merge.

## 7.2 Adjustments on amalgamation

Adjustments required in respect of unrecorded goodwill and asset revaluation are as follows:

(a) *Entries in old records*

(i) *unrecorded goodwill* is debited to goodwill account (and credited to the "old partners" in "old profit-sharing ratio" in the case of an existing partnership).

(ii) *assets are revalued* and the increase or decrease is credited or debited to capital accounts as for unrecorded goodwill above.

*Note:* Revaluation and realisation accounts should not be opened unless specifically required.

(b) *Entries in new partnership*

(i) *Assets to be recorded at new values*—partners' capital account balances brought forward from old partnerships and no adjustment necessary.

(ii) *Assets to be recorded at original values*—assets are written back to their original values, partners' capital accounts being debited (or credited) in new profit-sharing ratio.

*Note:* It will be noted that this is simply the same "credit at old—debit at new" rule.

### *Example*

QUESTION

Tick and Cross, each in sole practice as accountants, agreed to amalgamate their practices as on 31st December 19X4 under the name of Tick Cross & Co.

Their balance sheets as on that date were as follows:

| | Tick | Cross | | Tick | Cross |
|---|---|---|---|---|---|
| | £ | £ | | £ | £ |
| Capital accounts | 7,000 | 5,700 | Leasehold premises | 4,000 | — |
| Creditors | 800 | 500 | Motor vehicles | — | 600 |
| Bank overdraft | 3,800 | — | Office equipment | 600 | 400 |
| | | | Work in progress | 2,800 | 1,800 |
| | | | Debtors | 4,200 | 2,600 |
| | | | Balance at bank | — | 800 |
| | £11,600 | £6,200 | | £11,600 | £6,200 |

The amalgamation was carried out on the following terms:

(a) Profits and losses are to be shared: Tick two-thirds, Cross one-third.

(b) Goodwill is to be valued at one and a half years' purchase of the average profits of the previous three or five years, whichever is the lower. No account for goodwill is to be opened in the books, any adjustments necessary being made in the partners' capital accounts.

(c) Tick's leasehold premises, not being required by the new practice, were to be taken over by him personally. Their value was agreed at £3,600 and he paid this amount into the new firm on 1st January 19X5.

(d) Certain assets were to be revalued, the new values being as follows:

| | Tick | Cross |
|---|---|---|
| | £ | £ |
| Office equipment | 800 | 500 |
| Work in progress | 3,200 | 1,500 |
| Debtors | 4,200 | 2,400 |

(e) Tick's car, which was owned by him personally, is to be taken over by the new firm at a value of £750.

The profits of the two firms for the five years ended 31st December 19X4 were as follows:

| | Tick | Cross |
|---|---|---|
| | £ | £ |
| Year ended 31st December 19X0 | 3,800 | 4,600 |
| Year ended 31st December 19X1 | 4,200 | 3,400 |
| Year ended 31st December 19X2 | 6,000 | 3,500 |
| Year ended 31st December 19X3 | 5,800 | 3,800 |
| Year ended 31st December 19X4 | 4,700 | 3,200 |

You are required to prepare:

(a) partners' capital accounts recording these transactions, and

(b) balance sheet (in vertical form) of the new firm as on 1st January 19X5 after the adjustment of the partners' capital accounts.

ANSWER

(a)

Tick and Cross's Books
Partners' Capital Accounts

| | Tick | Cross | | Tick | Cross |
|---|---|---|---|---|---|
| | £ | £ | | £ | £ |
| Assets transferred to new firm: | | | Balances brought forward | 7,000 | 5,700 |
| Motor vehicles | 750 | 600 | Personal motor car | 750 | — |
| Office equipment | 800 | 500 | Liabilities taken over by new firm: | | |
| Work in progress | 3,200 | 1,500 | Creditors | 800 | 500 |
| Debtors | 4,200 | 2,400 | Bank overdraft | 3,800 | — |
| Balance at bank | — | 800 | Revaluation of assets: | | |
| | 8,950 | 5,800 | Office equipment | 200 | 100 |
| Leasehold premises retained | 4,000 | — | Work in progress | 400 | — |
| Provisions: | | | | | |
| Work in progress | — | 300 | | | |
| Bad debts (£2,600 − £2,400 | — | 200 | | | |
| | £12,950 | £6,300 | | £12,950 | £6,300 |

Partners' Capital Accounts
(Firm's Books)

| | Tick | Cross | | Tick | Cross |
|---|---|---|---|---|---|
| | £ | £ | | £ | £ |
| Liabilities taken over: | | | Assets introduced at valuations (above) | 8,950 | 5,800 |
| Creditors | 800 | 500 | Cash introduced | 3,600 | — |
| Bank overdraft | 3,800 | — | Goodwill | | |
| Goodwill written off in profit-sharing ratio (2:1) | 8,400 | 4,200 | (*see* working 1) | 7,350 | 5,250 |
| Balances carried down | 6,900 | 6,350 | | | |
| | £19,900 | £11,050 | | £19,900 | £11,050 |

Tick Cross & Co
Balance Sheet
as at 1st January 19X5

| | £ | £ | £ |
|---|---|---|---|
| Fixed assets: | | | |
| Motor vehicles | | 1,350 | |
| Office equipment | | 1,300 | |
| | | | 2,650 |
| Current assets: | | | |
| Work in progress | | 4,700 | |
| Debtors | 6,800 | | |
| *deduct:* Provision for bad debts | 200 | | |
| | | 6,600 | |
| Balance at bank | | 600 | |
| *deduct:* Current liabilities: | | 11,900 | |
| Creditors | | 1,300 | |
| | | | 10,600 |
| | | | £13,250 |
| Financed by: | | | |
| Partners' capital accounts: | | £ | £ |
| Tick | | 6,900 | |
| Cross | | 6,350 | |
| | | | £13,250 |

WORKINGS

(1) Calculation of goodwill

| | Tick £ | Cross £ |
|---|---|---|
| Average profits for previous years: | | |
| Year ended 31st December 19X2 | 6,000 | 3,500 |
| Year ended 31st December 19X3 | 5,800 | 3,800 |
| Year ended 31st December 19X4 | 4,700 | 3,200 |
| | £16,500 | £10,500 |
| Averages | £5,500 | £3,500 |
| Average profits for previous five years: | £ | £ |
| Year ended 31st December 19X0 | 3,800 | 4,600 |
| Year ended 31st December 19X1 | 4,200 | 3,400 |
| Year ended 31st December 19X2 | 6,000 | 3,500 |
| Year ended 31st December 19X3 | 5,800 | 3,800 |
| Year ended 31st December 19X4 | 4,700 | 3,200 |
| | £24,500 | £18,500 |
| Averages | £4,900 | £3,700 |

| | | |
|---|---|---|
| Tick: | $1\frac{1}{2}$ × lower of £5,500 and £4,900: | 7,350 |
| Cross: | $1\frac{1}{2}$ × lower of £3,500 and £3,700: | 5,250 |
| | Total value of goodwill: | £12,600 |

(2) Bank

| | £ | | £ |
|---|---|---|---|
| Cash introduced—Cross | 800 | Overdraft brought forward—Tick | 3,800 |
| Introduced by Tick—(paid 1st January) | 3,600 | Balance carried forward | 600 |
| | £4,400 | | £4,400 |

## 8.0 DEATH OR RETIREMENT OF A PARTNER

When a partner withdraws from the partnership, it is necessary to ascertain the amount of capital due to him or his estate. Assets, including goodwill, are therefore revalued and adjusting entries are made to the books of account as for the amalgamation of a partnership.

Money retained in the partnership by the outgoing partner is transferred from his capital and current accounts to a loan account. Interest is usually paid annually for the use by the partnership of this money.

Money withdrawn by the outgoing partner may be taken either in one transaction, or by a series of instalments. Interest is credited to the balance remaining.

*Example*

QUESTION

G, H and J were in partnership sharing profits and losses in the ratio 3:2:1. The balances on their capital accounts were:

| | |
|---|---|
| G | £5,000 |
| H | £3,000 |
| J | £1,000 |

At 31st December 19X1, G retired. The partners agreed to revalue certain assets as follows:

| | Book value at 31st December 19X1 | Revised value |
|---|---|---|
| | £ | £ |
| Furniture and fittings | 610 | 510 |
| Debtors | 2,700 | 2,500 |
| Goodwill | — | 2,000 |

G's current account at the date of retirement showed a debit balance of £165. Investments of £285 book value were transferred to G in part payment and £1,500 was settled in cash at the date of retirement.

The partnership agreement stated that the amount outstanding on retirement was to be transferred to a loan account and repaid (at the end of each year) in three equal instalments, plus interest at 6 per cent per annum on the annual balance.

After G's retirement, profits were to be shared equally, and all assets except goodwill were to remain in the books at their revised values.

Show the partnership accounts giving effect to these transactions.

ANSWER

Furniture and Fittings

| | £ | | £ |
|---|---|---|---|
| Balance brought down | 610 | Capital: Loss on revaluation in profit-sharing ratio: | |
| | | G $\frac{3}{6}$ × £100 | 50 |
| | | H $\frac{2}{6}$ × £100 | 33 |
| | | J $\frac{1}{6}$ × £100 | 17 |
| | | Balance carried down | 510 |
| | £610 | | £610 |

Debtors

| | £ | | £ |
|---|---|---|---|
| Balance brought down | 2,700 | Capital: Bad debts written off in profit-sharing ratio: | |
| | | G $\frac{3}{6}$ × £200 | 100 |
| | | H $\frac{2}{6}$ × £200 | 67 |
| | | J $\frac{1}{6}$ × £200 | 33 |
| | | Balance carried down | 2,500 |
| | £2,700 | | £2,700 |

Capital Accounts

| | G | H | J | | G | H | J |
|---|---|---|---|---|---|---|---|
| | £ | £ | £ | | £ | £ | £ |
| Loss on revaluation of furniture and fittings | 50 | 33 | 17 | Balances brought down | 5,000 | 3,000 | 1,000 |
| Bad debts written off | 100 | 67 | 33 | | | | |
| Goodwill | | 1,000 | 1,000 | Goodwill | 1,000 | 667 | 333 |
| Current account: To settle | 1,950 | | | | | | |
| Loan account: Transfer of balance | 3,900 | | | | | | |
| Balances carried down | | 2,567 | 283 | | | | |
| | £6,000 | £3,667 | £1,333 | | £6,000 | £3,667 | £1,333 |

G—Current Account

| | £ | | £ |
|---|---|---|---|
| Balance brought down | 165 | G—Capital account: | |
| Investments | 285 | *Amount settled to date of* | |
| Cash | 1,500 | *retirement* | 1,950 |
| | £1,950 | | £1,950 |

G—Loan Account

| | £ | | £ |
|---|---|---|---|
| Balance carried down | 3,900 | G—Capital account: | |
| | | *Amount transferred on G's* | |
| | | *retirement* | 3,900 |
| | £3,900 | | £3,900 |

G's loan account will be repaid in annual instalments as follows:

| | Principal £ | Interest £ | Total £ |
|---|---|---|---|
| Sum outstanding at 31st December 19X1 | 3,900 | | |
| Interest at 6% | | 234 | |
| Total repayment: | | | |
| $\frac{1}{3}$ × principal and loan interest to date | (1,300) | (234) | 1,534 |
| Sum outstanding at 31st December 19X2 | 2,600 | | |
| Interest at 6% | | 156 | |
| Total repayment: | | | |
| $\frac{1}{3}$ × total principal and loan interest to date | (1,300) | (156) | 1,456 |
| Sum outstanding at 31st December 19X3 | 1,300 | | |
| Interest at 6% | | 78 | |
| Total repayment: | | | |
| Final $\frac{1}{3}$ × total principal and final amount of loan interest | (1,300) | (78) | 1,378 |

*Note:* In this and other partnership problems it is sometimes necessary to arrive at the value of a partnership between accounting dates. In an examination question it may be necessary to do this by taking the opening net assets (from a balance sheet given in the question) and adding the proportion of profit accrued to the valuation date. To appreciate the logic of this calculation, think back to the fundamental principle you probably learnt at foundation level—that the profit earned by a business must necessarily be reflected in more assets or fewer liabilities. In other words:

Opening net assets + Profit = Closing net assets.

Naturally, it is necessary to allow for drawings and for fresh capital introduced from partners or from outside lenders.

## 9.0 DISSOLUTION OF PARTNERSHIP

### 9.1 Double entry

Table 18 shows the double entry involved in the dissolution of a partnership.

Table 18. DISSOLUTION OF A PARTNERSHIP—DOUBLE ENTRY

| *Transaction* | *Debit* | *Credit* |
|---|---|---|
| Book value of all assets being realised, including those taken over by partners (if any) | Realisation account | Sundry asset accounts |
| Creditors paid off | Creditors' account | Cash account |
| Creditors taken over by purchaser | Creditors' account | Purchaser's account |
| Partners' current accounts transferred to capital accounts | Current accounts | Capital accounts |
| Cash received as part of purchase consideration | Cash account | Purchaser's account |
| Shares issued to partners at agreed value as part of purchase consideration | Partners' capital account | Purchaser's account |
| Purchase consideration being balance on purchaser's account | Purchaser's account | Realisation account |
| Realisation expenses paid | Realisation account | Cash account |
| Profit on realisation divided between partners in profit-sharing ratio (reverse entries for a loss) | Realisation account | Capital accounts |
| Introduction of cash by partner with debit balance on his capital account | Cash account | Capital account |
| Distribution of remaining balance in bank to close partners' capital account | Capital accounts | Cash account |

### 9.2 *Garner* v. *Murray* rule (1904)

If any partner has a debit balance on his capital account, he must introduce sufficient cash to eliminate it. If unable to do this the debit balance must be written off to the other partners' capital accounts in capital account ratio, i.e. the ratio of balances on the capital accounts before the dissolution (*Garner* v. *Murray* (1904)).

## 9.3 Account outlines

A and B are in partnership sharing profits and losses in the ratio of 2:1. The last balance sheet of the business was as follows:

Balance Sheet

| | £ | £ | | £ | £ |
|---|---|---|---|---|---|
| Capital | | | Fixed assets | | 10,000 |
| A | 12,000 | | | | |
| B | 8,000 | | Current assets: | | |
| | | 20,000 | Stock | 3,000 | |
| | | | Debtors | 7,000 | |
| Current liabilities: | | | Bank | 2,000 | |
| Creditors | | 2,000 | | | 12,000 |
| | | £22,000 | | | £22,000 |

The partners agreed to sell the business other than stock and cash to a limited company for the sum of £17,400 to be satisfied as follows:

| | |
|---|---|
| Cash | 1,400 |
| Taking over some of creditors | 1,000 |
| Ordinary shares fully paid | 15,000 |
| | £17,400 |

Expenses of the realisation amounted to £600. B agreed to take over the stock at a valuation of £2,000. The partners agreed to take the ordinary shares in the same proportion as they share profit. The other creditors were duly paid off.

*Note:* In the following outlines, the letters B/S indicate the figures come from the partnership balance sheet.

Realisation Account

| | £ | | | £ |
|---|---|---|---|---|
| Asset accounts: *All partnership assets to be transferred at book value* | 20,000 B/S | Purchaser's account: *Purchase consideration* | | 17,400 C |
| Cash account: *Expenses of realisation* | 600 E | Capital account: *Assets taken over at agreed values* | | 2,000 D |
| | | Capital account: *Loss on realisation in profit-sharing ratio* | A | 800 F |
| | | | B | 400 F |
| | £20,600 | | | £20,600 |

Purchaser's Account

| | £ | | £ |
|---|---|---|---|
| Realisation account: *Purchase consideration* | 17,400 C | Creditors' account: *Taken over* | 1,000 B/S |
| | | Cash account: *Cash paid by purchaser* | 1,400 A |
| | | Shares account: *Shares issued by purchaser* | 15,000 |
| | £17,400 | | £17,400 |

Cash Account

| | £ | | | £ |
|---|---|---|---|---|
| Balance brought down | 2,000 B/S | Creditors' account: *Not taken over* | | 1,000 B/S |
| Purchaser's account: *Cash in discharge of purchase consideration* | 1,400 A | Realisation account: *Expenses of realisation* | | 600 E |
| | | Capital accounts: *To close the accounts* | A | 1,200 G |
| | | | B | 600 G |
| | £3,400 | | | £3,400 |

Partners' Capital Accounts

| | A | B | | A | B |
|---|---|---|---|---|---|
| | £ | £ | | £ | £ |
| Asset accounts: *Asset taken over* | | 2,000 D | Balances brought down | 12,000 | 8,000 B/S |
| Realisation account: *Loss on realisation* | 800 | 400 F | | | |
| Shares account: *Shares of purchasing company issued to partners* | 10,000 | 5,000 B | | | |
| Cash account: *To close the accounts* | 1,200 | 600 G | | | |
| | £12,000 | £8,000 | | £12,000 | £8,000 |

*Notes:*

(1) When shares or debentures are issued in discharge of the purchase consideration, they should be debited to the partners' capital accounts in *profit-sharing ratio* unless the question states otherwise.

(2) The balance on the cash account represents the remaining balances on the capital accounts and these will be closed off by cash payments to the respective partners.

## 10.0 PIECEMEAL REALISATION

Where assets are realised piecemeal the partners may wish to withdraw cash as soon as it is available, rather than wait for all the assets to be realised. It is very important, in these circumstances, to ensure that no partner receives more than he will be ultimately entitled to.

There are two methods by which the interim distributions between partners may be arrived at. These may be remembered as:

(a) the "safe method", and

(b) the "not-so-safe method".

### 10.1 The safe method

This method involves calculating the *maximum possible loss* after each individual realisation.

(a) *Procedure*

(i) Ascertain maximum possible loss by assuming that remaining assets are valueless and no more cash will be received.

(ii) Divide between partners in the normal way.

(iii) Apply *Garner* v. *Murray* if necessary.

(iv) Remaining balance on capital accounts represents amount to be distributed to each partner.

(v) Repeat process until final realisation has been distributed.

*Note:* Calculation and division of the maximum loss after each realisation is not part of the double entry, but is made in a statement in order to arrive at the distributions.

(b) *Pro-forma of the safe method*
A, B and C were in partnership showing profits in the ratio 3:1:1.

Balance Sheet at Date of Dissolution

| | | £ | £ | | £ |
|---|---|---|---|---|---|
| Capital accounts | | | | Sundry assets | 14,000 |
| | A | 8,000 | | | |
| | B | 4,000 | | Cash | 1,000 |
| | C | 1,000 | | | |
| | | | 13,000 | | |
| Creditors | | | 2,000 | | |
| | | | £15,000 | | £15,000 |

Proceeds of the first two realisations of sundry assets were (in order of receipt) (i) £3,000, (ii) £2,000.

| | Partners | | |
|---|---|---|---|
| | A | B | C |
| | £ | £ | £ |
| *First realisation* | | | |
| (i) Capital account balances | 8,000 | 4,000 | 1,000 |
| (ii) Maximum possible loss divided in profit-sharing ratio (£11,000) | 6,600 | 2,200 | 2,200 |
| | 1,400 | 1,800 | (1,200) |
| (iii) Deficiency divided in capital ratio | (800) | (400) | 1,200 |
| (iv) *First distribution* | £600 | £1,400 | — |
| *Second realisation* | | | |
| (v) Deduct (iv) from (i) to give new capital account balances | 7,400 | 2,600 | 1,000 |
| (vi) Maximum possible loss divided in profit-sharing ratio (£9,000) | 5,400 | 1,800 | 1,800 |
| | 2,000 | 800 | (800) |
| (vii) Deficiency divided in *opening* capital ratio | (534) | (266) | 800 |
| *Second distribution* | £1,466 | £534 | — |

*Third and subsequent realisations* follow the above pattern. Remember always to open the new working account with the revised balance on capital account and if the *Garner* v. *Murray* calculation has to be made this will be based on the original opening capital account balances.

## 10.2 The not-so-safe method

This method may lead to an over-distribution to one partner in cases where the solvency of some or all of the partners is in doubt. However, when the financial position of the partners is quite secure it is a perfectly valid approach.

The objective of the method is to bring the partners' capital accounts as rapidly as possible into the same ratio as their profit-sharing arrangements. The process is best explained by means of an illustration.

### *Illustration*

X Y and Z are in partnership sharing profits in the ratio 3:2:1.

Their capital accounts at 31st December 19X9 were:

X £12,000
Y £ 4,000
Z £ 1,000

It was agreed that the partnership should be dissolved at this date, and it was expected that the realisation of the assets would take some time.

Prepare a statement showing the manner in which the proceeds of disposal of the assets should be distributed among the partners, on the assumption that there is no doubt about the solvency of any of the partners.

DISCUSSION

The distribution must proceed by paying all moneys becoming available first to the partner with the highest capital per unit of profit share. When that partner's capital is reduced (by the repayments to him) to the point at which his capital per unit of profit share is the same as that of the partner with the next highest capital per unit of profit share, the two of them share further moneys in their profit-sharing ratio until they "catch up" with the partner with the least capital per unit of profit share.

The first step in the answer must be to calculate the capital per unit of profit share:
In this case Z has £1,000 capital per $\frac{1}{6}$ profit share,
Y has £2,000 capital per $\frac{1}{6}$ profit share,
X has £4,000 capital per $\frac{1}{6}$ profit share.

The first repayments must therefore go to X. He must receive the first £6,000 of realisations. This will reduce his capital to £6,000, at which point his capital will bear the same ratio to his profit share as Y's does to his:

X Capital £6,000, profit share $\frac{3}{6}$,
capital per $\frac{1}{6}$ unit of profit share £2,000;
Y Capital £4,000, profit share $\frac{2}{6}$,
capital per $\frac{1}{6}$ unit of profit share £2,000.

From this point on, X and Y share the proceeds in the ratio 3:2 until their capitals are reduced to £1,000 per $\frac{1}{6}$ of profit share. At this point all three partners can participate in further distribution in their profit-sharing ratios 3:2:1.

ANSWER

| | Partners | | |
|---|---|---|---|
| | X | Y | Z |
| Profit-sharing ratios | 3 | 2 | 1 |
| | £ | £ | £ |
| Opening capital | 12,000 | 4,000 | 1,000 |
| Distribution to equalise capital–profit ratios of X and Y: | 6,000 | | |
| | 6,000 | 4,000 | 1,000 |
| The capital accounts of X and Y are now in the same ratio as their profit shares | | | |
| Distribution to equalise capital–profit ratios of X and Y: | 3,000 | 2,000 | |
| | 3,000 | 2,000 | 1,000 |

The capital accounts of all partners are now in the same ratio as their profit shares, and all can participate in the ratio 3:2:1 in future realisations up to and beyond £17,000, the sum of their original capitals.

PROOF

(Not required to be given when answering a question.)

(a) Consider the position after the first distribution of £6,000 entirely to X. If this were the final distribution there would be a loss of £11,000 on the dissolution (£17,000 minus £6,000), and this would be shared among the partners in their profit-sharing ratios:

| | X | Y | Z |
|---|---|---|---|
| | £ | £ | £ |
| Opening capitals | 12,000 | 4,000 | 1,000 |
| *loss:* £11,000 3:2:1 | 5,500 | 3,667 | 1,833 |
| | 6,500 | 333 | (833) |
| Z's loss allocated between X and Y in profit-sharing ratio 3:2 | (500) | (333) | 833 |
| X's share as calculated above: | £6,000 | — | — |

(b) Next consider the position if the first and second stages totalling £11,000 were the final balance available:

| | X | Y | Z |
|---|---|---|---|
| | £ | £ | £ |
| Opening capitals | 12,000 | 4,000 | 1,000 |
| *loss:* £6,000 3:2:1 | 3,000 | 2,000 | 1,000 |
| Shares of X and Y as calculated above: | £9,000 | 2,000 | — |

## 11.0 CONVERSION OF A PARTNERSHIP TO A LIMITED COMPANY

This follows the same rules as a dissolution in the books of the partnership. In this case the limited company effectively buys the partnership as a going concern.

### 11.1 Additional accounts required

When the partnership is to be sold as a viable business, in addition to the normal accounts, the following are required:

(a) *Realisation account*
A "trading account" for the sale of a business. It records the book value of *assets*, the purchase consideration for the assets, and the profit or loss on realisation.

(b) *Account with purchaser*
A personal account showing the amount due from the purchaser for assets taken over, and the form in which payment is made (usually cash or shares, and creditors taken over).

*Detailed example*

QUESTION

Moore, Gate and Place were trading in partnership, sharing profits and losses in the ratio 5:4:3 respectively.

On 31st March 19X1 they formed a limited company with an authorised capital of £20,000 in shares of £1 each (to be divided into different classes) to take over the business of the partnership.

The trial balance of the partnership, subject to charging interest on partners' capital accounts, on 31st March 19X1 was:

| | £ | £ |
|---|---|---|
| Capital accounts as on 31st March 19X0: | | |
| Moore | | 6,300 |
| Gate | | 4,200 |
| Place | | 2,100 |
| Drawings: | | |
| Moore | 2,000 | |
| Gate | 2,000 | |
| Place | 1,500 | |
| Plant and machinery at cost | 8,500 | |
| Depreciation of plant and machinery | | 2,500 |
| Stocks and work in progress | 6,420 | |
| Debtors | 6,650 | |
| Creditors | | 8,470 |
| Bank balance | 8,830 | |
| Trading profit for the year | | 12,330 |
| | £35,900 | £35,900 |

The partnership deed provided for interest to be paid on partners' capital accounts at the rate of 5 per cent per annum on the balance at the beginning of the year.

You ascertain that:

(a) Plant and machinery is to be transferred at its written-down value for income tax, which is £6,600.

(b) To avoid having to value goodwill, shares in the company are to be issued to the partners, at par, in such numbers and such classes as will give the partners, by reason of their shareholdings alone, the same rights as regards interest on capital and the sharing of profits and losses as they had in the partnership.

(c) Before transferring the business the partners wish to draw from the partnership their profits to such an extent that the bank balance is reduced to £5,000. For this purpose, sufficient profits of the year are to be retained in profit-sharing ratio.

(d) All assets and liabilities, except plant and machinery and the bank balance, are to be transferred at their value in the books of the partnership as on 31st March 19X1.

*You are required to prepare:*

(a) the profit and loss appropriation account of the partnership for the year ended 31st March 19X1;

(b) the capital accounts (in columnar form), showing all the adjustments required to dissolve the partnership;

(c) your computation of the number of shares of each class to be issued by the company to each of the partners and details of the rights attaching to those shares; and

(d) the balance sheet of the company immediately after acquiring the business of the partnership and issuing the shares.

ANSWER

(a)

Moore, Gate and Place
Profit and Loss Appropriation Account
for the year ended 31st March 19X1

| | £ | £ | | £ |
|---|---|---|---|---|
| Interest on capital: | | | Net profit | 12,330 |
| Moore | 315 | | | |
| Gate | 210 | | | |
| Place | 105 | 630 | | |
| Share of profits: | | | | |
| Moore | 4,875 | | | |
| Gate | 3,900 | | | |
| Place | 2,925 | 11,700 | | |
| | | £12,330 | | £12,330 |

(b)

Capital Accounts

| | | Moore | Gate | Place | | | Moore | Gate | Place |
|---|---|---|---|---|---|---|---|---|---|
| | | £ | £ | £ | | | £ | £ | £ |
| 19X1 | | | | | 19X0 | | | | |
| Mar 31 | Drawings | 2,000 | 2,000 | 1,500 | Apr 1 | Balance | 6,300 | 4,200 | 2,100 |
| | Pref. shares | 6,300 | 4,200 | 2,100 | 19X1 | | | | |
| | Ord. shares | 1,500 | 1,200 | 900 | Mar 31 | Interest on capital | 315 | 210 | 105 |
| | Cash | 1,910 | 1,110 | 780 | | Share of profits | 4,875 | 3,900 | 2,925 |
| | | | | | | Profit on realisation | 250 | 200 | 150 |
| | | £11,740 | 8,510 | 5,280 | | | £11,740 | 8,510 | 5,280 |

(c)

Allocation of Shares

To preserve interest rights: 5 per cent preference shares to be issued in settlement of opening capital balance

To preserve shares of profit: Ordinary shares to be issued in profit-sharing ratio.

| | 5% Preference | Ordinary |
|---|---|---|
| Moore | 6,300 | 1,500 |
| Gate | 4,200 | 1,200 |
| Place | 2,100 | 900 |
| | 12,600 | 3,600 |

(d) Company Balance Sheet

| | £ | £ |
|---|---|---|
| Share capital | | |
| Authorised: | | |
| 15,000 5% preference shares of £1 each | 15,000 | |
| 5,000 ordinary shares of £1 each | 5,000 | |
| | 20,000 | |
| Issued: | | |
| 12,600 5% preference shares of £1 each fully paid | | 12,600 |
| 3,600 ordinary shares of £1 each fully paid | | 3,600 |
| | | 16,200 |
| Fixed assets: | | |
| Plant and machinery at cost | | 6,600 |
| Current assets: | | |
| Stock and work in progress | 6,420 | |
| Debtors | 6,650 | |
| Bank balance | 5,000 | |
| | 18,070 | |
| *deduct:* Current liabilities: | | |
| Creditors | 8,470 | 9,600 |
| | | £16,200 |

*Note:* Ordinary share distribution

| | £ |
|---|---|
| Net profit | 12,330 |
| Profit on realisation | 600 |
| | 12,930 |
| *less:* Drawings | 5,500 |
| | 7,430 |
| Agreed reduction on cash | 3,830 |
| Balance of profits retained | £3,600 |

| Share: | | |
|---|---|---|
| Moore | $\frac{5}{12} \times 3,600$: | 1,500 shares |
| Gate | $\frac{1}{3} \times 3,600$: | 1,200 shares |
| Place | $\frac{1}{4} \times 3,600$: | 900 shares |
| | | 3,600 |

## PROGRESS TEST 8

1. Draw a block diagram to illustrate partnership accounts. (1.0)
2. What types of partnership agreement exist? List the subject matter contained in a typical agreement. (2.1)

3. What are the duties of partners as laid down by the Partnership Act 1890. (2.2(b))
4. What are the two situations which must be distinguished in capital accounts? (3.2)
5. Describe the two ways in which profit may be split. (4.2)
6. Name five sources of goodwill. (6.2)
7. Draw a block diagram illustrating the various goodwill adjustments arising on changes in a partnership. (6.6)
8. What situations can arise in cases where an incoming partner pays cash for goodwill. (6.8)
9. What adjustments need to be made to a company's accounts in the case of an amalgamation with another company? (7.2)
10. What procedures govern the retirement or death of a partner. (8.0)
11. What is the safe method whereby the interim distributions between partners in the case of a piecemeal realisation of assets may be made? (10.1)
12. Outline the "not-so-safe" method? (10.2)
13. What additional accounts are required when a partnership is converted into a limited company? (11.1)

CHAPTER NINE

# Incomplete Records, Including the Accounts of Clubs and Societies

## 1.0 RECEIPTS AND PAYMENTS ACCOUNTS

### 1.1 Definition

A receipts and payments account is a summary of *actual* cash *received* and *paid* during the period:

(a) It is prepared by clubs, associations and non-profit-making organisations which do not prepare income and expenditure account and balance sheet.

(b) It is also used as a basis for preparing accounts for incomplete records.

### 1.2 Pro-forma account

| Receipts | | £ | Payments | £ |
|---|---|---|---|---|
| Opening bank (or cash) balance | | 990 | Bar purchases | 4,120 |
| Subscriptions received | | | Wages | 710 |
| Arrears for previous years | 30 | | Repairs to pavilion | 130 |
| Current year | 370 | | Group upkeep | 50 |
| In advance for future years | 10 | 410 | Secretary's expenses | 20 |
| | | | Coach hire | 40 |
| Bar sales | | 5,300 | Prizes | 10 |
| Donations | | 250 | Games equipment | 60 |
| Sale of refreshments | | 140 | Rent and rates | 230 |
| Sale of dance tickets | | 80 | Printing and stationery | 70 |
| Investment interest | | 40 | Purchase of investments | 340 |
| Competition fees | | 50 | Bank charges | 30 |
| Sale of old lawn mower | | 10 | Closing bank (or cash) balance | 2,220 |
| Entrance fees | | 60 | | |
| Sale of land | | 700 | | |
| | | £8,030 | | £8,030 |

### 1.3 Contents

(a) Opening bank (or cash) balance.

(b) Summary of amounts *actually* received or paid during the period. No adjustment is made for accrued income and expenditure.

(c) Deals with both capital and revenue items.

(d) Receipts entered on debit side (as in a normal cash book).

(e) Payments entered on credit side (as in a normal cash book).

(f) Closing balance represents bank balance (or cash in hand).

### 1.4 Sundry matters

To prepare an income and expenditure account from a receipts and payments account all the revenue items are adjusted for accruals and prepayments. Capital items appear in the balance sheet. Note that for a receipts and payments account, as there is no balance sheet, all items, whether capital or revenue, appear in the receipts and payments account.

## 2.0 INCOME AND EXPENDITURE ACCOUNTS

### 2.1 Definition

An income and expenditure account is the equivalent of the profit and loss account of a non-trading concern such as a club, association or school.

### 2.2 Pro-forma income and expenditure account and balance sheet

Income and Expenditure Account

| Expenditure | £ | Income | | £ |
|---|---|---|---|---|
| Wages | 710 | Subscriptions for year | | 500 |
| Repairs to equipment | 150 | Bar sales | 5,300 | |
| Rent and rates | 300 | *deduct:* Expenses | 4,000 | |
| Printing and stationery | 70 | *Bar profit* | | 1,300 |
| Loss on sale of lawn mower | 10 | Donations | | 250 |
| Depreciation of fixed assets | 150 | Competition fees | | 50 |
| Balance: | | Investment interest | | 40 |
| Excess of income over expenditure | 750 | | | |
| | £2,140 | | | £2,140 |

Balance Sheet

| | £ | £ | | £ | £ |
|---|---|---|---|---|---|
| General fund | | | Fixed assets | | |
| Balance brought forward | 1,400 | | Furniture and equipment at cost | 1,700 | |
| *add:* Excess of income over expenditure for the year | 750 | 2,150 | *deduct:* Depreciation | 280 | 1,420 |
| | | | Current assets | | |
| | | | Bar stock | 200 | |
| | | | Subscriptions due | 50 | |
| Current liabilities | | | Prepayments | 80 | |
| Expenses | 90 | | Cash at bank | 500 | |
| Competition | 10 | 100 | | | 830 |
| | | £2,250 | | | £2,250 |

## 2.3 Contents

The income and expenditure account:

(a) Summarises all items relating to income and expenditure on an accruals basis, taking into account outstanding income or expenses.

(b) Deals only with revenue items.

(c) Contains income entered on *Credit* side.

(d) Contains expenditure entered on *Debit* side.

(e) Shows a balance representing surplus or deficit for the period, which is taken to "general fund" or "accumulated fund" in the balance sheet.

## 2.4 Main forms of income

(a) *Subscriptions:* the figure shown in the income and expenditure account will be that of the subscriptions relating to the accounting period. Any subscriptions in arrears or advance at the balance sheet date will appear in the balance sheet.

(b) *Income from a bar, socials etc.* will be shown net, i.e. after expenses have been deducted. Very often a bar account (similar to a trading account) will be required.

(c) *Donations:*

(i) for general running expenses may be shown in the income and expenditure account;

(ii) for the immediate purchase of or in the form of capital equipment will be added to the "accumulated fund" or "general fund" in the balance sheet;

(iii) towards a specific fund, e.g. development fund will be shown as additions to the fund in the balance sheet (this fund will be shown separately from the "accumulated" or "general fund").

If donations are to be capitalised they should not appear in the income and expenditure account but should be added to the "accumulated fund".

## 2.5 Notes on balance sheet

(a) *Accumulated fund*
Normally the term capital will not be found but instead there will be an "accumulated fund" or a "general fund". This fund represents the net assets of the concern and is found in the same way as the capital. It is usually necessary to find the value of the fund at the start of the period by deducting the opening liabilities from the opening assets.

(b) *Special funds*
These funds may be set aside for a specific purpose and may represent a legacy given for that purpose, e.g. a prize fund. The fund should be represented by specific assets in the balance sheet. The fund will be shown as a separate item in the balance sheet.

Any income or expenditure in respect of the fund will not appear in the income and expenditure account but will be shown in a separate supporting statement or adjusted on the face of the balance sheet.

# 3.0 INCOMPLETE RECORDS

Accounting procedures for incomplete records are outlined in Fig. 7.

## 3.1 Examination technique

The following procedure should be adopted when dealing with this type of question:

(a) Study examiner's requirements.

(b) Open up accounts required by examiner which may include:

(i) trading account,

(ii) profit and loss account,

(iii) balance sheet.

(c) Glance through rest of question.

(d) Adjust the summary of bank statements for errors, omissions, outstanding cheques and uncredited items.

(e) Then work through the question line by line.

(f) Arrive at opening capital, if not given, by reconstructing the opening balance sheet.

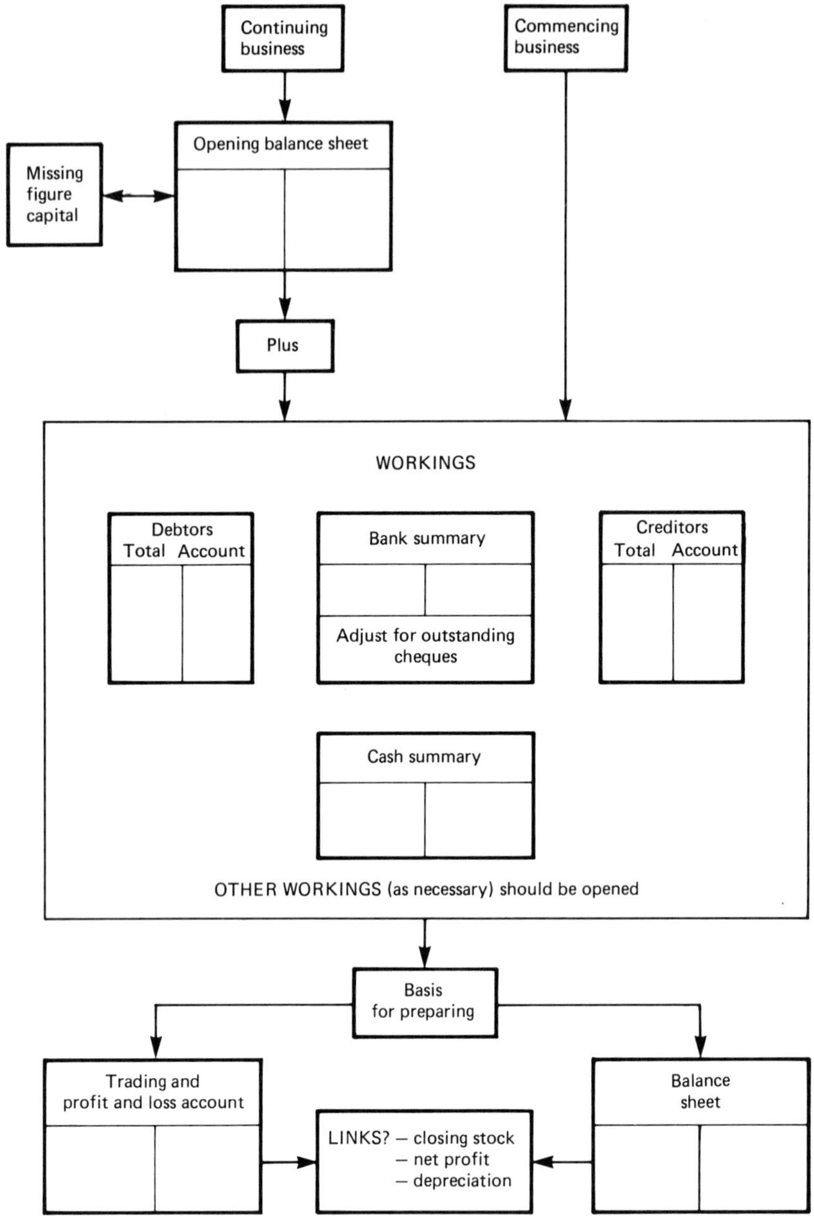


Fig. 7. *Accounting procedures for incomplete records.*

(g) Use the summary prepared at (d) above to post into the accounts, adjusting for opening or closing accruals at the same time.

(h) Where the figures require difficult adjustments, use "T" accounts on the working sheet.

(i) It is nearly always essential to open up a cash account in order to deal correctly with the cash position.

(j) Always aim at "building up" the whole of the answer, on a simultaneous basis rather than completing one account at a time.

## 3.2 Account outlines for workings

Cash Account

| | £ | | £ |
|---|---|---|---|
| Balance brought down | 200 | Cash purchases | 950 |
| Balance = Takings: | | Wages: *Debited in profit and* | |
| *Transferred to debtors account* | 2,360 | *loss account* | 460 |
| | | Expenses: *Debited in profit and* | |
| | | *loss account* | 680 |
| | | Drawings: *Debited to current* | |
| | | *account (or capital account)* | 300 |
| | | Balance carried down | 170 |
| | £2,560 | | £2,560 |

Total Debtors Account

| | £ | | £ |
|---|---|---|---|
| Balance brought down | 400 | Cash received | 2,360 |
| Balance = Total sales | 2,600 | Discounts allowed: *Debited in* | |
| | | *profit and loss account* | 200 |
| | | Bad debts: *Debited in profit* | |
| | | *and loss account* | 60 |
| | | Balance carried down | 380 |
| | £3,000 | | £3,000 |

Total Creditors Account

| | £ | | £ |
|---|---|---|---|
| Cash paid | 950 | Balance brought down | 350 |
| Discounts received: *Credited* | | Balance = purchases | 1,050 |
| *in profit and loss account* | 70 | | |
| Balance carried down | 380 | | |
| | £1,400 | | £1,400 |

## 3.3 Missing figures

A feature of all incomplete records questions is the concept of missing figures found by balancing accounts. The usual missing figures are listed in Table 19, also the means of finding them.

Table 19. INCOMPLETE RECORDS—USUAL FIGURES MISSING

| *Missing figure* | *How found* |
|---|---|
| (a) Opening capital | Prepare opening balance sheet |
| (b) Cash takings | Balance on cash account |
| (c) Sales | Balance on debtors account |
| (d) Purchases | Balance on creditors account |
| (e) Closing stock | Balance on trading account after entering gross profit based on usual percentage |

### *Example*

QUESTION

Jones is a retail trader who fails to keep proper books of account. His accounts are prepared annually to 31st December from his bank statements, vouchers, paying-in books and cheque book stubs.

His balance sheet at 31st December 19X3 was as follows:

| | | £ | | £ |
|---|---|---|---|---|
| Capital | | 2,500 | Fixtures | 500 |
| Creditors: | | | Stock | 480 |
| Goods | 310 | | Debtors | 86 |
| Electricity | 24 | 334 | Prepayment—rates | 20 |
| | | | Balance at bank | 1,703 |
| | | | Cash | 45 |
| | | £2,834 | | £2,834 |

A summary of his bank statements shows the following position:

| | £ | | £ |
|---|---|---|---|
| Balance at 1st January 19X4 | 1,703 | Goods for resale | 10,910 |
| Cash banked | 12,120 | Rent | 450 |
| Credit from customer paid | | Electricity | 218 |
| direct to bank | 106 | Rates: year to 31st March 19X5 | 96 |
| | | Sundry expenses | 90 |
| | | Private expenses | 405 |
| | | Balance: 31st December 19X4 | 1,760 |
| | £13,929 | | £13,929 |

The following further information is obtained from Jones:

(a) Cash takings are banked with the exception of cash used for the following weekly payments: wages £18, sundry expenses £1.50, goods for resale £12, drawings £25.

(b) £500 cash from the sale of private furniture was paid into the bank.

(c) Goods taken for private use during the year 19X4 by Jones were estimated to cost £520.

(d) At 31st December 19X4, debtors were £140, creditors for goods £610, creditors for electricity £51, rent £150. Cash in hand was £32, stock was valued at £575 and fixtures at £450.

Prepare the trading and profit and loss account for the year ended 31st December 19X4 and a balance sheet at that date.

ANSWER

Jones: Trading and Profit and Loss Account
for the year ended 31st December 19X4

| | | | |
|---|---|---|---|
| | | | £ |
| Sales | | | 14,705 |
| *deduct:* Cost of sales: | | £ | |
| Stock at 1st January 19X4 | | 480 | |
| Purchases | | 11,314 | |
| | | 11,794 | |
| *deduct:* Stock at 31st December 19X4 | | 575 | 11,219 |
| Gross profit | | | 3,486 |
| Wages | | 936 | |
| Rent | | 600 | |
| Rates | | 92 | |
| Electricity | | 245 | |
| Sundry expenses | | 168 | |
| Depreciation of fixtures | | 50 | 2,091 |
| Net profit | | | £1,395 |

Jones: Balance Sheet at 31st December 19X4

| | | | |
|---|---|---|---|
| Fixed assets: | | £ | £ |
| Fixtures | | 500 | |
| *less:* Depreciation | | 50 | 450 |
| Current assets: | | | |
| Stock | | 575 | |
| Debtors | | 140 | |
| Prepayment—rates | | 24 | |
| Balance at bank | | 1,760 | |
| Cash | | 32 | |
| | | 2,531 | |
| *deduct:* Current liabilities: | | | |
| Creditors trade | 610 | | |
| expenses | 201 | 811 | 1,720 |
| | | | £2,170 |

| | £ | £ |
|---|---|---|
| Capital: | | |
| At 1st January 19X4 | 2,500 | |
| Capital introduced | 500 | |
| Net profit | 1,395 | |
| | 4,395 | |
| *less:* Drawings | 2,225 | £2,170 |

WORKINGS

(a) Cash Book

| | £ | | £ |
|---|---|---|---|
| Balance brought forward | 45 | Bankings | 12,120 |
| Sales | 14,545 | Wages | 936 |
| Capital | 500 | Sundry expenses | 78 |
| | | Purchases | 624 |
| | | Drawings | 1,300 |
| | | Balance carried forward | 32 |
| | £15,090 | | £15,090 |

(b) Total Debtors Account

| | £ | | | £ |
|---|---|---|---|---|
| Balance brought forward | 86 | Cash received | 14,545 | |
| Sales: Trading account | 14,705 | Bank | 106 | 14,651 |
| | | Balance carried forward | | 140 |
| | £14,791 | | | £14,791 |

(c) Total Creditors Account

| | | £ | | £ |
|---|---|---|---|---|
| Cash paid | 624 | | Balance brought forward | 310 |
| Bank | 10,910 | 11,534 | Purchases | 11,834 |
| Balance carried forward | | 610 | | |
| | | £12,144 | | £12,144 |

(d) Purchases in trading account £11,834 − goods for private use £520 = £11,314.

(e) Electricity

| | £ | | £ |
|---|---|---|---|
| Bank | 218 | Balance brought forward | 24 |
| Balance carried forward | 51 | Profit and loss account | 245 |
| | £269 | | £269 |

(f) Rates

| | £ | | £ |
|---|---|---|---|
| Balance brought forward | 20 | Profit and loss account | 92 |
| Bank | 96 | Balance carried forward | 24 |
| | £116 | | £116 |

(g) Drawings

| | £ |
|---|---|
| Cash | 1,300 |
| Cheque | 405 |
| Goods | 520 |
| | £2,225 |

(h) Rent

| | £ | | £ |
|---|---|---|---|
| Bank | 450 | Profit and loss account | 600 |
| Balance carried forward | 150 | | |
| | £600 | | £600 |

TUTORIAL NOTE

Once experience has been gained at working through incomplete records questions, it will be possible not to use so many "T" accounts in the workings. Instead, the figures which would have appeared in the "T" accounts can be put on the face of the actual answer.

Example: for Sales in the above questions (Trading Account extract)

| | £ |
|---|---|
| Sales (−86 + 14,545 + 106 + 140) | 14,705 |

It is, however, important to master the principles of incomplete records before this method is used.

## PROGRESS TEST 9

1. What are receipts and payments accounts? (1.1)
2. What are income and expenditure accounts? (2.1)
3. What are taken to be the main forms of income that must be recorded in the accounts mentioned in question 2? (2.4)
4. Draw a diagram illustrating the accounting procedures used in the case of incomplete records. (3.0)
5. What technique should you employ when answering incomplete records questions? (3.1)

CHAPTER TEN

# Miscellaneous Accounts

## 1.0 SELLING AGENCY AND AUTONOMOUS BRANCHES

Figure 8 outlines two accounting systems which may be used for branch accounts.

### 1.1 System one—selling agency

(a) *Accounts required and their purposes*

(i) *Branch stock account:*

(1) maintained at estimated selling price (invoice price);

(2) controls branch stocks;

(3) balance should represent selling price of branch stocks in hand;

(4) any difference between physical stocks and the balance on the account must be investigated.

(ii) *Branch mark-up account:*

(1) opening balance represents provision for unrealised profit on stocks brought forward;

(2) this account records anticipated profits on goods sent to branch;

(3) balance carried forward, representing unrealised profit on closing stocks, is deducted from branch stock account balance, thus reducing stock to cost for balance sheet purposes;

(4) gross profit of the branch will be the balancing figure on the account.

(Hence it is *not* normally necessary to prepare trading account, although the examiner sometimes requires this.)

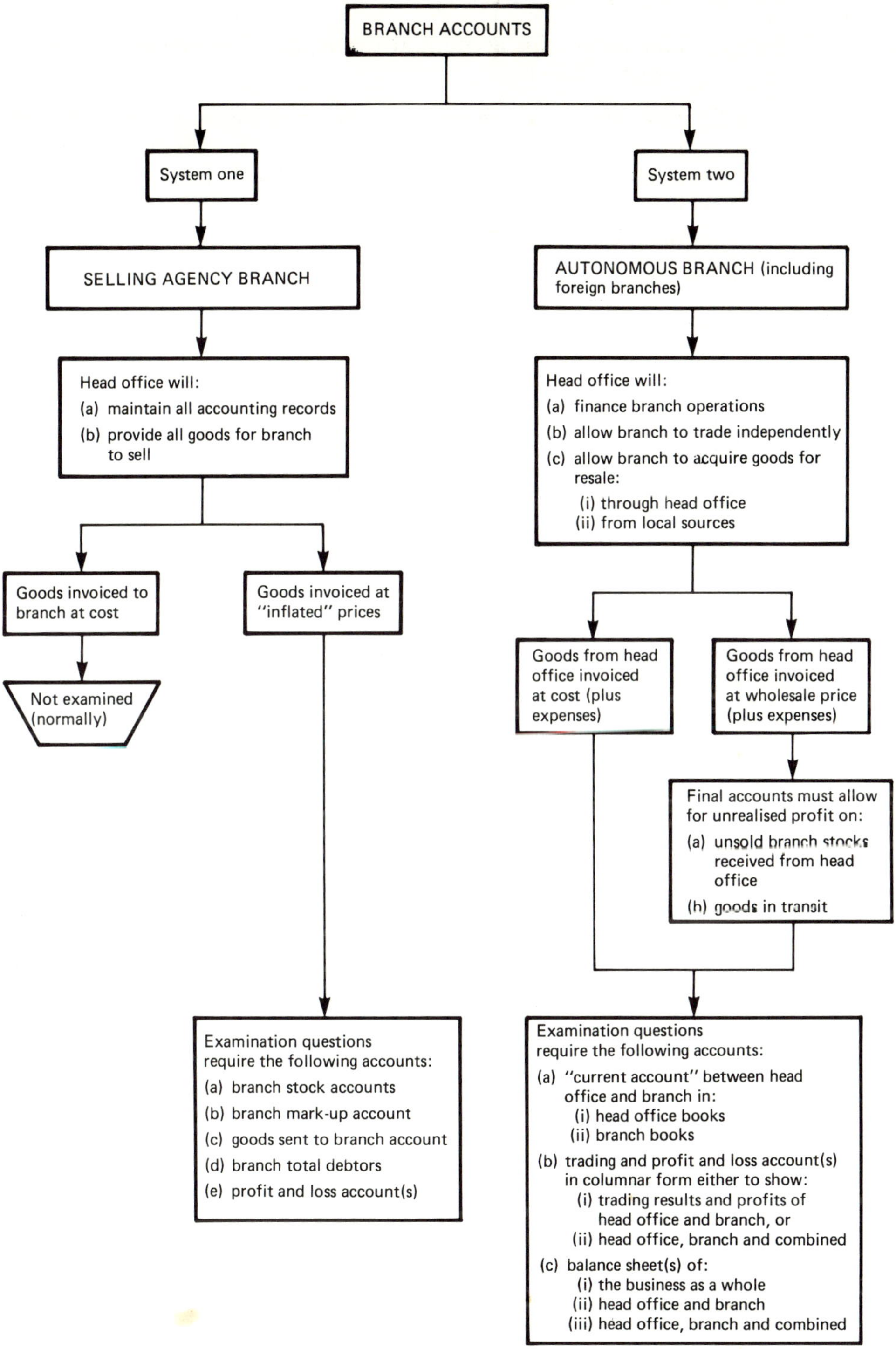


Fig. 8. *Accounting systems for branch accounts.*

(iii) *Goods sent to branch account:*

(1) amount on this account at the year end represents cost of goods sent to branch;

(2) this figure is credited to the purchases account to reduce purchases to goods dealt with by head office (or if head office is not a selling organisation, the stocks held on behalf of branches at the year end); this account has neither an opening nor a closing balance.

(iv) *Branch total debtors account:* used to control branch debtors.

(v) *Profit and loss account:* provides a useful way of breaking down profits and losses by branches and is normally prepared in columnar form where there is more than one branch. As the gross profit is shown in the mark-up account it is not necessary to prepare a trading account unless the examiner specifically requires this.

(vi) *Balance sheet:* not normally required by the examiner under this system. However, if it is required, stock is shown at cost, which is arrived at by deducting the balance carried down on the mark-up account from that on the branch stock account.

(b) *Sundry matters*

(i) Branch stock account is a practical means of controlling stock at branches. Supervisors can quickly ascertain the selling price of stocks at a branch and compare this with the balance shown in the head office books. Such spot checks will immediately bring to light:

(1) normal differences, e.g. wastage, evaporation, minor miscalculation of selling price, or errors in stocktaking;

(2) abnormal differences, e.g. goods or cash stolen.

(ii) This method prevents branch staff from knowing the cost of goods being sold and preserves secrecy with regard to profits.

(iii) Ascertaining the percentages or fraction to deduct from invoice price may cause some students difficulty. No doubt it is appreciated that the percentage to be deducted from selling price is not the same as that which is added to cost, e.g., if $33\frac{1}{3}$ per cent is added to cost to arrive at invoice price then 25 per cent must be deducted from selling price to get back to cost.

This calculation is necessary to arrive at:

(1) mark-up on closing stock;

(2) mark-up on returns to head office.

(iv) This accounting system is also appropriate to departmental accounts.

(c) *Double entry*

The double entry in selling agency accounts is shown in Table 20.

Table 20. SELLING AGENCY ACCOUNTS—DOUBLE ENTRY

| *Transactions* | *Debit* | *Credit* |
|---|---|---|
| Cost of goods sent to branch | Branch stock account | Goods sent to branch account |
| Mark-up on goods sent to branch | Branch stock account | Branch mark-up account |
| Cost of goods returned by branch to head office | Goods sent to branch account | Branch stock account |
| Mark-up on goods returned by branch to head office | Branch mark-up account | Branch stock account |
| Cash sales | Cash account | Branch stock account |
| Credit sales | Branch debtors account | Branch stock account |
| Returns from credit customers | Branch stock account | Branch debtors account |
| Discounts allowed to credit customers | Branch profit and loss account | Branch debtors account |
| Bad debts written off | Branch profit and loss account | Branch debtors account |
| Cost of stock lost from branch | Branch profit and loss account | Branch stock account |
| Mark-up on stock lost from branch | Branch mark-up account | Branch stock account |
| Amount of cash lost from branch | Branch profit and loss account | Branch stock account |
| Amount of normal stock loss of branch | Branch mark-up account | Branch stock account |
| Balance on branch mark-up account being gross profit of branch | Branch mark-up account | Branch profit and loss account |
| Balance on goods sent to branch account being cost of goods sent for period | Goods sent to branch account | Purchases account |

(d) *Account outlines*

The following figures are used to illustrate the outline accounts. All purchases are made by the head office and goods are invoiced to branch at selling price, which is cost plus $33\frac{1}{3}$ per cent.

At the beginning of the year, stock at the branch, at selling price amounted to £400 and debtors to £360.

During the year the following transactions took place at the branch:

| | £ |
|---|---:|
| Cash sales | 170 |
| Credit sales | 1,240 |
| Goods received from head office, at selling price | 1,200 |
| Goods returned to head office, at selling price | 80 |
| Goods returned by customers | 100 |
| Cash received from debtors | 1,210 |
| Bad debts written off | 20 |
| Discounts allowed to debtors | 80 |

At the end of the year the branch stock at selling price amounted to £200.

(i) Branch Stock Account (Selling Price)

| | £ | | £ |
|---|---|---|---|
| Balance brought down: *Being selling price of opening stocks* | 400 | Goods returned to head office: *At invoiced price* | 80 B |
| Goods sent to branch: *At invoiced price* | 1,200 A | Cash account: *Cash sales* | 170 |
| Branch debtors account: *Returns from customers* | 100 D | Branch debtors account: *Credit sales* | 1,240 C |
| | | Branch mark-up account: *Normal difference transferred* | 10 E |
| | | Balance carried forward: *Being selling price of closing stock* | 200 |
| | £1,700 | | £1,700 |

(ii) Branch Mark-Up Account

| | £ | | £ |
|---|---|---|---|
| Branch stock account: *Mark-up on goods returned to Head Office* | 20 B | Balance brought down: *Being mark-up on opening stock* | 100 |
| Branch stock account: *Difference* | 10 E | Branch stock account: *Mark-up on goods sent to branch* | 300 A |
| Profit and loss account: *Being the transfer of the balance of the account which is the actual gross profit earned* | 320 | | |
| Balance carried down: *Being mark-up on closing stock* | 50 | | |
| | £400 | | £400 |

(iii) Goods Sent to Branch Account

| | £ | | £ |
|---|---|---|---|
| Branch stock account: *Cost of goods returned by branch* | 60 B | Branch stock account: *Cost of goods sent to branch* | 900 A |
| Purchases: *Elimination from Head Office purchases of goods acquired for the branch* | 840 | | |
| | £900 | | £900 |

(This account will have neither an opening nor a closing balance.)

(iv) Branch Debtors Account

| | £ | | £ |
|---|---|---|---|
| Balance brought down: *Opening debtors at the branch* | 360 | Cash account: *Cash from debtors* | 1,210 |
| Branch stock account: *Credit sales* | 1,240 C | Profit and loss account: *Bad debts written off* | 20 |
| | | Profit and loss account: *Discounts allowed* | 80 |
| | | Branch stock account: *Returns* | 100 D |
| | | Balance carried down: *Closing debtors at the branch* | 190 |
| | £1,600 | | £1,600 |

## 1.2 System two—autonomous branch

(a) *Legal aspects*
There is no law relating to branch accounts but examination problems under this heading are frequently linked to either *partnership* or *company* account problems. Answering such problems will therefore require a knowledge of branch accounting as well as the legal matters appropriate to partnership or company accounting.

(b) *Accounts required and their purpose*

(i) *Branch current account* (head office books)

(1) records all transactions between head office and branch;

(2) the balance represents the investment made by head office in the branch.

(ii) *Head office current account* (branch books)

(1) records all transactions between branch and head office;

(2) the balance represents the branch's capital;

(3) profit and loss account balance must be transferred to this account at the end of the period.

(iii) *Final accounts*

(1) *Examination questions*. Two types of problem arise in examinations:

*either* (A) transfers between head office and branch are made at cost,

*or* (B) transfers between head office and branch are made at "wholesale" price which will include a small element of profit. In such cases, the examiner frequently requires the final columnar accounts to show in the *branch column* goods from head office and stocks at *invoiced price* but to reduce these to *cost* in the combined column.

(2) Trading account: *head office* column records transactions from point of view of head office. Shows all purchases made by head office, sales to customers and transfers to the branch at "wholesale" price.

(3) Trading account: *branch column* records transactions from point of view of branch. Shows goods received from head office at "wholesale" price and local purchases at cost. Stocks of goods from head office valued at "wholesale" price (i.e., includes an element of unrealised profit from the point of view of the business as a whole), stocks of local purchases valued at cost.

(4) Trading account: *combined column* shows transactions from point of view of business as a whole, profits between head office and branch being eliminated.

Gross profit figures will not cross-cast to the combined gross profit.

(5) Profit and loss account: provisions for unrealised profit on goods *received* by branch and on goods in transit entered in head office column.

Net profit figures will crosscast to the combined net profit.

(6) Balance sheet:

(A) Current accounts will appear in head office and branch columns but not in combined columns.

(B) Provision for unrealised profits on branch stock and goods in transit will appear under current liabilities in the head office column but will be deducted from the stock figures in the combined column.

(7) The "combined" column in the trading, profit and loss account and balance sheet is not a part of the double entry. The individual

columns of the head office and the branch should always be prepared first and the combined column prepared from these individual columns.

(c) *Sundry matters*

(i) Current accounts must always be equal and opposite.

(ii) Head office current account in the branch books should always have a credit balance.

(iii) Branch current account in head office books should always have a debit balance.

(iv) Goods in transit and cash in transit must always be adjusted in head office books (regardless of the direction in which it is in transit).

(v) The final entry to close the current account will be the transfer of branch profit to head office.

(d) *Double entry*
The double entry in autonomous branch accounts is shown in Table 21.

Table 21. AUTONOMOUS BRANCH ACCOUNTS—DOUBLE ENTRY

| *In Head Office Books* | | |
|---|---|---|
| *Transactions* | *Debit* | *Credit* |
| Invoice value of goods sent to branch (may be cost or "wholesale" price) | Branch current account | Goods sent to branch account |
| Cash received from branch | Cash account | Branch current account |
| Expenses of branch paid by head office (if any) | Branch current account | Cash account (or expense creditors account) |
| Profit of branch transferred into head office books | Branch current account | Profit and loss account |
| Provision for unrealised profit where goods are invoiced to branch at cost plus a mark-up | Profit and loss account | Provision for unrealised profit account |

| *In Branch Books* | | |
|---|---|---|
| *Transactions* | *Debit* | *Credit* |
| Invoice value of goods received by branch (will not be the same as goods sent by head office because of goods in transit) | Goods received from head office account | Head office current account |

*continued*

Table 21.—*cont.*

| *In Branch Books* | | |
|---|---|---|
| *Transactions* | *Debit* | *Credit* |
| Cash sent to head office (will not be the same as cash received by head office because of cash in transit) | Head office current account | Cash account |
| Expenses paid by head office on behalf of branch | Relevant expense account | Head office current account |
| Profit of branch transferred into head office books | Profit and loss account | Head office current account |

(e) *Account outlines*

(i) *Head office books*

Current Account with Branch

| | £ | | £ |
|---|---|---|---|
| Balance brought forward: *Representing the investment in the branch at the beginning of the year* | 20,000 | Goods sent to branch account: *Being invoiced value of goods returned by branch* | 6,000 |
| Goods sent to branch account: *Being invoiced value of goods sent to branch: may include a profit element* | 84,000 | Cash account: *Remittances* received *from the branch during the year* | 70,000 |
| Sundry expenses account: *Expense paid on behalf of the branch* | 4,000 | Balance carried forward: *Invoice value of goods not received by the branch until after the year end* | 4,000 |
| Profit and loss account: *Being branch profit for the year* | 16,000 | Balance carried forward: *Cash remitted by the branch before the year end but not received by head office until after the year end* | 2,000 |
| | | Balance carried forward: *Representing the year end investment in the branch* | 42,000 |
| | £124,000 | | £124,000 |

*Notes:*

(1) Adjustments for goods and cash in transit are always made in head office books.

(2) The balance on the current account is in fact represented by the branch fixed and current assets less liabilities (i.e., the head office has provided the branch with its capital).

(ii) *Branch books*

Current Account with Head Office

| | £ | | £ |
|---|---|---|---|
| Goods from head office account: *Being returns at invoiced price* | 6,000 | Balance brought forward: *Representing the capital of the branch at the beginning of year* | 20,000 |
| Cash account: *Remittances to head office* | 72,000 | Goods from head office account: *At invoiced price* | 80,000 |
| Balance carried forward: *Representing branch capital at year end* | 42,000 | Expenses account: *Branch expenses met by head office* | 4,000 |
| | | Branch profit and loss account: *Transfer of branch profit to head office* | 16,000 |
| | £120,000 | | £120,000 |

*Notes:*

(1) Goods and cash in transit are always adjusted in the head office books regardless of the direction of movement.

(2) The final entry in the account before balancing is the transfer of the profit to head office current account—normally in examination questions this must be worked out and entered before closing the current account.

(iii) Branch, Head Office and Combined Trading and Profit and Loss Accounts

| | Head office £ | Branch £ | Combined £ | | Head office £ | Branch £ | Combined £ |
|---|---|---|---|---|---|---|---|
| Opening stock: | | | | Sales | SP | SP | SP |
| Head office goods | C | C + % | C | Goods sent to branch: | | | |
| Local purchase | — | C | C | Received | C + % | — | (Contra) |
| Purchases | C | C | C | In transit | C + % | — | C |
| Goods from head office | — | C + % | (Contra) | Goods lost or destroyed | C | C + % | C |
| Gross profit carried down (to balance) | X | X | X | Closing stock: | | | |
| | | | | Head office goods | C | C + % | C |
| | | | | Local purchases | — | C | C |
| | £X | £X | £X | | £X | £X | £X |
| Expenses | X | X | X | Gross profit brought down | X | X | X |
| Goods lost or destroyed | C | C + % | C | | | | |
| Unrealised profits (on branch stocks received from head office or goods in transit) | X | — | — | | | | |
| Net profit | X | X | X | | | | |
| | £X | £X | £X | | £X | £X | £X |

*continued*

*continued*

| | £ | | £ |
|---|---|---|---|
| Balance carried down | X | Net profit brought down: | |
| | | Head office | X |
| | | Branch | X |
| | £X | | £X |

*Note:* Only the items in boxes cross-cast.

Balance Sheets

| | Head office £ | Branch £ | Combined £ | | Head office £ | Branch £ | Combined £ |
|---|---|---|---|---|---|---|---|
| Capital | X | — | X | Fixed assets | X | X | X |
| Head office current account | | X | (Contra) | Branch current account | X | | (Contra) |
| Loans | X | X | X | Current assets: | | | |
| | | | | Stocks: | | | |
| Current liabilities: | | | | Head office | C | | C |
| Provision for unrealised profits on branch stocks and goods in transit (deduct from stocks in combined column) | X | — | — | Branch | | C + % | |
| | | | | Goods in transit (in combined column deduct provision for unrealised profits) | C + % | | |
| Miscellaneous current liabilities | X | X | X | Miscellaneous current assets | X | X | X |
| | £X | £X | £X | | £X | £X | £X |

*Note:* Only the items in boxes cross-cast.

## 1.3 Selling agency branches compared with autonomous branches

(a) *Differences between systems*

Students should distinguish carefully the following differences between System One and System Two:

(i) Examination questions on "System One" always involve goods invoiced at a figure in excess of cost. Questions on "System Two" may involve invoicing at cost *or* cost plus a percentage.

(ii) The invoice price in "System One" represents the estimated *selling price* of the goods. If goods are invoiced at a figure in excess of cost under "System Two", this represents *wholesale price* so that some profit will be taken by the head office and some by the branch.

(iii) Under "System One", a trading account will not usually be required. Under "System Two" this is usually the most difficult aspect of an examination question.

(b) *Point to remember*

(i) *System One*
*Never* bring down balances on "Goods sent to branch account".

(ii) *System Two*
(1) Always make sure current accounts are *equal and opposite.*
(2) Always make provision for unrealised profit on branch stocks (*if any*) in *head office column.*
(3) Don't worry that the columns do not always cross-cast.

## 2.0 FOREIGN AUTONOMOUS BRANCHES

Figure 9 illustrates the treatment of foreign branch accounts.

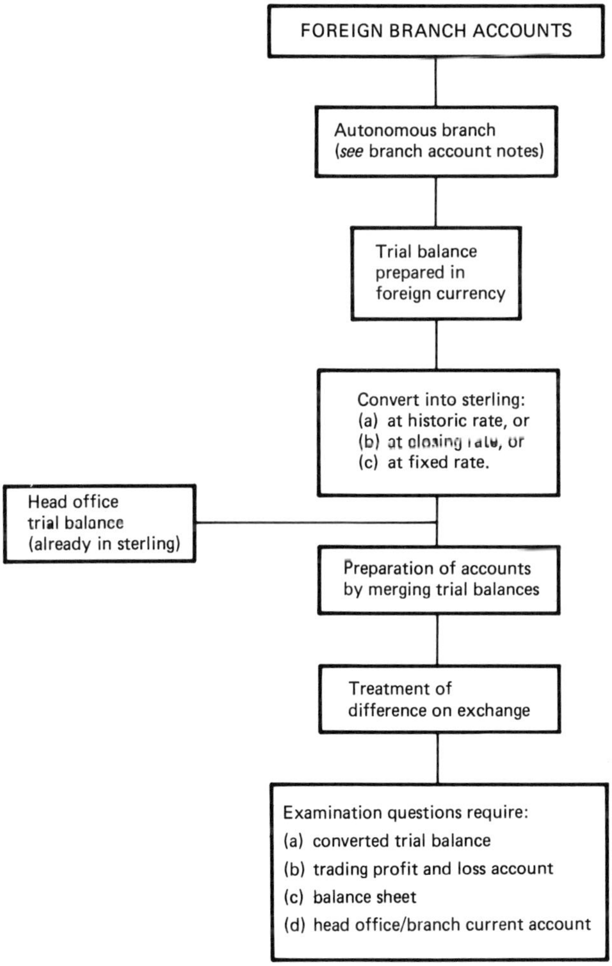


Fig. 9. *Foreign branch accounts.*

## 2.1 Conversion of trial balance

(a) *Introduction*

Before the balances appearing in the branch books can be combined with those in the head office books, they must be converted into sterling.

If the rate of exchange is fixed, all items in the branch trial balance will be converted at the fixed rate given.

In examinations, the rate of exchange is normally *fluctuating* and conversion may be at *historic rate* or *closing rate.*

(b) *Rules for conversion: historic rate*

| *Item* | *Rate to be used* |
|---|---|
| (i) *Trading account* | |
| Opening stock | average (or opening rate) |
| Purchases | average |
| Sales | average |
| Closing stock | average (or closing rate) |
| (ii) *Profit and loss account* | |
| All items | average |
| *except* | |
| Depreciation | same rate as relevant fixed asset (see below) |
| Provision for branch managers' commission | year end |
| (iii) *Balance sheet* | *either* |
| Fixed assets (the rate to be used will be one of the three mentioned and the question will have to be read very thoroughly to establish which one the examiner requires) | sterling cost of a specific remittance the whole proceeds of which are used to acquire the asset *or* rate of exchange ruling at date of acquisition *or* rate of exchange applicable to a general remittance part proceeds of which are used to acquire the asset |
| Current assets | year end |
| Current liabilities | year end |
| Debentures, mortgages and other long-term liabilities | as for fixed assets (unless there has been a permanent drop in the exchange rate when provision should be made for the increased cost of repaying the loan) |

| *Item* | *Rate to be used* |
|---|---|
| Head office current account | sterling equivalent of that balance appearing in head office books after any appropriate reconciliation has been made |
| Remittances | sterling equivalent of amounts received at head office |

(c) *Rules for conversion: closing rate*
All items are converted *at the rate ruling at the balance sheet date* except:

(i) head office current account: actual figure in HO books;

(ii) remittances from branch on account of profit: actual rate at which realised.

(d) *Historic rate and closing rate compared*
These methods are equally acceptable in practice. The historical rate has been more often required for examination questions but the closing rate method should be remembered as a simpler alternative, widely used in practice, to be referred to in any written questions on the subject.

(e) *Difference on exchange*
After converting all the branch figures into sterling in accordance with the above rules, there will be a difference between the totals of the two columns of the trial balance:

(i) in the *branch books* no entries are required because the accounts are maintained in the foreign currency;

(ii) in the *head office books* the entries are:

(1) *For a loss on exchange represented by a balance on the debit side:*

Debit: Profit and loss account *or* exchange equalisation account where it exists
Credit: Branch current account

(2) *For a profit on exchange represented by a balance on the credit side:*

Debit: Branch current account
Credit: Exchange equalisation account.

## 2.2 Devaluation

(a) *Definition*
Devaluation involves a major change in the parity rates of a foreign currency in relation to sterling.

The Institute of Chartered Accountants in England and Wales recommends that any profit or loss resulting from a devaluation should be shown as an extraordinary item unless there is a credit balance on a capital reserve set up on the revaluation of fixed assets. In this case, where there is a loss, it is debited first to capital reserve and any excess shown as an extraordinary item.

(b) *Calculation of profit or loss arising from devaluation*

| | £ |
|---|---|
| (i) Net assets at devaluation date converted at old exchange rate (100,000 koko dollars at 2 to £) | 50,000 |
| *deduct:* Net assets at devaluation date converted at new exchange rate (100,000 koko dollars at $2\frac{1}{2}$ to £) | 40,000 |
| Loss on devaluation | £10,000 |

| | |
|---|---|
| (ii) Net assets at devaluation are arrived at as follows: | koko dollars |
| Net assets at last balance sheet date | 65,000 |
| *add:* Profits from last balance sheet date to devaluation date | 35,000 |
| Net assets at devaluation date | kd 100,000 |

(c) *Accounting entries*

(i) In the *branch books* no entries are required because the accounts are maintained in the foreign currency.

(ii) In the *head office books* an entry must be made to record the increase or decrease in the investment of the head office in the branch (as shown by the branch current account) as follows:

(1) *For a profit on devaluation:*
Debit: Branch current account
Credit: Profit and loss account *OR*
reserve account
with the amount of the profit

(2) *For a loss on devaluation:*
Debit: Profit and loss account *OR*
reserve account
Credit: Branch current account
with the amount of the loss

(iii) After this adjustment, the branch current account will represent the net assets of the branch at their post-devaluation sterling values.

## 2.3 Sundry matters

(a) *Different bases of accounting*
An examination question may specify an alternative method of conversion to those set out above. For instance, current assets and all liabilities may be adjusted but fixed assets may be left at their historic cost.

(b) *Companies Acts 1967, 2nd Schedule*
Disclosure requirements of the 2nd Schedule are to show the basis of conversion of foreign currency where amounts involved are material.

### *Example*

QUESTION

On 1st January 19X4 Brooms Ltd, with its head office in London, opened a trading branch in Galatia. Goods are invoiced by Head Office and the Galatian Branch converts the sterling into local currency—Mints at a fixed exchange rate of 40. The average exchange rate during 19X4 was 45 and at 31st December 19X4 the exchange rate was 50. Fixtures and fittings were purchased locally on 1st January 19X4 when the exchange rate was 48.

Galatia submits the following trial balance as at 31st December 19X4 to Head Office:

| | Mints | Mints |
|---|---|---|
| Sales | | 1,003,500 |
| Goods from head office | 741,200 | |
| Local expenses | 124,200 | |
| Fixtures and fittings | 33,600 | |
| Debtors | 165,000 | |
| Creditors | | 71,750 |
| Bank balance | 72,400 | |
| Head office current account: | | |
| Goods | | 741,200 |
| Remittances | 680,050 | |
| | 1,816,450 | 1,816,450 |

A provision for depreciation at 10 per cent on fixtures and fittings is to be made.

On 31st December 19X4, stocks of goods (all from Head Office) amounted to 48,000 mints.

A remittance of 62,600 mints, which subsequently realised £1,240, was in transit at 31st December 19X4. Other remittances realised £13,420.

*You are required to:*

(i) convert the Galatian trial balance into sterling;

(ii) prepare a branch (memorandum) trading and profit and loss account;

(iii) prepare the branch current account in the Head Office ledger and show what the balance represents.

Convert stock at one rate only.

ANSWER

(i) Trial Balance at 31st December 19X4

| | Conversion rate | Mints | Mints | £ | £ |
|---|---|---|---|---|---|
| Sales | 45 | | 1,003,500 | | 22,300 |
| Goods from head office | 40 | 741,200 | | 18,530 | |
| Local expenses | 45 | 124,200 | | 2,760 | |
| Fixtures and fittings | 48 | 33,600 | | 700 | |
| Depreciation: Profit and loss account | 48 | 3,360 | | 70 | |
| Provision for depreciation | 48 | | 3,360 | | 70 |
| Debtors | 50 | 165,000 | | 3,300 | |
| Creditors | 50 | | 71,750 | | 1,435 |
| Bank balance | 50 | 72,400 | | 1,448 | |
| Head office current account: | | | | | |
| Goods | 40 | | 741,200 | | 18,530 |
| Remittances | actual | 680,050 | | 14,660 | |
| Difference on exchange: | | | | | |
| Loss | | | | 867 | |
| | | 1,819,810 | 1,819,810 | 42,335 | 42,335 |

*Note:* The balance of the currency columns in branch current account must agree with the balance on Head Office current account in the branch books before inserting the sterling equivalent in the trial balance.

(ii) Branch Current Account

| 19X4 | | Mints | £ | 19X4 | | Mints | £ |
|---|---|---|---|---|---|---|---|
| Dec 31 | Goods to branch | 741,200 | 18,530 | Dec 31 | Cash: Remittance | 617,450 | 13,420 |
| | Net profit | 182,740 | 1,900 | | Cash in transit | 62,600 | 1,240 |
| | | | | | Loss on exchange | | 867 |
| | | | | 31 | Balance carried down | 243,890 | 4,903 |
| | | 923,940 | 20,430 | | | 923,940 | 20,430 |

| 19X5 | | Mints | £ |
|---|---|---|---|
| Jan 1 | Balance brought down | 243,890 | 4,935 |

Branch Trading and Profit and Loss Account
for the year ended 31st December 19X4

| | Mints | £ | | Mints | £ |
|---|---|---|---|---|---|
| Goods from Head Office | 741,200 | 18,530 | Sales | 1,003,500 | 22,300 |
| *deduct:* Stock at 31st December 19X4 | 48,000 | 960 | | | |
| | 693,200 | 17,570 | | | |
| Gross profit | 310,300 | 4,730 | | | |
| | 1,003,500 | 22,300 | | 1,003,500 | 22,300 |
| Local expenses | 124,200 | 2,760 | Gross profit | 310,300 | 4,730 |
| Depreciation | 3,360 | 70 | | | |
| Net profit | 182,740 | 1,900 | | | |
| | 310,300 | 4,730 | | 310,300 | 4,730 |

COMMENT

Had the stock been shown at average rate in the trading account and closing rate at 31st December 19X4 for the balance sheet then it would have appeared in both sides of the trial balance as follows:

| | | Mints | Mints | £ | £ |
|---|---|---|---|---|---|
| Stock trading account | 45 | | 48,000 | | 1,067 |
| Stock balance sheet | 50 | 48,000 | | 960 | |

This would have reduced the loss on exchange by £107.

CHECK ON CURRENT ACCOUNT BALANCE

| | | Mints | £ |
|---|---|---|---|
| Branch: | Fixed assets *less:* Depreciation | 30,240 | 630 |
| | Stock | 48,000 | 960 |
| | Debtors | 165,000 | 3,300 |
| | Bank | 72,400 | 1,448 |
| | | 315,640 | 6,338 |
| | Creditors | 71,750 | 1,435 |
| Net assets | | 243,890 | £4,903 |

## 3.0 CONSIGNMENT ACCOUNTS

Figure 10 illustrates the treatment of accounts in the books of consignor and consignee.

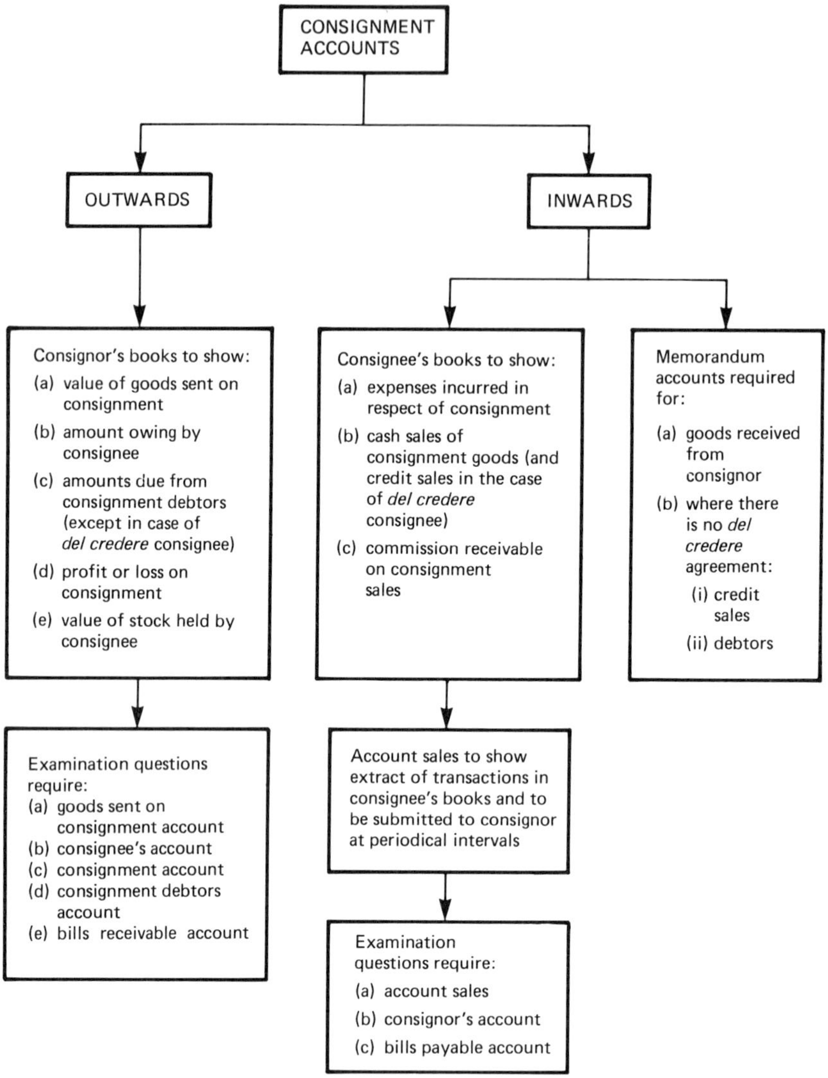


Fig. 10. *Accounts in the books of consignor and consignee.*

### 3.1 Legal aspects

(a) The *relationship* is that of principal and agent.

(b) The *ownership of goods* legally belongs to the consignor and are part of his stocks although physically in the hands of the consignee.

(c) The *rights of consignee* are to agreed commission and reimbursement of monies spent by him in the course of dealing with the consignment.

(d) A *del credere agent* is one who indemnifies the consignor against any loss arising through bad debts in respect of credit sales. The additional remuneration paid to such an agent is termed "*del credere* commission".

## 3.2 Consignor's books

(a) *Accounts required and their purposes*

(i) *Goods sent on consignment account*

(1) Records:

(A) cost of goods sent on consignment;

(B) cost of returns from consignee;

(C) balance transferred to purchases at the end of each accounting period.

(2) There is *never* an opening or closing balance on this account.

(ii) *Consignee's account*

(1) Credited with expenses incurred on behalf of consignment.

(2) Credited with commission on agreed scale.

(3) Credited with cash or bills sent to consignor.

(4) Debited with cash collected from sales (in the case of a *del credere* consignee all credit sales as well).

(5) Balance represents amount due to consignor.

(iii) *Consignment account*

(1) Is the *profit and loss account* of the consignment.

(2) Debited with *cost* of goods sent on consignment and expenses incurred thereon.

(3) Debited with consignee's expenses and commission (per account sales).

(4) Credited with cash and credit sales.

(5) Credited with value of unsold stock in the hands of the consignee at the end of the period.

(6) Balance of the account represents profit or loss on consignment for the accounting period.

(iv) *Consignment debtors account:* in cases where consignee is not a *del credere* agent this provides a control account on the consignment debtors.

(b) *Sundry matters*

(i) Stock is valued on the basis of the lower of "cost at destination" and "net realisable value". "Cost at destination" includes a proportion of all expenses incurred in getting the goods into the hands of the consignee and in a saleable condition, e.g. freight, insurance, landing charges, dock dues and customs duties.

(ii) Care needs to be taken in apportioning expenses when goods are lost in transit.

(iii) In examination questions the goods sent on consignment figure may be given at *pro-forma* invoice price and for the purposes of the ledger accounts must be reduced to cost.

(iv) Doubt sometimes arises in cases where there are bill charges when the consignee settles his account by bill of exchange. There is no definite ruling as to whether such charges should be debited to consignment account or to general profit and loss account.

(v) The amount of the consignee's commission is not normally given by the examiner but the information on which the calculation is to be made is given and you must remember to insert this figure in the account.

(c) *Double entry*
The double entry involved in the consignor's accounts is shown in Table 22.

Table 22. CONSIGNOR'S ACCOUNTS—DOUBLE ENTRY

| *Transaction* | *Debit* | *Credit* |
|---|---|---|
| Cost of goods sent on consignment | Consignment account | Goods sent on consignment account |
| Expenses paid by consignor | Consignment account | Cash account |
| Expenses paid by consignee | Consignment account | Consignee's account |
| Commission due to consignee on sales | Consignment account | Consignee's account |
| Cash sales and credit sales subject to a *del credere* agreement | Consignee's account | Consignment account |
| Credit sales not subject to a *del credere* agreement | Consignment debtors account | Consignment account |
| Insurance claim in respect of goods lost | Insurance claim account | Consignment account |
| Profit on consignment for period | Consignment account | Profit and loss account |

*continued*

Table 22.—*cont.*

| *Transaction* | *Debit* | *Credit* |
|---|---|---|
| Amount due from consignee settled by bill of exchange | Bills receivable account | Consignee's account |
| Cost of goods sent on consignment for period | Goods sent on consignment account | Purchases account |

(d) *Account outlines*

(i) Consignment Account

| | £ | | £ |
|---|---|---|---|
| Goods sent on consignment account: *Cost of goods sent to consignee* | 1,350 A | Consignee's account: *Cash sales for period* | 200 D |
| Cash account: *Expenses incurred by consignor* | 300 | Consignment debtors account: *Credit sales for period* | 200 E |
| Consignee's account: *Expenses incurred by consignee* | 80 B | Insurance claim account: *Claim on goods lost which are insured* | 275 |
| Consignee's account: *Agreed commission on sales* | 22 C | Stock carried down: *Unsold goods in hands of consignee valued at "cost at destination"* | 1,083 |
| Profit and loss account: *Profit for period* | 6 | | |
| | £1,758 | | £1,758 |

(ii) Consignee's Account

| | £ | | £ |
|---|---|---|---|
| Consignment account: *Cash sales for period* | 200 D | Consignment account: *Expenses incurred by consignee* | 80 B |
| Consignment debtors account: *Cash collected by consignee* | 200 F | Consignment account: *Commission due to consignee* | 22 C |
| | | Cash or bills receivable account: *Settlement of amount due to consignor* | 298 |
| | £400 | | £400 |

(iii) Goods Sent on Consignment Account

| | £ | | £ |
|---|---|---|---|
| Purchases account: *Write off at end of period* | 1,350 | Consignment account: *Cost of goods sent to consignee* | 1,350 A |

*Note:* There is never a balance on this account.

(iv) Consignment Debtors Account

| | £ | | £ |
|---|---|---|---|
| Consignment account: *Credit sales* | 200 E | Consignee's account: *Cash collected by consignee* | 200 F |

## 3.3 Consignee's accounts

(a) *Accounts required and their purpose*

(i) *Consignor's account*

(1) This is the only account required and simply shows amounts received in respect of cash sales, collections from credit sale debtors and payments made on behalf of the consignor.

(2) Commission due to the consignee is debited to the consignor's account and credited to commission received account.

(3) The balance on the consignor's account is the amount due to the consignor.

(ii) *Del credere consignee:* where the consignee has entered into a *del credere* arrangement he will also maintain a *memorandum* debtors account in respect of credit sales.

(b) *Sundry matters*
Examination questions sometimes require the preparation of an "account sales". This is simply a statement showing proceeds of sales received by the consignee, less expenses incurred and commission charged. The balance is the amount due from the consignee.

(c) *Double entry*
The double entry involved in the consignee's accounts is shown in Table 23.

Table 23. CONSIGNEE'S ACCOUNTS—DOUBLE ENTRY

| *Transaction* | *Debit* | *Credit* |
|---|---|---|
| Goods sent by consignor | *No entry* | *No entry* |
| Expenses paid by consignee | Consignor's account | Cash account |
| Sales made by consignee | Cash account | Consignor's account |
| Commission due to consignee | Consignor's account | Commission receivable account |
| Remittance of balance due to consignor by bill of exchange | Consignor's account | Bills payable account |

(d) *Account outlines*

(i) Consignor's Account

| | £ | | £ |
|---|---|---|---|
| Cash account: *Expenses paid* | 80 | Cash account: *Sales* | 200 |
| Commission received account: *Commission due to consignee* | 22 | Cash account: *Amounts received from consignment debtors (assuming consignee is not a del credere agent)* | 200 |
| Cash or bills payable account: *Settlement of amount outstanding* | 298 | | |
| | £400 | | £400 |

(ii) Account Sales

| | £ | £ | £ |
|---|---|---|---|
| 40 cases at £10 per case | | | 400 |
| *deduct:* Dock dues | 20 | | |
| Import duty | 30 | | |
| Insurance | 25 | | |
| Storage | 5 | | |
| | | 80 | |
| Commission: 5% of £400 | 20 | | |
| Del credere commission: 1% of £200 | 2 | | |
| | | 22 | |
| | | | 102 |
| Amount due to consignor | | | £298 |

## 4.0 JOINT VENTURES

Figure 11 illustrates two accounting systems which may be used for joint ventures.

### 4.1 Legal aspects

A joint venture is best regarded as a partnership in miniature and in the event of dispute will be subject to the provisions of the Partnership Act 1890.

### 4.2 Joint venture—system one—A

(a) *Accounts required and their purposes*

(i) *Joint venture account:* records payment and receipts of *all* joint venturers, and any assets taken over at end of joint venture; also shows eventual profit or loss.

(ii) *Current account* (one for each joint venturer): records all transactions detailed above relating to all joint venturers other than the "recording joint venturer". Since examination questions are not usually set on this subject the detailed entries are not dealt with.

## 4.3 Joint venture—system one—B

(a) *Accounts required and their purposes*

(i) *Joint venture with . . . account:* each joint venturer records only the transactions in which he himself has paid or received cash, or supplied

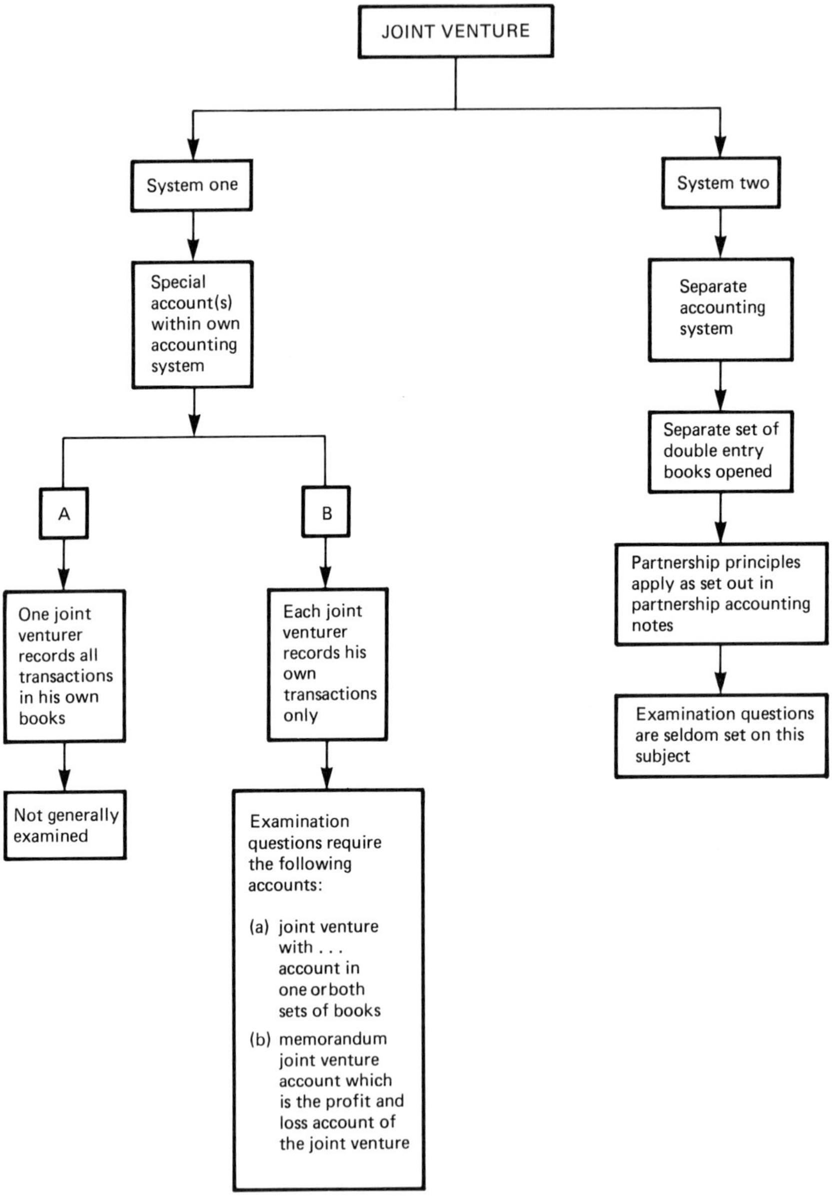


Fig. 11. *Two accounting systems for joint ventures.*

or taken assets. The individual joint venture accounts do *not* show the whole picture; it is necessary to add the various figures together in a "memorandum joint venture account" to show the profit or loss.

(ii) *Memorandum joint venture account:* forms no part of the double entry. It is compiled by adding together the details shown in each of the separate joint venture accounts except for cash and bills transferred between joint venturers.

(b) *Sundry matters*

(i) *Transfers of assets between joint venturers:* NO ENTRY is necessary where assets are transferred between joint venturers.

(ii) *Assets taken over by one of the joint venturers:* where a joint venturer takes over an asset he credits the joint venture with . . . account and debits his own assets account. The item is also credited in the memorandum joint venture account.

(c) *Double entry*
Double entry in joint ventures is shown in Table 24.

Table 24. JOINT VENTURES—DOUBLE ENTRY

| *Transaction* | *Debit* | *Credit* |
|---|---|---|
| Goods purchased | Joint venture with . . . account | Cash account |
| Expenses incurred | Joint venture with . . . account | Cash account |
| Cash received from sales | Cash account | Joint venture with . . . account |
| Transfer of cash to other joint venturer | Joint venture with . . . account | Cash account |
| Transfer of cash from other joint venturer | Cash account | Joint venture with . . . account |
| Transfer of goods between joint venturers | NO ENTRY | NO ENTRY |
| Asset taken over by joint venturer | Asset account | Joint venture with . . . account |
| Share of profit as shown by memorandum joint venture account | Joint venture with . . . account | Profit and loss account |
| Remaining balance on joint venture with . . . account (assumed to be owing to other joint venturer) | Joint venture with . . . account | Cash account |

(d) *Account outlines*

A's Books
Joint Venture with B Account

| | £ | | £ |
|---|---|---|---|
| Cash account: *Being purchase made by A* | 200 | Cash account: *Being sale proceeds received by A* | 350 |
| Cash account: *Being expenses incurred by A* | 70 | | |
| Profit and loss account: *Being profit due to A* | 50 | | |
| Balance carried down: *Being amount due to other joint venturer* | 30 | | |
| | £350 | | £350 |
| Cash account: *To settle* | £ 30 | Balance brought down | £ 30 |

B's Books
Joint Venture with A Account

| | £ | | £ |
|---|---|---|---|
| Cash account: *Being purchase made by B* | 300 | Cash account: *Being sale proceeds received by B* | 400 |
| Cash account: *Being expenses incurred by B* | 30 | Asset account: *Being asset taken over by B* | 50 |
| Profit and loss account: *Being profit due to B* | 150 | Balance carried down: *Being amount due from other joint venturer* | 30 |
| | £480 | | £480 |
| Balance brought down | £ 30 | Cash account: *To settle* | £ 30 |

Memorandum Joint Venture Account

| | £ | | £ |
|---|---|---|---|
| Purchases: *Total of purchases made by A and B* | 500 | Sales: *Total of sales proceeds received by A and B* | 750 |
| Expenses: *Total of expenses incurred by A and B* | 100 | Asset taken over: *Asset taken over by B* | 50 |
| Profit on joint venture: | | | |
| A 50 | | | |
| B 150 | 200 | | |
| | £800 | | £800 |

(e) *Sundry point*
Normally, joint venture questions cover the total period of the venture and therefore there are no balances (i.e. stock) to be carried forward. Where, in a question, the joint venture is *on-going*, stock is carried down in the books of the party buying that stock irrespective of who has possession of the stock at the end of the period.

## 4.4 Joint venture—system two

Examination questions are not normally set on this type of problem.

## 4.5 Foreign joint ventures

The same principles of conversion apply as explained in 2.0 above—foreign autonomous branches. An example of a foreign joint venture is given below.

*Question*

Kevin Ltd, a United Kingdom company, was a partner sharing profits and losses equally with Woolf in a trading venture operating in Woolfania.

Kevin Ltd supplied and invoiced goods to the Woolfanian partnership in that country's currency, namely ducats (d's). The goods were invoiced at cost of production and the current accounts of the partners on trading transactions were agreed at three-monthly intervals in accordance with the exchange rates operating at the end of each quarterly accounting period.

The initial capital investment made by Kevin Ltd in 19X2 had remained unaltered in the books of Kevin Ltd at £10,000.

The quarterly statements prepared by Woolf from the partnership's books showed:

| | 31st Dec. 19X6 d's | 31st March 19X7 d's | 30th June 19X7 d's | | 31st Dec. 19X6 d's | 31st March 19X7 d's | 30th June 19X7 d's |
|---|---|---|---|---|---|---|---|
| Proprietors' capital (equal shares) | 180,000 | 180,000 | 180,000 | Fixed assets at cost *less* depreciation | 120,000 | 116,000 | 132,000 |
| Current account: | | | | Stock | 150,000 | 140,000 | 120,000 |
| Kevin Ltd | 135,000 | 138,000 | 126,000 | Trade debtors | 280,000 | 330,000 | 350,000 |
| Bill payable | — | 60,000 | — | | | | |
| Creditors (including Woolf's current account) | 140,000 | 168,000 | 226,000 | | | | |
| Bank overdraft | 95,000 | 40,000 | 70,000 | | | | |
| | 550,000 | 586,000 | 602,000 | | 550,000 | 586,000 | 602,000 |

An analysis of Kevin Ltd's current account in the partnership's books showed:

| Three months ended | 31st March 19X7 | | 30th June 19X7 | |
|---|---|---|---|---|
| | d's | d's | d's | d's |
| Opening balance | | 135,000 | | 138,000 |
| Share of profit for quarter to date | | 68,000 | | 33,000 |
| Goods supplied, at cost | | 80,000 | | 60,000 |
| | | 283,000 | | 231,000 |
| Payments to Kevin Ltd | 85,000 | | 105,000 | |
| Bill of exchange drawn in ducats and paid as agreed on 1st May 19X7 | 60,000 | 145,000 | — | 105,000 |
| | | 138,000 | | 126,000 |

After receipt of the June quarterly statement, Kevin Ltd agreed to determine the partnership and to sell its half share therein to Woolf. The sale was deemed to have been effected as on 30th June 19X7. Owing to the trade depression it was further agreed to revalue stock at 99,000 ducats. Goodwill and trade marks were to be introduced at 240,000 ducats and fixed assets revalued at 120,000 ducats. All of these adjustments were to be reflected in the books of account as on 30th June 19X7.

The rate of exchange had remained constant at 9 ducats to £1 until 1st December 19X6, when it was altered to 10 ducats to £1. On 1st April 19X7, following the assassination of the Grand Duke, the ducat was devalued to 15 ducats to £1.

You are required to write up in the books of Kevin Ltd for the half year ended 30th June 19X7:

(a) the investment account,

(b) the current account (including a memorandum column in ducats), and

(c) the profit and loss on exchange account.

*Answer*

(a)

Kevin Ltd
Investment Account

| | ducats (000's) | £ | | ducats (000's) | £ |
|---|---|---|---|---|---|
| Balance brought forward at 1st Jan X7 | 90 | 10,000 | Profit and loss on exchange account devaluation of balance brought forward | | |
| Capital reserve: Profit on realisation on 30th June X7 (*see* working) | 103.5 | 6,900 | at 1st Dec X6 | — | 1,000 |
| | | | at 1st Apr X7 | — | 3,000 |
| Current account: Balance at 30th June X7 transferred | 126 | 8,400 | Total balance due on sale of share in business carried forward | 319.5 | 21,300 |
| | 319.5 | £25,300 | | 319.5 | £25,300 |

(b) Current Account

| | ducats (000's) | £ | | ducats (000's) | £ |
|---|---|---|---|---|---|
| Balance brought forward at 1st Jan X7 | 135 | 13,500 | Cash | 85 | 8,500 |
| Profit and loss account: share of profit for quarter to 31st Mar X7 | 68 | 6,800 | Bill receivable | 60 | 6,000 |
| Goods supplied | 80 | 8,000 | Balance carried down | 138 | 13,800 |
| | 283 | £28,300 | | 283 | £28,300 |
| Balance brought down at 1st Apr X7 | 138 | 13,800 | Profit and loss on exchange account devaluation of opening balance | — | 4,600 |
| Profit and loss account: share of profit for quarter to 30th June X7 | 33 | 2,200 | Cash | 105 | 7,000 |
| Goods supplied | 60 | 4,000 | Balance carried down | 126 | 8,400 |
| | 231 | £20,000 | | 231 | £20,000 |
| Balance brought down at 1st June X7 | 126 | 8,400 | Balance transferred to investment account | 126 | 8,400 |

(c) Profit and Loss on Exchange Account

| | £ | | £ |
|---|---|---|---|
| Devaluations relating to: | | Profit and loss account | 10,600 |
| Bills of exchange receivable | 2,000 | | |
| Investment account balance | 4,000 | | |
| Current account balance | 4,600 | | |
| | £10,600 | | £10,600 |

WORKINGS

| | + ducats 000's | − ducats 000's | | |
|---|---|---|---|---|
| Profit on realisation: | | | | |
| Goodwill and trademarks | 240 | | | |
| Fixed assets | | 12 | | |
| Stock | | 21 | | |
| | 240 | 33 | | |
| | 33 | | | |
| Profit | 207 at 15 ducats to £ | | = | £13,800 |
| Half share | | | | £ 6,900 |

*Notes to answer*

(1) In the books of Kevin Ltd the bills receivable account would have been debited from current account with £6,000 in the March quarter. On payment of the bill in the June quarter only £4,000 would have been received, as a result of devaluation, leaving £2,000 to be written off to profit and loss on exchange account.

(2) In arriving at the profit for the June quarter stock has been valued at 120,000 ducats. For the purpose of the sale of the half share in the business, it has been revalued at 99,000 ducats. The view could be taken that Kevin's half share of the loss on stock (£700) should be written off through the current account to the debit of profit and loss account, leaving a profit on realisation of £7,600 on the investment account.

## 5.0 ROYALTY ACCOUNTS

Figure 12 illustrates the treatment of royalty accounts.

### 5.1 Legal aspects

Royalties are subject to the normal law of contract and it is most important to note the various terms of the royalty agreement.

In particular, the royalty agreement will contain clauses dealing with:

(a) royalty per unit of output;

(b) minimum rent payable;

(c) recovery of "short workings";

(d) right to sub-let part or whole of royalty agreement.

### 5.2 Accounting for royalties

(a) *Definition of royalty*
The owner of some form of privilege or monopoly allows other firms to utilise this right by charging them a "royalty". Royalties may arise in respect of the following:

(i) extraction of mineral from the ground;

(ii) copyright (books and music);

(iii) use of patent.

(b) *Accounts required and their purposes*

(i) *Royalties payable account* shows the royalty payable on the *actual* extraction or production for the period, being the total of the tenant's and sub-tenant's production.

(ii) *Landlord's (lessor's) account* shows the actual amount paid to the landlord for the period which may be the *minimum rent* or if more, the royalty payable less short workings recouped.

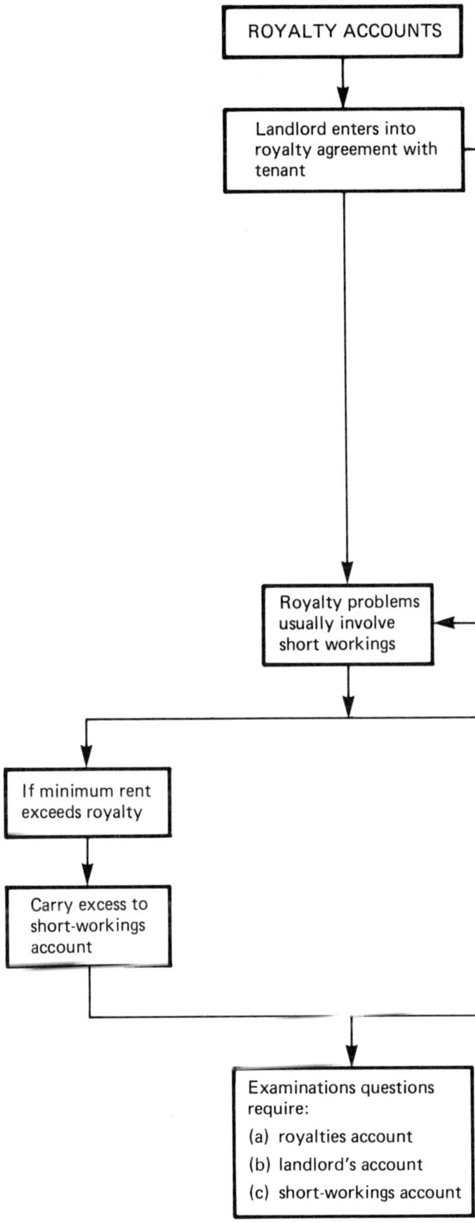


Fig. 12. *Royalty accounts.*

(iii) *Short workings account.* When production royalties are less than minimum rent this account is debited with the royalty on the "short working".

(iv) *Accounts for sub-tenants.* Where there is a sub-tenant, it is advisable to open a further three accounts, corresponding with the three mentioned above. These are:

(1) royalties receivable account;

(2) sub-tenant's account;

(3) short workings account (sub-tenant).

(c) *Sundry matters*

(i) Royalties are part of the cost of production or sales and should be transferred to production or manufacturing account or trading account, as appropriate, and *never* to profit and loss account.

(ii) Irrecoverable short workings are debited to profit and loss account and should be written off in the accounting period in which the right to recoupment expires.

(iii) Income tax is deducted from payments of mining royalties (not copyright) but is normally ignored for examination purposes.

(iv) Where a sub-lease is made at a royalty which will yield a profit to the lessee the amount receivable will consist of the sum payable by the tenant to the landlord calculated on the output of the sub-lessee, plus the profit to the lessee.

The sum payable by the tenant to the landlord will be transferred from royalties receivable account to royalties payable account, and the profit to the lessee will be transferred from royalties receivable account to profit and loss account.

(v) Balance sheet disclosure of short workings: normally any short workings recoverable will be included with debtors and prepayments. If the amount is material it would be disclosed separately.

(d) *Double entry*
Double entry in royalty accounts is shown in Table 25.

Table 25. ROYALTY ACCOUNTS—DOUBLE ENTRY

| | *Transaction* | *Debit* | *Credit* |
|---|---|---|---|
| *No provision for minimum rent* | Royalty based on actual production | Royalties payable account | Landlord's account |
| | Cash paid | Landlord's account | Cash account |
| *Where minimum rent exceeds royalty* | Royalty based on production | Royalties payable account | Landlord's account |
| | Short workings to be recovered in future | Short workings account | Landlord's account |
| | Cash paid to landlord | Landlord's account | Cash account |
| | Short workings irrecoverable (if any) | Profit and loss account | Short workings account |

*continued*

Table 25.—*cont.*

| | *Transaction* | *Debit* | *Credit* |
|---|---|---|---|
| *Where royalties exceed minimum rent* | Royalty based on actual production | Royalties payable account | Landlord's account |
| | Short workings recouped (if any) | Landlord's account | Short workings account |
| | Cash paid<br>*Note:* Cash paid to landlord must not be less than the minimum rent. | Landlord's account | Cash account |
| | Short workings irrecoverable | Profit and loss account | Short workings account |
| *Sub-tenant (additional entries to deal with sub-tenancy agreement)* | Royalty payable based on actual production (own + sub-tenant) | Royalties payable account | Landlord's account |
| | Royalties receivable (based on sub-tenant's production) | Sub-tenant's account | Royalties receivable account |
| | Short workings recoverable in future by sub-tenant | Sub-tenant's account | Short workings account (sub-tenant) |
| | Royalty payable by tenant on sub-tenant's production | Royalties receivable account | Royalties payable account |
| | Profit on sub-lease | Royalties receivable account | Profit and loss account |
| | Short workings irrecoverable by sub-tenant | Short workings account (sub-tenant) | Profit and loss account |

(e) *Account outlines*

Year 1 No sub-tenant

Year 2 Tenant sub-lets to sub-tenant

A leased mine from landlord in year 1, the terms being that A should pay a royalty of 10p per ton on ore extracted, with a minimum rent of £2,000 per annum and the right to recoup short workings up to the end of year 2.

A granted a sub-lease to sub-tenant in year 2 for a royalty of 12½p per ton merging into a minimum rent of £800 per annum and the right to recoup short workings up to the end of the second year of the sub-lease.

The amount of ore extracted was as follows:

| | By A | By sub-tenant |
|---|---|---|
| Year 1 | 11,000 tons | — |
| Year 2 | 17,400 tons | 5,600 tons |
| Year 3 | ? | 6,800 tons |

Royalties Payable Account

| | | £ | | | £ |
|---|---|---|---|---|---|
| Year 1 | Landlord's account: *Royalties based on own actual production* | 1,100 A | Year 1 | Production account: *Royalties charged to cost of production* | 1,100 |
| Year 2 | Landlord's account: *Royalties based on tenant's and sub-tenant's production* | 2,300 B | Year 2 | Royalties receivable account: *Royalty payable to landlord on sub-tenant's production* | 560 C |
| | | | | Production account: *Royalty payable on own production only* | 1,740 |
| | | £2,300 | | | £2,300 |

Landlord's Account

| | | £ | | | £ |
|---|---|---|---|---|---|
| Year 1 | Cash account: *Minimum rent* | 2,000 | Year 1 | Royalties payable account: *Based on own production* | 1,100 A |
| | | | | Short workings account: *Excess of minimum rent over royalties payable* | 900 D |
| | | £2,000 | | | £2,000 |
| Year 2 | Short workings account: *Excess of royalties payable over minimum rent* | 300 E | Year 2 | Royalties payable account: *Based on own and sub-tenant's production* | 2,300 B |
| | Cash account: *Not less than minimum rent* | 2,000 | | | |
| | | £2,300 | | | £2,300 |

Short Workings Account

| | | £ | | | £ |
|---|---|---|---|---|---|
| Year 1 | Landlord's account: *Royalties on own production less than minimum rent* | 900 D | Year 2 | Landlord's account: *Short workings recouped royalties exceed minimum rent* | 300 E |
| | | | | Profit and loss account: *Short workings irrecoverable* | 600 |
| | | £900 | | | £900 |

Royalties Receivable Account

| | | £ | | | £ |
|---|---|---|---|---|---|
| Year 2 | Royalties payable account: *Based on sub-tenant's production* | 560 C | Year 2 | Sub-tenant's account: *Royalty on sub-tenant's production* | 700 F |
| | Profit and loss account: *Excess of rate paid by sub-tenant over rate charged by landlord on sub-tenant's production* | 140 | | | |
| | | £700 | | | £700 |
| Year 3 | Royalties payable account | 680 | Year 3 | Sub-tenant's account | 850 G |
| | Profit and loss account | 170 | | | |
| | | £850 | | | £850 |

Sub-tenant's Account

| | | £ | | | £ |
|---|---|---|---|---|---|
| Year 2 | Royalties receivable account: *Based on sub-tenant's production* | 700 F | Year 2 | Cash received account: *Sub-tenant's minimum rent* | 800 |
| | Short workings (sub-tenant) account: *Sub-tenant's production less than minimum rent* | 100 H | | | |
| | | £800 | | | £800 |

*continued*

*continued*

| | £ | | £ |
|---|---|---|---|
| Year 3 Royalties receivable account | 850 G | Year 3 Short workings account (sub-tenant): *Sub-tenant's short workings recovered* | 50 J |
| | | Cash account: *Not less than minimum rent* | 800 |
| | £850 | | £850 |

Short Workings (Sub-tenant)

| | £ | | £ |
|---|---|---|---|
| Year 3 Sub-tenant's account: *Excess of sub-tenant's production over minimum rent* | 50 J | Year 2 Sub-tenant's account: *Excess of minimum rent over production* | 100 H |
| Profit and loss account: *Short workings no longer recoverable* | 50 | | |
| | £100 | | £100 |

## 6.0 CONTAINERS

Figure 13 illustrates the treatment of container accounts.

### 6.1 Legal aspects

The "sale or return" aspect must be considered: a sale being effective only when containers have not been returned within the stipulated period.

### 6.2 Accounts required and their purposes

(a) *Containers stock account*

(i) This account records *all* transactions relating to containers owned by the company.

(ii) The account shows the stock at book value at the commencement and close of the period and includes not only the containers in the warehouse but also those with customers for which the stipulated time for return has not expired.

(iii) Purchases and sales of containers including cost of repairs and containers scrapped are shown in this account.

(iv) In order to deal adequately with the above matters the account should be ruled with columns for quantity and value.

(v) Shows profit or loss on container transactions during accounting period.

(b) *Containers suspense account*

(i) This account shows the credit due on containers with customers for which the stipulated time for return has not expired.

(ii) The following transactions are dealt with through this account:

(1) containers charged to customers;

(2) hire profit on containers sent to customers is transferred to containers stock account;

(3) containers returned credited back to customers' accounts;

(4) containers retained (effectively sold) credited to stock account.

(iii) The account should be ruled with columns for quantity and value.

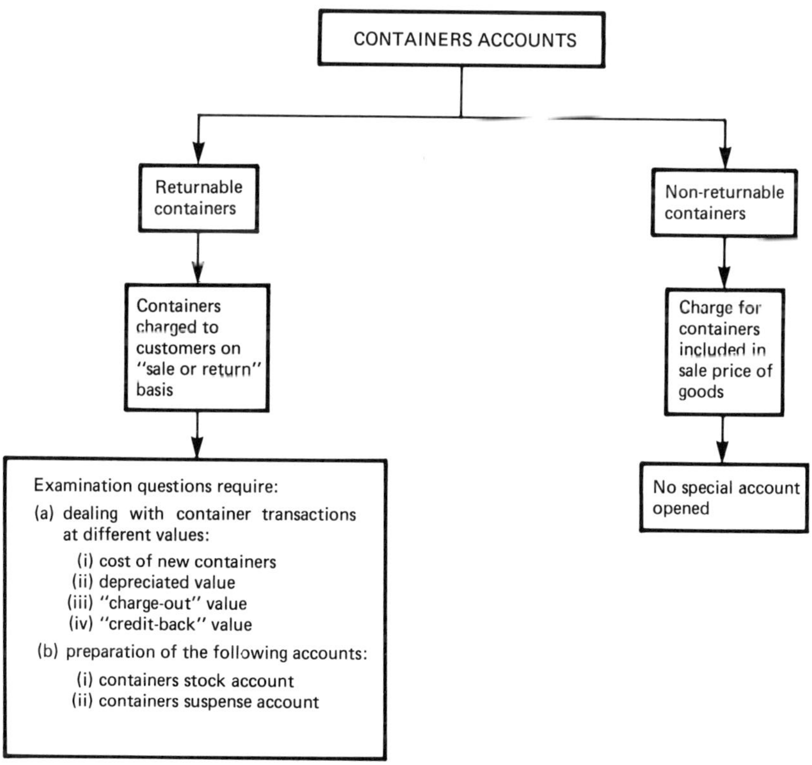


Fig. 13. *Containers accounts.*

## 6.3 Sundry matters

(a) When goods are sold in containers the personal accounts of customers are debited with the following:

(i) the selling price of the goods, and

(ii) the selling price of the containers ("charge out" price).

Periodically the total for goods sold is credited to sales account and the total for containers charged is credited to containers suspense account.

(b) When containers are returned by customers the containers suspense account is debited and the personal accounts of the customers credited with the "credit back" price.

(c) The containers suspense account represents the amount charged out in respect of returnable containers. Since this account is included in the balance of total debtors, for balance sheet purposes the credit balance on containers suspense account is deducted from total debtors.

(d) Containers are returnable within a stated period. The same containers may be sent to customers several times during the year. Therefore the number of containers sent out to customers during the year could be several times the number in stock.

(e) A balancing figure in the quantity column is generally required in examination problems. This figure may be containers retained by customers, stock in warehouse or with customers. By completing both quantity and value columns with the information given in the question, the missing information will be the balancing figure.

(f) *Definition of terms used:*

(i) *Cost:* the actual amount paid for containers purchased.

(ii) *Depreciated value:* the value of containers for stock purposes.

(iii) *"Charge-out" price:* the value at which containers are charged out to customers.

(iv) *"Credit back" price:* the value at which credit is given to customers for containers returned.

(v) *"Hire profit":* the difference between "charge out" price and "credit back" price.

## 6.4 Double entry

Double entry in container accounts is shown in Table 26.

Table 26. CONTAINER ACCOUNTS—DOUBLE ENTRY

| *Transactions* | *Debit* | *Credit* |
|---|---|---|
| "Charge out" price of containers sent to customers | Customers' personal accounts | Containers suspense account |
| Difference between "charge out" and "credit back" price of containers sent to customers being an immediate profit | Containers suspense account | Customers stock account |
| "Credit back" price of containers returned | Containers suspense account | Customers personal account |
| "Credit back" price of containers retained by customers | Containers suspense account | Containers stock account |
| Cost of purchases of new containers | Containers stock account | Cash account |
| Cost of repairs to containers | Containers stock account | Cash account |
| Cash received for containers scrapped | Cash account | Containers stock account |
| Profit on containers being balance on stock account | Containers stock account | Profit and loss account |

## 6.5 Balancing accounts at year end

Stocks of containers with customers and in the warehouse are carried down at the depreciated value on the containers stock account. The balance on the stock account represents the profit or loss on containers transactions during the year which may be proved as follows (based on the following example):

| | | £ | £ |
|---|---|---|---|
| | Profit on containers sent to customers | | 3,400 |
| | Additional profit on containers retained by customers (difference between "credit back" price and depreciated stock value) | | 320 |
| | | | 3,720 |
| *deduct:* | Container repairs | 100 | |
| | Depreciation (difference between cost and stock value) | 1,000 | |
| | Loss on containers scrapped | 80 | 1,180 |
| | Profit (or loss) | | £2,540 |

The balance on containers suspense account represents the containers with customers for which the stipulated time for return has not expired and is shown at the "credit back" price.

## 6.6 Account outlines

Containers dealt with at following values:

| | £ |
|---|---|
| Cost | 1.00 |
| Book value | 0.50 |
| Charged out at | 0.80 |
| Credit back at | 0.60 |

| | |
|---|---|
| Opening stock of containers: | |
| in warehouse | 1,000 |
| with customers | 3,000 |
| Containers sent to customers | 17,000 |
| Containers returned by customers | 16,000 |
| Containers retained by customers | 3,200 |
| Containers scrapped | 160 |
| Containers purchased | 2,000 |

Repairs to containers cost £100.

Containers Stock Account

| | quantity | £ | | quantity | £ |
|---|---|---|---|---|---|
| Balances brought forward: | | | Containers suspense account: | | |
| *In warehouse* | 1,000 | 500 | *Hire profit on containers sent* | — | 3,400 A |
| *With customers* | 3,000 D | 1,500 | Containers suspense account: | | |
| Cash account: *Containers purchased* | 2,000 | 2,000 | *Containers retained by customers* | 3,200 B | 1,920 B |
| Cash account: *Repairs* | — | 100 | Containers scrapped | 160 | — |
| Profit and loss account: | | | Balances carried forward: | | |
| | | | *In warehouse* | 1,840 | 920 |
| *Profit on container operations* | — | 2,540 | *With customers* | 800 C | 400 |
| | 6,000 | £6,640 | | 6,000 | £6,640 |

Containers Suspense Account

| | quantity | £ | | quantity | £ |
|---|---|---|---|---|---|
| Containers stock account: *Hire profit on container sent* | — | 3,400 A | Balance brought forward: *Containers with customers* | 3,000 D | 1,800 |
| Sales ledger control account: *Containers returned by customers* | 16,000 | 9,600 | Sales ledger control account: *Containers sent to customers* | 17,000 | 13,600 |
| Containers stock account: *Containers retained by customers* | 3,200 B | 1,920 B | | | |
| Balance carried forward: *Containers with customers* | 800 C | 480 | | | |
| | 20,000 | £15,400 | | 20,000 | £15,400 |

## 7.0 CONTRACT ACCOUNTS

### 7.1 Legal aspects

A contract is a legally binding agreement between two parties. The agreement deals with the following:

(a) contract price;

(b) completion date;

(c) penalties;

(d) terms;

(e) date of commencement;

(f) details of payments;

(g) details of contractee;

(h) contract number.

### 7.2 The contract account

(a) *Types of expenses*
A contract account is a form of trading, profit and loss account which is charged with all the expenses relating to the contract and credited on completion with the contract price.

The most important expenses are as follows:

(i) *Materials*

(1) Materials purchased specially for a contract will be charged direct to the contract account.

(2) Materials requisitioned from stores will be charged periodically to the contract.

(3) The cost of materials already charged to a contract which are sold, returned to stores or transferred to another contract must be credited to the original contract account.

(ii) *Labour*

(1) A considerable proportion of labour is engaged directly on the contract and is therefore charged direct to the contract account.

(2) Certain employees cannot be identified with any one particular contract—e.g. time-keepers, storemen, general foremen. Such wages are treated as indirect and apportioned on an equitable basis.

(iii) *Plant*

(1) The charge to the contract is dependent on the type of plant used and the period of time during which the plant will be used.

(2) Plant required for an extended period of time and purchased specially for the contract is charged direct to the contract account. At the end of each financial year plant is revalued and carried down to the next year. The depreciation in this case is automatically recorded.

On completion of the contract, if the plant is sold or found to be still serviceable, the contract account is credited with the sale proceeds or value of the plant.

(3) Plant required for a limited period on several contracts is charged to the contract account at an hourly, daily or weekly rate.

(iv) *Direct expenses*
These expenses are charged direct to the contract. Examples are electricity at site, insurance, telephone installed on site, architect's fees, sub-contracts etc.

(v) *Indirect expenses*

(1) Certain expenses cannot be allocated to any one particular contract, such as rent, rates, salaries and other establishment expenses. These must be charged to the contract account on an equitable basis.

(2) On small contracts indirect expenses are charged to the contract on the basis of a percentage of the value of prime cost.

(3) On large contracts which extend over a number of years either an

established hourly rate is charged to each contract or the indirect expenses are allocated in proportion to the total expenditure of each contract.

(b) *Progress payments*
On large contracts progress payments are often made by the contractee based on the value of work completed at "contract" price as certified by an architect or surveyor. A clause in the contract frequently entitles the customer to retain a proportion of the contract value with the object of giving him a right should there be faulty work or penalties become due for late completion. On satisfactory completion of the contract this "retention money" is paid over to the contractor.
The amount received is credited to the personal account of the customer.

## 7.3 Uncompleted contracts

(a) *Balances*
At the end of the accounting period if a contract is incomplete the following procedure should be adopted:

(i) debit the contract account with accrued expenses and carry down this amount to the next period;

(ii) credit the contract account with prepayments, stock on hand at site, plant on site at depreciated value and work in progress and carry down these amounts to the next period;

(iii) the balance remaining on the account represents the cost of work completed to date and is the basis for calculating the profit or loss to date.

(b) *Calculation of profit on uncompleted contracts*
Where a contract extends over several accounting periods, it is necessary to take credit for profit earned to date at the end of each period. If this were not done, the accounts of the contractor would probably show large fluctuations in the net profit figure.
Three situations arise:

(i) *Where a contract has just been started* it is not considered prudent to take credit for any profit and the work in progress should be carried forward at cost.

(ii) *Where the contract is well under way* a certain amount of profit may reasonably be taken to the credit of the profit and loss account. This profit is ascertained as follows:

| | £ |
|---|---|
| Architect's valuation of work to date, as shown on architect's certificates | 8,000 |
| *deduct:* Cost of work certified (being the work-in-progress figure less the cost of any work not certified) | 5,000 |
| Profit | £3,000 |

This profit figure may then be reduced by one or both of the following amounts, in order to take credit for only a part of the estimated profit:

(1) An arbitrary fraction—most usually one-third—so that only two-thirds of the estimated profit is taken.

(2) The percentage of the cash retention.

For example, if the basic profit were £3,000 and the contractee had made retentions of 10 per cent on the architect's certificates, the calculation might be as follows:

$$£3{,}000 \times \tfrac{2}{3} \times 90/100 = \underline{\underline{£1{,}800}}.$$

(iii) *Where the contract is substantially completed* it is possible to estimate the cost of completing the contract, and therefore the ultimate profit to be earned. The calculation is then as follows:

| | | £ |
|---|---|---|
| Contract price (being the total amount receivable on completion of the contract) | | 13,000 |
| | £ | |
| Cost of work in progress to date | 5,000 | |
| *add:* Estimated cost to complete contract | 4,000 | 9,000 |
| Total profit | | £4,000 |

Profit earned to date may be calculated by either of the following formulae:

$$\frac{\text{Work certified to date}}{\text{Contract price}} \times \text{Total profit } \textit{or}$$

$$\frac{\text{Cost of work to date}}{\text{Estimated total cost of contract}} \times \text{Total profit}$$

This will give the profit earned to date which may then be reduced by either or both the *one-third* fraction and the *cash received* fraction, as in the second fraction above.

*Note:* In most examination questions, the basis for computing profit to date will be given.

(c) *Treatment of profit on uncompleted contracts*
The final profit figure when calculated is *credited* to profit and loss account and *debited* to the contract account, thus increasing the value of the work in progress to be carried forward to the next period.

(d) *Losses on contracts*
Where a contract shows a loss the *full loss* to date should be debited in the profit and loss account *and* provision should be made for losses anticipated in future accounting periods.

(e) *Cash received from the contractee*
Cash received from the contractee should be credited to a debtor's account and *not* to the contract account. When the contract is completed, the debtors account is debited and the contract account credited with the full contract price.

(f) *Balance sheet disclosure*
The relevant items will appear in the balance sheet as shown in the following extract:

| | £ | £ |
|---|---|---|
| Current assets: | | |
| Stock of materials | | 200 |
| Work in progress valued on the basis of cost | 3,600 | |
| *add:* Proportion of eventually realisable profit | 400 | |
| | 4,000 | |
| *deduct:* Cash received on account | 1,000 | |
| | | 3,000 |
| Retention monies due on completed contracts | | 500 |

## 7.4 Account outline

Contract Account—No. 1

| | £ | | £ |
|---|---|---|---|
| Materials purchased | 800 | Sale of plant | 900 |
| Materials from stores | 100 | Sale of materials | 70 |
| Direct expenses | 750 | Plant transferred to another | |
| Wages | 990 | contract | 750 |
| Indirect expenses | 260 | Materials transferred to another | |
| Plant purchased | 3,500 | contract | 130 |
| Accrued expenses carried down: | | Stock of materials carried down | 200 |
| Wages | 150 | Plant carried down | 950 |
| Direct expenses | 50 | *(at written down value)* | |
| | 6,600 | Work in progress carried down: | 4,000 |
| Profit and loss account: | 400 | *Actual cost to date and profit* | |
| *Profit on contract* | | *taken into account* | |
| | £7,000 | | £7,000 |

## 7.5 Long-term contract work in progress—SSAP 9

SSAP 9 recommends that the gross amount of long-term contract work in progress should be stated, at:

> cost plus attributable profit, less foreseeable losses, less progress payments received and receivable.

The following reasons for the above are given:

(a) Owing to the length of time taken to complete long-term contracts, if profit were not taken into account until the contract were completed, the profit and loss account would not reflect a true and fair view of the *activities* of the company during the year, but only of the results relating to contracts completed by the year end.

(b) Profit should therefore be taken in proportion to work carried out by the accounting date, taking into account inequalities in profitability of the various parts of the contract, and also all contingencies, such as increased costs, penalties etc., which may arise before completion. Attributable profit should only be included when the contract is substantially complete and a profit may reasonably be forecast.

Many businesses such as construction and building companies carry out contracts whose outcome cannot reasonably be assessed before conclusion of the contract. In these cases, it is obviously prudent not to take any profit on uncompleted contracts, yet this point is overlooked in the statement of standard accounting practice. The practice of taking profit on uncompleted contracts has also been criticised as being inconsistent with the practice employed on "short-term" contracts.

## 8.0 HIRE PURCHASE ACCOUNTS—BUYER'S BOOKS AND GENERAL PRINCIPLES

### 8.1 Legal aspects of hire purchase, credit sale and rental agreements

(a) *Hire purchase*

Under a hire purchase agreement, there is a difference between the *legal position* of the contracting parties and their *true intentions*.

(i) The *true intention* of the parties is to effect the sale of an asset whereby the price is paid over a period of time with interest charged on the outstanding balance.

(ii) The *legal form* in which this transaction is clothed is for the vendor to *hire* the asset to the "purchaser" until the purchaser has paid hire charges equivalent to the purchase price plus interest on the outstanding balance. Throughout this period, the title to the goods remains with the vendor. The purchaser is then given an option to acquire the asset for a nominal sum (usually £2) and it is only at this stage that title passes to the purchaser.

From the above description it will be seen that, in default of payment at any time, the vendor is free to recover the goods from the hire purchaser and to terminate the "hiring agreement".

The right to repossession of goods is curtailed by the Hire Purchase Act 1965 which requires a Court Order for repossession once one-third of the instalments have been paid. The Act does not apply to agreements where the total purchase price exceeds £2,000 or where the purchaser is a body corporate.

(b) *Credit sale*
In a credit sale agreement, the title to the goods passes to the buyer immediately on delivery and the purchase price is payable in instalments. In the event of default in payment, the vendor can only sue for the unpaid instalments; he cannot repossess the goods.

(c) *Rental*
In a rental agreement, the supplier of the goods retains title thereto, the customer merely paying a hire charge or rental for as long as he possesses the goods.

(d) *Accounting treatment of hire purchase transactions*
Normal accounting policy is to treat hire purchase transactions from the point of view of the *true intention* of the parties and *not* the *legal form* of the agreement. Assets are therefore treated as acquired when delivered.
The main point of difficulty in all hire purchase accounting is in the treatment of hire purchase interest.

## 8.2 Hire purchase transactions in the purchaser's books

Figure 14 illustrates the treatment of hire purchase transactions in the purchaser's books.

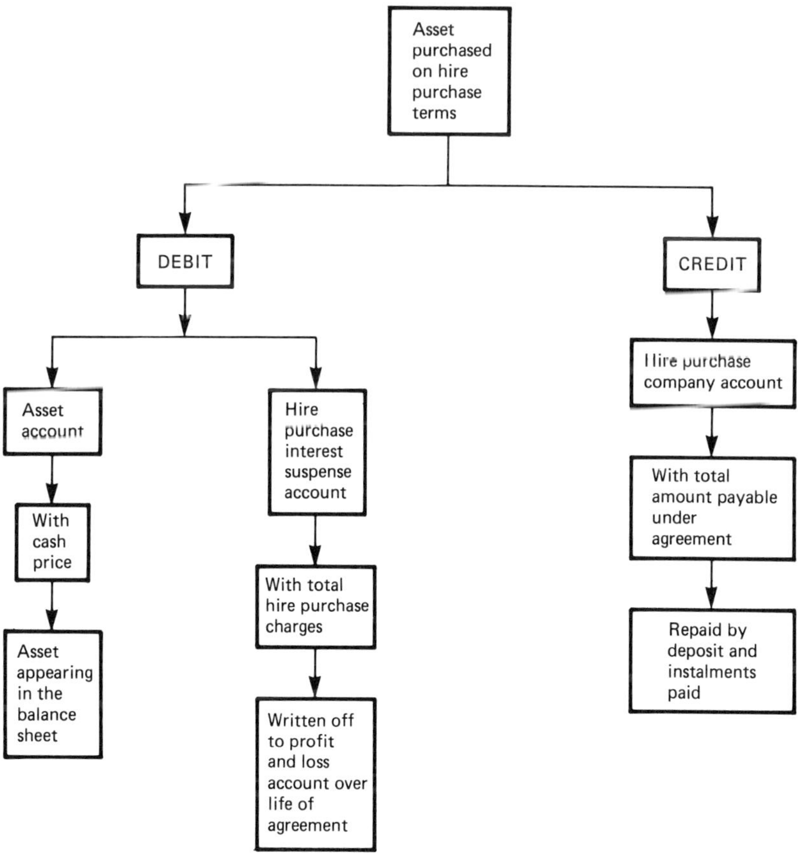


Fig. 14. *Treatment of HP transactions in the purchaser's books.*

(a) *Accounts required and their purpose*

(i) *Asset account:* Records the cash price of the goods purchased under the hire purchase agreement.
*Note:* Always maintain separate asset accounts in respect of:

(1) cost;

(2) depreciation;

(3) disposal.

(ii) *Hire purchase company account:* Shows the amount payable under the agreement in respect of both the cash price and the hire purchase interest.

(iii) *Hire purchase interest suspense account:* Records the interest included in the balance on the hire purchase company's account. The interest relating to any period is written off to profit and loss account; the balance, being interest not yet due, is carried forward.

Methods of determining the write-off to profit and loss account are detailed in paragraph (b).

(iv) *Balance sheet presentation:* The balance on the hire purchase company account *less* the balance on the interest suspense account is shown in current liabilities. This amount is *never* deducted from the asset being acquired on hire purchase terms.

(b) *Methods of writing off hire purchase interest*
There are three commonly accepted methods of writing off hire purchase interest charges. They are:

(i) actuarial (or reducing balance) method;

(ii) sum of the digits (or "rule of 78") method;

(iii) straight line (or equal instalment) method.

Each of these are considered in turn, with figures to illustrate their application.

(i) *Actuarial method.* In this method, the hire purchase interest is computed on the reducing balance. It is therefore necessary to strike a balance after each instalment has been paid and to compute the interest charge for the next period.

*Illustration*

Asset purchased on hire purchase terms:

| | £ |
|---|---|
| Cash price | 4,000 |
| Hire purchase price | 4,618 |
| Interest rate 10% | |
| Repayments: Deposit | 1,000 |
| Three annual payments of | 1,206 |

(All workings are to nearest £ and the option payment has been ignored.)

The position is as follows:

| | £ |
|---|---|
| Cash price | 4,000 |
| *deduct:* Deposit | 1,000 |
| Balance on hire purchase | 3,000 |
| *add:* 10% for one year | 300 |
| | 3,300 |
| *deduct:* First repayment | 1,206 |
| | 2,094 |
| *add:* 10% for one year | 209 |
| | 2,303 |
| *deduct:* Second repayment | 1,206 |
| | 1,097 |
| *add:* 10% for one year | 109 |
| | 1,206 |
| *deduct:* Third repayment | 1,206 |

Interest is therefore written off as follows:

| | £ |
|---|---|
| First year | 300 |
| Second year | 209 |
| Third year | 109 |
| | £618 |

Where the number of repayments is large, this method is cumbersome and is likely to be used only where the true rate of interest is known and the value of the transaction substantial.

(ii) *Sum of the digits method* (also known as "rule of 78"). This is an arithmetical method of apportioning the interest in approximate proportion to the amount outstanding at any time. The method is as follows:

(1) Number the instalments, giving the highest digit to the first instalment, and the digit 1 to the last instalment.

(2) Add up the digits.

(3) Apportion to each accounting period a proportion of the hire purchase interest for each instalment paid in the period. The fraction is the digit given to the instalment divided by the sum of the digits as indicated above.

*Illustration*

Asset purchased on hire purchase terms:

| | | £ |
|---|---|---|
| Cash price | | 2,500 |
| Hire purchase price | | 2,900 |
| Repayments: Deposit | | 500 |
| | 12 monthly instalments of | 200 |

(Work to the nearest £ and ignore the option payment.)

Assuming a calendar year, the instalments are numbered as follows:

| | | |
|---|---|---|
| January | — | 12 |
| February | — | 11 |
| March | — | 10 |
| April | — | 9 |
| May | — | 8 |
| June | — | 7 |
| July | — | 6 |
| August | — | 5 |
| September | — | 4 |
| October | — | 3 |
| November | — | 2 |
| December | — | 1 |
| | | 78 |

Total interest is £400.

Interest to be written off:

for January $= \frac{12}{78} \times £400 = \underline{\underline{£62}}$

for first quarter $= \frac{12 + 11 + 10}{78} \times £400 = \underline{\underline{£169}}$

for third quarter $= \frac{6 + 5 + 4}{78} \times £400 = \underline{\underline{£77}}$

for November $= \frac{2}{78} \times £400 = \underline{\underline{£10}}$

(iii) *Straight-line method.* In this method the hire purchase interest is written off on a straight line basis, over the life of the agreement.

*Illustration*

Asset purchased on hire purchase terms:

| | | £ |
|---|---|---|
| Cash price | | 4,000 |
| Hire purchase price | | 4,600 |
| Repayments: Deposit | | 1,000 |
| | 24 monthly instalments of | 150 |

(Work to the nearest £ and ignore the option payment.)

The position is as follows:

| | £ |
|---|---|
| Cash price | 4,000 |
| *deduct:* Deposit | 1,000 |
| Balance on hire purchase | 3,000 |
| *add:* Interest | 600 |
| | £3,600 |

Each instalment includes:

$$\text{Principal } \frac{3,000}{3,600} \times £150 = £125$$

$$\text{Interest } \frac{600}{3,600} \times £150 = £\ 25$$

$$£150$$

Interest is therefore written off at the rate of £25 per instalment paid.

(c) *Sundry matters*
Students should have no difficulty in determining how to write off the hire purchase interest in an examination question. The question will generally make it very clear which method is required. If there is no indication, adopt that which seems easiest and most appropriate.

(d) *Double entry*
Double entry in the purchaser's books is shown in Table 27.

Table 27. HIRE PURCHASE BUYER'S ACCOUNTS: DOUBLE ENTRY

| | *Transaction* | *Debit* | *Credit* |
|---|---|---|---|
| *Entries on acquisition of assets* | Cash price of asset | Asset account | Hire purchase company account |
| | Total hire purchase interest | Hire purchase interest suspense account | Hire purchase company account |
| *Repayments* | Deposit and instalments paid | Hire purchase company account | Bank account |
| *Year-end entry* | Interest to be written off in period | Profit and loss account | Hire purchase interest suspense account |

*continued*

Table 27.—*cont.*

| | *Transaction* | *Debit* | *Credit* |
|---|---|---|---|
| *Entries on disposal of asset* | Cost of asset to be sold | Disposal of asset account | Asset at cost account |
| | Provision for depreciation on asset to be sold | Asset depreciation account | Disposal of asset account |
| | Sale proceeds of asset sold | Bank account | Disposal of asset account |
| | Under-provision for depreciation on asset sold | Profit and loss account | Disposal of asset account |
| *Entries on early repayment of debt* | Amount paid on early termination of agreement | Hire purchase company account | Bank account |
| | Balance remaining on hire purchase company account which represents interest waived | Hire purchase company account | Hire purchase interest suspense account |
| | Balance remaining on hire purchase interest suspense account which represents the final interest charge | Profit and loss account | Hire purchase interest suspense account |

(e) *Account outlines*

The account outlines shown below illustrate the accounting entries for hire purchase accounts, based on the following example:

Asset acquired on hire purchase terms on 1st April Year 1.

| Details as follows: | £ |
|---|---|
| Cash price | 2,500 |
| Hire purchase price | 2,900 |
| Repayable as follows: | |
| Deposit | 500 |
| 24 monthly instalments of £100 each | 2,400 |

First instalment payable 30th April Year 1

Company makes up accounts to 31st December

Asset sold on 28th September Year 2 for £1,500. Hire purchase agreement terminated on that date for a final payment of £680.

Depreciation is calculated at the rate of 20 per cent per annum on cost.

Hire purchase interest to be written off on a straight-line basis.

Asset at Cost Account

| | £ | | £ |
|---|---|---|---|
| Year 1 | | Year 2 | |
| April 1 Hire purchase account: *Cash price of asset* | 2,500 | Sept 28 Asset disposal account: *Cost of asset sold* | 2,500 |

Asset Depreciation Account

| | £ | | £ |
|---|---|---|---|
| Year 2 | | Year 1 | |
| Sept 28 Asset disposal account: *Depreciation on asset sold* | 750 | Dec 31 Profit and loss account; *Provision for year* *20% × $\frac{9}{12}$ × £2,500* | 375 |
| | | Year 2 | |
| | | Sept 28 Profit and loss account: *Provision for year* *20% × $\frac{9}{12}$ × £2,500* | 375 |
| | £750 | | £750 |

Asset Disposal Account

| | £ | | £ |
|---|---|---|---|
| Year 2 | | Year 2 | |
| Sept 28 Asset at cost account: *Cost of asset sold* | 2,500 | Sept 28 Asset depreciation account: *Depreciation on asset sold* | 750 |
| | | Sept 28 Bank account: *Sale proceeds* | 1,500 |
| | | Sept 28 Profit and loss account: *Under-provision for depreciation* | 250 |
| | £2,500 | | £2,500 |

Hire Purchase Company Account

| | £ | | £ |
|---|---|---|---|
| Year 1 | | Year 1 | |
| April 1 Bank account: *Deposit* | 500 | April 1 Asset at cost account: *Asset purchased* | 2,500 |
| Dec 31 Bank account: *9 instalments* | 900 | April 1 Hire purchase interest suspense account: *Total interest payable* | 400 |
| Dec 31 Balance carried forward | 1,500 | | |
| | £2,900 | | £2,900 |

*continued*

*continued*

| | £ | | £ |
|---|---|---|---|
| Year 2 | | Year 2 | |
| Aug 31 Bank account: *8 instalments* | 800 | Jan 1 Balance brought forward | 1,500 |
| Sept 28 Bank account: *Final payment* | 680 | | |
| Hire purchase interest suspense account: *Interest waived* | 20 | | |
| | £1,500 | | £1,500 |

Hire Purchase Interest Suspense Account

| Year 1 | £ | Year 1 | £ |
|---|---|---|---|
| April 1 Hire purchase company account: *Interest included in hire purchase price* | 400 | Dec 31 Profit and loss account: *Interest charged for year* $\frac{9}{24} \times$ *£400* | 150 |
| | | Dec 31 Balance carried forward | 250 |
| | £400 | | £400 |
| Year 2 | | Year 2 | |
| Jan 1 Balance brought forward | 250 | Sept 28 Hire purchase company account: *Interest waived* | 20 |
| | | Sept 28 Profit and loss account: *Balance on account* | 230 |
| | £250 | | £250 |

(f) *Alternative accounting method*
Where the total HP interest cannot be calculated at the beginning of the HP agreement, it will not be possible to use an HP interest suspense account. (Where this is the case, the following answer would be applicable to part (e).)

There would be no change to the following:

(1) asset at cost account;

(2) asset depreciation account;

(3) asset disposal account.

Hire Purchase Company Account

| | | £ | | | £ |
|---|---|---|---|---|---|
| Year 1 | | | Year 1 | | |
| April 1 | Bank account: *Deposit* | 500 | April 1 | Asset at cost account: *Asset purchased* | 2,500 |
| Dec 31 | Bank account: *9 instalments* | 900 | Dec 31 | Profit and loss account: *Interest charged for year* | 150 |
| Dec 31 | Balance carried forward | 1,250 | | | |
| | | £2,650 | | | £2,650 |
| Year 2 | | | Year 2 | | |
| Aug 31 | Bank account: *8 instalments* | 800 | Jan 1 | Balance brought forward | 1,250 |
| Sept 28 | Bank account: *Final payment* | 680 | Sept 28 | Profit and loss account: *Balance on account* | 230 |
| | | £1,480 | | | £1,480 |

*Note:* Where the HP interest suspense account is not used, all entries are made in the HP company account as shown above.

## 9.0 HIRE PURCHASE ACCOUNTS—SELLER'S BOOKS

### 9.1 Hire purchase and credit sale transactions in the vendor's books

(a) *Introduction*
This section of the manual deals with the accounts of a retailer or other dealer who makes sales on hire purchase terms, and who therefore, as a matter of accounting policy, must decide when to take credit for the profit made on such transactions.

(b) *Distinction between gross profit and hire purchase interest*
A trader may distinguish between the normal gross profit, made on hire purchase sales, and interest earned on the debt outstanding.

*Illustration*

| | £ |
|---|---|
| Cost | 100 |
| Cash selling price | 120 |
| Hire purchase selling price | 156 |

A trader may distinguish:

| | £ |
|---|---|
| Normal gross profit | 20 |
| Interest | 36 |
| Total profit | £56 |

In many cases, particularly where a substantial proportion of sales is made on hire purchase terms, no distinction is made between the two elements of profit, and the profit in the above illustration is taken to be £56.

Whether the trader recognises one single profit figure or distinguishes between two profits, there are a number of ways of spreading the profit over the accounting periods covered by the hire purchase agreement.

(c) *The two accounting systems*
There are two methods of accounting for hire purchase and credit sale transactions in the vendor's accounts. These are:

(i) the *sales system* where gross profit and interest charged are accounted for separately;

(ii) the *stock system* where no distinction is made between gross profit and interest charged and the total profit is apportioned to successive profit and loss accounts in proportion to cash received.

The sales system is considered in 9.2 below and the stock system in 9.3.

## 9.2 The sales system in the vendor's books

(a) *The sales system—general principles*
This accounting system allows the trader to take credit for the gross profit at the time of delivery of the goods or to apportion it. The interest earned may be spread over a number of accounting periods on a suitable basis.

(i) *Accounts required and their purpose*

(1) *Sales account* is credited with the cash selling price. The balance on this account, including both cash, hire purchase and credit sales, is transferred to the trading account in the usual way.

(2) *Hire purchase interest suspense account* is credited with the total hire purchase interest. At the end of each accounting period, a proportion of the interest is credited to the profit and loss account and the balance carried forward as deferred income.

(3) *Hire purchase debtors account* is debited with the full hire purchase selling price. It is credited with cash payments as they are received.

*Note:* A moment's reflection will show that the above accounts are simply the reverse of the asset account, hire purchase interest suspense account and hire purchase company account in the purchaser's books.

(4) *Profit and loss account disclosure:* the profit and loss account is credited with

(A) gross profit on sales,

(B) profit on repossessions (if any),

(C) interest earned in current period.

(5) *Balance sheet disclosure:* current assets will include the hire purchase debtors *less* the unearned interest.

(ii) *Double entry*
Double entry in the general sales system is shown in Table 28.

Table 28. HIRE PURCHASE VENDOR: DOUBLE ENTRY IN GENERAL SALES SYSTEM

| | *Transactions* | *Debit* | *Credit* |
|---|---|---|---|
| *Entries at time of sale* | Cash selling price | Hire purchase debtors account | Sales account |
| | Total interest charge | Hire purchase debtors account | Hire purchase interest suspense account |
| *Payments received* | Deposit and instalments received | Bank account | Hire purchase debtors account |
| *Year-end entries* | Total sales for year | Sales account | Trading account |
| | Unearned gross profit carried forward to future periods (if any) | Trading account | Provision for unrealised profit account |
| | Interest to be credited to profit and loss account for period | Hire purchase interest suspense account | Profit and loss account |

(iii) *Account outlines*
The following account outlines show the method of accounting in a simple situation. Profit is taken *pro rata* to cash receivable (allowing for the deposit in year 1) while interest is spread evenly over the period of the agreement.

On 1st January Year 1, Q Ltd, a furniture retailer, sold items which had cost £960 to X on the following terms:

| | £ |
|---|---|
| Cash price | 1,200 |
| Deposit | 300 |
| | 900 |
| Interest over three years (36 × £10) | 360 |
| Payable by 36 monthly instalments of £35 each | £1,260 |

It is Q Ltd's practice to spread interest evenly over the life of an agreement and to take credit for profit proportionately to cash due in each accounting period. Q Ltd makes up its accounts to 31st December in each year.

Hire Purchase Debtors Account

| | £ | | £ |
|---|---|---|---|
| Year 1 | £ | Year 1 | £ |
| Jan 1 Sales account: *Cash selling price* | 1,200 | Jan 1 Bank account: *Deposit* | 300 |
| Jan 1 Hire purchase interest suspense account: *Total interest charge* | 360 | Dec 31 Bank account *(12 × £35)* | 420 |
| | | Balance carried forward | 840 |
| | £1,560 | | £1,560 |
| Year 2 | | Year 2 | |
| Jan 1 Balance brought forward | 840 | Dec 31 Bank account *(12 × £35)* | 420 |
| | | Balance carried forward | 420 |
| | £840 | | £840 |
| Year 3 | | Year 3 | |
| Jan 1 Balance brought forward | 420 | Dec 31 Bank account *(12 × £35)* | 420 |
| | £420 | | £420 |

Sales Account

| | £ | | £ |
|---|---|---|---|
| Year 1 | £ | Year 1 | £ |
| Dec 31 Trading account | 1,200 | Jan 1 Hire purchase debtors account: *Cash selling price* | 1,200 |

Hire Purchase Interest Suspense Account

| | £ | | £ |
|---|---|---|---|
| Year 1 | £ | Year 1 | £ |
| Dec 31 Profit and loss account *((12 ÷ 36) × £360)* | 120 | Jan 1 Hire purchase debtors account: *Total interest charge* | 360 |
| Balance carried forward | 240 | | |
| | £360 | | £360 |
| Year 2 | | Year 2 | |
| Dec 31 Profit and loss account *((12 ÷ 36) × £360)* | 120 | Jan 1 Balance brought forward | 240 |
| Balance carried forward | 120 | | |
| | £240 | | £240 |
| Year 3 | | Year 3 | |
| Dec 31 Profit and loss account | 120 | Jan 1 Balance brought forward | 120 |

Provision for Unrealised Profit Account

| | | £ | | | £ |
|---|---|---|---|---|---|
| Year 2 | | | Year 1 | | |
| Dec 31 | Trading account: *Profit to be credited in year 2* | 60 | Dec 31 | Trading account: *Unearned profit—see working* | 120 |
| | Balance carried forward | 60 | | | |
| | | £120 | | | £120 |
| Year 3 | | | Year 3 | | |
| Dec 31 | Trading account: *Profit to be credited in year 3* | 60 | Jan 1 | Balance brought forward | 60 |
| | | £60 | | | £60 |

Trading and Profit and Loss Account—Year 1

| | £ | | £ |
|---|---|---|---|
| Purchases account | 960 | Sales account | 1,200 |
| Provision for unrealised profit account *((£600 ÷ £1,200) × £240)* | 120 | | |
| Gross profit carried down | 120 | | |
| | £1,200 | | £1,200 |
| | | Gross profit brought down | 120 |
| | | Hire purchase interest | 120 |

The trading account for years 2 and 3 will be debited with purchases and credited with sales as in year 1. It will also be credited with the proportion of profit to be taken in each year from the provision for unrealised profit account.

WORKINGS

Calculation of unrealised profit

| Cash price is due as follows: | £ | £ |
|---|---|---|
| *Year 1* Deposit | 300 | |
| Instalments 12 × £(35 − 10) | 300 | |
| | | 600 |
| *Year 2* Instalments 12 × £(35 − 10) | | 300 |
| *Year 3* Instalments 12 × £(35 − 10) | | 300 |
| | | £1,200 |

Allocation of profit is therefore:

| | | £ |
|---|---|---|
| *Year 1* $\frac{£600}{£1,200} \times £240$ | = | 120 |
| *Year 2* $\frac{£300}{£1,200} \times £240$ | = | 60 |
| *Year 3* $\frac{£300}{£1,200} \times £240$ | = | 60 |
| | | £240 |

(b) *The sales system—treatment of repossessions*

(i) *Additional accounts required and their purpose*
*Repossessions account:* outstanding balances on

(1) hire purchase debtors account,

(2) hire purchase interest suspense account, and

(3) provision for unrealised profit account

as far as they relate to the repossessed goods are transferred to the repossessions account. The directors' valuation of the goods repossessed is then carried down as a stock balance (until the goods are sold) and the resulting balance transferred to profit and loss account as a profit/loss on repossessions.

(ii) *Double entry*
Double entry in accounting for repossessions is shown in Table 29.

Table 29. HIRE PURCHASE VENDOR: DOUBLE ENTRY IN ACCOUNTING FOR REPOSSESSIONS

| *Transaction* | *Debit* | *Credit* |
|---|---|---|
| Outstanding instalments on repossessed goods | Repossessions account | Hire purchase debtors account |
| Unearned interest on repossessed goods | Hire purchase interest suspense account | Repossessions account |
| Unrealised profit on repossessed goods | Provision for unrealised profit account | Repossessions account |
| Loss on repossessions (*reverse the entries if a profit*) | Profit and loss account | Repossessions account |

(iii) *Account outlines*
The following account outlines demonstrate the entries for a simple repossession. The next section of the book contains a comprehensive example on the sales system.

On 1st January Year 5, the following balances are brought forward in the accounts of N Ltd, a hire purchase dealer:

| | £ |
|---|---|
| Hire purchase debtors | 80,000 |
| Hire purchase interest suspense | 16,000 |
| Provision for unrealised profit | 12,000 |

On the same day, goods are repossessed. The original agreement relating to these goods was as follows:

| | £ |
|---|---|
| Cost | 400 |
| Cash selling price | 600 |
| Hire purchase price | 696 |
| Repayment by a deposit of £120 and 24 instalments of £24 each | |

At the time of repossession, 8 instalments had been paid. The company takes credit for gross profit in proportion to cash received and spreads interest evenly over the term of the agreement.

The directors value the repossessed goods at £160.

Hire Purchase Debtors Account

| Year 5 | £ | Year 5 | £ |
|---|---|---|---|
| Jan 1 Balance brought forward | 80,000 | Jan 1 Repossessions account: *Outstanding instalments in respect of repossessed goods—see workings* | 384 |

Hire Purchase Interest Suspense Account

| Year 5 | £ | Year 5 | £ |
|---|---|---|---|
| Jan 1 Repossessions account: *Unearned interest in respect of repossessed goods—see workings* | 64 | Jan 1 Balance brought forward | 16,000 |

Provision for Unrealised Profit Account

| Year 5 | £ | Year 5 | £ |
|---|---|---|---|
| Jan 1 Repossessions account: *Unearned profit in respect of repossessed goods—see workings* | 107 | Jan 1 Balance brought forward | 12,000 |

Repossessions Account

| Year 5 | £ | Year 5 | £ |
|---|---|---|---|
| Jan 1 Hire purchase debtors account: *Outstanding instalments* | 384 | Jan 1 Hire purchase interest suspense account: *Unearned interest* | 64 |
| | | Provision for unrealised profit account: *Unearned profit* | 107 |
| | | Purchases—trading account: *Directors' valuation of repossessed goods* | 160 |
| | | Profit and loss account: *Loss on repossessions* | 53 |
| | £384 | | £384 |

*Note:* If the repossessed goods are still in stock at the year end, they will be included in closing stock.

## Workings

1: *"Model" of agreement*

| | £ |
|---|---|
| Cost | 400 |
| Gross profit | 200 |
| Cash selling price | 600 |
| Deposit | 120 |
| Balance on credit | 480 |
| Interest charged | 96 |
| Repayable by 24 instalments of £24 | £576 |

2: *Outstanding instalments*

| | £ | £ |
|---|---|---|
| Hire purchase price | | 696 |
| *deduct:* Deposit | 120 | |
| 8 instalments | 192 | 312 |
| | | £384 |

3: *Unearned interest*

$$\frac{\text{Unpaid instalments}}{\text{Total instalments}} \times \text{Total interest}$$

$$= \frac{£384}{£576} \times £96 = £64$$

4: *Unearned profit*

$$\frac{\text{Unpaid instalments net of HP interest}}{\text{Cash selling price}} \times £200 =$$

$$\frac{£320}{£600} \times £200 = £107 \text{ (to nearest pound)}$$

(c) *The sales system—comprehensive account outlines*
The following account outlines illustrate the accounting entries for the sales system, based on two agreements; one continues, the other is subject to repossession as follows:

| | £ |
|---|---|
| Cost of each item | 840 |
| Gross profit | 240 |
| Cash selling price | 1,080 |
| Hire purchase interest | 288 |
| Hire purchase selling price | £1,368 |
| Repayable by: Deposit | 360 |
| 24 instalments of £42 | 1,008 |
| | £1,368 |

On one agreement, 12 instalments were received. On the other agreement only the deposit and 3 instalments were received. The goods were then repossessed and the directors valued them at £400. The company's policy is to take credit for gross profit in proportion to the cash received, and interest in proportion to instalments received.

### Trading Account

| | £ | | £ |
|---|---|---|---|
| Purchases account: *Cost of sales* | 1,680 | Hire purchase debtors account: *Cash selling price* | 2,160 |
| Provision for unrealised profit account: *Unearned gross profit included in outstanding instalments (working 2)* | 220 | | |
| Profit and loss account: *realised profit for year (working 4)* | 260 | | |
| | £2,160 | | £2,160 |

### Hire Purchase Debtors Account

| | £ | | £ |
|---|---|---|---|
| Trading account: *Cash selling price* | 2,160 | Bank account: *Deposits* | 720 |
| Hire purchase interest suspense account: *Hire purchase interest* | 576 | Bank account: | |
| | | *12 instalments* | 504 |
| | | *3 instalments* | 126 |
| | | Repossessed stock account: *Outstanding balance on stock repossessed—21 instalments* | 882 |
| | | Balance carried forward: *12 instalments* | 504 |
| | £2,736 | | £2,736 |

### Hire Purchase Interest Suspense Account

| | £ | | £ |
|---|---|---|---|
| Profit and loss account: *Interest earned for year (working 4)* | 180 | Hire purchase debtors account: *Interest on sales* | 576 |
| Repossessed stock account: *Interest element in outstanding instalments (working 3)* | 252 | | |
| Balance carried forward: *Unearned interest (working 3)* | 144 | | |
| | £576 | | £576 |

### Provision for Unrealised Profit Account

| | £ | | £ |
|---|---|---|---|
| Repossessed stock account: *Unrealised gross profit in instalments on repossessed item (working 2)* | 140 | Trading account: *Unrealised gross profit included in outstanding instalments (working 2)* | 220 |
| Balance carried forward: *Unrealised gross profit on continuing agreement* | 80 | | |
| | £220 | | £220 |
| | | Balance brought forward | 80 |

Repossessed Stock Account

| | £ | | £ |
|---|---|---|---|
| Hire purchase debtors account: *Outstanding balance on repossession* | 882 | Provision for unrealised profit account: *Unrealised gross profit in instalments outstanding on item repossessed (working 2)* | 140 |
| | | Hire purchase interest suspense account: *Interest element in outstanding instalments (working 3)* | 252 |
| | | Purchases—Main trading account: *Directors' valuation* | 400 |
| | | Profit and loss account: *Loss on repossessions* | 90 |
| | £882 | | £882 |
| Balance brought forward | 400 | | |

*Note:* If the repossessed goods are still in stock at the year end, they will be included in closing stock.

Profit and Loss Account (extract)

| | £ | | £ |
|---|---|---|---|
| Loss on repossessed goods | 90 | Gross profit | 260 |
| | | Hire purchase interest | 180 |

Balance Sheet (extract)

Current Assets

| | £ |
|---|---|
| Stock of repossessed goods at directors' valuation (if not resold) | 400 |
| Hire purchase debtors less provision for unrealised profit and hire purchase interest not earned | 280 |

WORKINGS

(1) *Analysis of deposits and instalments between cost, gross profit and interest*

| | Total | Cost | Gross profit | Interest |
|---|---|---|---|---|
| | £ | £ | £ | £ |
| Cash selling price | 1,080 | 840 | 240 | |
| *deduct:* Deposit (apportioned between cost and gross profit) | 360 | 280 | 80 | |
| | 720 | 560 | 160 | |
| *add:* Interest | 288 | — | — | 288 |
| | £1,008 | £560 | £160 | £288 |
| Each instalment apportioned between cost, gross profit and interest | £42 | £23.33 | £6.67 | £12 |

(2) *Unearned gross profit*

| | £ |
|---|---|
| Agreement still in operation | |
| 12 instalments outstanding including £6.67 gross profit each | 80 |
| Agreement terminated | |
| 21 instalments outstanding including £6.67 gross profit each | 140 |
| | £220 |

(3) *Unearned interest*

| | £ |
|---|---|
| Agreement still in operation | |
| 12 instalments outstanding including £12 interest each | 144 |
| Agreement terminated | |
| 21 instalments outstanding including £12 interest each | 252 |
| | £396 |

(4) *Proof of profit and interest figures*

| | | 1st agreement | | 2nd agreement |
|---|---|---|---|---|
| | | £ | | £ |
| Gross profit | | | | |
| Included in deposit (working 1) | | 80 | | 80 |
| Included in | | | | |
| 12 instalments (working 1) | | 80 | | |
| 3 instalments (working 1) | | | | 20 |
| | | £160 | | £100 |
| | Total | | £260 | |
| Interest | | | | |
| Included in (working 1) | | | | |
| 12 instalments | | 144 | | |
| 3 instalments | | | | 36 |
| | Total | | £180 | |

*Note:* These proofs are not an essential part of the answer but merely confirm the accuracy of the figures.

## 9.3 The stock system in the vendor's books

(a) *The stock system—general principles*
This accounting system is used where the trader intends to apportion the whole profit to successive periods in proportion to cash received.

(i) *Accounts required and their purpose*

(1) *Hire purchase trading account* is a separate account showing hire purchase gross profit only. (Cash sales are dealt with in a separate trading account.)
It is debited with the cost of goods sold.
It is credited with *cash received.*

At the end of the accounting period, a balance is carried forward in the form of a stock figure, representing the cost of outstanding instalments (see (ii) below).

*Note:* This trading account is unlike a normal one in that sales are not credited to the account, only cash as it is received.

(2) *Memorandum hire purchase debtors account* is not a part of the double entry.

Because sales are not recorded in the trading account, there is no debtors ledger within the double entry.

It is necessary, however, to maintain memorandum accounts for each customer and this account controls the individual customers' accounts.

(ii) *Valuation of stock out on hire* at the end of an accounting period, the cost element of outstanding instalments is carried forward as *stock out on hire.* It is calculated as follows:

$$\frac{\text{Outstanding instalments}}{\text{HP selling price}} \times \text{Cost} = \text{Stock out on hire}$$

(iii) *Double entry*

Double entry in the stock accounting system is shown in Table 30.

Table 30. HIRE PURCHASE VENDOR: DOUBLE ENTRY IN STOCK SYSTEM ACCOUNTS

| *Transaction* | *Debit* | *Credit* |
|---|---|---|
| Cost of goods sold on hire purchase | Hire purchase trading account | General trading account |
| Deposits and instalments received | Bank account | Hire purchase trading account |
| Stock out on hire being cost element of outstanding instalments | Next year's hire purchase trading account | This year's hire purchase trading account |
| Gross profit on hire purchase transactions being balance on the trading account | Hire purchase trading account | Profit and loss account |

(iv) *Account outline*

The following account outline illustrates a typical year's transactions but omits any reference to repossessions. Details are as follows:

| | £ |
|---|---|
| Cost of items sold during year on hire purchase terms | 20,000 |
| Hire purchase sales during year (all at uniform mark-up) | 30,000 |
| Cash collected during year | 12,000 |

Hire Purchase Trading Account

| | £ | | £ |
|---|---|---|---|
| General trading account: *Cost of goods sold on hire purchase terms* | 20,000 | Bank account: *Deposits and instalments received* | 12,000 |
| Gross profit carried down | 4,000 | Stock out on hire carried down: *Cost element of outstanding instalments (see working 2)* | 12,000 |
| | £24,000 | | £24,000 |

WORKINGS

(1) *Computation of outstanding instalments*

| | £ |
|---|---|
| Hire purchase sales | 30,000 |
| *deduct:* Cash collected | 12,000 |
| | £18,000 |

(2) *Computation of stock out on hire*

$$\frac{£18,000}{£30,000} \times £20,000 = £12,000.$$

(b) *The memorandum hire purchase debtors account*

A moment's reflection will show that in a conventional trading account sales are credited to the trading account and debited to a debtors ledger control account. The debtors ledger is thus a part of the double entry accounts.

In the hire purchase trading account *cash collected* is credited to the trading account and there is therefore no debtors ledger within the double-entry system. It is necessary to maintain ledger accounts for each customer, to record his indebtedness and this is controlled by a *memorandum* hire purchase debtors account. The word memorandum reflects the fact that the account *is not a part of the double entry.*

The following account outline is based on the figures used in (a)(iv) above.

Memorandum Hire Purchase Debtors Account

| | £ | | £ |
|---|---|---|---|
| Hire purchase sales | 30,000 | Deposits and instalments received | 12,000 |
| | | Balance carried forward | 18,000 |
| | £30,000 | | £30,000 |

(c) *Treatment of repossessions under the stock system*

(i) *Additional account required and its purpose*

*Repossessions account.* When goods are repossessed, the cost element of the outstanding instalments is transferred from the hire purchase trading account to the debit of the repossessions account. The directors' valuation of the repossessed goods is added back to main purchases and carried forward as a stock figure until sold. Any difference in value between the cost element of outstanding instalments and the directors' valuation is written off to profit and loss account as a loss/profit on repossessions.

(ii) *Double entry*
Double entry in the treatment of repossessions is shown in Table 31.

Table 31. HIRE PURCHASE VENDOR: DOUBLE ENTRY IN ACCOUNTING FOR REPOSSESSIONS

| *Transaction* | *Debit* | *Credit* |
|---|---|---|
| Cost element of outstanding instalments | Repossessions account | Hire purchase trading account |
| Sale proceeds of repossessed goods sold | Bank account | Repossessions account |
| Directors' valuation of goods repossessed and brought back into stock | Main purchases | Repossessions account |
| Loss (if any) on repossessed goods | Profit and loss account | Repossessions account |

(iii) *Account outline*
The following account outline illustrates a single repossession in respect of the following hire purchase agreement:

| | £ |
|---|---|
| Cost of goods | 400 |
| Hire purchase price | 480 |
| Instalments received until repossession | 120 |
| Directors' valuation of goods | 250 |

Repossessions Account

| | £ | | £ |
|---|---|---|---|
| Hire purchase trading account: *Cost element of outstanding instalments (see workings)* | 300 | Profit and loss account: *Loss on repossessions* | 50 |
| | | Main purchases: *Directors' valuation* | 250 |
| | £300 | | £300 |

WORKINGS

Cost element of outstanding instalments

$$\frac{£360}{£480} \times £400 = £300.$$

(d) *Comprehensive account outlines*

The following account outlines illustrate two transactions; one continuing, one subject to repossession, as follows:

| | £ | |
|---|---|---|
| Cost of each item | 1,000 | |
| Hire purchase price of each item | 1,500 | |

| | 1st agreement | 2nd agreement |
|---|---|---|
| Deposit received | £300 | £300 |
| Instalments received | | |
| 9 × £50 | £450 | |
| 3 × £50 | | £150 |

Goods in respect of 2nd agreement were repossessed and valued by directors at £750.

Hire Purchase Trading Account

| | £ | | £ |
|---|---|---|---|
| General trading account: *Cost of sales* | 2,000 | Bank account: *Deposits* | 600 |
| | | *Instalments* | 600 |
| Profit and loss account: *Gross profit* | 400 | Repossessed stock account: *Cost element of outstanding instalments (working 1)* | 700 |
| | | Balance carried forward: *Stock out on hire (working 2)* | 500 |
| | £2,400 | | £2,400 |

Repossessed Stock Account

| | £ | | £ |
|---|---|---|---|
| Hire purchase trading account: *Cost element of outstanding instalments* | 700 | Main purchases: *Directors' valuation* | 750 |
| Profit and loss account: *Profit on repossession* | 50 | | |
| | £750 | | £750 |
| Balance brought forward | 750 | | |

Memorandum Hire Purchase Debtors Account

| | £ | | £ |
|---|---|---|---|
| Hire purchase sales | 3,000 | Deposits | 600 |
| | | Instalments received | 600 |
| | | Repossessions: *Outstanding instalments* | 1,050 |
| | | Balance carried forward (15 × £50) | 750 |
| | £3,000 | | £3,000 |
| Balance brought forward | 750 | | |

WORKINGS

(1) *Repossessions*

$$\frac{\text{Outstanding instalments}}{\text{HP selling price}} \times \text{Cost}$$

$$= \frac{£1,050}{£1,500} \times £1,000 = £700.$$

(2) *Stock out on hire*

$$\frac{\text{Outstanding instalments}}{\text{HP selling price}} \times \text{Cost}$$

$$= \frac{£750}{£1,500} \times £1,000 = £500.$$

## 9.4 Hire purchase transactions in a finance company's books

(a) *Introduction*
In many hire purchase transactions, three parties are involved, namely seller, buyer and finance company. Two situations may be distinguished:

(i) *Customer* wishes to buy goods on credit from trader. *Trader* sells goods to *finance company* with whom he is associated and *finance company* enters into hire purchase agreement with *customer*;

(ii) *Customer* wishes to buy goods on credit from *trader*. Trader introduces customer to *finance company* which provides the cash selling price of the goods. Customer repays this to finance company together with interest.

In both cases the customer may not be aware of the true position and may believe he is dealing only with the trader. In many cases the trader will act as the agent of the finance company, collecting repayments on its behalf.

(b) *Accounting approach*
In situation (i) above, the *trader* has effectively made a sale and may take credit for the whole of his gross profit. This is subject to any liability in respect of guarantees he may have given to the finance company. The *finance company* has purchased goods which it is selling on hire purchase terms. The company is effectively trading and will follow one of the methods outlined in 9.2 and 9.3 above.

In situation (ii) above, the *finance company* has not purchased any goods but is merely lending money to the customer. It is this latter case which now requires consideration and, as before, the main problem revolves around the writing off of interest.

(c) *Accounts required and their purpose*
The type of finance company under consideration does not trade and therefore does not require a trading account or purchases or sales accounts.

(i) *Hire purchase debtors control account* shows the total amount owed by debtors, including original monies lent and the total hire purchase interest payable. The account controls the individual borrower's accounts.

(ii) *Hire purchase interest account* records the total interest receivable in respect of all hire purchase agreements. An appropriate proportion is transferred to profit and loss account in each period.

(iii) *Balance sheet disclosure*. Balance on the debtors account *less* the balance of unearned interest on the hire purchase interest account is shown under current assets.

(d) *Double entry*
Double entry in the finance company's accounts is shown in Table 32.

Table 32. HIRE PURCHASE FINANCE COMPANY—DOUBLE ENTRY

| | *Transactions* | *Debit* | *Credit* |
|---|---|---|---|
| *Entries at time of sale* | Money lent to debtor | Hire purchase debtors control account | Bank account |
| | Total interest to be charged | Hire purchase debtors control account | Hire purchase interest account |
| | Option payment payable at end of agreement (frequently ignored in examination questions) | Hire purchase debtors control account | Option charges account |
| *Repayments* | Repayments received | Bank account | Hire purchase debtors control account |
| *Year-end entries* | Interest to be credited for period | Hire purchase interest account | Profit and loss account |
| | Option charges in respect of agreements completed during period | Option charges account | Profit and loss account |
| *Early repayment by debtor* | Interest charges remitted on early repayment of loan | Hire purchase interest account | Hire purchase debtors control account |

The next two paragraphs, (e) and (f), deal with methods of determining the amount of interest to be credited to profit and loss account in any period.

(e) *Apportionment of hire purchase interest*
The interest charged on hire purchase transactions may be credited to the

profit and loss account in any of the ways listed in 8.2(b) above. The following points concerning the various methods should be noted:

(i) *Actuarial method* gives an accurate apportionment of interest charges but involves a formidable amount of computational work;

(ii) *"Sum of digits" method*, although only an approximation, requires less computational work than (i) above and produces reasonably accurate results;

(iii) *Straight-line method* is a relatively straightforward method and is frequently used. It ignores the primary nature of interest which, being a reward for money lent, should be related to the money outstanding at any time.

(f) *Short-cut methods used in the apportionment of interest*
It will be appreciated that where a company has many thousands of hire purchase agreements it would be impracticable to apply any of the above methods to each individual agreement. Short-cut methods have been developed to obtain approximately correct apportionments of interest with a minimum of computation. These are:

(i) batching, and

(ii) average date.

*Batching* involves the grouping together of transactions with similar terms and the application of the appropriate method of apportionment to the batch total. Monthly or quarterly totals provide suitable batches for computation.

*Average date*—where agreements are stated to have been entered into steadily throughout the year (as is frequently found in examination questions), a single date may be used to represent the commencement of all agreements during the year. The whole year's transactions may then be treated as one batch.

(g) *Account outlines*
The following account outlines illustrate the accounting entries, based on the following information and apportioning interest according to the "sum of digits" method.

Trial Balance year ended 31st December 19XX

| | £ | £ |
|---|---|---|
| Ordinary share capital | | 20,000 |
| Fixed assets | 20,000 | |
| General expenses | 1,500 | |
| Bank overdraft | | 17,371 |
| Hire purchase debtors | 22,369 | |
| Hire purchase interest | | 6,300 |
| Option charges | | 198 |
| | £43,869 | £43,869 |

Contracts during the first year of operations are as follows:

| | Cash price | Deposit | HP interest | Option charge |
|---|---|---|---|---|
| | £ | £ | £ | £ |
| January | 1,500 | 500 | 300 | 10 |
| February | 1,500 | 500 | 300 | 8 |
| March | 1,500 | 500 | 300 | 10 |
| April | 2,250 | 750 | 450 | 14 |
| May | 2,250 | 750 | 450 | 16 |
| June | 2,250 | 750 | 450 | 14 |
| July | 3,000 | 1,000 | 600 | 20 |
| August | 3,000 | 1,000 | 600 | 18 |
| September | 3,000 | 1,000 | 600 | 18 |
| October | 3,750 | 1,250 | 750 | 24 |
| November | 3,750 | 1,250 | 750 | 22 |
| December | 3,750 | 1,250 | 750 | 24 |
| | £31,500 | £10,500 | £6,300 | £198 |

Contracts are for 24 months, the first instalment payable on the last day of the month of the contract. All instalments are equal except the last one which includes an additional £2 option charge.
(All calculations are to nearest £.)

Profit and Loss Account for the year ended 31st December 19XX

| | £ | | £ |
|---|---|---|---|
| General expenses | 1,500 | Hire purchase charges | 2,371 |
| Net profit for year | 871 | (working 2) | |
| | £2,371 | | £2,371 |

Balance Sheet 31st December 19XX

| | £ | £ |
|---|---|---|
| Share capital | | 20,000 |
| Retained profits | | 871 |
| | | £20,871 |
| Fixed assets | | 20,000 |
| Hire purchase debtors (working 3) | 18,242 | |
| *deduct:* Bank overdraft | 17,371 | 871 |
| | | £20,871 |

WORKINGS

(1) *Apportionment of interest*

| Contract date | Hire purchase interest | Proportion unearned | Hire purchase interest unearned |
|---|---|---|---|
| | £ | | £ |
| January | 300 | 78/300 | 78 |
| February | 300 | 91/300 | 91 |
| March | 300 | 105/300 | 105 |
| April | 450 | 120/300 | 180 |
| May | 450 | 136/300 | 204 |
| June | 450 | 153/300 | 229 |
| July | 600 | 171/300 | 342 |
| August | 600 | 190/300 | 380 |
| September | 600 | 210/300 | 420 |
| October | 750 | 231/300 | 577 |
| November | 750 | 253/300 | 633 |
| December | 750 | 276/300 | 690 |
| | | | £3,929 |

The above working assumes the contracts to be entered into on the first day of each month.

*Sum of digits*

Sum of digits 24–1 equals 300.

The first repayment on the January contract will occur on 31st January, and there will be twelve repayments during the year and therefore twelve outstanding at the year end. The sum of the digits 1–12 is 78 and therefore the proportion of unearned interest is $\frac{78}{300}$. The calculations for the other months follow on logically from this first one.

(2) *Hire purchase interest*

| | £ |
|---|---|
| Per trial balance | 6,300 |
| *deduct:* Unearned (working 1) | 3,929 |
| | £2,371 |

(3) *Hire purchase debtors*

| | £ | £ |
|---|---|---|
| Per trial balance | | 22,369 |
| *deduct:* Unearned interest | 3,929 | |
| Unearned option charge | 198 | 4,127 |
| | | £18,242 |

*Note:* Since the option is exercisable at the end of the contract it is not considered appropriate to take credit for the option charges in this period.

## 9.5 Institute recommendation (N. 23)

(a) *Hire purchase and credit sale transactions*
The following is a brief summary of the recommendations of the Institute of Chartered Accountants in England and Wales on hire purchase and credit sale transactions.

(b) *Hire purchase finance companies*
The basis for apportioning interest should be appropriate to the business and applied consistently.

The most suitable method is either the actuarial or the "sum of the digits" method. The straight-line method may be suitable where the business is not subject to sharp fluctuations. The basis used should be disclosed in a note to the accounts.

Where the volume of hire purchase sales is large, it may be convenient to "batch" the transactions and make a single interest calculation for the agreements entered into a month or a quarter. This technique of batching may also be used by traders ((c) below).

The amount of interest carried forward as unearned should not be less than the rebates which would be allowed if the agreements were immediately terminated.

The interest should be shown as a deduction from the debtors in the balance sheet.

(c) *Dealers financing their own transactions*
Balance sheet should disclose:

(i) hire purchase debts outstanding

(ii) credit sale debts outstanding.

These should be shown net of any bad debt provision. The unearned interest carried forward should be shown as a separate figure in each case.

In respect of hire purchase sales, the trader should carry forward an appropriate amount of his gross profit and finance charges as not yet earned. The unearned gross profit should be related to instalments receivable. The unearned finance charge should be carried forward according to the actuarial or "sum of digits" method except where there are no sharp fluctuations, when the straight line method may be appropriate.

With regard to credit sales, the trader may take credit for the whole gross profit immediately.

(d) *Dealers financing their transactions by a finance company*
Where a dealer is not a party to a credit instalment agreement and is not responsible for the collection of instalments, he may treat the transaction as an outright sale.

Provision must be made for any guarantee given by the dealer to the finance company either to pay instalments in arrear or to repurchase the goods where customers have defaulted in payment.

(e) *Bad debts provision*
Bad debts provision should preferably be computed by reference to individual accounts. Where this is not practicable, the use of percentage provisions based on past experience and applied to different classes of account is suitable.

(f) *Change in basis of accounting*
Whatever method of accounting is chosen should be applied consistently. Where there is a change in the basis of accounting the effect of such change must be disclosed.

## 10.0 INVESTMENT ACCOUNTS

Figure 15 illustrates the problems which may be encountered in investment accounts.

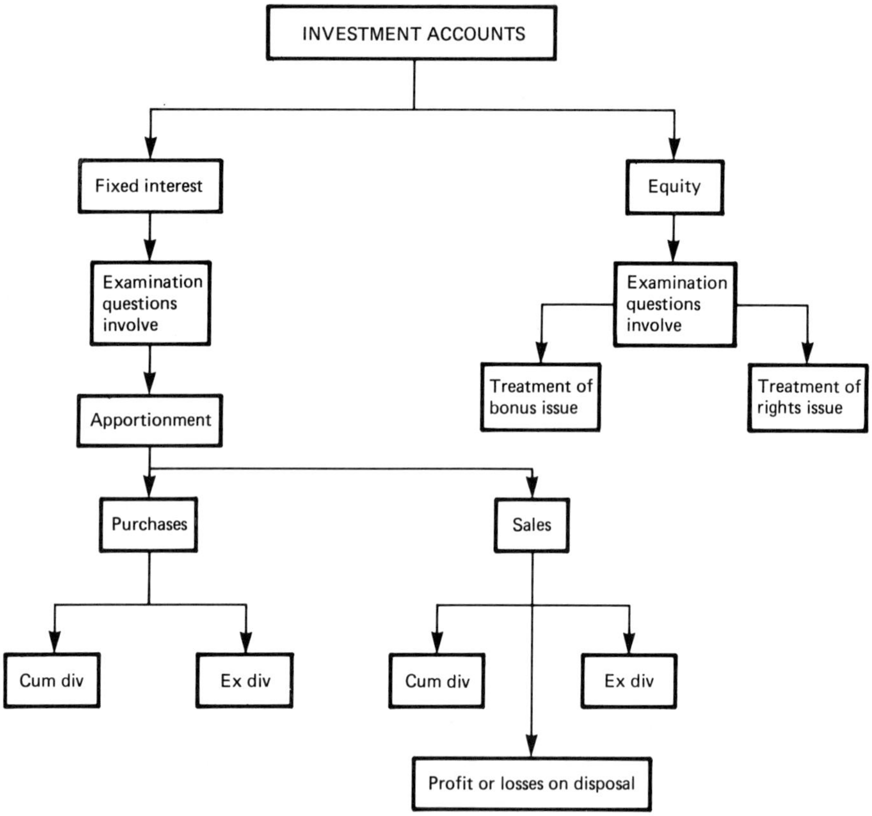


Fig. 15. *Problems encountered in investment accounts.*

### 10.1 Legal aspects

No legal considerations apply to examination problems on investment accounts but the disclosure provisions of the Companies Acts 1948 and 1967 with regard to presentation of investments in a company's accounts must be known.

## 10.2 Fixed interest securities

(a) *Purchase "cum div"*

(i) Work out the total cost of acquisition including stamp duty, brokerage, transfer fees, etc.

(ii) Calculate the dividend accrued from the date it was last paid to the date of purchase. This amount represents the income content in the purchase consideration.

(iii) Debit *income* columns with figure calculated in (ii) and the balance of purchase price to *cost* column.

(iv) Credit *income* column with income when received.

(b) *Purchase "ex div"*

(i) Debit *cost* column with total purchase price inclusive of all expenses.

(ii) Calculate the dividend from the date of purchase to the due date of payment. This amount represents the income deducted from the purchase consideration.

(iii) By means of journal entry debit *cost* column with figure arrived at in (ii) and credit *income* column with the same amount.

(c) *Sales "cum div"*

(i) Work out the net proceeds of sale, that is, after deducting brokerage and transfer fees etc. from the sale price.

(ii) Calculate the dividend due from the date it was last paid to the date of sale. This amount represents the income content in the sale proceeds.

(iii) Credit *income* column with figure arrived at in (ii) and credit *cost* column with balance of sale proceeds.

(iv) Calculate the profit or loss on sale and transfer this to profit and loss account.

(d) *Sale "ex div"*

(i) Calculate the net proceeds of sale, that is, after deducting brokerage and transfer fees etc. from the sale price.

(ii) Calculate the dividend on the securities sold from the date of sale to the due date of payment of the dividend. This amount represents the income deducted from the sale proceeds. On receipt of dividend, *credit* this to *cost* column and the balance to *income*.

(iii) Treat the profit or loss on sale as in (c)(iv) above.

## 10.3 Equity shares

The current practice is not to make an apportionment of dividend on purchase or sale of equities, either "cum" or "ex" dividend. The full cost of investment including expenses is debited to the *cost* column.

On a sale of investments it is necessary to calculate any *profit* or *loss* on sale. For this purpose the *average cost* at the date of sale is used for the calculation and not the capital gains tax rules.

(a) *Bonus issue*
An entry of the number of shares received is entered in the *nominal* column only since these shares have not cost anything.

(b) *Rights issue*

(i) *Rights taken up:* enter in *nominal* column the number of shares taken up and in *cost* column the cost of these shares.

(ii) *Rights sold:* credit proceeds of sale in *cost* column. This sale does not result in a profit or loss but does reduce the "average" cost of the share holding.

(c) *Sales*
In calculating the profit or loss on disposal a bonus issue or a rights issue will affect the average cost of the shares being sold.

## 10.4 Sundry matters

(a) *Market prices*
Where two prices are quoted, for example, 75p to 85p:

(i) selling price is the lower, i.e. 75p;

(ii) purchase price is the higher, i.e. 85p;

(iii) for calculating the market value for balance sheet purposes the mid-market price is taken, i.e. 80p.

(b) *Income tax*

(i) Examination questions on investment accounts normally state that income tax is to be ignored.

(ii) If income tax is to be taken into account then all apportionments for interest or dividends must be made on *net income*.

(iii) the *income tax account* is debited and the *income* column of the investment account credited with the income tax suffered by deduction at source.

(c) *Income from investment accounts*
At the end of the accounting period the total income received is transferred from the debit of the investment account to the credit of income from investments account which will be closed off to profit and loss account.

## 10.5 Account outlines

(a) *Fixed-interest securities*
A company bought £10,000 ABC 6 per cent stock on 31st January 19X2 when the quotation was 80–82. Brokerage etc. amounted to £136. Interest on the stock was paid half-yearly on 31st March and 30th September.

On 31st August 19X2 the company sold half its holding, at 85–87 ex div, brokerage amounted to £72.

Give the ledger account recording the stock in the company's books to 31st December 19X2 (ignore taxation).

Investment Account—ABC 6 per cent Stock

| | Nominal £ | Income £ | Cost £ | | Nominal £ | Income £ | Cost £ |
|---|---|---|---|---|---|---|---|
| Bank: *Purchase cum div* | 10,000 | 200 | 8,136 | Bank: *Interest received* | | 300 | |
| Investment income account | | 450 | | Bank: *Sale ex div* | 5,000 | | 4,178 |
| Profit and loss account: *Profit on sale* | | | 135 | Bank: *Half year's interest* | | 275 | 25 |
| | | | | Balance carried down | 5,000 | 75 | 4,068 |
| | £10,000 | £650 | £8,271 | | £10,000 | £650 | £8,271 |

| Proof: | Interest: | 7 months at 6% p.a. on £10,000 | 350 |
|---|---|---|---|
| | | 4 months at 6% p.a. on £ 5,000 | 100 |
| | | | £450 |

(b) *Equity shares*
A company bought 5,000 ordinary shares of £1 each fully paid in EDE Ltd on 1st April 19X2. The price paid was £1.50 per share cum div. On 1st July 19X2 EDE Ltd made a bonus issue of 1 share for every 5 shares held. On 10th August 19X2 a dividend (which applied to the bonus shares) of 8 per cent was received for the year ended 30th June 19X2. The company sold 1,000 of its shares on 31st August 19X2 for £1,350.

Prepare the ledger account recording the above in the books of the company and balance the account at 30th September 19X2, the end of the company's financial year.

Investment Account—EDE Ltd Ordinary Shares

| | Nominal £ | Income £ | Cost £ | | Nominal £ | Income £ | Cost £ |
|---|---|---|---|---|---|---|---|
| Bank: *Purchase £1.50 each* | 5,000 | | 7,500 | Bank: *Dividend on shares* | | 480 | |
| Bonus issue | 1,000 | | — | Bank: *Sale of shares* | 1,000 | | 1,350 |
| Investment income account | | 480 | | Balances carried forward | 5,000 | | 6,250 |
| Profit and loss account: *Profit on sale* | | | 100 | | | | |
| | £6,000 | £480 | £7,600 | | £6,000 | £480 | £7,600 |

| Proof of profit on sale: | | |
|---|---|---|
| | Cost of 1,000 shares (1,000 ÷ 6,000 × £7,500) | 1,250 |
| | Sale of proceeds | 1,350 |
| | Profit | £100 |

## 11.0 BILLS OF EXCHANGE

Figure 16 illustrates the treatment of bills of exchange.

### 11.1 Legal aspects

(a) *Bill of exchange*
A bill of exchange is "an unconditional *order* in writing, addressed by one person to another, signed by the person giving it, requiring the person to whom it is addressed to pay on demand, or at a fixed or determinable future time, a certain sum in money to or to the order of, a specified person or bearer".

(b) *Promissory note*
A promissory note is "an unconditional promise made in writing by one person to another, signed by the maker engaging to pay on demand or at a fixed or determinable future date, a certain sum in money for, or to the order of a specified person or bearer".

(c) *Cheque*
A cheque is "a bill of exchange drawn on a banker payable on demand".

(d) *Accommodation bill*
An accommodation bill is "a bill of exchange which has been accepted, drawn or endorsed by a person not in the course of ordinary business transactions, but for the specific object of enabling another person to raise funds by discounting the bill on the strength of the first person's name".

When the bill is discounted, the banker is entitled to hold the accommodating person liable on his acceptance, drawing or endorsement.

(e) *Parties to a bill*
*Drawer:* the party who draws the bill and signs it.
*Drawee:* the party to whom the bill is addressed.
*Payee:* the party to whom the bill is expressed to be payable.
*Acceptor:* the drawee after he has signed the bill.

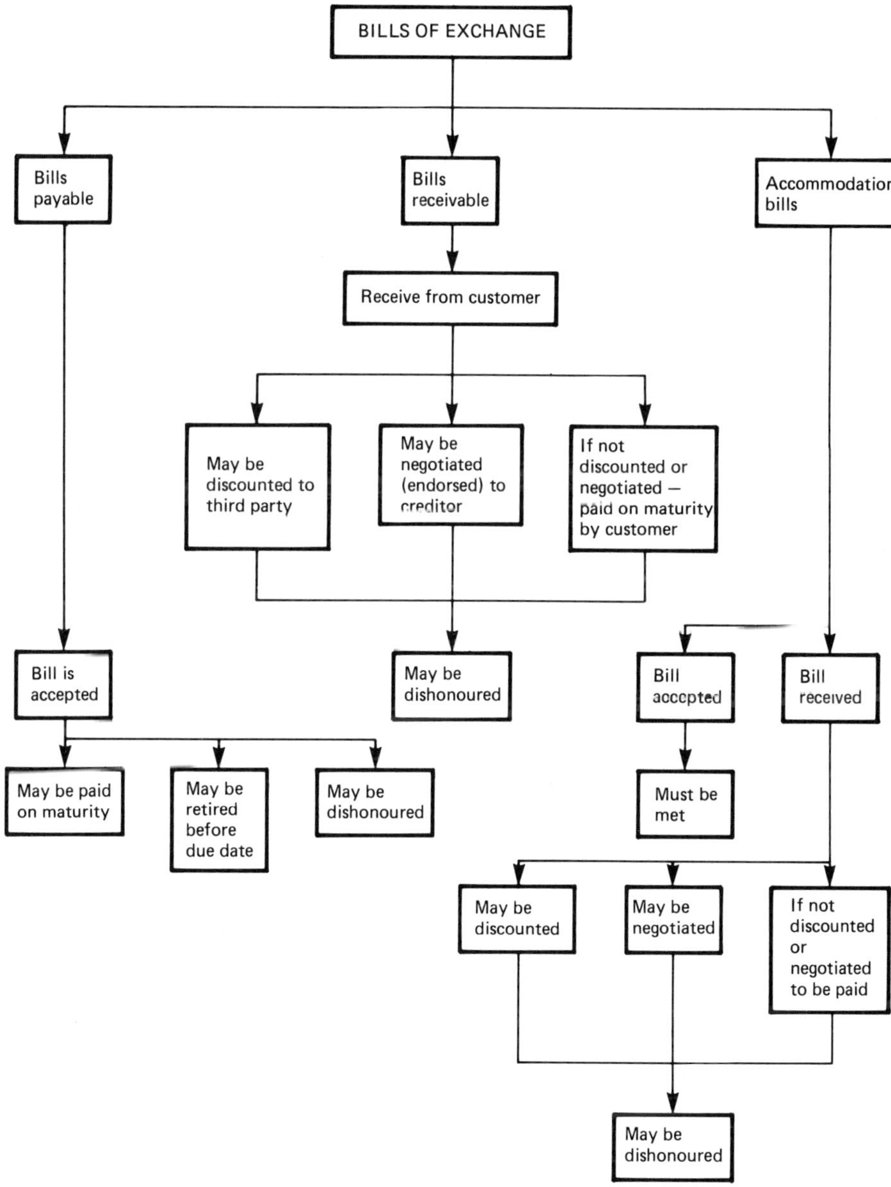


Fig. 16. *Bills of exchange.*

## 11.2 Discounting bills of exchange

When a bill receivable is discounted the bill is in effect sold to the banker for cash.

## 11.3 Bills receivable—double-entry principles

These are shown in Table 33.

Table 33. BILLS RECEIVABLE—DOUBLE ENTRY

| | *Transaction* | *Debit* | *Credit* |
|---|---|---|---|
| *Normal entries* | Bill of exchange received from a customer | Bills receivable account | Customer's account |
| | Bill paid on maturity by customer | Bank account | Bills receivable account |
| *Entries where bill is discounted with a bank* | Proceeds of discounting bill with bank rather than wait for maturity | Bank account | Bills receivable account |
| | Discounting charges of bank | Discounting charges account | Bills receivable account |
| *Entries where bill is endorsed to a creditor* | Face value of bill endorsed over to a creditor | Creditor's account | Bills receivable account |
| *Entries where bill is dishonoured* | Face value of bill dishonoured where it has not been discounted or endorsed | Customer's account | Bills receivable account |
| | Face value of bill dishonoured where it has been discounted with a bank | Customer's account | Bank account |
| | Face value of bill dishonoured where it has been endorsed over to a creditor | Customer's account | Creditor's account |
| *Entries where a bill is retired to avoid dishonour and new bill is issued* | Face value of bill retired | Customer's account | Bills receivable account |
| | Interest charged to customer as a result of retiring old bill and issuing a new one | Customer's account | Interest receivable account |
| | Amount of new bill being face value of old one plus interest charged | Bills receivable account | Customer's account |

*continued*

Table 33. *continued*

| | *Transaction* | *Debit* | *Credit* |
|---|---|---|---|
| *Normal entries* | Face value of bill of exchange accepted for payment to a creditor | Creditor's account | Bills payable account |
| | Face value of bill paid on maturity | Bills payable account | Bank account |
| *Entries where bill is dishonoured* | Face value of bill retired | Bills payable account | Creditor's account |
| | Interest charged by customer as a result of retiring old bill and issuing a new one | Interest payable account | Creditor's account |
| | Face value of new bill issued being face value of old one plus interest charged | Creditor's account | Bills payable account |

## 11.4 Accommodation bills

The principles involved in accommodation bills are exactly the same as for bills payable and bills receivable. In the place of a customer's account, each person will maintain a current account with the other party to the bill.

# 12.0 INSURANCE CLAIMS

## 12.1 Loss of profits claims

(a) *Introduction*

This type of insurance indemnifies the insured for losses arising from the suspension, wholly or in part, of the activities of the business caused by fire or the occurrence of some other insured risk.

Policies vary considerably, but most contain clauses relating to the following matters:

(i) period of indemnity;

(ii) computation of profit lost;

(iii) increased cost of working;

(iv) savings in insured standard charges;

(v) special circumstances clause;

(vi) average proviso.

(b) *Computation of claim*

The steps involved in computing a loss of profits claim are as follows:

(i) Fix the *period of the claim* by taking the shorter of the period of indemnity or the period of interruption.

(ii) Ascertain the *reduction in turnover* for the period as follows:

| | £ |
|---|---|
| Turnover of corresponding period (standard turnover) | 000 |
| *deduct:* Turnover of period of dislocation (actual turnover) | 000 |
| Reduction in turnover | £000 |

The "special circumstances clause" (*see* (vii) below) may affect the standard turnover and therefore the amount of reduction in turnover.

(iii) Ascertain the *rate of gross profit* to be used in the claim: this is the percentage of gross profit to turnover based on the last accounting period.

The "special circumstances clause" (*see* (vii) below) may affect the rate of gross profit.

(iv) The *profit lost* during the period of dislocation is found by multiplying the reduced turnover by the rate of gross profit.

(v) Where extra expense has been incurred in order to minimise the reduction in turnover, this increase in *cost of working* may be added to the claim. The amount to be claimed is the lowest of the three following items:

(1) actual expenditure;

(2) actual expenditure $\times \dfrac{\text{net profit plus } \textit{insured} \text{ standing charges}}{\text{net profit plus } \textit{all} \text{ standing charges}}$;

(3) rate of gross profit applied to the turnover which would have been lost if the extra cost of working had not been incurred.

The second and third of the above three may be affected by the "special circumstances" clause (*see* (vii) below).

(vi) Any *savings in insured standing charges* must be deducted *in full* from the amount of the claim.

(vii) Examples of *special circumstances clauses* include adjustments to be made to turnover and the rate of gross profit figures where it can be shown that:

(1) turnover during the period of dislocation was higher than in the corresponding period, and/or

(2) the rate of gross profit was higher during the period of dislocation than the year immediately preceding the date of dislocation.

If an adjustment is called for under this clause, it may affect the following items, mentioned above:

(ii) reduction in turnover

(iii) rate of gross profit

(v) limitations on additional cost of working.

The adjustment may also affect the "average clause" mentioned at (viii) below.

(viii) The *average clause* places a further limitation on the amount of the claim where the amount of the *indemnity* is less than the rate of gross profit (as adjusted by "special circumstances") applied to the annual turnover of the twelve months preceding the period of dislocation (as adjusted for "special circumstances").

The limitation is as follows:

$$\text{Amount of claim} \times \frac{\text{Amount insured}}{\text{Rate of gross profit} \times \text{Annual turnover}}.$$

(ix) It should be noted that the "special circumstances clause" is a "two-edged weapon"—it benefits the insured in calculating the loss of profits but may work against him in the average clause.

(c) *Summary*
The various steps involved may be summarised for convenience as follows:

(i) fix period of indemnity;

(ii) ascertain reduced turnover;

(iii) calculate rate of gross profit;

(iv) (ii) × (iii) = gross profit lost;

(v) add to (iv) additional cost of working (limitations);

(vi) deduct savings in insured standing charges;

(vii) amend (ii), (iii) and (v) in light of any special circumstances;

(viii) consider average clause.

## 12.2 Loss of stock claims

(a) *Loss of stock insurance*
Subject to verification of facts, an insurance company will, in consideration of a premium, agree to indemnify a trader in respect of loss of stock by fire or other causes.

(b) *Preparation of estimated trading account*
Where it is not possible to verify the actual stock lost, a frequent practice is to construct an estimated trading account assuming a given rate of gross profit on sales, and from this compute the stock which should have been in hand but for the fire. The difference between this figure and the actual stock is assumed to have been lost.

In preparing a claim for submission to the insurance company, where a trading account is to be used the following information must be given:

(i) basis of previous stocktakings, particularly as regards consistency of valuation;

(ii) the stock value at the date of the last balance sheet date (or a nearer date where interim accounts have been prepared);

(iii) the total purchases from the date used in (ii) above to the date of the fire, care being taken that goods invoiced but not delivered at the date of the fire are not included;

(iv) the total sales for the period;

(v) the value of any stock salvaged;

(vi) the average rate of gross profit in recent years, having regard to any factor likely to render the average unrealisable.

(c) *Average clause*
In addition to the above factors, the precise terms of the policy would have to be examined, particularly as regards any average clause which would operate to the disadvantage of the insured; e.g.

| | |
|---|---|
| Value of stock | £10,000 |
| Insurance cover for | £8,000 |

The insured could only claim for eight-tenths of the loss even though it is less than £8,000.

(d) *Double entry*
Double entry for loss of stock claims is shown in Table 34.

Table 34. INSURANCE CLAIMS FOR LOSS OF STOCK—DOUBLE ENTRY

| *Transaction* | *Debit* | *Credit* |
|---|---|---|
| Computed value of stock lost | Insurance claim account | Trading account |
| Expenses in respect of the claim and of repairing damaged stock | Insurance claim account | Bank account |
| Proceeds of claim received | Bank account | Insurance claim account |
| Loss on insurance claim (being balance on account, if any) | Profit and loss account | Insurance claim account |

# 13.0 CASH BUDGETS

## 13.1 Introduction

Cash budgets are prepared to enable an enterprise to work out how much surplus or deficit of cash it may have at any one time over the budgeting period. The budgeting period will depend on:

(a) the size of the enterprise;

(b) the exact purpose of the budget;

(c) how long the cash flow figures can be reasonably estimated for.

If the cash budget (sometimes called cash flow forecast) is accurate, it can be used so that any excess cash is utilised in the most beneficial way and that where there is an expected deficit, arrangements can be made to tide the business over. In a large company, it may be necessary to issue debentures or new shares.

## 13.2 Exam questions

In financial accounting papers, the questions generally involve the preparation of a cash budget together with a projected trading and profit and loss account and balance sheet.

Information such as expected sales, purchases and expenses is given and this has to be formulated in a table. From the table, the actual timing of the receipts and payments is put onto the cash budget.

## 13.3 Detailed example

*Question*

Star Ltd and Garter Ltd agree to enter into a joint venture on an equal basis for importing and selling electronic equipment. The bankers to the joint venture agree to provide overdraft facilities up to 50 per cent of the working capital required. Star Ltd and Garter Ltd are to provide working capital in proportion to their agreed sharing basis in the venture. After an initial contribution totalling £20,000 they are to pay into the bank at the beginning of each month any additional amount required, based on the position shown at the end of the previous month, after the bank has added interest at $1\frac{1}{4}$ per cent per month on the overdrawn balance at the month end.

The following information is available of the expected trading for the first six months of the venture:

(a) Sales in the first month are expected to reach £25,000 and in each subsequent month they are expected to increase by 10 per cent over the previous month.

(b) Wages will be £3,000 per month until the month when anticipated turnover is in excess of £35,000, when it will be necessary to engage additional staff at an additional charge of £600 monthly from and including that month.

(c) Overhead expenses will be £1,200 per month for the first three months, and then £1,100 per month thereafter. Overhead expenses, which accrue evenly, are paid half a month in arrear.

(d) Sales will be effected through agents who receive a commission of $2\frac{1}{2}$ per cent on selling price paid one month in arrear.

(e) The partnership makes a standard 25 per cent gross profit on sales before charging any commission.

(f) Debtors are expected to pay in the month following sale.

(g) Regular monthly supplies of goods will be imported and must be paid for immediately against shipping documents. It is intended to have sufficient stock at the end of each month to cover the next month's sales.

You are required to prepare:

(a) A statement showing the estimated bank balance at the end of each of the first six months together with the amounts to be provided by the partners based thereon.

(b) A budgeted trading and profit and loss account and balance sheet for the first six months.

Ignore *all* taxation.

ANSWER

(a) Star Ltd and Garter Ltd Joint Venture: Cash Budget for first 6 months

| | Month | | | | | |
|---|---|---|---|---|---|---|
| | 1 | 2 | 3 | 4 | 5 | 6 |
| Operating budget | £ | £ | £ | £ | £ | £ |
| Receipts from debtors | — | 25,000 | 27,500 | 30,250 | 33,275 | 36,602 |
| *Payments* | | | | | | |
| Wages | 3,000 | 3,000 | 3,000 | 3,000 | 3,600 | 3,600 |
| Overheads | 600 | 1,200 | 1,200 | 1,150 | 1,100 | 1,100 |
| Commission | — | 625 | 687 | 756 | 832 | 915 |
| Purchases | 39,375 | 22,687 | 24,956 | 27,455 | 30,196 | 33,216 |
| | 42,975 | 27,512 | 29,843 | 32,361 | 35,728 | 38,831 |
| Net operating cash flow | −42,975 | −2,512 | −2,343 | −2,111 | −2,453 | −2,229 |
| Finance budget | | | | | | |
| Balance brought forward | — | −23,262 | −25,021 | −27,128 | −29,399 | −32,250 |
| Capital introduced by: | | | | | | |
| Star Ltd | 10,000 | 531 | 285 | 102 | — | — |
| Garter Ltd | 10,000 | 531 | 286 | 101 | — | — |
| Balance before interest | −22,975 | −24,712 | −26,793 | −29,036 | −31,852 | −34,479 |
| Interest at $1\frac{1}{4}\%$ | −287 | −309 | −335 | −363 | −398 | −431 |
| Balance carried forward | −23,262 | −25,021 | −27,128 | −29,399 | −32,250 | −34,910 |
| Facility | 22,200 | 24,450 | 26,925 | 29,674 | 32,666 | 35,961 |
| Capital required by the Partners Star Ltd and Garter Ltd | 1,062 | 571 | 203 | — | — | — |

(b)

Star Ltd and Garter Ltd
Budgeted Trading and Profit and Loss Account
for first 6 months

| | £ | £ |
|---|---|---|
| Sales | | 192,889 |
| Purchases | 177,885 | |
| *deduct:* Closing stock | 33,216 | |
| | | 144,669 |
| Gross profit | | 48,220 |
| Wages | 19,200 | |
| Overheads | 66,900 | |
| Sales commission | 4,822 | |
| Bank interest | 2,123 | |
| | | 33,045 |
| Net profit | | £15,175 |

Budgeted Balance Sheet after first 6 months

| | £ | £ | £ |
|---|---|---|---|
| Capital introduced | | | 21,836 |
| *add:* Net profit | | | 15,175 |
| | | | £37,011 |
| Current assets | | | |
| Stock | | 33,216 | |
| Debtors | | 40,262 | |
| *deduct:* Current liabilities | | 73,478 | |
| Bank overdraft | 34,910 | | |
| Creditors (550 + 1,007) | 1,557 | 36,467 | £37,011 |

**Workings**

(1)

Table of Sales, Purchases and Expenses

| Month | 1 | 2 | 3 | 4 | 5 | 6 |
|---|---|---|---|---|---|---|
| | £ | £ | £ | £ | £ | £ |
| Sales | 25,000 | 27,500 | 30,250 | 33,275 | 36,602 | 40,262 |
| Cost of sales (75%) | 18,750 | 20,625 | 22,687 | 24,956 | 27,455 | 30,196 |
| | | | | | | (7 = 33,216) |
| Wages | 3,000 | 3,000 | 3,000 | 3,000 | 3,600 | 3,600 |
| Overheads | 1,200 | 1,200 | 1,200 | 1,100 | 1,100 | 1,100 |
| Sales commission | 625 | 687 | 756 | 832 | 915 | 1,007 |
| Purchases (month 1) | 18,750 | | | | | |
| (month 2) | 20,625 | 22,687 | 24,956 | 27,455 | 30,196 | 33,216 |
| | 39,375 | | | | | |

*continued*

| *continued* | 1 | 2 | 3 | 4 | 5 | 6 |
|---|---|---|---|---|---|---|
| Working capital | £ | £ | £ | £ | £ | £ |
| Debtors | 25,000 | 27,500 | 30,250 | 33,275 | 36,602 | 40,263 |
| Stock | 20,625 | 22,687 | 24,956 | 27,455 | 30,196 | 33,216 |
| Overhead creditor | −600 | −600 | −600 | −550 | −550 | −550 |
| Commission creditor | −625 | −687 | −756 | −832 | −915 | −1,007 |
| | 44,400 | 48,900 | 53,850 | 59,348 | 65,333 | 71,922 |
| Facility = 50% | 22,200 | 24,450 | 26,925 | 29,674 | 32,666 | 35,961 |

(2) Calculation of figures in budgeted accounts

(i) Sales: addition of the 6 months sales from table in working (1)

(ii) Purchases: addition of the purchases for the first 7 months (1 month stock)

(iii) Closing stock: month 7 purchases

(iv) Wages, overheads and sales commission: addition of the 6 months from the table in working (1)

(v) Bank interest: addition of the 6 months from the cash budget

(vi) Capital introduced: addition of the first 4 months from the cash budget (nothing introduced in months 5 and 6)

(vii) Debtors: month 6 sales

(viii) Bank overdraft: per cash budget at month 6

(ix) Creditors:

| | £ |
|---|---|
| (1) 50% of month 6 overheads (overheads being paid $\frac{1}{2}$ month in arrear) | 550 |
| (2) Sales commission of month 6 (paid 1 month in arrear) | 1,007 |
| | £1,557 |

Note that there are no creditors for purchases as these are paid for immediately.

TUTORIAL NOTE

It is not clear what is meant by working capital in the question. In this answer, the overdraft is not taken into account in calculating the working capital itself.

## 14.0 GOODS ON SALE OR RETURN

### 14.1 Introduction

In some trades, a substantial part of the business is conducted on terms which allow the customer to return them within a stipulated period. In these circumstances, it would obviously be foolhardy to count the transaction as a sale immediately. It would also be foolish to make no record at all, because this would probably result in loss to the business through failure to chase up the return of goods supplied on these terms.

The method of recording to use depends on the number of transactions. If the number of transactions is small, the addition of some memorandum columns to the sales day book will probably suffice (*see* 14.2 below), but if we have a large number of items with a high unit value, it may be necessary to have a separate set of double-entry records (*see* 14.3 below).

## 14.2 The memorandum system for small numbers of sale or return items

There is not much mileage for the examiner in this, because it is so simple! All that is required is a ruling along these lines:

Sale or Return Day Book

| Date | Customer | Value of goods sent on sale or return | Returns | | Sales | | SL Reference |
|---|---|---|---|---|---|---|---|
| | | | Value | Date | Value | Date | |
| (1) | (2) | (3) | (4) | (5) | (6) | (7) | (8) |
| | | £ | £ | | £ | | |

When goods are supplied on sale or return, a pro-forma invoice is prepared and the details entered in columns (1) to (3).

When goods are returned or sold, entries are made in columns (4) to (8).

Columns (6) to (8) function as a normal sales day book, while columns (3) to (5) provide memorandum information to keep the position under control and to allow sale or return customers to be reminded of their obligation to return the goods supplied.

## 14.3 The double-entry method

Under this method, we shall create a small self-balancing sub-system, consisting of three books and a total account.

The records required are:

(a) sale or return day book;

(b) goods sold or returned day book;

(c) sale or return ledger.

The procedure is:

(a) When goods are supplied on sale or return terms:
Enter details in sale or return day book and post to debit of customer's account in sale or return ledger.

(b) When goods are returned by customer:
Enter details in returns column of goods sold or returned day book and post to credit of customer's account in sale or return ledger.

(c) When goods are sold:

(i) Enter details in sales column in goods sold or returned day book and post to *credit* of customer's account in sale or return ledger.

(ii) And also:
Post the same figure to the *debit* of the customer's account in the conventional sales ledger.

(d) The total account:
We post to the *debit* of the total account the monthly total of the sale or return day book.

This gives us the total sales value of goods sent on sale or return for the month.

We post to the *credit* of the total account the monthly totals of the returns column and the sales column in the goods sold or returned day book.

That leaves as a balance the sales value of goods still with customers (i.e. not yet returned or acknowledged as sales).

(e) The sale or return ledger:
The sale or return ledger shows which customers still have goods on approval. The total of the balances in the sale or return ledger will equal the balance on the total account.

### *Illustration*

During January 19X2 the Bonanza Mail Order Company Limited sent the following goods to customers on sale or return terms:

| 19X2 | | £ |
|---|---|---|
| Jan 5 | Mrs B Smith | 86 |
| Jan 11 | Mr R Jones | 116 |
| Jan 15 | Mrs E Dell | 90 |
| Jan 24 | Mr B Roberts | 44 |
| Jan 31 | Mr J McTavish | 79 |

At 1st January 19X2 the following goods were outstanding, having been supplied during December 19X1:

| | £ |
|---|---|
| Mr B Roberts | 20 |
| Mr R Jones | 57 |

Goods returned during January were:

| 19X2 | | £ |
|---|---|---|
| Jan 4 | Mr B Roberts | 20 |
| Jan 27 | Mrs B Smith | 40 |
| Jan 8 | Mr R Jones | 116 (the goods supplied on Jan 11) |

Goods accepted by customers during January were:

| 19X2 | | £ |
|---|---|---|
| Jan 2 | Mr R Jones | 57 |
| Jan 22 | Mrs E Dell | 90 |

You are required to record these transactions in a double-entry sale or return bookkeeping system.

*Stage 1:* Recording the goods sent during the month:

Sale or Return Day Book

| 19X2 | | | £ |
|---|---|---|---|
| Jan 5 | Mrs B Smith | S.30 | 86 |
| Jan 11 | Mr R Jones | J.1 | 116 |
| Jan 15 | Mrs E Dell | D.27 | 90 |
| Jan 24 | Mr B Roberts | R.10 | 44 |
| Jan 31 | Mr J McTavish | M.2 | 79 |
| | | | £415 |
| | | | To total account |

Sale or Return Ledger Accounts

Mr B Roberts R.10

| 19X2 | | | £ | 19X2 | | | £ |
|---|---|---|---|---|---|---|---|
| Jan 1 | Balance | B/D | 20 | Jan 4 | Returns | GSR1 | 20 |
| Jan 24 | Goods | SR1 | 44 | Jan 31 | Balance | C/D | 44 |
| | | | £64 | | | | £64 |
| Feb 1 | Balance | B/D | 44 | | | | |

Mr R Jones J.1

| 19X2 | | | £ | 19X2 | | | £ |
|---|---|---|---|---|---|---|---|
| Jan 1 | Balance | B/D | 57 | Jan 2 | Sales | GSR1 | 57 |
| Jan 11 | Goods | SR1 | 116 | Jan 8 | Returns | GSR1 | 116 |
| | | | £173 | | | | £173 |

Mrs B Smith S.30

| 19X2 | | | £ | 19X2 | | | £ |
|---|---|---|---|---|---|---|---|
| Jan 5 | Goods | SR1 | 86 | Jan 27 | Returns | GSR1 | 40 |
| | | | | Jan 31 | Balance | C/D | 46 |
| | | | £86 | | | | £86 |
| Feb 1 | Balance | B/D | 46 | | | | |

Mrs E Dell D.27

| | | | | | | | |
|---|---|---|---|---|---|---|---|
| 19X2 | | | £ | 19X2 | | | £ |
| Jan 15 | Goods | SR1 | 90 | Jan 22 | Sales | GSR1 | 90 |

Mr J McTavish M.2

| | | | | | | | |
|---|---|---|---|---|---|---|---|
| 19X2 | | | £ | | | | £ |
| Jan 31 | Goods | SR1 | 79 | | | | |

Sale or Return Total Account

| | | | | | | | |
|---|---|---|---|---|---|---|---|
| 19X2 | | | £ | 19X2 | | | £ |
| Jan 31 | GSR Day Book R | GSR1 | 176 | Jan 1 | Balance | B/D | 77 |
| Jan 31 | GSR Day Book S | GSR1 | 147 | Jan 31 | S or R Day Book | SR1 | 415 |
| Jan 31 | Balance | C/D | 169 | | | | |
| | | | £492 | | | | £492 |
| | | | | Feb 1 | Balance | B/D | 169 |

*Stage 2:* Recording the goods returned or sold during the month:

Goods Sold or Returned Day Book

| | | | Returns | | Sales | | |
|---|---|---|---|---|---|---|---|
| Date | Name | S or R | SRL ref. | | SRL ref. | SL ref. | |
| 19X2 | | | | £ | | | £ |
| Jan 2 | Mr R Jones | S | | | J.1 | | 57 |
| Jan 4 | Mr B Roberts | R | R.10 | 20 | | | |
| Jan 8 | Mr R Jones | R | J.1 | 116 | | | |
| Jan 22 | Mrs E Dell | S | | | D.27 | | 90 |
| Jan 27 | Mrs B Smith | R | S.30 | 40 | | | |
| | | | | £176 | | | £147 |
| | | | | To total account | | | To total account |

*Conclusions*
At the end of January 19X2, the sale or return ledger balances total £169 and this is equal and opposite to the balance on the sale or return total account.

We have recorded all sale or return transactions for the month. One job remains—that of posting the £147 sale transactions to the sales ledger accounts concerned, and the total to sales ledger control account. Thus the sales column in the goods sold or returned day book functions to this extent in exactly the same way as the normal sales day book of the business.

Obviously the system could be mechanised or dealt with in other ways designed to suit a particular business. The object of the system used in the illustration is to enable you to cope with examination questions on this topic.

## PROGRESS TEST 10

1. Draw a diagram outlining the two accounting systems required for branch accounts. (1.1)
2. What accounts are required for the selling agency branch calculations? (1.1(a))
3. What accounts are required for the autonomous branch calculations? (1.2(b))
4. Compare selling agency branches and autonomous branches. (1.3)
5. Draw a diagram illustrating foreign branch accounts. (2.0)
6. Define the term "devaluation". (2.2)
7. Draw a diagram outlining the accounts in the books of consignor and consignee. (3.0)
8. Discuss the legal relationship between the two above (question 7). (3.1)
9. What accounts are required in the consignor's books? (3.2(a)) And what accounts are required in the consignee's books? (3.3(a))
10. Draw a diagram outlining the system for joint ventures. (4.0)
11. What accounts are required for the two systems outlined above for joint ventures? (4.2, 4.3)
12. Draw a diagram outlining the system for accounting for royalty accounts. (5.0)
13. What is a "royalty"? (5.2)
14. What accounts are required for the calculation of royalty accounts? (5.3(b))
15. Draw a diagram illustrating a container's account. (6.0)
16. What accounts are required for the calculation of royalty accounts? (6.2(a))
17. What are the most important expenses associated with contract accounts? (7.2)
18. How may profit be calculated on incomplete contracts? (7.3(b))
19. What does SSAP 9 recommend for the treatment of long-term contract work in progress? (7.5)
20. What legal considerations govern hire purchase accounts? (8.1)
21. Draw a diagram illustrating hire purchase transactions in the purchaser's books. (8.2)
22. What are the three methods of writing off hire purchase interest? (8.2(c))
23. What is the sales system in the vendor's books? (9.2)
24. Discuss the stock system in the vendor's books. (9.3)
25. What is the accounting approach to hire purchase transactions in a finance company's books? (9.4(b))
26. What methods govern the apportionment of hire purchase interest? (9.4(e), (f))
27. Draw a diagram illustrating the problems encountered in investment accounts. (10.0)
28. Discuss the treatment of fixed-interest securities "cum div" and "ex div". (10.3(a) and (b))
29. Explain bills of exchange by drawing a block diagram. (11.0)

30. What legal considerations govern:
    (a) bills of exchange;
    (b) promissory notes;
    (c) cheques;
    (d) accommodation bills; and
    (e) parties to a bill? (11.1)
31. Describe the features that may differ between various forms of loss of profit insurance schemes. (12.1)
32. Briefly outline the steps to be followed when calculating a claim under such a scheme. (12.1(b))
33. What are cash budgets? (13.1)
34. Discuss the double-entry method used to account for goods bought on a sale or return basis. (14.3)

CHAPTER ELEVEN

# Interpretation of Accounts

## 1.0 INTRODUCTION

It is important to realise when studying accountancy that the preparation of financial statements is only useful if the result is the reporting of relevant information to interested parties. We now turn to a detailed examination of the technique used to draw conclusions about the state of a company's affairs from the information contained in its annual accounts.

### 1.1 Reasons for interpretation

In examination questions, and indeed in practice, the three main reasons why a detailed interpretation exercise will be undertaken are:

(a) to enable a prospective purchaser of all or part of a business to decide whether to proceed;

(b) to enable a prospective lender to decide whether to make an advance;

(c) to assist management by identifying areas requiring attention.

## 2.0 AREAS TO BE EXAMINED

The emphasis to be placed on different aspects will vary according to the purpose of the review, but the main areas to be examined are:

(a) Profitability, in relation to turnover and in relation to capital employed.

(b) Liquidity.

(c) Management efficiency in controlling:

(i) stock levels;

(ii) collections from debtors;

(iii) payments to creditors;

(iv) asset utilisation.

(d) The degree of risk in the enterprise, in particular the proportion of capital provided by loan capital compared with that provided by equity. (The higher the proportion of loan capital, the greater the risk attaching to the equity.)

## 3.0 TECHNIQUES TO BE USED

Practically all interpretation involves *comparison*: comparison with previous periods for the same company, comparison with budgets, and comparison with corresponding figures for other companies.

To permit comparison, it is necessary to use *ratios* or *percentages* rather than absolute figures so that, for example, companies of differing size can be meaningfully compared.

This chapter concentrates on the use of ratios in interpretation. The use of funds statements in drawing conclusions about the affairs of a company has already been covered in a previous chapter. Always bear in mind when answering interpretation questions that as well as calculating and commenting on ratios a quick funds statement should be produced and commented upon, whenever two consecutive balance sheets are given in the question!

## 4.0 RATIOS: SOME GENERAL OBSERVATIONS ON THE MATHEMATICS

The less mathematically inclined candidate sometimes experiences difficulty with the arithmetic involved in ratios. This section is written mainly with these students in mind and may be skimmed by those who have no difficulty with the subject.

### 4.1 Calculating a ratio

To express one number as a ratio of another, simply write down the first-mentioned figure and divide it by the second.

Thus, to find the ratio "sales to net assets" simply divide "sales" by "net assets". So if sales are £4.8 million and net assets are £2 million, the ratio "sales to net assets" is £4.8m ÷ £2m = 2.4.

"Sales to net assets" may also be written "sales/net assets"; and all other ratios expressed in at least two ways.

To take another example: the "stock to sales" ratio is simply:

$$\frac{\text{Closing stock}}{\text{Sales}}.$$

So if stock is £960,000 and sales are £4.8 million, the "stock to sales" ratio is:

$$\frac{£960,000}{£4.8m} = 0.2.$$

This ratio can also be termed "stock/sales".

## 4.2 Upside-down ratios

It would be true to say that this last ratio was 1 : 5, but it would not be written like that in UK practice; and were it written that way in an examination marks could be lost.

## 4.3 Two ways of expressing the same relationship

Many ratios are conventionally expressed one way up, e.g. "current assets to current liabilities", never "current liabilities to current assets"; and an examiner would regard as "odd" the unconventional usage "current liabilities to current assets", though that ratio is quite meaningful and useful.

Other relationships *are* found in two forms. For example, some people use the ratio: sales/working capital; others working capital/sales. Neither is wrong; they simply have somewhat different uses.

Sales/working capital tells one the number of times working capital (i.e. stocks plus debtors plus cash and bank balances minus current liabilities) has been turned over during the period, i.e. it measures the working capital utilisation.

Working capital/sales, on the other hand, tells one how much working capital (in money terms) the business needs to support each pound's worth of sales.

If one is seeking to improve performance as regards capital utilisation, the first of these ratios will seem more immediately useful. If one is interested in the extra working capital likely to be needed if sales expand, say, by £120,000, it is the second ratio which is more obviously appropriate.

Both ratios can, however, be used for either purpose provided one understands them.

The important thing is to give the examiner the answer *he* asks for, not the inverse (i.e. the upside-down version of the same relationship).

If the choice of ratio is open, select the normal in preference to the unusual; and if, for good reason, a ratio is selected which is not in common use then the reason why must be explained.

## 4.4 The measurement of change: absolute amount

Past results, shown by accounts prepared on a consistent basis, form the solid base from which one can begin to assess the probable future of a business. The changes which they record are of two basic types:

(a) *Discrete* (i.e. step-like) changes of a once and for all nature, which may or may not be repeated in the future (e.g. a share issue).

(b) *Other movements* (e.g. increased turnover, increased employment costs) which may be indicative of a trend.

The most obvious way of measuring change is to set the accounts of two successive periods side by side and to show in a third column the amount by which the latest figures exceed those of the previous period:

| | 19X7 | 19X6 | Change |
|---|---|---|---|
| Sales | £163,412 | £141,308 | + £22,104 |

It is wrong to go mad and fill the answer, quite uncritically, with the amount of every change between one year and the next. It is necessary to sort out the wheat from the chaff, and to discuss the *significant* changes which have occurred.

It is important, on the other hand, to *look critically* at the absolute amount of all the changes which have occurred, so that it is clear what each represents, and that nothing is ignored which was significant.

Has there, for instance, been a change in share capital? If so, in what type of share? If it was an issue, was it a scrip issue? If so, reserves must have fallen by the nominal amount involved. Or was it a rights issue? If so, at what price? Has it caused a change in the share premium account? Or was it an acquisition issue? If so, when did the acquisition take place? What effect will it have on the ratios being worked with?

If, in an examination, candidates are asked to state what changes have occurred, they must keep a sense of balance:

In particular they must:

(a) omit the insignificant; on the other hand they must

(b) not be afraid to state the obvious.

A small variation is not necessarily insignificant because it is small. A 1 per cent increase in turnover when inflation is running at 20 per cent, and the industry as a whole is showing 25 per cent, is highly significant.

On the other hand, it would probably be quite in order to omit all mention of a 2 per cent increase in the expenditure on new fixed assets in a non-inflationary period *unless* it was significant for some other reason, e.g. it represented an upturn after three to four years of falling investment.

The obvious should be stated because what is obvious to the candidate may not be at all obvious to someone else. In any case, any advice is probably being given to a non-expert to whom it would not be obvious.

## 4.5 The measurement of change: use of ratios

Another way of expressing change is to use ratios. If sales in 19X7 are £2.400m, whereas those in 19X6 were £2.000m, one can say that 19X7 sales were:

$$\frac{£2.400\text{m}}{£2.000\text{m}} = 1.2 \text{ times those in 19X6.}$$

This is the normal way of expressing change: to put the current period figure on top, and that for the preceding period on the bottom line of the fraction. It would be equally true to say:

$$\text{19X6 sales were only } \frac{£2.000\text{m}}{£2,400\text{m}} = \text{five-sixths or 0.833 of those in 19X7,}$$

but one does not normally work this way.

If sales were £2.400m this year against £1.000m last year, it is proper to say that they were 2.4 times as great this year as last; but avoid using the form ". . . times greater than". Many people say "2.4 times *greater* than last year", when they mean "2.4 times as great as" or "1.4 times greater than"; so much so that the form "greater than" is in danger of being ambiguous; but if it is used wrongly in the examination then marks will certainly be lost.

## 4.6 The measurement of change: percentages

Yet another way of expressing change is to use percentages. Traditionally, one expresses either:

(a) the change; or

(b) the figure for the later period;

as a percentage of that for an earlier period.

Thus, if sales were £2.000m in 19X6, and £2.400m in 19X7, the increase (£0.400m) may be said to be:

$$\frac{\pounds 400{,}000}{\pounds 2.000\text{m}} \times 100 = 20 \text{ per cent.}$$

Alternatively, sales in 19X7 may be said to be:

$$\frac{\pounds 2.400\text{m}}{\pounds 2.00\text{m}} \times 100 = 120 \text{ per cent of those in 19X6.}$$

## 4.7 Horizontal analysis

Where figures are available for a series of years what is known as horizontal analysis can be performed. The figures can be linked (a) by percentage changes; or (b) by index numbers.

## 4.8 Percentage change over a series of years

*Illustration*

| | 19X3 | | 19X4 | | 19X5 | | 19X6 | | 19X7 |
|---|---|---|---|---|---|---|---|---|---|
| Sales(£000) | 220 | | 275 | | 330 | | 396 | | 455 |
| | | +25% | | +20% | | +20% | | +15% | |

## 4.9 Index numbers

If one of the years (usually but not necessarily the first) is taken as 100, a series can be linked by index numbers. Using the figures in 4.8:

| | 19X3 | 19X4 | 19X5 | 19X6 | 19X7 |
|---|---|---|---|---|---|
| Sales (19X3 = 100) | 100 | 125 | 150 | 180 | 207 |

To compute the index for any year, divide the data for that year by that for the year chosen as the base (19X3 in this case) and multiply by 100. Thus the index for 19X4 is:

$$\frac{275,000}{220,000} \times 100 = 125.$$

Annual figures of percentage change give a better idea of how the *rate of change* is moving (in this case it is clearly falling), whereas index numbers provide a better overall perspective of the data (it will be seen quite easily that sales a little more than doubled in four years). They increased by the same absolute amount in 19X4 and 19X5; by rather more in 19X6 (though less in percentage terms); and in 19X7, a little less than in 19X6.

### 4.10 Use of semi-logarithmic paper

It is sometimes convenient to plot data on semi-logarithmic graph paper, i.e. paper on which the horizontal scale is divided into equal parts, but on which the vertical scale is proportional to the logarithms of numbers, rather than to the numbers themselves.

It is beyond the scope of this manual to enter into the reasons, but where data are plotted over time on semi-logarithmic paper and they slope upwards in:

(a) a straight line, then the rate of growth is constant;

(b) a line curving upwards, then the (percentage) rate of growth is increasing;

(c) a line curving downwards, then the (percentage) rate of growth is declining.

If the line slopes downwards, then "growth" is negative. Once again, if the line is a straight line, the rate of (negative) growth is constant. If it curves away downwards, the rate of negative growth is accelerating; if it curves upwards, it is slowing down.

### 4.11 Percentages against ratios

Some financial measures are virtually always expressed as percentages. A trader who said that his profit ratio was 0.04 would be regarded as rather odd. Most people would say one of 4 per cent.

Profit is normally expressed in percentage terms. Asset-based ratios, on the other hand, e.g. sales/net assets, are normally expressed, in UK practice, as ratios. For example, in UK practice, the current ratio (i.e. current assets ÷ current liabilities) is expressed as a ratio. Some Americans talk of a ratio of 130 per cent; the British would say one of 1.3.

## 5.0 RATIOS: THE RATIOS THEMSELVES

### 5.1 Using ratios as a profit-improvement tool

Management will find ratios useful as a means of improving profitability. Ratios computed in respect of the current year may be compared with:

(a) those of previous periods;

(b) those of other companies either as part of an inter-firm comparison scheme or on the basis of published figures;

(c) industry averages.

A useful starting point for such an analysis is return on capital employed.

$$\frac{\text{Profit}}{\text{Capital employed}} = \frac{\text{Profit}}{\text{Sales}} \times \frac{\text{Sales}}{\text{Capital employed}}$$

and this makes it possible to examine separately (*see* Table 35) the two aspects:

(a) profit margins,

(b) asset utilisation.

A particular business may be producing a return on capital employed of 10 per cent. In present conditions this would be regarded as subnormal. A return of 18 to 25 per cent might be expected. One of only 10 per cent could arise in a number of quite different ways, as Table 35 shows.

Table 35. EXAMPLES OF 10 PER CENT RETURN ON CAPITAL EMPLOYED

| *Situation* | *Profit / Sales* % | *Sales / Capital employed* % | *Profit / Capital employed* % |
|---|---|---|---|
| A | 10 | 1.00 | 10 |
| B | 8 | 1.25 | 10 |
| C | $6\frac{2}{3}$ | 1.50 | 10 |
| D | 5 | 2.00 | 10 |
| E | 4 | 2.50 | 10 |
| F | 2.5 | 4.00 | 10 |
| G | 2.0 | 5.00 | 10 |
| H | 1.5 | $6\frac{2}{3}$ | 10 |

*Profit margin* (profit/sales) varies quite widely from industry to industry, and within an industry between one company and another.

In simple terms the profit margin depends upon three factors:

(a) *The level of selling prices which it is possible to set.* A monopoly situation, for instance, makes high selling prices possible, but when it comes to an end (e.g. when patents run out), this advantage is likely to be lost. Competition, on the other hand, will limit the ability to raise prices even if costs rise; and price controls are an obvious dampening factor at the present time.

(b) *Direct costs* of purchase or manufacture.

(c) *Overheads.*

The inefficient business tends to achieve low profit margins because its direct costs of purchase and manufacture are high, because, for instance, it does not take advantage of cash and/or quantity discounts, and uses its workforce inefficiently; and it has unnecessarily high overheads.

The efficient business tends to have a far better profit/sales ratio in times of normal or good business, but it may suffer in a slump; for high levels of mechanisation or automation involve high fixed costs, which it is difficult to recover if volume falls to low levels.

*Asset utilisation* (i.e. sales/capital employed) also varies widely from industry to industry. The highly mechanised, capital-intensive industry tends to have a relatively low sales/capital employed ratio; whereas one dependent upon personal skills with little investment in plant or stocks, tends to have a high one.

Asset utilisation increases in boom times (when plant is working to capacity), and falls in a depression.

Efficient management tends to produce higher levels of asset utilisation than less efficient; and the higher the sales/capital employed ratio achieved *with stability* the better.

But, as will be seen in a little while, this emphasis on stability is paramount. A high sales/capital employed ratio is itself often a warning that all is not well.

Returning to Table 35, can anything be said about what needs to be improved in situation A? B? C? . . . H?

Not a lot. The profit/sales ratio *looks* quite satisfactory in situation A, and the sales/capital employed ratio *looks* rather low. Conversely, in situation H, the profit/sales ratio *looks* rather unsatisfactory, whereas the sales/capital employed ratio could well be in order.

But there is nothing against which to compare the ratios. For example, if situation D prevails and the figures for last year and year before were:

| | Profit / Sales | Sales / Capital employed | Profit / Capital employed |
|---|---|---|---|
| Last year | 5% | 2.0 | 10% |
| Year before last | 4.8% | 2.2 | 10.56% |

Then, clearly, the position has deteriorated. While the profit/sales ratio improved marginally (by 0.2 per cent), sales/capital employed fell (by 0.2) and as a result the profit/capital employed ratio fell from 10.56 per cent to 10.0 per cent.

How does this information help?

There is a feeling, say, that the return on capital employed *ought* to be nearer 18 per cent. But is it possible by comparing the results of an admittedly inefficient business this last year with those of any equally (?) inefficient business the year before, to find where the improvement needs to come? Probably not.

That is why inter-firm comparison schemes are useful.

Suppose that it is discovered that the median company (the middle one if all the ratios are ranked in declining order) had these ratios:

| | Profit / Sales | Sales / Capital employed | Profit / Capital employed |
|---|---|---|---|
| Last year | 5.2% | 3.4 | 17.68% |
| Year before last | 4.7% | 4.0 | 18.8% |

There is now something to work on. The margins are about right, if it is desired to be average. It is the asset utilisation which is letting the company down. The median company turns over its assets 1.7 times as fast as this company.

There is a completely different sense of perspective too. Instead of patting themselves on the back because their profit/sales ratio is up from 4.8 per cent to 5.0 per cent, the company must ask itself: why other people improved not by 0.2 per cent, but by 0.5 per cent? And why have they slipped from above-average margins (strictly, above-median margins—but no one uses the term) to well below average?

Other companies are suffering from declining sales/capital employed ratios, but that is where this company has to improve if they are to obtain a reasonable return on capital employed.

But before beginning to study the problem, it is perhaps worth looking at the figures for the best of the rivals:

| | $\frac{\text{Profit}}{\text{Sales}}$ | $\frac{\text{Sales}}{\text{Capital employed}}$ | $\frac{\text{Profit}}{\text{Capital employed}}$ |
|---|---|---|---|
| Last year | 6.0% | 4.0 | 24% |

Note how a return on capital employed 2.4 times the companies was the result of a 20 per cent better margin (6 per cent instead of 5 per cent), and twice as good a sales/capital employed ratio.

## 5.2 Ratios which make up or contribute to capital employed

Figure 17 shows the ratios which make up, or contribute to, return on capital employed; and Figure 18 suggests the questions which management, or an outside accountant or analyst, might ask as a result of each.

## 5.3 Asset utilisation

If there are investments, it is advisable to consider them separately.

For most purposes, it is convenient to deduct intangible assets from reserves, and not to regard them as assets at all.

This leaves this simple balance sheet:

| | |
|---|---|
| Capital employed | Fixed assets (net after depreciation)<br>Net current assets |

It has already been seen that

$$\frac{\text{Profit}}{\text{Sales}} \times \frac{\text{Sales}}{\text{Capital employed}} = \frac{\text{Profit}}{\text{Capital employed}}$$

and that $\frac{\text{Sales}}{\text{Capital employed}}$ plays a major part in determining return on capital employed.

Although it is not too hard to envisage a business turning over its capital

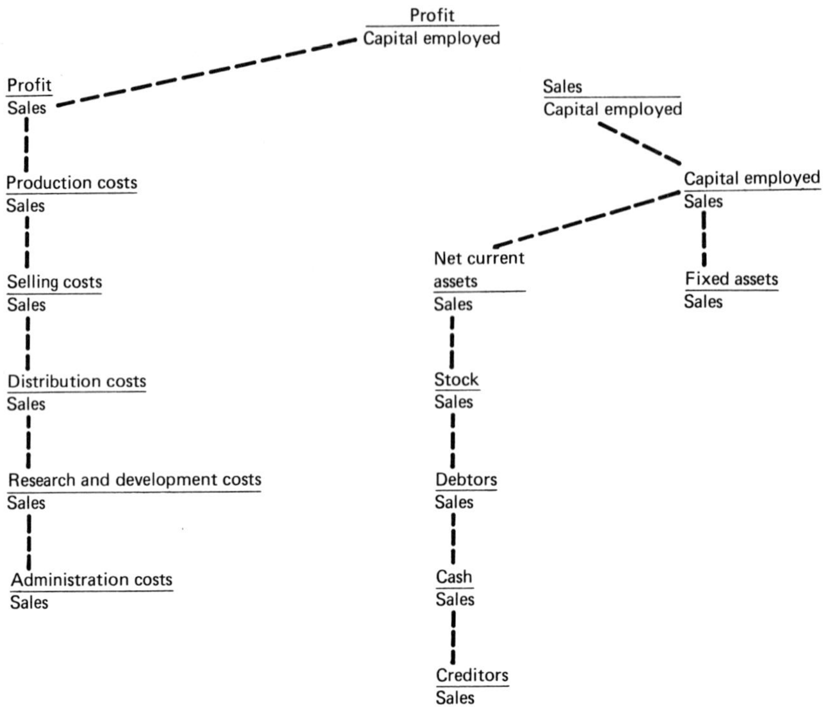


Fig. 17. *Ratios which contribute to return on capital employed.*

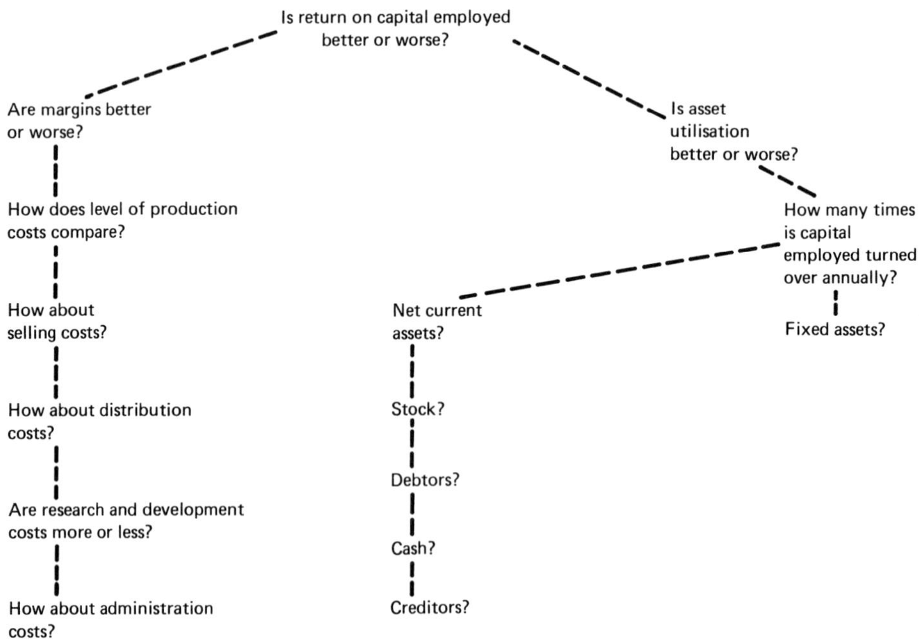


Fig. 18. *Questions management or the outside analyst might ask.*

employed—or for that matter improving its return by doing so more often—it is a somewhat abstract concept, and it is often easier to think in terms of the inverse of the ratio

$$\frac{\text{Capital employed}}{\text{Sales}},$$

i.e. of the capital it is necessary to employ to support each pound's worth of sales.

Looking back at the simple balance sheet, it is obvious that:

$$\frac{\text{Capital employed}}{\text{Sales}} = \frac{\text{Fixed assets (net after depreciation)}}{\text{Sales}} + \frac{\text{Net current assets}}{\text{Sales}}$$

and that if one is to improve the ratio capital employed/sales, this can only be done by improving either:

$$\frac{\text{Fixed assets (net after depreciation)}}{\text{Sales}} \text{ or } \frac{\text{Net current assets}}{\text{Sales}},$$

or both.

## 5.4 Fixed assets (net after depreciation)/sales

This is a difficult ratio to interpret. At first sight a low ratio might seem preferable to a high one, since it would indicate better utilisation of assets, but this is not necessarily true:

| *Situation* | *Fixed assets (net after depreciation)* | *Sales* | *Fixed assets / Sales* |
|---|---|---|---|
| A | £100,000 | £1m | 0.100 |
| B | £500,000 | £1m | 0.500 |
| C | £800,000 | £1m | 0.800 |
| D | £1,800,000 | £1m | 1.800 |

Which situation is to be preferred?

Without further information it is impossible to say.

Suppose that each represents precisely the same company, with exactly the same plant. The plant cost £1m in each of situations A, B and C and is being written off by the straight-line method over 10 years with no residual value. In situation A it is 9 years old, in B 5 years old, and in C 2 years old. As a result of a recent bout of inflation, the cost of the plant has doubled, and in situation D the plant is 1 year old.

Can one reasonably suggest that situation A is preferable to situation B or C? In some respects it is not: for instance, the plant will have to be replaced at a cost of £1,800,000 during the next year; whereas in situation B it will be another 5 years. Not only will this involve a sizeable cash flow outwards in situation A, it will affect future costs and profitability 4 years sooner than in situation B.

Be careful, therefore, and do not jump to hasty conclusions over differences in the fixed assets/sales ratio of different companies, or those of the same company at different times: examine the underlying situation.

## 5.5 Net current assets/sales

In simple terms, net current assets are:

| | | |
|---|---|---|
| Stocks and work in progress | xxxx | |
| Debtors | xxxx | |
| Bank | xxxx | |
| | | xxxx |
| *less:* Current liabilities | | xxxx |
| Net current assets | | xxxx |

The ratio net current assets/sales thus represents:

$$\frac{\text{Stocks and work in progress}}{\text{Sales}} + \frac{\text{Debtors}}{\text{Sales}} + \frac{\text{Bank}}{\text{Sales}} - \frac{\text{Current liabilities}}{\text{Sales}}.$$

To improve the ratio it is necessary to make it smaller, so that the company uses less in the way of net current assets to support each £ of sales. Each of the four components can play a part.

On the face of things, the net current assets/sales ratio will fall, other things being equal, if a business:

(a) reduces stocks and work in progress; and/or

(b) reduces debtors; and/or

(c) reduces cash at bank; and/or

(d) increases current liabilities.

This will not necessarily make it more profitable; indeed it may make it less so. This is a problem with ratios: ratios are interdependent; and what serves to improve one ratio may have an adverse effect on another equally important ratio.

Take current liabilities, for instance: a company may purchase in each 4-week period materials costing £80,000. If its supplier offers a choice of terms: cash in 7 days, $2\frac{1}{2}$ per cent discount; cash in 28 days, net; the company may take advantage of the discount, in which case it is likely to owe the supplier £20,000 at the end of a 4-week period. The alternative policy of paying each 28 days, and leaving the supplier owed on the last day of the period £80,000, would clearly require less working capital (£60,000 less at a typical period end) but it would increase costs by £80,000 × 13 × $2\frac{1}{2}$ per cent per annum = £26,000. It would improve the net current assets/sales ratio and the sales/capital employed ratio. But it would cut back profit/sales and in all probability profit/capital employed.

Earlier it was suggested that "on the face of things" it would appear that the sales/net current assets ratio would improve if, say, stocks (or debtors) were reduced. This is only true, of course, if the funds released are used elsewhere in the business and not:

(a) to swell debtors (or stocks); or

(b) to swell cash and bank balances; or

(c) to reduce current liabilities.

To sum up:

(a) Asset utilisation has a profound effect upon return on capital employed.

(b) Differences in the sales/capital employed (or in capital employed) are not necessarily due to efficiency or inefficiency.

(c) Given that a company has a low sales/capital employed ratio, it is relatively difficult to use the information directly to suggest ways in which it may be improved.

(d) It is normally easier to improve individual aspects of the business in the knowledge that an overall improvement in efficiency tends to improve the sales/capital employed ratio.

## 5.6 Collection period

$$\text{Collection period (days)} = \frac{\text{Trade debtors}}{\text{Credit sales} \div 365};$$

$$\text{Collection period (months)} = \frac{\text{Trade debtors}}{\text{Credit sales} \div 12}.$$

These are ideal formulae for use where the information is available. Published accounts generally do not distinguish credit sales from cash sales, and may not separate trade debtors from other debtors (say, proceeds of sale of a subsidiary) or prepayments, which may have a profound effect on the total debts, but again the necessary information is unlikely to be available.

Collection period provides an indicator of the quality of the debtors and of their ability and willingness to pay promptly.

Custom of the trade provides for normal credit terms, which differ from trade to trade. Individual companies may, as a matter of policy, offer a shorter or longer period to all or some of their customers.

Collection period is affected by a number of factors, not all of which are, perhaps, immediately obvious:

(a) *Delay in invoicing:* whether due to slow transmission of data to the accounts department, or delay in preparation or despatch by accounts, the result is the same: the customer does not know what to pay, and cannot begin the payment process.

(b) *Delay in sending statements; or failure to send them altogether:* although many companies pay scant regard to statements, enough customers do use them for any laxity to have some effect on collections. At the very least, failure to send statements provides an excuse for the debtor looking for one.

(c) *Weakness in debt chasing:* companies which are short of funds tend to pay: (i) those suppliers upon whom they are most dependent; and (ii) those who cause most fuss if they are not paid.

(d) *Poor credit control* will inevitably mean that credit is granted to customers who cannot obtain credit elsewhere. They are more likely to be the slow payers, and to become bad debts.

(e) *Statutory restrictions:* where companies sell by HP or on credit sale agreements, any change in the maximum period allowed and/or the minimum deposit required is likely to affect collection period.

Most businesses are to some extent seasonal. Often they deliberately select a year end falling in the low-activity period immediately following their seasonal peak. Thus a store may select 31st January as a year end. This can have a profound effect on collection period, which if calculated on the information available externally will be quite wrong.

*Illustration*

| | £000 |
|---|---|
| Annual sales | 4,800 |
| of which: | |
| December | 1,600 |
| Debtors at 31st December | 800 |

Collection period (calculated normally):

$$\frac{£800,000}{£48m \div 12} = 2 \text{ months.}$$

Collection period (based on December sales):

$$\frac{£800,000}{£1.6m} = 0.5 \text{ months.}$$

Internally, it may be useful to consider each month's sales separately, reporting from time to time the proportion of that month's credit sales which are still outstanding.

*Illustration*

| | Sales | Debtors | Decimal fraction of months' sales still outstanding |
|---|---|---|---|
| | £000 | £000 | |
| October | 400 | 40 | 0.100 |
| November | 800 | 120 | 0.150 |
| December | 1,600 | 640 | 0.400 |
| | | | 0.650 |

An external analyst cannot do this and can be misled.

Collection period (based on published accounts) varies widely from industry to industry. Typical figures are (it is not necessary to memorise them!):

| | Days |
|---|---|
| Building and civil engineering contractors | 30–35 |
| Chemical manufacturers | 70–85 |
| Rubber manufacturers | 80 |
| Brewers | 30–35 |
| Soft drinks manufacturers | 80–100 |
| Electronics manufacturers | 100–120 |
| Fruit and vegetable wholesalers | 20 |

Debtors typically represent 20 to 30 per cent of total assets. A reduction (or expansion) of collection period thus has a profound effect upon liquidity.

## 5.7 Stock ratios

Stocks form a major element in the balance sheet of most companies. They tend to be smallest in service industries, and highest where little more than stock-holding is involved. Typically figures are:

| | % of total assets |
|---|---|
| Newspaper publishers | 3–6 |
| Brewers | 10–12 |
| Plant hire | 10–14 |
| Grocery supermarkets | 25–30 |
| Car dealers | 25–30 |
| Domestic electrical appliance manufacturers | 25–33 |
| Builders merchants | 30 |
| Building and civil engineering contractors | 40 |
| Wine and spirit merchants | 40–50 |
| Distillers | 55 |
| Foreign car distributors | 60–70 |

In most companies, about one-third of total assets are tied up in stocks. Any reduction (or expansion) in stock levels has a profound effect on capital requirements.

Internally, management is likely to use the *stock turnover ratio:*

$$\text{Stock turnover} = \frac{\text{Cost of goods sold}}{\text{Average of opening and closing stocks}}.$$

*Illustration*

| | 19X6 | 19X7 |
|---|---|---|
| | £ | £ |
| Cost of goods sold | 1.200m | 1.400m |
| Stock: 1st January | 0.360m | 0.440m |
| 31st December | 0.440m | 0.560m |

Stock turnover: $\dfrac{1.200\text{m}}{\frac{1}{2}(0.360 + 0.440)\text{m}} = 3.0$ $\qquad \dfrac{1.400\text{m}}{\frac{1}{2}(0.440 + 0.560)\text{m}} = 2.8$

This ratio cannot be used in the UK by an external analyst, since cost of goods sold is not generally indicated separately in the accounts.

External analysts generally employ either:

(a) *stock/sales ratio*, i.e.: $\dfrac{\text{Closing stock}}{\text{Sales}}$, or

(b) *sales/stock ratio:* $\dfrac{\text{Sales}}{\text{Closing stock}}$

The stock/sales ratio indicates the stock necessary (on the indication of the closing balance sheet) to support £1 of sales.

In a seasonal business it gives no indication of the *peak* stock necessary immediately before or during the season, and there is no way an external analyst can discover this short of industrial espionage.

The sales/stock ratio gives *some indication* of the rate of stock turnover, but it does not *measure* it since sales are, by their nature, stated at selling price, whereas stocks are conventionally stated at cost (unless net realisable value is lower). This ratio tends to flatter the true rate of turnover; and is affected by any change in margins.

On the face of things, a high sales/stock ratio is preferable to a low one (or a low stock/sales ratio to a high one). In asset utilisation terms this is true, but as stocks are reduced, quality of service is likely to fall.

Costs of purchase increase if goods are bought in small lots: there is an optimum lot size, neither too big nor too small.

If raw materials are not available when required, production delays are likely to occur; penalties may be incurred; capacity utilisation may fall; staff may become discontented, and so on.

Similarly, if finished goods are not available ex stock where that has been the custom, potential purchasers will go elsewhere, and may not return. If spare parts are not held, and customers have to wait weeks or months for repairs, they will not buy that make again.

It is reasonable for a company's directors to ask: "*Why* is our stock turnover lower than other people's?" or to suggest: "If we acquire A Ltd there *could* be scope for stock reduction." But an in-depth investigation ought to be made *before* a decision is made: "Cut stocks × per cent."

SSAP 9 calls for the sub-classification in the balance sheet or notes of stocks and work in progress "in a manner which is appropriate to the business and so as to indicate the amounts held in each of the main categories".

Even if the total stock is much the same, and the sales/stock ratio virtually unchanged, any significant variation in composition could be a danger signal.

*Illustration*

Speculative Builders Ltd is a small business specialising in building houses as small developments, moving on from one site to the next as part of the work is completed.

| | 19X6 | 19X7 |
|---|---|---|
| | £ | £ |
| Sales of completed properties | 720,000 | 700,000 |
| Stocks: | | |
| Raw materials | 14,400 | 1,400 |
| Work in progress | 129,600 | 5,600 |
| Completed houses | 36,000 | 168,000 |
| | 180,000 | 175,000 |
| Sales/stock ratio | 4.0 | 4.0 |

Snap diagnosis: houses are not selling; bringing shortage of cash, layoff of workers and, probably, unwillingness on the part of suppliers to supply on credit. One would need to look elsewhere for confirmation of this hypothesis.

## 5.8 Vertical analysis of the profit and loss account

As was shown in 5.1, return on capital employed may be viewed as consisting of two components:

$$\frac{\text{Profit}}{\text{Capital employed}} = \frac{\text{Profit}}{\text{Sales}} \times \frac{\text{Sales}}{\text{Capital employed}}.$$

Previous sections have looked briefly at the sales/capital employed ratio, and at the ratios which lie behind it. It is now necessary to look at profitability in relation to turnover.

As shown in Table 35, it is possible to break down the profit/sales ratio. Assuming that the costs to be deducted from selling price are production costs, selling costs, distribution costs, research and development costs and administration costs:

| | |
|---|---|
| Production costs/sales | xxx |
| Selling costs/sales | xxx |
| Distribution costs/sales | xxx |
| Research and development costs/sales | xxx |
| Administration costs/sales | xxx |
| Profit/sales | xxx |

In an inter-firm comparison, or in comparing results of one year with those of another of the same company, it is possible to compare separately the five principal cost factors. This is rarely feasible with published accounts, there being no requirement to distinguish the components separately.

Even where comparative information is available, e.g. costs of a competitor (or competitors) are known, care should be taken not to jump to hasty conclusions. Company A could, for instance, have much higher selling costs than company B, because it has taken a strategic decision to advertise a new product widely with the intention of increasing its market share—a perfectly reasonable idea, which may or may not succeed.

Again, company X could have somewhat higher production costs than company Y, company X being antiquated in methods, and labour intensive, while company Y is heavily automated, with a considerable investment in capital equipment.

Each of these would produce a real and quite proper difference in costs.

## 5.9 Balance sheet structure ratios

In order to compare one balance sheet with another, it is useful to:

(a) produce a vertical analysis;

(b) compute two key working capital ratios:

 (i) the current ratio,

 (ii) the quick or acid-test ratio;

(c) compute the gearing, or debt ratio.

## 5.10 Vertical analysis of the balance sheet

Analysts frequently:

(a) re-state the balance sheet in standard form;

(b) express each item as a percentage of the balance sheet total;

(c) use the statements for a series of years, or compare them with those of other companies, to discover, and explain, the changes and differences which are apparent.

It is often useful to set alongside any comparison of one year's figures with another the absolute amount of the change which has occurred; and the increase or decrease in percentage terms, i.e. the increase or decrease expressed as a percentage of the figure for the earlier year.

*Example*

Balance Sheet as at 31st December

| | 19X6 | % of total | 19X7 | % of total | | |
|---|---|---|---|---|---|---|
| | £000 | | £000 | | £000 | % |
| Fixed assets | 45,000 | 56.3 | 47,250 | 53.7 | +2,250 | + 5.0 |
| Investments | 3,000 | 3.7 | 10,350 | 11.8 | +7,350 | +245.0 |
| Sub-total | 48,000 | 60.0 | 57,600 | 65.5 | +9,600 | +20.0 |
| Net current assets: | | | | | | |
| Stock | 40,000 | 50.0 | 66,100 | 75.1 | +26,100 | +65.3 |
| Debtors | 44,000 | 55.0 | 52,900 | 60.1 | +8,900 | +20.2 |
| Bank | 12,000 | 15.0 | 2,600 | 2.9 | −9,400 | −78.3 |
| | 96,000 | 120.0 | 121,600 | 138.1 | +25,600 | +26.7 |
| *less:* | | | | | | |
| Current liabilities | 64,000 | 80.0 | 91,200 | 103.6 | +27,200 | +42.5 |
| Sub-total | 32,000 | 40.0 | 30,400 | 34.5 | −1,600 | −5.0 |
| Capital employed | 80,000 | 100.0 | 88,000 | 100.0 | +8,000 | +10.0 |

If, in an examination or in real life, this form of analysis is used, then:

*Don't uncritically report all the information: be selective!*

Spend not more than *three* minutes studying the table. Select the *two* most important features evident from the analysis. Having done so, select the third most important; the *fourth* most important, and finally the *fifth* most important . . . given that sales increased in 19X7 by 10 per cent compared with 19X6.

SOLUTION

All interpretation problems involve professional judgement and opinion. If the selected order of importance is different from this solution don't worry; the important thing was to try to impose an order on a complex problem.

(a) Capital employed increased by 10 per cent, absolutely in line with sales growth; but working capital (net current assets) failed to keep pace (indeed it fell by 5 per cent over 19X7).

(b) This appears to have been largely due to an increase in investments (by £7,350,000), which itself absorbed almost the entire increase in capital employed (£8m).

(c) Stocks rose alarmingly during 19X7 (by 65.3 per cent or £26,100,000), which suggests sales resistance, or massive over-production.

(d) Debtors rose by 20.2 per cent (against an increase in sales of 10 per cent), which suggests there are also difficulties in collection.

(e) Cash at bank fell by 78.3 per cent (or £9,400,000), whereas current liabilities rose by 42.5 per cent (£27,200,000), which suggests very obvious liquidity problems.

## 5.11 The current ratio

The current ratio (or as it is sometimes termed "the working capital ratio" or occasionally "the liquidity ratio") is perhaps the most universally used of all accounting ratios.

$$\text{Current ratio} = \frac{\text{Current assets}}{\text{Current liabilities}}.$$

It is a useful quick indicator that something may be going wrong. Any violent, or continuing, change in the current ratio is worth investigating. But it is a relatively primitive guide.

Once upon a time it used to be suggested that a current ratio of 2 was sound, any less was a suggestion of weakness. Today, one of 1.5 would be normal; but the ratio tends to vary quite widely with the type of business. Typical figures are:

| | |
|---|---|
| Grocery wholesalers and supermarkets | 1.0 or less |
| Brewers | 1.2 |
| Car dealers | 1.2 |
| Construction | 1.5 |
| Chemical manufacturers | 1.5 |
| Domestic electrical appliance manufacture | 1.5 |
| Printers | 1.5 |
| Departmental stores | 1.7 |
| Machine tool manufacturers | 1.9 |
| Paper merchants | 2.0 |
| Distillers | 3.0 or over |

Businesses with a rapid turnover of stock (e.g. supermarkets, greengrocers and fish merchants) and few debtors will, provided they can themselves obtain normal trade credit, have a low current ratio. Supermarkets which are a household name manage to operate year after year on "other people's capital" with a current ratio of well under 1.

At the other extreme, companies which must retain stocks for months or years (e.g.

distillers with maturing whiskey) have heavy debtors, but few creditors, and tend to have a high current ratio.

The current ratio provides an indication of the extent to which current assets are sufficient to cover current liabilities. But do not carry this idea too far.

For each business there is a bare minimum of stock which must be maintained if it is to continue in its present form and at its existing size. Stock surplus to requirements could be sold (and not replaced) to pay creditors; but all stock could not be sold without liquidation, and normally this would mean its being sold well below cost.

Similarly, most businesses need to offer credit to some or all of their customers. They may bill efficiently and collect debts effectively, but unless the business ceases or is reduced in size, it cannot reduce debtors below the minimum which represents efficient operation.

What is important to a business is the ability to pay its debts as they fall due. Provided that is possible, the business is likely to survive. When it ceases to be, trouble, in the shape of restricted supplies, demands for cash with order, writs, and the appointment of receivers, comes all too swiftly.

In assessing the current asset/current liability situation, it is important to consider:

(a) the "quality" of the assets;

(b) the imminence of both assets and liabilities, but particularly liabilities.

It may be that doubtful debts, and stock which is difficult to dispose of, have been included in current assets, but would not easily be realisable to pay creditors. Similarly, prepaid rent, rates or insurance premiums are properly included as current assets, but cannot easily be "realised".

Conventionally, a liability is a current liability if it falls due within 12 months. But there is an enormous difference between the following two cases:

| | Balance sheet as at | |
|---|---|---|
| | 31st March 19X7 | 31st December 19X7 |
| Current liabilities: | £ | £ |
| Trade creditors | 4,350,000 | 4,350,000 |
| Current taxation (due 1st January 19X8) | 9,720,000 | 9,720,000 |
| | £14,070,000 | £14,070,000 |

In the first case, it is necessary to find £4,350m in the near future (the £9,720,000 is not due for 9 months); in the second, £14,070m.

Two difficulties are worth considering in some detail:

(a) the problem of bank overdrafts;

(b) window dressing.

A bank overdraft is a current liability and is treated as such in British practice when computing the current ratio.

In the United States overdrafts as such are unknown. Money is borrowed on a term loan for perhaps 3 to 5 years, for most of which it is not a current liability since it is not due within 12 months. At the same time the company is required to keep its current account in credit, and often a minimum balance is prescribed.

Imagine a company with the following working capital structure:

| | £ | £ | £ |
|---|---|---|---|
| Current assets: | | | |
| Stock | 170,000 | | |
| Debtors | 280,000 | | |
| Bank | — | 450,000 | |
| *less:* Current liabilities: | | | |
| Trade creditors | 300,000 | | |
| Bank overdraft | 60,000 | 360,000 | 90,000 |

$$\text{Current ratio} = \frac{£450,000}{£360,000} = 1.25.$$

It is impossible to tell from the accounts whether, say:

(a) the company's overdraft limit is £60,000, which the bank refuses to increase; or

(b) that the limit is £200,000, and relations with the bank over a long period have been good, and there is no reason to believe that the limit will be reduced.

Our view of the company would clearly be very different; but the current ratio would be the same.

A US company in circumstances similar to (b) above would show the bank loan as loan capital, and:

| | £ | £ | £ |
|---|---|---|---|
| Current assets: | | | |
| Stock | 170,000 | | |
| Debtors | 280,000 | | |
| Bank | 140,000 | 590,000 | |
| *less:* Current liabilities: | | | |
| Trade creditors | | 300,000 | 290,000 |

$$\text{Current ratio} = \frac{£590,000}{£300,000} = 1.97 \text{ and a much fairer indicator.}$$

Imagine a company with the current asset/current liability structure:

| | £ | £ | £ |
|---|---|---|---|
| Current assets: | | | |
| Stock | 170,000 | | |
| Debtors | 200,000 | | |
| Bank | 80,000 | 450,000 | |
| *less:* Current liabilities: | | | |
| Trade creditors | | 360,000 | 90,000 |

$$\text{Current ratio} = \frac{£450,000}{£360,000} = 1.25.$$

Which is rather low. Could the company have done anything to improve it? One thing it might have done was to pay the £80,000 to creditors on the last day of the period. Current assets would then have only been £370,000; but trade creditors would have been only £280,000:

$$\text{Current ratio} = \frac{\pounds 370{,}000}{\pounds 280{,}000} = 1.32,$$

which people guided largely by the current ratio might view as "better". But is a company with a zero bank balance "better" than one with £80,000 in the bank?

Now return to the British company whose current asset/current liability structure was shown above. Suppose that the company has an overdraft limit of £200,000, and that it is not happy to exhibit a current ratio of 1.25. What happens if on the last day of its accounting period it pays £80,000 to creditors? It might seem that this would improve its current ratio, but it would not. Its current ratio is unaffected. Current assets remain £450,000; and current liabilities (including bank overdraft) £360,000.

On the other hand, a company with a current ratio less than unity can improve it (provided it has cash at bank rather than an overdraft) by *not* paying its creditors.

Remember always, that a balance sheet shows the position on one day. A seasonal business is likely to have a very different working capital structure just before, during and immediately after its seasonal peak. Stocks and debtors are likely to be at their lowest, and cash at its highest, a couple of months after the season—just the date to which many such companies make up their accounts.

To sum up:

(a) Do not rely uncritically upon the current ratio as an indicator.

(b) The lower the current ratio a company lives with, the more efficient its use of working capital.

(c) The higher the current ratio, the less efficient the use of working capital, but the greater the security.

(d) Suspect companies with current ratios which are *too* high, or *too* low.

## 5.12 Quick or acid-test ratio

A second key ratio employed by analysts of all kinds is the quick (or "acid-test") ratio:

$$\text{Quick ratio} = \frac{\text{Current assets} - \text{Stock}}{\text{Current liabilities}}$$

$$= (\text{in simple terms}) \frac{\text{Debtors} + \text{Bank}}{\text{Current liabilities}}$$

Some analysts include quoted investments (at market value) as current assets regardless of where they appear in the accounts, for the purpose of computing both the current ratio and the quick ratio. This is entirely reasonable.

Others take the quick ratio to be:

$$\frac{\text{Debtors} + \text{Bank}}{\text{Immediate liabilities}}.$$

This is not the accepted definition. In any case it is difficult to implement without knowledge only available to those inside the organisation.

Traditionally, a quick ratio of 1 is regarded as normal; one substantially greater than this *could* mean over-long credit was being granted, or too much was being tied up in cash at bank; but it is quite proper to have cash available if there are plans for its early use.

A quick ratio well below 1—say, 0.6 or 0.7—*could* be a sign of weakness, and would generally be viewed with suspicion.

The quick ratio is an indicator of the extent to which it would be possible to meet current liabilities from existing cash and that collected from debtors without having to rely on further sales.

It is distorted in the same way as the current ratio by any bank overdraft: and there is the same need for care over imminence. There is all the difference in the world between current tax (or any other current liability) due next week, and that due, say, 11 months hence, but both are current liabilities for the purpose of the quick ratio.

Ignoring for the sake of simplicity any need for cash balances, businesses granting a long period of credit tend to have higher quick ratios than those offering a short period of credit, or selling for cash; and those to which long periods of credit are granted tend to have a lower ratio than those which are granted only a short period of credit.

## 5.13 Gearing

Gearing is the relationship between debt and equity. While it is universally agreed that a company with heavy borrowings in relation to equity is highly geared, and that one with little borrowed money is less highly geared, there is no universally accepted numerical measure of gearing.

The most primitive measures of gearing simply compare the book amounts of equity share capital and "prior charges" in the form of preference shares, debentures and loan stocks.

| | Company | | |
|---|---|---|---|
| | A | B | C |
| | £ | £ | £ |
| Share capital: | | | |
| 1,200,000 ordinary shares of 50p each | 600,000 | 600,000 | 600,000 |
| 100,000 6% preference shares of £1 | 100,000 | — | — |
| | 700,000 | 600,000 | 600,000 |
| 8% debentures | 250,000 | 300,000 | — |
| 12% unsecured loan stock | 50,000 | — | 60,000 |
| | 1,000,000 | 900,000 | 660,000 |
| which may be summarised: | | | |
| Equity | 600,000 | 600,000 | 600,000 |
| Prior charges | 400,000 | 300,000 | 60,000 |
| Total | £1,000,000 | £900,000 | £660,000 |

Leading authorities use these three pieces of information: equity, prior charges and the total, to give three commonly used measures of gearing:

| | | A | B | C |
|---|---|---|---|---|
| (a) | $\dfrac{\text{Prior charges}}{\text{Total}}$ | 40% | 33.33% | 9.09% |
| (b) | $\dfrac{\text{Prior charges}}{\text{Equity}}$ | 0.667 | 0.500 | 0.100 |
| (c) | $\dfrac{\text{Equity}}{\text{Prior charges}}$ | 1.5 | 2 | 10 |

Although everyone would accept that company A was more highly geared than company B; and company B more highly geared than company C, and methods (a) and (b) suggest this numerically, method (c) works in the reverse; a company with a gearing of 10 is *less* highly geared than one with a gearing of 2 or 1.5.

None of these measures pays any regard to the *form* of gearing, though in some respects debentures might seem "heavier" in gearing than an equivalent sum and coupon in unsecured loan stock; and similarly, unsecured loan stock might seem to be "heavier" than a similar sum and coupon in preference shares.

Nor do these measures pay any regard to the rate of coupon. It might seem that if companies A and B have these structures:

| | | A | B |
|---|---|---|---|
| | | £ | £ |
| Equity | | 1,000,000 | 1,000,000 |
| Prior charges: | 10% debentures | 600,000 | — |
| | 4% debentures | — | 600,000 |

then company B would be the less highly geared, but the commonly used measures do not suggest this.

All these primitive measures of gearing have one further failing in common: they ignore reserves. They also ignore deferred taxation.

A more sophisticated indicator of the gearing of a business is the *extent to which total assets have been financed by equity shareholders:*

$$\frac{\text{Equity shareholders' funds}}{\text{Total assets}} \times 100.$$

Clearly, the greater the percentage financed by equity shareholders, the lower the gearing.

The measures outlined so far have all been static measures, whereas the importance of gearing lies in its effect.

The *gearing factor* is a dynamic measure of gearing on earnings available to equity shareholders:

$$\text{Gearing factor} = \frac{\dfrac{\text{Profit after interest available}}{\text{to ordinary shareholders}} \div \text{Equity shareholders' funds}}{\text{Profit before interest} \div \text{Total assets}}.$$

*Illustration*

| | Balance sheet as at 31st December | |
|---|---|---|
| | Company A | Company B |
| | £ | £ |
| Equity shareholders' funds | 600,000 | 600,000 |
| Prior charges: | | |
| 10% debentures | 400,000 | — |
| 4% debentures | — | 400,000 |
| | £1,000,000 | £1,000,000 |

Table 36 shows how the gearing factor (a) differs between company A and company B, and (b) changes with the level of profit. Taxation is ignored.

Table 36. GEARING FACTOR DIFFERENCES AND CHANGES

| *Company A* | | | | | *Company B* | | | |
|---|---|---|---|---|---|---|---|---|
| *Profit before interest* | *% on capital with no gearing* | *Profit with gearing* | *% on equity with gearing* | *Gearing factor* | *% on capital with no gearing* | *Profit with gearing* | *% on equity with gearing* | *Gearing factor* |
| £000 | % | £000 | % | | % | £000 | % | |
| 0 | 0 | −40 | −6.67 | | 0 | −16 | −2.67 | |
| 10 | 1 | −30 | −5.00 | −5.00 | 1 | −6 | −1.00 | −1.00 |
| 20 | 2 | −20 | −3.33 | −1.67 | 2 | 4 | 0.67 | 0.33 |
| 30 | 3 | −10 | −1.67 | −0.56 | 3 | 14 | 2.33 | 0.78 |
| 40 | 4 | 0 | 0 | 0 | 4 | 24 | 4.00 | 1.00 |
| 50 | 5 | 10 | 1.67 | 0.33 | 5 | 34 | 5.67 | 1.13 |
| 60 | 6 | 20 | 3.33 | 0.56 | 6 | 44 | 7.33 | 1.22 |
| 80 | 8 | 40 | 6.67 | 0.83 | 8 | 64 | 10.67 | 1.33 |
| 100 | 10 | 60 | 10.00 | 1.00 | 10 | 84 | 14.00 | 1.40 |
| 120 | 12 | 80 | 13.33 | 1.11 | 12 | 104 | 17.33 | 1.44 |
| 200 | 20 | 160 | 26.67 | 1.33 | 20 | 184 | 30.67 | 1.53 |
| 500 | 50 | 460 | 76.67 | 1.53 | 50 | 484 | 80.67 | 1.61 |
| 5,000 | 500 | 4,960 | 826.67 | 1.65 | 500 | 4,984 | 830.67 | 1.66 |

Although both companies have identical gearing measured in static terms, the lower coupon of company B means that gearing factor is greater at all levels of profit.

Gearing factor is unity (i.e. gearing makes no difference) when the rate of profit before interest to total assets is equal to interest as a percentage of debt (in this simplified example, the coupon). It is less than unity (i.e. gearing is disadvantageous) when the rate of profit before interest to total assets is less than the interest as a percentage of debt; and more than unity (advantageous) when it is greater.

Notice how the gearing factor increases with profit before interest, but the rate of increase slows down. In mathematical terms, gearing factor tends towards a limit of:

$$\frac{\text{Equity shareholders' funds + Prior charges}}{\text{Equity shareholders' funds}}.$$

In this case:

$$\frac{£1,000,000}{£600,000} = 1.6667$$

irrespective of the rate of interest paid on prior charges.

Yet another dynamic measure of gearing is *gearing effect*.

Gearing effect = Change in profit after interest available for equity brought about by a 1 per cent increase in profit before interest.

Table 37. GEARING EFFECT

| *Profit before interest* | *Gearing effect* Company A | *Gearing effect* Company B |
|---|---|---|
| £000 | % | % |
| 20 | — | 5.00 |
| 30 | — | 2.14 |
| 40 | — | 1.67 |
| 50 | 5.00 | 1.47 |
| 60 | 3.00 | 1.36 |
| 80 | 2.00 | 1.25 |
| 100 | 1.67 | 1.19 |
| 120 | 1.50 | 1.15 |
| 200 | 1.25 | 1.09 |
| 500 | 1.09 | 1.03 |
| 5,000 | 1.008 | 1.003 |

Gearing effect is greatest when profit before interest barely covers the interest. Thus (Table 37) in the case of company A, if profit before interest was £41,000, then £40,000 would go in interest, and there would be £1,000 for equity shareholders. If the profit rose by 1 per cent (i.e. by £410) before tax then ordinary shareholders would get £1,410 (i.e. 41 per cent more).

Gearing effect is least when profits before interest vastly exceed the interest due. In mathematical terms it tends towards 1 as profits before tax increase.

## 5.14 Return on capital employed

Section 5.1 looked at ways in which the "return on capital employed" could be improved by using ratios. For that purpose capital employed was assumed to be closing tangible fixed assets (net of depreciation) *plus* net current assets. This is a frequently used definition, and one which it is comparatively simple to explain; but it is not the only "return on capital employed" measure commonly employed.

For a start, why employ the *closing* figure? Capital is employed day by day throughout the year: why pick on the figure for one day? And, especially if capital has been raised during the year, why treat it as though it had been employed throughout the year? Why treat retained profits of the year, too, as though they were available for the whole year?

It is impossible for an external analyst to measure capital employed from day to day, but some analysts do use for certain purposes:

(a) capital employed at the beginning of the period; or

(b) the average of opening and closing capital employed; or

(c) a weighted average where capital has been raised (or redeemed) during the period.

Some inter-firm comparisons take as their basis the *return on total assets* (rather than that on net assets). That is to say, they treat current liabilities as a part of capital employed. Some, to obtain more comparable results, include fixed assets at cost, rather than written down value. But once one starts on this process of adjustment, it becomes difficult to stop. Ought one to include a notional rent charge when premises are owned? And if a controlling director performs a management function, ought one to substitute for his actual salary, the hypothetical salary of a manager of similar age and experience? The list could go on and on.

One cannot say that one formula for return on capital employed is "right", and all others are wrong: everything depends upon the purpose of the calculation.

An equity shareholder could reasonably compute:

$$\text{Return on equity shareholders' funds employed} = \frac{\text{Profit attributable to ordinary shareholders}}{\text{Equity share capital} + \text{Reserves}}.$$

Management might look separately at:

(a) Return on funds used in operations =

$$\frac{\text{Profit before deducting interest (but excluding associated companies, and investment income)}}{\text{Net assets (excluding associated companies and investments)}}.$$

(b) Return on funds invested in associated companies =

$$\frac{\text{Profit of associated companies (before tax)}}{\text{Investment in associated companies (per consolidated balance sheet)}}.$$

(c) Return on other investments =

$$\frac{\text{Income from other investments (gross)}}{\text{Investment in other investments}}.$$

In some cases it may be worth considering:

(d) Return to minority shareholders =

$$\frac{\text{Profits attributable to minority shareholders}}{\text{Minority shareholders (per consolidated balance sheet)}}.$$

This latter ratio will help to explain the return to equity shareholders of the group. It may also, where the group is small, or consists almost entirely of wholly owned subsidiaries, pin-point an area where losses are being made; or where profits are above average. The external analyst has to be continually on the look-out for clues of this nature.

Many analysts, when comparing the performance of one company with another, automatically deduct goodwill (and other intangible assets) from equity shareholders' funds in computing return on capital employed.

Goodwill only appears in a company balance sheet where it has been purchased; and even then it may be written off over a period of years. This makes the balance sheet figure difficult to interpret.

Nevertheless, there are cases where goodwill should not be deducted. For instance, in assessing the return on a prospective subsidiary, goodwill cost of control, if the purchase consideration was fairly valued, is an essential part of the cost of the acquisition, and should be taken into account in assessing the possible return on the funds employed.

The important thing in computing return on capital employed is that the top line and bottom line of the ratio should be consistent. It would clearly be wrong (i.e. unfair) to compute:

$$\frac{\text{Profit after deducting interest paid}}{\text{Net assets}},$$

taking net assets to be: fixed assets (net of depreciation) + net current assets, since these are provided, in part at least, by borrowed money, the interest upon which has been deducted in arriving at the top line.

Shareholders tend to be more interested in after corporation tax returns; and managers in pre-tax figures—but this is not universally true. In comparing overseas investments, managers may be very interested in the effects of tax, and in the *net* returns.

## 5.15 Overtrading

Overtrading is a term used by bankers, credit rating organisations and analysts generally to denote a condition in which the resources—and in particular the liquid resources—of a business are insufficient to maintain the existing level of trading.

In colloquial terms, overtrading represents the failure on the part of management to cut their coat according to their cloth.

Overtrading may arise from internal factors or external.

It may be caused by the management of the business itself (i.e. internally) in a number of ways:

(a) *By expanding turnover* (e.g. by sales promotion schemes) without correspondingly increasing working capital. Clearly, if a business with an annual turnover of £12,000,000 and average debtors of £2,500,000 increases turnover by 30 per cent, offering the same credit terms on the new turnover, its debtors are likely to rise by 30 per cent too, i.e. by £750,000. That £750,000 *may* be found (i) from existing working capital resources (which previously were excessive); or (ii) from new money introduced. If neither of these occurs, the business will be overtrading.

(b) *By increased investment in land and buildings, machinery, vehicles or other fixed assets* without a corresponding increase in equity or borrowings. As already explained, net cash flow (basically retained earnings plus depreciation) is available to finance the acquisition of fixed assets, and any balance remaining will increase net current assets. On the other hand, expenditure on fixed assets which exceeds net cash flow will deplete net current assets by that excess.

(c) *By lending money* (whether to another business, say, a supplier, or to employees); or *acquiring investments* (whether in a subsidiary, in an associated company, for trade reasons or otherwise) when the resources are not available or specifically raised to do so.

(d) *By allowing exceptionally high stock levels.* If prices are likely to rise, it may be entirely reasonable to consider stocking up in anticipation. If strikes or lockouts, or other production difficulties are foreseen, either on the part of suppliers or in one's own organisation, again it may be entirely reasonable to think of stocking up in anticipation. But if the funds are not already available, or are not raised, to do so would involve overtrading, and be unwise.

(e) *By allowing exceptionally long credit.* Companies sometimes agree as a condition of the contract (which they would not otherwise obtain) to an exceptionally long period of credit, or agree to the deferment of payment as a favour to a valued customer. In either case, such an arrangement will involve factors other than overtrading, such as an increased risk of bad debts, the future levels of inflation, and due allowance for interest on the money borrowed; but it also brings a danger of overtrading.

Any increase in one component of working capital must involve a reduction in another, so that unless working capital is excessive (or, at least, more than adequate) to start with, it will be depleted below that necessary to maintain the existing level of turnover, and overtrading will be present.

(f) *By purchasing debentures and loan stocks in the open market for redemption*, without replacing them. It may be to a company's advantage, or be made to look in the accounts to be to its advantage, to purchase debentures and loan stocks in the open market for redemption before they are due to be redeemed. Thus, if a company's 4 per cent debentures, due to be redeemed at par in 10 years' time, stand at 60; to purchase in the open market debentures of a market value of £1,200,000 will reduce the 4 per cent debentures outstanding by £2,000,000 and show an extraordinary profit of £800,000. But it will at the same time reduce cash resources by £1,200,000—and *could* therefore result in overtrading.

(g) *Through trading losses.* Just as in the absence of any change in capital, net current assets increase by the excess of net cash flow, i.e. retained earnings plus depreciation over the cost of fixed assets acquired, so, if losses are made (or excessive dividend paid):

After tax loss + Dividends paid + Fixed assets acquired − Depreciation

will represent *the fall in net current assets.*

Unless turnover falls even faster, such a fall in net current assets will probably result in overtrading.

Losses shown as exceptional or among extraordinary items need to be considered carefully. Not all of them represent a drain on working capital resources—e.g. the destruction or abandonment of a fixed asset does not of itself reduce working capital, but redundancy payments, stock write-downs, provisions for bad and doubtful debts, additional contributions to pension funds, payments of damages, and all losses on exchange relating to current assets and liabilities (and those realised on medium and long-term liabilities) do reduce working capital.

Overtrading also arises from external factors:

(a) *Changes in taxation rates/systems.* Since net cash flow represents retained earnings (i.e. after tax profits less dividends), any increase in the proportion of pre-tax profits taken in taxation will reduce net cash flow, and hence the amount available to pay dividends and to purchase fixed assets; net current assets are likely to be less than they would otherwise have been.

(b) *Changes in date of payment of tax.* If the date on which tax is due is brought forward (by changing the system) working capital will fall, not throughout the year, but during the period between the new date of payment and the old. This could involve financial strain during that period.

(c) *Inflation.* Rising prices involve an increased investment simply to maintain the existing physical monetary stocks of raw materials, work in progress and finished goods. The physical turnover and credit policy also bring, in a period of rising prices, an increase in debtors. Unless sufficient is ploughed back by way of retained earnings (or money is raised in some other way) both involve a drain on liquidity, and a danger of overtrading.

(d) *Price controls.* Profits normally increase with inflation. But where government introduces legislation to control prices, or reduce margins, net cash flow is less than it otherwise would have been.

(e) *Cutbacks in bank lending.* Overtrading is essentially the inability to find the cash to meet trading needs. So long as a business has access to funds which enable it to meet its debts as they fall due, both currently and in the foreseeable future, it is not overtrading. Where, however, a company comes to depend upon overdraft facilities from its bankers, which may be withdrawn with little notice as a result either of a change in bank policy or of changed government policies on bank lending, there is always a danger that it may find itself in a situation where funds are no longer available, and it is, in consequence, overtrading.

*Overtrading has a number of consequences* all connected directly or indirectly with shortage of cash (rather than assets in general):

(a) *Difficulties with creditors.* It may be possible to persuade some creditors to draw bills of exchange (generally by offering a suitable consideration), or otherwise agree to deferral of payment. Once this avenue is exhausted, a trader who lacks the money to pay all his suppliers is forced to adopt delaying tactics (querying delivery, quality, quantity or price; asking for copy invoices etc.) in an effort to avoid early payment, on the one hand, and writs on the other. Whatever happens, there are likely to be interruptions in normal supply, and loss of goodwill of both customers and suppliers.

(b) *Increased purchase costs.* The company which is short of cash:

(i) will be unable to pay accounts promptly, and thus loses the (very considerable) benefit of cash discounts;

(ii) may be unable to buy in bulk, so losing valuable quantity discounts;

(iii) may be forced to select those sources of supply which give substantial periods of credit (or even credit at all) rather than on price or quality criteria.

(c) *Pressure on debtors.* While pressure upon debtors to comply with the usual terms of business is to be regarded as normal, the business which is itself under pressure may go too far in pressuring customers to pay.

Factoring of debtors may help the liquidity situation, but it is costly.

(d) *Reduction in effective turnover.* If it becomes essential to reduce stocks substantially to provide cash, this may be possible only by reducing prices drastically.

Similarly, if it becomes necessary to reduce debtors, this may involve liberal discounts to encourage prompt payment.

(e) *Inefficient working.* In the short term it may be possible to conserve cash by deferring the replacement of machinery, or by postponing the maintenance of facilities. In the long term this will bring inefficient working, interruption and delay.

(f) *Difficulty in finding wages.* While it is possible to postpone for a few days or even weeks the payment of all or some monthly trade accounts without irreparable damage, failure to pay wages at the end of the week, or salaries at the end of the month, will almost inevitably result in immediate collapse.

Bankers are often faced with urgent demands to find the week's wages to tide a customer over—the alternative being that of putting the customer out of business. The banker's preferential position in a liquidation as to advances for wages (s. 319(4) Companies Act 1948) gives him some protection, but it is not an easy task to decide on the spur of the moment how far it is prudent to go.

(g) *Difficulty in paying tax.* Mainstream corporation tax is due in a single sum (in long-standing businesses on 1st January 9 to 21 months after the end of the accounting year) and produces a very considerable overnight drain upon liquid resources (in the absence of stock relief and first year allowances)—a drain which leaves overtrading, where it already exists, all too apparent.

## 5.16 Detecting overtrading from a study of the accounts:

(a) *Turnover/equity shareholders' funds rises excessively.* Turnover/equity shareholders' funds is not an easy ratio to interpret. It may increase for a variety of reasons, not all of them bad.

Indeed, a maintained high turnover/equity shareholders' funds ratio, or one which edges upwards slowly over the years, is likely to be a good sign—an indication that the ordinary shareholders' investment is being used effectively to obtain sales.

But a high ratio of turnover/equity shareholders' funds, and especially one which rises rapidly, may indicate that the business is trying to do too much (i.e. overtrading), highly geared, subject to strains and liable to become unstable.

(b) *Progressive reduction in liquid resources.*

(c) *The charging of more and more assets to secure loans as more and more is borrowed.*

(d) *A falling ratio of working capital/sales*, indicating that working capital has not increased in line with turnover.

(e) *Trade creditors increasing faster than turnover.*

(f) *Appearance of bills payable* where not previously found and not normal in the trade, indicating accommodation (inevitably for a consideration) on the part of creditors.

(g) *Disappearance of bills receivable* accompanied by a note referring to the contingent liability in respect of bills discounted (a perfectly respectable thing to do, but further evidence of tighter liquidity).

(h) *Increase in stocks.* Where a business over-expands in a boom, a sign of imminent failure when trade turns down may be growth in stocks of materials, work in progress and finished goods far exceeding that in sales; suggesting that stocks are hanging fire and may be saleable only at a very considerable reduction, if at all.

An indication that this was the case would be a falling ratio of debtors/stocks and work in progress, suggesting over-production (overstocking) and static or falling sales.

(i) *Unstable debtors/creditors ratio.* In a business operating normally, debtors tend (at balance sheet date at least) to bear a fairly constant relationship to creditors. Different industries have quite different relationships, partly because of the different credit periods. Once a business runs into trouble, the relationship tends to change: debtors may be slower to pay; it may be impossible to take discounts from suppliers, and creditors may increase; debtors may be asked to accept a bill, which is promptly discounted—all of which will affect the ratio debtors/creditors. The important thing is not the direction of change, but that any movement in the ratio tends to denote fundamental differences in the trading pattern.

## 5.17 The cure

Overtrading is a painful, and all too frequently fatal, disease.

As explained earlier, it essentially consists of a failure on the part of management to cut its coat according to its cloth.

Put like this, the cure is obvious. *Either:*

(a) cut the coat smaller; *or*

(b) obtain some more cloth.

But the fact that the cure is obvious does not make it easy to accept or to execute.

If the disease has progressed too far, it will be difficult, if not impossible, to obtain more cloth. In any case, borrowing will be expensive.

Similarly, if the disease is far advanced, so that creditors are pressing, the cloth which is left after forced sales of stock and other asset may be sufficient only for a very small coat.

Overtrading is thus best avoided, *But* if it cannot be, being introduced by external factors (such as a major bad debt) early action should be taken to cure it—for it is a progressive disease.

## 5.18 Undertrading

Although undertrading does not receive the attention among business analysts received by overtrading, perhaps because the fatalities it brings are less spectacular, it is just as frequent.

Undertrading represents the state of affairs where the sales/equity shareholders' funds ratio is unduly low because of the lack of sales.

Undertrading may be brought about by:

(a) under-utilisation of fixed assets;

(b) imbalance of plant, or excess capacity;

(c) low productivity;

(d) failure to produce a product which meets a market need;

(e) lack of marketing effort or ability.

Undertrading may be associated with loss-making, though this is not necessarily the case.

A distinction should also be drawn between undertrading and over-capitalisation. They often, but not always, go hand in hand.

Over-capitalisation by itself is easy to cure provided the excess capital is represented by cash or marketable assets. If it is not—if, for instance, it is tied up in excessive stocks—the task may be difficult.

Whereas over-capitalisation and overtrading are primarily financial problems, undertrading is a problem for general management. Thousands of businesses go out of existence each year simply because their management cannot find a way of developing sufficient sales volume to operate profitably.

## 6.0 PUTTING IT ALL TOGETHER: HINTS ON ANSWERING INTERPRETATION QUESTIONS

1. *Study the instructions*
   What is highly significant for one purpose, or in one context, may be irrelevant in another.

2. *Read the data*
   Try to develop an inner "bell mechanism". If something stands out as peculiar, especially significant, or inconsistent with something said elsewhere, underline it, or mark it with a cross; and then continue the reading process.

3. *Think ratios as the question is read*
   Endeavour to visualise (i.e. do a rough mental calculation) the key ratios as the data is read.

   At first, it may be best to do this on a second reading, but as skill is acquired, it should prove possible at first reading.

   Look especially for the key changes:

   (a) in profitability;

   (b) in liquidity;

   (c) in capital structure;

   (d) in the nature of the business.

4. *Think:*
   — Is there a problem? If so, what is the heart of the problem?
   — Sort out mentally the important from the trivial. Concentrate largely on the important, emphasising why it appears to be significant.
   — Don't totally ignore the less important, but do not dwell unduly on it.
   — Consider the questions:

   (a) How did the business get into this position? i.e. the *past*.

   (b) What is happening currently? i.e. the *present*.

   (c) What are the prospects for the business? i.e. the *future*.

   — If any significant information is lacking:

   (a) Be prepared to say so, explaining briefly *why* the information could be important.

   (b) Consider whether, in the position posed by the question, there would be any means of obtaining that information.

   (c) Consider the possible consequences.

5. *Structure*
   Quickly list the key areas which need to be covered. If there is a logical order, choose that. If not, try to put things in order of importance.

6. *Write*
Remember to obey the instructions in the question. If asked to draft a report, do not write a letter, or vice versa. If asked for notes, produce notes, not a finished report.

7. *Support the answer with facts and figures*
By the time this stage is reached, a great deal should be known about the problem. Do not assume that the recipient of the report or letter knows as much. If he did, he would not need any advice.

Choose the ratios and financial data to be supplied. Do not overwhelm; be selective. Get to the heart of the problem. On the other hand, do not ignore significant side-issues. It is very much a matter of balance.

## PROGRESS TEST 11

1. What reasons are there behind the interpretation of accounts? (1.1)
2. What observations are made in this chapter concerning the mathematics used in calculating ratios? (4.0)
3. Discuss the use of semi-logarithmic paper in this context. (4.10)
4. How may ratios be used as a profit measurement tool? (5.1)
5. What are stock ratios? (5.7)
6. What two components can be said to make up the return on capital employed? (5.8)
7. How may one compare one balance sheet with another? (5.9)
8. Describe a vertical balance sheet analysis. (5.10)
9. What is "the current ratio" and what may it be used for? (5.11)
10. What may an acid-test ratio be used for? (5.12)
11. Discuss the term "overtrading". (5.15) How may overtrading be detected by examining a company's accounts? (5.16)
12. What is "undertrading"? (5.18)

CHAPTER TWELVE

# Inflation Accounting

## 1.0 INTRODUCTION

### 1.1 The need for inflation accounting

It is a truth universally acknowledged that a set of accounts prepared under the historical cost convention must be in want of adjustment for inflation.

What is by no means yet universally agreed is the method by which the inflation adjustments should be made.

### 1.2 The proposals made by the ASC

Four main proposals have so far been made:

(a) The current purhasing power method (CPP) was proposed by Provisional SSAP 7 in May 1974 but withdrawn in January 1978 (8.0 below).

(b) The current cost accounting (CCA) method was proposed by ED 18 issued in November 1976 based upon the report of the Sandilands Committee. This proposed that the CCA accounts should be the main accounts published. The ED 18 proposals, which were very complicated and ran to over 100 pages, were rejected in 1977 and replaced by a more modest and simplified version, the Hyde Guidelines ((c) below).

(c) In December 1977 the ASC issued an interim recommendation which came to be known as the Hyde Guidelines, suggesting that companies listed on the Stock Exchange should prepare a supplementary statement to accompany their published accounts showing a simplified version of the ED 18 proposals, confined to the profit and loss account only. This was always intended as an interim solution pending the production of a definitive standard.

(d) In April 1979 the ASC published ED 24, entitled current cost accounting and intended this to be the final solution to the problem. It is based upon the same general principles as ED 18, and became a standard (SSAP 16) in March 1980.

SSAP 16 applies to listed companies and to all other entities meeting at least two of the following three criteria:

(a) turnover £5m or more;

(b) balance sheet total in the historical cost accounts £2.5m or more;

(c) average number of employees in the UK 250 or more.

Exceptions are insurance companies, property investment and dealing entities, investment trusts, unit trusts, non-profit organisations like building societies, and wholly-owned subsidiaries of UK companies.

Under SSAP 16, annual financial statements would include, in addition to historical cost accounts, a current cost profit and loss account, a current cost balance sheet and explanatory notes.

The current cost profit and loss account would show:

(a) the current cost operating profit, being the historical cost based profit after making depreciation, cost of sales and monetary working capital adjustments;

(b) the current cost profit attributable to shareholders, after making a gearing adjustment.

The current cost balance sheet would show fixed assets and stock at their value to the business. This would normally be net current replacement cost.

Paragraphs 2 to 7 below explain the CCA system along the lines proposed by SSAP 16.

## 1.3 Two vital definitions

Before proceeding to a detailed coverage of inflation accounting methods it is necessary to establish definitions of two terms constantly encountered—"monetary" items and "non-monetary" items.

(a) *Monetary items*
A monetary item is one which retains the same money value regardless of inflation. As a result it obviously loses real value in a period of inflation. The most obvious example is cash. Other examples are debtors, creditors, debentures and loans.

(b) *Non-monetary items*
A non-monetary item is one which retains its real value regardless of inflation. As a result it gains in money value in a period of inflation if the general inflation applies to the particular item under review. Examples of non-monetary items are stock in trade and fixed assets.

Master these two definitions really clearly before reading further.

## 2.0 CURRENT COST ACCOUNTING

### 2.1 The basic principles of CCA

(a) *The current cost profit and loss account*
The current cost profit and loss account is intended to show the adjustments necessary to allow for the effects of inflation on the HC profit.
The main items to be adjusted are:

(i) *Depreciation*, which needs to reflect the values used in revising the balance sheet to show the value to the business of the assets concerned.

(ii) *Cost of sales*, which needs to be adjusted to charge against sales a cost which allows for the effect of inflation. This adjustment is referred to as the cost of sales adjustment (COSA).

(iii) *Monetary working capital*. Current cost profit needs to reflect the extent to which the effects of inflation are increased or reduced by the manner in which the trading is financed. For example, if trade debtors are low and trade creditors are high, as in a retailing business, the stock holding may well be largely financed by suppliers, so that it is they rather than the retailer who suffer the effects of inflation. The monetary working capital adjustment (MWCA) seeks to allow for this factor.

(iv) *Gearing*. If a company is partly financed by loans or debentures, it will enjoy a considerable benefit in a period of inflation, because the real value of the money needed to repay those loans will be reduced.
A gearing adjustment is made to allow for this factor whenever monetary liabilities exceed monetary assets. In calculating monetary liabilities and assets for the purpose of the gearing adjustment, creditors, debtors and other items already allowed for in the MWCA are ignored.

(b) *The current cost balance sheet*
The objective of the current cost balance sheet is to show the main non-monetary assets at their value to the business at the balance sheet date.

This may mean revaluing fixed assets by reference to movements in a specific index applicable to the industry concerned.

Current assets other than stocks and all liabilities remain stated at their value in the HC accounts.

## 3.0 ILLUSTRATIVE ACCOUNTS

In the detailed explanations which follow, the accounts of Y Ltd, as shown below together with necessary indices, are used throughout.

Y Ltd

Balance Sheets as at 31st December

| | | 19X7 | | 19X8 |
|---|---|---|---|---|
| | £ | £ | £ | £ |
| Share capital | | 10,000 | | 10,000 |
| Profit and loss account | | 14,000 | | 18,000 |
| | | 24,000 | | 28,000 |
| Debentures | | 10,000 | | 10,000 |
| | | £34,000 | | £38,000 |
| Represented by: | | | | |
| Fixed assets: | | | | |
| Land and buildings (cost 31st December 19X7) | | 20,000 | | 19,800 |
| Machinery | 11,000 | | 11,000 | |
| *less:* Depreciation | 4,400 | 6,600 | 5,500 | 5,500 |
| | | 26,600 | | 25,300 |
| Current assets: | | | | |
| Stock | 7,250 | | 19,500 | |
| Trade debtors | 8,000 | | 10,000 | |
| Cash | 6,550 | | 3,200 | |
| | 21,800 | | 32,700 | |
| *less:* Current liabilities: | | | | |
| Trade creditors | (10,200) | | (14,800) | |
| Taxation | (3,000) | | (4,000) | |
| Proposed dividend | (1,200) | 7,400 | (1,200) | 12,700 |
| | | £34,000 | | £38,000 |

## Y Ltd

### Profit and Loss Account for year ended 31st December 19X8

| | £ | £ |
|---|---|---|
| Sales | | £100,000 |
| *less:* Cost of sales: | | |
| Opening stock | 7,250 | |
| Purchases | 89,250 | |
| | 96,500 | |
| *less:* Closing stock | 19,500 | 77,000 |
| | | 23,000 |
| *less:* Sundry expenses: | 11,500 | |
| Depreciation | 1,300 | |
| Interest on debentures | 1,000 | 13,800 |
| | | 9,200 |
| *less:* Taxation | | 4,000 |
| | | 5,200 |
| *less:* Proposed dividend | | 1,200 |
| | | 4,000 |
| Retained profit brought forward | | 14,000 |
| Retained profit as per balance sheet | | £18,000 |

Indices

| | Machinery | Stock |
|---|---|---|
| 1st January 19X4 | 110 | |
| 31st October 19X7 (Average date of acquisition of opening stock) | | 145 |
| 31st December 19X7 | 160 | 160 |
| 31st October 19X8 (Average date of acquisition of closing stock) | | 195 |
| 31st December 19X8 | 180 | 200 |
| Average for year to 31st December 19X8: | | 180 |

*Notes:*

(1) The cost of land and buildings at 31st December 19X7 was:

| | £ |
|---|---|
| Land | 10,000 |
| Buildings | 10,000 |

The buildings are to be depreciated at 2 per cent per annum.

At 31st December 19X8 it was agreed that the value for the purpose of the CC accounts was:

| | £ |
|---|---|
| Land | 14,000 |
| Buildings | 11,000 |

(2) Depreciation on buildings and plant and machinery is to be calculated on the closing value of the assets in the CC accounts.

## 4.0 THE CURRENT COST BALANCE SHEET—DETAILED CALCULATIONS

### 4.1 Relationship with the HC balance sheet

It is a fundamental feature of CCA that the figures shown should be based on and easily reconcilable with the HC accounts.

The CC balance sheet will contain *three* points of difference:

(a) A current cost reserve will appear among the reserves to reflect the adjustments made to fixed assets and stock, and also the adjustments made to profit.

(b) Fixed assets will be revalued by the use of indices or otherwise.

(c) Stock will be revalued.

### 4.2 Current cost reserve

The current cost reserve appears in the balance sheet to reflect the net effect of all the adjustments made in converting the HC accounts to CCA.

The current cost reserve as it will appear for Y Ltd is fully analysed at the end of paragraph 5 below when the profit and loss account adjustments have been made.

In answering an examination question (or indeed in practice) it is necessary to calculate the opening current cost reserve and then to make the entries necessary to reflect the changes made in the current year. (If the company has already operated CCA for the previous year, the opening balance on current cost reserve will already be in existence, of course). The opening current cost reserve figure will be needed to calculate the gearing adjustment (*see* 5.5 below).

For Y Ltd the opening current cost reserve balance is calculated as follows:

| | £ | £ |
|---|---|---|
| Machinery | | |
| (£11,000 × 160 ÷ 110) | 16,000 | |
| Depreciation | | |
| (£4,400 × 160 ÷ 110) | 6,400 | |
| | 9,600 | |
| HC value | 6,600 | |
| | | 3,000 |
| Stock | | |
| (£7,250 × 160 ÷ 145) | 8,000 | |
| HC value | 7,250 | |
| | | 750 |
| | | £3,750 |

The current cost reserve in essence consists of two elements:

(a) the credit arising when assets are revalued upwards (debit asset account in CC balance sheet);

(b) the transfer from profit and loss account necessary to withhold from distribution the amounts charged in the CC profit and loss account to allow for the net effect of additional depreciation, the COSA, the MWCA and the gearing adjustment.

## 4.3 Fixed-asset adjustments

(a) *Basis of valuation*
As indicated in 2.1(a) above, most fixed assets are to be adjusted to their value to the business at the balance sheet date. Value to the business is normally the *net current replacement price*. In exceptional circumstances, where there has been a permanent drop in value to below replacement price, the *recoverable amount* should be substituted. The recoverable amount is the greater of the net realisable value if sold and the value recoverable from its further use if retained.

(b) *Arriving at net current replacement price*
"Net" current replacement price means the actual current replacement price of a new asset at the balance sheet date (the gross current replacement price) less depreciation based on the new figure.

It may be convenient to use appropriate indices to arrive at gross current replacement price. Indices for the purpose may be produced by trade associations for an industry, or may be developed by a company for its own use. It is to be expected, however, that considerable use will be made of cost indices prepared by the Government Statistical Service, which has published two lists, one covering UK assets and one giving price indices for overseas countries. Suppliers' price lists or quotations may also sometimes be used.

It is not thought that the use of indices will be appropriate for most types of land and buildings. These should be revalued by qualified internal or external valuers at least every five years. The directors (and, of course, auditors) should review the need to obtain professional advice to update the values between the valuation dates. Indices will accordingly be used mainly for plant and machinery and stocks.

When an asset is revalued, this will have two consequences as regards depreciation. First, an additional depreciation charge must be made for the current year, and second, a *backlog* depreciation adjustment is needed to reflect the fact that depreciation based on original cost is insufficient to depreciate current replacement price. The backlog depreciation is debited to current cost reserve, so that the net increase in current cost reserve is the difference between the credit arising on revaluation of the asset and the debit to allow for backlog depreciation.

The following calculation shows the use of indices in arriving at net current replacement price and depreciation adjustments. Figures and indices are taken from the details in 3.0 above:

Y Ltd plans to introduce CCA adjustments for its accounts to 31st December 19X8. On 1st January 19X4, five years previously, it had bought machinery for £11,000, depreciation being charged at 10 per cent per annum on the straight line basis.

Appropriate specific indices for the machinery were:

| | |
|---|---|
| At 31st December 19X7 | 160 |
| At 31st December 19X8 | 180 |
| At 1st January 19X4 | 110 |

Calculate the value of the machinery as it should appear in the CCA balance sheet at 31st December 19X8.

Value of machinery in CCA balance sheet at 31st December 19X8:

| | | £ |
|---|---|---|
| (i) | Gross current replacement cost:<br>180 ÷ 110 × £11,000 | 18,000 |
| (ii) | Depreciation based on £18,000 for five years | 9,000 |
| | Net current replacement price | £9,000 |

As the value in the HC balance sheet is £5,500 the net increase in value is £3,500 which must be credited to current cost reserve. As £3,000 already stands to the credit of the reserve at 31st December 19X7, an additional £500 must be credited for the change in value during 19X8.

Now for the calculation when an asset is revalued. The land and buildings of Y Ltd are revalued at £25,000 as at 31st December 19X8.

This means that there is an upward revaluation of £5,200 (£25,000 minus HC balance sheet value £19,800).

## 4.4 Stock adjustment

The stock should be stated in the balance sheet at its value to the business and it is accordingly necessary to ascertain the index at the average date of acquisition.

The historical cost balance sheet of Y Ltd at 31st December 19X8 showed stock at £19,500. The average date of acquisition of the stock was 31st October 19X8, when the relevant index stood at 195. The index at 31st December 19X8 was 200.

Stock should appear in the CCA balance sheet as:

| | |
|---|---|
| 200 ÷ 195 × £19,500 | £20,000 |

This represents a credit to current cost reserve of £500 (£20,000 minus £19,500). The opening current cost reserve figure for stock is £750. Accordingly a net debit of £250 must be made to current cost reserve.

The current cost reserve adjustments to reflect the changes for the balance sheet are:

| | £ | £ |
|---|---|---|
| Balance at 31st December 19X7: | | |
| Plant | 3,000 | |
| Stock | 750 | |
| | | 3,750 |
| Revaluation of plant | 3,500 | |
| *less:* Provided at 31st December 19X7 | 3,000 | |
| | | 500 |
| Revaluation of land and buildings | | 5,200 |
| Revaluation of stock | 500 | |
| *less:* Provided at 31st December 19X7 | 750 | |
| | | (250) |
| | | £9,200 |

It is important to proceed methodically and to adjust the balance sheet items first, because the figure of £9,200 will be used when calculating the gearing adjustment (*see* 5.5 below).

## 5.0 THE CURRENT COST PROFIT AND LOSS ACCOUNT

### 5.1 The adjustments required

The adjustments required are:

(a) depreciation adjustment;

(b) cost of sales adjustment;

(c) monetary working capital adjustment;

(d) gearing adjustment.

All are debited or credited in the CC profit and loss account, with a corresponding entry to current cost reserve.

### 5.2 The depreciation adjustment

The object of the depreciation adjustment is to charge against profits a figure for depreciation based on the *value to the business* of the asset rather than one based on cost.

Strictly speaking, the average value to the business should be taken, though it is convenient and acceptable to use the closing value.

(a) *Depreciation adjustment for plant*
Using the closing value, the depreciation adjustment for Y Ltd is:

| | £ |
|---|---|
| £18,000 (gross current replacement cost) at 10 % | 1,800 |
| HC depreciation provided | 1,100 |
| Depreciation adjustment | £700 |

This is the figure used in preparing Y Ltd's CC accounts.

If the average value had been taken, the adjustment would have been:

| | £ |
|---|---|
| Average gross current replacement cost: | |
| £16,000 + £18,000 ÷ 2 = £17,000: at 10% | 1,700 |
| HC depreciation provided | 1,100 |
| Depreciation adjustment | £600 |

No further adjustment for the £100 difference is required: all that happens is that current cost operating profit is reported at £100 more and current cost reserve is £100 less because it is credited with £600 instead of £700.

(b) *Depreciation adjustment for buildings*
The buildings are valued at £11,000 at 31st December 19X8. They were acquired one year earlier and are being depreciated at 2 per cent per annum.

| | £ |
|---|---|
| CC depreciation required is: | |
| 2 ÷ 98 × £11,000 | 225 |
| HC depreciation provided | 200 |
| Depreciation adjustment | £25 |

Depreciation adjustments of £700 and £25 are debited to CC profit and loss account and credited to current cost reserve.

## 5.3 Cost of sales adjustment (COSA)

The purpose of the COSA is to adjust the profit to what it would have been if items in the trading account were all restated on the basis of the average cost for the year.

If purchases and sales are assumed already to be expressed at a figure closely approximating to average (which they will be if sales are not markedly seasonal and the rate of inflation is reasonably steady), the only items requiring adjustment are opening and closing stock.

| | £ | £ |
|---|---|---|
| The COSA therefore equals: | | |
| Opening stock adjusted to average cost: | | |
| £7,250 × 180 ÷ 145 | 9,000 | |
| *less:* HC value of opening stock | 7,250 | |
| | | 1,750 |
| Closing stock adjusted to average cost: | | |
| £19,500 × 180 ÷ 195 | 18,000 | |
| *less:* HC value of closing stock | 19,500 | |
| | | 1,500 |
| | | £3,250 |

This is a "short cut" method of calculation and may be proved as follows:

| | Trading Accounts | | | |
|---|---|---|---|---|
| | HC | | CC | |
| | £ | £ | £ | £ |
| Sales | | 100,000 | | 100,000 |
| *less:* Cost of sales: | | | | |
| Opening stock | 7,250 | | 9,000 | |
| Purchases | 89,250 | | 89,250 | |
| | 96,500 | | 98,250 | |
| *less:* Closing stock | 19,500 | 77,000 | 18,000 | 80,250 |
| | | 23,000 | | 19,750 |

Difference £3,250

The entry to reflect the COSA is:

| | | £ | £ |
|---|---|---|---|
| Profit and loss account | Dr | 3,250 | |
| To current cost reserve | Cr | | 3,250 |

## 5.4 Monetary working capital adjustment (MWCA)

(a) *Purpose of the MWCA*

The MWCA is intended to adjust the profit for two related factors. First, inflation is likely to cause an increase in trade debtors, so inflicting a loss on the company as a result of its holding a monetary asset through a period of inflation. Second, inflation is likely to cause an increase in trade creditors, giving the company a gain because it has an additional monetary liability during a period of inflation.

If there is a material difference in the indices appropriate for debtors and creditors, two separate calculations should be made. Where the percentage changes in the two indices are similar, however, a single calculation should be made as shown below. It will be safe to assume in examination questions that only one calculation is required unless separate and different indices are given.

(b) *Calculation of the MWCA*

The calculation is:

| | | |
|---|---|---|
| Opening monetary working capital: | | |
| Trade debtors | £8,000 | |
| Trade creditors | £10,200 | minus £2,200 |
| Closing monetary working capital: | | |
| Trade debtors | £10,000 | |
| Trade creditors | £14,800 | minus £4,800 |
| Difference during year | | minus £2,600 |

The extent to which net creditors have financed the business during the year has increased by £2,600.

This is not the MWCA, however, because it is first necessary to eliminate the effect of the change in volume. In other words, it is necessary to restate the £2,200 and the £4,800 in terms of the average price for the period, using the same indices as those used in the COSA and subtract the resultant figure from the difference of £2,600.

| | £ | £ |
|---|---|---|
| £2,200 × 180 ÷ 160 = | 2,475 | |
| *less:* HC | 2,200 | |
| | | 275 |
| £4,800 × 180 ÷ 200 = | 4,320 | |
| *less:* HC | 4,800 | |
| | | 480 |
| | minus £1,845 | 755 |

The entry to reflect the MWCA is:

| | | £ | £ |
|---|---|---|---|
| Current cost reserve | Dr | 755 | |
| To profit and loss account | Cr | | 755 |

(c) *Some special points in making the MWCA*

(i) It is normal to include trade debtors and trade creditors only in the calculation and to exclude cash at bank or overdraft. SSAP 16 proposes that cash or overdrafts should only be included in special circumstances, as for example in the case of a chain of retail shops needing to hold considerable floats of cash to operate, or when fluctuations in trade debtors and creditors cause material fluctuations in cash at bank or overdraft.

(ii) If the MWCA is a credit to profit and loss account, it should be limited to the amount debited for the COSA.

(iii) Where the MWC is a net liability greater than the value of stock, the excess should be left out of account when calculating the MWC and should be included in the gearing adjustment (*see* 5.5 below).

## 5.5 The gearing adjustment

(a) *Purpose of the gearing adjustment*
It should already have become clear in your study of this chapter so far that a company gains by having monetary liabilities in a period of inflation.

If interest is paid on loans or debentures it will be appropriate to show the gearing adjustment as a subtraction from such interest in the current cost profit and loss account.

(b) *Calculation of the gearing adjustment*

(i) Ascertain the average net borrowing during the period. The average net borrowing will be:

all liabilities and provisions, including deferred taxation but excluding proposed dividends, other than those included in the monetary working capital adjustment,

*minus*

*all current assets other than those brought into the COSA or included within monetary working capital.**

If net borrowing is negative (i.e. assets exceed liabilities) no adjustment is made.

(ii) Ascertain the average shareholders' interest during the period. This will be:

average share capital and reserves,† including preference shares and minority interest, if any

*plus*

proposed dividends.

(iii) Calculate gearing ratio. This will be:

$$\frac{\text{(i)}}{\text{(i)} + \text{(ii)}}$$

(iv) Multiply the sum of the current cost adjustments made in converting HC profit to CC operating profit by this fraction. The result is the gearing adjustment which is added to the current cost operating profit.

Applying these stages to the figures in the accounts of Y Ltd we have:

| | Opening £ | Average £ | Closing £ |
|---|---|---|---|
| (i) *Average net borrowings* | | | |
| Debentures | 10,000 | | 10,000 |
| Taxation | 3,000 | | 4,000 |
| | 13,000 | | 14,000 |
| *less:* Cash | 6,550 | | 3,200 |
| | £6,450 | 8,625 | £10,800 |

**Note:* Although the phrase in italics is in accordance with SSAP 16, it is considered that non-depreciable investments and investments should be included here.

†Note that the figure needed is the reserves from the CCA accounts.

| | Opening | Average | Closing |
|---|---|---|---|
| | £ | £ | £ |
| (ii) *Average shareholders' interest* | | | |
| Share capital | 10,000 | | 10,000 |
| Profit and loss account | 14,000 | | 18,000 |
| Current cost reserve (asset revaluations only—*see* 4.4 above) | 3,750 | | 9,200 |
| Proposed dividend | 1,200 | | 1,200 |
| | £28,950 | 33,675 | £38,400 |
| | | £42,300 | |

(iii) *Gearing ratio is:*
8,625 ÷ 42,300

(iv) *The adjustments in Y Ltd are:*

| | £ |
|---|---|
| Depreciation | 725 |
| COSA | 3,250 |
| MWCA | (755) |
| | £3,220 |

Gearing adjustment is accordingly:

$$\frac{8,625}{42,300} \times £3,220 = £657$$

In the current cost profit and loss account £657 will be added to the current cost operating profit.

This may be done, if desired, by setting it off against interest payable (*see* specimen accounts in 6.0 below).

The entry to record the gearing adjustment is:

| | | £ | £ |
|---|---|---|---|
| Current cost reserve | Dr | 657 | |
| To profit and loss account | Cr | | 657 |

Note that when building up the figure for average shareholders' interest on a CC basis, it is only necessary to bring in the asset revaluation credits to current cost reserve, because the profit and loss account adjustments (depreciation, COSA, MWCA, gearing) are adjusted between the profit and loss account and current cost reserve, and so do not affect the total reserves.

## 5.6 Current cost reserve

After giving effect to the balance sheet changes the current cost reserve account was £9,200 (4.4 above).

The final figure needed for the CC balance sheet is:

| | £ |
|---|---|
| Balance as above | 9,200 |
| Depreciation | 725 |
| COSA | 3,250 |
| MWCA | (755) |
| Gearing | (657) |
| | £11,763 |

## 6.0 THE CURRENT COST ACCOUNTS COMPLETED

Y Ltd

Current Cost Balance Sheet as at 31st December 19X8

| | £ | £ | £ |
|---|---|---|---|
| Share capital | | | 10,000 |
| Current cost reserve | | | 11,763 |
| Retained profit | | | 15,437 |
| | | | 37,200 |
| Debentures | | | 10,000 |
| | | | £47,200 |
| Represented by: | | | |
| Fixed assets: | | | |
| Land and buildings | | | 25,000 |
| Machinery | | 18,000 | |
| *less:* Depreciation | | 9,000 | 9,000 |
| | | | 34,000 |
| Current assets: | | | |
| Stock | | 20,000 | |
| Trade debtors | | 10,000 | |
| Cash | | 3,200 | |
| | | 33,200 | |
| *less:* Current liabilities: | | | |
| Trade creditors | 14,800 | | |
| Taxation | 4,000 | | |
| Proposed dividend | 1,200 | 20,000 | 13,200 |
| | | | £47,200 |

Y Ltd

Current Cost Profit and Loss Account
for the year ended 31st December 19X8

| | £ | £ |
|---|---|---|
| Turnover | | 100,000 |
| Profit before interest and taxation as in the historical cost accounts | | 10,200 |
| *less:* Current cost operating adjustments: | | |
| Depreciation | 725 | |
| Cost of sales adjustment | 3,250 | |
| Monetary working capital adjustment | (755) | 3,220 |
| Current cost operating profit | | 6,980 |
| Gearing adjustment | (657) | |
| *less:* Interest payable | 1,000 | |
| | | 343 |
| Current cost profit before taxation | | 6,637 |
| Taxation | | 4,000 |
| Current cost profit attributable to shareholders | | 2,637 |
| Proposed dividend | | 1,200 |
| | | 1,437 |
| Retained current cost profit brought forward | | 14,000 |
| Retained current cost profit as per balance sheet | | £15,437 |

## 6.1 Notes on examination approach

(1) It is important to present the adjustments in the profit and loss account properly. Observe particularly the description and position of the items marked*:

The format is:

| | £ | £ |
|---|---|---|
| HC profit | | X |
| *less:* Current cost adjustments: | | |
| Depreciation | X | |
| COSA | X | |
| MWCA | X | |
| | | X |
| *Current cost operating profit | | X |
| *Gearing adjustment | X | |
| *Interest payable | X | |
| | | X |
| | | X |
| *less:* Taxation | | X |
| *Current cost profit attributable to shareholders | | X |
| Dividend | | X |
| Retained earnings | | X |

(2) Once you have a clear idea of the adjustments needed, it will be possible to develop a methodical approach:

(a) Draw up formats for CC balance sheet and profit and loss account (separate sheets, both in vertical form).

(b) Calculate opening current cost reserve figure if not given in the question.

(c) Calculate revised asset values (debit assets and credit current cost reserve working) and record in balance sheet.

(d) Calculate depreciation adjustment and insert in profit and loss account, crediting current cost reserve.

(e) Calculate COSA and insert in profit and loss account, crediting current cost reserve.

(f) Calculate MWCA and insert in profit and loss account, crediting or debiting current cost reserve.

(g) Calculate gearing adjustment if required, insert in profit and loss account, crediting or debiting current cost reserve.

(h) Complete casts of profit and loss account and enter closing retained profit to balance sheet.

(i) Enter final balance of current cost reserve to balance sheet.

(j) Cast balance sheet. If your double entry in (b) to (i) above has been correct, it will balance!

## 7.0 SOME FURTHER POINTS IN CCA

We have now worked through, with explanations, the typical detailed calculations necessary to produce a CCA balance sheet and profit and loss account. One or two further points which did not emerge in the illustration are dealt with below.

### 7.1 Wasting assets like mineral-bearing land or mineral rights

Where the cost is capitalised in the HC accounts, a current replacement cost should be calculated by revaluation or by the use of appropriate indices.

### 7.2 Patents and copyrights

If these assets are material to a business, they should be restated at current replacement cost where possible.

### 7.3 Research and development expenditure and other deferred revenue items

These should also be restated at current replacement cost.

### 7.4 Goodwill

(a) *Purchased goodwill or capitalised internally generated goodwill*
The figure in the HC accounts should be repeated in the CC accounts without adjustment.

(b) *Goodwill arising on consolidation*
If part of the goodwill figure represents revaluation surpluses existing at the date of acquisition of the subsidiary, that part should be offset against the capital maintenance reserve.

(Note that if SSAP 14 is followed, the tangible assets are consolidated on the basis of their fair value to the acquiring company, this problem cannot arise.)

### 7.5 Profits and losses on disposal of fixed assets

In the HC accounts, a considerable "profit" may be reported when an asset is sold. In the CC accounts the profit should be recalculated using net current cost instead of historical cost. For example, if an asset with an HC book value of £50,000 is sold for £100,000 at a time when its net current cost is £80,000, the HC profit of £50,000 must be reduced to £20,000.

The adjustment will be effected by debiting CC profit and loss account (immediately after COSA and MWCA) and crediting fixed asset working with £30,000.

## 7.6 Fully depreciated assets

Fully depreciated assets will by definition appear in the HC balance sheet at a nil value. If there are such assets with a material value at the time CCA is first applied, the net value should form part of the initial transfer to current cost reserve.

## 7.7 Depreciation and backlog depreciation

The charge for depreciation for a period should represent the estimated consumption of service potential during the period, evaluated at current costs. These, theoretically, should be those ruling at the date of consumption. However, for practical purposes, either average or period end costs will suffice.

*Assets other than land and buildings carried at open market value:* the restatement of the net current replacement cost due to price changes will be derived from a restatement of the gross current replacement cost. Consequently, the accumulated depreciation also requires to be restated. The difference arising on this restatement is known as *backlog depreciation* and is transferred to the current cost reserve. The transfer to or from current cost reserve is thus the net amount of the restatement of the gross current replacement cost and the restatement of the accumulated depreciation.

## 7.8 Modern equivalent assets

Fixed assets are seldom replaced by identical assets. It is implicit in CCA that the allowance for price changes should take technological change into account. It would be unrealistic to base current costs and depreciation on the current cost of a similar or nearly similar asset when an equivalent modern asset incorporating technological change could do the same work and perhaps cost only half as much.

The use of broadly based indices allows for some of the effects on current costs of gradual technological change. Nevertheless, it may sometimes be necessary to derive the equivalent current cost of an existing fixed asset from the cost of a modern asset.

In determining the gross current replacement cost of fixed assets, the object is to make a realistic estimate of what it would now cost to buy an asset which has the same service potential as that of the existing asset when acquired. If the design of the particular assets has not changed significantly, there is no problem, and an index of the current cost of those assets can be used. Even if there have been changes, either in the methods of manufacture or in the detailed design, it will commonly be found that application of an index for the industry or for the class of assets involved will give a result of acceptable accuracy.

However, it may happen that the technology has changed significantly so that a modern substitute for the existing asset would be markedly different in its:

(a) initial capital cost,

(b) operating costs,

(c) life, or

(d) output.

The effect of (d) is that the modern asset will probably have a different service potential from the existing asset. However, these differences may also have an effect on the initial capital cost of the modern substitute. In these situations it would be unrealistic to take the cost of the modern asset and use it without adjustment as the current cost of the existing asset. For example, the modern asset may have a higher capital cost (e.g. it may incorporate computer control) but lower operating costs per unit of output if the higher capital costs were adopted, the existing asset would have to bear a higher depreciation charge as well as the existing higher operating costs. The true position is that the capital cost of the modern substitute includes the cost of the improvements so that like is not being compared with like.

There are two ways of approaching the problem, either of which should give a reasonable approximation. The simpler way is to use a broadly based or general price index, which, because of its wider base, may reflect a gradual change in technology in the industries concerned. Alternatively, if the modern asset were included in a different index from the existing asset then changes in that index could be used as being more relevant to the current technology.

However, in extreme cases and where major assets are involved, it may be necessary to check the results against calculations which make allowances for the difference in service potential. This is achieved by eliminating that part of the current capital cost of the modern asset which gives rise to improvement in output (by quantity or quality), operating costs or life. The aim is to ensure that there is no double counting. The calculation may sometimes be made by direct apportionment of the current capital cost by reference to comparative outputs or life. Quantifying the capital cost of an operating cost saving is more difficult. However, recourse to the discounting back of operating cost saving is only needed where the potential savings are likely to be substantial and there is no other way of estimating that part of the capital cost in the modern asset attributable to the difference in operating costs.

*Illustration*

| | |
|---|---|
| Original cost of each existing asset | £100,000 |
| Price index for class of assets: | |
| When existing asset acquired | 120 |
| At the accounting date | 180 |
| Current cost of a modern asset | £220,000 |
| Output of each existing asset | 20,000 units p.a. |
| Output of a modern asset | 40,000 units p.a. |
| Operating costs per unit and asset lives identical: | |
| Indexed original cost £100,000 × 180 ÷ 120 = | £150,000 |
| Current cost of existing service potential: | |
| £220,000 × 20,000 ÷ 40,000 = | £110,000 |

The existing asset would be overvalued if either the indexed cost (£150,000) or the unadjusted cost of a modern asset (£220,000) were used. The current cost of replacing the service potential of each existing asset is £110,000, and this is the correct figure.

This reduction to the cost of a modern equivalent asset is effectively a reduction in the price of the service potential and does not represent a change in the volume of service potential remaining. Consequently, the resulting change in the net current replacement cost is charged against current cost reserve. The amount of the charge may be small if depreciation has previously been based on estimates of asset life which have allowed for likely changes in technology.

It must be emphasised that it is the current cost relating to the existing asset which is being estimated, and the cost of a modern equivalent asset is merely a guide to this objective. Even if the existing asset will not be replaced, it is necessary to attribute a current cost to it. Furthermore, it is current proven technology which should be considered, not future possible developments because the latter do not represent current costs. The current amount to be adopted should not exceed the current replacement cost of the actual existing asset.

## 7.9 Statements of source and application of funds

In current cost accounts the flows of funds imposed on the business by changes in its input prices are isolated leaving the remainder as the result of other factors. Changes in the volume at constant prices of the total net operating assets and of their constituent elements can thus be shown.

A number of possible formats exist for a statement of source and application of funds. Two suggestions follow, both starting with the current cost operating profit. Either format would comply with SSAP 10, *Statements of source and application of funds*, and may be used even if the current cost accounts are not regarded as the main accounts. The second format closely follows example 1 in SSAP 10. The first illustrates a different approach.

Neither format shows the gearing adjustment on the face of the statement although it is possible to modify either statement to include it.

*Illustration*

Statement of Source and Application of Funds
for the year to 31st December 19X9
(based on current cost accounts)

| 19X8 £000 | | 19X9 £000 | £000 |
|---|---|---|---|
| | Generated from operations | | |
| xx | Current cost operating profit | | 2,080 |
| | *less:* Profit and loss items associated with the movement of funds: | | |
| | Interest | (1,000) | |
| | Current taxation: paid | (750) | |
| | Change in provision | 50 | |
| | Charge for year | (700) | |
| | Dividend paid | (250) | |
| | Change in provision | (50) | |
| | Proposed for year | (300) | |
| | | | (2,000) |
| | Retained earnings of the period, excluding gearing credit | | 80 |

*continued*

*continued*

| 19X8 £000 | | 19X9 £000 | £000 |
|---|---|---|---|
| | **Application of funds** | | |
| | Fixed assets: | | |
| | Purchases | (2,700) | |
| | Proceeds on disposals | 2,000 | |
| | Current cost profit on disposal | (100) | |
| | | 1,900 | |
| | Depreciation (CC) | 1,850 | |
| | "Volume" decrease | | 1,050 |
| | Working capital: | | |
| | Increase in stock | (2,120) | |
| | Increase in MWC | (500) | |
| | | (2,620) | |
| | Current cost working capital adjustments | 1,370 | |
| | Change in revaluation surplus on stock | 120 | |
| | | 1,490 | |
| | "Volume" increase | | (1,130) |
| | Increase in net operating assets during the period | | (80) |
| | Change in net operating assets at constant prices, giving rise to external funding requirements* | | Nil |
| | Proceeds from issue of new shares | | 2,000 |
| | Decrease in net short term liabilities | | (1,700) |
| | Decrease in HP creditors | | (300) |
| | Decrease in provision for taxation | | (50) |
| | Increase in provision for dividend | | 50 |
| | | | Nil |

*A measure of the extent to which the business was self sustaining in the period. It is a coincidence that the value is nil.

*Notes:*

| 19X8 £000 | | 19X9 £000 | £000 |
|---|---|---|---|
| | (1) Movements in fixed assets | | |
| | Purchases | | (2,700) |
| | Proceeds on disposal | 2,000 | |
| | CC profit on disposal | (100) | |
| | | | 1,900 |
| | Depreciation | | 1,850 |
| | "Volume" decrease (Note 2) | | £1,050 |

| 19X8 £000 | | 19X9 £000 | £000 |
|---|---|---|---|
| | (2) Volume change in net operating assets during the period at constant prices | | |
| | Retained earnings in the period | 990 | |
| | Exclude gearing credit | 910 | 80 |
| | Invested as follows: | | |
| | In fixed assets (decrease) | 1,050 | |
| | In working capital (increase) | (1,130) | (80) |

*Illustration*

Statement of Source and Application of Funds
for the year to 31st December 19X9
(based on current cost accounts)

| 19X8 £000 | | 19X9 £000 | £000 |
|---|---|---|---|
| | Source of funds | | |
| xx | Current cost operating profit | | 2,080 |
| | Adjustments for items involving funds retained in the business: | | |
| | Depreciation (CC) (Note 1) | 1,850 | |
| | Current cost profit on fixed assets disposals (Note 1) | (100) | 1,750 |
| | Generated from operations (before interest and taxation) | | 3,830 |
| | Funds from other sources | | |
| | Issue of shares for cash | 2,000 | |
| | Proceeds on disposal of fixed assets (Note 1) | 2,000 | 4,000 |
| | | | 7,830 |
| | Application of funds | | |
| | Fixed assets purchased (Note 1) | (2,700) | |
| | Interest paid | (1,000) | |
| | Taxation paid | (750) | |
| | Dividends paid | (250) | (4,700) |
| | *carried forward* | | 3,130 |

| 19X8 | | 19X9 | |
|---|---|---|---|
| £000 | | £000 | £000 |
| | | *brought forward* | 3,130 |
| | Movements in current assets/current liabilities | | |
| | Increase in stock | (2,120) | |
| | Increase in MWC | (500) | |
| | | (2,620) | |
| | Current cost working capital adjustments | 1,370 | |
| | Change in revaluation surpluses on stock | 120 | |
| | | 1,490 | |
| | Volume increase in working capital (Note 2) | (1,130) | |
| | Decrease in HP creditors | (300) | |
| | Movements in net liquid funds: | | |
| | Increase in cash balances | (1,000) | |
| | Decrease in overdraft | (700) | |
| | | (1,700) | |
| | | | (3,130) |

## 7.10 Statement of changes in shareholders' equity interest

CCA does not deal with the maintenance of financial capital in general purchasing power terms. Some users may be interested in a statement of the change in shareholders' equity interest after allowing for the change in the general purchasing power of money. Such a statement may be particularly helpful in situations where there are excess monetary assets or where part of the group has activities exempt under SSAP 16.

*Illustration*

Statement of Change in Shareholders' Equity Interest After Allowing for Change in the General Purchasing Power of Money
for the year ended 31st December 19X9

| | £000 |
|---|---|
| Equity interest at the beginning of the year as shown in the current cost accounts | 18,540 |
| Share capital issued during the year (30th June) | 2,000 |
| | 20,540 |
| Amount required to compensate for the change in the general purchasing power of money during the year (*see* note) | 1,626 |
| | 22,166 |
| Equity interest before dividends at the end of the year as shown in the current cost accounts | 23,828 |
| Excess | 1,662 |

This indicates that reserves before dividends (£300,000) as measured by the current cost accounts have increased during the year by £1,662,000 more than that required to compensate the funds invested by the shareholders for the fall in the UK in the general purchasing power of money during the year.

The excess can be analysed as follows:

| | £000 |
|---|---|
| Current cost profit attributable to shareholders | 1,290 |
| Effect on equity interest of price changes experienced by the company being greater than the general rate of UK inflation | 372 |
| | 1,662 |

*Note:*
The price index used to calculate the £1,626,000 in the above calculation is the general index of changes in retail price, as follows:

| | |
|---|---|
| 31st December 19X8 | 188.4 |
| 30th June 19X9 | 197.2 |
| 31st December 19X9 | 204.2 |
| Percentage change in the year | 8.39% |

(The use of the retail price index is preferred but other general indices could be used. The index used should be disclosed.)

## 8.0 CURRENT PURCHASING POWER ACCOUNTING (CPP)

### 8.1 Introduction

Although PSSAP 7 dealing with CPP accounting was withdrawn in January 1978, it remains necessary for examination purposes to know the basic principles of this system.

PSSAP 7 provided that the HC accounts should remain, but that they should be supplemented by inflation-adjusted accounts in which all items except monetary items are adjusted according to the movement in the Retail Price Index (RPI) between the date of a transaction and the balance sheet date. Trading and profit and loss account items are generally adjusted by reference to the average rate for the period, though depreciation is adjusted at the rate applicable to the relevant asset and opening and closing stocks according to the changes in the index between their respective dates of acquisition and the closing balance sheet date.

One further calculation is necessary when the indexation of the items is complete. The gain or loss on net monetary items must be calculated. This is done by setting out a cash statement for the year in HC terms (working 3), then converting each item to what it would have been if it had taken place at the close of the year.

Opening net monetary items are converted according to the movement in the index during the year, while transactions during the year (purchases, sales and cash expenses) are converted according to the difference between the average index for the year and the closing index. Working 3 in the illustration below shows the process in detail.

The intention of CPP accounting is to show the current purchasing power at the balance sheet date of the funds expended to acquire the assets held on that date.

CPP accounting was rejected by the Sandilands Committee because it does not allow for differential rates of inflation (movements in the Retail Price Index, based mainly on household expenditure, may be greatly at variance with movements in the price of industrial plant) and because the balance sheet does not show the current value to the business of the assets held.

## 8.2 CPP illustrated

Study the illustration below:

The accounts of Cappa Ltd for the year ended 31st December 19X9 are given below:

Trading and Profit and Loss Account
for the year ended 31st December 19X9

| | £000 | £000 |
|---|---|---|
| Sales | | 3,100 |
| *less:* Cost of sales: | | |
| Opening stock | 270 | |
| Purchases | 2,015 | |
| | 2,285 | |
| Closing stock | 480 | 1,805 |
| Gross profit | | 1,295 |
| Trade expenses | 870 | |
| Depreciation | 200 | 1,070 |
| Net profit | | 225 |

Balance Sheets

| | 31st December 19X8 | | 31st December 19X9 | |
|---|---|---|---|---|
| | £000 | £000 | £000 | £000 |
| Fixed assets (acquired 1st January 19X7) | 2,000 | | 2,000 | |
| Depreciation to date | 400 | 1,600 | 600 | 1,400 |
| Current assets: | | | | |
| Stock | 270 | | 480 | |
| Debtors | 250 | | 300 | |
| Cash | 400 | | 650 | |
| | 920 | | 1,430 | |
| *less:* Current liabilities | 465 | 455 | 550 | 880 |
| | | 2,055 | | 2,280 |
| Ordinary share capital | | 1,800 | | 1,800 |
| Profit and loss account | | 255 | | 480 |
| | | 2,055 | | 2,280 |

*continued*

*continued*

Retail price indices:

| | |
|---|---|
| 1st January 19X7 | 100 |
| 31st December 19X7 | 120 |
| 31st December 19X8 | 140 |
| 31st December 19X9 | 170 |
| Average for: 19X9 | 155 |
| Last 2 months of 19X9 | 160 |
| Last 2 months of 19X8 | 135 |

Procedure:
(a) Construct CPP profit and loss account by applying the appropriate indices to the figures.

| | Historical cost | | Index adjustment | CPP | |
|---|---|---|---|---|---|
| | £000 | £000 | | £000 | £000 |
| Sales | | 3,100 | $\frac{170}{155}$ | | 3,400 |
| *less:* Cost of sales: | | | | | |
| Opening stock | 270 | | $\frac{170}{135}$ | 340 | |
| Purchases | 2,015 | | $\frac{170}{155}$ | 2,210 | |
| | 2,285 | | | 2,550 | |
| Closing stock | 480 | 1,805 | $\frac{170}{160}$ | 510 | 2,040 |
| | | 1,295 | | | 1,360 |
| Trade expenses | 870 | | $\frac{170}{155}$ | 954 | |
| Depreciation | 200 | 1,070 | $\frac{170}{100}$ | 340 | 1,294 |
| | | 225 | | | 66 |
| *less:* Loss on monetary items (*see* (c) below) | | | | | 61 |
| CPP net profit | | | | | 5 |

(b) Construct CPP balance sheet:

| | Historical cost £000 | £000 | Index adjustment | CPP £000 | £000 |
|---|---|---|---|---|---|
| Fixed assets | 2,000 | | 170/100 | 3,400 | |
| *less:* Depreciation | 600 | 1,400 | 170/100 | 1,020 | 2,380 |
| Current assets: | | | | | |
| Stock | 480 | | 170/160 | 510 | |
| Debtors | 300 | | — | 300 | |
| Cash | 650 | | — | 650 | |
| | 1,430 | | | 1,460 | |
| *less:* Current liabilities | 550 | 880 | — | 550 | 910 |
| | | 2,280 | | | 3,290 |
| Share capital and reserves | | 2,280 | | | 3,290 |

(c) Calculate loss on monetary items and subtract from CPP profit:

| | Historical cost £000 | £000 | Index adjustment | CPP £000 | £000 |
|---|---|---|---|---|---|
| Opening monetary position 1st January 19X9: | | | | | |
| Debtors | 250 | | | | |
| Cash | 400 | | | | |
| | 650 | | | | |
| *less:* Creditors | 465 | 185 | 170/140 | | 225 |
| Sales | | 3,100 | 170/155 | | 3,400 |
| | | 3,285 | | | 3,625 |
| *less:* Purchases | 2,015 | | 170/155 | 2,210 | |
| Expenses other than depreciation | 870 | | 170/155 | 954 | |
| | | 2,885 | | | 3,164 |
| Closing monetary position (Debtors plus cash less creditors) | | 400 | | | 461 |

As the net monetary position is actually 400, when the CPP adjusted figure is 461, there has been a "loss" on short-term monetary items of this amount, which is accordingly added to CPP profit in the profit and loss account.

## PROGRESS TEST 12

1. What need exists for systems of inflation accounting? (1.1)
2. What are the four main proposals made by the ASC concerning inflation accounting? (1.2)
3. Define (a) monetary items; (b) non-monetary items. (1.3)
4. Outline the basic principles of current cost accounting. (2.1)
5. What is the purpose of the MWCA? (5.4)

CHAPTER THIRTEEN

# Consolidation of Foreign Subsidiaries

## 1.0 INTRODUCTION

Although the AAP syllabus does not generally include exposure drafts, the Association has announced that consolidation of foreign subsidiaries is to be added to the syllabus, and the following material dealing mainly with Exposure Draft 27 is now included in this book to cover this ground.

The problem of accounting for foreign currency translation has proved to be an intractable one, and an exposure draft (ED 21) on the subject was first issued in 1977.

ED 21 allowed a company to adopt either the closing rate method or the temporal method (*see* 3.0 below) in spite of the fact that the vast majority of UK companies had adopted the closing rate method by 1977.

ED 27, published in December 1980, stipulates the closing rate method for the balance sheet (and the average rate for the profit and loss account), except where the trade of the overseas branch or subsidiary is a direct extension of the UK holding company.

## 2.0 DEFINITIONS

It is fundamental to an understanding of the subject to understand the terminology used, and in particular to distinguish between *translation*, which is the subject of ED 27, and *conversion*:

(a) *Translation* is defined in ED 27 as "the process whereby financial data denominated in one currency is expressed in terms of another currency. It includes both the expression of individual transactions in terms of another currency and the expression of a complete set of financial statements prepared in one currency in terms of another currency."

(b) *Conversion* is not defined in ED 27 but may be taken, following ED 21, as "the process of exchanging ownership of a sum of money in one currency, or the right thereto, for a sum of money in another currency, or the right thereto."

(c) *Exchange rate* is a rate at which two currencies may be exchanged for each other at a particular point in time; different rates apply for spot and forward transactions.

(d) *Monetary items* are money held and amounts to be received or paid in money. All other balance sheet items are non-monetary items.

(e) *Net investment*—the net investment which a company has in a foreign subsidiary is its effective equity stake and comprises its proportion of the subsidiary's share capital and reserves.

## 3.0 METHODS OF ACCOUNTING FOR FOREIGN CURRENCY TRANSLATION

(a) *The closing rate method/net investment method*

Under this method all the amounts in the balance sheet of a foreign subsidiary company should be translated into the reporting currency of the holding company using the rate of exchange ruling at the balance sheet date.

Amounts in the profit and loss account should be translated at an average rate for the accounting period.

Exchange gains or losses will arise if the rate of exchange at the balance sheet date is different from the rate of exchange ruling at the previous balance sheet date. A difference will also result where the average rate used to translate the profit and loss account differs from the closing rate.

The net investment approach recognises that the investment of the holding company is in the net worth of a foreign business enterprise rather than a direct investment in its individual assets and liabilities. The foreign business will normally have net current assets and fixed assets which may be financed partly by local currency borrowings. In its day-to-day operations the foreign subsidiary is not dependent on the reporting currency of the holding company. The holding company may look forward to a stream of dividends in the future but the net investment in the subsidiary will remain until the business is liquidated or the investment disposed of.

The best indication of the performance of a foreign business is the net profit shown in its local currency financial statements. Therefore it is this amount which should be reflected in the group profit and loss account without adjustment other than for normal consolidation adjustments, e.g. the elimination of unrealised intra group profits on stock and to bring the accounting policies of the subsidiary into line with those of the holding company. Exchange differences on the net investment may result from many factors unrelated to the trading performance of the subsidiary. If such differences are introduced into the profit and loss account the results may be distorted.

(b) *The temporal method*

Under the temporal method non-monetary assets and all revenues and expenses are translated at the rate of exchange ruling at the date on which the amount recorded in the financial statements was established or, where appropriate, at the rate of exchange at which it is contracted to settle the transaction in the future.

Under this method monetary assets and liabilities together with any assets carried at current values are translated at the rate of exchange ruling at the balance sheet date. An exchange difference will result if the rate of exchange at the balance sheet date differs from the rate of exchange used to translate the same items at the last balance sheet date or when the monetary items were first recorded.

It is appropriate when using the temporal method to take exchange differences on monetary items as part of the profit or loss for the year from ordinary operations because the cash flows of the subsidiary are reflected in cash flows between it and the holding company. All gains and losses on foreign monetary assets and liabilities should be expressed in the holding company's reporting currency without any offset for the unrealised gains and losses on non-monetary assets.

(c) *The ED 27 position*

As previously explained, ED 27 requires the closing rate method to be used except where the trade of the overseas branch or subsidiary is a direct extension of the UK holding company, when the temporal rate should be used.

In the explanation of the closing rate method in (a) above, it is stipulated that the average rate should be used for the translation of the profit and loss account. In fact, many UK companies currently using the closing rate method apply the closing rate to the profit and loss account also. ED 27 prefers the average rate for the following reasons:

(i) it more fairly reflects the profits and cash flows which arise throughout an accounting period;

(ii) the profits disclosed in quarterly statements do not have to be restated if the exchange rate is different at the year end from the rates prevailing during the year;

(iii) the exposure draft produced by the Financial Accounting Standards Board (FASB) in the USA make the use of an average rate mandatory.

## 4.0 PROPOSED STANDARD ACCOUNTING PRACTICE

The proposed standard accounting practice is reproduced below exactly as it appears in ED 27. The original paragraph numbers have been retained.

46. When preparing the financial statements of an individual company the procedures set out in paras. 47 to 50 should be followed. When preparing consolidated financial statements the procedures set out in paras. 51 to 58 should be followed.

## Individual companies

47. Subject to the provisions of para. 48 each asset, liability, revenue or cost arising from a transaction denominated in a foreign currency should be translated and recorded at the rate of exchange ruling at the date of the transaction; or at an average rate for the period.

48. At each balance sheet date, monetary assets and liabilities denominated in a foreign currency should be translated at the closing rate or the rate of exchange at which the transaction is contracted to be settled in the future.

49. All exchange differences should be reported as part of the profit for the year from ordinary operations unless they result from transactions which themselves would fall to be treated as extraordinary items; in such circumstances the exchange differences should be included as part of extraordinary items.

50. Where a foreign branch operates as if it were a separate business entity with local finance it should be accounted for in the same way as if it were a subsidiary company.

## Consolidated financial statements

51. When preparing group accounts for a company and its subsidiaries, or where the results of associated companies are incorporated into those of an investing company using the equity method of accounting, the closing rate method of translating foreign currency financial statements should normally be used.

52. Exchange differences arising from the re-translation of the opening net investment in a subsidiary or an associated company at the closing rate should be recorded as a movement on reserves.

53. The profit and loss account of a foreign subsidiary should be translated at an average rate for the period. The difference between the profit and loss account translated at an average rate and at the closing rate should be recorded as a movement on reserves.

54. In those relatively exceptional circumstances where the trade of the subsidiary is a direct extension of the trade of the holding company the temporal method should be used.

55. Translation differences arising from the use of the temporal method should be reported either as part of the profit for the year from ordinary operations or as an extraordinary item as the case may be.

56. The translation method chosen for translating the financial statements of each subsidiary should be used consistently from period to period unless the financial and other operational relationships which exist between the holding company and the subsidiary change.

57. Where the proceeds of foreign loans raised by a holding company have been used to finance equity investments in foreign subsidiaries or associated companies differences on the loans may be offset by differences arising on the re-translation of the opening net assets relating to the foreign equity investments provided that:

(a) the exchange difference arising on loans denominated in a particular currency in any accounting period may be offset only to the extent of the exchange difference arising on foreign equity investments in the same currency;

(b) the relationship between the holding company and the subsidiary or associated company justifies the use of the closing rate method;

(c) the accounting treatment is applied consistently from period to period.

58. Long-term loans and other inter-company balances between a holding company and a subsidiary or associated company which are in substance equity investments should be treated by the holding company as equity investments in the subsidiary or associated company.

**Disclosure**

59. The methods used in the translation of the financial statements of foreign based operations and the treatment accorded to exchange differences should be disclosed in financial statements.

60. Any movement on a reserve account arising from translation differences should be disclosed separately in the financial statements.

**Date from which effective**

61. The accounting and disclosure requirements set out in this statement should be regarded as standard in respect of financial statements relating to periods starting on or after (date to be inserted after exposure).

## 5.0 SPECIAL PROBLEMS

(a) *Equity investment in overseas subsidiary financed by foreign loans*
As indicated in para. 57 of the proposed standard accounting practice (*see* 4.0 above), it is proposed that translation differences on loans may generally be offset against differences arising on the re-translation of the opening net assets relating to the foreign equity investments.

The logic of this treatment is that the holding company is probably covered in economic terms against any movement in exchange rates, because any increase or decrease in the amount outstanding on the loan as a result of exchange movements is likely to be covered by a corresponding change in the value of the net investment. For this treatment to be acceptable it is, of course, necessary to stipulate, as ED 27 does, that the foreign loan must be denominated in the same currency as the investment.

(b) *Areas of hyper-inflation*
In countries in which very high rates of inflation exist it may not be possible to present fairly the financial position of a subsidiary simply by a translation process. In such circumstances it may be necessary to revalue fixed assets in the local currency financial statements before the translation process is undertaken.

(c) *Permanent impairment situations*
There may be circumstances in which the translation of the net investment in a particular subsidiary gives rise to continuing adverse exchange differences and it appears that this trend is unlikely to be reversed in the foreseeable future. In such cases it will be necessary to consider whether that investment has been permanently impaired and make provision accordingly in the financial statements of the holding company.

## 6.0 ARITHMETICAL EXAMPLES OF THE PROPOSALS IN ED 27

Appendix 1 to ED 27 provides some very useful arithmetical illustrations of some of the calculations necessary, and these are reproduced below:

### *Illustration 1—Fixed assets*

A UK company purchases plant and machinery for use in the UK from a German company for DM800,000 in September 19X9. The exchange rate was £1 = DM3.95. The company records the purchase price in its own accounting records as £202,532. Thereafter it will not be necessary to translate the asset again and no exchange differences will arise.

### *Illustration 2—Debtors*

A UK company sells goods to a Swiss company in May 19X9 for SwFc750,000. Payment is received in August 19X9.

In May the company will record a debtor in its records of the sterling equivalent of SwFc750,000 at the exchange rate in May 19X9 of 3.5544 or £211,006. When payment is received in August the exchange rate has moved to 3.7081 so that the actual amount received is £202,260. The loss on exchange of £211,006 − £202,260 = £8,746 should be reported in the profit and loss account as part of the profit from ordinary operations.

### *Illustration 3—Creditors*

A UK company purchases goods from a Belgian company in November 19X9 for BFc11,000,000 when the exchange rate was 61.29. At the UK company's year end at 31st December 19X9 the account had not been settled. The cost of goods purchased in November would be recorded as £179,475. At 31st December the exchange rate was 62.09 so that the creditor would be recorded at £177,162 in the balance sheet. The gain on exchange of £179,475 − £177,162 = £2,313 would be reported as part of the profit from ordinary operations for the year.

### *Illustration 4—Long-term loans*

A UK company takes out a ten-year loan from an American bank in February 19X9 for US $10,000,000. The proceeds of the loan are converted to sterling and remitted to the UK when the exchange rate was 2.0025; they amounted to £4,991,265. At the company's year end of 31st December 19X9 the exchange rate was 2.1978. The loan should be re-translated at the year end rate and shown in the balance sheet as £4,550,005. The gain on exchange of £4,991,265 − £4,550,005 = £441,260 should be reported in the profit and loss account as part of the profit from ordinary operations—if necessary as an exceptional item.

### *Illustration 5—Extraordinary items*

A company sold a property in Sweden in October 19X9 for Kr2,650,000 when the exchange rate was 9.029. Payment was received in December 19X9 when the exchange rate was 9.187. The loss on exchange of £293,499 − £288,451 = £5,048 should be included as part of the gain or loss on the sale of the property and included as an extraordinary item.

### *Illustration 6—Consolidation procedures*

(a) *The closing rate method for translation of balance sheet items*
A UK company owns 100 per cent of the share capital of an Italian company. At 31st December 19X8 the share capital and reserves of the Italian subsidiary amounted to 1,450 million lire. The exchange rate at 31st December 19X8 was 1,671. At 31st December 19X9 the exchange rate was 1,785. The UK company consolidates its interest in the Italian subsidiary using the closing rate method.

The share capital and reserves (the net investment) at the start of the year should be re-translated using the exchange rate at the end of the year and the difference disclosed as a reserve movement.

| | £ |
|---|---|
| The net investment at 31st December 19X9 translated at the exchange rate at 31st December 19X9 would be 1,450m lire ÷ 1,785 = | 812,325 |
| The net investment at 31st December 19X9 would be 1,450m lire ÷ 1,671 = | 867,744 |
| Reduction in net investment | (£55,419) |

The reduction in the net investment in the year would be shown as a deduction from reserves.

(b) *Profit and loss account treatment*
The same Italian company made a profit in the year of 167m lire. The UK company translates the profit for consolidation purposes at an average rate for the year of 1,761. The profit for the year in sterling therefore is £94,832.

The difference between the profit for the year translated at an average rate and the profit translated at the closing rate would be accounted for as a movement on reserves.

| | £ |
|---|---|
| Profit of 167m lire at average rate of 1,761 = | 94,832 |
| Profit of 167m lire at closing rate of 1,785 = | 93,557 |
| Movement on reserves | £1,275 |

(c) *Reconciliation of positions in (a) and (b) for the investments in the Italian subsidiary*

| | £ |
|---|---|
| Net investment at 31st December 19X8 1,450m lire ÷ 1,671 = | 867,744 |
| Reduction in net investment in 19X9 | (55,419) |
| Profit for 19X9 at average rate | 94,832 |
| Movement on reserves being the difference between profit at an average rate and at the closing rate | (1,275) |
| Net investment at 31st December 19X9 1,617m lire at 1,785 = | £905,882 |

### *Illustration 7—Intra-group loans*

A UK holding company borrows US $100m. From the proceeds it lends US $20m to its USA subsidiary, DM4m to its German subsidiary, £5m to its French subsidiary and the balance it invests in the UK. All loans are denominated in the currency stated and are made for a period of 5 years from 31st March 19X9. The year end of all companies is 31st December 19X9.

(a) *Holding company records*
The holding company will record the following:

| | Balances at | | |
|---|---|---|---|
| | 31st March 19X9 | 31st December 19X9 | Gain/(loss) |
| | £ | £ | £ |
| External US $100m loan | 49,062,900 | 45,500,050 | 3,562,850 |
| $20m loan to USA subsidiary | 9,812,580 | 9,100,010 | (712,570) |
| DM4m loan to German subsidiary | 1,055,409 | 1,049,042 | (6,367) |
| £5m loan to French subsidiary | 5,000,000 | 5,000,000 | — |
| Gain in year by holding company | | | £2,843,913 |

(b) *Subsidiary company records*
In the accounts of the USA and German subsidiaries no adjustments would need to be made as they have loans with the holding company denominated in the currencies in which they account. Therefore no gain or loss on exchange arises. In the case of the French subsidiary it has a sterling loan and will suffer an exchange difference in the year as follows:

| Balances at: 31st March 19X9 | 31st December 19X9 | Gain/(loss) |
|---|---|---|
| FrFc43,669,000 | FrFc44,701,000 | FrFc(1,032,000) |

£5m due to
holding company

The French subsidiary will therefore record an exchange loss on the sterling loan of FrFc1,032,000 which it will account for as part of the profit for the year from ordinary operations.

(c) *Consolidated accounts*
In the consolidated accounts the exchange differences by the holding company and the French subsidiary will both be taken as part of the profit for the year from ordinary operations, so the total gain from the loan finance scheme will be:

| | £ |
|---|---|
| Holding company | 2,843,913 |
| French subsidiary FrFc1,032,000 ÷ 8.9402 | (115,434) |
| | £2,728,479 |

*Illustration 8—Foreign loans used to purchase equity shares*

A UK company borrows FrFc20m in July 19X9 to purchase equity shares in a French business. The sterling cost amounted to FrFc20m ÷ 9.5957 = £2,084,267. At the year end of 31st December 19X9 the loan would be re-translated as FrFc20m ÷ 8.9402 = £2,237,086. The exchange loss on the loan would be £152,819. As the sterling equivalent of the net assets acquired in the French business would have increased by this same amount, the UK company would be allowed to offset the exchange difference on the loan against the gain in the assets which would be shown as a reserve movement on consolidating the French investment.

## 7.0 FURTHER CONSIDERATION OF BACKGROUND TO ED 27

(a) *History*
The original method adopted to translate foreign financial statements was the temporal method, the underlying assumption being that the pound sterling was a stable and dominant currency by reference to which other currencies fluctuated. Against such a background, the translation of fixed assets on the basis of the rate ruling at the time of their acquisition seemed reasonable.

In the post-war period sterling could no longer be viewed in this light, but the fact that exchange rates tended to remain fixed meant that the use of the (temporal) method, with major currency realignments being treated as extraordinary items, continued to be appropriate.

With the progressive abandonment of fixed exchange rates, the continuation of the temporal method gave rise to increasing exchange differences. As a result UK companies gradually moved to the closing rate method which is now used by almost all major UK companies with overseas interests.

(b) *Practice in the USA*
In the USA, companies were slower to abandon the temporal method, and FAS 8, issued by the Financial Accounting Standards Board (FASB) in October 1975, required the use of the temporal method. Growing

dissatisfaction with FAS 8 has led to the recent publication of an FASB exposure draft calling for a US treatment broadly similar to that proposed by ED 27. It is to be hoped that an agreed standard acceptable to both countries will be developed.

## 8.0 THE NET INVESTMENT CONCEPT

The net investment concept forms the basis of ED 27. It was considered, and rejected, for use in the USA at the time FAS 8 was developed.

The net investment concept is based on the approach that the accounting treatment adopted for translation purposes should reflect the manner in which a company operates.

Where a holding company carries the exchange risk in respect of its overseas operations this should be reflected by taking exchange differences into operating profit. Where an overseas business operation is semi-independent and self-financing the exchange risk exposure of the holding company is its net investment in the overseas operation taken as a whole and not a risk which can be identified with individual assets and liabilities.

The basic approach is as follows:

(a) Gains and losses in each individual company in a group arising from changes in relative values of currencies should be included in local currency operating profit and then into the consolidated profit figure.

(b) When consolidated accounts are prepared, the opening balances, being the net investments by the holding company in the subsidiaries, should be restated at the closing rate of exchange and the total differences shown as a movement on reserves.

Calculation (b) is shown in Illustration 7(a) above.

## PROGRESS TEST 13

1. Define the following terms:
   (a) translation;
   (b) conversion;
   (c) exchange rate;
   (d) monetary items;
   (e) net investment. (2.0)
2. What are three main methods of accounting for foreign currency translations? (3.0)
3. What is the net investment concept? (8.0)

APPENDIX ONE

# Index to Examination Questions and Suggested Answers

## 10. Miscellaneous accounts

APPENDIX TWO

# Examination Questions

The following are provided to enable you to practice answering examination questions under examination conditions. Many of the problems have been taken from actual papers and our thanks must go to the ACCA, the ICAEW and the ICMA for allowing us to reproduce their question material here.

Answer each question within 35 minutes. That is approximately how long you will have in most examinations—allowing time to read the paper and make rough calculations. Do *not* check the answer before you attempt the question. It is a better education to fail utterly at first than to preserve a false sense of security by supplementing your knowledge by means of covert glances at the model answers.

## 1 COMPANY ACCOUNTS—PUBLISHED ACCOUNTS

### 1 Profit and loss account disclosure

List eight items of expense or income required to be shown separately in a company's published profit and loss account or in notes to the accounts.

(8 marks)

### 2 Balance sheet disclosure

What information is required to be given in a company's balance sheet or in notes to the accounts for:

(a) goodwill (3 marks)

(b) investments (8 marks)

(c) stock (3 marks)

(d) creditors (5 marks)

(e) share capital? (4 marks)

Your answer should include in each case an indication of how the item is shown in the statutory balance sheet format.

(23 marks)

## 3 Directors' report

List twelve matters required to be disclosed separately in a company's published directors' report.

(12 marks)

## 4 Small and medium-sized companies

(a) What are the criteria for determining whether a company qualifies for the small and medium-sized companies exemptions?

(b) "The small or medium-sized company exemptions entitle a company to omit information from its published accounts." True or false?

(c) What modified accounts may be lodged with the Registrar by companies qualifying under the Companies Act 1981 as:

(i) small companies

(ii) medium-sized companies?

(20 marks)

## 5 Radical plc

After closing off the profit and loss account for the year ended 30th September 19X4, the following draft balance sheet was extracted from the nominal ledger of Radical plc:

Balance Sheet

| | £ | | £ |
|---|---|---|---|
| Ordinary share capital | 250,000 | Stocks: | |
| Preference share capital | 100,000 | Raw materials | 63,606 |
| $9\frac{1}{2}$% loan stock | 150,000 | Work in progress | 27,104 |
| Creditors—trade | 64,700 | Finished goods | 102,024 |
| Aggregate deprcciation: | | Debtors | 175,400 |
| Freehold property | 5,000 | Cash in hand | 2,146 |
| Plant and machinery | 165,230 | Balance at bank | 42,735 |
| Fixtures and fittings | 31,300 | Freehold property, at cost | 131,000 |
| Provision for bad debts | 13,420 | Plant and machinery, at cost | 341,195 |
| Profit and loss account | 89,642 | Fixtures and fittings, at cost | 65,600 |
| Share premium | 52,400 | Shares in Midland Bank PLC | |
| Corporation tax at 52% | 26,750 | at cost 10th August 19X2 | 7,400 |
| Proposed ordinary dividend | 25,000 | Shares in Shell Transport | |
| | | and Trading Co. PLC at | |
| | | cost 18th July 19X3 | 5,232 |
| | | Shares in Redfire Ltd at | |
| | | cost 18th May 19X3 | 10,000 |
| | £973,442 | | £973,442 |

You also obtain the following information:

(a) The company has an authorised and issued share capital of £350,000 divided into 200,000 8 per cent cumulative preference shares of 50p each, and 1,000,000 ordinary shares of 25p each.

(b) The $9\frac{1}{2}$ per cent loan stock is unsecured and repayable on 1st October 19X9.

(c) Of the balance on corporation tax account £16,750 was due for payment on 1st January 19X5 and the balance a year later.

(d) Freehold property includes payments made during the year of £26,000, being amounts paid for work certified on a new factory extension which will eventually cost a total of £75,000.

(e) Additional plant and machinery was purchased during the year at a cost of £40,450 but there have been no changes in fixtures and fittings.

(f) There were no disposals of any fixed assets.

(g) On 30th September 19X4 the market value of shares in Midland Bank PLC was £10,429, and Shell Transport and Trading Co. PLC £9,427. Both investments are listed and are held as current assets.

(h) Redfire Ltd is a private company incorporated in England with an issued share capital of £40,000 in £1 shares. Radical's investment was purchased at par. Redfire's balance sheet at 30th June 19X4, the latest available, showed reserves of £33,000. Its profit for the year ended on that date was £18,000. The investment in Redfire is held as a fixed asset.

(i) If the investments were realised at their market and directors' values respectively, it is estimated that taxation amounting to £14,000 would become payable.

(j) It is the company's policy to value stock at the lower of cost or net realisable value, calculated on a FIFO basis.

(k) Debtors are all trade with the exception of £12,750 of prepayments.

*Required:*
Prepare the company's balance sheet and notes as on 30th September 19X4 in a form suitable for presentation to members, indicating in your answer which of the permitted formats you have adopted.

Corresponding figures are not required and the information given may be taken as if it included all that is necessary to satisfy the requirements of the Companies Acts 1948 to 1981.

Assume income tax to be at the rate of 33 per cent.

(22 marks)

## 6 Thermal Ltd

Thermal Limited, a wholly-owned subsidiary of Heating PLC, has an authorised share capital of £250,000, divided into 100,000 7 per cent preference shares of £1 each and 300,000 ordinary shares of 50p each. The company makes up its accounts to 31st

December in each year, and the draft accounts for 19X0, presented by the directors for consideration, showed the following position:

Trading and Profit and Loss Account
for the year ended 31st December 19X0

| | £ | | £ |
|---|---|---|---|
| Materials used | 219,016 | Sales | 450,096 |
| Technical wages and salaries | 70,609 | | |
| Gross profit carried down | 160,471 | | |
| | £450,096 | | £450,096 |
| Office salaries | 48,358 | Gross profit brought down | 160,471 |
| Establishment expenses | 17,537 | | |
| Motor and travel expenses | 41,494 | Investment income received: | |
| Depreciation of motor vans | 5,048 | Unlisted | 420 |
| Advertising | 10,487 | Listed | 644 |
| General expenses | 4,625 | | |
| Audit fee (fixed by directors) | 420 | Rents receivable | 175 |
| Contribution to pension scheme | 3,496 | | |
| Pension to widow of former director | 500 | | |
| Provision for doubtful debts | 1,149 | | |
| Depreciation of fixtures and fittings | 430 | | |
| Corporation tax at 50% (based on the profits for the year) | 7,623 | | |
| Debenture interest (gross) paid 30th June 19X0 | 600 | | |
| Preference dividend paid on 31st December 19X0 | 3,500 | | |
| Net profit | 16,443 | | |
| | £161,710 | | £161,710 |

Thermal Limited—Balance Sheet as at 31st December 19X0

| | £ | £ | £ | £ |
|---|---|---|---|---|
| *Assets employed* | | | | |
| Fixed assets: | | | | |
| Freehold land and buildings | | | | 64,000 |
| Fixtures and fittings | | | | 3,840 |
| Motor vans | | | | 6,540 |
| | | | *carried forward* | 74,380 |

Thermal Limited—Balance Sheet as at 31st December 19X0

| | £ | £ | £ | £ |
|---|---|---|---|---|
| | | | *brought forward* | 74,380 |
| Current assets: | | | | |
| Stock, at cost: | | | | |
| Raw materials | | 16,380 | | |
| Work in progress | | 4,197 | | |
| Finished goods | | 40,919 | 61,496 | |
| Debtors: | | | | |
| trade | | 109,402 | | |
| prepayments and accrued income | | 3,005 | 112,407 | |
| Investments at cost | | | 14,000 | |
| Cash at bank and in hand | | | 103,787 | |
| | | | 291,690 | |
| Current liabilities: | | | | |
| Creditors—trade | 61,433 | | | |
| ACT | 1,044 | 62,477 | | |
| Taxation | | 26,146 | 88,623 | |
| Net current assets | | | | 203,067 |
| | | | | 277,447 |
| Deferred asset—ACT* | | | | 1,044 |
| | | | | £278,491 |
| *Financed by* | | | | |
| Share capital: | | | | |
| Preference shares | | | | 50,000 |
| Ordinary shares | | | | 100,000 |
| Share premium | | | | 25,000 |
| Profit and loss account | | | | 93,491 |
| 6% debentures 2002 | | | | 10,000 |
| | | | | £278,491 |

| | |
|---|---|
| *This figure is made up of ACT on preference dividend $\frac{3}{7} \times$ £3,500 = | 1,500 |
| *Less:* Tax credit on franked investment income | 456 |
| | £1,044 |

The following additional information is also available:

(a) The charge for technical wages and salaries includes the salary of the technical director amounting to £22,500, while office salaries include an amount of £26,000 for the salary of the chairman and managing director; pension scheme contributions include £651 on his behalf.

(b) There have been no additions to, or sales of, freehold land and buildings, motor vans or fixtures and fittings during the year, and the original cost of these assets was:

| | £ |
|---|---|
| Freehold land and buildings | 64,000 |
| Motor vans | 20,500 |
| Fixtures and fittings | 8,600 |

(c) Work has started on a new warehouse which it is estimated will cost £30,000 to complete, but no payments have been made by the company.

(d) The investments, all listed, had a market value on 31st December 19X0 of £18,369.

(e) The issued share capital is all fully paid.

(f) The directors recommend payment of an ordinary dividend of 5.25p per share.

*You are required:*

(a) To prepare, in a form suitable for issue to members to comply with the requirements of the Companies Acts 1948 to 1981, the profit and loss account for the year ended 31st December 19X0, and balance sheet as on that date, indicating in your answer which of the permitted formats you have adopted.

The auditors' and directors' reports and corresponding figures are not required.

Assume income tax to be at the rate of 30 per cent.

(b) To explain how the accounts you have prepared would be modified for lodging with the Registrar in accordance with the small companies rules. (You are not required to redraft the accounts, merely to indicate the items omitted or modified.)

(30 marks)

## 7 Machapuchare Ltd—deferred taxation

Machapuchare Ltd accounts for deferred taxation on the basis of the liability method. In the past the company has provided for deferred taxation on all timing differences in accordance with SSAP 11. A decision has been made to change the accounting policy to comply with SSAP 15 for the 19X8 accounts. The company is consistently profitable; there is no intention to sell its buildings which are required in the business.

Corporation tax is taken at 50 per cent (30 per cent on capital gains).

(a) The balance brought forward on the deferred tax account at 1st January 19X8 is as follows:

| | £000 |
|---|---|
| Revaluation of buildings (30% × £5m) | 1,500 |
| Stock appreciation relief (50% × £2.5m) | 1,250 |
| Excess of capital allowances over depreciation on plant (50% × £9.65m) | 4,825 |
| | 7,575 |

(b) At 31st December 19X8 the company wishes to make a general bad debt provision of 5 per cent on debtors of £2.65m.

(c) The company has interest receivable of £200,000 on a loan made during the year. The interest has been accrued for in the accounts.

(d) Depreciation charged in 19X8, £2.1m; capital allowances claimed, £2.5m.

(e) The following timing differences relating to plant and stock relief are foreseen (reversals in brackets) at 31st December 19X8:

| | 1 year ahead | 2 years ahead | 3 years ahead | Total |
|---|---|---|---|---|
| | £000 | £000 | £000 | £000 |
| Stock relief | — | 500 | 500 | 1,000 |
| Plant | (1,900) | 1,000 | 900 | — |
| | (1,900) | 1,500 | 1,400 | 1,000 |

A major plant is to be started in 19Y0 and will come on stream partly in 19Y1 and partly in 19Y2.

(f) The profit for 19X8 before taxation is £5m. Corporation tax on profits for the year at 50 per cent has been calculated at £2,300,000.

(g) Reserves brought forward amount to £9m.

(h) The provision for corporation tax on the unrealised gain on revaluation of buildings had originally been charged against the profit and loss account.

*You are required* on the basis of the information provided:

(a) to calculate the total tax charge for 19X8;

(b) to draft the accounting policy note in relation to deferred taxation and the change in accounting policy for the year;

(c) to draft the notes to the accounts to comply with the disclosure requirements of SSAP 15; and

(d) to comment on an SSAP 15 tax charge in the light of inflation adjusted statements.

(20 marks)

## 8 Value added statement

The following information has been extracted from the annual report of a public quoted company.

| | £000 |
|---|---|
| Dividends to stockholders | 59 |
| Depreciation | 182 |
| Employees pay, pension and national insurance | 816 |
| Exchange gain on net current assets of overseas subsidiaries | 29 |
| Extraordinary items, net loss | 1 |
| Government corporate taxes, less grants | 125 |

| | £000 |
|---|---|
| Interest paid on borrowings | 73 |
| Materials and services used | 1,842 |
| Minority shareholders in subsidiaries | 24 |
| Profit retained | 112 |
| Profit sharing bonus to employees | 17 |
| Royalties received and other trading income | 30 |
| Sales | 3,129 |
| Share of profits of principal associated companies and investment income | 63 |

*You are required* to prepare a "value added" statement and discuss briefly its purpose.
(10 marks)

## 2 STATEMENTS OF STANDARD ACCOUNTING PRACTICE

### 9 Disclosure

A limited company owns a chain of hotels on the South Coast. Examination of its accounts for the year 19X9 reveals that:

(a) publicity expenses incurred in connection with the opening of three large new motels have been charged to revenue, and the cost of training courses run for their new staff is being written off over four years;

(b) Tourist Board capital grants received have been deducted from the cost of fixed assets and depreciation has been calculated on the net amount;

(c) a surplus arising on the disposal of two hotels considered unsuitable for modernisation has been taken direct to reserves, as has also a surplus arising on the revaluation of the company's two remaining pre-war hotels;

*You are required* to state how these items should be dealt with in the published accounts of the company in order to comply with statutory and other requirements.
(12 marks)

### 10 Research and development

A recently established pharmaceutical company, of which you are the auditor, has set up a separate research department in its factory. The total cost to the company of the department for the year just ended was £55,000 made up as follows:

| | £ |
|---|---|
| Salaries: | |
| Chemists transferred to department | 25,000 |
| Additional technical staff appointed | 5,000 |
| Clerical labour | 1,000 |
| Consultants' fees: | |
| Introductory payment for drug "A" know-how | 5,000 |
| General consultancy work | 3,000 |
| | 39,000 |

| | | £ |
|---|---|---|
| | Brought forward | 39,000 |
| Direct costs: | | |
| Drugs, chemicals and materials | | 3,000 |
| Royalties and licences | | 1,000 |
| Miscellaneous | | 2,000 |
| Overheads, etc.: | | |
| General overheads | | 5,000 |
| Cost of special partitioning | | 3,000 |
| Depreciation of equipment | | 2,000 |
| | | £55,000 |

In the annual accounts of the company, one-fifth of the total cost of the department has been charged to revenue and the remainder carried forward in the balance sheet as "research and development in progress". A directors' minute dealing with this matter states that it is the Board's intention to adopt this basis consistently in future years.

On making further enquiries you ascertain:

(a) That the department carried out the following work on developing five potential new drugs:

| Drug | Approximate total cost £ |
|---|---|
| "A" (anticipated to be marketed in six months' time) | 9,000 |
| "B" (project now abandoned) | 5,000 |
| "C" (anticipated to be marketed in one to two years' time) | 6,000 |
| "D" (early stages of development) | 3,000 |
| "E" (early stages of development) | 1,000 |
| | £24,000 |

(b) that the department also undertook general testing and quality control of existing products (estimated total cost £16,000);

(c) that the balance of the department's expenditure related to general research designed to discover possible new lines for manufacture.

*You are required* to state whether or not the company's accounting treatment is acceptable to you and, if not, to set out an alternative treatment you would recommend. Give your reasons.

(16 marks)

## 11 SSAP 3

In assessing the worth of a company which has deferred capital, it is important to calculate both the "basic earnings per share" and the "fully diluted earnings per share".

*Required:*
Explain what is meant by the terms "basic earnings per share" and "fully diluted earnings per share" and write brief notes on how you would calculate the fully diluted earnings in the case of:

(a) deferred shares;

(b) convertible loan stock; and

(c) options or warrants.

(13 marks)

## 12 Goodwill

The following information relates to Expansion Limited, a quoted public company:

Expansion Limited
Group Balance Sheet Summary as at 31st March 19X9

| | £ | | £ |
|---|---|---|---|
| Issued share capital: | | Goodwill | 120,000 |
| 1 million ordinary shares | | Net tangible assets | |
| of 25 pence each fully paid | 250,000 | i.e. fixed assets plus | |
| Reserves | 750,000 | net current assets | 880,000 |
| Book value of | | | |
| shareholders' equity | £1,000,000 | | £1,000,000 |

*Notes:*

(1) The directors' report advises that the value of certain property and investments of its subsidiary at balance sheet date is £90,000 above the value shown in the books.

(2) The stock market price of the Expansion Ltd ordinary share on 31st March 19X9 is £0.75.

(3) The company's earnings per share and the dividend proposed for the year ended 31st March 19X9 are at the same level as for the previous year.

*You are required:*

(a) to make use of this information to describe the nature of goodwill and its relationship to earnings and the market value of the company's ordinary shares; and

(b) to summarise current accounting practices in relation to non-purchased and to purchased goodwill.

(16 marks)

## 13 Disclosure

Roller Ltd is a substantial manufacturing company.

The draft accounts for the year ended 30th April 19X9 include the following items:

(a) The company had purchased raw materials from Africa for £400,000 f.o.b. at the port. Due to a misunderstanding Roller Ltd omitted to insure the goods and the ship transporting them sank during a storm. The amount has been written off against profits.

(b) The directors have included an overhead charge of 25 per cent on prime cost in valuating the work in progress at £500,000, whereas this had previously been ignored. At the end of the previous year the work in progress had been included in the accounts at a valuation of £350,000.

(c) An amount of £200,000 was paid for the goodwill of another business some years ago. The basis of trading has now changed and it is considered that the goodwill no longer exists. The amount has been written off against profits.

*You are required* to state how these items should be dealt with in the published accounts presented to members.

(14 marks)

## 3 STATEMENTS OF SOURCE AND APPLICATION OF FUNDS

### 14 Plan Ahead Ltd

The balance sheet of Plan Ahead Ltd as at 31st March 19X6, together with its projected balance sheet as at 31st March 19X7 and profit and loss account for the year ending on that date, is as follows:

Plan Ahead Ltd

| | Balance Sheets as at | | | |
|---|---|---|---|---|
| | 31st March 19X6 | | 31st March 19X7 | |
| | £000 | £000 | £000 | £000 |
| Ordinary share capital in £1 shares fully paid | | 200 | | 250 |
| Capital reserve: Share premium a/c | | — | | 25 |
| Revenue reserves: General reserve | 30 | | 40 | |
| Profit and loss a/c | 40 | 70 | 68 | 108 |
| | | 270 | | 383 |
| Represented by: | | | | |
| Fixed assets: | | | | |
| Freehold premises—cost | | 60 | | 90 |
| Plant and machinery at cost *less:* depreciation | | 48 | | 125 |
| | | 108 | | 215 |
| Current assets: | | | | |
| Stock | 140 | | 170 | |
| Debtors | 100 | | 120 | |
| Cash | 1 | | 2 | |
| | 241 | | 292 | |

*continued*

*continued*

| | Balance Sheets as at | | | |
|---|---|---|---|---|
| | 31st March 19X6 | | 31st March 19X7 | |
| | £000 | £000 | £000 | £000 |
| *less:* Creditors: | | | | |
| Trade creditors | 40 | | 64 | |
| Accrued expenses | 1 | | 2 | |
| Corporation tax | 16 | | 26 | |
| Proposed dividends | 16 | | 20 | |
| Bank overdraft | 6 | | 12 | |
| | 79 | 162 | 124 | 168 |
| | | 270 | | 383 |

Budgeted Profit and Loss Account (Extract)
for the year ending 31st March 19X7

| | £000 | £000 |
|---|---|---|
| Trading profit for the year *after* charging all expenses including depreciation of plant and machinery (£28,000), but before taxation | | 84 |
| *less:* Corporation tax | | 26 |
| Profit after taxation | | 58 |
| *add:* Balance of profit unappropriated last year brought forward | | 40 |
| | | 98 |
| Appropriations: | | |
| Proposed dividends to ordinary shareholders | 20 | |
| Transfer to general reserve | 10 | |
| | | 30 |
| Profit unappropriated carried forward | | 68 |

*Note:* No disposals of fixed assets were anticipated for the year ending 31st March 19X7.

*You are required* to produce as part of the planning information, a sources and application of funds statement for the year ending 31st March 19X7. You should bear in mind the objectives of SSAP 10 and choose a presentation format which will demonstrate clearly the manner in which the operations of the business will be financed and the utilisation of its financial resources. You should highlight the excess or deficiency of internally generated funds over the disposition thereof and your statement with the variation in the company's liquid resources.

Marks will be awarded for form and presentation.

(18 marks)

## 15 Excelsior Ltd

The balance sheet of Excelsior Ltd as at 31st March 19X8 (with comparative figures as at 31st March 19X7) together with other pertinent information, are given below:

| | Balance Sheets as at | | | |
|---|---|---|---|---|
| | 31st March 19X8 | | 31st March 19X7 | |
| | £000 | £000 | £000 | £000 |
| Fixed assets: | | | | |
| Land and buildings at cost | | 3,500 | | 1,800 |
| Plant and machinery at cost | 6,100 | | 5,800 | |
| *less:* Depreciation | 3,900 | 2,200 | 3,850 | 1,950 |
| | | 5,700 | | 3,750 |
| Current assets: | | | | |
| Stock and work in progress | 3,435 | | 3,150 | |
| Debtors | 2,200 | | 1,900 | |
| Cash and bank balance | 160 | 5,795 | 500 | 5,550 |
| | | 11,495 | | 9,300 |
| Share capital: ordinary shares of £1 each fully paid | | 1,200 | | 1,000 |
| Reserves: Share premium | | 550 | | 600 |
| Retained profits | | 3,725 | | 3,500 |
| | | 5,475 | | 5,100 |
| Debentures: 8% £1 convertible | | 2,000 | | — |
| Creditors: | | | | |
| Bank overdraft | 1,750 | | 1,500 | |
| Creditors | 1,450 | | 1,550 | |
| Taxation | 820 | 4,020 | 1,150 | 4,200 |
| | | 11,495 | | 9,300 |

*Notes:*

(1) The profit for the year 19X8, after charging all expenses including the loss on the sale of the plant but before depreciation and taxation, was £1,715,000. The corporation tax of £820,000 charged in the profit and loss account on the profits for the year was reduced by the over-provision for corporation tax on the 19X7 profit, i.e. by £150,000. The ordinary dividend paid during the year and charged against the profit after tax was £180,000.

(2) During the year, plant and machinery which had cost £1,200,000 and in respect of which depreciation of £590,000 had been provided, was sold for £565,000. There had been a rights issue of ordinary shares at the rate of 1 for 10 at a price of £1.50 per share payable in full on 1st April 19X7. Subsequently, a scrip (bonus) issue of 1 for 11 had been made utilising share premium account. The convertible debentures had been issued at par on 1st April 19X7, payable in full. The conversion terms exercisable on 31st March 19Y1 are 1 ordinary share for every 4 £1 debentures. £1 million agreed corporation tax on the 19X7 profits had been paid on the due date.

*You are required to:*

(a) Prepare a sources and application of funds statement for the year ended 31st March 19X8 bearing in mind the recommendations of SSAP 10.

(14 marks)

(b) Tabulate briefly *seven* points of comment on the prepared statement.

(7 marks)

(c) Calculate (i) basic, and (ii) diluted earnings per share for the year ended 31st March 19X8.

(4 marks)

Your workings should be submitted.

(Total 25 marks)

## 16 KS Ltd

Consolidated Balance Sheet of KS Ltd and its Subsidiaries

| | 30th June 19X6 | | 30th June 19X5 | |
|---|---|---|---|---|
| | £m | £m | £m | £m |
| Capital and reserves | | | | |
| (1) Issued share capital: | | | | |
| £1 ordinary shares | | 247.0 | | 244.3 |
| £1 preference shares | | 2.4 | | 2.4 |
| (2) Reserves | | 229.3 | | 246.0 |
| Minority interests | | 58.0 | | 58.5 |
| | | 536.7 | | 551.2 |
| (3) Investment grants | | 44.5 | | 39.4 |
| Deferred taxation | | 34.0 | | 41.4 |
| (4) Loans | | 284.8 | | 218.1 |
| | | 900.0 | | 850.1 |
| Financing the following net assets: | | | | |
| (5) Fixed assets | | 593.5 | | 553.3 |
| (6) Goodwill | | 8.3 | | 19.9 |
| (7) Interest in associated companies | | 101.1 | | 95.9 |
| | | 702.9 | | 669.1 |
| Net current assets: | | | | |
| Stocks | 157.4 | | 145.6 | |
| Debtors | 193.2 | | 185.5 | |
| Cash and short-term investments | 65.7 | | 50.2 | |
| | 416.3 | | 381.3 | |
| *less:* Creditors | 98.0 | | 102.8 | |
| (8) Proposed ordinary dividends | 20.0 | | 17.0 | |
| (9) Taxation | 47.0 | | 35.9 | |
| (10) Short-term borrowings | 54.2 | | 44.6 | |
| | | 197.1 | | 181.0 |
| | | 900.0 | | 850.1 |

## Notes to the Accounts

(1) During the year KS Ltd purchased a controlling interest in NB Ltd.

| | £m | £m |
|---|---|---|
| Net assets acquired: | | |
| Fixed assets: | | |
| Land and buildings | | 20.0 |
| Plant and equipment | | 55.0 |
| Goodwill | | 8.3 |
| Current assets: | | |
| Stock | 10.0 | |
| Debtors | 4.0 | |
| | 14.0 | |
| *less:* Creditors | 7.3 | 6.7 |
| | | 90.0 |

The consideration was agreed as follows:

| | £m |
|---|---|
| Issue of ordinary shares, at par | 2.7 |
| Cash | 87.3 |
| | 90.0 |

(2) Reserves

| | £m |
|---|---|
| 1st July 19X5 | 246.0 |
| Goodwill written off | (19.9) |
| Loss on sale of fixed assets | (4.0) |
| Retained profit—KS Ltd current year | 12.0 |
| Retained profit—associated companies | 5.2 |
| Loss on exchange | (10.0) |
| | 229.3 |

(3) Investment grants
£10m was received in 19X6. Following the recommendations of SSAP 4, £4.9m of the balance brought forward was credited to the profit and loss account this year.

(4) Loans
Long-term capital finance via loans was increased by £66.7m in 19X6.

(5) Fixed assets

| | Land and buildings | | | Plant and equipment | | | Total |
|---|---|---|---|---|---|---|---|
| | Cost £m | Depn £m | NBV £m | Cost £m | Depn £m | NBV £m | £m |
| 1st July 19X5 | 189.6 | (66.5) | 123.1 | 771.1 | (340.9) | 430.2 | 553.3 |
| Additions | 27.3 | — | 27.3 | 92.7 | — | 92.7 | 120.0 |
| Disposals | (6.4) | 3.8 | (2.6) | (40.0) | 28.0 | (12.0) | (14.6) |
| Depreciation for year | — | (7.5) | (7.5) | — | (57.7) | (57.7) | (65.2) |
| 30th June 19X6 | 210.5 | (70.2) | 140.3 | 823.8 | (370.6) | 453.2 | 593.5 |

(6) The goodwill figure of £19.9m for 19X5 was written off against reserves this year.

(7) The investments of KS Ltd in associated companies has not increased in 19X6. The change is explained by the group's share of current retained profits of £5.2m. (Share of current profit £10m. Dividends received £4.8m.)

(8) The 19X5 proposed dividend on ordinary shares was paid in 19X6. A 10 per cent (net) dividend was paid on the preference shares in 19X6.

(9) Taxation is payable within 9 months of the balance sheet date.

(10) The loan of £44.6m from Guichy, a merchant bank in the City, was increased by £9.6m. This was used to purchase further freeholds in Holborn.

From the information given, prepare a funds flow statement, using one of the suggested layouts contained in SSAPs.

(30 marks)

## 17 Standard Products Ltd

The directors of Standard Products Ltd wish to prepare a consolidated statement of source and application of funds using a format designed to show changes in net liquid resources. They are uncertain how to deal with a number of items which are listed below:

(1) Consolidated profit after all charges but before taxation was £90,000.

(2) Consolidated creditors decreased by £5,000.

(3) Standard Products Ltd declared and distributed 50 per cent scrip issue on the share capital of £1 million, in fully paid ordinary shares of £1 each.

(4) The minority interest in the consolidated profit totalled £4,000.

(5) Standard Products Ltd declared and paid a cash dividend of 5p per share after the scrip issue.

(6) £2 million long-term convertible loan stock of Standard Products Ltd was converted to ordinary shares.

(7) Consolidated debtors increased by £3,000.

(8) Equipment, with a book value of zero, was sold outside the group for £15,000.

(9) Equipment costing £8,000 was purchased for cash from outside the group.

(10) Equipment costing £8,000 was purchased for cash by one subsidiary from another.

(11) Standard Products Ltd issued 5,000 ordinary shares in exchange for 80 per cent of the stock of the Nonconforming Co Ltd.

(12) Standard Products Ltd's share of the earnings of an associated company totalled £4,000. The associate did not pay any cash dividends during the year.

(13) Consolidated depreciation provision for the year was £10,000.

(14) Standard Products Ltd's share of a cash dividend declared and paid by a consolidated subsidiary totalled £4,000.

(15) The minority interest in a cash dividend declared and paid by a consolidated subsidiary totalled £1,000.

(16) Transferred to consolidated reserves £3,000 previously set aside as a provision for taxation.

(17) An increase of £200,000 in the bank overdraft facility.

In order to identify the appropriate treatment of these items, the directors have specified the following symbols:

AP = add in determining total generated from operations

SO = subtract in determining total generated from operations

OF = other sources of funds obtained

A = application of funds obtained

L = increase/decrease in net liquid resources

N = not separately disclosed or not included

*You are required* to indicate how each of the items 1 to 17 listed above should be disclosed in the consolidated source and application of funds statement of Standard Products Ltd and its subsidiaries, making use of the symbols specified by the directors.

You are not required to rewrite the questions. Merely list the items in sequence and opposite each item record the symbol(s) you think appropriate.

There may be more than one answer; if so, indicate all answers.

(17 marks)

# 4 COMPANY ACCOUNTING

## A Issue and forfeiture of shares

### 18 AB Co. Ltd

The AB Company Limited was registered with a capital of 100,000 ordinary shares of £1 each and 20,000 6 per cent preference shares of £1 each. No preference shares had been issued but 40,000 ordinary shares had been issued at par and were fully paid.

All the remaining authorised capital was then offered for subscription on the following terms:

| | Ordinary | Preference |
|---|---|---|
| On application | 25p | 12½p |
| On allotment | 37½p | 37½p (including premium) |
| On first call | 25p | 25p |
| On second call | 12½p | 37½p |

Applications were received for 73,120 ordinary shares and 18,200 preference shares. One application for 1,000 ordinary shares was refused; with the exception of the application money on these shares the excess application money was retained against the allotment money due.

The first and second call money on 600 preference shares was received with the allotment money.

All the sums due were received except the first and second call money on 800 ordinary shares.

Some time later those 800 ordinary shares were forfeited for non-payment of the first and second calls and 600 of the forfeited shares were then reissued as fully-paid for 75p each.

*You are required to:*
Prepare the ledger accounts (including bank account) recording the above, and illustrate how the share capital and other accounts affected would appear in a balance sheet prepared:

(a) before the second call was made,

(b) after forfeiture of the 800 ordinary shares and before the reissue, and

(c) after the reissue of 600 of the forfeited shares.

(25 marks)

## B Redemption of redeemable preference shares

### 19 Change plc

The issued share capital of Change plc included preference shares which were redeemable at a premium of 7½ per cent on 1st April 19X5. The shares had originally been issued at £1.10p each.

The company proposed to issue £300,000 8¾ per cent convertible loan stock at 99 to finance the redemption.

A summarised balance sheet showed the following position on 31st March 19X5:

| | £ | | £ |
|---|---|---|---|
| Issued share capital: | | Sundry assets | 888,500 |
| 200,000 8% redeemable preference shares of £1 each, fully paid | 200,000 | | |
| 1,000,000 ordinary shares of 25p each, fully paid | 250,000 | | |
| Share premium account | 12,500 | | |
| Profit and loss account | 396,700 | | |
| Sundry creditors | 27,900 | | |
| Bank overdraft | 1,400 | | |
| | £888,500 | | £888,500 |

The issue of the convertible loan stock was fully subscribed and the preference shares were redeemed on the due date.

*You are required to prepare:*

(a) the journal entries (including cash) necessary to record the above transactions, and

(b) a balance sheet showing the position after completion.

(18 marks)

## 20 Alter Ltd

The summarised balance sheet of Alter Ltd (a private limited company) as on 31st March 19X8, showed the following position:

| | £ |
|---|---|
| Authorised share capital | 750,000 |
| Issued share capital and reserves: | |
| 700,000 ordinary shares of 50p each, fully paid | 350,000 |
| 175,000 8% redeemable preference shares of £1 each, fully paid | 175,000 |
| Profit and loss account | 100,000 |
| | 625,000 |
| 9% unsecured convertible loan stock | 250,000 |
| | £875,000 |

*continued*

| *continued* | £ |
|---|---|
| Sundry assets | 866,500 |
| Investments | 50,000 |
| Balance at bank | 56,000 |
| | 972,500 |
| *less:* Sundry creditors | 97,500 |
| | £875,000 |

The preference shares are redeemable at a premium of 10p per share on 1st April 19X8. The shares were issued @ par after Companies Acts 1981.

The unsecured loan stock was issued on 1st April 19X5, and under the terms of the issue holders have the right on 1st April in each year to convert this stock into ordinary shares on a sliding scale. At the end of the first year each £100 loan stock was convertible into 160 ordinary shares, and this figure was reduced by 5 ordinary shares in each subsequent year. On 1st April 19X8 holders of £50,000 loan stock exercise their right to convert into ordinary shares.

In order to facilitate the redemption of the preference shares it was decided:

(a) to realise the investments for £45,000;

(b) to finance part of the redemption out of capital under the provisions of Companies Act 1981.

(c) to issue 135,000 ordinary shares at a premium of 20p per share to help finance the redemption.

*You are required to prepare:*

(a) the necessary journal entries (including cash) to record the above transactions, and

(b) the balance sheet as on completion.

Ignore taxation

(16 marks)

## C Redemption of debentures

## 21 Q Ltd

On 1st August 19X7, Q Ltd had in issue £82,000 5 per cent debentures, out of an original total issue of £100,000. The debenture trust deed provided that:

(a) interest was payable on 31st January and 31st July,

(b) a sinking fund for redemption of debentures was to be built up by an annual appropriation of:

(i) £1,000 and

(ii) 5 per cent of the total nominal amount of debentures already purchased and cancelled at the preceding 31st July,

which, together with any interest received on the investments of the sinking fund, were to be invested on 31st July in each year, and

(c) sinking fund investments could be realised at any time to purchase debentures in the open market at or below par for immediate cancellation.

You ascertain that:

(a) the sinking fund balance at 1st August 19X7 was £8,000, and

(b) sinking fund investments were realised on 31st May 19X8 for £815 (cost £790) and the proceeds were used to purchase debentures of a nominal value of £840, and

(c) interest on sinking fund investments for the year ended 31st July 19X8 amounted to £325 on which date the available funds were duly invested.

*You are required to:*

write up the following accounts for the year ended 31st July 19X8:

(a) sinking fund investments,

(b) sinking fund, and

(c) redemption of debentures.

Ignore income tax.

(14 marks)

## 22 Vesta Ltd

Vesta Ltd decides to issue on 1st January 19X6 £100,000 11 per cent debenture stock at 98, redeemable at par after 10 years. A redemption fund is to be created by the annual investment of £6,300, the first instalment being paid on 31st December 19X6. The rate of interest on the investment is 10 per cent p.a. (ignore tax).

*Required:*

Answer each of the following questions relating to the above circumstances or to the redemption of debentures generally.

(a) Indicate briefly why debentures might be issued at a discount. What does the discount represent, and how would it be treated in the accounts? (Actual accounts not required.)

(3 marks)

(b) Show the debenture redemption fund and debenture redemption fund investment accounts from 19X6 to 19X9 inclusive, indicating by your entries which other accounts would be involved. Show how the relevant balances would appear in the balance sheet at 31st December 19X9.

(6 marks)

(c) Show in journal form the book entries upon completion of the redemption, assuming that the investment yields exactly the amount required.

(3 marks)

(d) If the sale of the investments produced a greater or lesser amount than that required for the redemption, how would the balance be treated?

(2 marks)

(Total 14 marks)

# 5 ACQUISITIONS AND MERGERS

## 23 Knut and Bolt

Knut and Bolt, proprietors of two small garages, have decided to amalgamate. They propose to sell their separate businesses to Spanner Ltd, a new company formed for the purpose.

The accounts of the respective businesses as on 31st December 19X8 are as follows:

| | Knut | Bolt | | Knut | Bolt |
|---|---|---|---|---|---|
| | £ | £ | | £ | £ |
| Capital account | 19,000 | 7,000 | Freehold property | 6,500 | — |
| Loan at 7% | — | 5,000 | Plant and machinery at cost less depreciation | 3,800 | 2,500 |
| Creditors | 3,100 | 2,000 | Stocks | 5,400 | 3,600 |
| | | | Debtors | 2,900 | 1,400 |
| | | | Bank balance | 3,500 | 6,500 |
| | £22,100 | £14,000 | | £22,100 | £14,000 |

The company is to take over the assets and liabilities of the two businesses except for the bank balances and the loan.

Freehold property is valued at an agreed figure of £8,000 and the company will take over the premises at this figure.

Knut proposes that the company takes over the assets and liabilities of the businesses at book amounts (apart from the revised figure attributable to freehold property).

Bolt proposes that the sale consideration should consist of:

(a) the freehold property at the agreed figure of £8,000, and

(b) a figure equal to three years' purchase of the adjusted profit of 19X8 plus one year's purchase of the adjusted profits of the calendar years 19X6 and 19X7.

The following information is relevant:

(a)

| | Calendar year | | | | | |
|---|---|---|---|---|---|---|
| | Knut | | | Bolt | | |
| | 19X6 | 19X7 | 19X8 | 19X6 | 19X7 | 19X8 |
| | £ | £ | £ | £ | £ | £ |
| Profit as shown in the audited accounts, after deduction of expenditure shown below: | 2,000 | 2,200 | 4,500 | 1,800 | 1,900 | 2,000 |
| Rent | — | — | — | 800 | 800 | 800 |
| Loan interest | — | — | — | 350 | 350 | 350 |
| Depreciation of plant and machinery | 800 | 850 | 900 | 400 | 400 | 440 |

(b) It is agreed that rent and loan interest should not be deducted from profits and that depreciation be increased for Bolt's business by 50 per cent for each calendar year.

Both agree that the consideration should be satisfied by the issue of ordinary shares of £1 each at par.

*You are required to:*

(a) compute the number of shares to be issued by Spanner Ltd to each vendor on the basis of the proposals put forward by (i) Knut and (ii) Bolt;

(b) prepare a provisional balance sheet of Spanner Ltd on completion of the acquisition, showing in separate columns the appropriate figures under the proposals of (i) Knut and (ii) Bolt; and

(c) briefly compare, and comment on, the two bases of valuation in relation to Knut.

(19 marks)

## 24 Alpha Ltd and Beta Ltd

Alpha Ltd and Beta Ltd agreed to amalgamate their businesses. The scheme envisaged the formation of Gamma Ltd with a share capital equal to the combined capitals of Alpha Ltd and Beta Ltd for the purpose of acquiring the assets, liabilities, and undertakings of the two companies in exchange for shares in Gamma Ltd.

The balance sheets of Alpha Ltd and Beta Ltd as on 31st December 19X8, the date of amalgamation, are summarised below:

| | Alpha Ltd £ | Beta Ltd £ | | Alpha Ltd £ | Beta Ltd £ |
|---|---|---|---|---|---|
| Authorised and issued capital | 10,000 | 14,000 | Fixed assets (exclusive of goodwill) | 12,000 | 18,000 |
| Reserves | 17,000 | 10,000 | Stock | 6,000 | 11,000 |
| Creditors | 4,000 | 9,000 | Debtors | 8,000 | 13,000 |
| Bank overdraft | — | 9,000 | Balance with bank | 5,000 | — |
| | £31,000 | £42,000 | | £31,000 | £42,000 |

The consideration was to be based on the net assets of the companies as shown in their books on 31st December 19X8, but subject to an addition to compensate Alpha Ltd for its superior profit record. This addition was to be the weighted average of the net profits of Alpha Ltd for the three years ended 31st December 19X8. The weights for this purpose for the calendar years of 19X6, 19X7 and 19X8 were agreed, respectively, as 1, 2 and 3. The net profits had been:

| | | |
|---|---|---|
| Year ended 31st December: | 19X6 | £2,000 |
| | 19X7 | £8,000 |
| | 19X8 | £12,000 |

Shares in Gamma Ltd were to be issued to Alpha Ltd and Beta Ltd at a premium and in proportion to the agreed net asset values of those companies.

In order to raise working capital, Gamma Ltd increased its authorised share capital by £20,000 and proceeded to issue 12,000 shares of £1 each, at a price of £1.75 a share.

*You are required to:*

(a) calculate the number of shares issued to Alpha Ltd and Beta Ltd;

(b) show journal entries in the books of Alpha Ltd to reflect the takeover; and

(c) prepare the summarised balance sheet of Gamma Ltd after the final issue of shares.

(15 marks)

## 25 Blough

Blough had been in business for a number of years and on 1st July 19X4 his net assets at book value were:

| | £ |
|---|---|
| Freehold property | 10,000 |
| Plant | 12,000 |
| Net current assets | 13,000 |
| Blough—capital account | £35,000 |

On 31st December 19X4 a company, Blough Limited, was incorporated with an authorised capital of £50,000 in shares of £1 each, to take over Blough's business, excluding the freehold property, at book values as at 30th September 19X4, the purchase price of £28,500 to be satisfied by an issue to Blough of fully paid-up shares at par.

It was agreed that Blough should retain the freehold property, charging the company's rent of £1,600 per annum for its use, and that he should be appointed a part-time executive at a salary of £1,800 per annum. Both rent and salary were payable from 1st October 19X4.

On 31st March 19X5, Blough Limited purchased from Copper, the controlling shareholder, all the 20,000 fully paid ordinary shares of £1 each in Copper Ltd at a price of £1.50 per share. In satisfaction of the purchase price, it was agreed that Blough Limited should transfer to Copper a debenture in Copper Ltd for £5,000 (the repayment of which was to be guaranteed by Blough Limited) and the balance in fully paid shares in Blough Limited, to be issued to him at £1.25 per share. No cash was to be paid by Blough Limited in respect of this transaction. Blough Limited had acquired the debenture in Copper Limited at par on 1st March 19X5.

Blough Limited had taken over Blough's books of account and did not open a new ledger. No entries had been made in respect of any of the above transactions.

The following information was extracted from Blough's books of account for the year ended 30th June 19X5:

(a) Blough's drawings for the three months ended 30th September 19X4 were £2,000.

(b) Sales for the year totalled £60,000. Those for the six months ended 30th June 19X5 were twice those for the six months ended 31st December 19X4, in which period sales occurred at a uniform rate.

(c) The rate of gross profit to sales was 25 per cent.

(d) Fixed expenses amounted to £800 and selling expenses to £3,000 for the year.

(e) A debt in respect of a sale made on 1st November 19X4 was found to be bad to the extent of £50 and was written off.

(f) On 1st April 19X5 a dividend amounting to £3,000 was received from Copper Ltd. There were no other transactions with this company.

(g) There were no additions to plant or purchases of other fixed assets throughout the year.

Depreciation at 10 per cent per annum on the book value is to be written off plant for the year. For the purposes of the sale and purchase agreement between Blough and Blough Ltd this is to be regarded as accruing evenly throughout the year.

*You are required to:*

(a) prepare a profit and loss account of Blough and Blough Ltd for the year ended 30th June 19X5, and a balance sheet of Blough Ltd at 30th June 19X5; and

(20 marks)

(b) draft journal entries in the books acquired by Blough Ltd, recording:

(i) the purchase of the business from Blough and the satisfaction of the purchase price, leading to the elimination of Blough's capital account; and

(ii) the purchase of shares in the subsidiary company, Copper Limited, and the satisfaction of the purchase price.

(8 marks)

Ignore taxation and interest on debenture and submit all your workings.

(Total 28 marks)

## 26 Kris Ltd and Wren Ltd

The following are the summarised balance sheets of Kris Ltd and Wren Ltd as at 30th September 19X6.

Kris Ltd

| | £ | £ |
|---|---|---|
| Ordinary share capital in £1 shares fully paid | | 80,000 |
| Revenue reserves | | 33,480 |
| | | 113,480 |
| 9% debentures (secured) | | 20,000 |
| | | £133,480 |

*continued*

| *continued* | £ | £ |
|---|---|---|
| Fixed assets (net book value) | | 49,420 |
| Investment in Wren Ltd: 16,000 shares at cost | | 5,400 |
| Current account with Wren Ltd | | 28,560 |
| Current assets: | | |
| Stocks | 35,760 | |
| Debtors | 9,320 | |
| Cash | 22,920 | |
| | 68,000 | |
| *less:* Current liabilities: | | |
| Creditors | 17,900 | 50,100 |
| | | £133,480 |

Wren Ltd

| | £ | £ |
|---|---|---|
| Ordinary share capital in 25p shares: 20,000 shares fully paid | | 5,000 |
| *less:* Profit and loss account (debit balance) | | 3,340 |
| | | 1,660 |
| Current account with Kris Ltd | | 28,560 |
| | | £30,220 |

| | | |
|---|---|---|
| Fixed assets (net book value) | | 14,300 |
| £4,000 9% debentures in Kris Ltd: cost | | 4,200 |
| Current assets: | | |
| Stocks | 6,800 | |
| Debtors | 2,440 | |
| Cash | 7,400 | |
| | 16,640 | |
| *less:* Current liabilities: | | |
| Creditors | 4,920 | 11,720 |
| | | £30,220 |

A new company, Kriswren Ltd, has been formed with a capital of 100,000 £1 shares to be issued to the shareholders of Kris Ltd, and to the "outside" shareholders of Wren Ltd, for the acquisition of the two companies as at 30th September 19X6. Each company will pay off its creditors and the expenses of liquidation which were £3,800 for Kris Ltd and £840 for Wren Ltd. The new company is to take over the balances of cash, the goodwill and the assets of the two companies. For the purpose of the merger the assets were valued as follows:

| | Kris Ltd | Wren Ltd |
|---|---|---|
| | £ | £ |
| Fixed assets | 110,000 | 19,600 |
| Stocks | 33,400 | 5,600 |
| Debtors | 6,820 | 1,720 |
| Goodwill | 50,000 | 10,000 |

The "outside" debenture holders of Kris Ltd are to be issued with 10 per cent debentures in the new company at the same par value as their present holding.

*You are required:*

(a) to prepare ledger accounts showing the liquidation of the two companies as they would appear in the respective books;

(b) to prepare the outline balance sheet of Kriswren Ltd as it would appear immediately after the merger, indicating by way of note the number of shares in Kriswren Ltd held by the former outside shareholders of Wren Ltd.

(28 marks)

## 27 Axis Ltd

The balances on the books of Axis Ltd at 1st January 19X7 were as follows:

| | Dr | Cr |
|---|---|---|
| | £ | £ |
| Freehold property (cost £160,000) | 130,000 | |
| Plant and machinery (cost £120,565) | 67,285 | |
| Motor vehicles (cost £10,890) | 5,675 | |
| Quoted (sinking fund) investments (market value £12,000) | 10,000 | |
| Stock | 10,864 | |
| Debtors | 19,571 | |
| Cash at bank | 9,345 | |
| Authorised and issued share capital in fully paid shares of £1 each: | | |
| Ordinary | | 100,000 |
| 7% preference | | 50,000 |
| Sinking fund for the redemption of debentures | | 10,000 |
| Profit and loss account | | 40,290 |
| 7% debentures of £100 each (originally issued at £95 each) | | 21,000 |
| Creditors | | 31,450 |
| | £252,740 | £252,740 |

On that day, Axis Ltd acquired a controlling interest in Bude Ltd, which carried on a similar business, with the agreed following arrangements:

(a) Axis Ltd to sell to Bude Ltd a section of its business as follows:
The freehold property for £150,000.

Plant (cost £53,958, book value £28,464) for £30,000.
Motor vehicles (cost £3,981, book value £2,163) for £2,500.
Stock (book value £4,850) for £5,000.
Debtors to be taken over at book value of £4,682.
Goodwill for £7,000.

(b) Bude Ltd to sell to Axis Ltd the following assets:
Plant for £6,000.
Motor vehicles for £1,000.
Stocks for £3,000.
Debtors to be taken over at book value of £2,183.

(c) Bude Ltd to assume liability for creditors of Axis Ltd amounting to £7,681 and Axis Ltd to assume liability for creditors of Bude Ltd amounting to £2,478.

(d) The net purchase price to be satisfied by Bude Ltd as follows:

(i) A debt due from Axis Ltd to Bude Ltd amounting to £4,890 to be waived.

(ii) Ten £100 7 per cent debentures in Axis Ltd held by Bude Ltd to be cancelled.

(iii) For every £100 debenture held in Axis Ltd, holders to receive 105, 6 per cent debentures of £1 each (fully paid) in Bude Ltd issued at par.

(iv) Axis Ltd to be allotted as fully paid 120,000 ordinary shares of £1 each in Bude Ltd (a controlling interest) at £1.25 each.

(v) Any balance due to Axis Ltd to remain as a loan to Bude Ltd.

*You are required* to prepare the balance sheet of Axis Ltd at 1st January 19X7, after giving effect to the above arrangements. Ignore taxation.

Your workings in the form of ledger accounts in the books of Axis Ltd must be submitted and should include a reconstruction account supported by detail of the calculation of the net purchase price.

(24 marks)

## 28 Sponge Ltd

A new company, Sponge Ltd, was formed on the 30th April 19X8 to take over the business of each of the following companies, all of which went into voluntary liquidation on the following day. The new company was incorporated with a capital of £300,000 divided into 200,000 ordinary £1 shares and 100,000 10 per cent £1 cumulative preference shares.

Summary Balance Sheets as at 30th April 19X8

| | Almond Ltd | | Battenby Ltd | | Cherry Ltd | |
|---|---|---|---|---|---|---|
| | | £000 | | £000 | | £000 |
| Debit balances | | | | | | |
| Bank | | 15 | | | | |
| Investments | | 10 | | | | |
| Trade debtors | | 50 | | 48 | | 8 |
| Stock | | 33 | | 13 | | 8 |
| Plant and machinery | | 22 | | 8 | | 4 |
| Land and buildings | | 20 | | 6 | | |
| Goodwill | | 18 | | | | 4 |
| Preliminary expenses | | | | 1 | | |
| Profit and loss | | — | | 12 | | — |
| | | 168 | | 88 | | 24 |
| Credit balances | | | | | | |
| Trade creditors | | 35 | | 20 | | 2 |
| Bank overdraft | | | | 18 | | 1 |
| Issued and paid-up capital: | | | | | | |
| Ordinary £1 shares | 100 | | 50 | | 10 | |
| 10% cumulative preference | — | 100 | — | 50 | 10 | 20 |
| Profit and loss | | 13 | | | | 1 |
| Revenue reserve | | 20 | | — | | — |
| | | 168 | | 88 | | 24 |

The basis of absorption of the three companies was:

*Almond Ltd.* All assets and liabilities to be taken over at book value and settlement to be by 5 fully paid ordinary shares in Sponge Ltd, to be issued for every 4 shares held in Almond Ltd.

*Battenby Ltd.* All assets and liabilities to be taken over at book values and settlement to be by 1 fully paid ordinary share and 3 cumulative preference shares paid £0.50 each in Sponge Ltd, to be issued for every 5 shares held in Battenby Ltd. Sponge Ltd was to provide for doubtful debts of £9,000 and revalue the stock in hand at £10,000.

*Cherry Ltd.* Sponge Ltd to purchase the assets and goodwill for £20,000 cash. Trade creditors to be paid by Cherry Ltd. Cherry Ltd also to pay liquidation expenses of £1,000 and to provide for and pay the outstanding current preference dividend. Sponge Ltd was to provide £2,000 for doubtful debts and to revalue stock at £7,000.

40,000 cumulative preference shares in Sponge Ltd are offered to and subscribed for by the public, 50p being called and all but £1,000 being received by 30th June 19X8. All Sponge Ltd shares are issued at par.

*You are required to prepare:*

(a) The liquidation accounts and sundry shareholders' accounts of the three vendor companies with the addition in the case of Cherry Ltd of its bank account showing the distribution of the available cash among the creditors and respective classes of shareholders.

(9 marks)

(b) The balance sheet of Sponge Ltd, as at 30th June 19X8, there being no transactions other than those above between 30th April and 30th June 19X8.

(11 marks)

Workings must be submitted and should include the purchase of business account in the books of Sponge Ltd.

Taxation is ignored.

(Total 20 marks)

# 6 CAPITAL REDUCTIONS AND RECONSTRUCTIONS

## 29 Axed Ltd

The following is the balance sheet of Axed Limited as on 31st December:

| | £ | £ | | £ | £ | £ |
|---|---|---|---|---|---|---|
| Share capital: | | | Fixed assets: | | | |
| | | | | Cost | Depn. | NBV |
| Authorised | 500,000 | | Freeholds | 46,000 | 5,000 | 41,000 |
| | | | Plant | 85,000 | 6,000 | 79,000 |
| Issued: | | | Patents | 28,000 | — | 28,000 |
| | | | | £159,000 | £11,000 | 148,000 |
| 250,000 8½% cumulative redeemable preference shares of £1 each fully paid | | 250,000 | | | | |
| | | | Subsidiary company: | | | |
| | | | Shares at cost | | 85,000 | |
| 100,000 ordinary shares of £1 each, 75p paid | | 75,000 | Advances | | 46,000 | |
| | | | | | | 131,000 |
| | | 325,000 | | | | |
| | | | Current assets: | | | |
| *deduct:* Adverse balance on profit and loss account | | 167,000 | Stocks at cost | | 82,000 | |
| | | | Debtors and prepayments | | 57,000 | |
| | | 158,000 | | | | 139,000 |
| Current liabilities: | £ | | | | | |
| Trade creditors | 232,000 | | | | | |
| Bank overdraft | 28,000 | | | | | |
| | | 260,000 | | | | |
| | | £418,000 | | | | £418,000 |

*Notes:*

(1) There are contingent liabilities in respect of (i) a guarantee given to bankers to cover a loan of £18,000 made to the subsidiary and (ii) uncalled capital of 15p per share on the holding of 100,000 shares of £1 each in the subsidiary.

(2) The arrears of dividend on the preference shares amount to £126,000. The

following capital reconstruction scheme, to take effect as from 1st January next, had been duly approved and authorised:

(a) The unpaid capital on the ordinary shares to be called up forthwith.

(b) The ordinary shares thereupon to be reduced to shares of 25p each fully paid up by cancelling 75p per share and then, each fully paid share of 25p to be subdivided into five shares of 5p each fully paid.

(c) The holders to surrender four of such 5p shares out of every five held for reissue as set out below.

(d) The $8\frac{1}{2}$ per cent cumulative preference shares together with all arrears of dividend thereon to be surrendered and cancelled, the holders to subscribe to a new issue of convertible $7\frac{1}{2}$ per cent notes of £30 each on the terms that for every 50 preference shares held they shall:

(i) pay £20 in cash;

(ii) be issued with one £30 note; and

(iii) receive 80 fully paid ordinary shares of 5p each being a redistribution of those surrendered by the ordinary shareholders.

(e) The unpaid capital on the shares in the subsidiary to be called up and paid by the parent company whose guarantee to the bank should be cancelled.

(f) The book value of the freeholds to be written up to £60,000 being the amount of an independent valuation.

(g) The adverse balance on profit and loss account and the patents to be written off: £50,000 to be written off the shares in the subsidiary and the balance of the sums made available by the scheme to be used to write down the plant.

*You are required to show:*

(a) a capital reduction and reorganisation account; and

(b) the balance sheet of the company as it would appear immediately after completion of the scheme.

(18 marks)

## 30 PQ Ltd

*You are required* for PQ Limited to show:

(a) the entries reflecting the transactions for the period from 1st January to 31st March 19X8 as they would appear in the following:

(i) capital reserve account;

(ii) capital reduction account;

(iii) bank account;

(iv) debenture redemption account;

(v) final call account;

(vi) ordinary share capital account;

(vii) profit and loss account;

(b) the balance sheet as at 31st March 19X8, after the transactions have been recorded and assuming no other changes in assets or liabilities since 1st January 19X8.

Taxation is to be ignored.

The balance sheet of PQ Limited, which had recently returned to profitable trading after a period of heavy losses, at 31st December 19X7 was as follows:

| | £ | £ |
|---|---|---|
| Share capital: | | |
| Authorised, issued and fully paid: | | |
| 750,000 ordinary shares of £1 each | | 750,000 |
| 200,000 8% redeemable cumulative preference shares of £1 each | | 200,000 |
| | | 950,000 |
| Debit balance on profit and loss account | | 470,000 |
| | | 480,000 |
| 10% debenture stock (redeemable at 102 in 19X8: interest payable 30th June and 31st December) | | 250,000 |
| Creditors | | 330,000 |
| | | £1,060,000 |
| Fixed assets, at cost *less* depreciation: | | |
| Land and buildings | 120,000 | |
| Plant and machinery | 210,000 | |
| | | 330,000 |
| Current assets: | | |
| Stocks and work in progress | 390,000 | |
| Debtors | 275,000 | |
| Bank | 65,000 | |
| | | 730,000 |
| | | £1,060,000 |

In view of the necessity to repay the debentures in 19X8, the directors considered that a capital reorganisation was desirable and the following scheme was approved by the parties concerned and the Court:

(a) On 1st January 19X8 the ordinary shares of £1 to be written down to 25 pence fully paid.

(b) On 2nd January 19X8 a rights issue of 1,000,000 ordinary shares of 25 pence to be made at par, payable in two instalments, one of 15 pence on application on 10th January 19X8, and one of 10 pence on allotment on 1st March 19X8, the proceeds to be applied toward redeeming the redeemable preference shares and repaying the debentures with accrued interest.

(c) In addition, as a result of a professional valuation, the directors decided to place a value of £250,000 on the land and buildings.

The following transactions took place:

(a) On 1st January 19X8 the ordinary shares were reduced to 25 pence.

(b) All the new shares were taken up and the full amount due on application was received on 10th January 19X8.

(c) On 1st February 19X8 the whole of the issued redeemable preference shares were redeemed at par.

(d) On 1st March 19X8 all moneys due on the second instalment were received except in respect of one holding of 10,000 shares.

(e) On 31st March 19X8 the principal and three months' accrued interest on the 10 per cent debenture were repaid.

(25 marks)

## 31 Roberts Ltd

Roberts Ltd had incurred exceptional losses and a scheme of reconstruction involving a creditors voluntary liquidation was approved by all parties. The balance sheet of Roberts Ltd on 30th June 19X8 was as follows:

| | £ |
|---|---|
| Credit balances: | |
| Share capital, authorised, issued and fully paid: | |
| 6% cumulative preference shares of £1 each | 80,000 |
| Ordinary shares of £1 each | 200,000 |
| Bank overdraft (secured) | 200,000 |
| Creditors: Preferential | 10,000 |
| Ordinary | 240,000 |
| | £730,000 |

| | £ |
|---|---|
| Debit balances: | |
| Fixed assets at cost *less* depreciation | 300,000 |
| Stock at cost | 120,000 |
| Trade debtors | 160,000 |
| Profit and loss account | 150,000 |
| | £730,000 |

The scheme of reconstruction provided for:

(a) A new company, Grove Ltd, which was incorporated with an authorised capital of £500,000, divided into 250,000 7 per cent cumulative preference shares and 250,000 ordinary shares, all of £1 each, to take over as on 30th June 19X8, the assets and liabilities of Roberts Ltd.

(b) 40,000 ordinary shares of £1 each in Grove Ltd credited as 50p per share paid up, to be issued to the liquidator of Roberts Ltd for the benefit of that company's ordinary shareholders, who had agreed to pay up the balance of 50p per share immediately.

(c) 80,000 preference shares of £1 each in Grove Ltd credited as 75p per share paid up, to be issued to the liquidator of Roberts Ltd for the benefit of that company's preference shareholders, who had agreed to pay the balance of 25p per share immediately. In addition, £9,600 in 10 per cent unsecured loan notes 19Y4/5 to be issued as compensation for arrears of preference dividends.

(d) Grove Ltd to pay the liquidation expenses of Roberts Ltd of £2,000.

(e) Grove Ltd adopted the following values for the tangible assets acquired: £280,000 for the fixed assets, £100,000 for stock and £160,000 for trade debtors.

(f) £40,000 to be paid off the bank overdraft out of the proceeds of the share issues and the balance to be secured on the fixed assets of Grove Ltd.

(g) Grove Ltd immediately to discharge the preferential creditors in cash. Liabilities to ordinary creditors to be fully satisfied by cash payments of 50p in the £ and the issue of 10 per cent unsecured loan notes 19Y4/5 for the balance.

(h) The directors of Grove Ltd to introduce £140,000 in cash on loan on 1st July 19X8 for £140,000 unsecured loan notes 19Y4/5.

All of the above provisions of the scheme were carried out and the preliminary expenses of Grove Ltd of £4,000 were paid in cash.

*You are required:*

(a) to show the closing entries in the books of Roberts Ltd as recorded in (i) the realisation account (*see* note) and (ii) the sundry members account having separate columns for preference and ordinary shareholders;

(8 marks)

*Note:* The purchase consideration should be included in the realisation account as one figure and its detailed make up, shown by way of a note.

(b) to show (i) the journal entries (including cash items) in the books of Grove Ltd and (ii) the opening balance sheet of that company as it would appear assuming that the only transactions were those referred to above.

(17 marks)

(Total 25 marks)

# 7 GROUP ACCOUNTS

## A Consolidated balance sheets on formation

### 32 H Ltd

H Ltd had acquired shares in S Ltd as from the incorporation of S Ltd. From the following information prepare the consolidated balance sheet at 31st December 19X5.

| | H Ltd | S Ltd |
|---|---|---|
| | £ | £ |
| Tangible fixed assets | 50,000 | 18,000 |
| Investment in S Ltd: | | |
| 8,000 £1 ordinary shares at cost | 8,000 | — |
| Sundry net assets/(liabilities) | (6,000) | 8,000 |
| | £52,000 | £26,000 |
| Ordinary shares | 20,000 | 8,000 |
| Share premium | 8,000 | — |
| Profit and loss account | 4,000 | 14,000 |
| Debentures | 20,000 | 4,000 |
| | £52,000 | £26,000 |

### 33 H Ltd

H Ltd has owned its shares in S Ltd since the incorporation of S Ltd. Prepare the consolidated balance sheet at 30th June 19X5 from the following information:

| | H Ltd | S Ltd |
|---|---|---|
| | £ | £ |
| Tangible fixed assets | 54,000 | 25,000 |
| Investment in S Ltd: | | |
| 4,000 £1 ordinary shares at cost | 4,000 | — |
| Sundry net assets | 36,000 | 9,000 |
| | £94,000 | £34,000 |
| Ordinary shares | 40,000 | 6,000 |
| Preference shares | — | 10,000 |
| Share premium | 12,000 | — |
| Profit and loss account | 18,000 | 18,000 |
| Debentures | 24,000 | — |
| | £94,000 | £34,000 |

## 34 H Ltd

H Ltd has owned its shares in S Ltd since the incorporation of S Ltd. Prepare the consolidated balance sheet at 30th September 19X5 from the following information:

| | H Ltd | S Ltd |
|---|---|---|
| | £ | £ |
| Tangible fixed assets | 14,000 | 40,000 |
| Investment in S Ltd: | | |
| 6,000 £1 ordinary shares | 6,000 | |
| 4,000 £1 preference shares | 4,000 | |
| 10,000 £1 debentures | 10,000 | |
| Sundry net assets | 16,000 | 8,000 |
| | £50,000 | £48,000 |
| Ordinary shares | 24,000 | 8,000 |
| Preference shares | — | 6,000 |
| Profit and loss account | 12,000 | 16,000 |
| Debentures | 14,000 | 18,000 |
| | £50,000 | £48,000 |

## 35 H Ltd

H Ltd purchased shares in S Ltd on 31st December 19X5. The balance sheets of H Ltd and S Ltd on that date were as follows. Prepare a consolidated balance sheet at 31st December 19X5.

| | H Ltd | S Ltd |
|---|---|---|
| | £ | £ |
| Investment in S Ltd: | | |
| 2,000 £3 ordinary shares | 6,000 | — |
| Sundry net assets | 8,000 | 5,000 |
| | £14,000 | £5,000 |
| Ordinary shares | 8,000 | 2,000 |
| Profit and loss account | 2,000 | 1,000 |
| General reserves | 4,000 | 2,000 |
| | £14,000 | £5,000 |

## 36 H Ltd

| | H Ltd | S Ltd |
|---|---|---|
| | £ | £ |
| Investment in S Ltd: | | |
| 1,800 shares | 5,400 | — |
| Sundry net assets | 15,600 | 7,500 |
| | £21,000 | £7,500 |
| Ordinary shares | 12,000 | 3,000 |
| Reserves | 6,000 | 3,000 |
| Profit and loss account | 3,000 | 1,500 |
| | £21,000 | £7,500 |

H Ltd purchased 1,800 shares in S Ltd on 31st December 19X5. Prepare a consolidated balance sheet of H Ltd and its subsidiary at 31st December 19X5.

## B Consolidated balance sheets on purchase of whole company

## 37 H Ltd

| | H Ltd | S Ltd |
|---|---|---|
| | £ | £ |
| Tangible fixed assets | 25,000 | 16,000 |
| Investment in S Ltd: | | |
| 4,000 ordinary shares | 6,000 | — |
| Sundry net liabilities | (1,000) | (2,000) |
| | £30,000 | £14,000 |
| Ordinary shares | 20,000 | 4,000 |
| Profit and loss account | 10,000 | 10,000 |
| | £30,000 | £14,000 |

H Ltd acquired its shares in S Ltd when S Ltd's reserves were £1,000. Prepare the consolidated balance sheet at 31st July 19X5.

## C Consolidated balance sheets—percentage holdings

## 38 H Ltd

The balance sheets of H Ltd and S Ltd on 31st December 19X5 were as set out below.

When H Ltd acquired its shares in S Ltd, the reserves of S Ltd were £16,000. Prepare the consolidated balance sheet at 31st December 19X5.

| | H Ltd | S Ltd |
|---|---|---|
| | £ | £ |
| Tangible fixed assets | 66,000 | 40,000 |
| Investment in S Ltd: | | |
| 6,000 shares | 24,000 | — |
| Sundry net assets/(liabilities) | (8,000) | 10,000 |
| | £82,000 | £50,000 |
| Ordinary shares | 20,000 | 8,000 |
| Share premium | 10,000 | — |
| Profit and loss account | 12,000 | 24,000 |
| Debentures | 40,000 | 18,000 |
| | £82,000 | £50,000 |

## 39 H Ltd

The balance sheets of H Ltd and S Ltd on 31st December 19X5 were as follows:

| | H Ltd | S Ltd |
|---|---|---|
| | £ | £ |
| Investment in S Ltd: | | |
| 2,250 ordinary shares | 1,800 | — |
| Sundry net assets | 14,700 | 8,400 |
| | £16,500 | £8,400 |
| Ordinary shares | 6,000 | 3,000 |
| Reserves | 6,000 | 3,000 |
| Profit and loss account | 4,500 | 2,400 |
| | £16,500 | £8,400 |

When H Ltd acquired the shares in S Ltd, the latter had a credit balance on profit and loss account of £1,800 and reserves of £2,400. No dividends have been declared by the subsidiary company. Prepare a consolidated balance sheet at 31st December 19X5.

## 40 H Ltd

| | H Ltd | S Ltd |
|---|---|---|
| | £ | £ |
| Tangible fixed assets | 62,000 | 38,000 |
| Investment in S Ltd: | | |
| 10,000 ordinary shares | 12,000 | — |
| 6,000 preference shares | 6,000 | — |
| Sundry net assets | 12,000 | 6,000 |
| | £92,000 | £44,000 |

*continued*

| *continued* | H Ltd | S Ltd |
|---|---|---|
| | £ | £ |
| Ordinary shares | 30,000 | 12,000 |
| Preference shares | — | 8,000 |
| Share premium | 20,000 | — |
| Profit and loss account | 24,000 | 24,000 |
| Debentures | 18,000 | — |
| | £92,000 | £44,000 |

H Ltd purchased its shares in S Ltd when S Ltd's reserves were £12,000. Prepare the consolidated balance sheet at 31st March 19X5.

## D Consolidated balance sheets—percentage holdings (further aspects)

### 41 H Ltd

At the date of acquisition of the S Ltd's shares by H Ltd, the profit and loss account of the former stood at £1,000, before dividends and reserves at £6,000. S Ltd had paid a dividend out of pre-acquisition profits on 1st April 19X5, H Ltd's share of which was £400. The balance sheets of H Ltd and S Ltd on 31st December 19X5 were as follows. Prepare a consolidated balance sheet as at 31st December 19X5.

| | H Ltd | S Ltd |
|---|---|---|
| | £ | £ |
| Investment in S Ltd: | | |
| 8,000 ordinary shares | 15,000 | — |
| Sundry net assets | 29,400 | 18,000 |
| | £44,400 | £18,000 |
| Ordinary shares | 30,000 | 10,000 |
| Reserves | 10,000 | 6,000 |
| Profit and loss account | 4,400 | 2,000 |
| | £44,400 | £18,000 |

H Ltd has taken credit into its own profit and loss account of the dividend received from S Ltd.

### 42 H Ltd

From the following information, prepare a consolidated balance sheet for H Ltd and its subsidiary S Ltd as at 31st December 19X5.

| | H Ltd | | S Ltd | |
|---|---|---|---|---|
| | £ | £ | £ | £ |
| Fixed assets: | | | | |
| Intangible—goodwill | | 30,000 | | 24,000 |
| Tangible fixed assets: | | | | |
| Freehold land and buildings | | 200,000 | | — |
| Plant at cost | 144,000 | | 164,000 | |
| *less:* Depreciation | 24,000 | 120,000 | 24,000 | 140,000 |
| Investment in S Ltd: | | | | |
| Ordinary shares (80,000) | 80,000 | | | |
| Debentures (£24,000) | 24,000 | 104,000 | | — |
| | | 454,000 | | 164,000 |
| Current assets: | | | | |
| Stocks | 146,400 | | 70,400 | |
| Trade debtors | 164,200 | | 75,600 | |
| Due from subsidiary | 29,400 | | — | |
| Bills receivable | — | | 18,200 | |
| Bank and cash | 16,000 | | 41,800 | |
| | 356,000 | | 206,000 | |
| Creditors: amounts falling due within one year: | | | | |
| Due to holding company | — | | 20,000 | |
| Corporation tax | 77,000 | | 34,400 | |
| Creditors | 169,000 | | 65,600 | |
| | 246,000 | | 120,000 | |
| Net current assets | | 110,000 | | 86,000 |
| Total assets *less* current liabilities | | 564,000 | | 250,000 |
| Creditors: amounts falling due after more than one year: | | | | |
| 6% debentures | | — | | 40,000 |
| Net assets | | £564,000 | | £210,000 |
| Capital and reserves: | | | | |
| Called up share capital | | | | 100,000 |
| Ordinary shares of £1 each | | 500,000 | | |
| 5% preference shares of £1 each | | — | | 40,000 |
| Capital redemption reserve | | — | | 30,000 |
| Profit and loss account | | 64,000 | | 40,000 |
| | | £564,000 | | £210,000 |

The following information is relevant:

(a) The shares in S Ltd have been owned since the incorporation of S Ltd.

(b) You ascertain that the difference between the current accounts is represented by cash in transit from S Ltd to H Ltd.

(c) Ignore taxation, other than that which appears in the above balance sheets.

## 43 H Ltd

The balance sheets of H Ltd and S Ltd on 31st December 19X5 were as follows. At the date when H Ltd acquired shares in S Ltd, the profit and loss account of the latter stood at £1,000. No dividends have been paid since, and one year's dividend, although not provided for in the balance sheet, has become due to the preference shareholders. Prepare a consolidated balance sheet at 31st December 19X5.

| | H Ltd | S Ltd |
|---|---|---|
| | £ | £ |
| Investment in S Ltd: | | |
| 8,000 ordinary shares | 11,000 | — |
| Sundry net assets | 33,000 | 22,000 |
| | £44,000 | £22,000 |
| Ordinary shares | 30,000 | 10,000 |
| 6% preference shares | — | 4,000 |
| General reserves | 10,000 | 6,000 |
| Profit and loss account | 4,000 | 2,000 |
| | £44,000 | £22,000 |

## 44 H Ltd

From the following balance sheet of H Ltd and its subsidiary S Ltd, prepare a consolidated balance sheet at 31st December 19X5.

| | H Ltd | | S Ltd | |
|---|---|---|---|---|
| | £ | £ | £ | £ |
| Fixed assets: | | | | |
| Tangible fixed assets | | 60,000 | | 64,000 |
| Investment in S Ltd: | | | | |
| 60,000 ordinary shares | | 80,000 | | — |
| | | 140,000 | | 64,000 |
| Current assets: | | | | |
| Stock | 24,000 | | 28,000 | |
| Trade debtors | 20,000 | | 36,000 | |
| Due from subsidiary | 4,000 | | — | |
| Bills receivable | 8,000 | | — | |
| Bank | 21,000 | | 9,000 | |
| | 77,000 | | 73,000 | |

*continued*

| | H Ltd | | S Ltd | |
|---|---|---|---|---|
| | £ | £ | £ | £ |
| *brought forward* | 77,000 | 140,000 | 73,000 | 64,000 |
| Creditors: Amounts falling due within one year: | | | | |
| Trade creditors | 30,000 | | 16,000 | |
| Due to holding company | — | | 16,000 | |
| | 30,000 | | 32,000 | |
| Net current assets | | 47,000 | | 41,000 |
| Net assets | | £187,000 | | £105,000 |
| Capital and reserves: | | | | |
| Called-up share capital: | | | | |
| Ordinary shares of £1 each | | 160,000 | | 80,000 |
| General reserves | | 12,000 | | 11,000 |
| Profit and loss account | | 15,000 | | 14,000 |
| | | £187,000 | | £105,000 |

The following information is relevant:

(a) At the date when H Ltd acquired the shares of S Ltd, the general reserve and profit and loss account of the latter company stood at £7,000 and £6,000 respectively.

(b) The stock held by H Ltd includes stock purchased from S Ltd for £7,200, S Ltd having made a profit of 50 per cent on cost.

## 45 H Ltd

From the following balance sheets, prepare a consolidated balance sheet of H Ltd and its two subsidiaries S Ltd and Y Ltd at 31st December 19X5.

| | H Ltd | S Ltd | Y Ltd |
|---|---|---|---|
| | £ | £ | £ |
| Fixed assets: | | | |
| Investments: | | | |
| 9,000 shares in S Ltd | 9,000 | — | — |
| 6,000 shares in Y Ltd | — | 6,000 | — |
| Sundry net assets | 9,000 | 6,000 | 7,500 |
| | £18,000 | £12,000 | £7,500 |
| Capital and reserves: | | | |
| Called-up share capital | £18,000 | £12,000 | £7,500 |

## 46 H Ltd

| | H Ltd | S Ltd | Y Ltd |
|---|---|---|---|
| | £ | £ | £ |
| Fixed assets: | | | |
| Tangibles | 200,000 | 120,000 | 100,000 |
| Investments: | | | |
| 80,000 shares in S Ltd at cost | 100,000 | — | — |
| 60,000 shares in Y Ltd at cost | | | |
| *less:* Amounts written off | 70,000 | — | — |
| Sundry net assets | 130,000 | 60,000 | 12,000 |
| | £500,000 | £180,000 | £112,000 |
| Capital and reserves: | | | |
| Ordinary shares | 380,000 | 100,000 | 80,000 |
| Capital reserves | — | 20,000 | — |
| Profit and loss account | 120,000 | 60,000 | 32,000 |
| | £500,000 | £180,000 | £112,000 |

When H Ltd acquired its shares in S Ltd, there was a credit balance on that company's profit and loss account of £40,000 and on the capital reserve of £20,000.

Y Ltd had a credit balance on profit and loss account of £40,000 when H Ltd purchased its shares for £76,000, but has since paid a net dividend of £8,000.

The companies do not trade with each other.

Prepare the consolidated balance sheet at 31st December 19X5.

## 47 H Ltd

Balance Sheet at 31st December 19X5

| | H Ltd | | S Ltd | | Y Ltd | |
|---|---|---|---|---|---|---|
| | £ | £ | £ | £ | £ | £ |
| Fixed assets: | | | | | | |
| Tangibles | | 200,000 | | 200,000 | | 104,000 |
| Investments: | | | | | | |
| 80,000 ordinary shares in S Ltd | 110,000 | | | | | |
| 40,000 6 per cent preference shares in S Ltd | 42,000 | | | | | |
| 60,000 ordinary shares in Y Ltd | 52,000 | | | | | |
| | | 204,000 | | — | | — |
| | | 404,000 | | 200,000 | | 104,000 |
| Current assets: | | | | | | |
| Due from subsidiaries: | | | | | | |
| S Ltd | 16,000 | | — | | — | |
| Y Ltd | 6,000 | | — | | — | |
| Due from fellow subsidiary | — | | 10,000 | | — | |
| Debtors | 390,000 | | 114,000 | | 38,000 | |
| | 412,000 | | 124,000 | | 38,000 | |

*continued*

| | H Ltd | | S Ltd | | Y Ltd | |
|---|---|---|---|---|---|---|
| | £ | £ | £ | £ | £ | £ |
| *brought forward* | 412,000 | 404,000 | 124,000 | 200,000 | 38,000 | 104,000 |
| Creditors: Amounts falling due within one year: | | | | | | |
| Due to holding company | — | | 12,000 | | 6,000 | |
| Due to fellow subsidiary | — | | — | | 8,000 | |
| Creditors | 326,000 | | 72,000 | | 22,000 | |
| | 326,000 | | 84,000 | | 36,000 | |
| Net current assets | | 86,000 | | 40,000 | | 2,000 |
| Net assets | | £490,000 | | £240,000 | | £106,000 |
| Capital and reserves: | | | | | | |
| Called-up share capital: | | | | | | |
| Ordinary £1 shares | | 400,000 | | 120,000 | | 100,000 |
| 6% preference shares | | — | | 60,000 | | — |
| Profit and loss account | | 90,000 | | 60,000 | | 6,000 |
| | | £490,000 | | £240,000 | | £106,000 |

The following information is relevant:

(a) H Ltd purchased its shareholdings in S Ltd on 30th June 19X5, the ordinary shares costing £110,000.

(b) S Ltd has paid its preference dividend up to 31st December 19X4.

(c) When H Ltd purchased its shares in Y Ltd there was a debit balance on the latter company's revenue reserves of £10,000.

(d) The differences in the current account balances are due to cash in transit.

(e) The profit and loss account balance of S Ltd at 1st January 19X5 was £24,000.

*You are required* to prepare a draft consolidated balance sheet of H Ltd and its subsidiary companies as at 31st December 19X5.

## 48 H Ltd

The following are the balances which appear in the books of H Ltd and its two subsidiaries at 31st December 19X5. The shares in the subsidiaries were all acquired on the same day, and at the date of acquisition the reserves of S Ltd and Y Ltd stood at £6,000 and £8,000 respectively, and their respective profit and loss accounts showed credit balances of £4,000 and £3,000. The bills payable by S Ltd were accepted in favour of H Ltd and the stock of H Ltd was purchased from S Ltd, the cost to S Ltd being £12,000.

| | H Ltd | S Ltd | Y Ltd |
|---|---|---|---|
| | £ | £ | £ |
| Credit balances: | | | |
| Share capital | 20,000 | 12,000 | 8,000 |
| Reserves | 10,000 | 12,000 | 10,000 |
| Profit and loss account | 6,000 | 5,800 | 4,000 |
| Creditors | 10,800 | 5,800 | 6,600 |
| Bills payable | — | 8,000 | — |
| | £46,800 | £43,600 | £28,600 |
| Debit balances: | | | |
| Tangible fixed assets | 11,000 | 9,800 | 10,200 |
| Investments in S Ltd: | | | |
| 8,000 shares at cost | 9,200 | — | — |
| Investments in Y Ltd: | | | |
| 6,000 shares at cost | — | 7,200 | — |
| Debtors | 6,600 | 26,600 | 18,400 |
| Bills receivable | 2,000 | — | — |
| Stock | 18,000 | — | — |
| | £46,800 | £43,600 | £28,600 |

*You are required* to prepare a consolidated balance sheet at 31st December 19X5.

## E Consolidated balance sheets—foreign subsidiaries

### 49 Eirespan Hotels Ltd

Eirespan Hotels Ltd has two subsidiaries—Eirespan (Ireland) Ltd and Eirespan (Spain) Ltd.

Eirespan (Spain) Ltd is the wholly owned subsidiary of Eirespan Hotels Ltd, having been set up in 19X0 by that company when it expanded its business overseas.

Eirespan Hotels Ltd acquired 250,000 of the 400,000 £1 ordinary shares of Eirespan (Ireland) Ltd on 1st January 19X3 for £750,000. At that time the equity shareholders' funds of Eirespan (Ireland) Ltd were £880,000. No further shares have been issued by Eirespan (Ireland) Ltd but equity shareholders' funds at 31st December 19X5 were £1,280,000.

From the consolidated balance sheet of Eirespan Hotels Ltd as at 31st December 19X5, state precisely (using the figures given where applicable) what each of the following items will represent:

(a) Minority interest.

(b) Goodwill—cost of control.

(c) Reserves.

# F Consolidated profit and loss accounts

## 50 H Ltd

The draft profit and loss accounts of H Ltd and its subsidiary S Ltd on 31st December 19X5 were as follows:

| | H Ltd | S Ltd |
|---|---|---|
| | £ | £ |
| Operating profit | 400,000 | 340,000 |
| Dividends from S Ltd | 120,000 | — |
| | 520,000 | 340,000 |
| Corporation tax | 200,000 | 170,000 |
| | 320,000 | 170,000 |
| Dividend | 120,000 | 160,000 |
| Profit for the financial year | £200,000 | £10,000 |

H Ltd has owned 75 per cent of the capital of S Ltd since incorporation of S Ltd.
Prepare a consolidated profit and loss account for the year ended 31st December 19X5.

## 51 H Ltd

The draft profit and loss accounts of H Ltd and its subsidiary S Ltd for the year ended 31st December 19X5 were as follows:

| | H Ltd | S Ltd |
|---|---|---|
| | £ | £ |
| Operating profit | 160,000 | 120,000 |
| Corporation tax | 80,000 | 60,000 |
| | 80,000 | 60,000 |
| Proposed dividend | 70,000 | 24,000 |
| Profit for the financial year | £10,000 | £36,000 |

H Ltd purchased 75 per cent of the share capital in S Ltd on 31st August 19X5. Profits are deemed to accrue evenly throughout the year.
Prepare a consolidated profit and loss account for the year ended 31st December 19X5.

## 52 H Ltd

H Ltd acquired 75 per cent interest in S Ltd two years previously when the profit and loss account of the latter company was in credit of £4,000. The draft profit and loss accounts of H Ltd and its subsidiary S Ltd on 31st December 19X5 were as follows:

| | H Ltd | S Ltd | | H Ltd | S Ltd |
|---|---|---|---|---|---|
| | £ | £ | | £ | £ |
| Taxation | 10,000 | 6,000 | Balance brought forward | 24,000 | 8,000 |
| Reserves | 10,000 | 8,000 | | | |
| Balance carried forward | 44,000 | 18,000 | Operating profit for the year brought down | 40,000 | 24,000 |
| | £64,000 | £32,000 | | £64,000 | £32,000 |

In arriving at the operating profit for the year as shown, the following amounts had been charged in the accounts: directors' fees H Ltd £2,000, S Ltd £2,000 (directors of H Ltd are also the directors of S Ltd); depreciation, H Ltd £5,000, S Ltd £2,400, and auditors' fees, H Ltd £1,000, S Ltd £800.

*You are required* to prepare a consolidated profit and loss account of H Ltd for the year ended 31st December 19X5.

## 53 H Ltd

Below are the draft profit and loss accounts of H Ltd and S Ltd for the year ended 31st December 19X5.

The share capital of S Ltd consists of 400,000 ordinary shares of £1 each of which H Ltd acquired 300,000 on 1st January 19X5 at a cost of £400,000.

Draft Profit and Loss Account for the year ended 31st December 19X5

| | H Ltd | | S Ltd | |
|---|---|---|---|---|
| | £ | £ | £ | £ |
| Gross profit | | 600,000 | | 200,000 |
| *less:* | | | | |
| Directors' fees | 16,000 | | 4,000 | |
| Depreciation | 40,000 | | 20,000 | |
| Audit fees | 400 | | 200 | |
| Debenture interest | — | 56,400 | 10,000 | 34,200 |
| | | 543,600 | | 165,800 |
| *Add:* | | | | |
| Investment income | | | | |
| Dividend received from S Ltd | | 15,000 | | |
| Dividend receivable from S Ltd | | 30,000 | | |
| Debenture interest from S Ltd | | 4,000 | | |
| | | 592,600 | | |
| Taxation | | 217,440 | | 66,320 |
| Profit after tax | | 375,160 | | 99,480 |

*continued*

| | H Ltd | | S Ltd | |
|---|---|---|---|---|
| | £ | £ | £ | £ |
| *brought forward* | | 375,160 | | 99,480 |
| Appropriations | | | | |
| Transfer to reserves | 60,000 | | 30,000 | |
| Dividends paid | — | | 20,000 | |
| Dividends proposed | 300,000 | 360,000 | 40,000 | 90,000 |
| Retained profit for the financial year | | 15,160 | | 9,480 |
| Retained profits at 1st January 19X5 | | 164,000 | | 52,000 |
| Retained profits at 31st December 19X5 | | £179,160 | | £61,480 |

The following information is relevant:

(a) During the last month of the financial year, H Ltd sold goods to S Ltd, and made a profit of £12,000 thereon. These goods are included in the stocks of S Ltd at invoice value.

(b) The dividends paid and proposed are all out of current profits.

*You are required* to prepare a consolidated profit and loss account of H Ltd and its subsidiary, having regard to the fact that H Ltd does not propose to publish its separate profit and loss account. The directors of H Ltd are not directors of S Ltd.

## 54 H Ltd

H Ltd has owned 80 per cent of the capital of S Ltd and 40 per cent of the capital of A Ltd since their incorporations. From the following information prepare a consolidated profit and loss account incorporating the results of A Ltd.

Profit and Loss Account—year ended 31st December 19X5

| | H Ltd | S Ltd | A Ltd |
|---|---|---|---|
| | £ | £ | £ |
| Operating profit | 180,000 | 100,000 | 40,000 |
| Dividend from S Ltd | 16,000 | — | — |
| Dividend from A Ltd | 4,000 | — | — |
| | 200,000 | 100,000 | 40,000 |
| Corporation tax | 90,000 | 50,000 | 20,000 |
| | 110,000 | 50,000 | 20,000 |
| Proposed dividend | 60,000 | 20,000 | 10,000 |
| Retained profit for the financial year | £50,000 | £30,000 | £10,000 |

## 55 A Ltd

From the information given below you are required to prepare the consolidated profit and loss account of A Ltd for the year ended 31st December 19X5.

Detailed workings should be shown and any assumptions stated clearly.

The standard rate of corporation tax may be assumed to be 50 per cent.

A Ltd acquired 80 per cent of the ordinary shares in B Ltd when that company was formed five years ago.

A Ltd acquired 40 per cent of the ordinary shares in C Ltd as from 1st January 19X5.

The following balances were extracted from the books of A Ltd, B Ltd, and C Ltd for the year ended 31st December 19X5:

| | A Ltd | B Ltd | C Ltd |
|---|---|---|---|
| | £ | £ | £ |
| Turnover | 3,000,000 | 1,000,000 | 800,000 |
| Balance brought forward at 1st January 19X5 | 45,000 | 30,000 | 25,000 |
| Cost of sales | 2,410,000 | 690,500 | 562,750 |
| Distribution cost | 251,000 | 144,500 | 139,200 |
| Administrative expenses | 99,000 | 45,000 | 28,050 |
| Transfer to general reserve | 30,000 | — | 10,000 |
| Debenture interest | 20,000 | 5,000 | — |
| Tax charge on trading profits | 70,000 | 40,000 | 20,000 |
| Proposed dividends: Ordinary shares | 40,000 | 25,000 | 10,000 |
| Balance carried forward at 31st December 19X5 | 58,000 | 49,000 | 35,200 |

The following information is relevant:

(a) There were no intra-group trading activities.

(b) The following adjustments have to be reflected:

| | A Ltd | B Ltd | C Ltd |
|---|---|---|---|
| | £ | £ | £ |
| Directors' fees | 25,000 | 8,000 | 4,000 |
| Auditors' remuneration (including expenses) | 2,000 | 1,000 | 800 |
| Depreciation of fixed assets | 40,000 | 22,000 | 15,000 |
| Debenture interest payable | 20,000 | 5,000 | — |

(c) The directors of A Ltd are *not* directors of B Ltd or C Ltd.

*You are required* to prepare the consolidated profit and loss account for the year ended 31st December 19X5.

## G Consolidated balance sheets (examination standard)

### 56 Holdco Ltd

The following is a summary of the balances in the books of Holdco Ltd and Subco Ltd as on 31st March 19X5:

| | Holdco Ltd | Subco Ltd |
|---|---|---|
| | £ | £ |
| Credits: | | |
| Authorised and issued capital, fully paid: | | |
| Ordinary shares of £1 each | 300,000 | 100,000 |
| 7% non-cumulative preference shares of £1 each | — | 80,000 |
| General reserves | 50,000 | 40,000 |
| Profit and loss account | 98,500 | 44,400 |
| Provision for depreciation of fixed assets | 60,000 | 30,000 |
| 6% debentures | — | 20,000 |
| Proposed dividends: | | |
| On ordinary shares | 30,000 | 10,000 |
| On preference shares | — | 5,600 |
| Debenture interest accrued | — | 1,200 |
| Creditors | 87,000 | 32,200 |
| | £625,500 | £363,400 |
| | £ | £ |
| Debits: | | |
| Tangible fixed assets, at cost | 250,000 | 220,000 |
| 75,000 ordinary shares in Subco Ltd at cost | 165,000 | — |
| 60,000 preference shares in Subco Ltd at cost | 60,000 | — |
| £5,000 6% debentures of Subco Ltd | 5,000 | — |
| Debtors | 145,500 | 143,400 |
| | £625,500 | £363,400 |

You ascertain the following:

(a) Holdco Ltd acquired the shares in Subco Ltd, cum dividend, on 31st March 19X4.

(b) The general reserve of Subco Ltd was the same on 31st March 19X4 as on 31st March 19X5. The balance on the profit and loss account of Subco Ltd is made up as follows:

| | £ |
|---|---|
| Balance on 31st March 19X4 | 28,000 |
| Net profit, year ended 31st March 19X5 | 32,000 |
| | 60,000 |
| *less:* Provision for proposed dividends | 15,600 |
| | £44,400 |

(c) The stock in trade of Subco Ltd on 31st March 19X5 included £16,000 in respect of goods purchased from Holdco Ltd. These goods had been sold by Holdco Ltd to Subco Ltd at such a price as to give Holdco a profit of 20 per cent on the invoice price.

(d) The balance on the profit and loss account of Subco Ltd on 31st March 19X4 is after providing for the preference dividend of £5,600 and a proposed ordinary dividend of £5,000, both of which were subsequently paid but had been incorrectly credited to profit and loss account in the books of Holdco Ltd.

(e) No entries had been made in the books of Holdco Ltd in respect of the debenture interest due from, or the proposed dividend of, Subco Ltd for the year ended 31st March 19X5.

(f) On 31st March 19X5 the authorised and issued ordinary share capital of Subco Ltd had been increased by £20,000 by capitalising part of the general reserve and issuing 20,000 £1 shares to the existing shareholders in proportion to their existing holdings. This transaction has not yet been shown in the books of Subco Ltd or Holdco Ltd.

*You are required* to prepare the consolidated balance sheet of Holdco Ltd and its subsidiary company Subco Ltd, as on 31st March 19X5.

Ignore taxation.

Workings are to be shown.

Comparative figures are not required.

## 57 Edgemont Ltd

The summarised balance sheets as on 31st December 19X2 of Edgemont Ltd, Edgehill Ltd and Edgedale Ltd were:

| | Edgemont Ltd | Edgehill Ltd | Edgedale Ltd |
|---|---|---|---|
| | £ | £ | £ |
| Ordinary shares of £1 each | 300,000 | 200,000 | 100,000 |
| Profit and loss account: | | | |
| Balances before taking into account proposed dividends | 80,000 | 50,000 | 31,000 |
| Creditors | 10,000 | 12,000 | 5,000 |
| | £390,000 | £262,000 | £136,000 |
| Intangible—goodwill, at cost | 20,000 | | |
| Tangible fixed assets | 150,000 | 110,000 | 120,000 |
| Investments acquired on 1st January 19X2: | | | |
| 150,000 shares in Edgehill Ltd | 160,000 | | |
| 80,000 shares in Edgedale Ltd | | 100,000 | |
| Stocks | 30,000 | 10,000 | 5,000 |
| Debtors and bank balances | 30,000 | 42,000 | 11,000 |
| | £390,000 | £262,000 | £136,000 |

The following information is relevant:

(a) On 1st January 19X2 credit balances on profit and loss accounts before taking into account proposed dividends were: Edgemont Ltd £40,000, Edgehill Ltd £24,000 and Edgedale Ltd £2,000.

(b) On 31st March 19X2 dividends of 10 per cent in respect of the year 19X1 had been distributed by Edgemont Ltd and Edgehill Ltd.

(c) Edgemont Ltd had credited the dividend received from Edgehill Ltd to profit and loss account.

(d) Dividends proposed for 19X2 to be wholly paid out of that year's profits, are: Edgemont Ltd 10 per cent, Edgehill Ltd 5 per cent and Edgedale Ltd 6 per cent.

*You are required* to prepare a summarised consolidated balance sheet as on 31st December 19X2 of Edgemont Ltd and subsidiaries.

## 58 Spades Ltd, Clubs Ltd and Hearts Ltd

Spades Ltd, Clubs Ltd and Hearts Ltd make up accounts annually to 31st March.

On 1st April 19X5 Clubs Ltd purchased 25,000 shares in Hearts Ltd for £45,000.

On 31st March 19X6 Spades Ltd purchased the whole of the issued share capital of Clubs Ltd for £120,000 and on the same date bought from outside shareholders 25,000 shares in Hearts Ltd for £40,000.

Draft accounts of each of the companies were prepared in respect of the year ended 31st March 19X6 and the resultant balances showing in the books as on that date are summarised below:

| | Spades Ltd | Clubs Ltd | Hearts Ltd |
|---|---|---|---|
| | £ | £ | £ |
| Share capital | 200,000 | 100,000 | 75,000 |
| Reserves at 1st April 19X5 | 50,000 | 10,000 | 18,000 |
| Profit and loss account: | | | |
| At 1st April 19X5 | 16,500 | 8,000 | 3,900 |
| Year ended 31st March 19X6 | 52,000 | 16,200 | 9,900 |
| Provision for depreciation of plant to 31st March 19X6 | 12,500 | 11,100 | 6,300 |
| Overdraft at Town Bank Ltd | — | 13,000 | — |
| Trade creditors | 34,600 | 23,000 | 27,300 |
| Current accounts: Spades Ltd | — | 15,000 | 600 |
| Clubs Ltd | — | — | 1,300 |
| | £365,600 | £196,300 | £142,300 |

*continued*

| *continued* | Spades Ltd | Clubs Ltd | Hearts Ltd |
|---|---|---|---|
| | £ | £ | £ |
| Goodwill at cost | — | 20,000 | 12,000 |
| Cost of shares in Clubs Ltd | 120,000 | — | — |
| Cost of shares in Hearts Ltd | 40,000 | 45,000 | — |
| Plant at cost | 60,000 | 38,100 | 19,300 |
| Stocks at cost | 38,000 | 32,000 | 52,000 |
| Bank balances: City Bank Ltd | 16,000 | — | 14,000 |
| Trade debtors | 73,900 | 59,900 | 45,000 |
| Current accounts: Clubs Ltd | 15,000 | — | — |
| Hearts Ltd | 2,700 | 1,300 | — |
| | £365,600 | £196,300 | £142,300 |

The following information is relevant:

(a) The current account difference arises from a cheque being in transit as on 31st March 19X6.

(b) One quarter of the stocks of Clubs Ltd as on 31st March 19X6 had been invoiced to that company by Spades Ltd at cost plus $33\frac{1}{3}$ per cent.

(c) The estimated corporation tax liabilities for the year ended 31st March 19X6 are: Spades Ltd £22,000; Clubs Ltd £7,000; Hearts Ltd £4,200.

(d) The proposed dividend of Spades Ltd is at the rate of 10 per cent.

*You are required* to prepare the consolidated balance sheet of Spades Ltd and its subsidiary companies as on 31st March 19X6.

Your workings should be presented as supporting schedules to the balance sheet.

## 59 Llewellyn Ltd

The summarised balance sheets of Llewellyn Ltd and Grove Ltd as at 31st December 19X3 were as follows:

| | Llewellyn Ltd | Grove Ltd |
|---|---|---|
| | £ | £ |
| Authorised and issued share capital: | | |
| Ordinary shares of £1 each, fully paid | 240,000 | 120,000 |
| Share premium account | 36,000 | — |
| Capital reserve on 1st January 19X3 | 16,000 | 12,000 |
| Revenue reserve on 1st January 19X3 | 30,000 | 20,000 |
| Profit and loss account on 1st January 19X3 | 80,000 | 16,000 |
| Profit for 19X3 | 32,000 | 10,000 |
| Creditors | 70,000 | 22,000 |
| Current account Grove Ltd | 5,400 | — |
| | £509,400 | £200,000 |

*continued*

| *continued* | Llewellyn Ltd £ | Grove Ltd £ |
|---|---|---|
| Goodwill at cost | — | 15,000 |
| Plant and machinery at cost *less* depreciation | 144,000 | 90,000 |
| Fixtures and fittings at cost *less* depreciation | 26,000 | 11,400 |
| Stock | 36,000 | 24,000 |
| Debtors | 175,400 | 42,200 |
| Investment in P Ltd at cost | — | 5,000 |
| Balance at bank | 20,000 | 6,000 |
| Current account Llewellyn Ltd | — | 6,400 |
| Shares in Grove Ltd: 96,000 shares at cost | 108,000 | — |
| | £509,400 | £200,000 |

Other relevant information:

(a) Llewellyn Ltd had allotted 72,000 shares at a premium of 50 pence each in exchange for the 96,000 shares in Grove Ltd on 1st January 19X3.

(b) In determining, on 1st January 19X3, the consideration for the shares in Grove Ltd, plant and machinery was revalued at £108,000, the fixtures and fittings at £10,000 and the investment in P Ltd was considered to be of no value.

No adjustments had been made in the books in respect of these valuations but effect of the revaluations is to be given in the consolidated accounts, and in the computation of depreciation for the year.

(c) There were no purchases or sales of plant and machinery or fixtures and fittings during 19X3.

(d) The depreciated figures for plant and machinery and fixtures and fittings as at 31st December 19X3 are after providing depreciation for 19X3 on the book values at 1st January 19X3 at rates of 10 per cent and 5 per cent per annum respectively.

(e) A cheque for £1,000 from Llewellyn Ltd to Grove Ltd sent before 31st December 19X3 was not received by the latter company until January 19X4.

*You are required* to prepare the consolidated balance sheet of Llewellyn Ltd and its subsidiary Grove Ltd as at 31st December 19X3.

Your workings must be submitted.

## 60 Grip Ltd

Grip Ltd, which has an authorised and issued share capital of 100,000 ordinary shares of £1 each fully paid, had a balance on revenue reserve of £16,200 on 31st December 19X2, after paying a dividend for the year ended on that date.

You are also given the following information:

(a) On 31st October 19X3, Grip Ltd purchased 9,000 of the 10,000 issued ordinary shares of £1 each fully paid in Hand Ltd for £14,250. The balance on revenue reserve of Hand Ltd as on 31st December 19X2 had been £3,450 after paying a dividend for the year ended on that date.

(b) For the year ended 31st December 19X3, Grip Ltd made a trading profit of £18,640 and paid a dividend of 15 per cent while Hand Ltd made a trading profit of £4,000 and paid a dividend of 20 per cent.

(c) For the year ended 31st December 19X4 Grip Ltd made a trading profit of £26,540 and paid a dividend of 20 per cent while Hand Ltd incurred a trading loss of £4,100 and no dividend was paid.

(d) During the year ended 31st December 19X4 Hand Ltd had manufactured and sold to Grip Ltd an item of plant for £8,000 which included a profit on the selling price to Hand Ltd of 25 per cent. The plant had been included in the fixed assets of Grip Ltd and a full year's depreciation had been provided thereon at 20 per cent on cost.

*You are required* to show how the above items would be reflected in the consolidated balance sheet of Grip Ltd as on 31st December 19X4, together with corresponding figures for the preceding year, and to provide detailed schedules showing the compilation of the figures contained therein.

## 61 Roberts Ltd

The following is the summary of the balance sheet capitals of Roberts Limited, Grove Limited and Dillwyn Limited as at 30th September 19X3:

| | Roberts Ltd | Grove Ltd | Dillwyn Ltd |
|---|---|---|---|
| | £ | £ | £ |
| Issued share capital in ordinary shares of £1 each, fully paid | 40,000 | 32,000 | 20,000 |
| Profit and loss account | 104,700 | 40,020 | 51,880 |
| | £144,700 | £72,020 | £71,880 |

Roberts Limited purchased 20,000 shares in Grove Limited on 30th September 19W7 at a cost of £32,000; Grove Limited profit and loss account had a credit balance of £29,312 at that time.

Grove Limited purchased 18,000 shares in Dillwyn Limited on 31st March 19W8 at a cost of £30,000 when there was a debit balance of £8,000 on the latter's profit and loss account.

There has been no variation in the share capitals of the subsidiaries since these acquisitions.

*You are required* to prepare a summary consolidated balance sheet of the group as at 30th September 19X3, inserting therein a balancing figure representing the net assets. As a note to the consolidated balance sheet, show a reconciliation of this figure of group net assets with the net assets of the individual companies. You may assume that any premium on consolidation is written off against the reserves.

*Note:* Any date represented by a "W" should be taken to lie in the previous decade to a date represented by an "X".

Your workings must be submitted.

## 62 Fig Ltd

As on 30th June 19X3 the balance sheets of three companies showed the following position:

| | Fig Ltd | | Run Ltd | | Trot Ltd | |
|---|---|---|---|---|---|---|
| | £ | £ | £ | £ | £ | £ |
| Tangible fixed assets: | | | | | | |
| Freehold land and buildings, at cost | | 40,000 | | 100,000 | | 65,000 |
| Plant and machinery, at cost | 130,000 | | 56,000 | | 87,000 | |
| *less:* Aggregate depreciation | 50,000 | 80,000 | 22,000 | 34,000 | 60,000 | 27,000 |
| | | 120,000 | | 134,000 | | 92,000 |
| Investments: | | | | | | |
| Shares in Run Ltd, at cost | 115,000 | | | | | |
| Shares in Trot Ltd, at cost | 70,000 | 185,000 | | — | | — |
| Current assets: | | | | | | |
| Stocks | 57,000 | | 68,000 | | 54,140 | |
| Debtors | 96,340 | | 43,245 | | 42,190 | |
| Balances at bank | 44,250 | 197,590 | 110,425 | 221,670 | 11,409 | 107,739 |
| | | 502,590 | | 355,670 | | 199,739 |
| Creditors: due within one year: | | | | | | |
| Creditors | 32,396 | | 61,710 | | 34,287 | |
| Corporation tax | 72,450 | | 52,000 | | 24,400 | |
| Proposed dividends | 120,000 | 224,846 | 80,000 | 193,710 | 10,000 | 68,687 |
| | | £277,744 | | £161,960 | | £131,052 |
| Capital and reserves: | | | | | | |
| Called-up share capital | | 200,000 | | 80,000 | | 100,000 |
| Capital reserve | | 20,000 | | 40,000 | | — |
| Profit and loss account | | 57,744 | | 41,960 | | 31,052 |
| | | £277,744 | | £161,960 | | £131,052 |

You are also given the following information:

(a) Fig Ltd acquired 50,000 shares in Run Ltd in 19W8 when the balance on capital reserve had been £20,000 and on revenue reserve £16,000. A further 20,000 shares were purchased in 19X0 when the balances on capital reserve and revenue reserve had been £40,000 and £24,000 respectively.

(b) Fig Ltd had purchased 75,000 shares in Trot Ltd in 19W9 when there had been an adverse balance on revenue reserve of £6,000.

(c) During the year ended 30th June 19X3 Fig Ltd had purchased a machine from Run Ltd for £10,000 which had yielded a profit on selling price of 30 per cent to that company. Depreciation on the machine had been charged in the accounts at 20 per cent on cost.

(d) Run Ltd purchases goods from Fig Ltd, providing Fig Ltd with a standard gross profit on invoice price of 33⅓ per cent. On 30th June 19X3, the stock valuation of Run Ltd included an amount of £16,000 being goods purchased from Fig Ltd for £18,000.

(e) The proposed dividends from subsidiary companies have been included in the figure for debtors in the accounts of the parent company.

*You are required* to prepare the consolidated balance sheet of Fig Ltd and its subsidiaries as on 30th June 19X3, together with your consolidation schedules.

*Note:* Any date represented by a "W" should be taken to lie in the previous decade to a date represented by an "X".

## H Consolidated profit and loss accounts (examination standard)

### 63 Kestrel Ltd

The summarised profit and loss accounts of Kestrel Ltd, Sparrow Ltd, Thrush Ltd and Osprey Ltd for the year ended 31st March 19X3, and the issued share capital as on that date, were as follows:

| | Kestrel Ltd | Sparrow Ltd | Thrush Ltd | Osprey Ltd |
|---|---|---|---|---|
| | £ | £ | £ | £ |
| Balance brought forward 1st April 19X2 | 45,000 | 30,000 | | |
| Trading profits | 416,000 | 126,000 | 10,000 | 210,000 |
| Interim dividend received from Sparrow Ltd | 16,000 | | | |
| Proposed dividend from Osprey Ltd | 27,000 | | | |
| Directors' fees from Thrush Ltd | 6,000 | | | |
| Balance carried forward | | | 29,800 | |
| | £510,000 | £156,000 | £39,800 | £210,000 |

*continued*

| *continued* | Kestrel Ltd | Sparrow Ltd | Thrush Ltd | Osprey Ltd |
|---|---|---|---|---|
| | £ | £ | £ | £ |
| Balance brought forward 1st April 19X2 | | | 20,000 | |
| Directors' fees | 24,000 | 12,000 | 10,000 | 20,000 |
| Depreciation | 20,000 | 18,000 | 9,000 | 15,000 |
| Audit fees | 1,500 | 1,000 | 800 | 1,000 |
| Provision for corporation tax | 188,000 | 47,000 | | 87,000 |
| Transfer to reserve | 50,000 | | | |
| Written-off shares in Thrush Ltd | 8,000 | | | |
| Proposed dividends, actual | 150,000 | | | 60,000 |
| Interim dividend paid, actual | | 20,000 | | |
| Balance carried forward | 68,500 | 58,000 | | 27,000 |
| | £510,000 | £156,000 | £39,800 | £210,000 |
| | £ | £ | £ | £ |
| Issued ordinary share capital in £1 shares | 250,000 | 100,000 | 80,000 | 120,000 |

You also obtain the following information:

(a) Kestrel Ltd had acquired the following shares:
Sparrow Ltd 60,000 shares on 1st April 19X0
20,000 shares on 1st April 19X2
Thrush Ltd 60,000 shares on 1st April 19X1
Osprey Ltd 54,000 shares on 1st April 19X2

(b) Osprey Ltd commenced trading on 1st April 19X2.

(c) The profit and loss account of Sparrow Ltd had a debit balance of £40,000 on 1st April 19X0. On 1st April 19X1 the credit balance on the profit and loss account of Thrush Ltd had been £4,000.

(d) An election has been made for dividends between subsidiary companies and the holding company to be treated as group income without the incidence of advance corporation tax.

(e) During the year Kestrel Ltd had purchased goods from Sparrow Ltd which had yielded a profit of 25 per cent on selling price to Sparrow Ltd. Goods purchased by Kestrel Ltd from that company for £20,000 were included in the closing stock as on 31st March 19X3 at a valuation of £19,000.

(f) The directors of Sparrow Ltd and Thrush Ltd are also directors of the holding company.

*You are required* to prepare a consolidated profit and loss account of Kestrel Ltd and its subsidiary companies incorporating the results of its associated company for the year ended 31st March 19X3, together with your consolidation schedules.

## 64 Abstract Ltd

On 1st February 19X3 Abstract Ltd purchased 150,000 ordinary shares and 50,000 preference shares in Bran Ltd, and on 1st March 19X3 purchased 45,000 ordinary shares in Corn Ltd. All three companies make up their accounts to 30th June in each year. The following figures were extracted from the companies' records for the year ended 30th June 19X3:

| | Abstract Ltd | Bran Ltd | Corn Ltd |
|---|---|---|---|
| | £ | £ | £ |
| Sales | 900,000 | 850,000 | 500,000 |
| Purchases | 497,990 | 482,580 | 221,100 |
| Selling and distribution costs | 45,000 | 67,500 | 45,000 |
| Administration expenses | 115,000 | 52,500 | 65,000 |
| Interim dividends paid 1st January 19X3 on ordinary shares | 75,000 | 40,000 | |
| on preference shares | | 4,500 | |
| Stocks on hand as on 30th June 19X2 | 49,650 | 100,280 | 34,500 |
| Issued share capital: | | | |
| Ordinary shares of £1 each | 300,000 | 200,000 | 100,000 |
| 9% preference shares of £1 each | | 100,000 | |
| Revenue reserves as on 30th June 19X2 after deducting all dividends to that date | 26,750 | 32,000 | 48,000 |

You also obtain the following additional information:

(a) Profits of Bran Ltd and Corn Ltd accrued evenly throughout the year.

(b) Stocks on hand at 30th June 19X3 were: Abstract Ltd £87,640; Bran Ltd £92,860; and Corn Ltd £45,600.

(c) Provision for corporation tax based on the profits for the year at 42 per cent is to be made as follows:

| | |
|---|---|
| Abstract Ltd | £150,000 |
| Bran Ltd | £108,000 |
| Corn Ltd | £86,400 |

(d) Abstract Ltd proposes to pay a final dividend on ordinary shares of 25 per cent; Bran Ltd a half-year's dividend on the preference shares, and a final dividend on ordinary shares of 30 per cent; and Corn Ltd a dividend on ordinary shares of 60 per cent.

*You are required* to prepare a consolidated profit and loss account of Abstract Ltd and its subsidiary company incorporating the results of its associated company for the year ended 30th June 19X3 together with your consolidation schedules.

# 8 INCOMPLETE RECORDS

## 65 Mr G

Mr G commenced business as a retailer on 1st April 19X2. On the same date he opened a bank account, but he had not kept any proper accounting records. In May 19X4 you are called in to assist in the preparation of accounts for taxation purposes. The following balance sheet had been submitted to the Inland Revenue in the previous year:

Balance Sheet at 1st April 19X3

| | £ | | £ |
|---|---|---|---|
| Capital | 9,350 | Furniture and equipment | |
| Loan from J | 1,500 | (cost £5,400) | 3,800 |
| Bank overdraft | 1,000 | Motor vehicles (cost £2,800) | 2,100 |
| Sundry creditors | 3,200 | Goodwill | 2,000 |
| Accrued expenses | 650 | Stocks | 6,300 |
| | | Debtors | 1,000 |
| | | Prepaid expenses | 500 |
| | £15,700 | | £15,700 |

An analysis of G's bank account for the year ended 31st March 19X4 provides the following information:

| | £ | | £ |
|---|---|---|---|
| Receipts: | | Payments: | |
| Debtors | 5,200 | Cash purchases | 23,200 |
| Cash sales | 34,300 | Creditors | 8,900 |
| New loan from J | 5,500 | Expenses | 5,300 |
| | | Motor vehicle | 1,750 |
| | | Drawings | 5,200 |
| | £45,000 | | £44,350 |

The following additional information is available:

(a) Drawings:
Mr G has taken goods, cost £100, for his personal use during 19X3/X4.

(b) Debtors and creditors:
The amounts outstanding at the end of the current financial year were £1,300 and £3,800 respectively. Bad debts of £100 had been taken into account in arriving at the debtors figure.

(c) Expenses:
£450 was accrued and £520 prepaid at 31st March 19X4.

(d) Stock:
End of current year valuation was £5,850.

(e) Loans:
Interest of 10 per cent is to be provided for on both loans.

(f) Bank overdraft:
The agreed maximum is £5,000. £50 interest is outstanding.

(g) Fixed assets:
Depreciation of 20 per cent is to be provided for on the original cost of all furniture and equipment and motor vehicles.

*You are required to:*

(a) prepare trading and profit and loss accounts for the year ended 31st March 19X4, and a balance sheet at the same date, showing all relevant workings, and

(b) comment on the results as shown in the accounts.

(22 marks)

## 66 Fair Travel Agency

Green trades as Fair Travel Agency, effecting sales of tickets for Tour Operators Ltd, Air Lines and British Rail. The commissions earned thereon are at the rate of 10 per cent, $7\frac{1}{2}$ per cent and 7 per cent respectively.

The accounts are made up to 31st October in each year.

The balances as on 31st October 19X8 were as follows:

| | £ | £ |
|---|---|---|
| Capital | | 5,100 |
| Deposits from customers re Tour Operators Ltd | | 2,000 |
| PAYE | | 250 |
| Accountancy | | 150 |
| Advertising | | 100 |
| Rates | | 100 |
| Fixtures and fittings | 1,000 | |
| Motor car | 900 | |
| Debtors for rail tickets | 500 | |
| Debtors for air tickets | 100 | |
| Rent in advance | 125 | |
| Bank balance | 5,075 | |
| | £7,700 | £7,700 |

You obtained the following information:

(a) From bank statements, returned cheques and the paying-in slips for the year ended 31st October 19X9:

| | £ |
|---|---|
| Bankings (cheques and cash) | 82,000 |
| Payments for tickets: Tour Operators Ltd | 62,000 |
| Air Lines | 6,500 |
| British Rail | 7,000 |

*continued*

*continued*

| | £ |
|---|---|
| Rent (4 quarters) | 500 |
| Electricity | 90 |
| Rates | 300 |
| Accountancy | 150 |
| PAYE | 910 |
| Advertising | 625 |
| Bank balance on 31st October 19X9 | 9,000 |

(b) Weekly expenditure (52 weeks) defrayed from cash takings before banking:

| | |
|---|---|
| Staff wages | £40 (net) |
| Petty expenses | £1 |
| Drawings | £20 per week. |

(c) From audit statements the following liabilities at 31st October 19X9 were disclosed:

| | £ |
|---|---|
| Rates | 110 |
| Advertising | 50 |
| British Rail | 1,370 |
| Tour Operators Ltd | 550 |
| Air Lines | 160 |
| Accountancy | 150 |

(d) Customers' deposits on 31st October 19X9, all re Tour Operators Ltd, were £1,000 and debtors for rail tickets were £100.

(e) Depreciation of car and fixtures is calculated at 25 per cent per annum and 10 per cent per annum of the reducing balances respectively; and

(f) Green agrees that any cash difference should be transferred to his drawings account.

*You are required to prepare:*

(a) Profit and loss account for the year ended 31st October 19X9, showing separately the commission from each class of ticket sold; and

(b) balance sheet as on 31st October 19X9.

Ignore taxation.

(20 marks)

## 67 Able

On 1st October 19X0, Able went into business as a wholesaler of plastic household goods. He opened a separate business bank account and placed £5,000 to the credit thereof. On the same day, Able acquired for £6,500 a ten-year lease of a small warehouse, using the bank overdraft facilities, up to £4,000, which he had arranged for one year under a guarantee from Baker, who deposited securities as collateral. In consideration, Able agreed to pay Baker 5 per cent of the profit of the first year's trading. Able used his own estate car for business purposes and employed Charles from

1st October 19X0 at a salary of £800 per annum. Charles used his van on Able's business.

On 30th June 19X1, Able took Charles into partnership. Charles introduced £2,000 in cash and was to receive one-third of the available profits. His salary ceased as from that date. No interest was to be allowed on partners' capital accounts or charged on their drawings.

For purposes of allocating the profits, they were to be assumed to accrue evenly from day to day. On the same day, both vehicles became partnership assets and an assistant was engaged at a salary of £600 per annum.

The only records kept were bank statements, suppliers' statements, paid cheques and unpaid invoices for goods purchased, together with a notebook in which were recorded credit sales. All credit customers paid their accounts by cheque. The cash takings were banked each week after certain expenses had been paid therefrom and the cash float retained for the following week.

An analysis of the bank statements for the year ended 30th September 19X1 was as follows:

| | £ | | £ |
|---|---|---|---|
| Receipts: | | Payments: | |
| Cash introduced | 7,000 | Cash float | 20 |
| Allowance from suppliers | 25 | Suppliers for purchases | 9,000 |
| Credit customers | 2,050 | Insurance | 70 |
| Weekly bankings | 8,100 | Bank charges and interest | 210 |
| | | Purchase of lease | 6,500 |
| | | Balance on 30th September 19X1 | 1,375 |
| | £17,175 | | £17,175 |

You ascertain that:

(a) The items paid out of cash takings were:

| | £ |
|---|---|
| Sundry expenses | 650 |
| Vehicle expenses | 500 |
| Wages and drawings | 2,250 |

Able drew the same amount each month and Charles drew a like monthly amount when he became a partner.

(b) The cost of the premises is to be amortised over the period of the lease and depreciation is to be provided on the vehicles at 20 per cent per annum of the cost to the partnership.

(c) The values of the vehicles at 30th June 19X1 were:

| | £ |
|---|---|
| Estate car | 800 |
| Van | 600 |

On 30th September 19X1:

(a) Cheques totalling £45 from credit customers and paid into the bank on that date had not yet been credited by the bank.

(b) The amount paid for insurance included a premium of £20 for the year ending 30th September 19X2.

(c) The cost of the stock was £1,250 but items costing £250 had been so damaged as to render them worthless.

(d) The cash float consisted of £15 cash and Able's IOU for £5.

(e) Suppliers' unpaid invoices amounted to £560, and £34 was owing for sundry expenses.

(f) Credit customers owed £380.

*You are required* to prepare, showing your workings:

(a) The trading and profit and loss accounts of the business for the year ended 30th September 19X1, and

(b) the balance sheet as on that date.

Ignore taxation.

(25 marks)

## 9 PARTNERSHIP ACCOUNTING

### A Basic

### 68 Long, Tall and Short

Long, Tall and Short are partners in a manufacturing business sharing profits and losses: Long four-sevenths, Tall two-sevenths and Short one-seventh. Short's annual share of the net profit is to be a minimum of £5,000, any deficiency being borne by the other two partners in their profit-sharing ratios. No interest is allowed or charged on partners' current accounts but fixed capitals carry interest at 10 per cent per annum.

The firm's trial balance as on 31st December 19X4 was as follows:

| | £ | | £ | £ |
|---|---|---|---|---|
| Freehold premises at cost | 22,000 | Capital accounts: | | |
| Plant and machinery at cost | 16,000 | Long | 10,000 | |
| Motor vehicles at cost | 3,400 | Tall | 7,000 | |
| Purchases | 46,000 | Short | 3,000 | |
| Stock at 1st January 19X4 | 12,400 | | | 20,000 |
| Manufacturing wages | 14,400 | Current accounts: | | |
| Carriage inwards | 840 | Long | 2,400 | |
| Discounts allowed | 980 | Tall | 1,100 | |
| Salaries | 6,100 | | | 3,500 |
| Repairs | 1,210 | Sales | | 104,000 |
| C/f | 123,330 | C/f | | 127,500 |

| | £ | | £ |
|---|---|---|---|
| B/f | 123,330 | B/f | 127,500 |
| Office expenses | 2,450 | Motor vehicle proceeds of sale | 600 |
| Debtors | 9,400 | Creditors | 4,600 |
| Balance at bank | 2,360 | Provision for doubtful debts | |
| Current account—Short | 600 | 1st January 19X4 | 840 |
| | | Provision for depreciation | |
| | | 1st January 19X4: | |
| | | Plant and machinery | 3,200 |
| | | Motor vehicles | 1,400 |
| | £138,140 | | £138,140 |

You are given the following information:

(a) Stock on hand on 31st December 19X4 amounted to £13,600.

(b) Sales included £1,800 for goods sent out on sale or return, charged to customers at cost plus 25 per cent and which remained in their hands unsold as on 31st December 19X4.

(c) The following amounts included in salaries, had been drawn each month by the partners as salary:

Long £100 Tall £60 Short £40.

(d) Repairs included an amount of £600 for the reconditioning of a machine which it is agreed should be capitalised.

(e) Provision is to be made for bonuses as follows:

| | |
|---|---|
| Factory | £800 |
| Office | £1,400 |

(f) Depreciation on plant and machinery and on motor vehicles is to be provided at the rate of 10 per cent and 25 per cent per annum, respectively, calculated on cost at the end of the year.

(g) A debt of £210 is to be written off and the provision for doubtful debts increased to £1,000.

(h) The motor vehicle sold during the year for £600 had cost £1,400 and had been written down to £400. Any profit or loss on the sale is to be credited or charged in the profit and loss account.

*You are required to prepare:*

(a) trading and profit and loss account for the year ended 31st December 19X4;

(b) balance sheet as on that date; and

(c) partners' current accounts for the year.

(18 marks)

## B Admission of partner

### 69 Taylor and Clough

Taylor and Clough were in partnership sharing profits and losses: Taylor two-thirds, Clough one-third.

The partnership deed provided:

(a) Interest at the rate of 8 per cent per annum is to be allowed on fixed capital accounts. No interest is to be allowed on current accounts but 10 per cent per annum is to be charged on any debit balance at the commencement of the year.

(b) Goodwill is to be valued at $1\frac{1}{2}$ times the average annual profits of the previous four or five years, whichever is the lower.

The partners agreed to take Best into partnership as on 1st January 19X9 and he introduced £5,000 into the business. It was agreed that the fixed capital of the business should be £20,000, contributed by the partners in their profit-sharing ratio, any surplus or deficiency being transferred to their current accounts. Taylor was to be entitled to a prior share of the profits of £500 and the balance was to be shared: Taylor two-fifths, Clough two-fifths, and Best one-fifth. In addition it was agreed that Best's share of the residue should not be less than £3,500 per annum.

Agreed profits for goodwill purposes of the past five years were as follows:

| | £ |
|---|---|
| 19X4 | 10,420 |
| 19X5 | 11,760 |
| 19X6 | 9,400 |
| 19X7 | 13,820 |
| 19X8 | 14,600 |

No account for goodwill is maintained in the books, adjusting entries for transactions between the partners being made in their current accounts.

Partners' accounts as on 31st December 19X8 were as follows:

| | Fixed capital | Current |
|---|---|---|
| | £ | £ |
| Taylor | 10,000 | 3,400 (credit) |
| Clough | 6,000 | 1,200 (credit) |

The draft accounts for the year ended 31st December 19X9, before taking into account interest on partners' accounts, show a profit of £16,400. Partners' drawings during the year are:

Taylor £5,000, Clough £2,500, Best £1,500.

*You are required to prepare:*

(a) a statement showing the division of profits for the year ended 31st December 19X9; and

(b) the partners' current accounts for the year ended 31st December 19X9, recording therein the entries necessary upon Best's admission as a partner.

(18 marks)

## 70 Owen, Glen and Dower

Owen & Glen who have been in partnership together for several years in concrete block manufacturing share profits and losses in the ratio of 3:2 after charging salaries of £2,500 each.

On 1st August 19X4 Dower was admitted into partnership on the following terms:

(a) that he paid £3,400 to the original partners;

(b) he would be entitled to a salary of £2,000 per annum and a 10 per cent share of profits after charging all salaries.

Owen & Glen are to continue their old profit-sharing ratio, but guarantee Dower's 10 per cent share of profits at a minimum figure of £1,200 per annum.

On 31st March 19X5, the following balances were extracted from the partnership books:

| | £ | £ |
|---|---|---|
| Capital accounts: Owen | | 28,000 |
| Glen | | 23,400 |
| Current accounts: Owen | | 3,000 |
| Glen | | 3,400 |
| Amounts paid in by Dower | | 3,400 |
| Life assurance policy premiums paid to 31st March 19X4 | 8,000 | |
| Sales | | 248,000 |
| Purchases | 192,000 | |
| Wages | 20,000 | |
| Salaries | 10,000 | |
| General expenses | 9,000 | |
| Plant and machinery | 24,000 | |
| Motor vehicles | 9,400 | |
| Debtors | 18,000 | |
| Creditors | | 10,200 |
| Stock 1st April 19X4 | 16,000 | |
| Provision for doubtful debts | | 1,400 |
| Balance at bank | 1,600 | |
| Private bank account | 12,800 | |
| | £320,800 | £320,800 |

You are informed that:

(a) the life assurance policy was surrendered on 1st April 19X4 for £9,500 and the proceeds paid direct to Owen & Glen in their profit-sharing ratio.

(b) The details of the private bank account are:

| | £ |
|---|---|
| Cash at bank on private agreement on 1st April 19X4 | 600 |
| Paid in by Dower at per agreement | 3,400 |
| Receipts from general cash account | 8,800 |
| | £12,800 |

The actual balance on the private bank account at 31st March 19X5 was £400, the difference being drawings by Owen £3,400, Dower £1,200, Glen £3,000, together with income tax paid for the year 19X4/X5 of £4,800. The income tax allocated to the partners as Owen £2,400, Glen £2,000 and Dower £400.

(c) Stock at 31st March 19X5 was valued at or under cost at £19,000.

(d) Depreciation on plant and machinery is 10 per cent per annum and on motor vehicles 20 per cent per annum.

(e) Provision for doubtful debts should be maintained at 5 per cent on debtors.

*You are required* to prepare:

(a) the trading, profit and loss, and appropriation accounts for the year ended 31st March 19X5 accounting for Dower on a pro-rata time basis;

(b) the balance sheet at the above date; and

(c) the partners' current accounts for the above period.

*Note:* All workings should be taken to the nearest £.

(20 marks)

## 71 Sparrow, Finch and Wren

Sparrow and Finch, who make up their accounts annually to 30th September, are partners in a retail business sharing profits and losses: Sparrow three-fifths, Finch two-fifths.

On 31st March 19X4, Sparrow retired and Wren was admitted as a partner, profits and losses from that date being shared: Finch two-thirds, Wren one-third.

For the purpose of these changes, the value of the firm's goodwill was agreed at £9,000. No account for goodwill is maintained in the books, adjusting entries for the transactions between the partners being made in their current accounts.

Interest on fixed capitals is allowed at 6 per cent per annum, but no interest is charged or allowed on current accounts. The amount due to a retiring partner is payable as to £2,500 on retirement, the balance being payable in five equal annual instalments, commencing on the first anniversary of his retirement and carrying interest at the rate of 8 per cent per annum.

The trial balance of the partnership as on 30th September 19X4 was as follows:

| | £ | | £ | £ |
|---|---|---|---|---|
| Leasehold premises (purchased 1st October 19X3) | 8,000 | Fixed capital accounts: | | |
| Purchases | 20,400 | Sparrow | 5,000 | |
| Motor vehicles at cost 30th September 19X3 | 4,200 | Finch | 3,000 | 8,000 |
| Balance at bank | 1,480 | Current accounts: | | |
| Salaries including partners' drawings | 6,400 | Sparrow | 2,200 | |
| Stock 30th September 19X3 | 5,100 | Finch | 2,600 | 4,800 |
| Shop fittings at cost | 1,800 | Cash introduced Wren 1st April 19X4 | | 4,000 |
| Cash paid Sparrow 1st April 19X4 | 2,500 | Sales (£13,933 for 6 months to 31st March 19X4) | | 38,000 |
| Debtors | 800 | Provision for depreciation 30th September 19X3: | | |
| Professional charges | 540 | Motor vehicles | 1,800 | |
| Shop wages | 3,800 | Shop fittings | 600 | 2,400 |
| Rates, lighting and heating | 1,680 | Creditors | | 3,600 |
| General expenses (£1,720 for 6 months to 31st March 19X4) | 4,100 | | | |
| | £60,800 | | | £60,800 |

You are given the following additional information:

(a) Of the £4,000 introduced into the firm by Wren on 1st April 19X4, it was agreed that £1,000 should comprise his fixed capital, the balance being credited to his current account.

(b) The stock as on 30th September 19X4 amounted to £5,600.

(c) Provision is to be made for depreciation for the year on motor vehicles and shop fittings at the rate of 20 per cent and 10 per cent respectively, calculated on cost at the end of the year.

(d) A motor vehicle which had cost £1,200 and on which depreciation of £480 had been provided had been taken over by Sparrow on his retirement at its written-down value.

(e) The following partners' drawings are included above in salaries:
Sparrow £600, Finch £400, Wren £200.

(f) As on 30th September 19X4, rates paid in advance amounted to £220 and a provision of £80 for general expenses was required.

(g) A difference of £100 had been written off at 30th September 19X4 to general expenses but had later been found to be due to an undercast of that amount in the purchase journal.

(h) Professional charges include £200 paid in respect of the acquisition of the leasehold premises. These fees are to be capitalised as part of the cost of the lease, the total cost of which is to be written off in 50 equal annual instalments.

*You are required* to prepare:

(a) the trading and profit and loss account for the year ended 30th September

19X4 (gross profit being apportioned on the basis of turnover; and expenses, unless otherwise indicated, on a time basis);

(b) the balance sheet as on that date; and

(c) partners' current accounts.

(22 marks)

## C Retirement of partner

### 72 Oak, Ash and Beeche

Oak, Ash and Beeche were trading in partnership sharing profits and losses 4:3:3 respectively. The accounts of the firm were made up to 31st December each year.

On 30th June 19X4 Oak died.

The partnership deed provided that:

(a) interest was to be credited on capital accounts at 5 per cent per annum on the balance at the beginning of the year;

(b) no interest was to be charged on drawings accounts; and

(c) on the death of a partner:

(i) goodwill was to be valued at three years' purchase of average profits of the three years up to the date of death, after deducting interest on capital employed at 8 per cent and a fair remuneration for each of the partners,

(ii) the amount due to the deceased partner's estate was to receive interest at 6 per cent per annum from the date of death until paid,

(iii) land and buildings and fixtures and fittings were to be taken at book value, and

(iv) accounts were not to be drawn up to the date of death but the profit or loss of the year in which a partner died was to be apportioned on a time basis.

The balances on the books of the firm at 31st December 19X4, subject to final adjustment, were:

| | £ | £ |
|---|---|---|
| Capital and drawings accounts: | | |
| Oak | 1,600 | 10,000 |
| Ash | 2,400 | 5,000 |
| Beeche | 2,400 | 6,000 |
| Land and buildings | 8,000 | |
| Fixtures and fittings | 1,500 | |
| Stock | 12,500 | |
| Debtors | 2,000 | |
| Bank | 4,000 | |
| Creditors | | 3,000 |
| Profit of year before charging interest | | 10,400 |
| | £34,400 | £34,400 |

You ascertain that:

(a) the profits for the earlier years, before charging partners' interest, were,

| | £ |
|---|---|
| 19X1 | 11,200 |
| 19X2 | 12,600 |
| 19X3 | 12,000 |

(b) the independent valuations at the date of death were:

| | £ |
|---|---|
| Land and buildings | 10,000 |
| Fixtures and fittings | 1,000 |

(c) any adjustment for goodwill was to be made in the capital accounts, but goodwill was not to be shown as an asset of the firm at 31st December 19X4;

(d) the land and buildings and fixtures and fittings were to be shown at the valuation figures;

(e) Ash and Beeche would share profits equally from the date of death of Oak; and

(f) it was agreed that a fair remuneration for the work done by the partners would be £2,500 per annum each and that the capital employed in the business was to be taken as £26,000.

*You are required* to prepare:

(a) partners' capital accounts in columnar form for the year ended 31st December 19X4; and

(b) balance sheet of the firm as on 31st December 19X4.

Ignore taxation.

(20 marks)

## D Amalgamation

### 73 Tom and Gerry

Tom and Gerry were trading in partnership sharing profits in the ratio of 2:1. Butch was trading as a sole trader in the same class of business. Both businesses made up their accounts to 31st December in each year.

It was agreed that with effect from 1st January 19X6, the two businesses should be merged with Gerry and Butch sharing profits equally and Tom retiring.

For the purpose of the merger and retirement, goodwill was to be valued at two years' purchase of the average adjusted profits of the last three years but was not to be brought in as an asset in the new firm.

The summarised balance sheets of the businesses at 31st December 19X5 were:

| | Tom and Gerry | Butch |
|---|---|---|
| | £ | £ |
| Capital accounts: Tom | 10,000 | |
| Gerry | 5,000 | |
| Butch | | 8,500 |
| Current accounts: Tom | 1,500 | |
| Gerry | 3,200 | |
| Creditors | 14,000 | 12,000 |
| | £33,700 | £20,500 |
| Freehold premises at cost | 12,000 | 3,000 |
| Furniture, fixtures and fittings at cost, less depreciation to date | 3,500 | 1,200 |
| Stocks at cost | 9,000 | 6,000 |
| Debtors | 3,200 | 2,800 |
| Balance at bank | 6,000 | 7,500 |
| | £33,700 | £20,500 |

You ascertain that:

(a) In valuing goodwill, the profits were to be adjusted for the following:

(i) the surplus or deficiency arising on the valuation of the furniture, fixtures and fittings was to be adjusted over the life of the assets to date, on a straight-line basis

(ii) the salary of £500 per annum paid to Butch's wife was to be added back, and

(iii) obsolete stock and bad debts were to be eliminated.

(b) Premises and furniture, fixtures and fittings were to be taken into the new firm at the value placed on them by an independent valuer.

(c) Stocks were to be taken in at cost less £300 in respect of obsolete stock held by Tom and Gerry.

(d) Creditors, debtors and bank balances were to be taken in at book value less bad debts amounting to £150 in the case of Tom and Gerry and £100 in the case of Butch.

(e) The new firm was to take over the liability to Tom for his share in Tom and Gerry.

(f) The valuations by the independent valuer were:

| | Tom and Gerry | Butch |
|---|---|---|
| | £ | £ |
| Freehold premises | 18,000 | 10,000 |
| Furniture, fixtures and fittings all purchased ten years ago | | 1,000 |
| all purchased since 31st December 19X2 | 3,800 | |

(g) The profits of the businesses for the last three years were:

| | Tom and Gerry | Butch |
|---|---|---|
| | £ | £ |
| Year to 31st December 19X3 | 7,300 | 3,300 |
| Year to 31st December 19X4 | 6,100 | 3,800 |
| Year to 31st December 19X5 | 7,510 | 3,900 |

*You are required* to prepare in columnar form:

(a) the partners' accounts in each of the businesses showing the closing of the businesses, and

(b) the balance sheet of the new firm of Gerry and Butch on 1st January 19X6.

(22 marks)

## E Dissolution

### 74 Old, Sage and Wit

Old, Sage and Wit had traded for many years as antiquarian booksellers in Oxford. The partnership agreement provided that Old, who was registered as a limited partner, should contribute £2,000 as capital. Profits and losses were to be shared in the ratios of 4:6:6.

On 31st December 19X6 it was agreed that the partnership should be dissolved. A summarised balance sheet as on that date showed:

| Partners | Capital accounts | Current accounts | | | |
|---|---|---|---|---|---|
| | £ | £ | £ | | £ |
| Old | 2,000 | — | 2,000 | Furniture and fittings | 1,000 |
| Sage | 14,000 | 5,000 | 19,000 | Trade debtors | 8,000 |
| Wit | 14,000 | 5,000 | 19,000 | Stock of books | 35,000 |
| | | | | Balance with bank | 6,000 |
| | | | 40,000 | | |
| Trade creditors | | | 10,000 | | |
| | | | £50,000 | | £50,000 |

Cash transactions during dissolution comprised:

| 19X7 | | £ |
|---|---|---|
| 1st January | Purchase of annuity for retiring employee (cost to be borne by Sage) | 3,000 |
| 1st January | The trade debtors assigned to Old for agreed sum of | 5,000 |
| 1st January | Furniture and fittings sold by auction for | 400 |
| 1st February | Paid realisation expenses | 600 |
| 10th February | Effected adjusting cash transfers between partners | |
| 15th February | Paid trade creditors | 10,000 |

On 1st January 19X7 Sage and Wit formed a new partnership by merging their connections with those of Young and Keen of Cambridge. The partners in the Cambridge firm had shared equally in capital, profits and losses. The new firm, trading under the name of Rarities, took over all of the existing stocks of books and on 1st January 19X7 moved into larger premises at York.

Values acceptable to all parties were attributed to assets as follows:

| | Oxford business | Cambridge business |
|---|---|---|
| | £ | £ |
| Stock of books | 20,000 | 60,000 |
| Furniture | — | 3,000 |
| Cars | — | 1,000 |
| Goodwill | 4,000 | 20,000 |

The partnership agreement of Rarities directed that profits and losses should be shared as to: Sage 10 per cent, Wit 15 per cent, Young 35 per cent and Keen 40 per cent. Capital was to be contributed in the same proportions, and was to amount in aggregate to a sum sufficient to reflect the values attributable to the acquired assets and, in addition, to provide £8,000 for working capital. Goodwill is not to appear in the books of any of the firms.

*You are required to:*

(a) show the journal entries (including those relating to cash) for closing the books of the Oxford firm, and

(b) to prepare a summarised balance sheet of Rarities as on 1st January 19X7.

Ignore taxation.

(25 marks)

## 75 Keen, Eager and Proud

Keen, Eager and Proud were in partnership sharing profits and losses: Keen two-fifths, Eager two-fifths and Proud one-fifth.

The partnership balance sheet as on 31st December 19X4 was as follows:

| | £ | £ |
|---|---|---|
| Fixed assets: | | |
| Plant, machinery, fixtures and fittings | | 8,000 |
| Motor vehicles | | 2,000 |
| | | 10,000 |
| Current assets: | | |
| Stock | 2,800 | |
| Debtors | 6,000 | |
| Cash in hand | 150 | |
| | 8,950 | |
| *less:* Current liabilities: | | |
| Creditors | 4,000 | |
| Bank overdraft | 2,400 | |
| | 6,400 | |
| Excess of current assets over current liabilities | | 2,550 |
| | | £12,550 |

*continued*

*continued*

| Financed by: | | £ | £ |
|---|---|---|---|
| Fixed capital accounts: | Keen | 5,000 | |
| | Eager | 3,000 | |
| | Proud | 2,000 | |
| | | | 10,000 |
| Current accounts: | Keen | 500 | |
| | Eager | 1,500 | |
| | | 2,000 | |
| | Proud—debit balance | (450) | |
| | | | 1,550 |
| Loan account: | Biggs | | 1,000 |
| | | | £12,550 |

The three partners, who wished to retire from the business, had agreed to accept an offer from Betters Ltd to acquire the assets of their business for £13,000 with the exception of the debtors, the cash balance and one of the motor vehicles.

The consideration was to be satisfied as follows:

(a) 3,000 10 per cent preference shares of £1 each valued at par,

(b) 18,000 ordinary shares of 25p each valued at 50p each, and the balance in cash.

The debtors realised £4,200 and the creditors were settled at £3,900.

The partners agreed that the basis of distribution on the dissolution of the partnership was to be as follows:

(a) Eager to take over the motor vehicle retained by the partnership at a value of £1,400.

(b) The loan from Biggs to be taken over by Keen.

(c) The ordinary shares to be allotted in proportion to fixed capital accounts.

(d) The preference shares to be allotted in profit-sharing ratio.

(e) The balance due to or from the partners to be settled in cash.

*You are required to prepare:*

(a) a realisation account;

(b) a cash account; and

(c) the partners' capital and current accounts.

(18 marks)

## F Sale to company

### 76 X, Y and Z

X, Y and Z are in partnership sharing profits in the proportion of 5:3:2 respectively. The firm's balance sheet as at 31st March 19X4 was as follows:

| | £ | £ | | £ |
|---|---|---|---|---|
| Capital Accounts | | | Assets | 94,200 |
| X | 44,000 | | | |
| Y | 29,000 | | | |
| Z | 12,000 | 85,000 | | |
| Current accounts: | | | Cash | 3,900 |
| X | 2,950 | | | |
| Y | 1,450 | | | |
| Z | 950 | 5,350 | | |
| Creditors | | 7,750 | | |
| | | £98,100 | | £98,100 |

On 1st April 19X4 the business was sold to YXZ Ltd on the following terms:

(a) The partners were to withdraw £1,350 in cash divided equally between them.

(b) The company to take over the assets, cash and the liabilities, in consideration for a sum of £95,000 to be satisfied by the issue to the partners of £13,000 5 per cent debentures, 46,000 ordinary shares of £1 each at par and £36,000 7 per cent preference shares.

(c) The partners agreed that the purchase consideration should be divided as follows:

Debentures: X—£8,000
Y—£5,000 and,
Preference shares in the proportion of their original capital accounts after deducting debentures as above.

*You are required to:*

Prepare the accounts showing the dissolution of the partnership and show how the shares should be divided between the partners.

(20 marks)

## 77 Fairway Ltd

On 31st December 19X7 Fairway Ltd was incorporated with an authorised share capital of £100,000 in shares of £1 each to take over the business carried on at that date by the partnership of Par, Green and Bogey.

The balance sheet of the partnership as on 31st December 19X7, showed the following position:

| | Par | Green | Bogey | |
|---|---|---|---|---|
| | £ | £ | £ | £ |
| Capital | 24,000 | 18,000 | 15,000 | 57,000 |
| Current accounts: | | | | |
| Balances as on 31 December 19X6 | 11,940 | 8,480 | 6,000 | |
| *add:* Interest on capital accounts | 720 | 540 | 450 | |
| Share of profit for year | 6,126 | 6,126 | 4,084 | |
| | 18,786 | 15,146 | 10,534 | |
| *less:* Drawings | 8,926 | 8,726 | 4,064 | |
| | 9,860 | 6,420 | 6,470 | 22,750 |
| | | | | £79,750 |

| Represented by: | Cost | Depn. | |
|---|---|---|---|
| | £ | £ | £ |
| Fixed assets: | | | |
| Freehold land and buildings | 26,000 | — | 26,000 |
| Plant and machinery | 42,000 | 22,000 | 20,000 |
| Motor vehicles | 19,700 | 4,700 | 15,000 |
| | 87,700 | 26,700 | 61,000 |
| Current assets: | | | |
| Stocks | | 22,400 | |
| Debtors | | 12,200 | |
| Balance at bank | | 19,750 | |
| | | 54,350 | |
| *less:* Creditors | | 35,600 | 18,750 |
| | | | £79,750 |

You are also given the following information:

(a) Freehold land and buildings are to be transferred to the limited company at a valuation of £30,000 and plant and machinery at £15,000. Stocks, debtors and creditors are to be transferred to the company at book value as on 31st December 19X7.

(b) The motor vehicles are to be withdrawn from the business by the partners at the following valuations: Par £4,900, Green £3,500 and Bogey £3,600.

(c) It is estimated that the company will require an opening balance at bank of £15,000.

(d) Sufficient 9 per cent unsecured loan stock is to be issued by the company to the partners so that they will receive the same interest as they received on capital in the partnership for the year ended 31st December 19X7.

(e) Ordinary shares are to be issued at par to each partner in proportion to their share in the partnership profits.

(f) Any surplus or deficiency on partners' accounts on realisation after taking into account loan stock and shares issued is to be withdrawn or paid in, whichever the case may be.

*You are required to prepare:*

(a) your computation of the shares and loan stock in Fairway Ltd to be issued to each partner;

(b) partners' accounts in columnar form, showing all the necessary entries to dissolve the partnership; and

(c) a balance sheet of the company upon completion.

(20 marks)

## G Piecemeal realisation

### 78 A, B and C

A, B and C are in partnership sharing profits and losses in the ratio 5:3:2 respectively. It was decided to dissolve the firm on 30th June 19X4, on which date the balance sheet was as follows:

| | £ | £ | | £ | £ |
|---|---|---|---|---|---|
| Capital accounts: | | | Freehold | | 2,200 |
| A | 8,000 | | Equipment | | 5,300 |
| B | 5,000 | | Vehicles | | 1,300 |
| C | 2,000 | 15,000 | | | |
| Current accounts: | | | Stock | 6,285 | |
| A | 200 | | Debtors | 5,600 | |
| B | 600 | 800 | Current account C | 700 | |
| Loan account B | | 2,000 | Profit and loss account | 2,400 | 14,985 |
| Creditors | 4,220 | | | | |
| Bank | 1,765 | 5,985 | | | |
| | | £23,785 | | | £23,785 |

The assets take some time to realise and it is decided that cash should be distributed as it is received. C has no private assets. At the commencement of the realisation costs are estimated to be £1,000.

Realisations are as follows:

| | | | £ |
|---|---|---|---|
| August | 1st | Debtors | 4,700 |
| August | 20th | Part of stock sold for | 2,700 |
| September | 30th | Equipment sold for | 2,805 |
| October | 15th | Remainder of stock sold for | 2,600 |
| October | 30th | The vehicles, consisting of 2 cars, were taken over by A and B at an agreed value of | 600 each |
| October | 30th | The premises were sold for | 4,000 |

The realisation expenses amounting to £800 were paid on 30th October.

*You are required to:*

Show the accounts to record the dissolution of the partnership and the payments made to the partners.

(25 marks)

## 10 MISCELLANEOUS ACCOUNTS

## A Selling agency branch accounts

### 79 Norsea Ltd

Norsea Ltd has a head office in Hull, and operates a branch in Grimsby.

All purchases are made by the head office and goods for the branch are invoiced at selling price, being cost price plus 50 per cent.

On 30th April 19X3, stock of goods at the branch, at selling price, amounted to £4,020 and debtors £1,652.

During the year ended 30th April 19X4 the following transactions took place at the branch:

| | £ |
|---|---|
| Cash sales | 25,200 |
| Credit sales | 18,000 |
| Cash discounts allowed to debtors | 452 |
| Cash received from debtors | 17,156 |
| Debts written off as bad | 149 |
| Goods received by the branch at selling price | 45,000 |
| Goods returned to head office at selling price | 420 |

On 30th April 19X4 stock of goods at the branch, at selling price, amount to £5,250.

*You are required to:*

Write up the ledger accounts in the head office books to record the above transactions, and compute the branch gross profit for the year ended 30th April 19X4.

(15 marks)

## 80 Alpha Ltd

Alpha Limited, whose head office is in London, operates a branch at Swansea. All goods are purchased by head office and invoiced to and sold by the branch at cost plus $33\frac{1}{3}$ per cent.

Other than a sales ledger kept at Swansea, all transactions are recorded in the books at London.

The following particulars are given of the transactions at the branch during the year ended 28th February 19X1:

| | £ |
|---|---|
| Stock on hand 1st March 19X0 at invoice price | 4,400 |
| Debtors 1st March 19X0 | 3,946 |
| Stock in hand 28th February 19X1 at invoice price | 3,948 |
| Goods sent from London during the year at invoice price | 24,800 |
| Credit sales | 21,000 |
| Cash sales | 2,400 |
| Returns to head office at invoice price | 1,000 |
| Invoice value of goods stolen | 600 |
| Bad debts written off | 148 |
| Cash from debtors | 22,400 |
| Normal loss at invoice price due to wastage | 100 |
| Cash discount allowed to debtors | 428 |

*You are required to:*

Write up the branch stock account and branch total debtors account for the year ended 28th February 19X1 as they would appear in the head office books.

(15 marks)

## B Autonomous and foreign branches

## 81 J Ltd

J Limited, a retailing organisation, has its head office in Birmingham and a branch at Swansea which keeps its own books. Goods are invoiced to Swansea at selling price less 20 per cent and the company's policy is to fix its selling prices at 40 per cent on the cost of the goods to the company from outside suppliers.

The trial balances extracted for the year ended 31st March 19X5 are:

| | Birmingham | | Swansea | |
|---|---|---|---|---|
| | £ | £ | £ | £ |
| Share capital | | 45,000 | | |
| Outside purchases | 185,300 | | 9,600 | |
| Freehold premises | 26,000 | | 4,500 | |
| Motor vehicles | 3,600 | 1,800 | 1,700 | 700 |
| Branch account | 38,205 | | | |
| Administration expenses | 9,756 | | 1,734 | |
| C/f | 262,861 | 46,800 | 17,534 | 700 |

| | Birmingham | | Swansea | |
|---|---|---|---|---|
| | £ | £ | £ | £ |
| B/f | 262,861 | 46,800 | 17,534 | 700 |
| Debtors/creditors | 34,323 | 28,705 | 7,553 | 3,386 |
| Stock 1st April 19X4 | 24,300 | | 5,980 | |
| Selling expenses | 12,635 | | 2,477 | |
| Remittances | | 25,500 | 25,500 | |
| Profit and loss account | | 3,470 | | |
| Distribution expenses | 8,750 | | 2,460 | |
| Head office account | | | | 37,335 |
| Depreciation on vehicles | 554 | | 225 | |
| Goods to branch | | 26,040 | | |
| Stock provision—unearned profit in stocks at Swansea on 1st April 19X4 | | 480 | | |
| Sales to customers | | 224,000 | | 47,000 |
| Balance at bank | 11,572 | | 1,132 | |
| Goods from head office | | | 25,560 | |
| | £354,995 | £354,995 | £88,421 | £88,421 |

You are also informed that:

(a) Stocks of goods purchased direct from outside suppliers and held at the branch were valued at cost at £1,500 on 1st April 19X4 and £700 on 31st March 19X5.

(b) Goods sent by head office on 30th March 19X5 and not received by branch until 3rd April 19X5 amounted to £480.

(c) Swansea has paid £390 in settlement of a head office supplier's account, which has not yet been dealt with in the head office books.

(d) The manager of the Swansea branch is to receive a commission of 10 per cent on the branch profit before charging this commission. This profit is to be based on the prices at which goods are charged to the branch.

*You are required to:*
Prepare a columnar trading and profit and loss account for the year and a balance sheet as at the end of the year.

Calculations should be made to the nearest £.

(20 marks)

## 82 China Ltd

China Limited commenced trading as wholesalers of crockery and glassware on 1st January 19X4 with a head office in London and a branch at Cardiff. A separate set of books was opened at the branch. Goods sent to Cardiff by head office were charged at invoice cost plus 10 per cent.

Cardiff sales were all at a uniform gross profit to the branch of 25 per cent on selling price, while head office sales, other than those to Cardiff, were at a uniform gross profit of 33⅓ per cent on selling price.

During the year ended 31st December 19X4 the following transactions took place:

(a) Expenses paid were: London £18,500 and Cardiff £4,050; expenses accrued at 31st December 19X4 were: London £416 and Cardiff £209.

(b) Head office purchases totalled £95,000, returns were £2,750 and discount allowed by suppliers for prompt payment amounted to £1,422; head office sales, including £33,000 invoiced to Cardiff branch, were £102,000, and discounts allowed to outside customers amounted to £546.

(c) Goods invoiced to Cardiff for £2,200 in December 19X4 were not received or recorded in the Cardiff books until January 19X5.

(d) In addition to goods received from head office, Cardiff branch also purchased goods from outside sources. During the year the branch had paid outside suppliers £5,850, having received discounts amounting to £150, and on 31st December 19X4 owed such suppliers £2,000. Cardiff sales were £40,000, breakages (at cost price to Cardiff) £497, and discounts allowed to customers £306.

Stock at Cardiff on 31st December 19X4 included stock invoiced by head office at £5,500.

*You are required to:*
Prepare in columnar form the head office, branch, and combined trading and profit and loss accounts for the year ended 31st December 19X4.
Ignore taxation.

(18 marks)

## 83 Bargains Ltd

Bargains Ltd, a retail store, has two departments for each of which a memorandum stock account and memorandum "mark-up" account is kept. All goods supplied to each department are debited to the memorandum stock account of the department at cost plus "mark-up", which together represent normal selling price, to which account the sales of the department are credited. The "mark-up" is credited to the departmental "mark-up" account. If the selling price of any goods is reduced below the normal selling price, the reduction (mark-down) is entered in the stock account and in the "mark-up" account. The "mark-up" for department A is 33⅓ per cent of cost and for department B 50 per cent of cost.

The following figures relating to the year 19X7 have been taken from the books:

| | Department A | Department B |
|---|---|---|
| | £ | £ |
| Stock on 1st January, at cost | 12,300 | 17,400 |
| Purchases | 81,600 | 94,800 |
| Sales | 105,000 | 140,000 |

(a) The stock of department A on 1st January included goods which cost £2,700, the selling price of which had been marked down by £250. These goods were sold during 19X7 at the reduced prices.

(b) Goods purchased in 19X7 at a cost of £1,440 for department A were later in the year transferred to department B, and sold for £2,160. The cost and the sale proceeds are included respectively in the purchases of department A and the sales of department B given above, but no entries for the transfer have been made in the books.

(c) Goods purchased in 19X7 were marked down as follows:

| | Cost | Mark down |
|---|---|---|
| | £ | £ |
| Department A | 4,860 | 430 |
| Department B | 10,000 | 2,000 |

With the exception of certain items in stock in department B at the end of the year, which cost £5,000 and were marked down by £1,000, all goods marked down in 19X7 were sold during the year at the reduced prices.

(d) At the stocktaking on 31st December 19X7 it was found that goods which had cost £120 were missing from department A, and it was decided to regard this amount as irrecoverable.

(e) For the purpose of the annual accounts, the closing stock of both departments is to be valued at cost.

*You are required to:*
Prepare, in columnar form, for each department for the year 19X7:

(a) the trading account:

(b) the memorandum stock account: and

(c) the memorandum "mark-up" account. (18 marks)

## 84 OTL Ltd

OTL Ltd commenced business on 1st January 19X0. The head office is in London and there is a branch in Highland. The currency unit of Highland is the crown.

The following are the trial balances of the head office and the Highland branch as at 31st December 19X0:

| | Head office | | Highland branch | |
|---|---|---|---|---|
| | £ | £ | crowns | crowns |
| Branch account | 65,280 | | | |
| Balances at bank | 10,560 | | 66,000 | |
| Creditors | | 21,120 | | 92,400 |
| Debtors | 18,480 | | 158,400 | |
| Fixed assets (purchased 1st January 19X0) | 39,600 | | 145,200 | |
| Head office account | | | | 316,800 |
| Profit and loss account (net profit for the year) | | 52,800 | | 79,200 |
| Issued share capital | | 86,400 | | |
| Stocks | 26,400 | | 118,800 | |
| | £160,320 | £160,320 | 488,400 | 488,400 |

The trial balance of the head office was prepared before any entries had been made in respect of any profits or losses of the branch.

Remittances from head office to branch and from branch to head office were recorded in the books at the actual amounts paid and received.

The rates of exchange were:

| | |
|---|---|
| On 1st January 19X0 | 5 crowns = £1 |
| Average rate for year 19X0 | 4.4 crowns = £1 |
| On 31st December 19X0 | 4 crowns = £1 |

*You are required to prepare:*

(a) The trial balance of the Highland branch as at 31st December 19X0 in sterling.

(b) The closing entries as at 31st December 19X0 in the branch account in the books of the head office.

(c) A summary of the balance sheet of OTL Ltd as at 31st December 19X0.

Ignore depreciation of fixed assets.
Ignore taxation.

(18 marks)

## C Consignment accounts

### 85 Green

On 1st October 19X1 S. Green of London consigned to P. Hall of Kingston, Jamaica, 50 bales of merchandise per SS *Trader*.

The merchandise cost Green £780; carriage to port, paid by him, was £40. Hall paid freight at £3 per bale, dock dues and landing charges £35 and marine insurance £26. Brokerage was 2 per cent and commission $2\frac{1}{2}$ per cent.

On 31st January 19X2 Hall had completed sales of the whole of this merchandise realising £1,200. He settled the net proceeds by a bill at three months which Green discounted for £920. The bill was duly met on maturity.

*You are required to:*

(a) make out Hall's account sales, and

(b) write up the ledger accounts in Green's books to record the transactions and show the profit arising.

(10 marks)

### 86 Oliver

Messrs Oliver & Company of Manchester had goods, cost price £600, which they found difficult to sell on the local market. They therefore consigned the goods to Mr L. Armstrong of London, with a pro-forma invoice for £800, on 17th March.

Oliver & Company paid the following expenses in respect of the consignment: packing £12, freight £18.

Mr Armstrong received the goods on 20th March and incurred storage expenses of £13 before the goods were sold.

The whole consignment was sold by auction on 28th March for £830, less auctioneer's commission of 10 per cent. Armstrong's own commission was £40.

Armstrong paid the balance due to Oliver & Company on 31st March.

*You are required to:*

Prepare the accounts recording the above in the ledger of

(a) the consignor,

(b) the consignee.

(12 marks)

## D Joint ventures

### 87 Duke and Lord

Duke and Lord entered into a joint venture to buy and sell second-hand cars. Profits and losses were to be shared: Duke two-thirds and Lord one-third.

On 16th August 19X9 Duke purchased two cars for £320 and £480 respectively. He incurred expenditure of £120 on repairs and on 1st September 19X9 sold one of the cars for £400; on 10th September 19X9 he sold the other car for £620.

On 12th September 19X9 he purchased a further car for £600 which was sold on 20th September 19X9 for £800, which amount was paid to Lord who paid it into his own bank account.

On 12th August 19X9 Lord purchased a car for £400 which he sold for £500 on 15th August 19X9, having incurred expenses of £40 on it. On 20th August 19X9 this car was returned by the customer, who was allowed £480 for it. As this car was still unsold on 30th September 19X9 it was agreed it should be taken over by Duke at a valuation of £450.

On 30th September 19X9 the sum required in full settlement as between Duke and Lord was paid by the party accountable.

*You are required to prepare:*

(a) the joint venture account as it would appear in the books of Duke recording his transactions with the joint venture; and

(b) a memorandum account for the joint venture, showing the net profit.

(18 marks)

### 88 Tower and Castle

Tower and Castle entered into a joint venture to buy and sell a quantity of briar pipes. It was agreed that Tower should receive a commission of 2 per cent on all sales in consideration for which he was to bear all losses from bad debts. Subject to this arrangement, profits and losses were to be shared equally.

On 2nd January 19X0, Tower purchased goods for £6,800 for which he paid £4,800 in cash, and accepted bills of exchange for £800 and £1,200.

On 3rd January Tower sent to Castle goods which had cost £2,750, and Castle paid £3,500 to Tower.

On 9th January Tower sold goods to Brown for £420 and to Green for £250 and they accepted bills of exchange for the amounts respectively due from them. Tower endorsed both these bills over to Castle, who discounted them. (Ignore discounting charges.)

On 3rd February Tower sold goods for £1,800. On delivery the customer rejected goods invoiced at £90, and these goods were collected by Castle, who sold them to another customer for £110.

On 11th February Brown met his bill, but Green's bill was dishonoured. Green was insolvent with no assets.

On 5th March Castle paid the bill for £800 which had been accepted by Tower, and Tower paid the second bill, £1,200.

During March 19X0 Tower sold the remainder of the goods in his possession for £2,910, and Castle's sales amounted to £3,400. Bad debts (apart from the amount due from Green) were £42, of which £30 was in respect of sales by Tower, and £12 was in respect of sales by Castle.

On 30th April 19X0 the venture was closed. Castle took over the stock in his possession at a valuation of £500, and the sum required to settle accounts between the venturers was paid by the party accountable.

*You are required to show:*

(a) the accounts which would appear in the books of Tower and Castle respectively to record the joint venture, and

(b) a memorandum joint venture account, showing the net profit.

(20 marks)

## E Royalty accounts

### 89 W. Heal

W. Heal manufactures casters, and has leased two machines on which to make them. The lease provides that for each machine:

(a) A royalty of £6 for every 120 casters produced should be paid but such payment was not to be less than £720 per annum for each machine.

(b) Any short workings in the first year of leasing the machines should be recouped out of royalties payable in the second year. Each machine is to be treated separately.

The lease of machine No. 1 commenced on 1st April 19X4 and that of machine No. 2 on 1st April 19X5.

The following are the numbers of casters produced:

| | Machine No. 1 | Machine No. 2 |
|---|---|---|
| Year ended 31st March 19X5 | 13,000 | |
| Year ended 31st March 19X6 | 15,200 | 14,400 |
| Year ended 31st March 19X7 | 16,400 | 15,000 |
| Year ended 31st March 19X8 | 18,300 | 16,100 |

W. Heal's books are closed on 31st March each year.

*You are required:*
To write up the royalties account, the short-workings account and the account of the lessor, as they would appear in W. Heal's books, from 1st April 19X4 to 31st March 19X8.

(16 marks)

## 90 A

The lease of a plot of land is granted to A upon the basis of a royalty of 10p per ton on the clay extracted, subject to a minimum rent of £2,000 per annum. A has the right to recoup short workings during the first seven years of the lease but not afterwards.

A granted a sub-lease for five years from 1st January 19X1 to XY Ltd of one-half of the area for a royalty of 15p per ton merging in a minimum rent of £1,250 per annum. Under the terms of the sub-lease, XY Ltd can recoup short workings in any of the two years immediately following that in which short workings accrued. The output in tons for A and XY Ltd was as follows:

| | A | XY Ltd |
|---|---|---|
| 31st December 19X1<br>First year | 10,000 tons | 6,500 tons |
| 31st December 19X2<br>Second year | 16,000 tons | 8,000 tons |
| 31st December 19X3<br>Third year | 20,000 tons | 8,200 tons |
| 31st December 19X4<br>Fourth year | 25,000 tons | 9,000 tons |
| 31st December 19X5<br>Fifth year | 26,000 tons | 9,900 tons |
| 31st December 19X6<br>Sixth year | 20,000 tons | |
| 31st December 19X7<br>Seventh year | 22,000 tons | |
| 31st December 19X8<br>Eighth year | 30,000 tons | |

*You are required* to prepare from the figures above:

(a) royalty account—payable and receivable,

(b) landlord's account, and

(c) short workings account.

Ignore income tax.

(17 marks)

## F Container accounts

### 91 Betta Garments

Betta Garments Ltd despatch their goods to customers in returnable cases which remain the property of Betta Garments Ltd. A deposit charge is made, and when the cases are returned there is a partial refund.

The cases cost £1.20p each and they are charged to customers at £1.50p each. Upon return of the cases the customers are credited with £1 each.

For stocktaking purposes all cases are valued at 75p each.

Records reveal that on 1st January 19X4 there were 14,000 cases in stock on the company's premises and 5,000 cases in the possession of customers.

During the year ended 31st December 19X4 the following occurred:

(a) 47,000 cases were despatched to customers; 39,600 were returned by customers.

(b) 1,600 cases were damaged and scrapped. They were sold for £110.

(c) 19,000 new cases were purchased.

(d) The company paid £600 during the year in respect of repairs to cases.

On 31st December 19X4 there were 12,400 cases in the possession of customers. A physical check of those held by Betta Garments Ltd showed no discrepancy.

*You are required:*

To write up the cast stock account and the cases suspense account of Betta Garments Ltd for the year ended 31st December 19X4 to show the transactions for the year. Show the balance of cases both in physical quantity and in value as at 31st December 19X4 and the profit or loss for the year as a result of these transactions.

(15 marks)

### 92 LEC Ltd

LEC Ltd despatches its product in metal containers which are charged to customers at £5 each. Customers are credited with £4 for each container returned.

On 31st December 19X2, there were 140 containers on the company's premises and 408 containers were in the hands of customers.

During 19X3:

(a) LEC Ltd purchased 250 containers for £3 each.

(b) 1,430 containers were charged to customers.

(c) 1,270 containers were returned by customers and credited to them.

(d) Customers retained 42 containers, for which they paid the amount charged.

For purposes of the annual accounts of LEC Ltd, all stocks of containers on the company's premises and returnable containers in the possession of customers are valued at £3 each.

*You are required:*
To show the container stock account and the container suspense account for the year 19X3. These accounts should be provided with additional memorandum columns in which quantities are to be shown.

(15 marks)

## G Contract accounts

### 93 Contract 17B

The ledger of a contractor disclosed that the following expenditure had been charged to Contract 17B during 19X9:

| | £ |
|---|---|
| Materials | 62,000 |
| Wages | 85,300 |
| Plant | 8,600 |
| Establishment charges | 6,700 |

The contract, which was for £360,000, was signed and work commenced in January 19X9. By 31st December 19X9 cash had been received on account of work done amounting to £162,000 representing 90 per cent of the value of the work certified. On 31st December 19X9 the value of materials unused was £4,000 and the cost of work completed but not certified was £5,000.

*You are required:*

(a) to prepare the account for Contract 17B for the year to 31st December 19X9, charging 10 per cent depreciation on plant,

(b) to show what proportion of the profit disclosed might be taken to the credit of the general profit and loss account, giving your reasons for the principle you adopt,

(c) to illustrate how the contract should be shown in the balance sheet at 31st December 19X9.

(15 marks)

## 94 Sandcastles Ltd

The following are particulars of two contracts, X and Y, undertaken by Sandcastles Ltd.

| | X | | Y |
|---|---|---|---|
| Date commenced | 1st June 19X7 | | 1st July 19X8 |
| Date completed | 30th November 19X8 | | 30th April 19X9 |
| Contract price | £100,000 | | £160,000 |
| | In 19X7 | In 19X8 | In 19X8 |
| | £ | £ | £ |
| Direct expenditure: | | | |
| Materials | 14,632 | 25,891 | 33,270 |
| Wages | 16,237 | 31,248 | 40,865 |
| Direct expenses | 866 | 1,215 | 1,624 |
| Plant purchased for cash, at commencement of contract | 10,725 | — | 12,350 |
| Payments for plant acquired on hire-purchase terms | — | 5,200 | 2,600 |
| Penalty for failure to complete Contract X by 31st October 19X8 | — | 500 | — |
| Cash received | 36,000 | 63,500 | 72,000 |

The plant purchased in 19X7 for cash was sold on 30th November 19X8 for £2,750.

As regards the plant acquired on hire-purchase terms, an initial deposit of £2,600 was paid on 28th February 19X8. The hire-purchase agreement called for two further payments of £2,600 each, which included interest at the rate of 12 per cent per annum; these payments were made on the due dates, viz: 30th June 19X8 and 31st October 19X8. This plant, the cash price of which was £7,504, was used on Contract X until 30th June 19X8, when it was transferred to Contract Y. For depreciation purposes the value of this plant at the date of transfer was taken to be £6,000.

The cash received in each year represented the contract price of all work certified in that year, less, in the case of uncompleted contracts, 10 per cent retention money, and, in the case of cash received for Contract X in 19X8, the penalty.

When the annual accounts for 19X7 were prepared, it was expected that Contract X would be completed on 31st October 19X8, when the market value of the plant purchased for cash would be £3,925. At the time it was estimated that expenditure on Contract X in 19X8 would amount to £39,000, but the acquisition of additional plant in 19X8 was not then foreseen.

When the annual accounts for 19X8 were prepared, it was expected that Contract Y would be completed on 30th April 19X9, when the market values of the plant purchased for cash and of the plant transferred would be £9,000 and £4,250 respectively. At that time it was estimated that the further expenditure on Contract Y would amount to £46,041.

The following principles were adopted for the purposes of the annual accounts:

(a) All depreciation was charged to contracts by the straight-line method, and was calculated by reference to the expected market value of the relevant plant at the completion of each contract.

(b) Credit was taken for that proportion of the estimated profit on each uncompleted contract which the contract price of the work certified bore to the total contract price.

*You are required* to prepare summaries of the accounts for

(a) Contract X for the years 19X7 and 19X8, and

(b) Contract Y for the year 19X8,

showing in each case the transfer to profit and loss account at the end of the year.

(28 marks)

## 95 Brick and Tile

Brick and Tile Ltd, building contractors, commenced to trade on 31st January 19X2.

At 31st December 19X2 there were three contracts uncompleted, Numbers 15, 16 and 18, and the following details are available in respect of them:

| Contract No. | 15 | 16 | 18 |
|---|---|---|---|
| | £ | £ | £ |
| Wages | 12,000 | 10,000 | 6,000 |
| Add 50% for overheads | 6,000 | 5,000 | 3,000 |
| Materials | 5,500 | 6,500 | 2,500 |
| Plant hire | 500 | 600 | — |
| Expenses | 2,000 | 1,000 | 300 |
| Vehicle expenses | 700 | 800 | 200 |
| Plant expenses | 1,000 | 900 | 400 |
| Cost to date | 27,700 | 24,800 | 12,400 |
| Value of work to date agreed with client's architect | 35,000 | 20,000 | 13,000 |
| *less:* Retentions | 3,500 | 2,000 | 1,300 |
| Sale value to date | 31,500 | 18,000 | 11,700 |
| Progress payments invoiced at 31st December 19X2 | 30,000 | 16,000 | 10,000 |
| Progress payments received at 31st December 19X2 | 25,000 | 16,000 | 10,000 |
| Estimate of: | | | |
| final cost | 30,000 | 35,000 | 60,000 |
| final sale value | 38,000 | 28,000 | 80,000 |

All materials are purchased for specific contracts and any unused on site are included in the measure.

*You are required* to compute the value that should be included in work in progress at 31st December 19X2, using methods that you consider appropriate to the circumstances of each contract. Each calculation should be preceded by a brief justification of the method you decide to apply to it.

(14 marks)

## H Hire purchase accounts—buyer's books

### 96 Tractors

A firm acquired two tractors under hire purchase agreements, details of which were as follows:

| | Tractor A | Tractor B |
|---|---|---|
| Date of purchase | 30th April 19X3 | 30th September 19X3 |
| | £ | £ |
| Cash price | 1,400 | 1,900 |
| Deposit | 200 | 268 |
| Interest (deemed to accrue evenly over the period of the agreement) | 240 | 288 |

Both agreements provided for payment to be made in twenty-four monthly instalments, commencing on the last day of the month following purchase, all instalments being paid on due dates.

On 30th June 19X4 Tractor B was completely destroyed by fire. In full settlement on 10th July 19X4 an insurance company paid £1,500 under a comprehensive policy out of which £1,200 was paid to the hire purchase company in termination of the agreement. Any balance on the hire purchase company's account in respect of these transactions was to be written off.

The firm prepared accounts annually to 31st December and provided depreciation on tractors on a straight-line basis at a rate of 20 per cent per annum, apportioned as from the date of purchase and up to the date of disposal.

*You are required* to record these transactions in the following accounts, carrying down the balances on 31st December 19X3 and 31st December 19X4.

(a) Tractors on hire purchase.

(b) Provision for depreciation of tractors.

(c) Disposal of tractors.

(d) Hire purchase company.

(15 marks)

### 97 Cars

A firm was acquiring two cars under hire purchase agreements, details of which are as follows:

| | | |
|---|---|---|
| Registration number | UE 452 | XA 300 |
| Date of purchase | 30th June 19X2 | 31st January 19X3 |
| | £ | £ |
| Cash price | 850 | 910 |
| Deposit | 94 | 118 |
| Interest (deemed to accrue evenly over the period of the agreement) | 108 | 144 |

Both agreements provided for payment to be made in thirty-six equal monthly instalments commencing on the last day of the month following purchase.

On 1st August 19X3, vehicle UE 452 became a total loss. In full settlement on 10th August 19X3:

(a) an insurance company paid £700 under a comprehensive policy, and

(b) the hire purchase company accepted £500 for termination of the agreement.

The firm prepared accounts annually to 28th February and provided depreciation on a straight-line basis at a rate of 20 per cent for motor vehicles, with a full year's depreciation in the year of purchase, no depreciation being provided in the year of disposal.

All instalments were paid on the due dates.

*You are required* to record these transactions in the following accounts:

(a) motor vehicles,

(b) depreciation, and

(c) hire purchase company,

carrying down the balances as on 28th February 19X4.

(15 marks)

## I Hire purchase accounts—seller's books

### 98 T Ltd

On 1st January 19X4, T Ltd commenced business selling goods on hire purchase. Under the terms of the agreements, an initial deposit of 20 per cent is payable on delivery, followed by four equal quarterly instalments, the first being due three months after the date of sale.

During the year sales were made as follows:

| | Cost price | HP sales price |
|---|---|---|
| | £ | £ |
| 17th January | 300 | 450 |
| 10th March | 350 | 500 |
| 22nd May | 90 | 135 |
| 4th July | 200 | 350 |
| 10th September | 700 | 900 |
| 15th November | 200 | 300 |

The goods sold in July were returned in October, after payment of the first instalment. All other instalments were paid on the due dates.

*You are required* to prepare the relevant account to show the profit on hire purchase transactions for the year ended 31st December 19X4, on the assumption that gross profit and interest are credited to profit and loss account in the proportion that deposits and instalments received bear to the hire purchase price.

(16 marks)

## 99 Scott

Scott commenced business on 1st July 19X1. During the year ended 30th June 19X2, purchases amounted to £5,400 and ordinary sales to £6,200. In addition, the following sales were made under hire-purchase arrangements:

| Article | Cost | Sale price HP | Deposit paid | Monthly instalments | Number paid in year |
|---|---|---|---|---|---|
| | £ | £ | £ | | |
| Television set | 60 | 90 | 10 | 20 of £4 | 8 |
| Washing machine | 80 | 120 | 12 | 12 of £9 | 2 |
| Refrigerator | 70 | 100 | 10 | 18 of £5 | 4 |

Instalments on the refrigerator could not be kept up and it was returned on 20th June 19X2.

Stock-in-trade on 30th June 19X2 amounted to £700 (excluding the returned refrigerator).

*You are required* to prepare the following accounts in Scott's books to record the hire-purchase transactions:

(a) hire purchase trading account;

(b) general trading account;

(c) memorandum hire purchase debtors account.

(15 marks)

## 100 John

John commenced trading on 1st January 19X5 selling television sets and washing machines both for cash and on hire purchase. Hire purchase sales are made on the basis of a 20 per cent deposit with the balance payable in four quarterly instalments. The first instalment is payable at the beginning of the next calendar quarter following the sale. The hire purchase agreements provide that any person wishing to do so may complete the purchase by paying off the balance due when the second instalment is made, thereby obtaining a 5 per cent refund of the initial hire purchase sales price.

The following information is extracted from John's books as at 31st December 19X5:

| | £ |
|---|---|
| Cash sales | 6,274 |
| Purchases | 8,700 |
| Hire purchase instalments received, including complete payments | 608 |
| Hire purchase deposits received | 648 |
| Cash from the sale of goods returned | 100 |

Sales under hire purchase agreements for the year were:

| | At cost | At HP sales price |
|---|---|---|
| | £ | £ |
| February | 160 | 250 |
| April | 300 | 430 |
| June | 175 | 280 |
| July | 460 | 700 |
| September | 240 | 370 |
| November | 380 | 560 |
| December | 420 | 650 |

Included in these were:

(a) April sales of £150 (cost £110) were returned from hire in September after only one instalment had been paid in July. These items were sold for cash £100 in October;

(b) June sales of £200 (cost £130) were paid for completely in October;

(c) July sales of £250 (cost £180) were returned in November, no instalments having been paid. These goods were brought into stock at a valuation of £140.

A contingency provision of 20 per cent is to be made on instalments due but not yet received.

At 31st December 19X5 stock, excluding goods returned from hire, was valued at £1,760.

*You are required* to prepare for the year's trading the following:

(a) hire purchase trading account;

(b) general trading account;

(c) hire purchase sales ledger control account;

(d) statement of closing stock valuation.

(30 marks)

## J Investment accounts

### 101 AB

On 1st March 19X4 AB purchased £6,000 10 per cent debenture stock in Needy Ltd at 98.

On 31st August 19X4 AB sold one-third of his holding at $98\frac{1}{2}$ ex-div and on 30th November sold another £2,000 of his nominal holding at $97\frac{3}{4}$. Interest is payable on 31st March and 30th September.

*You are required to* write up the investment account, bringing down the balances on 31st December 19X4.

Ignorc taxation.

(10 marks)

## 102 Skipper

Skipper carried out during the year ended 30th June 19X5 the following transactions in the shares of Ringlet Ltd.

(a) On 1st July 19X4 he purchased 30,000 ordinary shares of 25p each fully paid for £52,800.

(b) On 15th August 19X4 he sold 5,000 shares cum div for £10,250.

(c) On 30th September 19X4 he received an interim dividend of 2.5p per share from Ringlet Ltd.

(d) On 10th October 19X4, the company made by way of capitalisation of reserves a bonus issue of 1 fully paid share for every 5 shares held on 1st October 19X4, such shares to rank for the final dividend for the year ended 31st March 19X5.

Skipper renounced his right to 2,000 of these bonus shares which he sold for 180p per share, receiving the proceeds on 5th November 19X4.

(e) On 30th November 19X4 he sold 4,000 shares for £6,000.

(f) On 15th January 19X5 the company gave its members the right to apply for 1 share for every 6 held on 31st December 19X4 at a price of 125p per share payable on or before 31st January 19X5, such shares not to rank for the final dividend for the year ended 31st March 19X5.

Skipper took up half his entitlement under this issue, paying the amount due on 25th January 19X5, and sold the remaining rights for 25p per share, receiving the proceeds on 31st January 19X5.

(g) On 15th June 19X5 Skipper received a final dividend of 5p per share.

*You are required* to show the investment account in Skipper's books for the year ended 30th June 19X5, transferring any profits or losses on sales as they occur and the income balance at the end of the year.

Expenses and taxation are to be ignored.

(17 marks)

## K Bills of exchange

## 103 A

On 1st January 19X1, A drew, and B accepted, a bill at three months for £1,000. On 4th January, A discounted the bill at 6 per cent per annum and remitted half the proceeds to B. On 1st February, B drew and A accepted a bill at 3 months for £400. On 4th February, B discounted the bill at 6 per cent per annum and remitted half the proceeds to A. A and B agreed to share the discounts equally. At maturity A met his acceptance but B failed to meet his and the holder had recourse to A. A drew and B accepted a new bill at three months for the amount of the original bill, plus interest at 5 per cent per annum.

On 1st July 19X1, B became bankrupt. A first and final dividend of 50p in the £ was paid by his trustee in bankruptcy on 31st October 19X1. B obtained his discharge on 5th December 19X1 and agreed to pay A the unsatisfied balance of his account. This was paid on 10th February 19X2.

*You are required to* write up B's account in the books of A. Calculations to be made in months.

(18 marks)

## L Cash budgets

### 104 Forest Ltd

Woodcock and Bowyer agree to form a limited company called Forest Ltd to take over part of an existing business. They are to contribute £25,000 each for ordinary shares issued at par and Cranstone is to supply any additional amount required to finance the business during the first six months without recourse to an overdraft. Cranstone is to be given 5 per cent debentures, to the nearest £1,000 above the amount required, secured on the freehold premises.

The company is to purchase freehold premises for £25,000, stock £8,000 and plant, fittings and motor vans for an additional £6,000. Settlement is to be made in the month of incorporation.

The following estimates are made of transactions for the six months commencing 1st April 19X7.

Sales: April, £14,500; May, £16,000; June, £18,000 and £24,000 for each of the following four months. Gross profit on sales to be at the rate of 20 per cent.

Purchases: to be sufficient to secure stock at the end of each month adequate to supply the sales of the following month.

Debtors: to settle their accounts net by the end of the second month after the month of sale.

Creditors: to be paid at the end of the month following the month of purchase.

Expenses:

(a) preliminary expenses, £800, to be paid in May;

(b) general expenses, £600 per month, payable at the end of each month;

(c) wages and salaries, £800 payable on the last day of each month for the first four months, and £900 thereafter;

(d) rates, £400 per annum, due six-monthly on 31st March and 30th September, to be paid in the month following that in which they are due.

Assume shares and debentures are issued on 1st April.

*You are required to:*

(a) Prepare a monthly cash budget for the six months commencing 1st April 19X7.

(b) Prepare budgeted trading and profit and loss accounts for the 6 months ended 30th September 19X7 together with a balance sheet on that date.
(20 marks)

## M Insurance claims

### 105 Cinder Ltd

Cinder Ltd, which operates a wholesale warehouse, had a fire on the premises on 31st January 19X5, which destroyed most of the building, although stock to the value of £396 was salvaged.

The company has an insurance policy covering the stock for £60,000, the building for £80,000 and loss of profits including standing charges for £25,000, with a six-month period of indemnity.

The company's last annual accounts for the year ended 31st December 19X4 showed the following position:

| | £ | £ | | £ |
|---|---|---|---|---|
| Opening stock | 41,250 | | Sales | 200,000 |
| Purchases | 181,250 | | | |
| | 222,500 | | | |
| *less:* Closing stock | 52,500 | 170,000 | | |
| Gross profit carried down | | 30,000 | | |
| | | £200,000 | | £200,000 |
| Variable expenses | | 8,000 | Gross profit, brought down | 30,000 |
| Standing charges | | 16,750 | | |
| Net profit for year | | 5,250 | | |
| | | £30,000 | | £30,000 |

The company's records show that the turnover for January 19X5 had been the same as for the corresponding month in the previous year at £10,000, payments made in January 19X5 to trade creditors were £10,668 and at the end of that month the balances owing to trade creditors had increased by £332.

The company's business was disrupted until the end of April, during which period the turnover fell by £18,000 compared with the same period in the previous year.

It was agreed that three-quarters of the value of the building had been lost and that at the time of the fire it had been worth £100,000.

*You are required* to prepare statements showing the amounts to be claimed by the company from its insurers for:

(a) loss of stock,

(b) the building, and

(c) loss of profits.

(15 marks)

## 11 INTERPRETATION OF ACCOUNTS

### 106 Construction of accounts

Statistics in respect of a quoted company include the following:

| | | |
|---|---|---|
| (a) | Net current assets : fixed assets ratio | 0.7 : 1 |
| (b) | Working capital ratio | 1.6 : 1 |
| (c) | Liquid ratio | 1.1 : 1 |
| (d) | Stock turnover ratio | 6 |
| (e) | Debtors' turnover ratio | 4 |
| (f) | Net equity income : equity capital employed percentage | 10% |
| (g) | Ordinary dividend cover | 1.1 times |
| (h) | Taxation charge in profit and loss account | £385,000 |
| (i) | Debtors are ten times cash in hand. | |

The capital structure of the company is:

| | £ |
|---|---|
| 5 per cent preference shares of £1 each | 700,000 |
| Ordinary shares of £1 each | 1,200,000 |
| Reserves | 3,200,000 |
| | £5,100,000 |

*You are required* to draft the balance sheet and trading and profit and loss account of the company in brief form, inserting as necessary balancing figures in the balance sheet for cash, and in the profit and loss account for (a) expenses other than purchases, and (b) taxation.

(10 marks)

## 107 Spark Ltd

Spark Ltd is an expanding private company in the electric trade with ten shareholders, most of whom belong to the same family. Business commenced in 19W7 and activities have been concentrated on one large store in the Croydon area. Accounts prepared in January 19X9 included the following information:

Profit Statement for the year ended 31st December

| | 19X7 | 19X8 |
|---|---|---|
| | £000 | £000 |
| Sales | 2,000 | 3,200 |
| *less:* Cost of goods sold | 1,100 | 1,800 |
| Gross profit | 900 | 1,400 |
| *less:* Trading expenses | 450 | 550 |
| Trading profit | 450 | 850 |
| *less:* Debenture interest | 25 | 25 |
| Net profit before taxation | 425 | 825 |
| *less:* Corporation tax | 160 | 320 |
| Net profit after taxation | 265 | 505 |
| *less:* Ordinary dividends | 125 | 175 |
| Undistributed profit for year | 140 | 330 |

(continued)

## Balance Sheet as at 31st December

| | 19X7 £000 | 19X8 £000 |
|---|---|---|
| Sources of capital: | | |
| Ordinary share capital | | |
| authorised and issued (£1 shares) | 500 | 500 |
| Undistributed profits | 350 | 680 |
| | 850 | 1,180 |
| 10% debentures | 250 | 110 |
| | 1,100 | 1,290 |

| | 19X7 £000 | 19X7 £000 | 19X7 £000 | 19X8 £000 | 19X8 £000 | 19X8 £000 |
|---|---|---|---|---|---|---|
| Uses of capital: | | | | | | |
| Fixed assets at cost | | | 1,000 | | | 1,400 |
| *less:* Depreciation | | | 200 | | | 250 |
| | | | 800 | | | 1,150 |
| Current assets: | | | | | | |
| Stock | 400 | | | 550 | | |
| Debtors | 250 | | | 350 | | |
| Cash | 80 | | | — | | |
| | | 730 | | | 900 | |
| *less:* Current liabilities: | | | | | | |
| Creditors | 145 | | | 200 | | |
| Taxation | 160 | | | 320 | | |
| Proposed dividends | 125 | | | 175 | | |
| Bank overdraft | — | | | 65 | | |
| | | 430 | | | 760 | |
| | | | 300 | | | 140 |
| | | | 1,100 | | | 1,290 |

*You are required to:*

(a) calculate six accounting ratios—for both 19X7 and 19X8—which you feel would be of particular value in assessing the profitability and liquidity performance of Spark Ltd;

(b) comment on the current position of Spark Ltd, with the aid of the accounting ratios previously selected, and any other information you consider to be relevant.

(20 marks)

## 108 Northern Manufacturers Ltd

The following are financial statements provided by Northern Manufacturers Ltd:

Comparative Statements of Profit and Loss

| | 19X4 | 19X5 |
|---|---|---|
| | £ | £ |
| Gross sales | 1,091,400 | 1,604,125 |
| *less:* Discounts | 21,400 | 39,125 |
| | £1,070,000 | £1,565,000 |
| Cost of goods sold: | | |
| Opening inventory | 50,500 | 65,000 |
| Raw materials | 225,000 | 293,000 |
| Direct labour | 485,000 | 795,000 |
| Factory overhead | 64,000 | 117,000 |
| Depreciation | 50,000 | 60,000 |
| Closing inventory | (65,000) | (105,000) |
| | £809,500 | £1,225,000 |
| Gross margin | 260,500 | 340,000 |
| Selling expenses | 84,500 | 121,000 |
| General and administrative expenses | 64,930 | 73,310 |
| | £111,070 | £145,690 |
| Other income (expenses) | (20,000) | 5,675 |
| Tax | 40,982 | 68,114 |
| Net profit | £50,088 | £83,251 |

Reconciliation of Surplus

| | 19X4 | 19X5 |
|---|---|---|
| | £ | £ |
| Earned surplus | 90,912 | 116,000 |
| *plus:* Net profit | 50,088 | 83,251 |
| | 141,000 | 199,251 |
| *less:* Dividends | 5,000 | 15,000 |
| Application to reserve for asset replacement | 20,000 | 25,000 |
| Balance | £116,000 | £159,251 |

Comparative Balance Sheets

| | 19X4 | 19X5 |
|---|---|---|
| | £ | £ |
| Current assets: | | |
| Cash | 1,000 | 11,500 |
| Debtors | 52,500 | 95,000 |
| Inventory | 65,000 | 105,000 |
| Prepaid expenses | 4,000 | 6,000 |
| | 122,500 | 217,500 |
| Fixed assets | 485,000 | 544,000 |
| *less:* Depreciation | 342,000 | 402,000 |
| | 143,000 | 142,000 |
| Other assets | 20,000 | 15,000 |
| Goodwill | 50,000 | 50,000 |
| | £335,500 | £424,500 |
| Current liabilities: | | |
| Creditors | 35,000 | 78,000 |
| Bank overdraft | 16,000 | — |
| Accrued expenses | 40,000 | 60,750 |
| Dividends payable | 2,000 | 3,000 |
| Taxes due | 1,500 | 6,499 |
| | 94,500 | 148,249 |
| Bills of exchange | 40,000 | — |
| Provision for claims | 10,000 | 10,000 |
| Reserve for asset replacement | 40,000 | 65,000 |
| | 90,000 | 75,000 |
| Net worth: | | |
| Preference shares | 4,000 | 4,000 |
| Ordinary shares | 26,000 | 28,000 |
| Capital surplus | 5,000 | 10,000 |
| Earned surplus | 116,000 | 159,251 |
| | 151,000 | 201,251 |
| | £335,500 | £424,500 |

Northern Manufacturers Ltd is seeking additional finance which your company is considering providing.

*You are required:*

(a) using ratio analysis, to advise your company; and

(b) to state, with reasons, what additional statements you would ask for.

(20 marks)

## 109 Go-Go Products Ltd and Numerous Inventions Ltd

The following is an extract from *Accountancy*, March 1977, p. 50:

> Take profit before tax divided by current liabilities; current assets as a proportion of total liabilities; current liabilities as a proportion of tangible assets; take into account the no-credit interval; mix them in the right proportions and you can tell whether a company will go bust.

The no-credit interval is defined as (current assets − current liabilities) ÷ (operating costs excluding depreciation).

The following are the summarised accounts of Go-Go Products Ltd and Numerous Inventions Ltd for the years ended 30th April 19X7 and 19X6:

| | Go-Go Products | | Numerous Inventions | |
|---|---|---|---|---|
| | 19X7 | 19X6 | 19X7 | 19X6 |
| | £ | £ | £ | £ |
| Turnover | 30,067 | 25,417 | 9,734 | 8,044 |
| | | | | |
| Costs: Depreciation | 311 | 284 | 331 | 195 |
| Other | 28,356 | 24,198 | 8,313 | 6,571 |
| Profit before tax | 1,400 | 935 | 1,090 | 1,278 |
| | 30,067 | 25,417 | 9,734 | 8,044 |
| | | | | |
| Intangible assets | 918 | 937 | — | — |
| Fixed assets | 4,644 | 5,228 | 1,950 | 1,530 |
| Stock | 6,243 | 6,773 | 986 | 1,257 |
| Debtors | 4,042 | 4,580 | 3,234 | 2,236 |
| Bank | 516 | 184 | 2,578 | 1,366 |
| | 16,363 | 17,702 | 8,748 | 6,389 |
| | | | | |
| Creditors | 5,261 | 5,144 | 1,297 | 972 |
| Current taxation | 312 | 379 | 483 | 321 |
| Short-term borrowing | 2,357 | 4,447 | 2,577 | 1,174 |
| Long-term loans | 1,409 | 1,168 | 55 | 38 |
| Capital and reserves | 7,024 | 6,564 | 4,336 | 3,884 |
| | £16,363 | £17,702 | £8,748 | £6,389 |

*You are required to:*

(a) calculate three of the stated factors for the two companies and two others you consider relevant to their going-concern status;

(15 marks)

(b) compare the two companies stating clearly which of your calculated ratios have moved in an unfavourable direction; and

(5 marks)

(c) describe and discuss the limitations of ratio analysis as a predictor of failure.

(5 marks)
(Total 25 marks)

## 110 General interpretation

*You are required* to give your interpretation of the following, which has been extracted from the published accounts of a company whose year ends on 31st March. Where possible, your comments should be supported by ratios and grouped under the following "user" groups: management, shareholders, creditors and employees. You may assume that prices have remained stable over the four-year period, advance corporation tax payable on proposed dividends is included with current tax and advance corporation tax recoverable on proposed dividends is included in debtors.

| Year | 1 | 2 | 3 | 4 |
|---|---|---|---|---|
| | £000 | £000 | £000 | £000 |
| Sales | 220,000 | 240,000 | 260,000 | 280,000 |
| Profit before tax | 28,000 | 32,600 | 32,360 | 38,450 |
| After charging: | | | | |
| Directors' emoluments | 560 | 560 | 570 | 580 |
| Depreciation | 18,000 | 14,800 | 12,240 | 12,554 |
| And crediting: | | | | |
| Gross dividends | 2,000 | 4,200 | 5,600 | 8,000 |
| Profit on sale of plant | — | — | — | 8,000 |
| Taxation on profits | 13,000 | 14,200 | 13,380 | 11,200 |
| Taxation on dividends | 600 | 1,260 | 1,680 | 2,400 |
| Profit after tax | 14,400 | 17,140 | 17,300 | 24,850 |
| Employee remuneration | 33,000 | 37,000 | 41,000 | 44,000 |
| Assets employed: | | | | |
| Leasehold property, at cost | 20,000 | 20,000 | 20,000 | 20,000 |
| Depreciation | 4,000 | 6,000 | 8,000 | 10,000 |
| | 16,000 | 14,000 | 12,000 | 10,000 |
| Plant and machinery, at cost | 100,000 | 100,000 | 100,000 | 100,000 |
| Depreciation | 36,000 | 48,800 | 59,040 | 57,786 |
| | 64,000 | 51,200 | 40,960 | 42,214 |
| Total fixed assets | 80,000 | 65,200 | 52,960 | 52,214 |
| Investment at cost | 20,000 | 40,000 | 50,000 | 70,000 |
| Sub-total | 100,000 | 105,200 | 102,960 | 122,214 |

*continued*

*continued*

| | Year 1 | 2 | 3 | 4 |
|---|---|---|---|---|
| | £000 | £000 | £000 | £000 |
| Current assets: | | | | |
| Stock | 48,210 | 55,800 | 65,600 | 73,700 |
| Debtors | 36,670 | 44,780 | 53,850 | 62,890 |
| Cash | 18,720 | 15,290 | 10,510 | 1,246 |
| | 103,600 | 115,870 | 129,960 | 137,836 |
| Current liabilities: | | | | |
| Trade creditors | 28,600 | 38,700 | 49,500 | 66,300 |
| Current tax | 13,000 | 15,230 | 13,380 | 13,260 |
| Proposed dividends | 12,000 | 14,400 | 14,400 | 18,000 |
| | 53,600 | 68,330 | 77,280 | 97,560 |
| Net current assets | 50,000 | 47,540 | 52,680 | 40,276 |
| | 150,000 | 152,740 | 155,640 | 162,490 |
| Share capital | 120,000 | 120,000 | 120,000 | 120,000 |
| Reserves | 30,000 | 32,740 | 35,640 | 42,490 |
| | £150,000 | £152,740 | £155,640 | £162,490 |
| Number of employees | 16,000 | 18,000 | 20,000 | 22,000 |

(30 marks)

## 12 INFLATION ACCOUNTING

### 111 Monetary and non-monetary items

(a) Explain the difference between monetary items and non-monetary items, indicating clearly why in all systems of inflation accounting they are treated differently.

(b) Identify the following items as monetary or non-monetary, and explain how each would be treated in (i) current purchasing power accounting (CPP); (ii) current cost accounting (CCA):

stock in trade (opening and closing);
debentures;
depreciation.

(16 marks)

## 112 Nimbus Ltd

The following information relates to Nimbus Ltd:

Summarised Balance Sheets

| | As on 30th June 19X7 | | As on 30th June 19X8 | |
|---|---|---|---|---|
| | £000 | £000 | £000 | £000 |
| Fixed asset at cost | | 600 | | 600 |
| *less:* Depreciation | | 270 | | 360 |
| | | 330 | | 240 |
| Net current assets: | | | | |
| Stock at cost | 150 | | 235 | |
| Debtors | 120 | | 160 | |
| Cash | 70 | | 120 | |
| | 340 | | 515 | |
| *less:* Creditors | 90 | | 80 | |
| | | 250 | | 435 |
| | | 580 | | 675 |
| Financed by: | | | | |
| Ordinary shares | | 100 | | 100 |
| Reserves | | 200 | | 295 |
| 10% loan stock | | 280 | | 280 |
| | | 580 | | 675 |

Summarised Trading and Profit and Loss Account
for the year ended 30th June 19X8

| | £000 | £000 |
|---|---|---|
| Sales | | 1,300 |
| Cost of sales: | | |
| Opening stock | 150 | |
| Purchases | 1,040 | |
| | 1,190 | |
| *less:* Closing stock | 235 | |
| | | 955 |
| Gross profit | | 345 |
| Expenses (excluding interest) | 132 | |
| Interest | 28 | |
| Depreciation | 90 | |
| | | 250 |
| | | 95 |

*Notes:*

(1) There was only one fixed asset which was purchased on 1st July 19X4. To purchase the same asset new on 30th June 19X8 would cost £987,500, while its replacement cost on 30th June 19X7 was £812,500.

(2) Transactions occur evenly throughout the year.

(3) On average stock was acquired three months before the year end.

(4) The price index for the stock at the end of each month was as follows:

| | | |
|---|---|---|
| March | 19X7 — | 115 |
| April | 19X7 — | 120 |
| June | 19X7 — | 126 |
| Dec. | 19X7 — | 138 |
| March | 19X8 — | 141 |
| April | 19X8 — | 145 |
| June | 19X8 — | 147 |

Average for the year ended 30th June 19X8: 138.

(5) The retail price index was 130 on 30th June 19X7 and 156 on 30th June 19X8. You may assume that the index rose evenly during the year.

*You are required* to prepare a current cost profit and loss account and balance sheet for Nimbus Ltd in respect of the year ended 30th June 19X8 in accordance with SSAP 16.

(35 marks)

### 113 Current cost accounting adjustments

In current cost accounting as proposed in SSAP 16 the following main adjustments to the profit shown by the historical cost accounts are required:

(a) cost of sales adjustment;

(b) depreciation adjustment;

(c) monetary working capital adjustment;

(d) gearing adjustment.

*You are required* to explain the purpose and normal method of calculating each adjustment for a trading concern.

(20 marks)

## 13 CONSOLIDATION OF FOREIGN SUBSIDIARIES

### 114 Rostov Ltd

Rostov Limited purchased the whole of the share capital of a French company, Oublier SA on 1st January 19X1. The agreed price of £55,000 was paid in cash. Fixed assets and stocks of Oublier were revalued for the purpose of the acquisition and the current valuations have been included in the balance sheet on 1st January 19X1:

Oublier SA

Balance Sheet on 1st January 19X1

| | French francs |
|---|---|
| Share capital | 100,000 |
| Revaluation reserve | 40,000 |
| Retained profits | 130,000 |
| | 270,000 |
| | |
| Fixed assets (at current value): | |
| Premises | 280,000 |
| Machinery | 100,000 |
| | 380,000 |
| Net current assets (at current value) | 40,000 |
| | 420,000 |
| *less:* Long-term loan | 150,000 |
| | 270,000 |

The summarised accounts for 19X1 of Rostov and Oublier are as follows:

Summarised Profit and Loss Accounts

| | Rostov | | Oublier | |
|---|---|---|---|---|
| | £000 | £000 | Fr000 | Fr000 |
| Operating profit before depreciation | | 72 | | 50 |
| *less:* Depreciation: Premises | 2 | | 4 | |
| Machinery | 16 | 18 | 12 | 16 |
| Profit before taxation | | 54 | | 34 |
| *less:* Taxation | | 21 | | 10 |
| | | 33 | | 24 |
| *add:* Retained profits brought forward | | 152 | | 130 |
| Retained profits | | 185 | | 154 |

Summarised Balance Sheets

| | Rostov | | Oublier | |
|---|---|---|---|---|
| | £000 | £000 | Fr000 | Fr000 |
| Share capital | | 200 | | 100 |
| Revaluation reserve | | — | | 40 |
| Retained profits | | 185 | | 154 |
| | | 385 | | 294 |

*continued*

| *continued* | Rostov | | Oublier | |
|---|---|---|---|---|
| | £000 | £000 | Fr000 | Fr000 |
| Fixed assets: | | | | |
| Premises—at cost to group | 300 | | 280 | |
| *less:* Depreciation | 40 | 260 | 4 | 276 |
| Machinery—at cost to group | 180 | | 100 | |
| *less:* Depreciation | 60 | 120 | 12 | 88 |
| | | 380 | | 364 |
| Investment in Oublier—at cost | | 55 | | — |
| Net current assets | | 150 | | 80 |
| | | 585 | | 444 |
| *less:* Long-term liabilities | | 200 | | 150 |
| | | 385 | | 294 |

Relevant rates of exchange are:

| | French francs to £1 |
|---|---|
| 1st January 19X1 | 9 |
| Average for year 19X1 | 10 |
| 31st December 19X1 | 11 |

*You are required:*

(a) To prepare a set of consolidated accounts for Rostov and its subsidiary Oublier using the *temporal* method of translation. (Stocks included in the net current assets of Oublier on 31st December 19X1 may be translated at the closing rate of exchange.)

(15 marks)

(b) To prepare a set of consolidated accounts for Rostov and its subsidiary using the *closing rate* method of translation. Follow the provisions of ED 27 and, in particular, use the average rate of exchange for translation of the profit and loss account.

(15 marks)

Work to the nearest £1 in so far as this is possible.

*Note:*
It is suggested that you calculate the goodwill on consolidation at the date of acquisition and confirm that this is the figure which appears in your consolidated balance sheets prepared in answer to (a) and (b).

## 115 Zhdanov Ltd

Zhdanov Limited is a UK company which makes up its accounts annually to 31st December. In September 19X2 it raised the following long-term loans:

| | |
|---|---|
| In Germany | 500,000 deutschmarks |
| In France | 1,000,000 francs |

On the date the loans were raised rates of exchange were 5 deutschmarks to £1 and 10 francs to £1 respectively.

The proceeds of the above loans were used to acquire a wholly owned French subsidiary, Vairon SA, at a cost of £200,000. At the date of acquisition the share capital and reserves of Vairon SA were 1,000,000 francs and 400,000 francs respectively while the rate of exchange was 10 francs to £1.

Summarised accounts of Zhdanov Limited and Vairon SA for the year to 31st December 19X5 are as follows:

Summarised Profit and Loss Accounts
for the year ended 31st December 19X5

| | Zhdanov | Vairon |
|---|---|---|
| | £ | francs |
| Operating profit | 270,300 | 160,000 |
| *less:* Taxation | 130,100 | 40,000 |
| | 140,200 | 120,000 |
| *less:* Dividends | 75,000 | — |
| | 65,200 | 120,000 |

Summarised Balance Sheets on 31st December 19X5

| | Zhdanov | Vairon |
|---|---|---|
| | £ | francs |
| Share capital | 500,000 | 1,000,000 |
| Reserves | 588,000 | 610,000 |
| | 1,088,000 | 1,610,000 |
| Long-term loans: | | |
| German loan (500,000 deutschmarks) | 108,696 | |
| French loan (1,000,000 francs) | 105,263 | |
| Others | 300,000 | 200,000 |
| | 1,601,959 | 1,810,000 |
| Fixed assets—at cost *less* depreciation | 730,300 | 890,000 |
| Investment in Vairon SA—at cost | 200,000 | — |
| Net current assets | 671,659 | 920,000 |
| | 1,601,959 | 1,810,000 |

In the summarised balance sheet of Zhdanov Limited the German and French loans are shown at the amounts at which they were translated on 31st December 19X4, namely:

| | |
|---|---|
| German loan | 500,000 deutschmarks at 4.6 deutschmarks to £1 |
| French loan | 1,000,000 francs at 9.5 francs to £1 |

Exchange rates have moved as follows:

| | Deutschmarks to £1 | Francs to £1 |
|---|---|---|
| 1st January 19X5 | 4.6 | 9.5 |
| 31st December 19X5 | 4.0 | 9.0 |
| Average for year to 31st December 19X5 | 4.3 | 9.3 |

The directors of Zhdanov Limited wish to prepare consolidated accounts for 19X5 using the closing rate method as proposed by Exposure Draft 27.

*You are required to:*

(a) Explain clearly the treatment of exchange differences on foreign loans used to finance equity investments in foreign subsidiaries or associated companies.

(5 marks)

(b) Translate the summarised account of Vairon SA using the closing rate method as preliminary to consolidation.

(10 marks)

(*Note:* You are advised to (i) translate share capital and pre-acquisition reserves at the historic rate to maintain goodwill on consolidation at its "cost"; (ii) translate post-acquisition reserves on 1st January 19X5 in a manner consistent with the figure used in preparing the consolidated accounts for the previous year.)

(c) Prepare the summarised consolidated accounts for 19X5 of Zhdanov Limited and its subsidiary Vairon SA, using the cover method of treating differences on long-term loans to the extent permitted by ED 27.

(15 marks)
(Total 30 marks)

Work to nearest £1.

APPENDIX THREE

# Suggested Answers to Examination Questions

## 1 COMPANY ACCOUNTS—PUBLISHED ACCOUNTS

### 1 Profit and loss account disclosure

(a) Distribution costs

(b) Administration expenses

(c) Depreciation

(d) Interest payable, distinguishing between interest on:

loans, including bank loans repayable within five years;

other loans

(e) Auditors' remuneration, including expenses

(f) Taxation

(g) Charge for hire of plant and machinery

(h) Rent receivable, less outgoings, if substantial

### 2 Balance sheet disclosure

(a) *Goodwill*
Goodwill may only appear in the balance sheet if it was originally purchased. It is shown separately under the subheading "intangible assets" which in turn appears under "fixed assets".

The cost and aggregate depreciation must be shown, with details of additions and disposals during the year.

The period over which it is being written off must be disclosed, with the directors' reasons for choosing that period.

(b) *Investments*

(i) A heading "investments" appears under both "fixed assets" and "current assets" in the statutory formats.

(ii) "Fixed asset" type investments must be classified into:

shares in group companies;

loans to group companies;

shares in related companies (i.e. companies in which 20 per cent or more of the voting share capital is held);

loans to related companies;

other investments other than loans;

other loans;

own shares (nominal value must be disclosed).

(iii) "Current asset" type investments must be classified into:

shares in group companies;

own shares (nominal value must be disclosed);

other investments.

(iv) For both fixed and current asset investments there must be shown:

total listed investments and their market value.

(v) If the investment in any one company exceeds:

10 per cent of its allotted equity capital, or

10 per cent of its allotted total capital, or

10 per cent of the total assets of the investing company,

then there must be disclosed:

name of company;

country of incorporation if outside Great Britain;

description and proportion of nominal value of allotted shares held.

(vi) If the investment in any one company exceeds 20 per cent of the allotted share capital of that company, there must also be disclosed:

its aggregate share capital and reserves in its latest accounts;

its latest profit or loss.

The details shown in (vi) are not required if the investment is valued on the equity basis or if the company is included in the reporting company's group accounts.

(c) *Stock*
Stock must be shown analysed under three headings:

(i) Raw materials and consumables.

(ii) Work in progress.

(iii) Finished goods and goods for resale.

Payments on account must also be disclosed separately, probably as a deduction from (say) work in progress.

The basis of valuation must be shown. Permissible methods of valuation are:

FIFO;

LIFO (unlikely to be used in view of SSAP 9);

weighted average;

any other similar method.

Any material difference between the stock as valued and replacement cost must also be disclosed.

(d) *Creditors*
The term "creditors" appears as a main heading in the formats.

Primary separation is between amounts falling due within one year and amounts falling due after more than one year. Those due within one year are deducted from current assets in Format 1 while the others are grouped with share capital and reserves.

Within each group, a further analysis is required so as to show separately:

Debenture loans (with separate details of any convertible loans).

Bank loans and overdrafts.

Payments received on account (insofar as not shown as deduction from stocks).

Trade creditors.

Bills of exchange payable.

Amounts owed to group companies.

Amounts owed to related companies.

Other creditors (including, separately detailed, taxation and social security).

Accruals and deferred income.

The aggregate amount of secured liabilities must be disclosed, with an indication of the general nature of the security given.

Where creditors are due after more than five years, the aggregate amount must be given, with repayment terms and rate of interest.

The proposed dividend must also be shown separately.
Arrears of cumulative preference dividend must be shown by note.

(e) *Share capital*

(i) Authorised capital.

(ii) Number and aggregate nominal value of allotted shares of each class, showing separately amount paid up.

(iii) Redeemable shares:

earliest and latest date of redemption;

whether redemption mandatory or at the company's option;

details of any premium on redemption.

(iv) Shares allotted during the year:

reasons for allotment;

number, nominal value and class of shares allotted;

consideration received.

(v) Details of any contingent rights to the allotment of shares.

(vi) Called-up share capital not paid.

## 3 Directors' report

Any twelve from:

| | | *Statutory references* |
|---|---|---|
| (a) | A fair review of the development of the business of the company and its subsidiaries during the financial year ending with the balance sheet date and of their position at the end of it. | s. 13 CA 1981 |
| (b) | Proposed dividend. | s. 157 CA 1948 |
| (c) | Proposed transfers to reserves. | s. 157 CA 1948 |
| (d) | Names of directors who held office at any time in the period. | s. 16 CA 1967 |
| (e) | Principal activities of the company and its subsidiaries and any significant changes in those activities. | s. 16 CA 1967 |
| (f) | Details of significant changes in fixed assets of the company or its subsidiaries. | s. 16 CA 1967 |
| (g) | Indication of difference between book and market value of land and buildings of company (or any of its subsidiaries) if significant. | s. 16 CA 1967 |

*continued*

*continued*

| | *Statutory references* |
|---|---|
| (h) Details of significant contracts with the company in which director interested. | s. 16 CA 1967 |
| (i) Directors' interests in shares or debentures of group companies at beginning of period (or later date of appointment) and at end of period. (This information may now be given by note to the accounts (s. 13(4) CA 1981).) | s. 16 CA 1967 |
| (j) Particulars of any important events affecting the company or any of its subsidiaries which have occurred since the end of that year. | s. 13 CA 1981 |
| (k) An indication of likely future developments in the business of the company and of its subsidiaries. | s. 13 CA 1981 |
| (l) An indication of the activities (if any) of the company and its subsidiaries in the field of research and development. | s. 13 CA 1981 |
| (m) Details of any acquisition by the company of its own shares, including acquisition by forfeiture and acquisition by nominees. | |
| The full details required are:<br>(i) number and nominal value of shares acquired in any way, the aggregate consideration paid and the reasons for purchase;<br>(ii) number and nominal value of shares charged, and the amount of the charge;<br>(iii) maximum number and nominal value of shares held during the year;<br>(iv) number and nominal value of shares held which were disposed of during the year, and the amount of consideration for the sale in each case;<br>(v) for all disclosures (i) to (iv) above, the percentage of called-up share capital involved. | s. 14 CA 1981 introducing s. 16A CA 1967 |
| (n) Totals of UK political and charitable contributions of the company (or, if any made by subsidiaries, of the group), unless together not more than £200. The amount and name of political party or person paid must be disclosed for each political contribution over £200. Wholly owned subsidiaries of UK companies are exempt. | s. 19 CA 1967 |

*continued*

*continued* | *Statutory references*

(o) Report on employment policy. Companies with 250 or more employees must include a statement as to the company's policy for the employment, training, career development and promotion of disabled people. —

## 4 Small and medium-sized companies

(a) A company is small or medium-sized for the purpose of determining eligibility for the CA 1981 disclosure exemptions if in the year under review and the preceding year it meets any two of the following three requirements:

| | *Small* | *Medium-sized* |
|---|---|---|
| Turnover | Not over £1.4m | Not over £5.75m |
| Balance sheet total | Not over £0.7m | Not over £2.8m |
| Average number of employees | Not over 50 | Not over 250 |

Certain companies cannot qualify for the exemptions:

(i) public companies;

(ii) banking, insurance or shipping companies (remember that they remain subject to the old disclosure requirements and are entitled to the exemptions given to them by those requirements);

(iii) members of an "ineligible group". (A group is ineligible if any of its members is within categories (i) or (ii) above, or if the group includes a body corporate (other than a company) which may issue shares or debentures to the public or operate as a banking or insurance company.)

(b) False. Only the accounts lodged with the Registrar are modified.

(c) (i) *The exemptions for small companies (s. 6)*
The exemptions for small companies are pretty extensive—they need to submit to the Registrar:

(1) A modified balance sheet (consisting of total figures for headings with Roman numerals I, II, III etc. in pro formas).

(2) No profit and loss account.

(3) Notes to the balance sheet on the following matters only:

accounting policies;

share capital;

allotments of shares;

analysis of creditors and indication as to whether secured;

analysis of debtors falling due after more than one year;

basis of translating foreign currency;

comparative figures.

(4) No details of directors'/employees' remuneration under s. 196 CA 1948 and ss. 6, 7 and 8 CA 1967.

(5) No director's report.

(ii) *The exemptions for medium-sized companies (s. 6)*
The exemptions for medium-sized companies are rather modest:

(1) No turnover figure need be given.

(2) Certain items in the profit and loss account can be ignored:

in Format 1: items 1, 2, 3, 6

in Format 2: items 1 to 5

in Format 3: items A1, B1, B2

in Format 4: items A1, A2, B1 to B4.

## 5 Radical plc

Balance Sheet 30th September 19X4 (using Format 1)

| | *Notes* | £ |
|---|---|---|
| Fixed assets: | | |
| Tangible assets | 2 | 336,265 |
| Investments: | | |
| Shares in related companies | 3(a) | 10,000 |
| | | 346,265 |
| Current assets: | | |
| Stocks | 4 | 192,734 |
| Debtors | 5 | 161,980 |
| Investments | 3(b) | 12,632 |
| Cash at bank and in hand | | 44,881 |
| | | 412,227 |
| Prepayments and accrued income: | | |
| Advance corporation tax recoverable after more than one year (see Working) | | 12,313 |
| | | 424,540 |
| Creditors: amounts falling due within one year | 6 | 118,763 |
| Net current assets | | 305,777 |
| Total assets less current liabilities | | £652,042 |

*continued*

*continued*

| | *Notes* | £ |
|---|---|---|
| Creditors: amounts falling due after more than one year | 7 | 160,000 |
| Capital and reserves: | | |
| Called-up share capital | 8 | 350,000 |
| Share premium account | 9 | 52,400 |
| Profit and loss account | 9 | 89,642 |
| | | £652,042 |

*Notes*

(1) Accounting policies:
*Stocks*. The basis of valuation of all stock items is first in first out (FIFO) (other policies not detailed).

(2) Tangible assets:

| | Freehold land and buildings | Plant and machinery | Fixtures and fittings | Buildings in course of construction | Total |
|---|---|---|---|---|---|
| | £ | £ | £ | £ | £ |
| Cost: | | | | | |
| As at 1st October 19X3 | 105,000 | 300,745 | 65,600 | — | 471,345 |
| Additions | — | 40,450 | — | 26,000 | 66,450 |
| As at 30th September 19X4 | 105,000 | 341,195 | 65,600 | 26,000 | 537,795 |
| Depreciation: | | | | | |
| As at 1st October 19X3 | ? | ? | ? | — | ? |
| Provided during year | ? | ? | ? | — | ? |
| As at 30th September 19X4 | 5,000 | 165,230 | 31,300 | — | 201,530 |
| Net book amounts at: | | | | | |
| 30th September 19X4 | 100,000 | 175,965 | 34,300 | 26,000 | 336,265 |
| 30th September 19X3 | ? | ? | ? | ? | ? |

(3) Investments:

(a) The shares in related companies are held in Redfire Ltd and are shown at cost. The company holds 10,000 £1 ordinary shares, being 25 per cent of the allotted share capital of Redfire Ltd.

At 30th June 19X4 the share capital and reserves of Redfire Ltd amounted to £73,000. Its profit for the year ended on that date was £18,000.

(b) The investments included under current assets are shown at cost. All are listed and they had a market value at 30th September 19X4 of £19,856. There were no purchases or sales of investments during the year.

Taxation on potential capital gain if all investments sold at valuation: £14,000.

(4) Stocks:

| Stock consisted of: | £ |
|---|---|
| Raw materials and consumables | 63,606 |
| Work in progress | 27,104 |
| Finished goods and goods for resale | 102,024 |
| | 192,734 |

(5) Debtors:

| | |
|---|---|
| Trade debtors | 149,230 |
| Prepayments and accrued income | 12,750 |
| | 161,980 |

(6) Creditors: amounts falling due within one year:

| | |
|---|---|
| Trade creditors | 64,700 |
| Taxation and social security (*see* Working) | 29,063 |
| Proposed ordinary dividend | 25,000 |
| | 118,763 |

(7) Creditors: amounts falling due after more than one year:

| | |
|---|---|
| Debenture loans: | |
| $9\frac{1}{2}$ per cent unsecured loan stock repayable on 1st October 19Y9 | 150,000 |
| Taxation | 10,000 |
| | 160,000 |

(8) Called-up share capital:

| | |
|---|---|
| Authorised, allotted, issued and fully paid: | |
| 1,000,000 ordinary shares of 25p each | 250,000 |
| 200,000 8 per cent cumulative preference shares | 100,000 |
| | 350,000 |

(9) Reserves:
Movements on reserves during the year would have been shown if the information had been provided.

(10) Capital commitments:
The company has entered into a contract for the erection of a new factory extension. The balance payable is estimated at £49,000.

**Working**

| Taxation | £ |
|---|---|
| Corporation tax payable 1st January 19X6 | 16,750 |
| Advance corporation tax $\frac{33}{67}$ × £25,000 | 12,313 |
| | 29,063 |

## 6 Thermal Ltd

(a) Profit and Loss Account
year ended 31st December 19X0
(using Format 1)

| | Notes | £ | £ |
|---|---|---|---|
| Turnover | | | 450,096 |
| Cost of sales | 1 | | 289,625 |
| Gross profit | | | 160,471 |
| Distribution costs (*see* Working 1) | 1 | 57,029 | |
| Administrative expenses (*see* Working 1) | 1 | 76,340 | 133,369 |
| | | | 27,102 |
| Interest receivable and similar income (*see* Working 2) | 3 | | 1,520 |
| | | | 28,622 |
| Interest payable (on loan not repayable within five years) | | | 600 |
| Profit on ordinary activities before taxation | 1 | | 28,022 |
| Tax on profit on ordinary activities (*see* Working 3) | | | 8,079 |
| Profit on ordinary activities after taxation | | | 19,943 |
| Dividends | | | |
| Preference | | 3,500 | |
| Ordinary—proposed | | 10,500 | 14,000 |
| Retained profit for year | | | £5,943 |

Balance Sheet at 31st December 19X0
(using Format 1)

| | Note | £ |
|---|---|---|
| Fixed assets: | | |
| Tangible assets | 4 | 74,380 |
| Current assets: | | |
| Stocks | 5 | 61,496 |
| Debtors | 6 | 112,407 |
| Investments | 7 | 14,000 |
| Cash at bank and in hand | | 103,787 |
| | | 291,690 |
| Prepayments and accrued income: | | |
| Advance corporation tax recoverable after more than one year | | 4,500 |
| | | 296,190 |
| Creditors: amounts falling due within one year | 8 | (96,000) |
| Net current assets | | 200,190 |
| Total assets *less* current liabilities | | £274,570 |

*continued*

*continued*

| | Notes | £ |
|---|---|---|
| Creditors: amounts falling due after more than one year | 9 | 16,579 |
| Capital and reserves: | | |
| Called-up share capital | 10 | 150,000 |
| Share premium account | 11 | 25,000 |
| Profit and loss account | 11 | 82,991 |
| | | £274,570 |

*Notes*

(Accounting policies note not given as information not in question.)

(1) Profit on ordinary activities:
Profit on ordinary activities before taxation includes the following expenses which have been charged where appropriate in computing cost of sales, distribution costs and administrative expenses:

| | £ |
|---|---|
| Directors' remuneration (*see* Note 2) | 49,651 |
| Auditors' remuneration | 420 |
| Depreciation | 5,478 |
| Interest payable | 600 |
| Staff costs (separate social security and pension figures not shown) | 69,816 (*see* Working 1) |

(2) Directors' remuneration:

| | £ |
|---|---|
| Remuneration | 49,151 |
| Pension to widow of former director | 500 |
| | 49,651 |

Your chairman's remuneration amounted to £26,000.
One other director received remuneration in the range £20,001 to £25,000.

(3) Interest receivable and similar income:

| | £ |
|---|---|
| Income from investments: | |
| Listed | 920 |
| Unlisted | 600 |
| | 1,520 |

(4) Tangible assets:

| | Freehold land and buildings £ | Plant and machinery £ | Fixtures and fittings £ | Total £ |
|---|---|---|---|---|
| Cost: | | | | |
| As at 1st January 19X0 | 64,000 | 20,500 | 8,600 | 93,100 |
| As at 31st December 19X0 | 64,000 | 20,500 | 8,600 | 93,100 |

*continued*

*continued*

| | Freehold land and buildings | Plant and machinery | Fixtures and fittings | Total |
|---|---|---|---|---|
| | £ | £ | £ | £ |
| Depreciation: | | | | |
| As at 1st January 19X0 | Nil | 8,912 | 4,330 | 13,242 |
| Provided during year | Nil | 5,048 | 430 | 5,478 |
| As at 31st December 19X0 | Nil | 13,960 | 4,760 | 18,720 |
| Net book amounts at: | | | | |
| 31st December 19X0 | 64,000 | 6,540 | 3,840 | 74,380 |
| 1st January 19X0 | 64,000 | 11,588 | 4,270 | 79,858 |

(5) Stocks:

Stocks consist of:

| | £ |
|---|---|
| Raw materials and consumables | 16,380 |
| Work in progress | 4,197 |
| Finished goods | 40,919 |
| | 61,496 |

(6) Debtors:

| | £ |
|---|---|
| Trade debtors | 109,402 |
| Prepayments and accrued income | 3,005 |
| | 112,407 |

(7) Investments:

The investments, all listed, are shown in the balance sheet at cost, and had a market value at 31st December 19X0 of £18,369. There were no purchases or sales of investments during the year.

(8) Creditors: amounts falling due within one year:

| | £ |
|---|---|
| Trade creditors | 61,433 |
| Taxation and social security | 24,067 |
| Proposed ordinary dividend | 10,500 |
| | 96,000 |

(9) Creditors: amounts falling due after more than one year:

| | £ |
|---|---|
| Debenture loans: 6% debentures 2002 | 10,000 |
| Taxation (*see* Working 4) | 6,579 |
| | 16,579 |

(10) Called-up share capital:

| | Authorised | Allotted, issued and fully paid |
|---|---|---|
| | £ | £ |
| 7% preference shares of £1 each | 100,000 | 50,000 |
| Ordinary shares of 50p each | 150,000 | 100,000 |
| | 250,000 | 150,000 |

(11) Reserves:

| | Share premium account | Profit and loss account |
|---|---|---|
| | £ | £ |
| At 1st January 19X0 | 25,000 | 77,048 |
| Retained profit for year | | 5,943 |
| At 31st December 19X0 | 25,000 | 82,991 |

(12) Capital commitments:
At 31st December 19X0 the company had entered into a contract for the construction of a new warehouse estimated to cost £30,000.

(13) The company's ultimate holding company is Heating PLC.

Notes giving segmental information regarding turnover and employees would have been added if the question had given the information.

## Workings

(1) Distribution costs and administrative expenses:

| | Distribution costs | Administrative expenses |
|---|---|---|
| | £ | £ |
| Office salaries | | 48,358 |
| Establishment expenses | | 17,537 |
| Motor and travel expenses | 41,494 | |
| Depreciation of motor vans | 5,048 | |
| Advertising | 10,487 | |
| General expenses | | 4,625 |
| Audit fee | | 420 |
| Contribution to pension scheme | | 3,496 |
| Pension to widow of former director | | 500 |
| Provision for doubtful debts | | 1,149 |
| Depreciation of fixtures and fittings | | 430 |
| | 57,029 | 76,515 |
| *less:* Rents receivable (not shown separately as not "substantial") | | 175 |
| | 57,029 | 76,340 |

Staff costs are £69,816, being total salaries and wages £118,967 *less* £49,151 included for directors.

(2) Interest receivable and similar income:

| | £ |
|---|---|
| Income from: Listed investments £644 × $\frac{10}{7}$ | 920 |
| Unlisted investments £420 × $\frac{10}{7}$ | 600 |
| | 1,520 |

(3) Taxation in profit and loss account:

| | £ |
|---|---|
| Corporation tax per question | 7,623 |
| Tax attributable to investment income: £920 + £600 = £1,520 at 30% | 456 |
| | 8,079 |

(4) Taxation in balance sheet:

| | £ |
|---|---|
| As per draft accounts | 26,146 |
| *less:* Charge for year ended 31st December 19X0 | 7,623 |
| | 18,523 |
| ACT due | 1,044 |
| ACT on proposed dividend $\frac{3}{7}$ × £10,500 | 4,500 |
| Due within one year | 24,067 |
| Due after more than one year as above | 7,623 |
| *less:* ACT | 1,044 |
| | 6,579 |

(b) If the company claimed the right to lodge modified accounts with the Registrar, there would be the following changes to the accounts presented in (a) above:

(i) The profit and loss account would be omitted entirely.

(ii) The balance sheet as presented would remain the same. All the notes except Note 10 would be omitted and the information in Notes 8 and 9 would be abridged as follows:

Creditors: amounts falling due after more than one year:

The total of £16,579 includes £10,000 repayable more than five years from the balance sheet date.

(iii) The directors would have to state on the face of the balance sheet that they have relied on the exemption for individual accounts on the grounds that the company is a small company.

## 7 Machapuchare Ltd—deferred taxation

(a) *The tax charge for 19X8:*
SSAP 15 basis:

(i) Provide for all short-term timing differences.

(1) General provision for bad debts
5% × 2.65m = £132,500
at 50% = £66,250

Debit: Deferred taxation
Credit: Profit and loss account—tax charge.

(2) Interest receivable £200,000
at 50% = £100,000

Credit: Deferred taxation
Debit: Profit and loss account—tax charge.

(ii) Provide for other timing differences only if a liability is expected to crystallise in the next three accounting periods, or foreseeably thereafter.

Note 5 indicates that no reversal of timing differences is foreseen in relation to stock relief and a provision is not considered necessary.

On plant, however, a total provision needs to be maintained on the deferred taxation account on the timing differences of £1.9m which are expected to reverse in the subsequent accounting period.

No account is taken of the further originating timing differences in the second and third years since (unless the capital allowances are sufficient to result in a tax loss available to be carried back) they will not be available to reduce the tax charge in the first year.

As the total provision required in relation to capital allowances/depreciation (50 per cent × £1.9m = £950,000) exceeds the originating timing difference of the current year and would have been provided for in any event if SSAP 15 had been applicable in previous periods, £950,000 previously charged against revenue brought forward in the deferred tax account, is retained as a provision brought forward on this category of timing difference being released to revenue as a prior year adjustment—provision brought forward no longer considered necessary.

Accordingly, the tax charge for the year would amount to:

| | £ |
|---|---|
| Per Note 6: | |
| CT at 50% on profit for the year | 2,300,000 |
| Deferred taxation (£100,000−£66,250) | 33,750 |
| | 2,333,750 |

(b) *Accounting policies*

(i) Deferred taxation
Provision is made for deferred taxation at the rate of corporation tax ruling at the year end (the liability method), except in respect of any tax reductions which can reasonably be expected to continue for the future. The amounts provided, the full potential liability and the major factors contributing to the reduction in the provision brought forward from previous years are set out in the appropriate notes to the balance sheet.

(ii) Change in accounting policy
The company's accounting policy in respect of deferred taxation has been changed in order to comply with SSAP 15 issued during the year. Previously, full provision was made for deferred taxation regardless of whether the tax reduction was expected to continue. The effect of the change has been to decrease the deferred taxation provision brought forward by £6,625,000 and to increase retained profits brought forward of £9,000,000 by £6,625,000.

(c) *Disclosure requirements*
Balance sheet
The provision made in the accounts for deferred taxation, and the full potential liability, are set out below:

| | Full potential liability £000 | Provision made/ (tax recoverable) £000 |
|---|---|---|
| Accelerated tax allowances on plant (4,825) + (50% × 400) | 5,025 | 950 |
| Stock appreciation relief | 1,250 | — |
| Tax payable if properties were disposed of at their revalued amounts | 1,500 | — |
| General bad debt provision | (66.25) | (66.25) |
| Interest receivable | 100 | 100 |
| | 7,808.75 | 983.75 |

## 8 Value added statement

Group Statement of Value Added for the year ended 19XX

| | £000 | £000 |
|---|---|---|
| Turnover | | 3,129 |
| *less:* Bought-in materials and services (*see* Workings) | | 1,813 |
| | | 1,316 |
| *add:* Royalties | | 30 |
| Group share of profits of associated companies and investment income | | 63 |
| Value added | | 1,409 |

*continued*

*continued*

| | £000 | £000 |
|---|---|---|
| Applied in the following way: | | |
| To pay employees: | | |
| Salaries, wages and pensions | 816 | |
| Profit sharing bonus | 17 | 833 |
| To pay providers of capital: | | |
| Interest on loans | 73 | |
| Dividends to shareholders | 59 | |
| Share of minority interests | 24 | 156 |
| To pay government: | | |
| Taxes on profits | | 125 |
| To provide for maintenance and expansion of assets: | | |
| Depreciation | 182 | |
| Retained profits | 112 | 294 |
| To provide for extraordinary item | | 1 |
| | | 1,409 |

### Workings

| | £000 |
|---|---|
| Bought-in materials and services: | |
| Materials and services used | 1,842 |
| Exchange gain | (29) |
| | 1,813 |

It was suggested in *The Corporate Report*, a discussion paper issued by the Accounting Standards Committee in July 1975, that a statement of added value should be one of the financial statements published annually by companies. It is based on the concept that the activities of a business "add value" to the raw materials and services which are the inputs. The fundamental change in approach compared with the traditional profit statement is to regard wages and salaries as a share of the value added which the employees have helped to create, rather than as a cost to the business. Depreciation is not classified as a cost, but as a retention of value added to provide for the maintenance and expansion of the business.

Value added per employee is an indicator of performance increasingly adopted.

The purpose of a value added statement is to show how the value added generated by a company's activities is shared among those who have contributed to its creation:

employees who contribute their work, remunerated by wages and salaries;

shareholders and lenders who contribute their capital, remunerated by dividend and interest;

the State, which contributes an organised environment in which the company can operate, "remunerated" by taxes.

# 2 STATEMENTS OF STANDARD ACCOUNTING PRACTICE

## 9 Disclosure

(a) (i) *Publicity expenses incurred in opening three new motels*

Having regard to the prudence concept, the immediate write-off of these expenses would be appropriate:

(1) if no further benefit were likely to accrue from the publicity after this first year, or

(2) if it were not possible to quantify the benefit accruing from the publicity in this and subsequent years.

In this particular case, immediate write-off of publicity expenditure is probably justified for the second reason given. Though initial publicity of motels is common "to put them on the map", subsequent bookings by independent motorists are generally made because they can see the motels are there, not because they have been told they are there.

(ii) *Training courses for new staff*

Following the accruals (revenue/cost matching) concept, an attempt should be made to link the cost of staff training to the benefits derived from their subsequent expertise. The turnover of hotel staff is generally rather more frequent than four years. If a proportion of training costs are to be carried forward, it should be linked to the length of time that staff spend in the employment of each hotel.

(b) *Tourist board capital grant*

Though this is not a grant under the Industry Act 1972 (these apply mainly to manufacturing industries in depressed areas), SSAP 4 *The Accounting Treatment of Government Grants* provides some guidelines as to appropriate accounting treatment.

Deduction of the grant from the cost of fixed assets is one of the two accounting treatments recognised by SSAP 4. It has the advantage of simplicity, but distorts the comparability of these assets with similar items for which grants were not provided. This disadvantage is counteracted in the alternative accounting treatment recognised, i.e. credit the grant to a suspense account and write off a proportion of this to profit and loss account each year at the same rate as depreciation is provided. This is not an application of the "accruals" concept, as the income from the grant is not a "profit" or "benefit" but a reduction of cost.

(c) The practice of carrying surpluses and deficits on disposal direct to reserves without passage through the profit and loss account is not recommended in SSAP 6 *Accounting for extraordinary and prior year items.*

Disclosure in the profit and loss account should be recommended in this case, so that shareholders, in examining the accounts, may consider the results of all the company's activities.

It is permissible to carry the surplus on revaluation of the hotels direct to reserves. To maintain consistency of accounting treatment, all hotels should be revalued, and the surplus or deficit on each carried to reserves.

## 10 Research and development

Applying the principles laid down in SSAP 13, research and development expenditure should only be carried forward if it can be matched against probable future profits. All other research and development expenditure should be written off as soon as incurred, except for capital expenditure or the provision of research and development facilities.

The company's policy of writing off one-fifth of all research and development expenditure regardless of the stage reached in development is not to be recommended. It is a requirement of the Companies Act 1981 that research expenditure should always be written off as incurred. If development expenditure is capitalised, the reason for doing so and the period over which it is being written off must be disclosed.

The following analysis indicates the accounting treatment recommended for each class of expenditure.

Analysis of Research and Development Expenditure

| Item | | Accounting treatment Write off | Carry forward | Comments |
|---|---|---|---|---|
| | | £ | £ | |
| Development of specific drugs | £ | | | |
| A | 9,000 | | 9,000 | £5,000 "know-how" capital cost, £4,000 general research (to be matched with revenue in next year). |
| B | 5,000 | 5,000 | | Project abandoned—no further benefits. |
| C | 6,000 | | 6,000 | To be matched with revenue in one to two years. |
| D | 3,000 | 3,000 | | The most prudent accounting treatment. No evidence of when or whether revenue will result from this research. |
| E | 1,000 | 1,000 | | (D and E together) |
| | 24,000 | 9,000 | 15,000 | |
| General testing | 16,000 | 16,000 | | Normal cost of maintaining a competitive position in the drugs market. |
| General research | 15,000 | 15,000 | | Normal cost of remaining a going concern. As results of this research materialise, items will be categorised in the same way as drugs A to E and costs treated accordingly. |
| | 55,000 | 40,000 | 15,000 | |

## 11 SSAP 3

"Basic earnings per share" means the profit in pence attributable to each equity share, based on the consolidated profit of the period after tax and after deducting minority interests and preference dividends, but before taking into account extraordinary items, divided by the number of equity shares in issue and ranking for dividend in respect of the period.

Where a company has at the balance sheet date contracted to issue further shares after the end of the period, or where it has already issued shares which will rank for dividend later, the effect may be to dilute future earnings per share. In addition, therefore, to the basic earnings per share, as set out above, the fully diluted earnings per share should be considered in assessing the worth of the equity shares in the following circumstances:

(a) where the company has issued a separate class of equity shares which do not rank for any dividend in the period under review, but which will do so in the future;

(b) where the company has issued debentures or loan stock (or preference shares) convertible into equity shares of the company;

(c) where the company has granted options or issued warrants to subscribe for equity shares of the company.

(i) Where a quoted company has in issue a class of equity shares not yet ranking for dividend but which will do so in the future (by conversion or otherwise), the fully diluted earnings per share should be calculated on the assumption that this class of shares ranked for dividends from the beginning of the period.

(ii) Where a company has convertible loan stock in issue at any time during the period, the fully diluted earnings per share should be calculated on the assumption that the maximum number of new equity shares had been issued on conversion and that this conversion had taken place on the first day of the period (or on the date of issue of the convertible loan stock if later). The earnings for the period should be adjusted by adding back the assumed saving of interest on the stock so converted, net of corporation tax.

(iii) Where a company has granted options or issued warrants to subscribe for equity shares of the company, the fully diluted earnings per share should be calculated on the assumption that the maximum number of new shares had been issued under the terms of the options or warrants and that these had been exercised on the first day of the period (or the date of issue if later). The earnings for the period should be adjusted on the basis that the proceeds of subscription had been invested in $2\frac{1}{2}$ per cent consolidated stock on the first day of the period at the closing price of the previous day.

## 12 Goodwill

(a) The goodwill of a business is the additional value brought into existence because of its ability to earn "super profits"—profits in addition to a reasonable return on the tangible assets. It represents the extra amount which a possible purchaser of the business would be prepared to pay in return for the right to receive the future super profits.

As goodwill can only be realised if all or part of a business is sold, it is customary not to include it in the balance sheet unless it has been purchased along with the other assets of another business acquired as a going concern. It can therefore be presumed that the figure of £120,000 appearing for goodwill in the balance sheet of Expansion Limited represents a premium over tangible assets arising on the purchase of another company.

The extent to which goodwill is reflected in the market value of a company will vary considerably, since stock exchange prices tend to reflect capitalised earnings or dividends rather than underlying assets. If a takeover is in prospect, the price of the share is likely to rise because the price to be paid by the purchaser is normally in excess of the current market price. It might be that this increase will be due to the agreed existence of unrecorded goodwill. The excess of the purchase price over the fair value of net tangible assets will, as indicated in the previous paragraph, be accounted for as goodwill by the purchasing company.

In the case of Expansion, the current market price of 75p values the company at £750,000 and thus values the assets of the business (£1,090,000) at a discount of £340,000. This reflects the company's static earnings and dividend and is not necessarily an accurate measure of the worth of the company if a bid were to be made.

(b) (i) *Accounting treatment for non-purchased goodwill*
As indicated in (a) above, it contravenes the Companies Act 1981 to include non-purchased goodwill in the balance sheet, except for goodwill arising on consolidation.

(ii) *Accounting treatment of purchased goodwill*
There are three possible methods of treating purchased goodwill:

(1) Write off immediately in the year in which it arises. To comply with SSAP 6 this must be passed through the profit and loss account, though some major companies (Spillers, for example) have debited such sums direct to reserves and received a qualified audit report as a result.

(2) Retained indefinitely as an asset in the balance sheet.

(3) Write off to profit and loss account by regular annual instalments.

The third treatment is the one stipulated by Companies Act 1981, with the requirement that goodwill should be written off over its economic life, with disclosure of the period chosen and the reason for choosing it.

## 13 Disclosure

(a) The loss of £400,000 is correctly written off to profit and loss account. It cannot be an extraordinary item because the purchase and transportation of raw materials is well within the ordinary activities of Roller Limited.

The amount should be disclosed as an exceptional item if, as will probably be the case, the amount is regarded as material. This will comply with the requirements of the Companies Acts and SSAP 6 as to the disclosure of such items.

(b) SSAP 9 requires "attributable" overheads to be included in arriving at the cost of work in progress.

The charge represents a change of accounting policy and so may, in compliance with SSAP 6, be accounted for as a prior year adjustment.

The amount included for overheads in the closing work in progress valuation is £100,000. £12,500 of this sum relates to the increase in work in progress during the year, so that the prior year adjustment is the overhead content of the opening work in progress or £87,500. (It is assumed that the percentage of overhead reasonably attributable to the opening work in progress is also 25 per cent.) The remaining £12,500 has the effect of increasing the reported profit for the year.

(c) The writing off of goodwill is one of the examples of extraordinary items given in SSAP 6. The £200,000, net of attributable taxation, should therefore be disclosed as such in the profit and loss account as a subtraction from profit after taxation.

## 3 STATEMENTS OF SOURCE AND APPLICATION OF FUNDS

### 14 Plan Ahead Ltd

Budgeted Sources and Application of Funds Statement
year ended 31st March 19X7

| | £000 | £000 | £000 |
|---|---|---|---|
| Budgeted internal sources of funds | | | |
| Profit before taxation | 84 | | |
| *add:* Depreciation of plant and machinery | 28 | | 112 |
| Funds generated from operations | | | 112 |
| Budgeted application of funds | | | |
| Dividends paid | 16 | | |
| Corporation tax paid | 16 | 32 | |
| Increase in fixed assets: | | | |
| Premises | 30 | | |
| Plant and machinery | 105 | 135 | 167 |
| Immediate deficiency of internal funds | | | 55 |
| Budgeted changes in working capital | | | |
| Additional finance for: | | | |
| Increase in debtors | 20 | | |
| Increase in stock | 30 | 50 | |
| *less:* Increase in credit received: | | | |
| From trade creditors | 24 | | |
| From expense creditors | 1 | | |
| | | 25 | 25 |
| Total deficiency of internally generated funds | | *carried forward* | 80 |

| | £000 | £000 | £000 |
|---|---|---|---|
| | | *brought forward* | 80 |
| *less:* Externally raised funds: | | | |
| Proceeds of issue of ordinary shares | | | 75 |
| Reduction in liquid resources—being increase in bank overdraft £6,000 *less* increase in cash in hand of £1,000 | | | 5 |

## 15 Excelsior Ltd

(a) Statement of Sources and Application of Funds
year ended 31st March 19X8
(comparative figures for 19X7 would be given)

| | £000 | £000 |
|---|---|---|
| Sources of funds | | |
| Funds from operations: | | |
| Profit before tax | | 1,120 |
| Depreciation for the year | | 640 |
| | | 1,760 |
| Funds from other sources: | | |
| Rights issue of shares | 150 | |
| Convertible debentures issued | 2,000 | |
| | | 2,150 |
| Proceeds of sale of plant | | 565 |
| | | 4,475 |
| Applications of funds: | | |
| Dividend paid | 180 | |
| Taxation paid | 1,000 | |
| Purchase of land and buildings | 1,700 | |
| Purchase of plant and machinery | 1,500 | |
| | | 4,380 |
| | | 95 |
| Net increase in working capital | | |

| | Sources | Applications | |
|---|---|---|---|
| Stocks etc. | — | 285 | |
| Debtors | — | 300 | |
| Creditors | — | 100 | |
| | | | 685 |
| Net decrease in liquid position being: | | | 590 |
| Increase in overdrafts | | 250 | |
| Decrease in cash | | 340 | |
| | | | 590 |

(b) Seven points of comment:

(i) The heavy investment in new premises and plant indicate a planned expansion of activities in 19X8/9.

(ii) The investment referred to in (i) has mainly been financed from the issue of convertible debentures and from retained profits.

(iii) Liquidity remains poor (*see* (iv)) shown by the movements in working capital and net liquid funds.

(iv) The acid-test ratio has remained at a very tight level (0.59:1 for 19X8; 0.57:1 for 19X7), indicating that too little capital was raised to finance the activities of the company adequately.

(v) The issue of the debentures affects the gearing of the company and may affect control after the conversion rights are exercised.

(vi) Following from comments (iii) and (iv) above, it is clear that the company is presently overtrading.

(vii) In view of previous comments it is surprising that the creditors show a reduction, and this point should be investigated.

(c) 19X8 earnings after taxation attributable to equity:

| | | | | |
|---|---|---|---|---|
| £1,715,000 less £1,460,000* | | | = | £255,000 |
| Number of shares | | | = | 1,200,000 |
| | | | = | 21.25 pence per share (basic earnings per share) |
| Earnings as above | | | = | £255,000 |
| *add:* Back interest on convertible loan | = | £160,000 | | |
| *less:* Corporation tax (52%) | = | 83,200 | | 76,800 £331,800 |
| Number of shares | | | = | 1,200,000 |
| plus 500,000 | | | = | 1,700,000 |
| | | | = | 19.52 pence per share (diluted earnings per share) |

* Depreciation £640,000 plus tax £820,000.

## Workings

(1) For statement of source and application of funds:

Share Capital

| | £000 | | £000 |
|---|---|---|---|
| | | Opening balance | 1,000 |
| | | Share premium account (bonus issue) | 100 |
| Closing balance | 1,200 | Cash (rights issue) | 100 |

Share Premium

| | £000 | | £000 |
|---|---|---|---|
| | | Opening balance | 600 |
| Share capital account | | Cash (rights issue) | 50 |
| (bonus issue) | 100 | | |
| Closing balance | 550 | | |
| | 650 | | 650 |

Plant

| | £000 | | £000 |
|---|---|---|---|
| Opening balance | 5,800 | Plant: Disposal account | 1,200 |
| New plant acquired (balancing figure) | 1,500 | Closing balance | 6,100 |
| | 7,300 | | 7,300 |

Plant—Depreciation

| | £000 | | £000 |
|---|---|---|---|
| | | Opening balance | 3,850 |
| Plant disposal account | 590 | Profit and loss account | |
| Closing balance | 3,900 | (balancing figure) | 640 |
| | 4,490 | | 4,490 |

Plant—Disposal

| | £000 | | £000 |
|---|---|---|---|
| | | Plant—Depreciation account | 590 |
| Plant account—cost | 1,200 | Proceeds of sale | 565 |
| | | Profit and loss account—loss | 45 |
| | 1,200 | | 1,200 |

Taxation

| | £000 | | £000 |
|---|---|---|---|
| Cash paid (balancing figure) | 1,000 | Opening balance | 1,150 |
| Closing balance | 820 | Profit and loss account | 670 |
| | 1,820 | | 1,820 |

Profit Working

| | £000 | £000 |
|---|---|---|
| | + | − |
| Increase in retained profit per question | 225 | |
| Dividend charged | 180 | |
| Tax charged | 670 | |
| Loss on disposal of plant added back | 45 | |
| Profit before charging above items | 1,120 | |

(2) For EPS calculation:

| | £ | |
|---|---|---|
| Rights issue: number of shares 19X7 | 1,000,000 | |
| Rights issue 1 for 10 | 100,000 | at £1.50 = £150,000 cash received |
| | 1,100,000 | (£50,000 share premium) |
| Scrip issue 1 for 11 utilising share premium | 100,000 | |
| Number of shares 19X8 | 1,200,000 | |

| | £ |
|---|---|
| Share premium 19X7 | 600,000 |
| Plus rights issue premium | 50,000 |
| | 650,000 |
| *less:* Scrip issue | 100,000 |
| Share premium 19X8 | 550,000 |

## 16 KS Ltd

Statement of Source and Application of Funds
year ended 30th June 19X6

| | £m | £m |
|---|---|---|
| Source of funds | | |
| Profit for year before tax | | 61.84 |
| *add:* Adjustments for non-monetary items: | | |
| Depreciation | 65.2 | |
| Investment grant credited | (4.9) | |
| Retained profits re minority interest | (0.5) | 59.80 |
| Total generated from operations | | 121.64 |
| Funds from other sources | | |
| Investment grants received | 10.0 | |
| Long-term loans | 66.7 | |
| Issue of shares* | 2.7 | |
| Sale of fixed assets (*see* Working 3) | 10.6 | 90.00 |
| | | 211.64 |
| Application of funds | | |
| Purchase of fixed assets* | 120.00 | |
| Tax paid (*see* Working 2) | 35.90 | |
| Dividends paid | 17.24 | |
| Goodwill purchased* | 8.30 | 181.44 |
| | *carried forward* | 30.20 |

| | £m | £m |
|---|---|---|
| | *brought forward* | 30.20 |
| Increase in working capital | | |
| Stocks* | 11.8 | |
| Debtors* | 7.7 | |
| Creditors* | 4.8 | |
| Short-term borrowings | (9.6) | |
| | 14.7 | |
| Change in net liquid funds: | | |
| Cash and short-term investments* | 15.5 | 30.20 |

* *Summary of effects of acquiring NB Ltd:*

| | £m | | £m |
|---|---|---|---|
| Net assets acquired | | Discharged by | |
| Fixed assets | 75.0 | Shares issued | 2.7 |
| Goodwill | 8.3 | Cash | 87.3 |
| Stock | 10.0 | | |
| Debtors | 4.0 | | |
| | 97.3 | | |
| *less:* Creditors | 7.3 | | |
| | 90.0 | | 90.0 |

**Workings**

(1) Profit for the Year

| | | £m |
|---|---|---|
| Retained profits KS Ltd | | 12.00 |
| *add:* Tax charged (*see* 2) | | 39.60 |
| Dividends of the year: | | |
| Ordinary dividend | 20.00 | |
| Preference dividend | 0.24 | 20.24 |
| | | 71.84 |
| *less:* Loss on exchange | | (10.00) |
| | | 61.84 |

(2) Tax Account

| | £m | | £m |
|---|---|---|---|
| Carried back | 35.9 | Brought down | 35.9 |
| Carried down | 47.0 | Deferred taxation | 7.4 |
| | | ∴ Profit and loss | 39.6 |
| | 82.9 | | 82.9 |

Deferred Tax Account

| | £m | | £m |
|---|---|---|---|
| Corporation tax | 7.4 | Brought down | 41.4 |
| Carried down | 34.0 | | |
| | 41.4 | | 41.4 |

(3) Disposal of Fixed Assets Account

| | £m | | £m |
|---|---|---|---|
| Book value | 14.6 | Loss—charged to reserves | 4.0 |
| | | Proceeds | 10.6 |
| | 14.6 | | 14.6 |

## 17 Standard Products Ltd

(1) AP
(2) L
(3) N
(4) N
(5) A
(6) OF and A
(7) L
(8) OF and SO
(9) A
(10) N
(11) OF and A
(12) SO
(13) AP
(14) N
(15) A
(16) N
(17) N

*Note:* It is assumed that increase/decrease in net liquid resources means that part of the statement devoted to working capital changes and which ends with the increase/decrease in net liquid resources.

# 4 COMPANY ACCOUNTING

## A Issue and forfeiture of shares

## 18 AB Co. Ltd

Ordinary Share Capital Account

| | £ | | £ |
|---|---|---|---|
| Forfeited shares account | 800 | Balance brought forward | 40,000 |
| Balance carried down | 99,800 | Application and allotment account | 37,500 |
| | | Calls account | 15,000 |
| | | Calls account | 7,500 |
| | | Forfeited shares reissued | 600 |
| | 100,600 | | 100,600 |
| | | Balance brought down | 99,800 |

Preference Share Capital Account

| | £ | | £ |
|---|---|---|---|
| Balance carried down | 18,200 | Application and allotment account | 6,825 |
| | | Calls account | 4,550 |
| | | Calls account | 6,825 |
| | 18,200 | | 18,200 |
| | | Balance brought down | 18,200 |

Application and Allotment Accounts

| | Ordinary £ | Preference £ | | Ordinary £ | Preference £ |
|---|---|---|---|---|---|
| Share capital account | 37,500 | 6,825 | Cash | 18,280 | 2,275 |
| Share premium account | — | 2,275 | Cash | 19,470 | 6,825 |
| Cash | 250 | — | | | |
| | 37,750 | 9,100 | | 37,750 | 9,100 |

Share Premium Account

| | £ | | £ |
|---|---|---|---|
| Balance carried down | 2,500 | Application and allotment account | 2,275 |
| | | Forfeited shares reissued | 225 |
| | 2,500 | | 2,500 |

Cash Book (Extract)

| | £ | | £ |
|---|---|---|---|
| Application and allotment ordinary | 18,280 | Application and allotment refund to ordinary share applications | 250 |
| Application and allotment preference | 2,275 | | |
| Application and allotment ordinary | 19,470 | | |
| Application and allotment preference | 6,825 | | |
| Calls account preference | 375 | | |
| Calls account ordinary | 14,800 | | |
| Calls account preference | 4,400 | | |
| Calls account ordinary | 7,400 | | |
| Calls account preference | 6,600 | | |
| Forfeited shares reissued | 450 | | |

Calls Account

| | Ordinary | Preference | | Ordinary | Preference |
|---|---|---|---|---|---|
| | £ | £ | | £ | £ |
| Share capital | 15,000 | 4,550 | Cash | 14,800 | 375 |
| Balance: Calls in advance carried down | | 225 | Cash | — | 4,400 |
| | | | Balance: Calls in arrear carried down | 200 | — |
| | 15,000 | 4,775 | | 15,000 | 4,775 |
| Balance brought down | 200 | | Balance brought down | | 225 |
| Share capital | 7,500 | 6,825 | Cash | 7,400 | 6,600 |
| | | | Balance: Calls in arrear carried down | 300 | |
| | 7,700 | 6,825 | | 7,700 | 6,825 |
| Balance brought down | 300 | | Forfeited shares account | 300 | |

Forfeited Shares Account

| | £ | | £ |
|---|---|---|---|
| Calls account | 300 | Share capital account | 800 |
| Forfeited shares reissued $\frac{6}{8} \times 500$ | 375 | | |
| Balance carried down | 125 | | |
| | 800 | | 800 |
| | | Balance brought down | 125 |

Forfeited Shares Reissued Account

| | £ | | £ |
|---|---|---|---|
| Share capital account | 600 | Forfeited shares account | 375 |
| Share premium account | 225 | Cash | 450 |
| | 825 | | 825 |

## Balance Sheet Extracts

(a) AB Co. Ltd (before second call was made)

| Share capital | Authorised | | Issued |
|---|---|---|---|
| | £ | £ | £ |
| 6% preference shares of £1 each 62½p called | 20,000 | | 11,375 |
| *add:* Calls in advance | | | 225 |
| | | | 11,600 |
| 40,000 ordinary shares of £1 each fully paid | | 40,000 | |
| 60,000 ordinary shares of £1 each 87½p called | 100,000 | 52,500 | |
| | | 92,500 | |
| *deduct:* Calls in arrear | | 200 | 92,300 |
| | | | 103,900 |
| Share premium account | | | 2,275 |

(b) AB Co. Ltd (after forfeiture)

| Share capital | Authorised | Issued |
|---|---|---|
| | £ | £ |
| 6% preference shares of £1 each | 20,000 | 18,200 |
| Ordinary shares of £1 each | 100,000 | 99,200 |
| | 120,000 | 117,400 |
| Share premium account | | 2,275 |
| Forfeited shares account | | 500 |

(c) AB Co. Ltd (after reissue of forfeited shares)

| Share capital | Authorised | Issued |
|---|---|---|
| | £ | £ |
| 6% preference shares of £1 each | 20,000 | 18,200 |
| Ordinary shares of £1 each | 100,000 | 99,800 |
| | 120,000 | 118,000 |
| Share premium account | | 2,500 |
| Forfeited shares account | | 125 |

## B Redemption of redeemable preference shares

### 19 Change plc

(a) Journal

| | | Dr | Cr |
|---|---|---|---|
| | | £ | £ |
| Bank | Dr | 297,000 | |
| Discount on debentures | Dr | 3,000 | |
| $8\frac{3}{4}$% convertible loan stock | Cr | | 300,000 |
| (being issue at 99 of £300,000 $8\frac{3}{4}$% convertible loan stock) | | | |
| 8% redeemable preference share capital | Dr | 200,000 | |
| Share premium account | Dr | 12,500 | |
| Profit and loss account | Dr | 2,500 | |
| 8% redeemable preference shares redemption account | Cr | | 215,000 |
| (being transfer of 200,000 £1 redeemable preference shares redeemable at a premium of $7\frac{1}{2}$%) | | | |
| 8% redeemable preference shares redemption account | Dr | 215,000 | |
| Bank | Cr | | 215,000 |
| (being redemption of 200,000 8% preference shares at a premium of $7\frac{1}{2}$%) | | | |
| Profit and loss account | Dr | 200,000 | |
| Capital redemption reserve fund | Cr | | 200,000 |
| (being creation of CRRF, out of profits equal to nominal amount of shares redeemed otherwise than out of the proceeds of a new issue) | | | |
| Profit and loss account | Dr | 3,000 | |
| Discount on debentures | Cr | | 3,000 |
| (being debenture discount written off) | | | |

(b) Balance Sheet 1st April 19X5

| | £ | £ |
|---|---|---|
| Capital employed | | |
| Issued share capital: | | |
| 1,000,000 ordinary shares of 25p each fully paid | | 250,000 |
| Reserves: | | |
| Capital redemption reserve | 200,000 | |
| Profit and loss account | 191,200 | 391,200 |
| | | 641,200 |
| $8\frac{3}{4}$% convertible loan stock | | 300,000 |
| | | 941,200 |

*continued*

*continued*

| | £ | £ |
|---|---|---|
| Represented by | | |
| Sundry assets | 888,500 | |
| Balance at bank | 80,600 | |
| | | 969,100 |
| *deduct:* Creditors | | 27,900 |
| | | 941,200 |

## 20 Alter Ltd

(a) Journal

| | | Dr | Cr |
|---|---|---|---|
| | | £ | £ |
| 9% unsecured convertible loan stock | Dr | 50,000 | |
| To ordinary share capital | Cr | | 37,500 |
| Share premium | Cr | | 12,500 |
| Conversion rights exercised by loan stock holders (150 50p shares per £100 loan stock). | | | |
| Cash | Dr | 45,000 | |
| Profit and loss account | Dr | 5,000 | |
| To Investments | Cr | | 50,000 |
| Sale of investments. | | | |
| Cash | Dr | 94,500 | |
| To Ordinary share capital | Cr | | 67,500 |
| Share premium | Cr | | 27,000 |
| Issue of 135,000 ordinary 50p shares at 70p per share to finance redemption of redeemable preference shares (*see* next entry). | | | |
| 8% redeemable preference share capital | Dr | 175,000 | |
| Profit and loss account | Dr | 17,500 | |
| To Cash | Cr | | 192,500 |
| Redemption of 175,000 redeemable shares at premium of 10p per share, premium being written off against profit and loss account as per s. 45 CA 1981. | | | |
| Profit and loss account | Dr | 77,500 | |
| To Capital redemption reserve (*see* Working 2) | Cr | | 77,500 |
| Under the provisions of s. 54 CA 1981 private limited companies can redeem redeemable shares partly out of capital. However, a capital redemption reserve is required if the nominal value of the shares redeemed exceeds the permissible capital payment plus the proceeds (if any) of a new issue made in order to finance the redemption. | | | |

(b) Balance Sheet 1st April 19X8

| | £ | £ |
|---|---|---|
| Share capital: | | |
| Authorised | 750,000 | |
| Issued and fully paid | | |
| 910,000 ordinary shares of 50p | | 455,000 |
| Capital redemption reserve | | 77,500 |
| Share premium account | | 39,500 |
| | | 572,000 |
| 9% unsecured convertible loan stock | | 200,000 |
| | | 772,000 |
| Represented by: | | |
| Sundry assets | | 866,500 |
| Balance at bank (*see* Working 4) | | 3,000 |
| | | 869,500 |
| *less:* Sundry creditors | | 97,500 |
| | | 772,000 |

## Workings

(1) Calculation of permissible capital payment:

| | £ | £ |
|---|---|---|
| Full cost of redemption: | | |
| 175,000 redeemable preference shares at £1.10 | | 192,500 |
| *less:* Available profit | | |
| (£100,000 − £5,000 loss on sale of investments) | 95,000 | |
| Proceeds of new issue (135,000 at 70p) | 94,500 | |
| | | 189,500 |
| Permissible capital payment | | 3,000 |

(2) Calculation of capital redemption reserve:

| | £ | £ |
|---|---|---|
| Nominal value of shares redeemed | | 175,000 |
| *less:* Proceeds of new issue | 94,500 | |
| Permissible capital payment | 3,000 | |
| | | 97,500 |
| Capital redemption reserve required | | 77,500 |

(3) Calculation of profit and loss account balance:

| | £ | £ |
|---|---|---|
| Balance per question | | 100,000 |
| *less:* Loss on sale of investments | 5,000 | |
| Premium on redemption | 17,500 | |
| Capital redemption reserve | 77,500 | |
| | | 100,000 |
| | | — |

*Note:* The profit and loss account balance will always be nil, as the redemption must first be made out of available profits, unless the premium on redemption can be debited to share premium account in accordance with s. 45(6) Companies Act 1981, in which case the profit and loss account balance will be in credit to the extent that the premium is debited to share premium.

(4) Calculation of balance at bank:

| | £ | £ |
|---|---|---|
| Balance per question | | 56,000 |
| *add:* Sale proceeds of investments | 45,000 | |
| Proceeds from issue of shares | 94,500 | 139,500 |
| | | 195,500 |
| *less:* Redemption of preference shares | | 192,500 |
| | | 3,000 |

## C Redemption of debentures

### 21 Q Ltd

Sinking Fund Investment Account

| | | | £ | £ | | | £ |
|---|---|---|---|---|---|---|---|
| 19X7 | | | | | 19X8 | | |
| Aug 1 | Balance brought forward | | | 8,000 | May 31 | Cash | 815 |
| 19X8 | | | | | | | |
| May 31 | Sinking fund a/c (being profit on sale) | | | 25 | | | |
| | Cash: | | | | | | |
| | Appropriation | | 1,900 | | | | |
| | Interest | 325 | | | | | |
| | | 14 | 339 | 2,239 | July 31 | Balance carried forward | 9,449 |
| | | | | 10,264 | | | 10,264 |

Sinking Fund Account

| | | £ | | | £ |
|---|---|---|---|---|---|
| 19X8 | | | 19X7 | | |
| Jul 31 | Transfer to general reserve | 840 | Aug 1 | Balance brought forward | 8,000 |
| | | | | Sinking fund investment account | 25 |
| | | | | Profit on redemption | 39 |
| | | | | Interest received | 325 |
| | | | 19X8 | | |
| Jul 31 | Balance carried forward | 9,449 | Jul 31 | Profit and loss appropriation a/c | 1,900 |
| | | 10,289 | | | 10,289 |

Redemption of Debentures Account

| | | £ | | £ |
|---|---|---|---|---|
| Cash | | 815 | Debentures account | 840 |
| Profit on redemption: | | | | |
| Interest | 14 | | Debenture interest account | 14 |
| Profit | 25 | | | |
| | | 39 | | |
| | | 854 | | 854 |

## 22 Vesta Ltd

(a) Debentures might be issued at a discount in order to make the issue more attractive to investors. On redemption, the gain could be taxable at a lower rate than the increased interest for which it is a substitute. Also, the use of a discount in conjunction with the interest rate allows the return offered to investors to be adjusted very precisely.

The discount represents the difference between the nominal value of the debentures and the price at which they were issued.

The discount could be shown in the accounts as a debit balance (subtracted from the total of share capital and reserves). Section 56 Companies Act 1948 allows it to be written off against share premium account if desired. Alternatively, the discount should be written off in the profit and loss account over the life of the debentures (or a shorter period).

(b) Debenture Redemption Fund

| | | £ |
|---|---|---|
| | 19X6 | |
| | Dec 31 Profit and loss account | 6,300 |
| | 19X7 | |
| | Dec 31 Cash: Interest | 630 |
| | Profit and loss account | 6,300 |
| | 19X8 | |
| | Dec 31 Cash: Interest | 1,323 |
| | Profit and loss account | 6,300 |
| | 19X9 | |
| | Dec 31 Cash: Interest | 2,085 |
| | Profit and loss account | 6,300 |
| | | 29,238 |

Debenture Redemption Fund Investment Account

| | £ | |
|---|---|---|
| 19X6 | | |
| Dec 31 Cash | 6,300 | |
| 19X7 | | |
| Dec 31 Cash | 6,930 | |
| | 13,230 | |
| 19X8 | | |
| Dec 31 Cash | 7,623 | |
| | 20,853 | |
| 19X9 | | |
| Dec 31 Cash | 8,385 | |
| | 29,238 | |

At 31st December 19X9 the relevant balances would be shown in the balance sheet as follows:

| | |
|---|---|
| Liabilities side: | |
| Reserves: | |
| Debenture redemption reserve fund | 29,238 |
| Assets side: | |
| Debenture redemption fund investments (shown separately from other assets) | 29,238 |

(c) Journal

| | | Dr | Cr |
|---|---|---|---|
| | | £ | £ |
| Cash | Dr | 100,000 | |
| To Debenture redemption fund investment account | Cr | | 100,000 |
| Sale of investments to finance redemption of debentures. | | | |
| 11% debentures | Dr | 100,000 | |
| To Debenture redemption account | Cr | | 100,000 |
| Redemption of debentures at par. | | | |
| Debenture redemption account | Dr | 100,000 | |
| To Cash | Cr | | 100,000 |
| Repayment of cash to debentureholders on redemption. | | | |
| Debenture redemption fund account | Dr | 100,000 | |
| To General reserve | Cr | | 100,000 |
| Transfer to reserves of debenture redemption fund on redemption of debentures. | | | |

(d) Any excess would be credited to profit and loss account and a shortfall debited to profit and loss account for the year in which the redemption took place.

# 5 ACQUISITIONS AND MERGERS

## 23 Knut and Bolt

(a) Number of shares to be issued at par:

| | Knut | Bolt |
|---|---|---|
| | £ | £ |
| (i) Knut's proposal: | | |
| Net assets, equivalent to capital account | 19,000 | 7,000 |
| Adjustments: | | |
| Increase in valuation of freehold property | 1,500 | |
| Loan not taken over | | 5,000 |
| | 20,500 | 12,000 |
| *less:* Bank balance retained by vendors | 3,500 | 6,500 |
| 22,500 shares of £1 each at par | 17,000 | 5,500 |
| (ii) Bolt's proposal: | £ | £ |
| Freehold property | 8,000 | |
| Valuation of business, per computation | 17,700 | 14,390 |
| 40,090 shares of £1 each at par | 25,700 | 14,390 |

Valuation of business for Bolt's proposal:

| | 19X6 | 19X7 | 19X8 | Total |
|---|---|---|---|---|
| | £ | £ | £ | £ |
| Knut's business: | | | | |
| Profit per accounts | 2,000 | 2,200 | 4,500 | |
| Valuation in accordance with Bolt's proposal: | | | | |
| 1 year's purchase of 19X6 and 19X7 | 2,000 | 2,200 | | 4,200 |
| 3 years' purchase of 19X8 | | | 13,500 | 13,500 |
| | | | | 17,700 |
| Bolt's business: | | | | |
| Profit per accounts | 1,800 | 1,900 | 2,000 | |
| *add:* Rent | 800 | 800 | 800 | |
| Loan interest | 350 | 350 | 350 | |
| | 2,950 | 3,050 | 3,150 | |
| *less:* Increase in depreciation | 200 | 200 | 220 | |
| Adjusted profit | 2,750 | 2,850 | 2,930 | |

*continued*

*continued*

| | 19X6 | 19X7 | 19X8 | Total |
|---|---|---|---|---|
| | £ | £ | £ | £ |
| Valuation in accordance with Bolt's proposal: | | | | |
| 1 year's purchase of 19X6 and 19X7 | 2,750 | 2,850 | | 5,600 |
| 3 years' purchase of 19X8 | | | 8,790 | 8,790 |
| | | | | 14,390 |

(b) Provisional Balance Sheet on Completion of Acquisition Proposals

| | (i) Knut | | (ii) Bolt | |
|---|---|---|---|---|
| | £ | £ | £ | £ |
| Issued share capital: | | | | |
| Ordinary shares of £1 each | | 22,500 | | 40,090 |
| Represented by: | | | | |
| Fixed assets: Freehold at valuation | | 8,000 | | 8,000 |
| Plant | | 6,300 | | 6,300 |
| Goodwill | | — | | 17,590 |
| Current assets: Stock | 9,000 | | 9,000 | |
| Debtors | 4,300 | | 4,300 | |
| | 13,300 | | 13,300 | |
| *less:* Current liabilities | 5,100 | 8,200 | 5,100 | 8,200 |
| | | 22,500 | | 40,090 |

*Note:* It is assumed that, under proposal (ii) above, Bolt's plant is to be taken into the new company's books at its book value without adjustment for additional depreciation.

(c) A comparison of the two bases of valuation in terms of individual shareholdings is as follows:

| | Total shares | Holdings | | | |
|---|---|---|---|---|---|
| | | % | Shares | % | Shares |
| (i) Knut | 22,500 | 75.6 | 17,000 | 24.4 | 5,500 |
| (ii) Bolt | 40,090 | 64.1 | 25,700 | 35.9 | 14,390 |

The difference between the two bases of valuation is accounted for by the fact that Knut's proposal ignores the profitability of the assets to be acquired by the new company, and based on the weighted figure of profit used under Bolt's proposal the profitability of Knut's assets is considerably lower than that of Bolt's, viz:

| | Knut | Bolt |
|---|---|---|
| | £ | £ |
| Total "weighted" profits | 17,700 | 14,390 |
| Average—one-fifth | 3,540 | 2,878 |
| Capital employed (excluding bank balance) | 17,000 | 5,500 |
| Return on capital | 20.8% | 52.3% |

Although proposal (i) is clearly more favourable to Knut, Bolt's proposal is not unreasonable from Knut's viewpoint, as Knut's share of future profits is greater at 64.1 per cent than either of the following figures:

| | % | £ |
|---|---|---|
| (i) Knut's proportion of the average profits used to calculate the consideration | 55.2 | 3,540 |
| (ii) Knut's proportion of the total profits of the two businesses for 19X8 | 60.6 | 4,500 |

No information is available on the question of directors' remuneration. It is assumed that this would be related to the amount of work done by each of the partners.

## 24 Alpha Ltd and Beta Ltd

(a) Calculation of the number of shares issued to:

| | Alpha Ltd | Beta Ltd |
|---|---|---|
| | £ | £ |
| Net assets, equivalent to: | | |
| Share capital | 10,000 | 14,000 |
| Reserves | 17,000 | 10,000 |
| | 27,000 | 24,000 |
| *add:* Weighted average of net profits for the years ended 31st December: | | |
| 19X6 2,000 × 1 = 2,000 | | |
| 19X7 8,000 × 2 = 16,000 | | |
| 19X8 12,000 × 3 = 36,000 | | |
| 6 ÷ 54,000 = | 9,000 | |
| | 36,000 | 24,000 |
| Shares issued by Gamma Ltd: | | |
| 24,000 £1 shares in the ratio 36:24 | 14,400 | 9,600 |

(b) Journal of Alpha Ltd

| | Dr | Cr |
|---|---|---|
| | £ | £ |
| Realisation account | 31,000 | |
| Fixed assets | | 12,000 |
| Stock | | 6,000 |
| Debtors | | 8,000 |
| Bank | | 5,000 |
| | 31,000 | 31,000 |
| Transfer to realisation account of book value of assets sold to Gamma Ltd. | | |

*continued*

*continued*

| | Dr | Cr |
|---|---|---|
| | £ | £ |
| Creditors | 4,000 | |
| Realisation account, Gamma Ltd | | 4,000 |
| Transfer to realisation account of liabilities taken over by Gamma Ltd. | | |
| Purchaser's account | 36,000 | |
| Realisation account | | 36,000 |
| Transfer to net purchase consideration. | | |
| Ordinary share capital | 10,000 | |
| Reserves | 17,000 | |
| Realisation account | 9,000 | |
| Sundry members' account | | 36,000 |
| Transfer to sundry members of capital, reserves, and profit on realisation. | | |
| Sundry members' account | 36,000 | |
| Purchaser's account | | 36,000 |
| Discharge of purchase consideration by issue of 14,400 shares of £1 each in Gamma Ltd, valued at £2.50 each. | | |

(c)

Balance Sheet of Gamma Ltd
after the final issue of shares

| | Authorised | Issued and fully paid |
|---|---|---|
| Capital employed | | |
| Share capital: | £ | £ |
| Shares of £1 each | 44,000 | 36,000 |
| Share premium account | | 45,000 |
| | | 81,000 |
| Employment of capital | | |
| Fixed assets: | | |
| Goodwill | | 9,000 |
| Others | | 30,000 |
| | | 39,000 |
| Net current assets: | | |
| Stock | 17,000 | |
| Debtors | 21,000 | |
| Balance at bank | 17,000 | |
| | 55,000 | |
| *deduct:* Creditors | 13,000 | |
| | | 42,000 |
| | | 81,000 |

**Working**

Balance at Bank

| | £ | | £ |
|---|---|---|---|
| Balance of Alpha Ltd | 5,000 | Balance of Beta Ltd | 9,000 |
| Proceeds of share issue | 21,000 | Balance | 17,000 |
| | 26,000 | | 26,000 |

## 25 Blough

(a) Profit and Loss Accounts

| | Blough | | Blough Ltd | | | |
|---|---|---|---|---|---|---|
| | 1st July 19X4 to 30th Sept 19X4 | | 1st Oct 19X4 to 31st Dec 19X4 | | 1st Jan 19X5 to 30th June 19X5 | |
| | 3 | | 3 | | 6 (×2) | |
| | £ | £ | £ | £ | £ | £ |
| Sales | | 10,000 | | 10,000 | | 40,000 |
| *less:* Cost of sales | | 7,500 | | 7,500 | | 30,000 |
| Gross profit | | 2,500 | | 2,500 | | 10,000 |
| *less:* | | | | | | |
| Rent | | | 400 | | 800 | |
| Salary | | | 450 | | 900 | |
| Fixed expenses | 200 | | 200 | | 400 | |
| Selling expenses | 500 | | 500 | | 2,000 | |
| Bad debt | | | 50 | | | |
| Depreciation | 300 | 1,000 | 300 | 1,900 | 600 | 4,700 |
| Net profit | | 1,500 | | 600 | | 5,300 |

Balance Sheet
Blough Limited 30th June 19X5

| | £ Cost | £ Depreciation | £ WDV |
|---|---|---|---|
| Fixed assets: | | | |
| Plant | 11,700 | 900 | 10,800 |
| Goodwill (*see* Working 1) | | | 4,000 |
| | | | 14,800 |
| Shares in subsidiary (*see* Working 2) | | | 27,000 |
| Net current assets (balancing figure but *see* Working 3) | | | 17,600 |
| | | | 59,400 |

| | £ | £ |
|---|---|---|
| Representing: | | |
| Share capital: | | |
| Authorised: 50,000 ordinary shares of £1 each | 50,000 | |
| Issued: 48,500 ordinary shares of £1 each, fully paid | | 48,500 |
| Reserves: | | |
| Share premium account | 5,000 | |
| Non-distributable—pre-acquisition profit | 600 | |
| Profit and loss account | 5,300 | 10,900 |
| | | 59,400 |

## Workings

| | £ | £ | £ |
|---|---|---|---|
| (1) Goodwill: | | | |
| Purchase consideration | | | 28,500 |
| Assets acquired: | | | |
| Plant: as at 1st July 19X4 | 12,000 | | |
| *less:* Depreciation to 30th September 19X4 | 300 | 11,700 | |
| Net current assets as at 1st July 19X4 | 13,000 | | |
| *add:* Profit to 30th September 19X4 | 1,500 | | |
| Depreciation charged in profit (no cash outflow) | 300 | | |
| | 14,800 | | |
| *less:* Drawings by Blough | 2,000 | 12,800 | 24,500 |
| Balance: Goodwill | | | 4,000 |

| | | £ |
|---|---|---|
| (2) | Shares in subsidiary: | |
| | Purchase price | 30,000 |
| | *less:* Dividend received out of pre-acquisition profits | 3,000 |
| | | 27,000 |

| | | £ |
|---|---|---|
| (3) | Net current assets: | |
| | As at 1st October 19X4 (*see* Working 2) | 12,800 |
| | Profit to 30th June 19X5 (£5,300 + £600) | 5,900 |
| | Depreciation charged in profit (no cash outflow) | 900 |
| | Dividend received | 3,000 |
| | | 22,600 |
| | *less:* Cost of debenture in Copper Ltd | 5,000 |
| | | 17,600 |

(b) Blough Limited: Journal

| | | | Dr | Cr |
|---|---|---|---|---|
| (i) | | | £ | £ |
| | Blough capital account | Dr | 10,000 | |
| | Freehold property | Cr | | 10,000 |
| | Freehold property retained by Blough. | | | |
| | Goodwill | Dr | 4,000 | |
| | Blough capital account | Cr | | 4,000 |
| | Excess of purchase consideration over net assets acquired from Blough. | | | |
| | Profit and loss account | Dr | 1,500 | |
| | Blough capital account | Cr | | 1,500 |
| | Net profit for quarter ending 30th September 19X4. | | | |
| | Blough capital account | Dr | 28,500 | |
| | Ordinary share capital | Cr | | 28,500 |
| | Fully paid £1 ordinary shares issued in satisfaction of purchase consideration. | | | |
| (ii) | | | | |
| | Shares in subsidiary | Dr | 30,000 | |
| | Ordinary share capital | Cr | | 20,000 |
| | Share premium account | Cr | | 5,000 |
| | Debenture in Copper Ltd | Cr | | 5,000 |
| | Purchase of 20,000 fully paid £1 ordinary shares in Copper Ltd at £1.50 each and payment by the issue of 20,000 £1 ordinary shares at £1.25 each and transfer of £5,000 debenture in Copper Ltd. | | | |

## 26 Kris Ltd and Wren Ltd

**Wren Ltd Books**

Realisation Account

| | £ | | £ |
|---|---|---|---|
| Assets taken over: | | Kriswren Ltd (*see* Note 2): | |
| Stocks | 6,800 | Purchase price | 38,560 |
| Debtors | 2,440 | | |
| Fixed assets | 14,300 | | |
| Cash (*see* Note 1) | 1,640 | | |
| 9% debentures in Kris (loss) | 200 | | |
| Expenses of realisation: Cash | 840 | | |
| Sundry members account: | | | |
| Profit on realisation | 12,340 | | |
| | 38,560 | | 38,560 |

*Notes:*

(1) Cash £1,640 is made up of £7,400 *less* creditors £4,920 *less* expenses £840.

Sundry Members Account

| | £ | | £ |
|---|---|---|---|
| Profit and loss account | 3,340 | Share capital account | 5,000 |
| Current account Kris Ltd: | | Realisation account: Profit | 12,340 |
| Proportion of credit balance | | | |
| attributable to 16,000 shares | 11,200 | | |
| | 14,540 | | |
| Kriswren Ltd: Value of | | | |
| shares issued to outside | | | |
| members in settlement | 2,800 | | |
| | 17,340 | | 17,340 |

Current Account Kris Ltd

| | £ | | £ |
|---|---|---|---|
| 9% debentures Kris Ltd | 4,000 | Balance brought forward | 28,560 |
| Balance transferred to | | Sundry members account | 11,200 |
| Kriswren Ltd | 35,760 | Investment by Kris Ltd | |
| | 39,760 | (*see* Note 3) | 39,760 |

9% Debentures in Kris Ltd

| | £ | | £ |
|---|---|---|---|
| Balance brought forward | 4,200 | Current account Kris Ltd | 4,000 |
| | | Realisation account: Loss | 200 |
| | 4,200 | | 4,200 |

Kriswren Ltd

| | £ | | £ |
|---|---|---|---|
| Realisation account | 38,560 | Sundry members account: | |
| | | Shares issued to outside | |
| | | shareholders in settlement | 2,800 |
| | | Current account Kris Ltd | 35,760 |
| | 38,560 | | 38,560 |

*Notes (cont.):*

| | | £ |
|---|---|---|
| (2) | Fixed assets | 19,600 |
| | Stocks | 5,600 |
| | Debtors | 1,720 |
| | Goodwill | 10,000 |
| | | 36,920 |
| | Cash | 1,640 |
| | | 38,560 |

| | | £ |
|---|---|---|
| (3) | Total consideration | 17,340 |
| | *less* Profit and Loss Account | 3,340 |
| | | 14,000 |

$$\frac{16,000}{20,000} \times £14,000 = £11,200$$

**Kris Ltd Books**

Realisation Account

| | £ | | £ |
|---|---|---|---|
| Assets taken over: | | Kriswren Ltd (purchase | |
| Fixed assets | 49,420 | price) (*see* Note 2) | 201,440 |
| Stocks | 35,760 | | |
| Debtors | 9,320 | | |
| Cash (*see* Note 1) | 1,220 | | |
| Expenses of realisation: Cash | 3,800 | | |
| Sundry members account: | | | |
| Profit on realisation | 101,920 | | |
| | 201,440 | | 201,440 |

*Notes:*

(1) Cash £1,220 is made up of £22,920 *less* creditors £17,900 *less* expenses £3,800.

| | | £ | £ |
|---|---|---|---|
| (2) | Fixed assets | 110,000 | |
| | Stock | 33,400 | |
| | Debtors | 6,820 | |
| | Goodwill | 50,000 | |
| | | 200,220 | |
| | Cash | 1,220 | 201,440 |

Sundry Members Account

| | £ | | £ |
|---|---|---|---|
| Kriswren Ltd: Value of shares issued in settlement | 221,200 | Share capital account | 80,000 |
| | | Revenue reserves | 33,480 |
| | | Profit on realisation | 101,920 |
| | | Investment in Wren Ltd | 5,800 |
| | 221,200 | | 221,200 |

Current Account Wren Ltd

| | £ | | £ |
|---|---|---|---|
| Balance brought forward | 28,560 | 9% debentures account | 4,000 |
| Investment in Wren Ltd account (*see* Note 3) | 11,200 | Balance transferred to Kriswren Ltd | 35,760 |
| | 39,760 | | 39,760 |

Kriswren Ltd

| | £ | | £ |
|---|---|---|---|
| Realisation account | 201,440 | 9% debentures account: Debentures in settlement | 16,000 |
| Current account Wren Ltd | 35,760 | Sundry members account: Shares in settlement | 221,200 |
| | 237,200 | | 237,200 |

Investment in Wren Ltd

| | £ | | £ |
|---|---|---|---|
| Balance brought forward | 5,400 | Current account Wren Ltd Amount due on liquidation (*see* Note 3) | 11,200 |
| Sundry members account: Profit on investment | 5,800 | | |
| | 11,200 | | 11,200 |

9% Debentures Account

| | £ | | £ |
|---|---|---|---|
| Current account Wren | 4,000 | Balance brought forward | 20,000 |
| Kriswren Ltd | 16,000 | | |
| | 20,000 | | 20,000 |

*Notes (cont.):*
(3) *See* Note 3 Wren Ltd books.

Kriswren Limited
Balance Sheet at 30th September 19X6

| | | £ |
|---|---|---|
| Share capital: Authorised, issued and fully paid in £1 ordinary shares | | 100,000 |
| Capital reserve: Share premium account | | 124,000 |
| | | 224,000 |
| 10% debentures | | 16,000 |
| | | 240,000 |
| | £ | £ |
| Fixed assets | | 129,600 |
| Goodwill | | 60,000 |
| Current assets: Stocks | 39,000 | |
| Debtors | 8,540 | |
| Cash | 2,860 | 50,400 |
| | | 240,000 |

*Note:* The shares in Kriswren are valued at £2.24 each. The former outside shareholders in Wren Ltd now hold: $\frac{£2,800}{£2.24} = 1,250$ shares.

## 27 Axis Ltd

Balance Sheet 1st January 19X7

| | | £ | £ |
|---|---|---|---|
| Share capital: Authorised, issued and fully paid: | | | |
| 50,000 £1 7% preference shares fully paid | | | 50,000 |
| 100,000 £1 ordinary shares fully paid | | 100,000 | |
| Capital reserve | | 27,873 | |
| General revenue reserve | | 10,000 | |
| Profit and loss account | | 40,440 | 178,313 |
| | | | 228,313 |
| Fixed assets: | Cost | Depreciation | |
| | £ | £ | £ |
| Plant and machinery | 72,607 | 27,786 | 44,821 |
| Motor vehicles | 7,909 | 3,397 | 4,512 |
| | 80,516 | 31,183 | 49,333 |
| Investment in subsidiary company (Bude Ltd): | | | |
| Shares at cost | | 150,000 | |
| Loan account | | 4,906 | 154,906 |
| Quoted investments (market value £12,000) | | | 10,000 |
| | *carried forward* | | 214,239 |

| | £ | £ |
|---|---|---|
| *brought forward* | | 214,239 |
| Current assets: | | |
| Stock | 9,014 | |
| Debtors | 17,072 | |
| Cash at bank | 9,345 | |
| | 35,431 | |
| *less:* Current liabilities: | | |
| Sundry creditors | 21,357 | 14,074 |
| | | 228,313 |

*Notes*

(1) As the credit balance on sinking fund account is no longer required for the redemption of the debentures it is transferred to general reserve (alternatively capital reserve) and the sinking fund investments become general investments of the company.

(2) Calculation of net purchase price to be paid by Bude Ltd:

| | £ | £ |
|---|---|---|
| Fixed assets: | | |
| Freehold property | 150,000 | |
| Plant | 30,000 | |
| Motor vehicles | 2,500 | |
| Goodwill | 7,000 | 189,500 |
| Stock | | 5,000 |
| Debtors | | 4,682 |
| Value of Axis Ltd assets transferred to Bude Ltd | | 199,182 |
| *less:* Value of Bude Ltd assets transferred to Axis Ltd: | | |
| Plant | 6,000 | |
| Motor vehicles | 1,000 | |
| Stocks | 3,000 | |
| Debtors | 2,183 | 12,183 |
| | | 186,999 |
| *less:* Axis Ltd liabilities taken over by Bude Ltd | 7,681 | |
| *plus:* Bude Ltd liabilities taken over by Axis Ltd | 2,478 | 5,203 |
| Net purchase price | | 181,796 |

(3) The surplus of £28,873 on the realisation of fixed assets sold to Bude Ltd is transferred from reconstruction account to capital reserve.

Calculation:

| Asset: | Book value | Sale price | Surplus |
|---|---|---|---|
| | £ | £ | £ |
| Freehold property | 130,000 | 150,000 | 20,000 |
| Plant | 28,464 | 30,000 | 1,536 |
| Motor vehicles | 2,163 | 2,500 | 337 |
| Goodwill | nil | 7,000 | 7,000 |
| | | | 28,873 |

## Axis Ltd Books

### Reconstruction Account

| | £ | | £ |
|---|---|---|---|
| Freehold property account | 130,000 | Plant and machinery account | 6,000 |
| Plant and machinery account | 28,464 | Motor vehicles account | 1,000 |
| Motor vehicles account | 2,163 | Stock account | 3,000 |
| Debtors account | 4,682 | Debtors account | 2,183 |
| Stock account | 4,850 | Axis Ltd creditors account (taken over by Bude Ltd) | 7,681 |
| Bude Ltd creditors taken over by Axis Ltd: Sundry creditors account | 2,478 | Bude Ltd account: Purchase consideration (*see* Note 2) | 181,796 |
| Capital reserve: Net surplus transferred (*see* Note 3) | 28,873 | | |
| Profit and loss account: Profit on sale of stock (£5,000 less £4,850) | 150 | | |
| | 201,660 | | 201,660 |

### Bude Limited Account

| | £ | | £ |
|---|---|---|---|
| Reconstruction account: Purchase price | 181,796 | Sundry creditors account (debt due to Bude Ltd waived) | 4,890 |
| | | 7% debentures account | 1,000 |
| | | 7% debentures account | 21,000 |
| | | Investment in subsidiary account (cost of shares) | 150,000 |
| | | Loan account: Bude Ltd—balance transferred | 4,906 |
| | 181,796 | | 181,796 |

### Capital Reserve

| | £ | | £ |
|---|---|---|---|
| 7% debentures account | 1,000 | Reconstruction account | 28,873 |
| Balance carried down | 27,873 | | |
| | 28,873 | | 28,873 |
| | | Balance brought down | 27,873 |

Plant and Machinery

| | £ | | £ |
|---|---|---|---|
| Balance brought down (cost) | 120,565 | Balance brought down (depreciation) | 53,280 |
| Reconstruction account (depreciation) | 25,494 | Reconstruction account (cost) | 53,958 |
| Reconstruction account (cost) | 6,000 | Balance carried down (cost) | 72,607 |
| Balance carried down (depreciation) | 27,786 | | |
| | 179,845 | | 179,845 |
| Balance brought down (cost) | 72,607 | Balance brought down (depreciation) | 27,786 |

Motor Vehicles

| | £ | | £ |
|---|---|---|---|
| Balance brought down (cost) | 10,890 | Balance brought down (depreciation) | 5,215 |
| Reconstruction account (depreciation) | 1,818 | Reconstruction account (cost) | 3,981 |
| Reconstruction account (cost) | 1,000 | Balance carried down (cost) | 7,909 |
| Balance carried down (depreciation) | 3,397 | | |
| | 17,105 | | 17,105 |
| Balance brought down (cost) | 7,909 | Balance brought down (depreciation) | 3,397 |

Stock

| | £ | | £ |
|---|---|---|---|
| Balance brought down | 10,864 | Reconstruction account | 4,850 |
| Reconstruction account | 3,000 | Balance carried down | 9,014 |
| | 13,864 | | 13,864 |
| Balance brought down | 9,014 | | |

Sundry Debtors

| | £ | | £ |
|---|---|---|---|
| Balance brought down | 19,571 | Reconstruction account | 4,682 |
| Reconstruction account | 2,183 | Balance carried down | 17,072 |
| | 21,754 | | 21,754 |
| Balance brought down | 17,072 | | |

Sundry Creditors

| | £ | | £ |
|---|---|---|---|
| Reconstruction account | 7,681 | Balance brought down | 31,450 |
| Bude Ltd account | 4,890 | Reconstruction account | 2,478 |
| Balance carried down | 21,357 | | |
| | 33,928 | | 33,928 |
| | | Balance brought down | 21,357 |

Profit and Loss

| | | | £ |
|---|---|---|---|
| | | Balance brought down | 40,290 |
| | | Reconstruction account | 150 |
| | | Balance brought down | 40,440 |

7% Debentures

| | £ | | £ |
|---|---|---|---|
| Bude Ltd account | 1,000 | Balance brought down | 21,000 |
| Bude Ltd account | 21,000 | Capital reserve, premium on redemption | 1,000 |
| | 22,000 | | 22,000 |

## 28 Sponge Ltd

(a) (i) **Almond Ltd Books**

Liquidation Account

| | £000 | | £000 |
|---|---|---|---|
| Sundry asset accounts | 168 | Sponge Ltd | 125 |
| | | Sundry creditor accounts | 35 |
| | | Sundry shareholders: Loss | 8 |
| | 168 | | 168 |

Sundry Shareholders Account

| | £000 | | £000 |
|---|---|---|---|
| Liquidation account: Loss | 8 | Share capital account | 100 |
| Sponge Ltd | 125 | Profit and loss account | 13 |
| | | Revenue reserve account | 20 |
| | 133 | | 133 |

(ii) **Battenby Ltd Books**

Liquidation Account

| | £000 | | £000 |
|---|---|---|---|
| Sundry asset accounts | 76 | Sundry liability accounts | 38 |
| | | Sponge Ltd | 25 |
| | | Sundry shareholders: Loss | 13 |
| | 76 | | 76 |

Sundry Shareholders Account

| | £000 | | £000 |
|---|---|---|---|
| Liquidation account: Loss | 13 | Share capital account | 50 |
| Profit and loss account | 12 | | |
| Sponge Ltd | 25 | | |
| | 50 | | 50 |

(iii) **Cherry Ltd Books**

Liquidation Account

| | £000 | | £000 |
|---|---|---|---|
| Sundry assets accounts | 24 | Sponge Ltd | 20 |
| Bank: Liquidation expenses | 1 | Sundry ordinary shareholders: Loss | 5 |
| | 25 | | 25 |

Sundry Ordinary Shareholders Account

| | £000 | | £000 |
|---|---|---|---|
| Liquidation account: Loss | 5 | Share capital account | 10 |
| Bank | 5 | Profit and loss account (after providing preference dividend) | nil |
| | 10 | | 10 |

Sundry Preference Shareholders Account

| | £000 | | £000 |
|---|---|---|---|
| Bank | 11 | Share capital account | 10 |
| | | Profit and loss: Dividend | 1 |
| | 11 | | 11 |

Bank Account

| | £000 | | £000 |
|---|---|---|---|
| Sponge Ltd | 20 | Balance: Overdraft | 1 |
| | | Liquidation account: Expenses | 1 |
| | | Trade creditors | 2 |
| | | Sundry preference shareholders | 11 |
| | | Sundry ordinary shareholders | 5 |
| | 20 | | 20 |

(b)

Sponge Ltd
Balance Sheet 30th June 19X8

| | £000 | £000 | £000 |
|---|---|---|---|
| Authorised share capital: | | | |
| 100,000 10% cumulative preference £1 shares | | 100 | |
| 200,000 ordinary £1 shares | | 200 | 300 |
| Issued share capital: | | | |
| 70,000 10% cumulative preference £1 shares, 50p called | | 35 | |
| 135,000 ordinary £1 shares, fully paid | | 135 | |
| | | 170 | |
| *less:* Calls in arrear | | 1 | 169 |
| Capital employed | | | 169 |
| Represented by: | | | |
| Fixed assets, at cost: | | | |
| Plant and machinery | | 34 | |
| Land and buildings | | 26 | |
| Investments | | 10 | 70 |
| Goodwill | | | 13 |
| | | | 83 |
| Current assets: | | | |
| Stock | | 50 | |
| Sundry debtors *less* provision | | 95 | |
| Bank | | 14 | |
| | | 159 | |
| *less:* Current liabilities: Trade creditors | 55 | | |
| Bank overdraft | 18 | 73 | |
| Net assets | | | 86 |
| | | | 169 |

## Workings
## Sponge Ltd Books

Purchase of Business Account

| | | £000 | | Almond £000 | Battenby £000 | Cherry £000 | Total £000 |
|---|---|---|---|---|---|---|---|
| Sundry liabilities | | | Sundry assets | | | | |
| A Ltd: Creditors | | 35 | Bank | 15 | | | 15 |
| B Ltd: Creditors | | 20 | Investments | 10 | | | 10 |
| Overdraft | | 18 | Debtors | 50 | 48 | 8 | 106 |
| Prov. doubtful debts | 9 | | Stock | 33 | 10 | 7 | 50 |
| C Ltd: Prov. doubtful debts | 2 | 11 | Plant and machinery | 22 | 8 | 4 | 34 |
| | | 84 | Land and buildings | 20 | 6 | | 26 |
| | | | | 150 | 72 | 19 | 241 |
| Purchase price | | | Goodwill | | | | 13 |
| Almond Ltd account | | 125 | | | | | |
| Battenby Ltd account | | 25 | | | | | |
| Cherry Ltd account | | 20 | | | | | |
| | | 254 | | | | | 254 |

Bank Accounts

| | £000 | | £000 |
|---|---|---|---|
| Almond Ltd balance | 15 | Battenby Ltd balance | 18 |
| Cum. pref. shareholders account | 19 | Cherry Ltd account | 20 |
| | 34 | | 38 |
| Balance carried down | 18 | Balance carried down | 14 |
| | 52 | | 52 |
| Balance brought down | 14 | Balance brought down | 18 |

Almond Ltd Account

| | £000 | | £000 |
|---|---|---|---|
| Ordinary share capital account: 125,000 £1 shares | 125 | Purchase of business account | 125 |

Battenby Ltd Account

| | £000 | | £000 |
|---|---|---|---|
| Ordinary share capital account: 10,000 £1 shares | 10 | Purchase of business account | 25 |
| 10% cum. preference shares account: 30,000 × 50p | 15 | | |
| | 25 | | 25 |

Cherry Ltd Account

| | £000 | | £000 |
|---|---|---|---|
| Bank | 20 | Purchase of business account | 20 |

## 6 CAPITAL REDUCTIONS AND RECONSTRUCTIONS

### 29 Axed Ltd

Capital Reduction and Reorganisation Account

| | £ | | £ |
|---|---|---|---|
| $7\frac{1}{2}$% notes | 50,000 | Ordinary share capital | 75,000 |
| Ordinary shares | 20,000 | Ordinary share capital | 20,000 |
| Profit and loss account | 167,000 | Redeemable preference shares | 250,000 |
| Patents | 28,000 | Freehold property | 19,000 |
| Shares in subsidiary | 50,000 | | |
| | 315,000 | | |
| Plant (balance) | 49,000 | | |
| | 364,000 | | 364,000 |

Balance Sheet as on 1st January

| | £ | £ |
|---|---|---|
| Ordinary share capital | | 25,000 |
| $7\frac{1}{2}$% notes | | 150,000 |
| | | 175,000 |
| Fixed assets: | | |
| Freehold property | | 60,000 |
| Plant | | 30,000 |
| | | 90,000 |
| Subsidiary company: | | |
| Shares | 50,000 | |
| Advances | 46,000 | 96,000 |
| Current assets: | | |
| Stock | 82,000 | |
| Debtors | 57,000 | |
| Bank | 82,000 | |
| | 221,000 | |
| Current liabilities: | | |
| Creditors | 232,000 | (11,000) |
| | | 175,000 |

## Workings

(1) Ordinary Share Capital

| | £ | | £ |
|---|---|---|---|
| Capital reduction | 75,000 | Opening balance | 75,000 |
| Capital reduction | 20,000 | Cash | 25,000 |
| Balance carried forward | 25,000 | Reissue | 20,000 |
| | 120,000 | | 120,000 |

(2) Cash

| | £ | | £ |
|---|---|---|---|
| Ordinary share capital | 25,000 | Opening balance | 28,000 |
| $7\frac{1}{2}$% notes | 100,000 | Shares in subsidiary | 15,000 |
| | | Balance carried forward | 82,000 |
| | 125,000 | | 125,000 |

(3) $7\frac{1}{2}$ per cent Notes

| | £ | | £ |
|---|---|---|---|
| Balance carried forward | 150,000 | Cash | 100,000 |
| | | Capital reduction | 50,000 |
| | 150,000 | | 150,000 |

## 30 PQ Ltd

(a) **Accounts**

Capital Reserve

| 19X8 | | £ | 19X8 | | £ |
|---|---|---|---|---|---|
| Mar 31 | Balance carried forward | 211,250 | — | Revaluation of land and buildings | 130,000 |
| | | | Mar 3 | Capital reduction | 81,250 |
| | | 211,250 | | | 211,250 |

Capital Reduction

| 19X8 | | £ | 19X8 | | £ |
|---|---|---|---|---|---|
| Mar 31 | Profit and loss account | 481,250 | Jan 1 | Ordinary share capital | 562,500 |
| | Transfer to capital reserve | 81,250 | | | |
| | | 562,500 | | | 562,500 |

Cash

| 19X8 | | £ | 19X8 | | £ |
|---|---|---|---|---|---|
| Jan 1 | Balance brought forward | 65,000 | Feb 1 | Redemption of preference shares | 200,000 |
| Jan 10 | Application and allotment | 150,000 | Mar 3 | Redemption of debentures | 261,250 |
| Mar 1 | First call | 99,000 | | | |
| Mar 31 | Balance carried forward | 147,250 | | | |
| | | 461,250 | | | 461,250 |

Debenture Redemption

| 19X8 | | £ | 19X8 | | £ |
|---|---|---|---|---|---|
| Mar 31 | Cash | 261,250 | Mar 31 | 10% debenture stock | 250,000 |
| | | | Mar 31 | Profit and loss account: Premium on redemption | 5,000 |
| | | | Mar 31 | Profit and loss account: Accrued interest | 6,250 |
| | | 261,250 | | | 261,250 |

Final Call

| 19X8 | | £ | 19X8 | | £ |
|---|---|---|---|---|---|
| Mar 1 | Ordinary share capital | 100,000 | Mar 1 | Cash | 99,000 |
| | | | Mar 31 | Balance carried forward | 1,000 |
| | | 100,000 | | | 100,000 |

Ordinary Share Capital

| 19X8 | | £ | 19X8 | | £ |
|---|---|---|---|---|---|
| Jan 1 | Reduction of capital | 562,500 | Jan 1 | Balance brought forward | 750,000 |
| Mar 31 | Balance carried forward | 437,500 | Jan 10 | Application and allotment | 150,000 |
| | | | Mar 1 | Final call | 100,000 |
| | | 1,000,000 | | | 1,000,000 |

Profit and Loss

| 19X8 | | £ | 19X8 | | £ |
|---|---|---|---|---|---|
| Jan 1 | Balance brought forward | 470,000 | Mar 31 | Capital reduction | 481,250 |
| Mar 31 | Debenture redemption: | | | | |
| | Premium on redemption | 5,000 | | | |
| | Debenture interest | 6,250 | | | |
| | | 481,250 | | | 481,250 |

(b) Balance Sheet 31st March 19X8

| | £ | | £ | £ | £ |
|---|---|---|---|---|---|
| Share capital: | | Fixed assets: | | | |
| 1,750,000 ordinary shares of 25p—issued | 437,500 | Land and buildings at valuation | | | 250,000 |
| *less:* Calls in arrears | 1,000 | Plant and machinery at cost *less:* Depreciation | | | 210,000 |
| | 436,500 | | | | 460,000 |
| | | Current assets: | | £ | |
| Capital reserves | 211,250 | Stocks and work in progress | | 390,000 | |
| | | Debtors | | 275,000 | |
| | | | | 665,000 | |
| | | Current liabilities: | £ | | |
| | | Creditors | 330,000 | | |
| | | Bank overdraft | 147,250 | 477,250 | 187,750 |
| | 647,750 | | | | 647,750 |

## 31 Roberts Ltd

(a) **Roberts Ltd Books**

(i) Realisation Account

| 19X8 | | £ | 19X8 | | £ | £ |
|---|---|---|---|---|---|---|
| Jun 30 | Sundry assets: | | Jun 30 | Grove Ltd: | | |
| | Fixed assets | 300,000 | | Purchase consideration (*see* Working) | | 541,600 |
| | Stock | 120,000 | | | | |
| | Trade debtors | 160,000 | | | | |
| | *carried forward* | 580,000 | | *carried forward* | | 541,600 |

| 19X8 | | £ | 19X8 | | £ |
|---|---|---|---|---|---|
| *brought forward* | | 580,000 | *brought forward* | | 541,600 |
| Creditors | | | Sundry members account | | |
| Liquidation expenses | | 2,000 | Loss on realisation | | 50,000 |
| Preference shareholders: | | | Preference shareholders | 20,000 | |
| Compensation for arrears of dividend | | 9,600 | Ordinary shareholders | 30,000 | |
| | | 591,600 | | | 591,600 |

**Working**

Purchase Consideration

| | £ | £ |
|---|---|---|
| Ordinary shares | | 20,000 |
| Preferential shares | | 60,000 |
| 10% unsecured loan notes | | 9,600 |
| Creditors taken over: | | |
| Bank | 200,000 | |
| Preferential | 10,000 | |
| Ordinary | 240,000 | |
| | | 450,000 |
| Liability for liquidation expenses | | 2,000 |
| | | 541,600 |

(ii) Sundry Members Account

| 19X8 | | Pref. £ | Ord. £ | 19X8 | | Pref. £ | Ord. £ |
|---|---|---|---|---|---|---|---|
| Jun 30 | Profit and loss account transferred | — | 150,000 | Jun 30 | Share capital transferred | 80,000 | 200,000 |
| | Grove Ltd account: | | | | Realisation account compensation for arrears of dividend | 9,600 | |
| | 10% unsecured loan notes | 9,600 | | | | | |
| | 80,000 £1 pref. shares, 75p paid | 60,000 | | | | | |
| | 40,000 £1 ord. shares, 50p paid | | 20,000 | | | | |
| | Balances: | | | | | | |
| | Losses to realisation account | 20,000 | 30,000 | | | | |
| | | 89,600 | 200,000 | | | 89,600 | 200,000 |

(b) **Grove Ltd Books**

(i) Journal

| | | | Dr | Cr |
|---|---|---|---|---|
| 19X8 | | | £ | £ |
| Jun 30 | Preliminary expenses | Dr | 4,000 | |
| | To Cash | Cr | | 4,000 |
| | Payment of formation expenses: | | | |
| | Fixed assets | Dr | 280,000 | |
| | Stock | Dr | 100,000 | |
| | Trade debtors | Dr | 160,000 | |
| | To liquidator of Roberts Ltd: | | | |
| | Purchase consideration | Cr | | 541,600 |
| | Goodwill (balance) | Dr | 1,600 | |
| | Assets taken over on reconstruction and goodwill arising. | | | |
| 19X8 | | | | |
| Jun 30 | Liquidator of Roberts Ltd | Dr | 541,600 | |
| | To Creditors: Preferential | Cr | | 10,000 |
| | Ordinary | Cr | | 240,000 |
| | Liquidation expenses | Cr | | 2,000 |
| | Bank overdraft | Cr | | 200,000 |
| | 10% unsecured loan notes 1994/5 | Cr | | 9,600 |
| | Share capital: | | | |
| | 80,000 7% preference shares of £1 each—75p paid | Cr | | 60,000 |
| | 40,000 ordinary shares of £1 each—50p paid | Cr | | 20,000 |
| | Creditors taken over and purchase consideration paid. | | | |
| 19X8 | | | | |
| Jun 30 | Application and allotment account | | | |
| | Preference shares, 25p per 80,000 shares called | Dr | 20,000 | |
| | Ordinary shares, 50p per 40,000 shares called | Dr | 20,000 | |
| | To Preference shares capital account | Cr | | 20,000 |
| | Ordinary share capital account | Cr | | 20,000 |
| | Cash | Dr | 40,000 | |
| | To Application and allotment account: | | | |
| | Preference shares | Cr | | 20,000 |
| | Ordinary shares | Cr | | 20,000 |
| | Amounts called and received as agreed. | | | |
| | Cash | Dr | 140,000 | |
| | To 10% unsecured loan notes | Cr | | 140,000 |
| | Loans by directors as agreed. | | | |

*continued*

| *continued* | | Dr | Cr |
|---|---|---|---|
| | | £ | £ |
| Creditors: Preferential | Dr | 10,000 | |
| Ordinary | Dr | 240,000 | |
| Liquidation expenses | Dr | 2,000 | |
| Bank overdraft | Dr | 40,000 | |
| To Cash | Cr | | 172,000 |
| 10% unsecured loan notes 1994/5 | Cr | | 120,000 |
| Payment of creditors and reduction in bank overdraft per reconstruction scheme. | | | |

(ii) Balance Sheet at 1st July 19X8 after reconstruction

| | Authorised | Issued |
|---|---|---|
| Share capital: | £ | £ |
| 7% £1 cumulative preference shares | 250,000 | 80,000 |
| Ordinary £1 shares | 250,000 | 40,000 |
| | 500,000 | 120,000 |
| 10% unsecured loan notes 19Y4/5 | | 269,600 |
| Bank overdraft (secured) | | 160,000 |
| | | 549,600 |
| Fixed assets at cost | | 280,000 |
| Goodwill at cost | | 1,600 |
| Current assets: | | |
| Stock at cost | 100,000 | |
| Trade debtors | 160,000 | |
| Bank balance (*see* Working) | 4,000 | |
| | | 264,000 |
| Preliminary expenses | | 4,000 |
| | | 549,600 |

**Working**

Bank Balance

| | £ | £ |
|---|---|---|
| Receipts | | |
| Cash received from preference shareholders | | 20,000 |
| Cash received from ordinary shareholders | | 20,000 |
| 10% loan notes (directors) | | 140,000 |
| | | 180,000 |
| Payments | | |
| Preferential creditors | 10,000 | |
| Ordinary creditors | 120,000 | |
| Liquidation expenses | 2,000 | |
| Bank overdraft | 40,000 | |
| Preliminary expenses | 4,000 | |
| | | 176,000 |
| | Balance | 4,000 |

# 7 GROUP ACCOUNTS

## A Consolidated balance sheets on formation

### 32 H Ltd

Consolidated Balance Sheet at 31st December 19X5

| | £ |
|---|---|
| Fixed assets: | |
| Tangibles | 68,000 |
| Sundry net assets | 2,000 |
| Creditors: Amounts falling due after more than one year: | |
| Debentures | (24,000) |
| Net assets | 46,000 |
| Capital and reserves: | |
| Called-up share capital: | |
| Ordinary | 20,000 |
| Share premium account | 8,000 |
| Profit and loss account | 18,000 |
| Shareholders' funds | 46,000 |

### 33 H Ltd

Consolidated Balance Sheet at 30th June 19X5

| | £ |
|---|---|
| Fixed assets: | |
| Tangibles | 79,000 |
| Sundry net assets | 45,000 |
| Creditors: Amounts falling due after more than one year: | |
| Debentures | (24,000) |
| Net assets | 100,000 |
| Capital and reserves: | |
| Called-up share capital: | |
| Ordinary | 40,000 |
| Share premium account | 12,000 |
| Profit and loss account | 30,000 |
| Shareholders' funds | 82,000 |
| Minority interests | 18,000 |
| Total capital employed | 100,000 |

**Workings**

Minority Interest

| | £ |
|---|---|
| Ordinary shares in S Ltd | 2,000 |
| Preference shares | 10,000 |
| Reserves ($\frac{1}{3}$ × £18,000) | 6,000 |
| | 18,000 |

Reserves

| | |
|---|---|
| H Ltd | 18,000 |
| $\frac{2}{3}$ S Ltd's £18,000 | 12,000 |
| | 30,000 |

## 34 H Ltd

Consolidated Balance Sheet at 30th September 19X5

| | £ |
|---|---|
| Fixed assets: | |
| Tangibles | 54,000 |
| Sundry net assets | 24,000 |
| | 78,000 |
| Creditors: Amounts falling due after more than one year: | |
| Debentures | (22,000) |
| Net assets | 56,000 |
| Capital and reserves: | |
| Called-up share capital: | |
| Ordinary | 24,000 |
| Profit and loss account | 24,000 |
| Shareholders' funds | 48,000 |
| Minority interests | 8,000 |
| Total capital employed | 56,000 |

**Workings**

Minority Interest

| | £ |
|---|---|
| Ordinary shares in S Ltd | 2,000 |
| Preference shares in S Ltd | 2,000 |
| Reserves in S Ltd: $\frac{1}{4}$ × £16,000 | 4,000 |
| | 8,000 |

Reserves

| | £ |
|---|---|
| H Ltd | 12,000 |
| $\frac{3}{4}$ × £16,000 share of S Ltd's reserves | 12,000 |
| | 24,000 |

## 35 H Ltd

Consolidated Balance Sheet at 31st December 19X5

| | £ |
|---|---|
| Fixed assets: | |
| Intangibles: Goodwill on consolidation | 1,000 |
| Sundry net assets | 13,000 |
| Net assets | 14,000 |
| Capital and reserves: | |
| Called-up share capital: | |
| Ordinary | 8,000 |
| General reserves | 4,000 |
| Profit and loss account | 2,000 |
| Shareholders' funds | 14,000 |

**Workings**

Cost of Control

| | £ | | £ |
|---|---|---|---|
| 1,000 shares in S Ltd at cost | 6,000 | Share capital | 2,000 |
| | | Pre-acquisition: | |
| | | Reserves | 2,000 |
| | | Profit and loss account | 1,000 |
| | | Goodwill at consolidation | 1,000 |
| | 6,000 | | 6,000 |

## 36 H Ltd

Consolidated Balance Sheet at 31st December 19X5

| | £ |
|---|---|
| Fixed assets: | |
| Intangibles: Goodwill on consolidation | 900 |
| Sundry net assets | 23,100 |
| Net assets | 24,000 |
| Capital and reserves: | |
| Called-up share capital: | |
| Ordinary | 12,000 |
| Reserves | 6,000 |
| Profit and loss account | 3,000 |
| Shareholders' funds | 21,000 |
| Minority interests | 3,000 |
| Total capital employed | 24,000 |

**Workings**

Cost of Control

| | £ | | £ |
|---|---|---|---|
| 1,800 shares in S Ltd at cost | 5,400 | Share capital ($\frac{3}{5}$) | 1,800 |
| | | Pre-acquisition: | |
| | | Reserves | 1,800 |
| | | Profit and loss account | 900 |
| | | Goodwill on consolidation | 900 |
| | 5,400 | | 5,400 |

Minority Interests

| | £ | | £ |
|---|---|---|---|
| Consolidated balance sheet | 3,000 | Share capital ($\frac{2}{5}$) | 1,200 |
| | | Reserves | 1,200 |
| | | Profit and loss account | 600 |
| | 3,000 | | 3,000 |

## B Consolidated balance sheets on purchase of whole company

### 37 H Ltd

Consolidated Balance Sheet at 31st July 19X5

| | £ |
|---|---|
| Fixed assets: | |
| Intangibles: Goodwill on consolidation | 1,000 |
| Tangibles | 41,000 |
| | 42,000 |
| Sundry net liabilities | (3,000) |
| Net assets | 39,000 |
| Capital and reserves: | |
| Called-up share capital: | |
| Ordinary | 20,000 |
| Profit and loss account | 19,000 |
| Shareholders' funds | 39,000 |

**Workings**

Cost of Control

| | £ | | £ |
|---|---|---|---|
| 4,000 shares in S Ltd at cost | 6,000 | Share capital | 4,000 |
| | | Reserves | 1,000 |
| | | Goodwill on consolidation | 1,000 |
| | 6,000 | | 6,000 |

Reserves

| | £ | £ |
|---|---|---|
| H Ltd | | 10,000 |
| S Ltd | 10,000 | |
| *less:* Pre-acquisition transfer to cost of control | 1,000 | |
| | | 9,000 |
| Consolidated balance sheet | | 19,000 |

## C Consolidated balance sheets—percentage holding

### 38 H Ltd

Consolidated Balance Sheet at 31st December 19X5

| | £ |
|---|---|
| Fixed assets: | |
| Intangibles: Goodwill on consolidation | 6,000 |
| Tangibles | 106,000 |
| | 112,000 |
| Sundry net assets | 2,000 |
| Creditors: Amounts falling due after more than one year: | |
| Debentures | (58,000) |
| Net assets | 56,000 |
| Capital and reserves: | |
| Called-up share capital: | |
| Ordinary | 20,000 |
| Share premium account | 10,000 |
| Profit and loss account | 18,000 |
| Shareholders' funds | 48,000 |
| Minority interests | 8,000 |
| Total capital employed | 56,000 |

**Workings**

Cost of Control

| | £ | | £ |
|---|---|---|---|
| Investment in S Ltd: | | Share capital ($\frac{3}{4}$) | 6,000 |
| 6,000 shares at cost | 24,000 | Pre-acquisition reserves | |
| | | ($\frac{3}{4}$ × £16,000) | 12,000 |
| | | Goodwill on consolidation | 6,000 |
| | 24,000 | | 24,000 |

Reserves

| | H Ltd | S Ltd | | H Ltd | S Ltd |
|---|---|---|---|---|---|
| | £ | £ | | £ | £ |
| Minority interest ($\frac{1}{4}$) | | 6,000 | Balances | 12,000 | 24,000 |
| Cost of control | | | S Ltd | 6,000 | |
| ($\frac{3}{4}$ × £16,000) | | 12,000 | | | |
| H Ltd post-acquisition | | 6,000 | | | |
| Consolidated balance sheet | 18,000 | | | | |
| | 18,000 | 24,000 | | 18,000 | 24,000 |

Minority Interest

| | £ | | £ |
|---|---|---|---|
| Consolidated balance sheet | 8,000 | Shares in S Ltd | 2,000 |
| | | Reserves | 6,000 |
| | 8,000 | | 8,000 |

## 39 H Ltd

Consolidated Balance Sheet 31st December 19X5

| | £ | £ |
|---|---|---|
| Sundry net assets | | 23,100 |
| Capital and reserves: | | |
| Called-up share capital: | | |
| Ordinary | | 6,000 |
| Reserves: | | |
| General | 6,450 | |
| On consolidation | 3,600 | |
| | | 10,050 |
| Profit and loss account | | 4,950 |
| Shareholders' funds | | 21,000 |
| Minority interests | | 2,100 |
| Total capital employed | | 23,100 |

**Workings**

Cost of Control

| | £ | | £ |
|---|---|---|---|
| 2,250 shares in S Ltd at cost | 1,800 | Share capital | 2,250 |
| Consolidated balance sheet | 3,600 | Pre-acquisition: | |
| | | Reserves | 1,800 |
| | | Profit and loss account | 1,350 |
| | 5,400 | | 5,400 |

Reserves

| | H Ltd | S Ltd | | H Ltd | S Ltd |
|---|---|---|---|---|---|
| | £ | £ | | £ | £ |
| Minority interest | | | Balances | 6,000 | 3,000 |
| ($\frac{1}{4}$ × £3,000) | | 750 | S Ltd | 450 | |
| Cost of control | | | | | |
| ($\frac{3}{4}$ × £2,400) | | 1,800 | | | |
| H Ltd post-acquisition | | 450 | | | |
| Consolidated balance sheet | 6,450 | | | | |
| | 6,450 | 3,000 | | 6,450 | 3,000 |

Profit and Loss Account

| | H Ltd | S Ltd | | H Ltd | S Ltd |
|---|---|---|---|---|---|
| | £ | £ | | £ | £ |
| Minority interest | | | Balances | 4,500 | 2,400 |
| ($\frac{1}{4}$ × £2,400) | | 600 | S Ltd | 450 | |
| Cost of control | | | | | |
| ($\frac{3}{4}$ × £1,800) | | 1,350 | | | |
| H Ltd post-acquisition | | 450 | | | |
| Consolidated balance sheet | 4,950 | | | | |
| | 4,950 | 2,400 | | 4,950 | 2,400 |

Minority Interest

| | £ | | £ |
|---|---|---|---|
| Consolidated balance sheet | 2,100 | Share capital ($\frac{1}{4}$) | 750 |
| | | Reserves | 750 |
| | | Profit and loss account | 600 |
| | 2,100 | | 2,100 |

## 40 H Ltd

Consolidated Balance Sheet 31st March 19X5

| | £ |
|---|---|
| Fixed assets: | |
| Tangibles | 100,000 |
| Sundry net assets | 18,000 |
| | 118,000 |
| Creditors: Amounts falling due after more than one year: | |
| Debentures | 18,000 |
| Net assets | 100,000 |

*continued*

*continued*

| | £ |
|---|---|
| Capital and reserves: | |
| Called-up share capital: | |
| Ordinary | 30,000 |
| Share premium account | 20,000 |
| Reserve on consolidation | 8,000 |
| Profit and loss account | 34,000 |
| Shareholders' funds | 92,000 |
| Minority interests | 8,000 |
| Total capital employed | 100,000 |

## Workings

Cost of Control

| | £ | | £ |
|---|---|---|---|
| 10,000 ordinary shares at cost | 12,000 | Ordinary shares in S Ltd | 10,000 |
| 6,000 preference shares at cost | 6,000 | Preference shares in S Ltd | 6,000 |
| Reserve on consolidation | 8,000 | Pre-acquisition reserves | 10,000 |
| | 26,000 | | 26,000 |

Reserves

| | H Ltd | S Ltd | | H Ltd | S Ltd |
|---|---|---|---|---|---|
| | £ | £ | | £ | £ |
| Minority interest ($\frac{1}{6}$) | | 4,000 | Balances | 24,000 | 24,000 |
| Cost of control pre-acquisition ($\frac{5}{6}$ × £12,000) | | 10,000 | S Ltd | 10,000 | |
| H Ltd post-acquisition | | 10,000 | | | |
| Consolidated balance sheet | 34,000 | | | | |
| | 34,000 | 24,000 | | 34,000 | 24,000 |

Minority Interest

| | £ | | £ |
|---|---|---|---|
| Consolidated balance sheet | 8,000 | Ordinary shares in S Ltd | 2,000 |
| | | Preference shares in S Ltd | 2,000 |
| | | Reserves | 4,000 |
| | 8,000 | | 8,000 |

# D Consolidated balance sheets—percentage holdings (further aspects)

## 41 H Ltd

Consolidated Balance Sheet at 31st December 19X5

| | £ |
|---|---|
| Fixed assets: | |
| Intangibles—Goodwill on consolidation | 1,400 |
| Sundry net assets | 47,400 |
| Net assets | 48,800 |
| Capital and reserves: | |
| Called-up share capital: | |
| Ordinary | 30,000 |
| Reserves | 10,000 |
| Profit and loss account | 5,200 |
| Shareholders' funds | 45,200 |
| Minority interests | 3,600 |
| Total capital employed | 48,800 |

**Workings**

Cost of Control

| | £ | | £ |
|---|---|---|---|
| 8,000 shares in S Ltd at cost | 15,000 | Share capital | 8,000 |
| | | Profit and loss account: | |
| | | Dividend out of pre-acquisition profit | 400 |
| | | Profit and loss account: | |
| | | Pre-acquisition profit | 400 |
| | | Reserves: Pre-acquisition | 4,800 |
| | | Goodwill on consolidation | 1,400 |
| | 15,000 | | 15,000 |

Reserves

| | H Ltd | S Ltd | | H Ltd | S Ltd |
|---|---|---|---|---|---|
| | £ | £ | | £ | £ |
| Minority interest ($\frac{1}{5}$ × £6,000) | | 1,200 | Balances | 10,000 | 6,000 |
| Cost of control ($\frac{4}{5}$ × £6,000) | | 4,800 | | | |
| Consolidated balance sheet | 10,000 | | | | |
| | 10,000 | 6,000 | | 10,000 | 6,000 |

Profit and Loss Account

| | H Ltd | S Ltd | | H Ltd | S Ltd |
|---|---|---|---|---|---|
| | £ | £ | | £ | £ |
| Transfer cost of control dividend out of pre-acquisition profit | 400 | | Balances | 4,400 | 2,000 |
| Minority interest ($\frac{1}{5}$ × £2,000) | | 400 | S Ltd | 1,200 | |
| Cost of control pre-acquisition profit ($\frac{4}{5}$ × £1,000 − £400) | | 400 | | | |
| H Ltd post-acquisition | | 1,200 | | | |
| Consolidated balance sheet | 5,200 | | | | |
| | 5,600 | 2,000 | | 5,600 | 2,000 |

Minority Interest

| | £ | | £ |
|---|---|---|---|
| Consolidated balance sheet | 3,600 | Share capital ($\frac{1}{5}$) | 2,000 |
| | | Profit and loss account | 400 |
| | | Reserves | 1,200 |
| | 3,600 | | 3,600 |

## 42 H Ltd

Consolidated Balance Sheet at 31st December 19X5

| | £ | £ |
|---|---|---|
| Fixed assets: | | |
| Intangible: Goodwill | | 54,000 |
| Tangibles: | | |
| Freehold land and buildings | 200,000 | |
| Plant | 260,000 | 460,000 |
| | | 514,000 |
| Current assets: | | |
| Stocks | 216,800 | |
| Trade debtors | 239,800 | |
| Bills receivable | 18,200 | |
| Bank and cash | 67,200 | |
| *carried forward* | 542,000 | |

| | | £ | £ |
|---|---|---|---|
| | *brought forward* | 542,000 | 514,000 |
| Creditors: Amounts falling due within one year: | | | |
| Corporation tax | | 111,400 | |
| Creditors | | 234,600 | |
| | | 346,000 | |
| Net current assets | | | 196,000 |
| Total assets *less* current liabilities | | | 710,000 |
| Creditors: Amounts falling due after more than one year: | | | |
| 6% debentures | | | 16,000 |
| Net assets | | | 694,000 |

| | £ |
|---|---|
| Capital and reserves: | |
| Called-up share capital | 500,000 |
| Capital redemption reserve | 24,000 |
| Profit and loss account | 96,000 |
| Shareholders' funds | 620,000 |
| Minority interest | 74,000 |
| | 694,000 |

**Workings**

(1) Minority Interest

| | £ |
|---|---|
| Shares in S Ltd | 20,000 |
| 5% preference shares | 40,000 |
| Capital redemption reserve ($\frac{1}{5}$) | 6,000 |
| Revenue reserves ($\frac{1}{5}$) | 8,000 |
| Consolidated balance sheet | 74,000 |

(2) Cancel 6 per cent debentures worth £24,000 held by H Ltd in S Ltd out of £40,000 and show the balance of £16,000 held outside the group on the consolidated balance sheet.

(3) To agree the current account,

| | | | |
|---|---|---|---|
| Debit: | H Ltd bank account | £9,400 | |
| Credit: | S Ltd current account | | £9,400 |

## 43 H Ltd

Consolidated Balance Sheet at 31st December 19X5

| | £ |
|---|---|
| Fixed assets: | |
| Intangibles: Goodwill on consolidation | 2,200 |
| Sundry net assets | 54,760 |
| Net assets | 56,960 |
| Capital and reserves: | |
| Called-up share capital: | |
| Ordinary | 30,000 |
| Reserves | 14,800 |
| Profit and loss account | 4,608 |
| Shareholders' funds | 49,408 |
| Minority interests | 7,552 |
| Total capital employed | 56,960 |

**Workings**

Cost of Control

| | £ | | £ |
|---|---|---|---|
| 8,000 shares in S Ltd at cost | 11,000 | Share capital | 8,000 |
| | | Pre-acquisition profit | 800 |
| | | Goodwill on consolidation | 2,200 |
| | 11,000 | | 11,000 |

Reserves

| | H Ltd | S Ltd | | H Ltd | S Ltd |
|---|---|---|---|---|---|
| | £ | £ | | £ | £ |
| Minority interest ($\frac{1}{5}$ × £6,000) | | 1,200 | Balances | 10,000 | 6,000 |
| H Ltd post-acquisition | | 4,800 | S Ltd | 4,800 | |
| Consolidated balance sheet | 14,800 | | | | |
| | 14,800 | 6,000 | | 14,800 | 6,000 |

Profit and Loss Account

| | H Ltd | S Ltd | | H Ltd | S Ltd |
|---|---|---|---|---|---|
| | £ | £ | | £ | £ |
| Minority interest ($\frac{1}{5}$ × £1,760) | | 352 | Balances | 4,000 | 1,760 |
| Cost of control pre-acquisition ($\frac{4}{5}$ × £1,000) | | 800 | S Ltd | 608 | |
| H Ltd post-acquisition | | 608 | | | |
| Consolidated balance sheet | 4,608 | | | | |
| | 4,608 | 1,760 | | 4,608 | 1,760 |

Minority Interest

| | £ | | £ |
|---|---|---|---|
| Consolidated balance sheet | 7,552 | Share capital: | |
| | | Ordinary ($\frac{1}{5}$) | 2,000 |
| | | Preference | 4,000 |
| | | Reserves | 1,200 |
| | | Profit and loss account | 352 |
| | 7,552 | | 7,552 |

## 44 H Ltd

Consolidated Balance Sheet at 31st December 19X5

| | £ | £ |
|---|---|---|
| Fixed assets: | | |
| Intangibles: Goodwill on consolidation | | 10,250 |
| Tangibles | | 124,000 |
| | | 134,250 |
| Current assets: | | |
| Stock | 49,600 | |
| Trade debtors | 56,000 | |
| Bank | 30,000 | |
| | 135,600 | |
| Creditors: Amounts falling due within one year: | | |
| Trade creditors | 42,000 | |
| Bills payable | 8,000 | |
| | 50,000 | |
| Net current assets | | 85,600 |
| Net assets | | 219,850 |

*continued*

| *continued* | £ |
|---|---|
| Capital and reserves: | |
| Called-up share capital | 160,000 |
| General reserves | 15,000 |
| Profit and loss account | 19,200 |
| Shareholders' funds | 194,200 |
| Minority interest | 25,650 |
| | 219,850 |

## Workings

Cancellation:

(a) Unrealised profits:
S Ltd has taken credit for £2,400 in respect of sales to H Ltd which are still held in stock. Make the following adjustment in your question paper:

| | | |
|---|---|---|
| Debit: | S Ltd profit and loss account | £2,400 |
| Credit: | H Ltd stock | £2,400 |

being elimination of unrealised profit.

(b) Inter-group debtors/creditors:
Cancel £4,000 debtors in the books of H Ltd with £4,000 in the creditors of S Ltd. (It is assumed that this is included in the £16,000 creditors in S Ltd.)

(c) Bills receivable/payable:
Cancel £8,000 bills receivable in H Ltd against £8,000 (out of £16,000) bills payable in S Ltd. The remaining bills payable of £8,000 will be shown on the consolidated balance sheet.

Cost of Control

| | £ | | £ |
|---|---|---|---|
| 60,000 shares in S Ltd at cost | 80,000 | Share capital | 60,000 |
| | | Pre-acquisition: | |
| | | Reserves | 5,250 |
| | | Profit and loss account | 4,500 |
| | | Goodwill on consolidation | 10,250 |
| | 80,000 | | 80,000 |

Reserves

| | H Ltd | S Ltd | | H Ltd | S Ltd |
|---|---|---|---|---|---|
| | £ | £ | | £ | £ |
| Minority interest | | | Balances | 12,000 | 11,000 |
| ($\frac{1}{4}$ × £11,000) | | 2,750 | S Ltd | 3,000 | |
| Cost of control | | | | | |
| ($\frac{3}{4}$ × £7,000) | | 5,250 | | | |
| H Ltd post-acquisition | | 3,000 | | | |
| Consolidated balance sheet | 15,000 | | | | |
| | 15,000 | 11,000 | | 15,000 | 11,000 |

Profit and Loss Account

| | H Ltd | S Ltd | | H Ltd | S Ltd |
|---|---|---|---|---|---|
| | £ | £ | | £ | £ |
| Minority interest | | | Balances | 15,000 | 11,600 |
| ($\frac{1}{4}$ × £11,600) | | 2,900 | S Ltd | 4,200 | |
| Cost of control | | | | | |
| ($\frac{3}{4}$ × £6,000) | | 4,500 | | | |
| H Ltd post-acquisition | | 4,200 | | | |
| Consolidated balance sheet | 19,200 | | | | |
| | 19,200 | 11,600 | | 19,200 | 11,600 |

Minority Interest

| | £ | | £ |
|---|---|---|---|
| Consolidated balance sheet | 25,650 | Share capital ($\frac{1}{4}$) | 20,000 |
| | | Reserves | 2,750 |
| | | Profit and loss account | 2,900 |
| | 25,650 | | 25,650 |

## 45 H Ltd

Consolidated Balance Sheet at 31st December 19X5

| | £ |
|---|---|
| Sundry net assets | 22,500 |
| Capital and reserves: | |
| Called-up share capital | 18,000 |
| Minority interest | 4,500 |
| | 22,500 |

**Workings**

| | S Ltd | Y Ltd | |
|---|---|---|---|
| Minority interest: | £ | £ | £ |
| Called-up share capital | 3,000 | 1,500 | 4,500 |

## 46 H Ltd

Consolidated Balance Sheet at 31st December 19X5

| | £ |
|---|---|
| Fixed assets: | |
| Tangibles | 420,000 |
| Sundry net assets | 202,000 |
| Net assets | 622,000 |
| Capital and reserves: | |
| Called-up share capital | 380,000 |
| Reserve on consolidation | 42,000 |
| Profit and loss account | 136,000 |
| Shareholders' funds | 558,000 |
| Minority interest | 64,000 |
| | 622,000 |

**Workings**

Cost of Control

| | £ | | £ |
|---|---|---|---|
| 80,000 ordinary shares in S Ltd at cost | 100,000 | Ordinary shares in S Ltd | 80,000 |
| 60,000 ordinary shares in Y Ltd at cost | 70,000 | Ordinary shares in Y Ltd | 60,000 |
| Reserve on consolidation | 42,000 | Revenue reserves Y Ltd | 24,000 |
| | | Revenue reserves S Ltd | 32,000 |
| | | Capital reserves S Ltd | 16,000 |
| | 212,000 | | 212,000 |

Revenue Reserves

| | H Ltd | S Ltd | Y Ltd | | H Ltd | S Ltd | Y Ltd |
|---|---|---|---|---|---|---|---|
| | £ | £ | £ | | £ | £ | £ |
| Minority interest Y Ltd ($\frac{1}{4}$) | | | 8,000 | Balances | 120,000 | 60,000 | 32,000 |
| Cost of control ($\frac{3}{4}$ × £32,000) | | | 24,000 | S Ltd | 16,000 | | |
| Minority interest S Ltd ($\frac{1}{5}$) | | 12,000 | | | | | |
| Cost of control ($\frac{4}{5}$ × £40,000) | | 32,000 | | | | | |
| H Ltd post-acquisition | | 16,000 | | | | | |
| Consolidated balance sheet | 136,000 | | | | | | |
| | 136,000 | 60,000 | 32,000 | | 136,000 | 60,000 | 32,000 |

Minority Interest

| | £ | | £ |
|---|---|---|---|
| Consolidated balance sheet | 64,000 | Ordinary shares in S Ltd | 20,000 |
| | | Ordinary shares in Y Ltd | 20,000 |
| | | Revenue reserves Y Ltd | 8,000 |
| | | Revenue reserves S Ltd | 12,000 |
| | | Capital reserves | 4,000 |
| | 64,000 | | 64,000 |

## 47 H Ltd

Consolidated Balance Sheet at 31st December 19X5

| | £ | £ |
|---|---|---|
| Fixed assets: | | |
| Intangibles: Goodwill on consolidation | | 2,000 |
| Tangibles | | 504,000 |
| | | 506,000 |
| Current assets: | | |
| Debtors | 548,000 | |
| Creditors: Amounts falling due within one year: | | |
| Creditors | 421,200 | |
| Net current assets | | 126,800 |
| Net assets | | 632,800 |

| | £ |
|---|---|
| Capital and reserves: | |
| Called-up share capital | 400,000 |
| Profit and loss account | 111,600 |
| Shareholders' funds | 511,600 |
| Minority interests | 121,200 |
| | 632,800 |

**Workings**

Cost of Control

| | £ | | £ |
|---|---|---|---|
| Investment in S Ltd: | | Ordinary shares in S Ltd | 80,000 |
| Ordinary shares at cost | 110,000 | Preference shares in S Ltd | 40,000 |
| Preference shares at cost | 42,000 | Ordinary shares in Y Ltd | 60,000 |
| Investment in Y Ltd: | | Preference dividend S Ltd | 1,200 |
| Ordinary shares at cost | 52,000 | Revenue reserves S Ltd | 26,800 |
| Revenue reserves Y Ltd | 6,000 | Goodwill on consolidation | 2,000 |
| | 210,000 | | 210,000 |

Revenue Reserves

| | H Ltd | S Ltd | Y Ltd | | H Ltd | S Ltd | Y Ltd |
|---|---|---|---|---|---|---|---|
| | £ | £ | £ | | £ | £ | £ |
| Minority interest (40%) | | | 2,400 | Balance | 90,000 | 60,000 | 6,000 |
| H Ltd post-acquisition | | ¢ | 9,600 | Cost of control ($\frac{3}{5}$ × £10,000) | | | 6,000 |
| Preference dividend: | | | | Y Ltd ¢ | 9,600 | | |
| Minority interest ($\frac{1}{3}$ × £3,600) | | 1,200 | | S Ltd preference dividend ¢ | 1,200 | | |
| Cost of control ($\frac{1}{2}$ × £2,400) | | 1,200 | | | | | |
| Post-acquisition | ¢ | 1,200 | | | | | |
| Balance carried down | | 56,400 | | | | | |
| | | 60,000 | | | | 60,000 | |
| Minority interest ($\frac{1}{3}$) | | 18,800 | | Balance brought down | | 56,400 | |
| Cost of control [$\frac{2}{3}$ × (24,000 + $\frac{1}{2}$ × 32,400)] | | 26,800 | | Post-acquisition S Ltd | 10,800 | | |
| Post-acquisition | | 10,800 | | | | | |
| Consolidated balance sheet | 111,600 | | | | | | |
| | 111,600 | 56,400 | 12,000 | | 111,600 | 56,400 | 12,000 |

Minority Interest

| | £ | | £ |
|---|---|---|---|
| Consolidated balance sheet | 121,200 | Ordinary shares in S Ltd | 40,000 |
| | | Preference shares in S Ltd | 20,000 |
| | | Ordinary shares in Y Ltd | 40,000 |
| | | Revenue reserves Y Ltd | 2,400 |
| | | Revenue reserves S Ltd | 18,800 |
| | 121,200 | | 121,200 |

## 48 H Ltd

Consolidated Balance Sheet at 31st December 19X5

| | £ | £ |
|---|---|---|
| Fixed assets: | | |
| Tangibles | | 31,000 |
| Current assets: | | |
| Stock | 12,000 | |
| Debtors | 51,600 | |
| | 63,600 | |
| Creditors: Amounts falling due within one year: | | |
| Creditors | 23,200 | |
| Bills payable | 6,000 | |
| | 29,200 | |
| Net current assets | | 34,400 |
| Net assets | | 65,400 |
| Capital and reserves: | | |
| Called-up share capital | | 20,000 |
| Reserve on consolidation | | 10,167 |
| General reserves | | 15,000 |
| Profit and loss account | | 3,700 |
| Shareholders' funds | | 48,867 |
| Minority interests | | 16,533 |
| | | 65,400 |

### Workings

(1) (a) *Unrealised profit on stock*

| | | | |
|---|---|---|---|
| Debit: | Profit and loss account | S Ltd | £6,000 |
| Credit: | Stock | H Ltd | £6,000 |

being elimination of unrealised profit on stock.

(b) Cancel bills receivable and bills payable by £2,000.

(2) Cost of Control

| | H Ltd £ | S Ltd £ | | H Ltd £ | S Ltd £ |
|---|---|---|---|---|---|
| 8,000 shares in S Ltd at cost | 9,200 | | Share capital: | | |
| | | | S Ltd | 8,000 | |
| 6,000 shares in Y Ltd at cost | | 7,200 | Y Ltd | | 6,000 |
| | | | Pre-acquisition reserves | 4,000 | 6,000 |
| Minority interest ($\frac{1}{3}$ × £7,050) | | 2,350 | Pre-acquisition profits | 2,667 | 2,250 |
| H Ltd ($\frac{2}{3}$ × £7,050) | | 4,700 | S Ltd | 4,700 | |
| Consolidated balance sheet | 10,167 | | | | |
| | 19,367 | 14,250 | | 19,367 | 14,250 |

(3) Reserves

| | H Ltd | S Ltd | Y Ltd | | H Ltd | S Ltd | Y Ltd |
|---|---|---|---|---|---|---|---|
| | £ | £ | £ | | £ | £ | £ |
| Minority interest ($\frac{1}{4}$ × £10,000) | | | 2,500 | Balances | 10,000 | 12,000 | 10,000 |
| Cost of control ($\frac{3}{4}$ × £8,000) | | | 6,000 | Y Ltd | | 1,500 | |
| S Ltd post-acquisition | | | 1,500 | S Ltd | 5,000 | | |
| Minority interest ($\frac{1}{3}$ × £13,500) | | 4,500 | | | | | |
| Cost of control ($\frac{2}{3}$ × £6,000) | | 4,000 | | | | | |
| H Ltd post-acquisition | | 5,000 | | | | | |
| Consolidated balance sheet | 15,000 | | | | | | |
| | 15,000 | 13,500 | 10,000 | | 15,000 | 13,500 | 10,000 |

Profit and Loss Account

| | H Ltd | S Ltd | Y Ltd | | H Ltd | S Ltd | Y Ltd |
|---|---|---|---|---|---|---|---|
| | £ | £ | £ | | £ | £ | £ |
| Balance | | 200 | | Balances | 6,000 | — | 4,000 |
| Minority interest ($\frac{1}{4}$ × £4,000) | | | 1,000 | Y Ltd | | 750 | |
| Cost of control ($\frac{3}{4}$ × £3,000) | | | 2,250 | S Ltd post-acquisition loss | | 2,300 | |
| S Ltd post-acquisition | | | 750 | | | | |
| Minority interest ($\frac{1}{3}$ × £550) | | 183 | | | | | |
| Cost of control ($\frac{2}{3}$ × £4,000) | | 2,667 | | | | | |
| S Ltd | 2,300 | | | | | | |
| Consolidated balance sheet | 3,700 | | | | | | |
| | 6,000 | 3,050 | 4,000 | | 6,000 | 3,050 | 4,000 |

Minority Interest

| | £ | | £ |
|---|---|---|---|
| Consolidated balance sheet | 16,533 | Share capital: | |
| | | S Ltd ($\frac{1}{3}$) | 4,000 |
| | | Y Ltd ($\frac{1}{4}$) | 2,000 |
| | | Reserves: | |
| | | Y Ltd | 2,500 |
| | | S Ltd | 4,500 |
| | | Profit and loss account: | |
| | | Y Ltd | 1,000 |
| | | S Ltd | 183 |
| | | Cost of control capital reserve | 2,350 |
| | 16,533 | | 16,533 |

## E Consolidated balance sheets—foreign subsidiaries

### 49 Eirespan Hotels Ltd

(a) Minority interest:
The minority interest shows the total equity funds or net assets belonging to shareholders of subsidiary companies outside the group.

Minority interest:

In Eirespan (Spain) Ltd: none, as this company is the wholly owned subsidiary of Eirespan Hotels Ltd.

In Eirespan (Ireland) Ltd:
Equity shareholders' funds at 31st December 19X5: £1,280,000
Minority interest: $\frac{3}{8}$ × £1,280,000 = £480,000

(b) Goodwill—cost of control:
This shows the excess of the amount paid for 250,000 £1 ordinary shares in Eirespan (Ireland) Ltd over the net assets attributable to those shares at the time of acquisition.

| | £ |
|---|---|
| Amount paid | 750,000 |
| Net assets attributable $\frac{5}{8}$ × £880,000 | 550,000 |
| Goodwill | 200,000 |

(c) Reserves:
Reserves figures will show the total amount of reserves attributable to the members of Eirespan Hotels Ltd.

| This will be made up as follows: | £ |
|---|---|
| Eirespan Hotels Ltd | X |
| Eirespan (Spain) Ltd: | |
| Total profits earned since incorporation (being wholly owned and the shares having been purchased on incorporation, so that there are no pre-acquisition profits) | X |
| Eirespan (Ireland) Ltd: | |
| $\frac{5}{8}$ of the post-acquisition profits (£1,280,000 − £880,000) = £400,000 × $\frac{5}{8}$ | 250,000 |
| | X |

## F Consolidated profit and loss accounts

### 50 H Ltd

Consolidated Profit and Loss Account
year ended 31st December 19X5

| | £ |
|---|---|
| Operating profit | 740,000 |
| Corporation tax | 370,000 |
| | 370,000 |
| Minority interest | 42,500 |
| Profit attributable to members of H Ltd (of which £320,000 has been dealt with in the accounts of H Ltd) | 327,500 |
| Proposed dividend | 120,000 |
| Profit for the financial year | 207,500 |

**Workings**

| | H Ltd | S Ltd | Total |
|---|---|---|---|
| | £ | £ | £ |
| Operating profit | 400,000 | 340,000 | 740,000 |
| Taxation | 200,000 | 170,000 | 370,000 |
| | 200,000 | 170,000 | 370,000 |
| Minority interest | | ($\frac{1}{4}$) 42,500 | 42,500 |
| | | 127,500 | 327,500 |
| Dividends: | | | |
| From S Ltd | 120,000 | (120,000) | |
| | 320,000 | 7,500 | |
| H Ltd | 120,000 | | 120,000 |
| | 200,000 | 7,500 | 207,500 |

## 51 H Ltd

Consolidated Profit and Loss Account
year ended 31st December 19X5

| | £ |
|---|---|
| Operating profit | 200,000 |
| Corporation tax | 100,000 |
| | 100,000 |
| Minority interest | 5,000 |
| Profit attributable to members of H Ltd (of which £80,000 has been dealt with in the accounts of H Ltd) | 95,000 |
| Proposed dividend | 70,000 |
| Profit retained | 25,000 |

**Workings**

| | H Ltd | S Ltd | S Ltd × $\frac{4}{12}$ | Consolidated |
|---|---|---|---|---|
| | £ | £ | £ | £ |
| Trading profit | 160,000 | 120,000 | 40,000 | 200,000 |
| Corporation tax | 80,000 | 60,000 | 20,000 | 100,000 |
| | 80,000 | 60,000 | 20,000 | 100,000 |
| Minority interest ($\frac{1}{4}$) | | | (5,000) | (5,000) |
| | | | 15,000 | 95,000 |
| Dividend | (70,000) | | (8,000) | (70,000) |
| | 10,000 | | 7,000 | 25,000 |

## 52 H Ltd

Consolidated Profit and Loss Account
year ended 31st December 19X5

| | £ |
|---|---|
| Operating profit (*see* Note 1) | 64,000 |
| Corporation tax | 16,000 |
| | 48,000 |
| Minority interest | 4,500 |
| Profit attributable to members of H Ltd (of which £30,000 has been dealt with in the accounts of H Ltd) | 43,500 |
| Transfer to reserves | 16,000 |
| Retained profit for the year | 27,500 |
| Retained profits at 1st January 19X5 | 27,000 |
| Retained profits at 31st December 19X5 (*see* Note 2) | 54,500 |

*Notes*

(1) Operating profit has been computed after charging the following items:

| | £ |
|---|---|
| Directors' fees | 4,000 |
| Depreciation | 7,400 |
| Auditors' fees | 1,800 |

(2) Balance carried forward:

| | £ |
|---|---|
| In: H Ltd | 44,000 |
| S Ltd | 10,500 |
| | 54,500 |

## Workings

| | | H Ltd | S Ltd | Total |
|---|---|---|---|---|
| | | £ | £ | £ |
| Operating profit | | 40,000 | 24,000 | 64,000 |
| Taxation | | 10,000 | 6,000 | 16,000 |
| | | 30,000 | 18,000 | 48,000 |
| Minority interest | | | (¼) 4,500 | 4,500 |
| | | | 13,500 | 43,500 |
| Transfer to reserves: | | | | |
| | £ | | | |
| H Ltd | | 10,000 | | |
| S Ltd | 8,000 | | | |
| *less:* Minority interest | (¼) 2,000 | | 6,000 | 16,000 |
| | | 20,000 | 7,500 | 27,500 |
| Profits brought forward: | | | | |
| H Ltd | | 24,000 | | |
| S Ltd | 8,000 | | | |
| *less:* Minority interest | (¼) 2,000 | | | |
| | 6,000 | | | |
| *less:* Pre-acquisition (¾ × £4,000) | 3,000 | | 3,000 | 27,000 |
| | | 44,000 | 10,500 | 54,500 |

## 53 H Ltd

Consolidated Profit and Loss Account
year ended 31st December 19X5

| | £ | £ |
|---|---|---|
| Operating profit (*see* Note 1) | | 701,400 |
| Corporation tax | | 283,760 |
| Profit after tax | | 417,640 |
| Minority interest | | 24,870 |
| Profit attributable to members of H Ltd (of which £363,160 has been dealt with in the accounts of H Ltd) | | 392,770 |
| Proposed dividend | 300,000 | |
| Transfer to reserves | 82,500 | |
| | | 382,500 |
| Retained profit for the financial year | | 10,270 |
| Retained profits at 1st January 19X5 | | 164,000 |
| Retained profits at 31st December 19X5 (*see* Note 2) | | 174,270 |

*Notes*

(1) Operating profit has been computed after charging the following items:

| | £ |
|---|---|
| Directors' fees | 16,000 |
| Depreciation | 60,000 |
| Audit fees | 600 |
| Debenture interest | 6,000 |

(2) Balance carried forward:

| | £ |
|---|---|
| In: H Ltd | 167,160 |
| S Ltd | 7,110 |
| | 174,270 |

### Workings

| | H Ltd | | S Ltd | | Total |
|---|---|---|---|---|---|
| | £ | £ | £ | £ | £ |
| Gross profit | | 600,000 | | 200,000 | |
| Directors' fees | 16,000 | | 4,000 | | |
| Depreciation | 40,000 | | 20,000 | | |
| Audit fees | 400 | | 200 | | |
| Debenture interest | (4,000) | | 10,000 | | |
| Unrealised profit on stock | 12,000 | 64,400 | — | 34,200 | |
| | | 535,600 | | 165,800 | 701,400 |
| Taxation | | 217,440 | | 66,320 | 283,760 |
| *carried forward* | | 318,160 | | 99,480 | 417,640 |

| | H Ltd | | S Ltd | | Total |
|---|---|---|---|---|---|
| | £ | £ | £ | £ | £ |
| *brought forward* | | 318,160 | | 99,480 | 417,640 |
| Minority interest | | | | (¼) 24,870 | 24,870 |
| | | | | 74,610 | 392,770 |
| Dividends: | | | | | |
| From: S Ltd | | 45,000 | | (45,000) | |
| | | 363,160 | | 29,610 | |
| H Ltd | | 300,000 | | | 300,000 |
| | | 63,160 | | | 92,770 |
| Transfer to reserves: | | | | | |
| In H Ltd | | 60,000 | | | |
| In S Ltd (¾ × £30,000) | | | | 22,500 | 82,500 |
| | | 3,160 | | 7,110 | 10,270 |
| Profits brought forward | | 164,000 | | | 164,000 |
| | | 167,160 | | 7,110 | 174,270 |

TUTORIAL NOTE

Since S Ltd was acquired on the first day of the accounting period to which the profit and loss accounts relate, all its brought-forward profits are pre-acquisition and the holding company will transfer its share to cost of control.

## 54 H Ltd

Consolidated Profit and Loss Account
year ended 31st December 19X5

| | £ | £ |
|---|---|---|
| Operating profit | | 280,000 |
| Associated company | | 16,000 |
| | | 296,000 |
| Corporation tax: | | |
| Group | 140,000 | |
| Associated company | 8,000 | |
| | | 148,000 |
| Profit after tax | | 148,000 |
| Minority interest | | 10,000 |
| Profit attributable to members of H Ltd (of which £110,000 has been dealt with in the accounts of H Ltd) | | 138,000 |
| Proposed dividend | | 60,000 |
| Retained profit for the financial year | | 78,000 |
| Profit retained for the year comprises: | | |
| In: H Ltd | 50,000 | |
| Subsidiary (S Ltd) | 24,000 | |
| Associate (A Ltd) | 4,000 | |
| | 78,000 | |

## Workings

| | H Ltd | S Ltd | Total | A Ltd |
|---|---|---|---|---|
| | £ | £ | £ | £ |
| Trading profit | 180,000 | 100,000 | 280,000 | 40,000 |
| Associated company | | | 16,000 | 16,000 |
| | | | 296,000 | |
| Taxation | 90,000 | 50,000 | 148,000 | 8,000 |
| | 90,000 | 50,000 | 148,000 | 8,000 |
| Minority interest | | (20%)10,000 | 10,000 | |
| | | 40,000 | 138,000 | |
| Dividends: | | | | |
| From S Ltd | 16,000 | (16,000) | | |
| From A Ltd | 4,000 | | | (4,000) |
| | 110,000 | 24,000 | 138,000 | 4,000 |
| H Ltd | 60,000 | | 60,000 | |
| | 50,000 | 24,000 | 78,000 | 4,000 |

## 55 H Ltd

Consolidated Profit and Loss Account
year ended 31st December 19X5

| | £ | £ |
|---|---|---|
| Turnover | | 4,000,000 |
| Cost of sales | | 3,100,500 |
| Gross profit | | 899,500 |
| Distribution costs | 395,500 | |
| Administrative expenses | 242,000 | 637,500 |
| Operating profit | | 262,000 |
| Debenture interest | | 25,000 |
| Profit on ordinary activities | | 237,000 |
| Share of profit of associated company | | 20,080 |
| | | 257,080 |
| Taxation: Group | 110,000 | |
| Associated company | 8,000 | 118,000 |
| | | 139,080 |
| Minority interest | | 8,800 |
| Profit for the financial year | | 130,280 |
| Appropriations: | | |
| Transfer to reserves | 30,000 | |
| Proposed dividend | 40,000 | 70,000 |
| Retained for the financial year | | 60,280 |
| Retained profits at 1st January 19X5 | | 69,000 |
| Retained profits at 31st December 19X5 | | 129,280 |

*Notes*

(1) Trading profit has been computed after charging the following items:

| | £ |
|---|---|
| Directors' fees | 25,000 |
| Auditors' fees | 3,000 |
| Depreciation | 62,000 |

(2) A Ltd owns 40 per cent of the ordinary share capital of C Ltd.

(3) Profit dealt with in the accounts of A Ltd: £83,000.

(4) Balance carried forward:

| | | £ |
|---|---|---|
| In: Holding company | A Ltd | 62,000 |
| Subsidiary | B Ltd | 59,200 |
| Associated Co. | C Ltd | 8,080 |
| | | 129,280 |

## Workings

| | | A Ltd | B Ltd | Group | C Ltd |
|---|---|---|---|---|---|
| | | £ | £ | £ | £ |
| Turnover | | 3,000,000 | 1,000,000 | 4,000,000 | 800,000 |
| Cost of sales | | 2,410,000 | 690,500 | 3,100,500 | 562,750 |
| Gross profit | | 590,000 | 309,500 | 899,500 | 237,250 |
| Distribution costs | | (251,000) | (144,500) | (395,500) | (139,200) |
| Administrative expenses | | (166,000) | (76,000) | (242,000) | (47,850) |
| Operating profit | | 173,000 | 89,000 | 262,000 | 50,200 |
| Debenture interest | | 20,000 | 5,000 | 25,000 | — |
| Profit on ordinary activities | | 153,000 | 84,000 | 237,000 | 50,200 |
| Share of profit of Associated Co. (40% × £50,200) | | | | 20,080 | 20,080 |
| | | | | 257,080 | |
| Taxation | | 70,000 | 40,000 | 118,000 | 8,000 |
| | | 83,000 | 44,000 | 139,080 | 12,080 |
| Minority interest | | | ($\frac{1}{5}$) 8,800 | 8,800 | |
| | | | 35,200 | 130,280 | |
| Dividend from C Ltd | | 4,000 | | | (4,000) |
| | | 87,000 | | | 8,080 |
| | £ | | | | |
| Transfer to reserves | 30,000 | | | | |
| Proposed dividend | 40,000 | 70,000 | | 70,000 | |
| | | 17,000 | | 60,280 | |
| Balance brought forward | | 45,000 | 24,000 | 69,000 | |
| | | 62,000 | 59,200 | 129,280 | 8,080 |

*continued*

| *continued* | A Ltd | B Ltd | Group | C Ltd |
|---|---|---|---|---|
| | £ | £ | £ | £ |
| Administration expenses | 99,000 | 45,000 | | 28,050 |
| Directors' fees | 25,000 | 8,000 | | 4,000 |
| Auditors' remuneration | 2,000 | 1,000 | | 800 |
| Depreciation | 40,000 | 22,000 | | 15,000 |
| | 166,000 | 76,000 | | 47,850 |

## G Consolidated balance sheets (examination standard)

### 56 Holdco Ltd

Consolidated Balance Sheet at 31st March 19X5

| | £ | £ |
|---|---|---|
| Fixed assets | | |
| Intangibles: Premium on consolidation | | 31,050 |
| Tangibles | | 380,000 |
| | | 411,050 |
| Current assets | | |
| Debtors | 285,700 | |
| Creditors: Amounts falling due within one year | | |
| Creditors | 119,200 | |
| Accruals | 900 | |
| Proposed dividend: Minority shareholders | 3,900 | |
| Company shareholders | 30,000 | |
| | 154,000 | |
| Net current assets | | 131,700 |
| Total assets *less* current liabilities | | 542,750 |
| Creditors: Amounts falling due after more than one year | | |
| 6% debentures | | (15,000) |
| Net assets | | 527,750 |
| Capital and reserves | | |
| Called-up share capital | | 300,000 |
| General reserves | | 50,000 |
| Profit and loss account | | 111,650 |
| Shareholders' funds | | 461,650 |
| Minority shareholders | | 66,100 |
| | | 527,750 |

## Workings

Accounting adjustments

(a) Unrealised profit. The full amount of unrealised profit (£16,000 × 20%), £3,200, has been eliminated by debiting the profit and loss account of Holdco Ltd and crediting stock of Subco Ltd.

*Note:* Some accountants would adjust only for the holding company's share: i.e. $\frac{3}{4}$ of £3,200 = £2,400.

(b) Capitalisation of general reserve

| | | | | |
|---|---|---|---|---|
| General reserve | Dr | £20,000 | | |
| Share capital | | | Cr | £20,000 |

The above adjustments can be done on the question paper.

Cost of Control

| | £ | | £ |
|---|---|---|---|
| Investment in Subco Ltd: | | Ordinary shares in | |
| 90,000 ordinary shares | | Subco Ltd | 90,000 |
| at cost | 165,000 | Preference shares in | |
| 60,000 preference shares | | Subco Ltd | 60,000 |
| at cost | 60,000 | General reserves, Subco Ltd | 15,000 |
| | | Profit and loss account: | |
| | | Subco Ltd | 21,000 |
| | | Holdco Ltd | |
| | | (Ordinary dividend) | 3,750 |
| | | (Preference dividend) | 4,200 |
| | | Premium on consolidation | 31,050 |
| | 225,000 | | 225,000 |

General Reserves

| | Holdco Ltd £ | Subco Ltd £ | | Holdco Ltd £ | Subco Ltd £ |
|---|---|---|---|---|---|
| Minority interest ($\frac{1}{4}$) | | 5,000 | Balances | 50,000 | 20,000 |
| Cost of control pre-acquisition ($\frac{3}{4}$ × £20,000) | | 15,000 | | | |
| Consolidated balance sheet | 50,000 | | | | |
| | 50,000 | 20,000 | | 50,000 | 20,000 |

Profit and Loss Account

| | Holdco Ltd £ | Subco Ltd £ | | Holdco Ltd £ | Subco Ltd £ |
|---|---|---|---|---|---|
| Minority interest ($\frac{1}{4}$) | | 11,100 | Balances | 95,300 | 44,400 |
| Cost of control pre-acquisition ($\frac{3}{4}$ × £28,000) | | 21,000 | Subco Ltd | 12,300 | |
| Dividend out of pre-acquisition profit | | | Proposed dividend | | |
| (O) $\frac{3}{4}$ × £5,000 | 3,750 | | Ordinary | 7,500 | |
| (P) $\frac{3}{4}$ × £5,600 | 4,200 | | Preference | 4,200 | |
| Holdco Ltd post-acquisition | | 12,300 | Debenture interest | 300 | |
| Consolidated balance sheet | 111,650 | | | | |
| | 119,600 | 44,400 | | 119,600 | 44,400 |

Minority Interest

| | £ | | £ |
|---|---|---|---|
| Consolidated balance sheet | 66,100 | Ordinary shares | 30,000 |
| | | Preference shares | 20,000 |
| | | General reserves | 5,000 |
| | | Profit and loss account | 11,100 |
| | 66,100 | | 66,100 |

Proposed Dividends

| | £ | | £ |
|---|---|---|---|
| Creditors | | Ordinary shares | 10,000 |
| Dividends payable to minority shareholders | | Preference shares | 5,600 |
| Pref. div. ($\frac{1}{4}$ × £5,600) | 1,400 | | |
| Ord. div. ($\frac{1}{4}$ × £10,000) | 2,500 | | |
| Profit and loss account | | | |
| Holdco Ltd | | | |
| Ord. dividend | 7,500 | | |
| Pref. dividend | 4,200 | | |
| | 15,600 | | 15,600 |

Debenture Interest Accrued

| | £ | | £ |
|---|---|---|---|
| Creditors | | Balance | 1,200 |
| Debenture interest accrued | 900 | | |
| Profit and loss account | | | |
| Holdco Ltd | 300 | | |
| | 1,200 | | 1,200 |

## 57 Edgemont Ltd

Consolidated Balance Sheet at 31st December 19X2

| | £ | £ |
|---|---|---|
| Fixed assets | | |
| Intangible assets: Goodwill | | 20,000 |
| Tangible assets | | 380,000 |
| | | 400,000 |
| Current assets | | |
| Stocks | 45,000 | |
| Debtors and bank | 83,000 | |
| | 128,000 | |
| Creditors: Amounts falling due within one year | | |
| Trade creditors | 27,000 | |
| Proposed dividends: | | |
| Company shareholders | 30,000 | |
| Minority shareholders | 4,900 | |
| | 61,900 | |
| Net current assets | | 66,100 |
| Net assets | | 466,100 |
| Capital and reserves | | |
| Called-up share capital | | 300,000 |
| Profit and loss account | | 86,900 |
| Reserve on consolidation | | 9,200 |
| Shareholders' funds | | 396,100 |
| Minority interests | | 70,000 |
| | | 466,100 |

## Workings

Holdings:

| | Edgehill Ltd | | Edgedale Ltd |
|---|---|---|---|
| Group | 75% | (75% × 80%) | 60% |
| Minority | 25% | | 40% |
| | 100% | | 100% |
| Pre-acquisition reserves: | £24,000 | | £2,000 |

Cost of Control

| | £ | | £ |
|---|---|---|---|
| Cost of investment: | | Shares in Edgehill Ltd | |
| Edgehill Ltd | 160,000 | (75% × £200,000) | 150,000 |
| Edgedale Ltd | | Shares in Edgedale Ltd | |
| (60% × £100,000) | 60,000 | (60% × £100,000) | 60,000 |
| Reserve on consolidation | 9,200 | Edgemont Ltd reserves | |
| | | Pre-acquisition dividend | 15,000 |
| | | Pre-acquisition profits | |
| | | Edgehill Ltd | 3,000 |
| | | Edgedale Ltd | 1,200 |
| | 229,200 | | 229,200 |

Edgehill Ltd Reserves

| | £ | | £ |
|---|---|---|---|
| Cost of control | | Brought down | 50,000 |
| pre-acquisition | | | |
| [75% × £(24,000 − 20,000)] | 3,000 | | |
| Consolidation reserves | | | |
| [75% × £(50,000 − 4,000)] | 34,500 | | |
| Minority interest | | | |
| (25% × £50,000) | 12,500 | | |
| | 50,000 | | 50,000 |

Edgedale Ltd Reserves

| | £ | | £ |
|---|---|---|---|
| Cost of control | | Brought down | 31,000 |
| pre-acquisition | | | |
| (60% × £2,000) | 1,200 | | |
| Consolidation reserves | | | |
| 60% × £(31,000 − 2,000) | 17,400 | | |
| Minority interest | | | |
| (40% × £31,000) | 12,400 | | |
| | 31,000 | | 31,000 |

Consolidated Reserves

| | £ | | £ |
|---|---|---|---|
| Cost of control: Dividend out of pre-acquisition profits | 15,000 | Brought down | 80,000 |
| Proposed dividend | 30,000 | Edgehill Ltd | 34,500 |
| Carried down | 86,900 | Edgedale Ltd | 17,400 |
| | 131,900 | | 131,900 |

Minority Interest

| | £ | | £ |
|---|---|---|---|
| Cost of investment in Edgedale Ltd (40% × £100,000) | 40,000 | Shares in Edgehill Ltd (25% × £200,000) | 50,000 |
| Dividend proposed | | Shares in Edgedale Ltd (40% × £100,000) | 40,000 |
| Edgehill Ltd 25% | 2,500 | Reserves: | |
| Edgedale Ltd 40% | 2,400 | Edgehill Ltd | 12,500 |
| Carried down | 70,000 | Edgedale Ltd | 12,400 |
| | 114,900 | | 114,900 |

## 58 Spades Ltd, Clubs Ltd and Hearts Ltd

Consolidated Balance Sheet at 13th March 19X5

| | £ | £ |
|---|---|---|
| Fixed assets | | |
| Intangible assets: Goodwill | | 32,000 |
| Premium on consolidation | | 9,400 |
| Tangible assets | | 87,500 |
| | | 128,900 |
| Current assets | | |
| Stocks | 120,000 | |
| Debtors | 32,100 | |
| Bank and cash balances | 178,800 | |
| | 330,900 | |
| Creditors: Amounts falling due within one year: | | |
| Bank overdraft | 13,000 | |
| Trade creditors | 84,900 | |
| Corporation tax | 33,200 | |
| Proposed dividends: | | |
| Company shareholders | 20,000 | |
| | 151,100 | |
| Net current assets | | 179,800 |
| Net assets | | 308,700 |

*continued*

| *continued* | £ |
|---|---|
| Capital and reserves | |
| Called-up share capital | 200,000 |
| Profit and loss account | 24,500 |
| Reserves | 50,000 |
| Shareholders' funds | 274,500 |
| Minority interests | 34,200 |
| | 308,700 |

## Workings

(1) Holdings:

| | Clubs Ltd | | Hearts Ltd |
|---|---|---|---|
| Group | 100% | Directly | $\frac{1}{3}$ |
| | | Indirectly | $\frac{1}{3}$ |
| | | | $\frac{2}{3}$ |
| Minority | — | | $\frac{1}{3}$ |
| | 100% | | 100% |

(2) Current account:

| | | |
|---|---|---|
| Hearts Ltd: Debit: | Bank | £2,100 |
| Credit: | Current account with Spades Ltd | £2,100 |

The current accounts of Hearts Ltd and Spades Ltd now agree to £2,700.

*Note:* This adjustment could have equally been made in Spades Ltd by debiting Spades Ltd's bank and crediting its current account with Hearts Ltd with £2,100, thus agreeing the current accounts to £600 which can then be eliminated.

(3) Unrealised profit on stock:
Unrealised profit on stock: $\frac{1}{4}$ ($\frac{1}{4}$ × £32,000) = £2,000

Debit: The profit and loss account of Spades Ltd, the company which made the unrealised profit.
Credit: The stock of Clubs Ltd with £2,000.

(4) Corporation tax liabilities:

| | | |
|---|---|---|
| Debit: | Profit and loss account: Spades Ltd | £22,000 |
| | Clubs Ltd | £ 7,000 |
| | Hearts Ltd | £ 4,200 |
| Credit: | Corporation tax payable | £33,200 |

(5) Proposed dividend:
Debit profit and loss account of Spades Ltd, and credit dividend payable with £20,000, being dividend proposed by Spades Ltd.

(6)

Cost of Control

| | £ | | £ |
|---|---|---|---|
| | | Share capital: | |
| | | C Ltd | 100,000 |
| | | H Ltd (⅔) | 50,000 |
| Cost of shares: | | Reserves: | |
| Clubs Ltd | 120,000 | Clubs Ltd | 10,000 |
| Hearts Ltd | 85,000 | Hearts Ltd | 12,000 |
| | | Profit and loss account: | |
| | | Clubs Ltd | 17,200 |
| | | Hearts Ltd | 6,400 |
| | | Premium on consolidation | 9,400 |
| | 205,000 | | 205,000 |

Reserves

| | Clubs | Hearts | | Clubs | Hearts |
|---|---|---|---|---|---|
| | £ | £ | | £ | £ |
| Cost of control | 10,000 | | Brought down | 10,000 | 18,000 |
| Cost of control (⅔) | | 12,000 | | | |
| Minority interest (⅓) | | 6,000 | | | |
| | | 18,000 | | | 18,000 |

Consolidated Reserves

| | £ | | £ |
|---|---|---|---|
| Consolidated balance sheet | 50,000 | Brought down: Spades Ltd | 50,000 |

Clubs Ltd Profit and Loss Account

| | £ | | £ |
|---|---|---|---|
| Corporation tax | 7,000 | Brought down | 8,000 |
| Cost of control | 17,200 | For 19X6 | 16,200 |
| | 24,200 | | 24,200 |

Hearts Ltd Profit and Loss Account

| | £ | | £ |
|---|---|---|---|
| Corporation tax | 4,200 | Brought down | 3,900 |
| Cost of control (⅔) | 6,400 | For 19X6 | 9,900 |
| Minority interest (⅓) | 3,200 | | |
| | 13,800 | | 13,800 |

Consolidated Profit and Loss Account

| | £ | | £ |
|---|---|---|---|
| Corporation tax | 22,000 | Brought down | 16,500 |
| Provision for unrealised profit | 2,000 | For 19X6 | 52,000 |
| Dividend | 20,000 | | |
| Carried down | 24,500 | | |
| | 68,500 | | 68,500 |

Minority Interest

| | £ | | £ |
|---|---|---|---|
| Carried down | 34,200 | Share capital | |
| | | H Ltd | 25,000 |
| | | Reserves | |
| | | C Ltd | — |
| | | H Ltd | 6,000 |
| | | Profit and loss account | |
| | | H Ltd | 3,200 |
| | 34,200 | | 34,200 |

## 59 Llewellyn Ltd

Consolidated Balance Sheet at 31st December 19X3

| | £ | £ |
|---|---|---|
| Fixed assets | | |
| Tangible assets | | 276,700 |
| Current assets | | |
| Stocks | 60,000 | |
| Debtors | 217,600 | |
| Bank | 27,000 | |
| | 304,600 | |
| Creditors: Amounts falling due within one year: | | |
| Trade creditors | 92,000 | |
| Net current assets | | 212,600 |
| Net assets | | 489,300 |
| Capital and reserves | | |
| Called-up share capital | | 240,000 |
| Share premium | | 36,000 |
| Reserves: Capital | | 31,200 |
| Revenue reserves | | 149,440 |
| Shareholders' funds | | 456,640 |
| Minority interests | | 32,660 |
| | | 489,300 |

*Note:* The purchase price of £108,000 for the four-fifths interest in Grove Ltd was less than the net assets acquired and a reserve of £27,200 arose. It was, therefore, considered that the goodwill of £15,000 in the Grove Ltd balance sheet at 31st December 19X3 had no real value and for the purpose of consolidation has been written off against reserve on consolidation and minority interest.

## Workings

Current account adjustment:

| | | |
|---|---|---|
| Grove Ltd: Bank account | Dr £1,000 | |
| Grove Ltd: Current account with Llewellyn Ltd | | Cr £1,000 |

Cost of Control

| | £ | | £ |
|---|---|---|---|
| Investment in G Ltd | 108,000 | Shares in G Ltd | 96,000 |
| Balance (reserve) carried down | 27,200 | Pre-acquisition | |
| | | Capital reserve | 10,400 |
| | | Revenue reserve | 16,000 |
| | | Profit and loss account | 12,800 |
| | 135,200 | | 135,200 |
| Goodwill write-off ($\frac{4}{5}$ × £15,000) | 12,000 | Balance (reserve) brought down | 27,200 |
| Reserve on consolidation | 15,200 | | |
| | 27,200 | | 27,200 |

Minority Interest

| | £ | | £ |
|---|---|---|---|
| Goodwill write-off ($\frac{1}{5}$ × £15,000) | 3,000 | Shares in G Ltd | 24,000 |
| Consolidated balance sheet | 32,660 | Capital reserve | 2,600 |
| | | Revenue reserve | 4,000 |
| | | Profit and loss account | 5,060 |
| | 35,660 | | 35,660 |

Capital Reserve

| | L Ltd £ | G Ltd £ | | L Ltd £ | G Ltd £ |
|---|---|---|---|---|---|
| Fixtures and fittings Revaluation | | 2,000 | Balance at 1st January 19X3 | 16,000 | 12,000 |
| Investment in P Ltd Write-off | | 5,000 | Plant and machinery: Revaluation | | 8,000 |
| Balance carried down | 16,000 | 13,000 | | | |
| | 16,000 | 20,000 | | 16,000 | 20,000 |

*continued*

| *continued* | L Ltd | G Ltd | | L Ltd | G Ltd |
|---|---|---|---|---|---|
| | £ | £ | | £ | £ |
| Minority interest ($\frac{1}{5}$) | | 2,600 | Balance brought down | 16,000 | 13,000 |
| Cost of control ($\frac{4}{5}$) | | 10,400 | | | |
| Consolidated balance sheet | 16,000 | | | | |
| | 16,000 | 13,000 | | 16,000 | 13,000 |

Revenue Reserve

| | L Ltd | G Ltd | | L Ltd | G Ltd |
|---|---|---|---|---|---|
| | £ | £ | | £ | £ |
| Minority interest ($\frac{1}{5}$) | | 4,000 | Balance at 1st January 19X3 | 30,000 | 20,000 |
| Cost of control ($\frac{4}{5}$) | | 16,000 | | | |
| Consolidated balance sheet | 30,000 | | | | |
| | 30,000 | 20,000 | | 30,000 | 20,000 |

Profit and Loss Account

| | L Ltd | G Ltd | | L Ltd | G Ltd |
|---|---|---|---|---|---|
| | £ | £ | | £ | £ |
| Plant and machinery: | | | Balance at 1st January 19X3 | 80,000 | 16,000 |
| Additional depreciation | | 800 | Year ended 31st December 19X3 | 32,000 | 10,000 |
| Balances carried down: | | | Fixtures and fittings: | | |
| At 1st January 19X3 | 80,000 | 16,000 | Depreciation written back | | 100 |
| Year ended 31st December 19X3 | 32,000 | 9,300 | | | |
| | 112,000 | 26,100 | | 112,000 | 26,100 |
| | | | Balances brought down: | | |
| Minority interest ($\frac{1}{5}$ × £25,300) | | 5,060 | At 1st January 19X3 | 80,000 | 16,000 |
| Cost of control ($\frac{4}{5}$ × £16,000) | | 12,800 | Year ended 31st December 19X3 | 32,000 | 9,300 |
| Post-acquisition ($\frac{4}{5}$ × £9,300 contra) | | 7,440 | Contra | 7,440 | |
| Consolidated balance sheet | 119,440 | | | | |
| | 119,440 | 25,300 | | 119,440 | 25,300 |

## 60 Grip Ltd

Consolidated Balance Sheet at 31st December 19X4
(extracts)

| | 19X4 £ | 19X4 £ | 19X3 £ | 19X3 £ |
|---|---|---|---|---|
| Capital and reserves | | | | |
| Called-up share capital | | 100,000 | | 100,000 |
| Reserves: | | | | |
| Reserve arising on consolidation | 855 | | 855 | |
| Revenue reserves | 21,890 | 22,745 | 20,440 | 21,295 |
| Shareholders' funds | | 122,745 | | 121,295 |
| Minority interest | | 935 | | 1,545 |
| | | 123,680 | | 122,840 |

*Note:* The whole amount of the unrealised profit on the plant has been provided.

### Workings

Revenue Reserves

| | G Ltd £ | H Ltd £ | | G Ltd £ | H Ltd £ |
|---|---|---|---|---|---|
| Cash: Dividend | 15,000 | | 31st December 19X2 | 16,200 | 3,450 |
| Cash: Dividend | | 2,000 | Year ended 31st December 19X3 | 18,640 | 4,000 |
| Minority interest ($\frac{1}{10} \times$ £5,450) | | 545 | Cash: Post-acquisition dividend ($\frac{9}{10} \times \frac{2}{12} \times$ £2,000) | 300 | |
| Cost of control ($\frac{9}{10} \times$ £3,450) | | 3,105 | Post-acquisition: Contra | 300 | |
| Cost of control ($\frac{9}{10} \times \frac{10}{12} \times$ £2,000) | | 1,500 | | | |
| Post-acquisition: Contra | | 300 | | | |
| Balance carried down | 20,440 | | | | |
| | 35,440 | 7,450 | | 35,440 | 7,450 |
| Cash: Dividend | 20,000 | | Balance brought down | 20,440 | |
| Year ended 31st December 19X4 | | 4,100 | Year ended 31st December 19X4 | 26,540 | |
| Unrealised profit on plant | | 2,000 | Depreciation adjustment on plant | 400 | |
| Contra | 5,490 | | Minority interest ($\frac{1}{10} \times$ £6,100) | | 610 |
| Consolidated balance sheet | 21,890 | | Post-acquisition loss Contra | | 5,490 |
| | 47,380 | 6,100 | | 47,380 | 6,100 |

Cost of Control

| | £ | | | £ |
|---|---|---|---|---|
| Investment in Hand Ltd | 14,250 | Shares in Hand Ltd | | 9,000 |
| Reserve on consolidation | 855 | Cash: Pre-acquisition dividend ($\frac{9}{10} \times \frac{10}{12} \times$ £2,000) | | 1,500 |
| | | Pre-acquisition profits | 3,105 | |
| | | Pre-acquisition profits | 1,500 | 4,605 |
| | 15,105 | | | 15,105 |

Minority Interest

| | £ | | £ |
|---|---|---|---|
| 19X3 | | 19X3 | |
| Dec 31 Balance carried down | 1,545 | Shares in Hand Ltd | 1,000 |
| | | Dec 31 Shares of profit | 545 |
| | 1,545 | | 1,545 |
| 19X4 | | | |
| Dec 31 Share of loss | 610 | Balance brought down | 1,545 |
| Balance carried forward | 935 | | |
| | 1,545 | | 1,545 |

## 61 Roberts Ltd

Consolidated Balance Sheet at 30th September 19X3
(extracts)

| | £ | £ |
|---|---|---|
| Capital and reserves | | |
| Called-up share capital | | 40,000 |
| Profit and loss account | | 145,075 |
| | | 185,075 |
| *less:* Premium on consolidation written off | | 3,805 |
| Shareholders' funds | | 181,270 |
| Minority interest | | 42,330 |
| | | 223,600 |
| Reconciliation of assets | | |
| Roberts Ltd | 144,700 | |
| *less:* Investment in Grove Ltd | 32,000 | 112,700 |
| Grove Ltd | 72,020 | |
| *less:* Investment in Dillwyn Ltd | 30,000 | 42,020 |
| Dillwyn Ltd | | 68,880 |
| Group net assets | | 223,600 |

## Workings

Cost of Control

| | £ | | £ |
|---|---|---|---|
| Cost of investments | | Share capital | |
| G | 32,000 | G ($62\frac{1}{2}\%$ × £32,000) | 20,000 |
| D ($56\frac{1}{4}\%$ × £30,000) | 16,875 | D ($56\frac{1}{4}\%$ × £20,000) | 11,250 |
| Pre-acquisition | | Pre-acquisition | |
| D | 4,500 | G | 18,320 |
| | | Premium on consolidation | 3,805 |
| | 53,375 | | 53,375 |

Grove Ltd Profit and Loss Account

| | £ | | £ |
|---|---|---|---|
| Cost of control | | Brought down | 40,020 |
| Pre-acquisition | | | |
| ($62\frac{1}{2}\%$ × £29,312) | 18,320 | | |
| Consolidated reserves | | | |
| [$62\frac{1}{2}\%$ × £(40,020 − 29,312)] | 6,693 | | |
| Minority interest | | | |
| ($37\frac{1}{2}\%$ × £40,020) | 15,007 | | |
| | 40,020 | | 40,020 |

Dillwyn Ltd Profit and Loss Account

| | £ | | £ |
|---|---|---|---|
| Consolidated reserves | 33,682 | Brought down | 51,880 |
| Minority interest | | Pre-acquisition | |
| ($43\frac{3}{4}\%$ × £51,880) | 22,698 | ($56\frac{1}{4}\%$ × £8,000) | 4,500 |
| | 56,380 | | 56,380 |

Consolidated Reserve Account

| | £ | | £ |
|---|---|---|---|
| Carried down | 145,075 | Brought down | 104,700 |
| | | G | 6,693 |
| | | D | 33,682 |
| | 145,075 | | 145,075 |

| Holdings | Grove Ltd | | Dillwyn Ltd |
|---|---|---|---|
| Group | $62\frac{1}{2}\%$ | ($62\frac{1}{2}$ × 90)% | $56\frac{1}{4}\%$ |
| Minority | $37\frac{1}{2}\%$ | | $43\frac{3}{4}\%$ |
| Pre-acquisition reserves | £29,312 Cr | | £(8,000) Dr |

Minority Interest

| | £ | | £ |
|---|---|---|---|
| Cost of investments | | Share capital | |
| D ($43\frac{3}{4}$% × £30,000) | 16,125 | G $37\frac{1}{2}$% | 12,000 |
| Carried down | 42,330 | D $43\frac{3}{4}$% | 8,750 |
| | | Profit and loss account | |
| | | G | 15,007 |
| | | D | 22,698 |
| | 58,455 | | 58,455 |

## 62 Fig Ltd

Consolidated Balance Sheet at 30th June 19X3

| | £ | £ |
|---|---|---|
| Fixed assets | | |
| Intangible assets: Premium on consolidation | | 6,000 |
| Tangible assets | | 343,600 |
| | | 349,600 |
| Current assets | | |
| Stocks | 175,140 | |
| Debtors | 104,275 | |
| Bank and cash balances | 166,084 | |
| | 445,499 | |
| Creditors: Amounts falling due within one year | | |
| Creditors | 128,393 | |
| Corporation tax | 148,850 | |
| Proposed dividends | | |
| Company shareholders | 120,000 | |
| Minority shareholders | 12,500 | |
| | 409,743 | |
| Net current assets | | 35,756 |
| Net assets | | 385,356 |
| Capital and reserves | | |
| Called-up share capital | | 200,000 |
| Reserves | | 32,500 |
| Profit and loss account | | 100,223 |
| Shareholders' funds | | 332,723 |
| Minority interests | | 52,633 |
| | | 385,356 |

## Workings

*Note:* The following consolidation adjustments are required:

| | Dr | Cr |
|---|---|---|
| Revenue reserves:* Run Ltd | 3,000 | |
| Plant and machinery | | 3,000 |
| Aggregate depreciation* | 600 | |
| Revenue reserves: Fig Ltd | | 600 |
| Revenue reserves:* Fig Ltd | 4,000 | |
| Stock | | |
| ($\frac{1}{3}$ × £18,000 = £6,000 − £2,000) | | 4,000 |
| Proposed dividends: Run Ltd | 70,000 | |
| Trot Ltd | 7,500 | |
| Debtors: Fig Ltd | | 77,500 |

* Some accountants would adjust only for the holding company's share.

Cost of Control—Fig Ltd

| | £ | | £ |
|---|---|---|---|
| Investment in Run Ltd | 115,000 | Shares in Run Ltd | 70,000 |
| Investment in Trot Ltd | 70,000 | Shares in Trot Ltd | 75,000 |
| Pre-acquisition: | | Pre-acquisition: | |
| Revenue reserves (T) | 4,500 | Capital reserves | |
| | | £(12,500 + 10,000) | 22,500 |
| | | Revenue reserves | |
| | | £(10,000 + 6,000) | 16,000 |
| | | Goodwill on consolidation | 6,000 |
| | 189,500 | | 189,500 |

Minority Interest

| | £ | | £ |
|---|---|---|---|
| Consolidated balance sheet | 52,633 | Shares in Run Ltd | 10,000 |
| | | Shares in Trot Ltd | 25,000 |
| | | Capital reserves: Run Ltd | 5,000 |
| | | Revenue reserves | |
| | | Trot Ltd | 7,763 |
| | | Run Ltd | 4,870 |
| | 52,633 | | 52,633 |

Capital Reserves

| | £ | £ | | £ | £ |
|---|---|---|---|---|---|
| Minority interest ($\frac{1}{8}$) | | 5,000 | Balances | 20,000 | 40,000 |
| Cost of control | | | | ¢ 12,500 | |
| ($\frac{5}{8}$ × £20,000) | | 12,500 | | | |
| ($\frac{2}{8}$ × £40,000) | | 10,000 | | | |
| Post-acquisition | | ¢ 12,500 | | | |
| Consolidated balance sheet | 32,500 | | | | |
| | 32,500 | 40,000 | | 32,500 | 40,000 |

Revenue Reserves

| | £ | £ | £ | | £ | £ | £ |
|---|---|---|---|---|---|---|---|
| Plant adjustment | | 3,000 | | Balances | 57,744 | 41,960 | 31,052 |
| Stock adjustment | 4,000 | | | Depreciation adjustment | 600 | | |
| Balance carried down | 54,344 | 38,960 | 31,052 | | | | |
| Minority interest (T) ($\frac{1}{4}$) | | | 7,763 | Balance brought down | 54,344 | 38,960 | 31,052 |
| Post-acquisition | | | ¢ 27,789 | Cost of control | | | |
| Minority interest (R) ($\frac{1}{8}$) | | 4,870 | | ($\frac{3}{4}$ × £6,000) | | | 4,500 |
| Cost of control | | | | | ¢ 27,789 | | |
| ($\frac{5}{8}$ × £16,000) | | 10,000 | | | ¢ 18,090 | | |
| ($\frac{2}{8}$ × £24,000) | | 6,000 | | | | | |
| Post-acquisition | | ¢ 18,090 | | | | | |
| Consolidated balance sheet | 100,223 | | | | | | |
| | 100,223 | 38,960 | 35,552 | | 100,223 | 38,960 | 35,552 |

## 63 Kestrel Ltd

Consolidated Profit and Loss Account
year ended 31st March 19X3

| Note | | £ | £ |
|---|---|---|---|
| 1 | Operating profit | | 457,700 |
| | Share of profits of Associated Company | | 78,300 |
| | | | 536,000 |
| | Corporation tax: | | |
| | Group | 235,000 | |
| | Associated Company | 39,150 | 274,150 |
| | Profit after tax | | 261,850 |
| | Minority interest | | 6,350 |
| 2 | Profit attributable to members of Holding Co. | *carried forward* | 255,500 |

| Notes | | £ | £ |
|---|---|---|---|
| | *brought forward* | | 255,500 |
| 3 | Amount written off investment in subsidiary | 8,000 | |
| | Transfer to reserves | 50,000 | |
| | Proposed dividends | 150,000 | |
| | | | 208,000 |
| | Retained profits for the financial year | | 47,500 |
| | Retained profits at 1st April 19X2: | | |
| | Group | 69,000 | |
| | Associated Company | — | |
| | | | 69,000 |
| 4 | Retained profits at 31st March 19X3 | | 116,500 |

Note 1: (a) Trading profit has been arrived at after charging:

| | £ |
|---|---|
| Directors' fees | 40,000 |
| Depreciation | 47,000 |
| Audit Fees | 3,300 |

(b) Accounting policy: Provision has been made for the whole of the unrealised inter-company profit without reference to minority interest.

Note 2: Profit dealt with in the accounts of Kestrel Ltd: £231,500.

Note 3: In view of losses in the subsidiary Thrush Ltd, the directors of Kestrel Ltd are of the opinion that £8,000 be written off its investment in that company.

Note 4: Retained profits at 31st March 19X3:

| | £ | £ |
|---|---|---|
| In: Holding Company | | 68,500 |
| Subsidiaries: Sparrow Ltd | 61,200 | |
| Thrush Ltd | (25,350) | |
| | | 35,850 |
| Associated Company | | 12,150 |
| | | 116,500 |

## Workings

| | Kestrel Ltd | Sparrow Ltd | Thrush Ltd | Total | Osprey Ltd |
|---|---|---|---|---|---|
| | £ | £ | £ | £ | £ |
| Trading profits | 416,000 | 126,000 | 10,000 | 552,000 | 210,000 |
| *less:* | | | | | |
| Directors' fees | 24,000 | 12,000 | 10,000 | | 20,000 |
| Inter-company fees | (6,000) | | | | |
| Depreciation | 20,000 | 18,000 | 9,000 | | 15,000 |
| Audit fees | 1,500 | 1,000 | 800 | | 1,000 |
| Unrealised profit (25% × £20,000 − £1,000) | | 4,000 | | | |
| | 39,500 | 35,000 | 19,800 | 94,300 | 36,000 |
| Operating profit | 376,500 | 91,000 | (9,800) | 457,700 | 174,000 |

*continued*

| | | Kestrel Ltd £ | Sparrow Ltd £ | Thrush Ltd £ | Total £ | Osprey Ltd £ |
|---|---|---|---|---|---|---|
| *brought forward* | | | | | | |
| Operating profit | | 376,500 | 91,000 | (9,800) | 457,700 | 174,000 |
| Share of profits of Associated Company ($\frac{9}{20}$ × £174,000) | | | | | 78,300 | 78,300 |
| | | | | | 536,000 | |
| Taxation | | 188,000 | 47,000 | — | 274,150 | 39,150 |
| | | 188,500 | 44,000 | (9,800) | 261,850 | 39,150 |
| Minority Interest | | | ($\frac{1}{5}$) 8,800 | ($\frac{1}{4}$)(2,450) | 6,350 | |
| | | | 35,200 | (7,350) | 255,500 | |
| Inter-company dividends | | 43,000 | (16,000) | | | (27,000) |
| | | 231,500 | 19,200 | | | 12,150 |
| | £ | | | | | |
| Amount written off | 8,000 | | | | | |
| Transfer to reserves | 50,000 | | | | | |
| Proposed dividend | 150,000 | 208,000 | | | 208,000 | |
| | | 23,500 | | | 47,500 | |
| Balance brought forward | | | | | | |
| Kestrel Ltd | | 45,000 | | | | |
| Sparrow Ltd (60% × £70,000) | | | 42,000 | | | |
| Thrush Ltd (75% × £24,000) | | | | (18,000) | 69,000 | |
| | | 68,500 | 61,200 | (25,350) | 116,500 | 12,150 |

## 64 Abstract Ltd

Consolidated Profit and Loss Account
year ended 30th June 19X3

| Note | | £ | £ |
|---|---|---|---|
| 1 | Sales | | 1,254,167 |
| | Cost of sales | | 664,167 |
| | | | 590,000 |
| | Selling and distribution costs | 73,125 | |
| | Administration expenses | 136,875 | 210,000 |
| | Operating profit, before taxation | | 380,000 |
| 2 | Share of associated company's profit | | 27,000 |
| | | | 407,000 |
| | Corporation tax: | | |
| | Group | 195,000 | |
| | Associated company | 12,960 | 207,960 |
| | *carried forward* | | 199,040 |

| Note | | £ | £ |
|---|---|---|---|
| | *(brought forward)* | | 199,040 |
| | Minority shareholders' interest | | 14,687 |
| 3 | Profit attributable to Abstract Ltd | | 184,353 |
| | Ordinary dividends: paid | 75,000 | |
| | proposed | 75,000 | 150,000 |
| | Retained profit: | | 34,353 |
| | Retained: | | |
| | By Abstract Ltd | 22,125 | |
| | By Subsidiary | 7,188 | |
| | In associated company | 5,040 | 34,353 |
| | Balance at 1st July 19X2 | | 26,750 |
| | Balance at 30th June 19X3 | | 61,103 |

*Notes to the accounts*

(1) This represents the turnover of the holding company and its subsidiary. The turnover of the associated company was £500,000.

(2) Abstract Ltd acquired 45 per cent of the ordinary share capital of Corn Ltd on 1st March 19X3.

(3) £172,125 has been dealt with in the separate accounts of Abstract Ltd.

(4) The accounting policy of Abstract Ltd is to take account of all dividends from subsidiary and associated companies as soon as they have been declared.

| | Abstract Ltd | Bran Ltd | $\times \frac{5}{12}$ | Consolidated | Corn Ltd |
|---|---|---|---|---|---|
| | £ | £ | £ | £ | £ |
| Sales | 900,000 | 850,000 | 354,167 | 1,254,167 | 500,000 |
| Opening stock | 49,650 | 100,280 | | | 34,500 |
| Purchases | 497,990 | 482,580 | | | 221,100 |
| | 547,640 | 582,860 | | | 255,600 |
| Closing stock | 87,640 | 92,860 | | | 45,600 |
| Cost of sales | 460,000 | 490,000 | 204,167 | 664,167 | 210,000 |
| Gross profit | 440,000 | 360,000 | 150,000 | 590,000 | 290,000 |
| Selling and distribution costs | (45,000) | (67,500) | (28,125) | (73,125) | (45,000) |
| Administration expenses | (115,000) | (52,500) | (21,875) | (136,875) | (65,000) |
| Operating profit | 280,000 | 240,000 | 100,000 | 380,000 | 180,000 |
| Share of profits of associated company (£180,000 × $\frac{4}{12}$ × 45%) | | | | 27,000 | 27,000 |
| | | | | 407,000 | |
| Taxation | 150,000 | 108,000 | 45,000 | 195,000 | |
| | 130,000 | 132,000 | 55,000 | 212,000 | |

*continued*

| | Abstract Ltd | Bran Ltd | $\times \frac{5}{12}$ | Consolidated | Corn Ltd |
|---|---|---|---|---|---|
| | £ | £ | £ | £ | £ |
| *brought forward* | 130,000 | 132,000 | 55,000 | 212,000 | 27,000 |
| Share of associated company taxation (£86,400 $\times \frac{4}{12} \times$ 45%) | | | | 12,960 | 12,960 |
| | | | | 199,040 | 14,040 |
| Pref. dividend (*see* Working 1) | 1,875 | | 1,875 | | |
| | 131,875 | | 53,125 | | |
| Minority interest (*see* Working 2) | | | 14,687 | (14,687) | |
| | | | 38,438 | 184,353 | |
| Inter-company dividend | 31,250 | | 31,250 | | |
| (*see* Working 3) | 9,000 | | | | (9,000) |
| | 172,125 | | 7,188 | | 5,040 |
| Proposed dividend | 150,000 | | | 150,000 | |
| | 22,125 | | 7,188 | 34,353 | 5,040 |

## Workings

(1) Preference dividends:

| | £ | | £ |
|---|---|---|---|
| Paid on account 1st January 19X3 | | | 4,500 |
| Final dividend 30th June 19X3 | | | 4,500 |
| | | | 9,000 |
| Minority interest 50% in preference shares | | | 4,500 |
| | | | 4,500 |
| Pre-acquisition | | ($\frac{7}{12}$) | 2,625 |
| Post-acquisition | | | 1,875 |

(2) Minority interest:

| | | | Minority interest |
|---|---|---|---|
| Profit after taxation | 132,000 | | |
| Preference dividend | 9,000 | 50% $\times \frac{5}{12}$ | 1,875 |
| | 123,000 | | |
| 25% $\times \frac{5}{12}$ thereof | | | 12,812 |
| | | | 14,687 |

(3) Inter-company dividends (ordinary shares):

| | £ |
|---|---|
| Bran Ltd: | |
| Dividends paid on account on the ordinary shares on 1st January 19X3 | 40,000 |
| Final dividend on 30th June 19X3 | 60,000 |
| Total dividend paid for the year | 100,000 |

*continued*

*continued*

| | | | £ |
|---|---|---|---|
| Holding Co's share $\frac{3}{4}$ × £100,000 | | | 75,000 |
| *less:* Pre-acquisition | | ($\frac{7}{12}$) | 43,750 |
| Post-acquisition | | | 31,250 |
| Corn Ltd: | | | |
| Dividend on 30th June 19X3 | £60,000 | | |
| Holding Co's share since the acquisition of shares in Corn Ltd (45% × $\frac{4}{12}$ × £60,000) | | | 9,000 |
| | | | 40,250 |

TUTORIAL NOTE

The disclosure requirements as indicated in SSAP 1 necessitate a note as to how much of the consolidated retained profit is dealt with in the separate accounts of holding company, subsidiary and associated company. For this purpose it is necessary to compute the post-acquisition dividends that Abstract Ltd would credit to its profit and loss account for the period. The calculation of the post-acquisition portion of the dividend must be made in respect of the total dividends for the period, both paid and proposed. The proportion attributable to the pre-acquisition period is then reduced by the dividend actually paid before acquisition and not therefore received by Abstract Ltd.

## 8 INCOMPLETE RECORDS

### 65 Mr G

(a) Trading and Profit and Loss Account
year ended 31st March 19X4

| | £ | £ | £ |
|---|---|---|---|
| Sales | | | 39,900 |
| *deduct:* Cost of sales | | | |
| Stock at 1st April 19X3 | | 6,300 | |
| Purchases | | 32,600 | |
| | | 38,900 | |
| *less:* Stock at 31st March 19X4 | | 5,850 | 33,050 |
| | | | 6,850 |
| Expenses | | 5,130 | |
| Loan interest | | 700 | |
| Depreciation: | | | |
| Furniture and equipment | 1,080 | | |
| Motor vehicle | 910 | 1,990 | |
| Bad debts | | 100 | 7,920 |
| Net loss | | | 1,070 |

Balance Sheet 31st March 19X4

| | £ | £ | £ |
|---|---|---|---|
| Capital | | | |
| As at 1st April 19X3 | | 9,350 | |
| *less:* Loss | 1,070 | | |
| Drawings | 5,300 | 6,370 | 2,980 |
| Loan J. | | | 7,000 |
| | | | 9,980 |
| Fixed assets | | | |
| Goodwill | | | 2,000 |
| Furniture and equipment at cost | | 5,400 | |
| *less:* Depreciation | | 2,680 | 2,720 |
| Motor vehicles at cost | | 4,550 | |
| *less:* Depreciation | | 1,610 | 2,940 |
| | | | 7,660 |
| Current assets | | | |
| Stock | | 5,850 | |
| Debtors | | 1,300 | |
| Prepayments | | 520 | |
| | | 7,670 | |
| *deduct:* Current liabilities | | | |
| Creditors | 3,800 | | |
| Bank overdraft | 350 | | |
| Accrued expenses | 1,200 | 5,350 | 2,320 |
| | | | 9,980 |

Accrued expenses include:

| | £ |
|---|---|
| Loan interest | 700 |
| Bank interest | 50 |
| Other expenses | 450 |
| | 1,200 |

(b)

Results: Unsatisfactory.

Profitability: Gross profit 17 per cent approximately: £6,850. Net loss £1,070; major causes high expenditure and depreciation.

Solvency: Current ratio 1.4:1 but liquid position is tight. Loan from J. has

| | |
|---|---|
| | enabled bank overdraft to be reduced but terms of repayment not stated. Immediate repayment would cause business to close unless further assistance available. Drawings are very high and restriction should be considered. |
| Financing: | Investment of J. much greater than owner's interest, J's loan at risk unless the firm's trading position improves. Purchase of additional motor vehicle seems to be somewhat extravagant. |
| General: | The reason for the loss should be investigated. |

## Workings

(1) Bank summary:

| | £ | £ |
|---|---|---|
| Balance overdrawn at 1st April 19X3 | | (1,000) |
| Receipts | 45,000 | |
| *less:* Payments | 44,350 | |
| | | 650 |
| Balance overdrawn at 31st March 19X4 | | (350) |

(2) Sales:

Total Debtors

| | £ | | £ |
|---|---|---|---|
| Balance brought forward | 1,000 | Cash | 5,200 |
| Sales | 5,600 | Bad debts | 100 |
| | | Balance carried forward | 1,300 |
| | 6,600 | | 6,600 |

Credit sales £5,600 + Cash sales £34,300 = £39,900

(3) Purchases:

Total Creditors

| | £ | | £ |
|---|---|---|---|
| Cash | 8,900 | Balance brought forward | 3,200 |
| Balance carried forward | 3,800 | Purchases | 9,500 |
| | 12,700 | | 12,700 |

| | £ |
|---|---|
| Credit purchases | 9,500 |
| Cash purchases | 23,200 |
| | 32,700 |
| *less:* Drawings | 100 |
| | 32,600 |

(4) Expenses:

Total Expenses

| | | £ | | | £ |
|---|---|---|---|---|---|
| 19X3 | | | 19X3 | | |
| Apr 1 | Balance brought forward | 500 | Apr 1 | Balance brought forward | 650 |
| 19X4 | | | 19X4 | | |
| Mar 31 | Cash | 5,300 | Mar 31 | Balance carried forward | 520 |
| Mar 31 | Balance carried forward | 450 | | Profit and loss account | 5,130 |
| | Bank interest carried forward | 50 | | | |
| | | 6,300 | | | 6,300 |

## 66 Fair Travel Agency

Profit and Loss Account
year ended 31st October 19X9

| | | £ | | £ |
|---|---|---|---|---|
| Wages | | 2,740 | Commission | |
| Rent | | 500 | Tour Operators | 6,950 |
| Rates | | 310 | British Rail | 630 |
| Electricity | | 90 | Airlines | 540 |
| Accountancy | | 150 | | |
| Advertising | | 575 | | |
| Sundry expenses | | 52 | | |
| Depreciation: | | | | |
| Motor car | 225 | | | |
| Fixtures and fittings | 100 | | | |
| | | 325 | | |
| Net profit | | 3,378 | | |
| | | 8,120 | | 8,120 |

Balance Sheet 31st October 19X9

| | £ | £ | | £ | £ |
|---|---|---|---|---|---|
| Capital at | | | Fixed assets | | |
| 1st November 19X8 | 5,100 | | Fixtures and fittings | 1,000 | |
| *add:* Net profit | 3,378 | | *less:* Depreciation | 100 | |
| | | | | | 900 |
| | 8,478 | | Motor car | 900 | |
| *deduct:* Drawings | 1,068 | | *less:* Depreciation | 225 | |
| | | 7,410 | | | 675 |
| Current liabilities: | | | | | 1,575 |
| Creditors | 2,390 | | Current assets | | |
| Deposits | 1,000 | | Debtors | 100 | |
| | | 3,390 | Prepayment | 125 | |
| | | | Balance at bank | 9,000 | |
| | | | | | 9,225 |
| | | 10,800 | | | 10,800 |

## Workings

| *Income* | £ | £ |
|---|---|---|
| Commission | | |
| Tour Operators Ltd | | |
| Cash paid | 62,000 | |
| Amount owing 31st October 19X9 | 550 | |
| 90% of charge | 62,550 | |
| 10% of charge | 6,950 | 6,950 |
| | 69,500 | |
| British Rail | | |
| Cash paid | 7,000 | |
| Creditor 31st October 19X9 | 1,370 | |
| 93% of charge | 8,370 | |
| 7% of charge | 630 | 630 |
| | 9,000 | |
| Airlines | | |
| Cash paid | 6,500 | |
| Creditor 31st October 19X9 | 160 | |
| $92\frac{1}{2}$% of charge | 6,660 | |
| $7\frac{1}{2}$% of charge | 540 | 540 |
| | 7,200 | |

*Expenses*

Wages

| | £ | | £ |
|---|---|---|---|
| Cash | 2,080 | Balance brought forward PAYE | 250 |
| Balance carried forward PAYE | 910 | Profit and loss account | 2,740 |
| | 2,990 | | 2,990 |

Rates

| | £ | | £ |
|---|---|---|---|
| Cash | 300 | Balance brought forward | 100 |
| Balance carried forward | 110 | Profit and loss account | 310 |
| | 410 | | 410 |

Advertising

| | £ | | £ |
|---|---|---|---|
| Cash | 625 | Balance brought forward | 100 |
| Balance carried forward | 50 | Profit and loss account | 575 |
| | 675 | | 675 |

Cash Account

| | £ | | £ |
|---|---|---|---|
| Charges | | Bankings | 82,000 |
| Tour Operators | 68,500 | Wages | 2,080 |
| British Rail | 9,400 | Sundries | 52 |
| Airlines | 7,300 | Drawings | 1,040 |
| | | Difference to drawings | 28 |
| | 85,200 | | 85,200 |

| | £ |
|---|---|
| Tour Operators | |
| Total charge | 69,500 |
| *less:* Deposits 19X7/8 | 2,000 |
| | 67,500 |
| *add:* Deposits at 31st October 19X9 | 1,000 |
| | 68,500 |
| British Rail | |
| Total charge | 9,000 |
| *less:* Debtors at end | 100 |
| | 8,900 |
| *add:* Debtors at start | 500 |
| | 9,400 |
| Airlines | |
| Total charge | 7,200 |
| *add:* Debtor at start | 100 |
| Cash received | 7,300 |

## 67 Able

(a)

Trading and Profit and Loss Accounts
year ended 30th September 19X1

| | £ | £ | £ |
|---|---|---|---|
| Sales: Cash | | | 11,500 |
| Credit | | | 2,475 |
| | | | 13,975 |
| *less:* Cost of sales: | | | |
| Purchases | | 9,535 | |
| Closing stock | 1,000 | | |
| Damaged stock | 250 | | |
| | | 1,250 | |
| | | | 8,285 |
| Gross profit | | *carried forward* | 5,690 |

| *brought forward* | £ | £ |
|---|---|---|
| | | 5,690 |
| *less:* Wages | 750 | |
| Sundry expenses | 684 | |
| Vehicle expenses | 500 | |
| Insurance | 50 | |
| Bank charges and interest | 210 | |
| Depreciation | 70 | |
| Amortisation | 650 | |
| Damaged stock | 250 | |
| Commission (5% × £2,526) | 126 | |
| | | 3,290 |
| Net profit before appropriations | | 2,400 |

| | 9 months to 30th June 19X1 | 3 months to 30th September 19X1 | |
|---|---|---|---|
| | £ | £ | |
| | 1,800 | 600 | |
| Divided: | | | |
| Able | 1,800 | 400 | ($\frac{2}{3}$) |
| Charles | — | 200 | ($\frac{1}{3}$) |

(b) Balance Sheet 30th September 19X1

| | Cost | Depreciation | Net book value |
|---|---|---|---|
| | £ | £ | £ |
| Fixed assets | | | |
| Lease | 6,500 | 650 | 5,850 |
| Motor vehicles | 1,400 | 70 | 1,330 |
| | 7,900 | 720 | 7,180 |
| Current assets | | | |
| Stock | | 1,000 | |
| Debtors and prepayments | | 405 | |
| Cash at bank and in hand | | 1,435 | |
| | | 2,840 | |
| Current liabilities | | | |
| Creditors and accrued charges | | 720 | |
| | | | 2,120 |
| | | | 9,300 |

*continued*

*continued*

| | Depreciation £ | Net book value £ |
|---|---|---|
| Capital accounts | | |
| Able | | 5,800 |
| Charles | | 2,600 |
| | | 8,400 |
| Current accounts | | |
| Able (2,200 − 1,200) | 1,000 | |
| Charles (200 − 300) | (100) | 900 |
| | | 9,300 |

## Workings

Cash Book

| | Cash £ | Bank £ | | Cash £ | Bank £ |
|---|---|---|---|---|---|
| Able | | 5,000 | Bank ¢ | 8,100 | |
| Charles | | 2,000 | Cash ¢ | | 20 |
| Purchase control | | 25 | Purchase control | | 9,000 |
| Sales control | | 2,095 | Insurance | | 70 |
| Cash ¢ | | 8,100 | Bank charges | | 210 |
| Bank ¢ | 20 | | Lease | | 6,500 |
| Cash sales | | | Sundry expenses | 650 | |
| (balancing figure) | 11,500 | | Motor expenses | 500 | |
| | | | Wages | 750 | |
| | | | Drawings | 1,500 | |
| | | | Able: IOU | 5 | |
| | | | Balances carried down | 15 | 1,420 |
| | 11,520 | 17,220 | | 11,520 | 17,220 |

Sales Control

| | £ | | £ |
|---|---|---|---|
| Trading account | 2,475 | Bank | 2,095 |
| | | Balance carried down | 380 |
| | 2,475 | | 2,475 |

Purchase Control

| | £ | | £ |
|---|---|---|---|
| Bank | 9,000 | Bank | 25 |
| Balance carried down | 560 | Trading account | 9,535 |
| | 9,560 | | 9,560 |

# 9 PARTNERSHIP ACCOUNTING

## A Basic

### 68 Long, Tall and Short

(a) Trading and Profit and Loss Account
year ended 31st December 19X4

| | £ | £ | | £ |
|---|---|---|---|---|
| Stock at 1st January 19X4 | | 12,400 | Sales | 102,200 |
| Purchases | | 46,000 | | |
| Carriage | | 840 | | |
| | | 59,240 | | |
| *deduct:* Stock at 31st December 19X4. (£13,600 + £1,440 on sale or return) | | 15,040 | | |
| | | 44,200 | | |
| Manufacturing wages (£14,400 + bonus £800) | | 15,200 | | |
| Depreciation on plant and machinery ($\frac{1}{10}$ × 16,600) | | 1,660 | | |
| Gross profit carried down | | 41,140 | | |
| | | 102,200 | | 102,200 |
| | £ | £ | | £ |
| Salaries and bonus (£6,100 + £1,400 − £2,400) | | 5,100 | Gross profit brought down | 41,140 |
| Repairs (£1,210 − £600 capitalised) | | 610 | Profit on sale of motor vehicle | 200 |
| Bad debts | | | | |
| Written off | 210 | | | |
| Provision for increase | 160 | 370 | | |
| Depreciation of motor vehicles ($\frac{1}{4}$ × £2,000) | | 500 | | |
| Office expenses | | 2,450 | | |
| Discounts allowed | | 980 | | |
| Net profit carried down | | 31,330 | | |
| | | 41,340 | | 41,340 |

Profit and Loss Appropriation Account

| | | £ | £ | | £ |
|---|---|---|---|---|---|
| Interest on capital | | | | Net profit brought down | 31,330 |
| Long | | 1,000 | | | |
| Tall | | 700 | | | |
| Short | | 300 | 2,000 | | |
| Salaries | | | | | |
| Long | | 1,200 | | | |
| Tall | | 720 | | | |
| Short | | 480 | 2,400 | | |
| Share of profit | | | | | |
| Long ($\frac{4}{7}$) | | 15,388 | | | |
| *deduct:* | | | | | |
| Contribution to Short | | 248 | 15,140 | | |
| Tall ($\frac{2}{7}$) | | 7,694 | | | |
| *deduct:* | | | | | |
| Contribution to Short | | 124 | 7,570 | | |
| Short ($\frac{1}{7}$) | | 3,848 | | | |
| From: Long | 248 | | | | |
| Tall | 124 | 372 | 4,220 | | |
| | | | 31,330 | | 31,330 |

(b) Balance Sheet at 31st December 19X4

| | Cost | Depreciation | NBV |
|---|---|---|---|
| Fixed assets | £ | £ | £ |
| Freehold premises | 22,000 | — | 22,000 |
| Plant and machinery | 16,600 | 4,860 | 11,740 |
| Motor vehicles | 2,000 | 900 | 1,100 |
| | 40,600 | 5,760 | 34,840 |
| Current assets | | | |
| Stock | | 15,040 | |
| Debtors | 7,390 | | |
| *less:* Provision for doubtful debts | 1,000 | 6,390 | |
| Balance at bank | | 2,360 | |
| | | 23,790 | |
| *less:* Current liabilities | | | |
| Creditors | 4,600 | | |
| Accrued expenses | 2,200 | 6,800 | 16,990 |
| | | | 51,830 |

*continued*

*continued*

| | Long | Tall | Short | |
|---|---|---|---|---|
| Financed by | £ | £ | £ | |
| Partners | | | | |
| Capital accounts | 10,000 | 7,000 | 3,000 | |
| Current accounts | 18,540 | 9,370 | 3,920 | |
| | 28,540 | 16,370 | 6,920 | 51,830 |

(c) Partners' Current Accounts

| | Long | Tall | Short | | Long | Tall | Short |
|---|---|---|---|---|---|---|---|
| | £ | £ | £ | | £ | £ | £ |
| Balance brought forward | | | 600 | Balances brought forward | 2,400 | 1,100 | |
| Drawings | 1,200 | 720 | 480 | Interest on capital | 1,000 | 700 | 300 |
| Balances carried forward | 18,540 | 9,370 | 3,920 | Salaries | 1,200 | 720 | 480 |
| | | | | Share of profit | 15,140 | 7,570 | 4,220 |
| | 19,740 | 10,090 | 5,000 | | 19,740 | 10,090 | 5,000 |

## Workings

| | £ | £ |
|---|---|---|
| (1) Debtors: Per trial balance | | 9,400 |
| *deduct:* Sent out on sale or return | 1,800 | |
| Bad debts written off | 210 | |
| | | 2,010 |
| Balance 31st December 19X4 | | 7,390 |

(2) Adjustments to motor vehicles accounts:

| | Cost | Depreciation | Net book value |
|---|---|---|---|
| | £ | £ | £ |
| Per trial balance | 3,400 | 1,400 | 2,000 |
| Sale in year | 1,400 | 1,000 | 400 (sold for £600) |
| | 2,000 | 400 | 1,600 |
| Depreciation for year (profit and loss account) | | 500 | (500) |
| Balances carried forward | 2,000 | 900 | 1,100 |

| (3) Short's share of profits: | £ |
|---|---|
| Interest | 300 |
| Salary | 480 |
| Normal share of profits ($\frac{1}{7}$) | 3,848 |
| *carried forward* | 4,628 |

| | £ | |
|---|---|---|
| | *brought forward* | 4,628 |
| Shortfall contributed in profit-sharing ratio | | |
| Long = £($\frac{2}{3}$ × (5,000 − 4,628)) = | 248 | |
| Tall = £($\frac{1}{3}$ × (5,000 − 4,628)) = | 124 | |
| | | 372 |
| Minimum sum guaranteed | | 5,000 |

## B Admission of partner

## 69 Taylor and Clough

(a) Statement Showing the Division of Profit
year ended 31st December 19X9

| | £ | £ |
|---|---|---|
| Profit as per draft accounts | | 16,400 |
| *less:* Interest on fixed capitals | | |
| Taylor | 640 | |
| Clough | 640 | |
| Best | 320 | 1,600 |
| | | 14,800 |
| *add:* Interest charged on debit balances | | |
| Clough | 200 | |
| Best | 260 | 460 |
| | | 15,260 |
| Division of profit | | |
| Profit available | | 15,260 |
| Prior share: Taylor | | 500 |
| | | 14,760 |
| Best's guaranteed share (*see* note) | | 3,500 |
| | | 11,260 |
| Taylor | 5,630 | |
| Clough | 5,630 | 11,260 |
| | | Nil |

Summary of Division

| | £ |
|---|---|
| Taylor (500 + 5,630) | 6,130 |
| Clough | 5,630 |
| Best | 3,500 |
| | 15,260 |

*Note:* Since Best's share of $\frac{1}{5}$ × £14,760 (£2,952) is less than his guaranteed amount, he must be given first the amount due to him before splitting the remainder of the profits.

(b)

## Partners' Current Account

| 19X9 | | Taylor | Clough | Best | 19X9 | | Taylor | Clough | Best |
|---|---|---|---|---|---|---|---|---|---|
| | | £ | £ | £ | | | £ | £ | £ |
| Jan 1 | Goodwill ¢ | 7,200 | 7,200 | 3,600 | Jan 1 | Balances brought down | 3,400 | 1,200 | — |
| | Capital accounts* | — | 2,000 | — | | Goodwill ¢ | 12,000 | 6,000 | — |
| | Balance carried down | 10,200 | — | — | | Capital accounts* | 2,000 | — | 1,000 |
| | | | | | | Balances carried down | — | 2,000 | 2,600 |
| | | 17,400 | 9,200 | 3,600 | | | 17,400 | 9,200 | 3,600 |
| | | £ | £ | £ | | | £ | £ | £ |
| Jan 1 | Balances brought down | — | 2,000 | 2,600 | Jan 1 | Balance brought down | 10,200 | — | — |
| Dec 31 | Interest on debit balances | — | 200 | 260 | Dec 31 | Interest on fixed capitals | 640 | 640 | 320 |
| | Drawings | 5,000 | 2,500 | 1,500 | | Share of profits | 6,130 | 5,630 | 3,500 |
| | Balances carried down | 11,970 | 1,570 | — | | Balances carried down | — | — | 540 |
| | | 16,970 | 6,270 | 4,360 | | | 16,970 | 6,270 | 4,360 |

* *See* workings.

## Workings

Calculation of Goodwill

| | 4-year method | 5-year method |
|---|---|---|
| | £ | £ |
| Profits: 19X4 | — | 10,420 |
| 19X5 | 11,760 | 11,760 |
| 19X6 | 9,400 | 9,400 |
| 19X7 | 13,820 | 13,820 |
| 19X8 | 14,600 | 14,600 |
| | 49,580 | 60,000 |
| Annual average profit | 12,395 | 12,000 |
| Therefore goodwill is valued at: $1\frac{1}{2} \times$ £12,000 = | £18,000 | |

*Note:* Goodwill is to be valued on the *lower* of the two methods for computing the annual average profit.

Partners' Capital Accounts

| | Original capitals | New capitals |
|---|---|---|
| | £ | £ |
| Taylor | 10,000 | 8,000 ($\frac{2}{5}$) |
| Clough | 6,000 | 8,000 ($\frac{2}{5}$) |
| Best | 5,000 | 4,000 ($\frac{1}{5}$) |
| | | 20,000 |

Transfer to/(from) Current Accounts

| | £ |
|---|---|
| Taylor | 2,000 |
| Clough | (2,000) |
| Best | 1,000 |

## 70 Owen, Glen and Dower

Trading Profit and Loss and Appropriation Accounts
year ended 31st March 19X5

| | £ | £ | | £ |
|---|---|---|---|---|
| Stock at 1st April 19X4 | | 16,000 | Sales | 248,000 |
| Purchases | | 192,000 | | |
| | | 208,000 | | |
| *less:* Stock at 31st March 19X5 | | 19,000 | | |
| | | 189,000 | | |
| Gross profit carried down | | 59,000 | | |
| | | 248,000 | | 248,000 |
| Wages | | 20,000 | Gross profit brought down | 59,000 |
| Salaries | | 10,000 | | |
| General expenses | | 9,000 | Decrease in provision for doubtful debts | 500 |
| Depreciation | | | | |
| Plant and machinery | 2,400 | | | |
| Motor vehicles | 1,880 | | | |
| | | 4,280 | | |
| Net profit carried down | | 16,220 | | |
| | | 59,500 | | 59,500 |

*continued*

*continued*

| | 1st April 19X4 to 31st July 19X4 | | | 1st August 19X4 to 31st March 19X4 | | 1st April 19X4 to 31st July 19X4 | 1st August 19X4 to 31st March 19X5 |
|---|---|---|---|---|---|---|---|
| | £ | | £ | £ | | £ | £ |
| Salaries | | | | | Net profit brought down | 5,407 | 10,813 |
| Owen | 833 | | | 1,667 | | | |
| Glen | 833 | | | 1,667 | | | |
| Dower | — | | | 1,333 | | | |
| Share of profits | | | | | | | |
| Owen (60%) | 2,245 | (54%) | 3,319 | | | | |
| *less:* Guarantee to Dower | | | 111 | 3,208 | | | |
| Glen (40%) | 1,496 | (36%) | 2,212 | | | | |
| *less:* Guarantee to Dower | | | 74 | 2,138 | | | |
| Dower | | (10%) | 615 | | | | |
| *add:* Guaranteed amounts | | | 185 | 800 | | | |
| | *5,407 | | | 10,813 | | 5,407 | 10,813 |

Balance Sheet at 31st March 19X5

| | £ | £ | £ |
|---|---|---|---|
| Capital accounts | | | |
| Owen | | 28,000 | |
| Glen | | 23,400 | 51,400 |
| Current accounts | | | |
| Owen | | 2,393 | |
| Glen | | 2,694 | |
| Dower | | 533 | 5,620 |
| | | | 57,020 |
| Fixed assets | | | |
| Plant and machinery | | 24,000 | |
| *less:* Depreciation | | 2,400 | 21,600 |
| Motor vehicles | | 9,400 | |
| *less:* Depreciation | | 1,880 | 7,520 |
| | | | 29,120 |
| Current assets | | | |
| Stock | | 19,000 | |
| Debtors | 18,000 | | |
| *less:* Provision for doubtful debts | 900 | 17,100 | |
| Balance at bank | | 2,000 | |
| | | 38,100 | |
| *deduct:* | | | |
| Current liabilities | | | |
| Creditors | | 10,200 | 27,900 |
| | | | 57,020 |

Current Accounts

| Date | | Owen £ | Glen £ | Dower £ | Date | | Owen £ | Glen £ | Dower £ |
|---|---|---|---|---|---|---|---|---|---|
| 19X4 | | | | | 19X4 | | | | |
| Apr 1 | Proceeds of life policy | 5,700 | 3,800 | | Apr 1 | Balance brought forward | 3,000 | 3,400 | |
| 19X5 | | | | | 1 | Share of profit on life policy | 900 | 600 | |
| Mar 31 | Drawings | 3,400 | 3,000 | 1,200 | Jul 31 | Salary | 833 | 833 | |
| | Income tax | 2,400 | 2,000 | 400 | | Share of profit | 2,245 | 1,496 | |
| 31 | Balance carried forward | 2,393 | 2,694 | 533 | Aug 1 | Cash share of goodwill | 2,040 | 1,360 | |
| | | | | | 19X5 | | | | |
| | | | | | Mar 31 | Salary | 1,667 | 1,667 | 1,333 |
| | | | | | | Share of profits | 3,208 | 2,138 | 800 |
| | | 13,893 | 11,494 | 2,133 | | | 13,893 | 11,494 | 2,133 |

# 71 Sparrow, Finch and Wren

(a)

Trading and Profit and Loss Account
year ended 30th September 19X4

| | £ | | £ |
|---|---|---|---|
| Stock 1st October 19X3 | 5,100 | Sales | 38,000 |
| Purchases (£20,400 + £100 difference) | 20,500 | | |
| | 25,600 | | |
| *Deduct:* Stock 30th September 19X4 | 5,600 | | |
| | 20,000 | | |
| Gross profit carried down | 18,000 | | |
| | 38,000 | | 38,000 |

| | 6 months to 31st March 19X4 | 6 months to 30th September 19X4 | | 6 months to 31st March 19X4 | 6 months to 30th September 19X4 |
|---|---|---|---|---|---|
| | £ | £ | | £ | £ |
| Salaries (£6,400 − £1,200) | 2,600 | 2,600 | Gross profit brought down (apportioned on the basis of turnover) | 6,600 | 11,400 |
| Shop wages | 1,900 | 1,900 | Net loss carried down | 992 | |
| Rates, lighting and heating (£1,680 − £220 prepaid) | 730 | 730 | | | |
| Professional charges (£540 − £200 capitalised) | 170 | 170 | | | |
| General expenses (£4,100 − £100 + £80) = £4,080 | 1,720 | 2,360 | | | |
| Amortisation of lease ($\frac{1}{50}$ × £8,000 + £200) = £164 | 82 | 82 | | | |
| Depreciation: | | | | | |
| Motor vehicles | 300 | 300 | | | |
| Shop fittings | 90 | 90 | | | |
| Sparrow loan account: | | | | | |
| Interest | — | 328 | | | |
| Net profit carried down | — | 2,840 | | | |
| | 7,592 | 11,400 | | 7,592 | 11,400 |

| | £ | £ | | £ | £ |
|---|---|---|---|---|---|
| Net loss brought down | 992 | | Net profit brought down | | 2,840 |
| Interest on capital: | | | Share of loss: | | |
| Sparrow | 150 | | Sparrow ($\frac{3}{5}$) | 739 | |
| Finch | 90 | 90 | Finch ($\frac{2}{5}$) | 493 | |
| Wren | | 30 | | | |
| Share of profits: | | | | | |
| Finch ($\frac{2}{3}$) | | 1,813 | | | |
| Wren ($\frac{1}{3}$) | | 907 | | | |
| | 1,232 | 2,840 | | 1,232 | 2,840 |

## (b) Balance Sheet 30th September 19X4

| | £ | £ |
|---|---|---|
| Partners' capital accounts | | |
| Finch | 3,000 | |
| Wren | 1,000 | 4,000 |
| Partners' current accounts | | |
| Finch | 1,300 | |
| Wren | 737 | 2,037 |
| Sparrow: Loan account | | 8,519 |
| | | 14,556 |
| Current liabilities | | |
| Creditors | 3,600 | |
| Accrual | 80 | 3,680 |
| | | 18,236 |

| | Cost £ | Depreciation £ | Net book value £ |
|---|---|---|---|
| Fixed assets | | | |
| Leasehold premises | 8,200 | 164 | 8,036 |
| Motor vehicles | 3,000 | 1,920 | 1,080 |
| Shop fittings | 1,800 | 780 | 1,020 |
| | 13,000 | 2,864 | 10,136 |
| Current assets | | £ | |
| Stock | | 5,600 | |
| Debtors | | 800 | |
| Prepayment | | 220 | |
| Balance at bank | | 1,480 | 8,100 |
| | | | 18,236 |

## (c) Partners' Current Accounts

| | Sparrow £ | Finch £ | Wren £ |
|---|---|---|---|
| Drawings | 600 | 400 | 200 |
| Transfer to loan account | 6,411 | | |
| Goodwill adjustments per contra* | | 6,000 | 3,000 |
| Share of loss | 739 | 493 | |
| Balances carried down | | 1,300 | 737 |
| | 7,750 | 8,193 | 3,937 |

| | Sparrow £ | Finch £ | Wren £ |
|---|---|---|---|
| Balance 1st October 19X3 | 2,200 | 2,600 | |
| Goodwill adjustments per contra* | 5,400 | 3,600 | |
| Cash | | | 3,000 |
| Interest on capitals | 150 | 180 | 30 |
| Share of profit | | 1,813 | 907 |
| | 7,750 | 8,193 | 3,937 |

* *See* Working 2.

## Workings

(1) Sparrow: Loan Account

| | £ | | £ |
|---|---|---|---|
| Motor vehicle: Acquired | 720 | Transferred from: | |
| Cash | 2,500 | Capital account: balance | 5,000 |
| Balance carried down | 8,191 | Current account: balance | 6,411 |
| | 11,411 | | 11,411 |
| | £ | | £ |
| Balance carried forward | 8,519 | Balance brought down | 8,191 |
| | | Interest to 30th September 19X4 ($\frac{8}{100} \times \frac{1}{2} \times$ £8,191) | 328 |
| | 8,519 | | 8,519 |

(2) Goodwill Adjustments

| | | £ |
|---|---|---|
| Dispersed by Sparrow and Finch in old profit-sharing ratio | | |
| Sparrow ($\frac{3}{5} \times$ £9,000) | | 5,400 |
| Finch ($\frac{2}{5} \times$ £9,000) | | 3,600 |
| | (Credit) | 9,000 |
| Purchased by Finch and Wren in new profit-sharing ratio | | |
| Finch ($\frac{2}{3} \times$ £9,000) | | 6,000 |
| Wren ($\frac{1}{3} \times$ £9,000) | | 3,000 |
| | (Debit) | 9,000 |

(3) Motor Vehicles

| | Cost £ | Depreciation £ |
|---|---|---|
| Balance 1st October 19X3 | 4,200 | 1,800 |
| *less:* Vehicle acquired by Sparrow | 1,200 | 480 |
| | 3,000 | 1,320 |
| Depreciation for the year: profit and loss account | — | 600 |
| Balances 30th September 19X4 | 3,000 | 1,920 |

## C Retirement of partner

## 72 Oak, Ash and Beeche

(a)

Capital Accounts

| | | Oak | Ash | Beeche | | | Oak | Ash | Beeche |
|---|---|---|---|---|---|---|---|---|---|
| | | £ | £ | £ | | | £ | £ | £ |
| 19X4 | | | | | 19X4 | | | | |
| Jun 30 | Goodwill adjustment | | 1,332 | 1,332 | Jan 1 | Balance brought | | | |
| | Loss on revaluation | | | | | forward | 10,000 | 5,000 | 6,000 |
| | Fixtures and fittings | 200 | 150 | 150 | Jun 30 | Goodwill adjustment | 2,664 | | |
| Jun 30 | Drawings | 1,600 | | | | Surplus on revaluation | | | |
| | Loan account | 13,784 | | | | Land and buildings | 800 | 600 | 600 |
| Dec 31 | Drawings | | 2,400 | 2,400 | Jun 30 | Interest on capital | 250 | 125 | 150 |
| | Balance carried | | | | | Share of profits | 1,870 | 1,403 | 1,402 |
| | forward | | 5,627 | 6,675 | Dec 31 | Interest on capital | | 125 | 150 |
| | | | | | | Share of profits | | 2,256 | 2,255 |
| | | 15,584 | 9,509 | 10,557 | | | 15,584 | 9,509 | 10,557 |

(b) Ash and Beeche Balance Sheet 31st December 19X4

| | £ | £ |
|---|---|---|
| Capital | | |
| Ash | 5,627 | |
| Beeche | 6,675 | 12,302 |
| Loan: Executors of Oak deceased | | 14,198 |
| | | 26,500 |
| Fixed assets | | £ |
| Land and buildings | | 10,000 |
| Fixtures and fittings | | 1,000 |
| | | 11,000 |
| Current assets | | |
| Stock | 12,500 | |
| Debtors | 2,000 | |
| Bank | 4,000 | |
| | 18,500 | |
| *deduct:* | | |
| Current liabilities | | |
| Creditors | 3,000 | 15,500 |
| | | 26,500 |

**Workings**

(1) Goodwill Calculation

| | £ | £ |
|---|---|---|
| Profits: 1st July 19X1 to 31st December 19X1 | | 5,600 |
| 19X2 | | 12,600 |
| 19X3 | | 12,000 |
| 1st January 19X4 to 30th June 19X4 | | 5,200 |
| | | 35,400 |
| Salaries: 3 × £7,500 | 22,500 | |
| Interest: 8% on £26,000 = £2,080<br>3 years | 6,240 | 28,740 |
| | | 6,660 |

(2) Goodwill Allocation

| | Oak | Ash | Beeche | Total |
|---|---|---|---|---|
| | £ | £ | £ | £ |
| Old partnership | 2,664 | 1,998 | 1,998 | 6,660 |
| New partnership | | 3,330 | 3,330 | 6,660 |
| | −2,664 | +1,332 | +1,332 | |

(3) Profit Division

| | 1st January to 30th June 19X4 | | 1st July to 31st December 19X4 | |
|---|---|---|---|---|
| | £ | £ | £ | £ |
| Profit | | 5,200 | | 5,200 |
| *deduct*: Interest on capital | | | | |
| 5% × £21,000 | | 525 | | |
| 5% × £11,000 | | | | 275 |
| | | 4,675 | | 4,925 |
| Interest on loan: | | | | |
| Estate of Oak deceased | | | | 414 |
| | | | | 4,511 |
| Share of profit: Oak | 1,870 | | | |
| Ash | 1,403 | | 2,256 | |
| Beeche | 1,402 | 4,675 | 2,255 | 4,511 |

## 73 Tom and Gerry

(a)

Partner's Capital Accounts

| 19X6 | | Tom and Gerry Tom £ | Gerry £ | Butch £ | 19X6 | | Tom and Gerry Tom £ | Gerry £ | Butch £ |
|---|---|---|---|---|---|---|---|---|---|
| Jan 1 | Goodwill written off | | 11,033 | 11,033 | Jan 1 | Balance brought forward | 10,000 | 5,000 | 8,500 |
| | Loan account | 24,627 | | | | Current account | 1,500 | 3,200 | |
| | Balance carried forward | | 3,730 | 12,393 | | Surplus on revaluation | 3,900 | 1,950 | 6,700 |
| | | | | | | Goodwill | 9,227 | 4,613 | 8,226 |
| | | 24,627 | 14,763 | 23,426 | | | 24,627 | 14,763 | 23,426 |

(b)

Gerry and Butch: Balance Sheet 1st January 19X6

| | £ | £ |
|---|---|---|
| Capital accounts | | |
| Gerry | 3,730 | |
| Butch | 12,393 | |
| | | 16,123 |
| Loan account: Tom | | 24,627 |
| | | 40,750 |
| Fixed assets | | |
| Freehold premises | 28,000 | |
| Furniture, fixtures and fittings | 4,800 | |
| | | 32,800 |
| Current assets | | |
| Stock | 14,700 | |
| Debtors | 5,750 | |
| Balance at bank | 13,500 | |
| | 33,950 | |
| *deduct:* | | |
| Current liabilities | | |
| Creditors | 26,000 | |
| | | 7,950 |
| | | 40,750 |

**Workings**

Valuation of Goodwill

| | Tom and Gerry | | Butch | |
|---|---|---|---|---|
| | £ | £ | £ | £ |
| Profits: Year to 31st December 19X3 | | 7,300 | | 3,300 |
| Year to 31st December 19X4 | | 6,100 | | 3,800 |
| Year to 31st December 19X5 | | 7,510 | | 3,900 |
| | | 20,910 | | 11,000 |
| *add:* Wife's wages | | | | 1,500 |
| Reduction in depreciation (£3,800 − £3,500) | | 300 | | |
| | | 21,210 | | 12,500 |
| *less:* Bad debts | 150 | | 100 | |
| Obsolete stock | 300 | | | |
| Increase in depreciation [(£200 ÷ 10) × 3] | — | 450 | 60 | 160 |
| Adjusted aggregate profits | | 20,760 | | 12,340 |
| Average profits | | 6,920 | | 4,113 |
| Goodwill: 2 years' purchase of adjusted average profits | | 13,840 | | 8,226 |
| Division in old partnership | | | | |
| Tom ($\frac{2}{3}$) | | 9,227 | | |
| Gerry ($\frac{1}{3}$) | | 4,613 | | |
| Butch | | | | 8,226 |
| Goodwill total | | 13,840 | | 8,226 = £22,066 |

Division (new partnership)

| | |
|---|---|
| Gerry | £11,033 |
| Butch | £11,033 |

Adjustments on Revaluation of Assets

| | Tom and Gerry | | Butch | |
|---|---|---|---|---|
| | £ | £ | £ | £ |
| Surplus on revaluation of premises | | 6,000 | | 7,000 |
| Surplus on revaluation of fixtures | | 300 | | |
| | | 6,300 | | |
| Loss on revaluation of fixtures | | | 200 | |
| Bad debts | 150 | | 100 | |
| Obsolete stock | 300 | 450 | — | 300 |
| Surplus on revaluation | | 5,850 | | 6,700 |

| | |
|---|---|
| Division: Tom ($\frac{2}{3}$) | £3,900 |
| Gerry ($\frac{1}{3}$) | £1,950 |

## E Dissolution

### 74 Old, Sage and Wit

(a) Journal

| | | | Dr | Cr |
|---|---|---|---|---|
| 19X7 | | | £ | £ |
| Jan 1 | Realisation account | Dr | 44,000 | |
| | Furniture and fittings | Cr | | 1,000 |
| | Debtors | Cr | | 8,000 |
| | Stocks | Cr | | 35,000 |
| | Transfer of assets on dissolution | | | |
| | Capital accounts: Old £ / Sage £ / Wit £ — Annuity: – / 3,000 / –; Debtors: 5,000 / – / –; Stocks: – / 10,000 / 10,000; Goodwill: – / 2,000 / 2,000; Totals: 5,000 / 15,000 / 12,000 | Dr | 32,000 | |
| | Cash | Cr | | 3,000 |
| | Realisation account | Cr | | 29,000 |
| | Purchase of annuity and acquisition of sundry assets by the partners | | | |
| | Cash | Dr | 400 | |
| | Realisation account | Cr | | 400 |
| | Proceeds of sale of furniture | | | |
| Feb 1 | Realisation account | Dr | 600 | |
| | Cash | Cr | | 600 |
| | Payment of realisation expenses | | | |
| Feb 10 | Current accounts: Sage | Dr | 5,000 | |
| | Wit | Dr | 5,000 | |
| | Capital accounts: Sage | Cr | | 5,000 |
| | Wit | Cr | | 5,000 |
| | Transfer of balances | | | |
| | Capital accounts: Old | Dr | 2,000 | |
| | Sage | Dr | 6,600 | |
| | Wit | Dr | 6,600 | |
| | Realisation account | Cr | | 15,200 |
| | Loss on realisation | | | |
| | Cash | Dr | 7,200 | |
| | Wit | Dr | 400 | |
| | Old | Cr | | 5,000 |
| | Sage | Cr | | 2,600 |
| | Cash withdrawn and paid in by the partners | | | |

Capital accounts breakdown (Jan 1):

| | Old | Sage | Wit |
|---|---|---|---|
| | £ | £ | £ |
| Annuity | | 3,000 | |
| Debtors | 5,000 | | |
| Stocks | | 10,000 | 10,000 |
| Goodwill | | 2,000 | 2,000 |
| | 5,000 | 15,000 | 12,000 |

*continued*

*continued*

| | | | Dr | Cr |
|---|---|---|---|---|
| | | | £ | £ |
| Feb 15 | Creditors | Dr | 10,000 | |
| | Cash | Cr | | 10,000 |
| | Settlement of creditors | | | |

*Note:* It is assumed that payment for the debts assigned to Old was made with the other cash adjustments on 10th February.

(b) Rarities

| Summarised balance sheet at 1st January 19X7 | £ | £ |
|---|---|---|
| Fixed assets at valuation | | |
| Furniture | | 3,000 |
| Cars | | 1,000 |
| | | 4,000 |
| Current assets | | |
| Stock | 80,000 | |
| Cash | 8,000 | 88,000 |
| | | 92,000 |
| Representing: | | |
| Partners' capital accounts | | |
| Sage | | 9,200 |
| Wit | | 13,800 |
| Young | | 32,200 |
| Keen | | 36,800 |
| | | 92,000 |

**Workings**

Partners' Capital Accounts—Oxford Firm

| | Old | Sage | Wit | | Old | Sage | Wit |
|---|---|---|---|---|---|---|---|
| | £ | £ | £ | | £ | £ | £ |
| Annuity and assets taken over | 5,000 | 15,000 | 12,000 | Balances brought forward | 2,000 | 14,000 | 14,000 |
| Loss on realisation | 2,000 | 6,600 | 6,600 | Current accounts | | 5,000 | 5,000 |
| Cash | | | 400 | Cash | 5,000 | 2,600 | |
| | 7,000 | 21,600 | 19,000 | | 7,000 | 21,600 | 19,000 |

Bank Account

| | £ | | £ |
|---|---|---|---|
| Balance brought forward | 6,000 | Expenses | 600 |
| Furniture | 400 | Annuity | 3,000 |
| Old | 5,000 | Wit | 400 |
| Sage | 2,600 | Creditors | 10,000 |
| | 14,000 | | 14,000 |

Partners' Capital Accounts—Rarities

| | Sage £ | Sage £ | Wit £ | Wit £ | Young £ | Young £ | Keen £ | Keen £ |
|---|---|---|---|---|---|---|---|---|
| Credit: | | | | | | | | |
| Assets introduced: | | | | | | | | |
| Stocks | | 10,000 | | 10,000 | | 30,000 | | 30,000 |
| Furniture | | | | | | 1,500 | | 1,500 |
| Cars | | | | | | 500 | | 500 |
| Goodwill | | 2,000 | | 2,000 | | 10,000 | | 10,000 |
| | | 12,000 | | 12,000 | | 42,000 | | 42,000 |
| Debit: | | | | | | | | |
| Goodwill written off in new profit ratio | 2,400 | | 3,600 | | 8,400 | | 9,600 | |
| Balances carried forward in new ratio (£92,000) | 9,200 | 11,600 | 13,800 | 17,400 | 32,200 | 40,600 | 36,800 | 46,400 |
| Cash introduced | | | | 5,400 | | | | 4,400 |
| Cash withdrawn | | 400 | | | | 1,400 | | |

(Net cash introduced £8,000.)

## 75 Keen, Eager and Proud

(a) Realisation Account

| 19X4 | | £ | 19X4 | | | £ |
|---|---|---|---|---|---|---|
| Dec 31 | Plant, machinery, fixtures and fittings | 8,000 | Dec 31 | Creditors Discount received | | 100 |
| | Motor vehicles | 2,000 | | Eager: Motor vehicle taken over | | 1,400 |
| | Stock | 2,800 | | Betters Ltd: Purchase consideration | | 13,000 |
| | Loss on realisation: Debtors | 1,800 | | Loss on realisation (in profit-sharing ratio) | | |
| | | | | Keen ($\frac{2}{5}$) | 40 | |
| | | | | Eager ($\frac{2}{5}$) | 40 | |
| | | | | Proud ($\frac{1}{5}$) | 20 | 100 |
| | | 14,600 | | | | 14,600 |

(b) Cash Account

| 19X4 | | £ | 19X4 | | £ |
|---|---|---|---|---|---|
| Dec 31 | Debtors | 4,200 | Dec 31 | Balance brought forward | 2,400 |
| | Cash in hand | 150 | | Creditors: Paid | 3,900 |
| | Betters Ltd | 1,000 | | Keen: Capital account | 760 |
| | Capital account | | | | |
| | Eager | 840 | | | |
| | Proud | 870 | | | |
| | | 7,060 | | | 7,060 |

(c) Partners' Capital Accounts

| | Keen £ | Eager £ | Proud £ | | Keen £ | Eager £ | Proud £ |
|---|---|---|---|---|---|---|---|
| Realisation account: Motor vehicle taken over | | 1,400 | | Balances brought forward | 5,000 | 3,000 | 2,000 |
| Current account | | | 470 | Loan account: Biggs | 1,000 | — | — |
| Betters Ltd (*see* workings) | | | | Current accounts | 460 | 1,460 | — |
| Ordinary shares | 4,500 | 2,700 | 1,800 | Cash introduced | | 840 | 870 |
| Preference shares | 1,200 | 1,200 | 600 | | | | |
| Cash repaid | 760 | | | | | | |
| | 6,460 | 5,300 | 2,870 | | 6,460 | 5,300 | 2,870 |

Partners' Current Accounts

| | Keen £ | Eager £ | Proud £ | | Keen £ | Eager £ | Proud £ |
|---|---|---|---|---|---|---|---|
| Balance brought forward | | | 450 | Balances brought forward | 500 | 1,500 | |
| Loss on realisation | 40 | 40 | 20 | Capital account | | | 470 |
| Capital account | 460 | 1,460 | | | | | |
| | 500 | 1,500 | 470 | | 500 | 1,500 | 470 |

**Workings**

Betters Ltd

| | £ | | £ | £ |
|---|---|---|---|---|
| Realisation account: Purchase consideration | 13,000 | Partners' capital accounts: Ordinary shares in proportion to fixed capitals | | |
| | | Keen ($\frac{5}{10}$) | 4,500 | |
| | | Eager ($\frac{3}{10}$) | 2,700 | |
| | | Proud ($\frac{2}{10}$) | 1,800 | 9,000 |
| | | Preference shares—in profit-sharing ratio | | |
| | | Keen ($\frac{2}{5}$) | 1,200 | |
| | | Eager ($\frac{2}{5}$) | 1,200 | |
| | | Proud ($\frac{1}{5}$) | 600 | 3,000 |
| | | Cash to balance | | 1,000 |
| | 13,000 | | | 13,000 |

## 76 X, Y and Z

Realisation Account

| 19X4 | | | | 19X4 | | |
|---|---|---|---|---|---|---|
| | | £ | £ | | | £ |
| Apr 1 | Sundry assets | | 94,200 | Apr 1 | Creditors | 7,750 |
| | Cash | | 2,550 | | XYZ Ltd | 95,000 |
| | Profit on realisation | | | | | |
| | X 50% | 3,000 | | | | |
| | Y 30% | 1,800 | | | | |
| | Z 20% | 1,200 | 6,000 | | | |
| | | | 102,750 | | | 102,750 |

Capital Accounts

| 19X4 | | | | | 19X4 | | | | |
|---|---|---|---|---|---|---|---|---|---|
| | | £ | £ | £ | | | £ | £ | £ |
| Apr 1 | Cash | 450 | 450 | 450 | Apr 1 | Balance brought forward | 44,000 | 29,000 | 12,000 |
| | Debentures | 8,000 | 5,000 | | | Current accounts | 2,950 | 1,450 | 950 |
| | 7% preference shares | 18,000 | 12,000 | 6,000 | | Profit on realisation | 3,000 | 1,800 | 1,200 |
| | Ordinary shares | 23,500 | 14,800 | 7,700 | | | | | |
| | | 49,950 | 32,250 | 14,150 | | | 49,950 | 32,250 | 14,150 |

XYZ Limited

| 19X4 | | | 19X4 | | |
|---|---|---|---|---|---|
| | | £ | | | £ |
| Apr 1 | Realisation Account | 95,000 | Apr 1 | Debentures in XYZ Ltd | 13,000 |
| | | | | Ordinary shares in XYZ Ltd | 46,000 |
| | | | | Preference shares in XYZ Ltd | 36,000 |
| | | 95,000 | | | 95,000 |

Debentures in XYZ Limited

| 19X4 | | £ | 19X4 | | | £ |
|---|---|---|---|---|---|---|
| Apr 1 | XYZ Ltd | 13,000 | Apr 1 | Capital accounts | X | 8,000 |
| | | | | | Y | 5,000 |
| | | 13,000 | | | | 13,000 |

7% Preference Shares in XYZ Limited

| 19X4 | | £ | 19X4 | | | £ |
|---|---|---|---|---|---|---|
| Apr 1 | XYZ Ltd | 36,000 | Apr 1 | Capital accounts | X | 18,000 |
| | | | | | Y | 12,000 |
| | | | | | Z | 6,000 |
| | | 36,000 | | | | 36,000 |

Ordinary Shares in XYZ Limited

| 19X4 | | £ | 19X4 | | | £ |
|---|---|---|---|---|---|---|
| Apr 1 | XYZ Ltd | 46,000 | Apr 1 | Capital accounts | X | 23,500 |
| | | | | | Y | 14,800 |
| | | | | | Z | 7,700 |
| | | 46,000 | | | | 46,000 |

## 77 Fairway Ltd

(a) Computation of shares and loan stock to be issued

(i) Shares:

Net assets taken over by Fairway Ltd

| | £ |
|---|---|
| Freehold land and buildings | 30,000 |
| Plant and machinery | 15,000 |
| Stocks | 22,400 |
| Debtors | 12,200 |
| Cash | 15,000 |
| | 94,600 |
| *less:* Creditors | 35,600 |
| | 59,000 |
| *less:* Loan stock issued (*see* (ii) below) | 19,000 |
| | 40,000 |

| Issued in profit-sharing ratios: | Shares at par |
|---|---|
| Par $\frac{3}{8}$ | 15,000 |
| Green $\frac{3}{8}$ | 15,000 |
| Bogey $\frac{2}{8}$ | 10,000 |
| | 40,000 |

(ii) Loan stock:

| | Interest on capital £ | 9% loan stock required to produce same amount | £ |
|---|---|---|---|
| Par | 720 | $720 \times \frac{100}{9}$ | 8,000 |
| Green | 540 | $540 \times \frac{100}{9}$ | 6,000 |
| Bogey | 450 | $450 \times \frac{100}{9}$ | 5,000 |
| | | | 19,000 |

(b) Partners' Accounts

| | Par £ | Green £ | Bogey £ | | Par £ | Green £ | Bogey £ |
|---|---|---|---|---|---|---|---|
| Realisation account | | | | Capital accounts | 24,000 | 18,000 | 15,000 |
| Cars taken over | 4,900 | 3,500 | 3,600 | Current accounts | 9,860 | 6,420 | 6,470 |
| Loss | 1,500 | 1,500 | 1,000 | | | | |
| Fairway Ltd | | | | | | | |
| Loan stock | 8,000 | 6,000 | 5,000 | | | | |
| Shares | 15,000 | 15,000 | 10,000 | | | | |
| Cash (balance) | 4,460 | — | 1,870 | Cash (balance) | — | 1,580 | — |
| | 33,860 | 26,000 | 21,470 | | 33,860 | 26,000 | 21,470 |

## Workings

Realisation Account

| | £ | | £ | £ |
|---|---|---|---|---|
| Sundry assets at book value | | Creditors | | 35,600 |
| Freehold land and buildings | 26,000 | Fairway Ltd | | |
| Plant and machinery | 20,000 | Purchase consideration: | | |
| Motor vehicles | 15,000 | Loan stock | 19,000 | |
| Stock | 22,400 | Shares | 40,000 | 59,000 |
| Debtors | 12,200 | Partner's accounts | | |
| Cash (amount taken over) | 15,000 | Cars taken over | | |
| | | Par | 4,900 | |
| | | Green | 3,500 | |
| | | Bogey | 3,600 | 12,000 |
| | | Partners' accounts | | |
| | | Loss on realisation | | |
| | | Par ($\frac{3}{8}$) | 1,500 | |
| | | Green ($\frac{3}{8}$) | 1,500 | |
| | | Bogey ($\frac{2}{8}$) | 1,000 | 4,000 |
| | 110,600 | | | 110,600 |

(c) Balance Sheet at 1st January 19X8

| | £ | £ |
|---|---|---|
| Share capital | | |
| Authorised: 100,000 shares of £1 each | 100,000 | |
| Issued: 40,000 ordinary shares of £1 each, fully paid | | 40,000 |
| 9% unsecured loan stock | | 19,000 |
| | | 59,000 |
| Represented by: | | |
| Fixed assets | | |
| Freehold land and buildings | | 30,000 |
| Plant and machinery | | 15,000 |
| | | 45,000 |
| Current assets | | |
| Stocks | 22,400 | |
| Debtors | 12,200 | |
| Cash | 15,000 | |
| | 49,600 | |
| *less:* Current liabilities | 35,600 | 14,000 |
| | | 59,000 |

# G Piecemeal realisation

## 78 A, B and C

### Realisation Account

| 19X4 | | £ | 19X4 | | | £ |
|---|---|---|---|---|---|---|
| Jun 30 | Freehold premises | 2,200 | Aug 1 | Cash: Debtors | | 4,700 |
| | Equipment | 5,300 | 20 | Cash: Proceeds of stock | | 2,700 |
| | Vehicles | 1,300 | Sep 30 | Cash: Proceeds of equipment | | 2,805 |
| | Stock | 6,285 | Oct 15 | Cash: Proceeds of stock | | 2,600 |
| | Debtors | 5,600 | 30 | Capital account | | |
| Oct 30 | Cash: Expenses | 800 | | A | | 600 |
| | | | | B | | 600 |
| | | | | Cash: Proceeds of premises | | 4,000 |
| | | | | Capital account | | |
| | | | | Loss on realisation | | |
| | | | | A | 1,740 | |
| | | | | B | 1,044 | |
| | | | | C | 696 | 3,480 |
| | | 21,485 | | | | 21,485 |

### Cash Bank Account

| 19X4 | | £ | 19X4 | | £ |
|---|---|---|---|---|---|
| | Realisation proceeds | | Jun 30 | Balance brought forward | 1,765 |
| Aug 1 | Debtors | 4,700 | Aug 20 | Creditors | 4,220 |
| 20 | Stock | 2,700 | | Loan: B | 2,000 |
| Sep 30 | Equipment | 2,805 | Sep 30 | Capital: A | 352 |
| Oct 15 | Stock | 2,600 | | B | 868 |
| 30 | Premises | 4,000 | Oct 15 | Capital: A | 1,620 |
| | | | | B | 980 |
| | | | 30 | Realisation expenses | 800 |
| | | | | Capital: A | 2,688 |
| | | | | B | 1,388 |
| | | | | C | 124 |
| | | 16,805 | | | 16,805 |

### Capital Accounts

| | | A | B | C | | | A | B | C |
|---|---|---|---|---|---|---|---|---|---|
| 19X4 | | £ | £ | £ | 19X4 | | £ | £ | £ |
| Jun 30 | Share of loss | 1,200 | 720 | 480 | Jun 30 | Balance brought forward | 8,000 | 5,000 | 2,000 |
| | Current account | | | 700 | | Current accounts | 200 | 600 | |
| Sep 30 | Cash | 352 | 868 | | | | | | |
| Oct 15 | Cash | 1,620 | 980 | | | | | | |
| 30 | Realisation account Motor vehicles | 600 | 600 | | | | | | |
| 30 | Loss on realisation | 1,740 | 1,044 | 696 | | | | | |
| | Cash | 2,688 | 1,388 | 124 | | | | | |
| | | 8,200 | 5,600 | 2,000 | | | 8,200 | 5,600 | 2,000 |

## Workings

| | | | Total | A | B | C |
|---|---|---|---|---|---|---|
| | £ | £ | £ | £ | £ | £ |
| Capital accounts | | | 15,000 | 8,000 | 5,000 | 2,000 |
| Current accounts | | | 100 | 200 | 600 | (700) |
| | | | 15,100 | 8,200 | 5,600 | 1,300 |
| *deduct:* Adverse balance on profit and loss account | | | (2,400) | (1,200) | (720) | (480) |
| | | | 12,700 | 7,000 | 4,880 | 820 |
| *Proceeds:* | | | | | | |
| Aug 1 | | 4,700 | | | | |
| Aug 20 | | 2,700 | | | | |
| Sep 30 | | 2,805 | | | | |
| | | 10,205 | | | | |
| *deduct:* Creditors | 4,220 | | | | | |
| Bank overdraft | 1,765 | | | | | |
| Loan B | 2,000 | | | | | |
| Provision for realisation expenses | 1,000 | 8,985 | | | | |
| Available for partners | | | 1,220 | | | |
| Notional loss | | | 11,480 | | | |
| (shared in profit-and-loss-sharing ratio) | | | | 5,740 | 3,444 | 2,296 |
| | | | | 1,260 | 1,436 | (1,476) |
| Deficit of C shared by A and B in their capital proportions £8,000:£5,000 | | | | (908) | (568) | 1,476 |
| Distribution | | | 1,220 | 352 | 868 | — |
| Revised balances (original *less* distribution) | | | 11,480 | 6,648 | 4,012 | 820 |
| Proceeds Oct 15 Stock | | | 2,600 | | | |
| | | | 8,880 | 4,440 | 2,664 | 1,776 |
| | | | | 2,208 | 1,348 | (956) |
| Deficit of C shared by A and B in capital proportions 8:5 | | | | (588) | (368) | 956 |
| Second distribution | | | 2,600 | 1,620 | 980 | — |

*continued*

*continued*

| | £ | Total £ | A £ | B £ | C £ |
|---|---|---|---|---|---|
| Revised balances | | 8,880 | 5,028 | 3,032 | 820 |
| Proceeds Oct 30 | | | | | |
| Premises | 4,000 | | | | |
| Motor vehicles | 1,200 | | | | |
| Realisation expenses over-provided | 200 | 5,400 | | | |
| | | 3,840 | 1,740 | 1,044 | 696 |
| | | | 3,288 | 1,988 | 124 |
| *less:* Motor vehicles taken over | | | 600 | 600 | — |
| Final distribution | | 4,200 | 2,688 | 1,388 | 124 |

# 10 MISCELLANEOUS ACCOUNTS

## A Selling agency branch accounts

### 79 Norsea Ltd

Goods Sent to Branch Account

| 19X4 | | £ | 19X4 | | £ |
|---|---|---|---|---|---|
| Mar 31 | Branch stock | | Mar 31 | Branch stock | 30,000 |
| | Returns | 280 | | | |
| | Trading account | 29,720 | | | |
| | | 30,000 | | | 30,000 |

Branch Stock Account

| | | Memo £ | £ | | | Memo £ | £ |
|---|---|---|---|---|---|---|---|
| 19X3 | | | | 19X3 | | | |
| Apr 1 | Balance brought forward | 4,020 | 2,680 | Mar 31 | Returns to Head Office | 420 | 280 |
| 19X4 | | | | | Cash sales | 25,200 | 25,200 |
| Mar 31 | Goods from Head Office | 45,000 | 30,000 | | Credit sales | 18,000 | 18,000 |
| | Gross profit | | 14,300 | | Stock shortage | | |
| | | | | | Normal wastage | 150 | |
| | | | | | Balance carried forward | 5,250 | 3,500 |
| | | 49,020 | 46,980 | | | 49,020 | 46,980 |

Branch Debtors Account

| | | £ | | | £ |
|---|---|---|---|---|---|
| 19X3 | | | | | |
| Apr 1 | Balance brought forward | 1,652 | | | |
| 19X4 | | | 19X4 | | |
| Mar 31 | Sales | 18,000 | Mar 31 | Bank | 17,156 |
| | | | | Bad debts | 149 |
| | | | | Balance carried forward | 2,347 |
| | | 19,652 | | | 19,652 |

## 80 Alpha Ltd

Branch Stock Account

| | £ | | £ |
|---|---|---|---|
| Stock brought forward | 4,400 | Sales: Credit | 21,000 |
| Goods | 24,800 | Cash | 2,400 |
| | | Returns | 1,000 |
| | | Goods stolen: Transfer to profit and loss account (abnormal loss) | 600 |
| | | Normal loss due to wastage | 100 |
| | | Shortage: Balancing figure | 152 |
| | | Stock carried forward | 3,948 |
| | 29,200 | | 29,200 |

Branch Total Debtors Account

| | £ | | £ |
|---|---|---|---|
| Balance brought forward | 3,946 | Cash received from debtors | 22,400 |
| Credit sales | 21,000 | Bad debts | 148 |
| | | Cash discount | 428 |
| | | Balance carried forward | 1,970 |
| | 24,946 | | 24,946 |

**Workings**

Goods Sent to Branch Account

| | £ | | £ |
|---|---|---|---|
| Returns | 750 | Goods | 18,600 |
| Purchases | 17,850 | | |
| | 18,600 | | 18,600 |

Branch Mark-up Account

| | £ | | £ |
|---|---|---|---|
| Returns | 250 | Balance brought forward | 1,100 |
| Normal loss | 100 | Goods | 6,200 |
| Shortages | 152 | | |
| Mark up on goods stolen | 150 | | |
| Gross profit (balancing figure) | 5,661 | | |
| Balance carried forward ($\frac{1}{4}$ × £3,948) | 987 | | |
| | 7,300 | | 7,300 |

**Proof**

Trading and Profit and Loss Account

| | £ | £ |
|---|---|---|
| Sales: Credit | 21,000 | |
| Cash | 2,400 | |
| | | 23,400 |
| Cost of goods sold | | |
| Opening stock (at cost to business) | 3,300 | |
| Purchases (£17,850 – £450 abnormal loss) | 17,400 | |
| | 20,700 | |
| *less:* Closing stock (at cost to business) | 2,961 | |
| | | 17,739 |
| Gross profit as per mark-up account | | 5,661 |
| Bad debts | 148 | |
| Discounts | 428 | |
| Goods stolen | 450 | |
| | | 1,026 |
| Net profit | | 4,635 |

*Note:* So as to show as true a gross profit as possible, the abnormal loss has been shown after gross profit. Double entry:

Debit: Goods stolen.
Credit: Purchases.

# B Autonomous and foreign branches

## 81 J Ltd

Trading and Profit and Loss Account
year ended 31st March 19X5

| | Swansea | Birming-ham | Firm | | Swansea | Birming-ham | Firm |
|---|---|---|---|---|---|---|---|
| | £ | £ | £ | | £ | £ | £ |
| Stock 1st April 19X4 | 5,980 | 24,300 | 29,800 | Sales | 47,000 | 224,000 | 271,000 |
| Purchases | 9,600 | 185,300 | 194,900 | Goods to branch | | 26,040 | |
| Goods from head office | 25,560 | | | | | | |
| | 41,140 | 209,600 | 224,700 | | | | |
| *less:* Stock 31st March 19X5 | 4,788 | 26,350 | 31,129 | | | | |
| | 36,352 | 183,250 | 193,571 | | | | |
| Gross profit carried down | 10,648 | 66,790 | 77,429 | | | | |
| | 47,000 | 250,040 | 271,000 | | 47,000 | 250,040 | 271,000 |
| Administration expenses | 1,734 | 9,756 | 11,490 | Gross profit brought down | 10,648 | 66,790 | 77,429 |
| Distribution expenses | 2,460 | 8,750 | 11,210 | | | | |
| Selling expenses | 2,477 | 12,635 | 15,112 | | | | |
| Provision for unrealised profit | | 9 | | | | | |
| Depreciation | 225 | 554 | 779 | | | | |
| Commission | 375 | | 375 | | | | |
| Net profit carried down | 3,377 | 35,086 | 38,463 | | | | |
| | 10,648 | 66,790 | 77,429 | | 10,648 | 66,790 | 77,429 |
| Balance carried forward | | | 41,933 | Net profit brought down | | | 38,463 |
| | | | | Balance brought forward | | | 3,470 |
| | | | 41,933 | | | | 41,933 |

Balance Sheet 31st March 19X5

| | £ | £ | £ |
|---|---|---|---|
| Share capital | | | |
| Issued and fully paid | | | 45,000 |
| Reserves | | | |
| Profit and loss account | | | 41,933 |
| | | | 86,933 |

*continued*

*continued*

| | Cost | Depreciation | NBV |
|---|---|---|---|
| Fixed assets | £ | £ | £ |
| Freehold premises | 30,500 | — | 30,500 |
| Motor vehicles | 5,300 | 2,500 | 2,800 |
| | 35,800 | 2,500 | 33,300 |
| Current assets | | | |
| Stock | | 31,129 | |
| Debtors | | 41,876 | |
| Balance at bank | | 12,704 | |
| | | 85,709 | |
| *deduct:* Current liabilities | | | |
| Creditors | 31,701 | | |
| Commission due | 375 | | |
| | | 32,076 | |
| | | | 53,633 |
| | | | 86,933 |

## Workings

(1) Opening Stock

| | £ | £ |
|---|---|---|
| Head office | | 24,300 |
| Branch | 5,980 | |
| *less:* Unrealised profit | 480 | |
| | | 5,500 |
| | | 29,800 |

Gross Profit

| | £ |
|---|---|
| Head office: Sales to outsiders: $\frac{40}{140} \times \frac{224,000}{1}$ | 64,000 |
| Goods to branch<br>Selling price: 140% of cost<br>Price to branch: (140 − 28)%<br>= 112% of cost | |
| $\frac{12}{112} \times \frac{26,040}{1}$ | 2,790 |
| | 66,790 |

(2) Branch

| | £ | £ |
|---|---|---|
| Goods from outside suppliers | | |
| Stock 1st April 19X4 | 1,500 | |
| Purchases | 9,600 | |
| | 11,100 | |
| *less:* Stock 31st March 19X5 | 700 | |
| | 10,400 | |
| Gross profit 40% | 4,160 | 4,160 |
| | 14,560 | |
| Goods from head office | | |
| Total sales | 47,000 | |
| *less:* Ex outside suppliers | 14,560 | |
| | 32,440 | |
| Gross profit 20% | | 6,488 |
| | | 10,648 |

(3) Closing Stock

| | £ | £ |
|---|---|---|
| Head office | | 26,350 |
| Branch: Ex other suppliers | | 700 |
| Ex head office | 4,088 | |
| Goods in transit | 480 | |
| | 4,568 | |
| *less:* Unrealised profit ($\frac{12}{112}$) | 489 | 4,079 |
| | | 31,129 |

(4) Unrealised Profit

| | £ |
|---|---|
| Provision at 1st April 19X4 | 480 |
| 31st March 19X5 | 489 |
| Charge in head office profit and loss account | 9 |

(5) Commission

| | £ |
|---|---|
| Gross profit | 10,648 |
| Expenses | 6,896 |
| | 3,752 |
| 10% | 375 |

(6) Creditors

| | £ |
|---|---|
| Head office | 28,705 |
| Branch | 3,386 |
| | 32,091 |
| *less:* Payment by branch to Head Office creditors | 390 |
| | 31,701 |

(7) Current Accounts

Head Office

| | | | £ |
|---|---|---|---|
| | | Balance | 37,335 |

Branch

| | £ | | £ |
|---|---|---|---|
| Balance | 38,205 | Payment of creditor by branch | 390 |
| | | Goods in transit | 480 |
| | | Balance | 37,335 |
| | 38,205 | | 38,205 |

## 82 China Ltd

Trading and Profit and Loss Account
year ended 31st December 19X4

| | Cardiff | London | Firm | | Cardiff | London | Firm |
|---|---|---|---|---|---|---|---|
| | £ | £ | £ | | £ | £ | £ |
| Purchases | 8,000 | 92,250 | 100,250 | Sales | 40,000 | 69,000 | 109,000 |
| Goods from head office | 30,800 | | | Goods to branch | | 33,000 | |
| | | | | Breakages | 497 | | 497 |
| | 38,800 | 92,250 | 100,250 | | | | |
| *less:* Stock at 31st December 19X4 | 8,303 | 16,250 | 26,053 | | | | |
| | 30,497 | 76,000 | 74,197 | | | | |
| Gross profit carried down | 10,000 | 26,000 | 35,300 | | | | |
| | 40,497 | 102,000 | 109,497 | | 40,497 | 102,000 | 109,497 |
| Expenses | 4,259 | 18,916 | 23,175 | Gross profit brought down | 10,000 | 26,000 | 35,300 |
| Discounts allowed | 306 | 546 | 852 | Discounts received | 150 | 1,422 | 1,572 |
| Breakages | 497 | | 497 | | | | |
| Provision for unrealised profit | | 700 | | | | | |
| Net profit | 5,088 | 7,260 | 12,348 | | | | |
| | 10,150 | 27,422 | 36,872 | | 10,150 | 27,422 | 36,872 |

*Note:* It has been assumed that all breakages were of goods bought locally.

## Workings

| | | £ |
|---|---|---|
| (1) Gross Profit: | | |
| Head Office | | |
| External sales ($33\frac{1}{3}\%$ × £69,000) | | 23,000 |
| Goods to branch ($\frac{1}{11}$ × £33,000) | | 3,000 |
| | | 26,000 |
| Branch | | |
| 25% of £40,000 | | 10,000 |

Having inserted the gross profit in the London and Cardiff columns, one may work back to find the stock.

| | £ | £ |
|---|---|---|
| (2) Closing stock: | | |
| Head Office | | 16,250 |
| Branch | | |
| from external suppliers | | 2,803 |
| from head office | 5,500 | |
| Goods in transit | 2,200 | |
| | 7,700 | |
| *less:* Provision for unrealised profit ($\frac{1}{11}$) | 700 | |
| | | 7,000 |
| | | 26,053 |

| | £ |
|---|---|
| (3) Purchases: | |
| Branch: Cash paid | 5,850 |
| Discounts | 150 |
| Creditors | 2,000 |
| | 8,000 |

## 83 Bargains Ltd

(a) Trading Account
Year Ended 31st December 19X7

| | Department A | Department B | | Department A | Department B |
|---|---|---|---|---|---|
| | £ | £ | | £ | £ |
| Opening stock, at cost | 12,300 | 17,400 | Sales | 105,000 | 140,000 |
| Purchases | 81,600 | 94,800 | Transfer to Dept B | 1,440 | |
| Transfer from Dept A | | 1,440 | Goods lost | 120 | |
| | 93,900 | 113,640 | Closing stock, at cost | 13,080 | 19,640 |
| Gross profit: carried down | 25,740 | 46,000 | | | |
| | 119,640 | 159,640 | | 119,640 | 159,640 |

(b) **Memorandum Stock Account**

| | Department A | Department B | | Department A | Department B |
|---|---|---|---|---|---|
| | £ | £ | | £ | £ |
| Stock brought forward | 16,400 | 26,100 | Reduction of selling price of goods included in opening stock brought forward | 250 | |
| Purchases | 108,800 | 142,200 | Sales | 105,000 | 140,000 |
| Goods transferred from Dept A | | 2,160 | Goods transferred to Dept B | 1,920 | |
| Reduction in selling price of goods still in stock, carried down | | 1,000 | Reduction in selling price of goods purchased during year | 430 | 2,000 |
| | | | Goods lost | 160 | |
| | | | Stock carried forward | 17,440 | 29,460 |
| | 125,200 | 171,460 | | 125,200 | 171,460 |

(c) **Memorandum Mark-up Account**

| | Department A | Department B | | Department A | Department B |
|---|---|---|---|---|---|
| | £ | £ | | £ | £ |
| Reduction in selling price of goods included in opening stock brought forward | 250 | | Mark-up on stock brought forward | 4,100 | 8,700 |
| Mark-up on goods transferred to Dept B | 480 | | Mark-up on purchases | 27,200 | 47,400 |
| Reduction of selling price of goods purchased in 19X7 | 430 | 2,000 | Mark-up on goods transferred from Dept A | | 720 |
| Mark-up on goods lost | 40 | | Reduction in selling price of goods still in stock carried down | | 1,000 |
| Gross profit | 25,740 | 46,000 | | | |
| Balance carried forward | 4,360 | 9,820 | | | |
| | 31,300 | 57,820 | | 31,300 | 57,820 |

## 84 OTL Ltd

(a) Highland Branch Trial Balance
31st December 19X0

| | Crowns | Crowns | Rate of translation | £ | £ |
|---|---|---|---|---|---|
| Balance at bank | 66,000 | | 4 | 16,500 | |
| Creditors | | 92,400 | 4 | | 23,100 |
| Debtors | 158,400 | | 4 | 39,600 | |
| Fixed assets | 145,200 | | 5 | 29,040 | |
| Head office account | | 316,800 | | | 65,280 |
| Profit and loss account | | 79,200 | 4.4 | | 18,000 |
| Stocks | 118,800 | | 4 | 29,700 | |
| Profit on exchange | | | | | 8,460 |
| | 488,400 | 488,400 | | 114,840 | 114,840 |

(b) Branch Current Account

| | | Crowns | £ | | | Crowns | £ |
|---|---|---|---|---|---|---|---|
| 19X0 | | | | 19X0 | | | |
| Dec 31 | Balance brought forward | 316,800 | 65,280 | Dec 31 | Balance brought forward | 396,000 | 91,740 |
| | Profit on exchange | | 8,460 | | | | |
| | Net profit | 79,200 | 18,000 | | | | |
| | | 396,000 | 91,740 | | | 396,000 | 91,740 |

(c) Balance Sheet as at 31st December 19X0

| | £ | £ |
|---|---|---|
| Issued share capital | | 86,400 |
| Reserves | | |
| Profit on exchange | | 8,460 |
| Profit and loss account | | 70,800 |
| | | 165,660 |
| Fixed assets | | 68,640 |
| Current assets | | |
| Stock | 56,100 | |
| Debtors | 58,080 | |
| Balance at bank | 27,060 | |
| | 141,240 | |
| *deduct:* Current Liabilities | | |
| Creditors | 44,220 | 97,020 |
| | | 165,660 |

## C Consignment accounts

### 85 Green

(a) Account Sales: Hall

| | | | £ |
|---|---|---|---|
| 50 bales sold for | | | 1,200 |
| *deduct:* | | | |
| Expenses | | 150 | |
| Marine insurance | | 26 | |
| Dock dues | | 35 | |
| | | 211 | |
| Brokerage 2% | 24 | | |
| Commission $2\frac{1}{2}$% | 30 | 54 | 265 |
| Bill enclosed for balance of | | | 935 |

(b) Consignment Account

| | £ | | £ |
|---|---|---|---|
| Goods at cost | 780 | Sales | 1,200 |
| Carriage | 40 | | |
| Freight: Hall | 150 | | |
| Dock dues: Hall | 35 | | |
| Insurance: Hall | 26 | | |
| Commissions: Hall | 54 | | |
| Profit | 115 | | |
| | 1,200 | | 1,200 |

Bills Receivable

| | £ | | £ |
|---|---|---|---|
| Consignee | 935 | Cash | 920 |
| | | Discount | 15 |
| | 935 | | 935 |

Goods Sent on Consignment Account

| | £ | | £ |
|---|---|---|---|
| Purchases | £780 | Goods | £780 |

Consignee's Account

| | £ | | £ |
|---|---|---|---|
| Sales | 1,200 | Freight | 150 |
| | | Dock dues | 35 |
| | | Insurance | 26 |
| | | Commissions | 54 |
| | | Bill | 935 |
| | 1,200 | | 1,200 |

## 86 Oliver

(a)

**Consignor's Books**

Consignment Account

| | £ | | £ |
|---|---|---|---|
| Mar 17 Goods at cost | 600 | Mar 28 Sales | 830 |
| Packing | 12 | | |
| Freight | 18 | | |
| 20 Storage | 13 | | |
| 28 Auction | 83 | | |
| Commission | 40 | | |
| Profit | 64 | | |
| | 830 | | 830 |

Consignee's Account

| | £ | | £ |
|---|---|---|---|
| Mar 28 Sales | 830 | Mar 20 Storage | 13 |
| | | 28 Auction | 83 |
| | | Commission | 40 |
| | | 31 Cash | 694 |
| | 830 | | 830 |

Goods Sent on Consignment Account

| | | | |
|---|---|---|---|
| Mar 31 Purchases | £600 | Mar 17 Consignment Account | £600 |

(b)

**Consignee's Books**

Consignor's Account

| | £ | | £ |
|---|---|---|---|
| Mar 20 Storage | 13 | Mar 28 Sales | 830 |
| 28 Auction | 83 | | |
| Commission | 40 | | |
| 31 Cash | 694 | | |
| | 830 | | 830 |

## D Joint ventures

### 87 Duke and Lord

**Books of Duke**

Joint Venture with Lord Account

| | | £ | | | £ |
|---|---|---|---|---|---|
| 19X9 | | | 19X9 | | |
| Aug 16 | Purchases | 800 | Sep 1 | Sales | 400 |
| Sep 1 | Repairs | 120 | 10 | Sales | 620 |
| 12 | Purchases | 600 | 30 | Car to Duke | 450 |
| | Profit and loss account | 220 | 30 | Cash | 270 |
| | | 1,740 | | | 1,740 |

Memorandum Joint Venture Account

| | £ | £ | | £ |
|---|---|---|---|---|
| Purchases | | 1,800 | Sales | 1,840 |
| Expenses | | 160 | Car to Duke | 450 |
| Profit: | £ | | | |
| Lord | 110 | | | |
| Duke | 220 | 330 | | |
| | | 2,290 | | 2,290 |

### 88 Tower and Castle

**Tower's Books**

(a) Joint Venture Account with Castle

| 19X0 | | | £ | 19X0 | | | £ |
|---|---|---|---|---|---|---|---|
| Jan 2 | Purchases | £ | | Jan 3 | Cash received from Castle | | 3,500 |
| | Cash | 4,800 | | Jan 9 | Sales: | £ | |
| | Bills payable | 800 | | | Bills receivable | 420 | |
| | Bills payable | 1,200 | 6,800 | | Bills receivable | 250 | 670 |
| Jan 9 | Bills endorsed over to Castle | | 670 | Feb 3 | Sales: Cash | | 1,800 |
| Feb 3 | Goods returned: Cash | | 90 | Feb 11 | Bad debts: Green | | 250 |
| Apr 30 | Commission receivable | | 176 | Mar 5 | Bill paid by Castle | | 800 |
| | Share of profit on joint venture | | 1,162 | March | Sales: Cash | | 2,910 |
| | Cash to settle | | 1,044 | March | Bad debts transferred from Castle | | 12 |
| | | | 9,942 | | | | 9,942 |

**Castle's Books**

Joint Venture Account with Tower

| 19X0 | | £ | 19X0 | | £ |
|---|---|---|---|---|---|
| Jan 3 | Cash paid to Tower | 3,500 | Jan 9 | Bill transferred from Tower | 670 |
| Feb 11 | Bill dishonoured | 250 | Feb 3 | Sales: Cash | 110 |
| Mar 5 | Bill paid by Castle | 800 | March | Sales: Cash | 3,400 |
| March | Bad debts to be borne by Tower | 12 | Apr 30 | Stock taken over | 500 |
| Apr 30 | Share of profit on joint venture | 1,162 | Apr 30 | Cash received in settlement | 1,044 |
| | | 5,724 | | | 5,724 |

(b) Memorandum Joint Venture Account

| | | £ | | £ |
|---|---|---|---|---|
| Purchases | | 6,800 | Sales | 8,800 |
| Commission | | 176 | Stock | 500 |
| Profit on joint venture | £ | | | |
| Tower | 1,162 | | | |
| Castle | 1,162 | 2,324 | | |
| | | 9,300 | | 9,300 |

## E Royalty accounts

### 89 W Heal

Royalties Account

| | £ | | £ |
|---|---|---|---|
| 19X5 | | 19X5 | |
| Mar 31 Lessor | 650 | Mar 31 Manufacturing account | 650 |
| 19X6 | | 19X6 | |
| Mar 31 Lessor | 1,480 | Mar 31 Manufacturing account | 1,480 |
| 19X7 | | 19X7 | |
| Mar 31 Lessor | 1,570 | Mar 31 Manufacturing account | 1,570 |
| 19X8 | | 19X8 | |
| Mar 31 Lessor | 1,720 | Mar 31 Manufacturing account | 1,720 |

Short Workings Account

| 19X5 | | Machine No. 1 | Machine No. 2 | 19X5 | | Machine No. 1 | Machine No. 2 |
|---|---|---|---|---|---|---|---|
| | | £ | | | | £ | |
| Mar 31 | Lessor | 70 | | Mar 31 | Balance carried down | 70 | |
| 19X5 | | | | 19X6 | | | |
| Apr 1 | Balance brought down | 70 | | Mar 31 | Lessor Short working recovered | 40 | |
| | | | | | Profit and loss account | 30 | |
| | | 70 | | | | 70 | |

Lessor's Account

| 19X5 | | £ | 19X5 | | £ |
|---|---|---|---|---|---|
| Mar 31 | Cash | 720 | Mar 31 | Royalty | 650 |
| | | | | Short working | 70 |
| | | 720 | | | 720 |
| 19X6 | | | 19X6 | | |
| Mar 31 | Short workings recovered | 40 | Mar 31 | Royalty | 1,480 |
| | Cash | 1,440 | | | |
| | | 1,480 | | | 1,480 |
| 19X7 | | | 19X7 | | |
| Mar 31 | Cash | 1,570 | Mar 31 | Royalty | 1,570 |
| 19X8 | | | 19X8 | | |
| Mar 31 | Cash | 1,720 | Mar 31 | Royalty | 1,720 |

## 90 A

(a) Royalty Account

| 19X1 | | £ | 19X1 | | £ |
|---|---|---|---|---|---|
| Dec 31 | Landlord | 1,650 | Dec 31 | XY Ltd receivable | 975 |
| | Profit and loss account | 325 | | Operating account | 1,000 |
| | | 1,975 | | | 1,975 |
| 19X2 | | | 19X2 | | |
| Dec 31 | Landlord | 2,400 | Dec 31 | XY Ltd | 1,200 |
| | Profit and loss account | 400 | | Operating account | 1,600 |
| | | 2,800 | | | 2,800 |

*continued*

*continued*

| | £ | | £ |
|---|---|---|---|
| 19X3 | | 19X3 | |
| Dec 31 Landlord | 2,820 | Dec 31 XY Ltd | 1,230 |
| Profit and loss account | 410 | Operating account | 2,000 |
| | 3,230 | | 3,230 |
| 19X4 | | 19X4 | |
| Dec 31 Landlord | 3,400 | Dec 31 XY Ltd | 1,350 |
| Profit and loss account | 450 | Operating account | 2,500 |
| | 3,850 | | 3,850 |
| 19X5 | | 19X5 | |
| Dec 31 Landlord | 3,590 | Dec 31 XY Ltd | 1,485 |
| Profit and loss account | 495 | Operating account | 2,600 |
| | 4,085 | | 4,085 |
| 19X6 | | 19X6 | |
| Dec 31 Landlord | 2,000 | Dec 31 Operating account | 2,000 |
| 19X7 | | 19X7 | |
| Dec 31 Landlord | 2,200 | Dec 31 Operating account | 2,200 |
| 19X8 | | 19X8 | |
| Dec 31 Landlord | 3,000 | Dec 31 Operating account | 3,000 |

(b) Landlord

| | £ | | £ |
|---|---|---|---|
| 19X1 | | 19X1 | |
| Dec 31 Cash | 2,000 | Dec 31 Royalty | 1,650 |
| | | Short workings | 350 |
| | 2,000 | | 2,000 |
| 19X2 | | 19X2 | |
| Dec 31 Cash | 2,050 | Dec 31 Royalty | 2,400 |
| Short workings | 350 | | |
| | 2,400 | | 2,400 |
| 19X3 | | 19X3 | |
| Dec 31 Cash | 2,820 | Dec 31 Royalty | 2,820 |
| 19X4 | | 19X4 | |
| Dec 31 Cash | 3,400 | Dec 31 Royalty | 3,400 |
| 19X5 | | 19X5 | |
| Dec 31 Cash | 3,590 | Dec 31 Royalty | 3,590 |

*continued*

*continued*

| | £ | | £ |
|---|---|---|---|
| 19X6 | | 19X6 | |
| Dec 31 Cash | 2,000 | Dec 31 Royalty | 2,000 |
| 19X7 | | 19X7 | |
| Dec 31 Cash | 2,200 | Dec 31 Royalty | 2,200 |
| 19X8 | | 19X8 | |
| Dec 31 Cash | 3,000 | Dec 31 Royalty | 3,000 |

## F Container accounts

### 91 Betta Garments

Cases Stock Account

| 19X4 | | Q | £ | 19X4 | | Q | £ |
|---|---|---|---|---|---|---|---|
| Jan 1 | Balance brought forward | | | Dec 31 | Cost: Cases scrapped | 1,600 | 110 |
| | Premises | 14,000 | 10,500 | | Cases suspense account | | |
| | With customers | 5,000 | 3,750 | | Profit on hire | | 23,500 |
| Dec 31 | Purchases | 19,000 | 22,800 | | Balance carried down | | |
| | Repairs | | 600 | | Premises | 24,000 | 18,000 |
| | Profit and loss account | | 13,260 | | Customers | 12,400 | 9,300 |
| | | 38,000 | 50,910 | | | 38,000 | 50,910 |

Cases Suspense Account

| 19X4 | | Q | £ | 19X4 | | Q | £ |
|---|---|---|---|---|---|---|---|
| Dec 31 | Cases returned | 39,600 | 39,600 | Jan 1 | Balance brought forward | 5,000 | 5,000 |
| | Cases: Stock | | | Dec 31 | Cases to customers | 47,000 | 70,500 |
| | Profit on hire | | 23,500 | | | | |
| Dec 31 | Balance carried down | 12,400 | 12,400 | | | | |
| | | 52,000 | 75,500 | | | 52,000 | 75,500 |

| *Check* | £ | £ |
|---|---|---|
| Profit on hire | | 23,500 |
| Loss on cases scrapped (1,600 at 75p − £110) | 1,090 | |
| Repairs | 600 | |
| Depreciation of cases (19,000 × 45p) | 8,550 | |
| | | 10,240 |
| | | 13,260 |

The missing figure was the cases on the firm's premises at the end of the period; this is found by reconciling the quantity columns in the stock account.

## 92 LEC Ltd

Containers Stock Account

| 19X3 | | Q | £ | 19X3 | | Q | £ |
|---|---|---|---|---|---|---|---|
| Jan 1 | Balance brought forward | | | Dec 31 | Containers suspense account | | |
| | Containers stock on premises | 140 | 420 | | Containers retained by customers | 42 | 168 |
| | Customers | 408 | 1,224 | | Profit on hire | | 1,430 |
| Dec 31 | Purchases | 250 | 750 | | Balance carried forward | | |
| | Profit and loss account | | | | Containers stock | | |
| | Profit on containers | | 1,472 | | Premises | 230 | 690 |
| | | | | | Customers | 526 | 1,578 |
| | | 798 | 3,866 | | | 798 | 3,866 |

Containers Suspense Account

| 19X3 | | Q | £ | 19X3 | | Q | £ |
|---|---|---|---|---|---|---|---|
| Dec 31 | Containers returned | 1,270 | 5,080 | Jan 1 | Balance brought forward | 408 | 1,632 |
| | Containers stock account | | | Dec 31 | Containers charged to customers | 1,430 | 7,150 |
| | Containers retained by customers | 42 | 168 | | | | |
| | Profit on hire | | 1,430 | | | | |
| | Balance carried forward | 526 | 2,104 | | | | |
| | | 1,838 | 8,782 | | | 1,838 | 8,782 |

*Check*

| | £ |
|---|---|
| Profit on hire | 1,430 |
| Profit on sale 42 × £1 | 42 |
| | 1,472 |

# G Contract accounts

## 93 Contract 17B

(a) Account

| | £ | | £ |
|---|---|---|---|
| Materials | 62,000 | Stocks carried forward | 4,000 |
| Wages | 85,300 | Plant carried forward | 7,740 |
| Plant | 8,600 | Work in progress carried forward | 166,344 |
| Establishment charges | 6,700 | Work not yet invoiced carried forward | 5,000 |
| Profit and loss account | 20,484 | | |
| | 183,084 | | 183,084 |

(b) Calculation of Profit to Date

| | £ | £ | £ |
|---|---|---|---|
| Work certified = 162,000 × $\frac{10}{9}$= | | | 180,000 |
| *deduct:* Costs to date | | 162,600 | |
| *deduct:* Stocks carried forward | 11,740 | | |
| Cost of work not certified | 5,000 | 16,740 | 145,860 |
| Estimated profit to date | | | 34,140 |

Adopting the usual basis of taking two-thirds of the realised profit the calculation is as follows:

$$£34{,}140 \times \tfrac{2}{3} \times \tfrac{90}{100} = £20{,}484.$$

TUTORIAL NOTE

Standard accounting practice is to reduce the total estimated profit by the proportion which has actually been realised and then to reduce this figure by an arbitrary amount. The most usual fraction is two-thirds.

(c) Balance Sheet Extracts

| | £ | £ |
|---|---|---|
| Current assets | | |
| Work in progress | 171,344 | |
| *deduct:* Cash received on account | 162,000 | 9,344 |
| Stock | | 11,740 |

## 94 Sandcastles Ltd

(a) Contract X Account

| | | £ | | | £ |
|---|---|---|---|---|---|
| 19X7 | | | 19X7 | | |
| Dec 31 | Materials | 14,632 | Dec 31 | Plant carried down | 7,925 |
| | Wages | 16,237 | | Work in progress carried down | 43,521 |
| | Direct expenses | 866 | | | |
| | Plant | 10,725 | | | |
| | | 42,460 | | | |
| | Profit and loss account | 8,986 | | | |
| | | 51,446 | | | 51,446 |
| 19X8 | | £ | 19X8 | | £ |
| Jan 1 | Plant brought down | 7,925 | Jun 30 | Plant transferred to Contract Y | 6,000 |
| | Work in progress brought down | 43,521 | Nov 30 | Cash: Sale of plant | 2,750 |
| Nov 30 | Materials | 25,891 | | Contract price | 100,000 |
| | Wages | 31,248 | Dec 31 | Profit and loss account: Loss | 9,250 |
| | Direct expenses | 1,215 | | | |
| | Plant | 7,504 | | | |
| | Hire purchase interest | 196 | | | |
| | Penalty | 500 | | | |
| | | 118,000 | | | 118,000 |

(b) Contract Y Account

| 19X8 | | £ | 19X8 | | £ |
|---|---|---|---|---|---|
| Jul 1 | Plant transferred from Contract X | 6,000 | Dec 31 | Plant carried down | 15,290 |
| Dec 31 | Materials | 33,270 | | Work in progress carried down | 95,419 |
| | Wages | 40,865 | | | |
| | Direct expenses | 1,624 | | | |
| | Plant | 12,350 | | | |
| | Hire purchase interest | 100 | | | |
| | | 94,209 | | | |
| | Profit and loss account | 16,500 | | | |
| | | 110,709 | | | 110,709 |
| 19X9 | | | | | |
| Jan 1 | Plant brought down | 15,290 | | | |
| | Work in progress brought down | 95,419 | | | |

## Workings

Contract X

| | | |
|---|---|---|
| (1) Plant, carried down at 31st December 19X7 | | £ |
| Cost at 1st June 19X7 | | 10,725 |
| Estimated market value at 31st October 19X8 | | 3,925 |
| Depreciation over seventeen months | | 6,800 |
| Cost 1st June 19X7 | | 10,725 |
| *deduct:* $\frac{7}{17}$ × £6,800 | | 2,800 |
| | | 7,925 |

| | | |
|---|---|---|
| (2) Work in progress, carried down at 31st December 19X7 | | £ |
| Total expenditure to date | | 42,460 |
| *deduct:* Estimated residual value of plant | | 3,925 |
| | | 38,535 |
| *add:* Estimated future expenditure | | 39,000 |
| | | 77,535 |
| Total profit on contract | | 22,465 |
| Contract price | | 100,000 |
| Cash received | 36,000 | |
| 10% retention | 4,000 | |
| Work certified | 40,000 | |
| Profit taken: $\frac{40,000}{100,000}$ × £22,465 | | 8,986 |
| Net expenditure to date | | 34,535 |
| | | 43,521 |

Contract Y

(1) Plant carried down at 31st December 19X8

| | £ |
|---|---|
| Market value of transfer from Contract X | 6,000 |
| Cost at 1st July 19X8 | 12,350 |
| | 18,350 |
| Estimated market value at 30th April 19X9 | 13,250 |
| Depreciation over ten months | 5,100 |
| | |
| Cost to contract | 18,350 |
| *deduct:* $\frac{6}{10}$ × £5,100 | 3,060 |
| | 15,290 |

(2) Work in progress carried down at 31st December 19X7

| | £ | £ |
|---|---|---|
| Total expenditure to date | | 94,209 |
| *deduct:* Estimated residual value of plant | | 13,250 |
| | | 80,959 |
| *add:* Estimated future expenditure | | 46,041 |
| | | 127,000 |
| Total profit on contract | | 33,000 |
| Contract price | | 160,000 |
| Cash received | | 72,000 |
| 10% retention | | 8,000 |
| Work certified | | 80,000 |
| Profit taken: $\frac{80{,}000}{160{,}000}$ × £33,000 | | 16,500 |
| | | 78,919 |
| Net expenditure to date | | 95,419 |

## 95 Brick and Tile

*Contract No. 15:* This contract is substantially completed, and it should therefore be reasonable to take credit for the proportion of total profit which the work certified (less retentions) bears to the total contract price. As a matter of prudence, this figure should then be reduced by (say) one-third. The work in progress valuation on this basis would be:

| | £ |
|---|---|
| Costs to date | 27,700 |
| *add:* Profit: $\frac{2}{3} \times \frac{£31{,}500}{£38{,}000}$ × profit on completion £(38,000 − 30,000) | 4,400 |
| | 32,100 |

*Contract No. 16:* Contract No. 16 is expected to show a loss on completion. SSAP 9 requires that such a loss should be provided for in full as soon as it becomes clear that a loss will be made. The work in progress valuation of the contract is accordingly:

| | £ |
|---|---|
| Costs to date | 24,800 |
| *less:* Provision for loss £(35,000 − 28,000) | 7,000 |
| | 17,800 |

*Contract No. 18:* At a fairly early state and for this reason it would be inappropriate to take credit for any profit yet. In any case little or no profit appears to have accrued. The work in progress valuation should therefore be taken as:

| | £ |
|---|---|
| Costs to date | £12,400 |

## H Hire purchase accounts—buyer's books

### 96 Tractors

(a) Tractors on Hire Purchase

| | | £ | | | £ |
|---|---|---|---|---|---|
| 19X3 | | £ | 19X3 | | £ |
| Apr 30 | Cash price: HP Co. Tractor A | 1,400 | Dec 31 | Balance carried down | 3,300 |
| Sep 31 | Cash price: HP Co. Tractor B | 1,900 | | | |
| | | 3,300 | | | 3,300 |
| 19X4 | | £ | 19X4 | | £ |
| Jan 1 | Balance brought down | | Jun 30 | Transfer to disposal of tractors account | 1,900 |
| | Tractor A | 1,400 | Dec 31 | Balance carried down | 1,400 |
| | Tractor B | 1,900 | | | |
| | | 3,300 | | | 3,300 |
| 19X5 | | £ | | | |
| Jan 1 | Balance brought down | 1,400 | | | |

(b) Provision for Depreciation of Tractors

| | | £ | | | | £ |
|---|---|---|---|---|---|---|
| 19X3 | | £ | 19X3 | | | £ |
| Dec 31 | Balance carried down | 282 | Dec 31 | Year-end provisions: | | |
| | | | | Tractor A | 187 | |
| | | | | Tractor B | 95 | 282 |
| | | 282 | | | | 282 |
| 19X4 | | £ | 19X4 | | | £ |
| Jun 30 | Transfer to disposal of Tractor account Tractor B | 285 | Jan 1 | Balance brought down | | 282 |
| | | | Jun 30 | Profit and loss account Tractor A | | 190 |
| Dec 31 | Balance carried down | 467 | Dec 31 | Profit and loss account Tractor A | | 280 |
| | | 752 | | | | 752 |
| | | | 19X5 | | | £ |
| | | | Jan 1 | Balance brought down | | 467 |

(c) Disposal of Tractors

| 19X4 | | £ | 19X4 | | £ |
|---|---|---|---|---|---|
| Jun 30 | Transfer from tractors on hire purchase Tractor B | 1,900 | Jun 30 | Transfer from provision for depreciation of tractor: Tractor B | 285 |
| | | | Jul 10 | Cash: Insurance | 1,500 |
| | | | Dec 31 | Profit and loss account: Loss | 115 |
| | | 1,900 | | | 1,900 |

(d) Hire Purchase Company

| | | Tractor A | Tractor B | | | Tractor A | Tractor B |
|---|---|---|---|---|---|---|---|
| 19X3 | | £ | £ | 19X3 | | £ | £ |
| Apr 30 | Cash (deposit) | 200 | | Apr 30 | Tractors on hire purchase | 1,400 | |
| Sep 30 | Cash (deposit) | | 268 | Sep 30 | Tractors on hire purchase | | 1,900 |
| Dec 31 | Cash (instalments) £60 × 8 | 480 | | Dec 31 | Hire purchase interest payable: £10 × 8 | 80 | |
| | £80 × 3 | | 240 | | £12 × 3 | | 36 |
| Dec 31 | Balances carried down | 800 | 1,428 | | | | |
| | | 1,480 | 1,936 | | | 1,480 | 1,936 |
| 19X4 | | £ | £ | 19X4 | | £ | £ |
| Jun 30 | Cash (instalments): £80 × 6 | | 480 | Jan 1 | Balances brought down | 800 | 1,428 |
| Jul 10 | Cash: Termination of agreement | | 1,200 | Jun 30 | Hire purchase interest: £12 × 6 | | 72 |
| Dec 31 | Cash (instalments): £60 × 12 | 720 | | Dec 31 | Hire purchase interest: £10 × 12 | 120 | |
| Dec 31 | Balance carried down | 200 | | Dec 31 | Profit and loss account: Loss | | 180 |
| | | 920 | 1,680 | | | 920 | 1,680 |
| | | | | 19X5 | | £ | |
| | | | | Jan 1 | Balance brought down | 200 | |

## 97 Cars

Motor Vehicles Account

| 19X2 | | £ | 19X3 | | £ |
|---|---|---|---|---|---|
| Jun 30 | HP company UE452 | 850 | Feb 28 | Balance carried down | 1,760 |
| 19X3 | | | | | |
| Jan 31 | HP company XA300 | 910 | | | |
| | | 1,760 | | | 1,760 |

*continued*

*continued*

| | | £ | | | £ |
|---|---|---|---|---|---|
| 19X3 | | | 19X3 | | |
| Mar 1 | Balance brought down | 1,760 | Aug 1 | Depreciation (20% of £850) | 170 |
| 19X4 | | | 10 | Bank: Proceeds from insurance company | 700 |
| Feb 28 | Profit and loss account: Profit on disposal | 20 | 19X4 | | |
| | | | Feb 28 | Balance carried forward | 910 |
| | | 1,780 | | | 1,780 |

Provision for Depreciation of Motor Vehicles

| | | £ | | | £ |
|---|---|---|---|---|---|
| 19X3 | | | 19X3 | | |
| Feb 28 | Balance carried down | 352 | Feb 28 | Profit and loss account (20% of £1,760) | 352 |
| | | 352 | | | 352 |
| 19X3 | | | 19X3 | | |
| Aug 1 | Motor vehicle (accumulated depreciation on vehicle lost) | 170 | Mar 1 | Balance brought down | 352 |
| 19X4 | | | 19X4 | | |
| Feb 28 | Balance carried forward | 364 | Feb 28 | Profit and loss account (20% of £910) | 182 |
| | | 534 | | | 534 |

Hire Purchase Company

| | | UE452 | XA300 | | | UE452 | XA300 |
|---|---|---|---|---|---|---|---|
| 19X2 | | £ | £ | 19X2 | | £ | £ |
| Jun 30 | Bank deposit | 94 | | Jun 30 | Motor vehicles | 850 | |
| 19X3 | | | | 19X3 | | | |
| Jan 31 | Bank deposit | | 118 | Jan 31 | Motor vehicles | | 910 |
| Feb 28 | Bank instalments | | | Feb 28 | Hire purchase interest | | |
| | 8 × £24 | 192 | | | 8 × £3 | 24 | |
| | 1 × £26 | | 26 | | 1 × £4 | | 4 |
| | Balance carried down | 588 | 770 | | | | |
| | | 874 | 914 | | | 874 | 914 |
| 19X3 | | £ | £ | 19X3 | | £ | £ |
| Aug 1 | Bank instalments | | | Mar 1 | Balance brought down | 588 | 770 |
| | 5 × £24 | 120 | | Aug 1 | Hire purchase interest | | |
| 10 | Bank settlement | 500 | | | 5 × £3 | 15 | |
| 19X4 | | | | 10 | Hire purchase charge | 17 | |
| Feb 28 | Bank instalments | | | 19X4 | | | |
| | 12 × £26 | | 312 | Feb 28 | Hire purchase interest | | |
| | Balance carried forward | | 506 | | 12 × £4 | | 48 |
| | | 620 | 818 | | | 620 | 818 |

## I Hire purchase accounts—seller's books

### 98 T Ltd

Hire Purchase Trading Account
year ended 31st December 19X4

| | £ | | £ |
|---|---|---|---|
| Cost of goods sold on hire purchase | 1,840 | Cash | 1,401 |
| Gross profit on hire purchase | 427 | Goods repossessed | 120 |
| | | Stock on hire at 31st December 19X4 | 746 |
| | 2,267 | | 2,267 |

**Workings**

| 19X4 | Cost price £ | HP selling £ | Cash received £ | Balance outstanding £ | Stock at cost £ | Profit £ | Repossessions at cost £ |
|---|---|---|---|---|---|---|---|
| Jan 17 | 300 | 450 | 360 | 90 | 60 | 120 | |
| Mar 10 | 350 | 500 | 400 | 100 | 70 | 120 | |
| May 22 | 90 | 135 | 81 | 54 | 36 | 27 | |
| Jul 4 | 200 | 350 | 140 | | | 60 | 120 |
| Sep 10 | 700 | 900 | 360 | 540 | 420 | 80 | |
| Nov 15 | 200 | 300 | 60 | 240 | 160 | 20 | |
| | 1,840 | | 1,401 | | 746 | 427 | 120 |

### 99 Scott

(a) Hire Purchase Trading Account

| | £ | | £ |
|---|---|---|---|
| Cost of goods | 210 | Deposits received | 32 |
| Hire purchase | | Instalments received | 70 |
| Goods profit | 33 | Repossessions | 49 |
| | | Stock carried down | 92 |
| | 243 | | 243 |

(b) General Trading Account

| | £ | £ | | £ |
|---|---|---|---|---|
| Purchases | 5,400 | | Sales | 6,200 |
| *deduct:* | | | | |
| Cost of goods sold on hire purchase | 210 | 5,190 | | |
| Closing stock | | 700 | | |
| | | 4,490 | | |
| Gross profit carried down | | 1,710 | | |
| | | 6,200 | | 6,200 |

(c) Hire Purchase Memorandum Debtors' Account

| | £ | | £ |
|---|---|---|---|
| Sales | 310 | Deposits | 32 |
| | | Instalments | 70 |
| | | Repossession | 70 |
| | | Balance carried down | 138 |
| | 310 | | 310 |
| Balance brought down | 138 | | |

## Workings

Calculation of stock out on hire purchase:

$$\frac{\text{Instalments outstanding}}{\text{Selling price}} \times \text{cost} = \frac{138}{210} \times 140 = £92.$$

Calculation of repossessions:

$$\frac{\text{Instalments outstanding}}{\text{Selling price}} \times \text{cost} = \frac{70}{100} \times 70 = £49.$$

## 100 John

(a) Hire Purchase Trading Account

| | £ | | | £ |
|---|---|---|---|---|
| General trading account | | HP sales | | |
| Cost of HP sales | 2,135 | Deposits | | 648 |
| *less:* Cost equivalent of outstanding instalments on goods returned (*see* Working 2) | 174 | Instalments received | | 608 |
| | | Instalments due (*see* Working 1) | 80 | |
| | | *less:* Contingency provision | 16 | |
| | 1,961 | | | 64 |
| Profit and loss account | 437 | | | 1,320 |
| | | Stock on hire carried down (*see* (d) below) | | 1,078 |
| | 2,398 | | | 2,398 |

(b) General Trading Account

| | £ | | £ |
|---|---|---|---|
| Purchases | 8,700 | Cash sales | 6,274 |
| *less:* Cost of HP sales | 2,135 | | |
| | 6,565 | | |
| *less:* Closing stock | 1,760 | | |
| | 4,805 | | |
| Gross profit | 1,469 | | |
| | 6,274 | | 6,274 |

*See* Tutorial Note 1.

(c) Hire Purchase Sales Ledger Control Account

| | £ | | | £ |
|---|---|---|---|---|
| HP sales account (*see* Working 1) | 3,240 | Cash: Deposits | | 648 |
| | | Instalments | | 608 |
| | | HP sales account: Discount re October completion of June sale | | 10 |
| | | HP sales account: Cancellation of amounts outstanding on goods returned (*see* Working 1) | | 240 |
| | | Balance carried down | | |
| | | Not yet due (*see* Working 1) | 1,654 | |
| | | Due (*see* Working 1) | 80 | 1,734 |
| | 3,240 | | | 3,240 |

(d) Statement of closing stock valuation

| Balances outstanding (per Working 1) | | Reduction factor (per question) | Stock valuation |
|---|---|---|---|
| | £ | | £ |
| February | 50 | 160/250 | 32 |
| April | 112 | 190/280 | 76 |
| June | 32 | 45/80 | 18 |
| July | 270 | 280/450 | 168 |
| September | 222 | 240/370 | 144 |
| November | 448 | 380/560 | 304 |
| December | 520 | 420/650 | 336 |
| | | Stock on hire purchase | 1,078 |
| | | General stock | 1,760 |
| | | Returned stock at valuation | 140 |
| | | | 2,978 |

## Workings

(1) Analysis of monthly HP sales

| Month | Sales | Deposits | Instalments | | | Balance on transactions terminated | |
|---|---|---|---|---|---|---|---|
| | | | No. | Due | Not due | | |
| | £ | £ | | £ | £ | | |
| February | 250 | 50 | 3 | 150 | 50 | | |
| April | 280 | 56 | 2 | 112 | 112 | | |
| April returns | 150 | 30 | 1 | 30 | | 90 | |
| June | 80 | 16 | 2 | 32 | 32 | | |
| June settled | 200 | 40 | 1 | 110 } | | | £10 discount allowed |
| | | | | 40 } | | | |
| July | 450 | 90 | 1 | 90 | 270 | | |
| July returns | 250 | 50 | 1 | 50 | | 150 | |
| September | 370 | 74 | 1 | 74 | 222 | | |
| November | 560 | 112 | | | 448 | | |
| December | 650 | 130 | | | 520 | | |
| | 3,240 | 648 | | 688 | 1,654 | 240 | |
| Instalments received | | | | 608 | | | |
| Instalments due but outstanding | | | | 80 | | | |

(2) Calculation of cost equivalent of instalments outstanding on goods returned.

| | £ | £ |
|---|---|---|
| (a) April: balance outstanding per Working 1 | 90 | |
| cost equivalent $£90 \times \frac{£110}{£150}$ | | 66 |

*continued*

| *continued* | | £ | £ |
|---|---|---|---|
| | *brought forward* | | 66 |
| (b) July: balance outstanding per Working 1 | | 150 | |
| cost equivalent £150 × $\frac{£180}{£250}$ | | | 108 |
| | | | 174 |

TUTORIAL NOTES

(1) It is frequently easier in examination questions to omit from the general trading account all transactions involving goods returned from HP companies. This is the method adopted in part (b) above.

The profit or loss on goods returned from hire is separately calculated and transferred to profit and loss account from a goods returned from HP customers account:

Goods Returned from HP Customers

| | £ | | £ |
|---|---|---|---|
| HP trading account | | Cash | 100 |
| Cost equivalent of | | Balance carried down | 140 |
| outstanding instalments | 174 | | |
| Profit and loss account | | | |
| Profit | 66 | | |
| | 240 | | 240 |
| Balance brought down | 140 | | |
| Stock at valuation | | | |

(2) A difficult question which will repay study. Note the importance of Working 1, which contributes to parts (a), (c) and (d). An orderly set-up for this working was absolutely essential for an accurate answer.

# J Investment accounts

## 101 AB

10% Debenture Stock: Needy Ltd

| 19X4 | | Nominal £ | Income £ | Capital £ |
|---|---|---|---|---|
| Mar 1 | Bank | 6,000 | 250 | 5,630 |
| Aug 31 | Transfer to capital: Interest on £2,000 sold ex dividend in September | | 17 | |
| | Profit and loss account Profit on sale | | | 110 |
| Nov 30 | Profit on sale | | | 45 |
| Dec 31 | Profit and loss account Investment income | | 416 | |
| | | 6,000 | 683 | 5,785 |

| 19X4 | | Nominal £ | Income £ | Capital £ |
|---|---|---|---|---|
| Mar 31 | Bank interest | | 300 | |
| Aug 31 | Bank sale proceeds | 2,000 | | 1,970 |
| | Transfer from income: Interest on £2,000 for September | | | 17 |
| Sep 30 | Bank interest 6 months on £6,000 | | 300 | |
| Nov 30 | Bank: Sale cum. div. dividend | 2,000 | 33 | 1,922 |
| Dec 31 | Balance Accrued interest 3 months carried down | 2,000 | 50 | 1,876 |
| | | 6,000 | 683 | 5,785 |

## Workings

| | |
|---|---:|
| Purchase 1st March: Interest last paid 30th September cum. div. | £ |
| ∴ Five months interest accrued, i.e. | 250 |
| Price apportioned: Accrued income | 250 |
| Capital | 5,630 |
| | 5,880 |

| | |
|---|---:|
| Sale 31st August ex div.: Full proceeds to capital | £ |
| Sale 30th November: | |
| Interest accrued 2 months, i.e. | 33 |
| Price apportioned: Income | 33 |
| Capital | 1,922 |
| | 1,955 |

| | |
|---|---:|
| | £ |
| Profit on sale 31st August: Proceeds | 1,987 |
| *less:* Cost $\frac{1}{3} \times 5,630$ | 1,877 |
| | 110 |
| 30th November: Proceeds | 1,922 |
| Cost | 1,877 |
| | 45 |

| | |
|---|---:|
| Check on interest: | £ |
| £2,000 held for 10 months | 166 |
| £2,000 held for 6 months | 100 |
| £2,000 held for 9 months | 150 |
| | 416 |

Investment Account
Ordinary Shares of 25p Each in Ringlet Ltd

| Date | Details | No. of Shares | Income £ | Capital £ |
|---|---|---|---|---|
| 19X4 | | | | |
| Jul 1 | Cash: Shares purchased | 30,000 | | 52,800 |
| Aug 15 | Profit on sale of investments | | | 1,450 |
| Oct 10 | Bonus issue (one for every five held) | 5,000 | | |
| Nov 5 | Profit on sale of investments | | | 667 |
| Nov 30 | Profit on sale of investments | | | 133 |
| 19X5 | | | | |
| Jan 25 | Cash: Shares taken up under rights issue (125p paid) | 2,000 | | 2,500 |
| Jun 30 | Profit and loss account Income for year | | 1,825 | |
| | | 37,000 | 1,825 | 57,550 |

| Date | Details | No. of Shares | Income £ | Capital £ |
|---|---|---|---|---|
| 19X4 | | | | |
| Aug 15 | Cash: Shares sold cum. div. | 5,000 | | 10,250 |
| Sep 30 | Cash: Interim dividend of 2.5p on 25,000 shares | | 625 | |
| Nov 5 | Cash: Sale of bonus shares | 2,000 | | 3,600 |
| Nov 30 | Cash: Sale of shares | 4,000 | | 6,000 |
| 19X5 | | | | |
| Jan 31 | Cash: Sale of 200 rights at 25p per share | | | 500 |
| Jun 15 | Cash: Final dividend of 5p on 24,000 shares | | 1,200 | |
| Jun 30 | Balance carried down | 26,000 | | 37,200 |
| | | 37,000 | 1,825 | 57,550 |

**Workings**

| | £ |
|---|---|
| Profit on sale of 5,000 shares | |
| Sale proceeds | 10,250 |
| *deduct:* Cost of shares sold: | |
| $\frac{5,000}{30,000} \times £52,800$ | 8,800 |
| | 1,450 |

| | £ |
|---|---|
| Profit on sale of 2,000 shares | |
| Sale proceeds | 3,600 |
| *deduct:* Cost of shares sold: | |
| $\frac{2,000}{30,000} \times £44,000\ (52,800 - 8,800)$ | 2,933 |
| | 667 |

| | £ |
|---|---|
| Profit on sale of 4,000 shares | |
| Sale proceeds | 6,000 |
| *deduct:* Cost of shares sold: | |
| $\frac{4,000}{28,000} \times £41,067\ (52,800 - 8,800 - 2,933)$ | 5,867 |
| | 133 |

## K Bills of exchange

### 103 A

Account with B

| 19X1 | | £ | 19X1 | | £ |
|---|---|---|---|---|---|
| Jan 4 | Cash<br>One half of proceeds of bill | 492.50 | Jan 1 | Bills receivable<br>3-month bill from B | 1,000.00 |
| Feb 1 | Bill payable<br>3-month bill to B | 400.00 | Feb 2 | Cash<br>One half of proceeds of bill | 197.00 |
| Feb 4 | Charges<br>Adjustment of discounting charges<br>(£15 Suffered by A<br>£ 6 Suffered by B<br>£ 9 ½ chargeable to B) | 4.50 | Apr 4 | Bill receivable<br>3-month bill from B for £1,000 + interest at 5% for 3 months | 1,012.50 |
| Apr 1 | Bill dishonoured<br>B's bill met by A | 1,000.00 | Oct 31 | Cash: First and final dividend 50p in £ from B's trustee in bankruptcy | 356.25 |
| Apr 4 | Interest: Chargeable to B on new bill | 12.50 | Oct 31 | Bad debt account<br>Balance on B's account now irrecoverable | 356.25 |
| Jul 1 | Bill dishonoured: Due to B's bankruptcy | 1,012.50 | | | |
| | | 2,922.00 | | | 2,922.00 |

*continued*

| *continued* | £ | | £ |
|---|---|---|---|
| 19X2 | | 19X2 | |
| Dec 5 Bad debts account Amount agreed to be paid by B after his discharge | 356.25 | Feb 10 Cash: From B | 356.25 |
| | 356.25 | | 356.25 |

## Workings

### Bills Receivable Account

| | £ | | £ | £ |
|---|---|---|---|---|
| B: 3-month bill | 1,000.00 | Cash | 985.00 | |
| | | Discounting charges | 15.00 | 1,000.00 |
| Cash: B's bill dishonoured | 1,000.00 | B: Bill dishonoured | | 1,000.00 |
| B: 3-month bill | 1,012.50 | B: Bill dishonoured | | 1,012.50 |
| | 3,012.50 | | | 3,012.50 |

### Bills Payable Account

| | £ | | £ |
|---|---|---|---|
| Cash | 400.00 | B: 3-month bill | 400.00 |
| | 400.00 | | 400.00 |

### Interest Receivable Account

| | £ | | £ |
|---|---|---|---|
| Profit and loss account | 12.50 | B: Interest on bill (5% × £1,000 × $\frac{3}{12}$) | 12.50 |
| | 12.50 | | 12.50 |

### Discounting Charges Account

| | £ | | £ |
|---|---|---|---|
| Bills receivable (6% × £1,000 × $\frac{3}{12}$) | 15.00 | B: Adjustment for charges | 4.50 |
| | | Profit and loss account | 10.50 |
| | 15.00 | | 15.00 |

# L Cash budgets

## 104 Forest Ltd

(a)

Cash Budget
Six Months Ending 30th September 19X7

| | April | May | June | July | August | September | Total |
|---|---|---|---|---|---|---|---|
| Receipts | £ | £ | £ | £ | £ | £ | £ |
| Shares issued | 50,000 | | | | | | 50,000 |
| Debtors | | | 14,500 | 16,000 | 18,000 | 24,000 | 72,500 |
| | 50,000 | — | 14,500 | 16,000 | 18,000 | 24,000 | 122,500 |
| Payments | | | | | | | |
| Fixed and current assets | 39,000 | | | | | | 39,000 |
| Preliminary expenses | | 800 | | | | | 800 |
| Wages and salaries | 800 | 800 | 800 | 800 | 900 | 900 | 5,000 |
| Expenses | 600 | 600 | 600 | 600 | 600 | 600 | 3,600 |
| Creditors (*see* workings) | — | 16,400 | 14,400 | 19,200 | 19,200 | 19,200 | 88,400 |
| Rates | 200 | | | | | | 200 |
| | 40,600 | 18,600 | 15,800 | 20,600 | 20,700 | 20,700 | 137,000 |
| Cumulative balance before issue of debentures (overdraft shown in brackets) | 9,400 | (9,200) | (10,500) | (15,100) | (17,800) | (14,500) | |
| Debentures issued | 18,000 | — | — | — | — | — | |
| Cumulative balance after issue of debentures | 27,400 | 8,800 | 7,500 | 2,900 | 200 | 3,500 | |

(b)

Budgeted Trading and Profit and Loss Account
Six Months Ending 30th September 19X7

| | £ | | £ |
|---|---|---|---|
| Stock purchased | 8,000 | Sales | 120,500 |
| Purchases | 107,600 | | |
| | 115,600 | | |
| *deduct:* Closing stock | 19,200 | | |
| | 96,400 | | |
| Gross profit carried down | 24,100 | | |
| | 120,500 | | 120,500 |
| Wages and salaries | 5,000 | Gross profit brought down | 24,100 |
| Rates | 200 | | |
| Expenses | 3,600 | | |
| Debenture interest | 450 | | |
| Net profit carried down | 14,850 | | |
| | 24,100 | | 24,100 |

Budgeted Balance Sheet 30th September 19X7

| *Employment of capital* | £ | £ | £ |
|---|---|---|---|
| Fixed assets | | | |
| Freehold premises | | | 25,000 |
| Plant and fittings | | | 6,000 |
| | | | 31,000 |
| Current assets | | | |
| Stock | | 19,200 | |
| Debtors | | 48,000 | |
| Bank | | 3,500 | |
| | | 70,700 | |
| *deduct:* Current liabilities | | | |
| Creditors | 19,200 | | |
| Debenture interest | 450 | 19,650 | 51,050 |
| | | | 82,050 |
| *Capital employed* | | | £ |
| Share capital | | | 50,000 |
| Retained profits | | | 14,850 |
| | | | 64,850 |
| *deduct:* Preliminary expenses | | | 800 |
| | | | 64,050 |
| 5% debentures | | | 18,000 |
| | | | 82,050 |

## Workings

Creditors

| | £ | Purchased in | Paid for in |
|---|---|---|---|
| Sales: April | 14,500 | | |
| May | 16,000 | | |
| | 30,500 | | |
| *deduct:* 20% | 6,100 | | |
| Cost of sales | 24,400 | | |
| *deduct:* Stock purchased | 8,000 | | |
| | 16,400 | April | May |
| Sales: June | 18,000 | | |
| *deduct:* 20% | 3,600 | | |
| Cost of sales | 14,400 | May | June |

*continued*

*continued*

| | £ | Purchased in | Paid for in |
|---|---|---|---|
| Sales: July | 24,000 | | |
| *deduct:* 20% | 4,800 | | |
| Cost of sales | 19,200 | June | July |
| August | 19,200 | July | August |
| September | 19,200 | August | September |
| October | 19,200 | September | October |

TUTORIAL NOTE

Preliminary expenses could have been written off to profit and loss account.

## M Insurance claims

### 105 Cinder Ltd

Statement Showing Amounts to be Claimed by the Company from Its Insurers

| | | £ | £ |
|---|---|---|---|
| (a) | Loss of stock: | | |
| | Estimated stock at the time of the fire (*see* workings) | 55,000 | |
| | *deduct:* Salvaged stock | 396 | |
| | Claim receivable (adequate insurance cover) | | 54,604 |
| (b) | Building: | | |
| | Loss to the company being $\frac{3}{4} \times$ £100,000 | 75,000 | |
| | As the building was under-insured, the insurance cover being £80,000 only, the amount to be claimed is $\frac{4}{5} \times$ £75,000 | | 60,000 |
| (c) | Loss of profits. | | |
| | Period of disruption 1st February to 30th April (3 months) | | |
| | Basis year: year ended 31st December 19X4 | | |
| | Percentage on turnover: | | |
| | Net profit | 5,250 | |
| | Add insured standing charges | 16,750 | |
| | | 22,000 | |
| | Being 11 per cent on the turnover of £200,000. (Both the amount of insurance cover and the period of indemnity are adequate.) | | |
| | Amount to be claimed: 11 per cent of £18,000, which was the shortfall in turnover during the period of disruption | | 1,980 |

**Workings**
Trading Account (Estimated)
Month Ended 31st January 19X5

| | £ | | £ |
|---|---|---|---|
| Stock at 1st January | 52,500 | Sales (January turnover) | 10,000 |
| Purchases (£10,668 + 332) | 11,000 | Balance: Estimated stock at | |
| Estimated gross profit | | date of fire | 55,000 |
| ($\frac{15}{100}$ × £10,000) | 1,500 | | |
| | 65,000 | | 65,000 |

Gross profit:
The estimated gross profit is calculated as based on the company's latest accounts for the year ended 31st December 19X4 $= \frac{30{,}000}{200{,}000} \times 100 = 15\%$.

## 11 INTERPRETATION OF ACCOUNTS

### 106 Construction of accounts

| | £ |
|---|---|
| Ordinary shares in issue | 1,200,000 |
| Reserves | 3,200,000 |
| Equity capital employed | 4,400,000 |

Per 6: Net equity income 10% $= 440{,}000$

Per 7: Ordinary dividend cover $\frac{1}{1.1}$ $= 400{,}000$

Dividend rate $= 33.33\%$

Net current assets and fixed assets $= 5{,}100{,}000$

Per 1: Net current assets $= \frac{0.7}{1.7}$ $= 2{,}100{,}000$

Fixed assets $= \frac{1.0}{1.7}$ $= 3{,}000{,}000$

Per 2: Working capital ratio of 1.6:1 means that

$$\frac{\text{Gross current assets}}{\text{Current liabilities}} = \frac{1.6}{1}$$

and net current assets = 0.6 thereof

Hence, gross current assets

$$= £2{,}100{,}000 \times \frac{1.6}{0.6} = 5{,}600{,}000$$

*continued*

| | | £ |
|---|---|---|
| and gross current liabilities | | |
| | $= £5,600,000 \times \frac{1}{1.6}$ | = 3,500,000 |
| Per 3: Current ratio of 1.1:1 means that | | |
| Cash and debtors | $= £3,500,000 \times \frac{1.1}{1}$ | = 3,850,000 |
| Whereof, cash is | | 350,000 |
| and debtors | | 3,500,000 |
| Per 5: Debtors' turnover ratio of 4 means that turnover is £3,500,000 × 4 | | = 14,000,000 |
| Current assets of £5,600,000 is therefore made up of: | | |
| Cash | | 350,000 |
| Debtors | | 3,500,000 |
| Stock | | 1,750,000 |
| Per 4: Stock turnover ratio of 6 means that Purchases are £1,750,000 × 6 | | = 10,500,000 |

Draft Balance Sheet

| | £ | £ | £ |
|---|---|---|---|
| Net fixed assets | | | 3,000,000 |
| Gross current assets | | 5,600,000 | |
| made up of: Stock | 1,750,000 | | |
| Debtors | 3,500,000 | | |
| Cash | 350,000 | | |
| *less:* Current liabilities (including taxation) | | 3,500,000 | |
| Net current assets | | | 2,100,000 |
| | | | 5,100,000 |
| Capital employed | | | |
| Made up of: | | | |
| 5% Preference shares of £1 each | | 700,000 | |
| Ordinary shares of £1 each | | 1,200,000 | |
| Reserves | | 3,200,000 | 5,100,000 |

Draft Trading and Profit and Loss Account

| | £ | £ |
|---|---|---|
| Sales turnover | | 14,000,000 |
| *less:* Cost of sales | | 13,140,000 |
| Purchases | 10,500,000 | |
| Expenses other than purchases | 2,640,000 | |
| Trading profit before taxation | | 860,000 |
| *less:* Taxation on profits of the year | | 385,000 |
| Trading profits after taxation | | 475,000 |
| *less:* Preference dividend (gross) | | 35,000 |
| Profits available for equity | | 440,000 |
| *less:* Ordinary dividend of 33.33% (gross) | | 400,000 |
| Unappropriated profit carried forward | | 40,000 |

## 107 Spark Ltd

(a) Six accounting ratios which would be of particular value in assessing the profitability and liquidity performance of Spark Ltd could be selected from the ratios and percentages shown below:

| | 19X7 | 19X8 |
|---|---|---|
| (i) Gross profit/sales | 45.0% | 43.7% |
| (ii) Trading expenses/sales | 22.5% | 17.1% |
| (iii) Trading profit/sales | 22.5% | 26.6% |
| (iv) Trading profit/net assets (or capital employed) | 40.9% | 65.9% |
| (v) Current assets/current liabilities | 1.7 | 1.2 |
| (vi) Quick assets/current liabilities | 0.8 | 0.5 |
| (vii) Stocks: Average period held in weeks: $\frac{\text{Year-end stock}}{\text{Cost of goods sold}} \times 52$ | 18.9 | 15.9 |
| (viii) Debtors: Credit period, in weeks: $\frac{\text{Debtors}}{\text{Sales}} \times 52$ | 6.5 | 5.7 |
| (ix) Fixed assets/total assets | 52.3% | 56.1% |

Clearly, there are a number of other ratios which could be calculated but the ones shown above are considered to be the most important.

*Notes on Ratios*

Capital employed:
It could also be argued that gross assets should have been used in (iv) above (the

answer uses net assets). This of course would depend on the duration of the liabilities in the question.

Credit taken by debtors:
As credit sales are not indicated in the question, the debtors calculation is based on the total sales figure.

Stock turnover:
As it is not possible to calculate average stock from the facts given in the question, year-end stock figures have been used to represent average stock.

(b) Comments on the current position of Spark Ltd, could include the following observations:

(i) Liquidity:

(1) An examination of the assets of the two years show that the current and quick asset ratios (*see* (v) and (vi) above) have deteriorated substantially. The percentage increase of current liabilities between 19X7 and 19X8 is clearly in excess of the percentage increase of current assets for the same period—thus causing the deterioration of the current and quick ratios.

(2) Stock ratios and credit taken by debtors (*see* ratios (vii) and (viii) above) have improved, and thus it would appear that the main reasons for the present financial difficulties can be attributed to the excessive expenditure in fixed assets, and the repayment of part of the 10 per cent debentures.

(ii) Profitability:

(1) Though sales have shown a substantial increase (60 per cent), the gross profit percentage (*see* ratio (i)) on the sales has deteriorated. This decrease in the gross profit percentage may be the result of reduced prices, or increased costs (more likely the latter during periods of inflation).

(2) The increase of trading profit of sales (*see* ratio (iii)) appears to be caused by the fact that trading expenses have only increased by 22 per cent. It would appear therefore that there is a significant element of relatively fixed trading expenses.

(3) Trading profit to net assets (*see* ratio (iv)) have increased substantially (increase of 25 per cent) showing better utilisation of fixed assets by the company.

*Conclusions:*
Though the business is extremely profitable, there is an urgent need for increased capital. In view of its profitability, it should not be difficult to obtain the required capital, and for the short-term requirements a bank loan could easily be arranged.

Taking the view that it is more permanent funds which are required, the company could consider the following:

(i) a new issue of debentures

(ii) a rights issue—though an increase in the authorised capital would be required for this.

The financial situation of the company suggests that a takeover is a distinct possibility, though the attitude of the members and directors would be relevant if this possibility were to be pursued further.

## 108 Northern Manufacturers Ltd

### Report to the Board of Directors

*Purpose:* Additional financial requirements of Northern Manufacturers Ltd.

(1) *Introduction*
The request for financial assistance from Northern Manufacturers Ltd was supported by financial statements for the year 19X4 and 19X5.
Your attention is now directed to the points set out below.

(2) *Sales and operating profit*
The accounts for 19X5 show an increase of 47 per cent in money turnover. It is not known to what extent this is due to increased selling prices as opposed to increased sales volume.
The additional sales turnover has been achieved with some reduction of gross margin (*see* Schedule A, 1.1) but operating profit as a percentage of net sales was down by only 1.1 per cent as compared with 19X5.
With a net operating margin of 9.3 per cent the company can offer reasonable cover for future interest payments.
The company's earnings before tax give a return on capital employed (net worth) of 56.7 per cent for 19X5. This rate is no doubt deceptive as it is based on a total which includes fixed assets presumably stated at historical cost, and apparently bought some years ago (total depreciation is approximately 75 per cent of cost). It would perhaps be more significant to express the earnings as a percentage of gross asset values (ignoring accumulated depreciation).
However, despite the limitations of this profitability ratio, the fact remains that at 56.7 per cent it represents an increase of 9 per cent over 19X4 (*see* Schedule A, 1.2).

(3) *Working capital*
A movement of funds statement is attached (Schedule B). This shows that expenditure on fixed assets has been approximately covered by depreciation retentions for the year, and the retained profit after dividends has been largely absorbed into working capital.
Current and liquidity ratios are low (*see* Schedule A, 2.1 and 2.2) but have improved during 19X5 due to profit retentions.
During 19X5 the company may have achieved a slightly higher rate of stock turnover but a valid calculation cannot be made without knowing the finished stock figures (*see* Schedule A, 2.3).
Debtors appear to be taking a longer period of credit (*see* Schedule A, 2.4) but again this cannot be conclusively determined without knowing the trend of sales over 19X5.
The company is clearly taking long credit from trade suppliers which at £78,000

for 19X5 have more than doubled from 19X4. During 19X5, however, the company had to meet £40,000 of bills payable.

(4) *Conclusion*
No conclusive advice can be given without a great deal more information (*see* Schedule C).

In general, however, it would seem that the company is in a satisfactory trading position. Expansion of sales has been achieved without substantial reduction in margins and without disproportionate inflation of stock and debtor inventories.

It seems clear that substantial replacement of fixed assets must be necessary and for this purpose the company has a reserve of £65,000 in addition to its accumulated depreciation. Quite apart from capital expenditure requirements, the company is in a difficult liquid position. It is not known to what extent creditors are pressing for payment. Moreover, with dividends covered nearly four times by available earnings, shareholders may be dissatisfied.

*Schedule A*

Interpretation of Accounts: Northern Manufacturers Ltd

(1) Sales and operating profit

1.1 Trading position

| | 19X4 | | 19X5 | | |
|---|---|---|---|---|---|
| | £000 | % | £000 | % | Change |
| Net sales | 1,070 | 100 | 1,565 | 100 | + 47% |
| Gross margin | 260.50 | 24.3 | 340.00 | 21.7 | −2.6% |
| Selling and administrative costs | 149.43 | 13.9 | 194.31 | 12.4 | −1.5% |
| | 111.07 | 10.4 | 145.69 | 9.3 | +1.1% |

1.2 Return on capital
Operating profit plus (minus) other income (expenses) as a percentage of total capital employed—net worth plus fixed asset replacement reserve.

19X4

$$\frac{£91{,}700}{191{,}000} \times 100 = 47.7\%$$

19X5

$$\frac{£151{,}365}{266{,}251} \times 100 = 56.7\%$$

Change = +9%

(2) Working capital

2.1 Current assets to current liabilities, bills and provisions.

| 19X4 | 19X5 | Change |
|---|---|---|
| 0.85 to 1 | 1.3 to 1 | +0.45 |

2.2 Liquidity ratio
Current assets excluding inventories to current liabilities, bills and provisions.

| 19X4 | 19X5 | Change |
|---|---|---|
| 0.40 to 1 | 0.71 to 1 | +0.31 |

2.3 Stock turnover ratio
Cost of sales divided by average of opening/closing inventory.

| | 19X4 | 19X5 | Change |
|---|---|---|---|
| Number of times turned over | 14.02 | 14.4 | +0.38 |

(This may be extremely misleading, as no information is given of the extent to which raw material and partly finished stocks enter into the total inventories.)

2.4 Debtors to sales, expressed as number of weeks' sales.

19X4

$$\frac{£52,500}{1,070,000} \times 52 = 2.5 \text{ weeks}$$

19X5

$$\frac{£95,000}{1,565,000} \times 52 = 3.15 \text{ weeks}$$

Change = 0.65 weeks.

*Schedule B*

Movement of Funds Statement

| | £ | £ |
|---|---|---|
| Opening bank and cash balances (deficit) | | 15,000 |
| Closing bank and cash balances | | 11,500 |
| | | 26,500 |
| Favourable movement explained by: | | |
| Sources of funds | | |
| Profit | | 83,251 |
| Retained depreciation | | 60,000 |
| | | 143,251 |
| Cash from sale of other assets (*see* note) | | 10,000 |
| Proceeds of ordinary shares issued | | 2,000 |
| | | 155,251 |
| *less:* Application of funds | | |
| Expenditure on fixed assets | 59,000 | |
| Increase in stock and debtors *less* current liabilities and provisions | 54,751 | |
| Dividends paid and payable | 15,000 | 128,751 |
| | | 26,500 |

*Note:* It is assumed that other assets were sold for a £5,000 surplus which was transferred to capital surplus account.

*Schedule C*

Schedule of Additional Statements Required

| *Statement* | *Reasons* |
|---|---|
| (i) Accounts covering the three previous years. | So that the trend of results and of cash flows can be examined. |
| (ii) Sales analyses for the past five years, showing units as well as turnover. | In order to examine changes in the mix of products and selling prices, and changes in sales outlets. |
| (iii) Analysis of stock and debtors. | To determine stock categories and the ageing of debtors. |
| (iv) Numbers of customers and suppliers. | To ensure that the company has an adequate range of sales outlets and sources of supply. |
| (v) Cost breakdown for the last two years. | To examine changes in cost structure. It is noticeable that in 19X5 as opposed to 19X4 there have been the following increases:<br>Raw material 30% (subject to stock adjustment)<br>Direct labour 64%<br>Factory overhead 83%<br>These figures indicate that there may have been material changes in manufacturing processes or in the nature of products manufactured. |
| (vi) Statement from the board of Northern Manufacturers Ltd setting out clearly the purposes for which finance required, supported by forward budgets, with particular reference to:<br>(a) sales budgets and market research reports;<br>(b) cash budget, including detailed capital expenditure budget;<br>(c) working capital budgets;<br>(d) profit forecasts. | To ensure that management are competent and forward-looking, and to assess the feasibility of the proposition. |

*continued*

| *continued* *Statement* | *Reasons* |
|---|---|
| (vii) Statement of proposed security or guarantees (if any) for finance raised. | To estimate the risk involved. |
| (viii) Statement from management of any known present or anticipated future difficulties. | To ensure that the forward budgets are realistic. |
| (ix) Auditors' reports and letters of weakness. | To assess any qualifications or major weaknesses notified. |
| (x) Summaries showing the rights of shareholders, and the borrowing powers of the company. Also a distribution summary of shares issued. | Information of this nature must be considered before steps are taken either to purchase shares or to make loans. Major shareholders must also be identified. |

## 109 Go-Go Products Ltd and Numerous Inventions Ltd

(a) Calculation of ratios (all four given, three only required for answer)

| | Go-Go Products Ltd 19X7 £ | Go-Go Products Ltd 19X6 £ | Numerous Inventions Ltd 19X7 £ | Numerous Inventions Ltd 19X6 £ |
|---|---|---|---|---|
| (i) $\frac{\text{Profit before tax}}{\text{Current liabilities}}$ | $\frac{1,400}{7,930} = 0.18$ | $\frac{935}{9,970} = 0.09$ | $\frac{1,090}{4,357} = 0.25$ | $\frac{1,278}{2,467} = 0.52$ |
| (ii) $\frac{\text{Current assets}}{\text{Total liabilities}}$ | $\frac{10,801}{9,339} = 1.16$ | $\frac{11,537}{11,138} = 1.04$ | $\frac{6,798}{4,412} = 1.54$ | $\frac{4,859}{2,505} = 1.94$ |
| (iii) $\frac{\text{Current liabilities}}{\text{Total tangible assets}}$ | $\frac{7,930}{15,445} = 0.51$ | $\frac{9,970}{16,765} = 0.59$ | $\frac{4,357}{8,748} = 0.50$ | $\frac{2,467}{6,389} = 0.39$ |
| (iv) No-credit interval: | | | | |
| $\frac{\text{Net current assets}}{\text{Operational costs } \textit{less} \text{ depreciation}}$ (decimals of a year) | $\frac{2,871}{28,356} = 0.10$ | $\frac{1,567}{24,198} = 0.06$ | $\frac{2,441}{8,313} = 0.29$ | $\frac{2,392}{6,571} = 0.36$ |
| Two additional ratios | | | | |
| (v) Acid test: | | | | |
| $\frac{\text{Current assets } \textit{less} \text{ stock}}{\text{Current liabilities}}$ | $\frac{4,558}{7,930} = 0.57$ | $\frac{4,764}{9,970} = 0.48$ | $\frac{5,812}{4,357} = 1.33$ | $\frac{3,602}{2,467} = 1.46$ |
| (vi) Long-term solvency: | | | | |
| $\frac{\text{Liabilities and loans}}{\text{Total tangible assets}}$ | $\frac{9,339}{15,445} = 0.60$ | $\frac{11,138}{16,765} = 0.66$ | $\frac{4,412}{8,748} = 0.50$ | $\frac{2,505}{6,389} = 0.39$ |

(b) The movements in the ratios have been all favourable for Go-Go Products Ltd (GG) and all unfavourable for Numerous Inventions Ltd (NI). However, it is also necessary to consider the absolute sizes of the ratios.

For example, ratio (v), the acid test, shows that GG must be under considerable pressure in attempting to pay its creditors as they fall due. It may be presumed that an overdraft facility could be arranged, but what GG probably needs is additional long-term capital to finance further expansion. The expansion achieved between 19X6 and 19X7 has been financed by a tight control over stock and debtors (both have decreased slightly while turnover has risen by 21 per cent). It is unlikely that further tightening is possible in the future. There has been some increase in GG's profitability between the two years, but margins are still tight. The possibility of increasing prices should be considered.

In contrast to GG, NI has a rather slack liquid ratio, ratio (v). Furthermore, the level of debtors in relation to sales is high, indicating relatively poor credit control. Stock levels in NI are much lower than GG which is surprising but may be accounted for by the fact that the two companies are in different trades or influenced by differing seasonal factors.

In conclusion, both companies seem sound. GG needs more capital to finance further expansion, while NI needs tighter credit control and has in fact some spare finance. Perhaps NI should lend its surplus resources to GG!

(c) Ratio analysis can help in assessing a company's situation and hence in predicting possible failure.

The limitations of ratio analysis for this purpose are that other factors, often difficult to discover or quantify, are also relevant to a company's failure. Examples of such factors are:

(i) The extent to which overdraft facilities, while nominally short-term finance, are in fact long-term.

(ii) The distorting effect of seasonal factors.

(iii) The economic situation and possible government action to regulate the economy, perhaps by putting pressure on banks to limit overdrafts or by increasing interest rates.

(iv) The willingness of creditors to grant extended credit to assist a company in overcoming a short-term difficulty.

(v) The inability of ratio analysis to predict the collapse of a major customer.

In spite of these limitations, the trend of ratios, monthly or annually, could be a valuable indication of increasing difficulty, or of the need to change policies to reverse an unfavourable trend.

## 110 General interpretation

*Shareholders* are likely to be pleased with what they see on the surface:

| | Year 1 | Year 2 | Year 3 | Year 4 |
|---|---|---|---|---|
| *Earnings* (£000) | 14,400 | 17,140 | 17,300 | 28,850 |

It is necessary to make some assumption with regard to the share capital. Let us assume it consisted throughout entirely of ordinary shares of £1 each in the absence of any suggestion to the contrary.

| | | | | |
|---|---|---|---|---|
| *Earnings per share* | 12.0p | 14.28p | 14.42p | 20.71p |
| Growth | | + 19.0% | + 0.9% | + 43.6% |

A hiccup in year 3, but basically sound—or so it seems.

The proof of the pudding is in the eating: how have shareholders fared when it comes to dividends?

| | | | | |
|---|---|---|---|---|
| *Total dividends* (£000) | 12,000 | 14,400 | 14,400 | 18,000 |
| *Dividend per share* | 10p | 12p | 12p | 15p |
| Index | 100 | 120 | 120 | 150 |

A 50 per cent increase in dividend in three years—during which price remained stable—which cannot be bad. Or can it?

Dividend cover (taken as earnings per share−dividend per share) if anything improved:

| | | | | |
|---|---|---|---|---|
| *Cover* | 1.20 | 1.19 | 1.20 | 1.38 |

but if shareholders thought this, they would be deceiving themselves.

*Creditors* would be less happy.

They would not appreciate the deteriorating current ratio:

| | | | | |
|---|---|---|---|---|
| *Current ratio* | 1.93 | 1.70 | 1.68 | 1.41 |

(The ratio itself looks satisfactory in year 1 and 2, mediocre in year 3 and weak in year 4, but it is difficult to say without knowing what industry the company is in.)

and the much weaker (and now unsatisfactory) quick ratio:

| | | | | |
|---|---|---|---|---|
| *Quick ratio* | 1.03 | 0.88 | 0.83 | 0.66 |

and the much weaker cash position:

| | | | | |
|---|---|---|---|---|
| *Cash* (£000) | 18,720 | 15,290 | 10,510 | 1,245 |

including the massive fall in year 4.

The more sophisticated creditors (e.g. bankers) will no doubt examine the ratio:

| | | | | |
|---|---|---|---|---|
| *Debtors/creditors* | 1.28 | 1.16 | 1.09 | 0.95 |

any significant change in which suggests a fundamental change in trading pattern, instability, possibly over-trading; and

| | | | | |
|---|---|---|---|---|
| *Net current assets/sales* | 22.7% | 19.8% | 20.3% | 14.4% |

which suggests weakness in working capital, particularly in year 4, and possible over-trading.

*Employees* are likely to be disturbed by the falling average remuneration per employee:

| | | | | |
|---|---|---|---|---|
| *Average remuneration (£)* | 2,062.5 | 2,055.6 | 2,050 | 2,000 |

which suggests the use of more unskilled or young workers, or less overtime.

The number of employees has risen:

| | | | | |
|---|---|---|---|---|
| *Number of employees* | 16,000 | 18,000 | 20,000 | 22,000 |
| Growth | | + 12.5% | + 11.1% | + 10.0% |
| Index | 100 | 112.5 | 125 | 137.5 |

Faster throughout than sales:

| | | | | |
|---|---|---|---|---|
| *Sales* (£000) | 220,000 | 240,000 | 260,000 | 280,000 |
| Growth | | + 9.09% | + 8.33% | + 7.69% |
| Index | 100 | 109.1 | 118.2 | 127.3 |

So, taking productivity to be index of sales ÷ index of number of employees, productivity has fallen:

| | | | | |
|---|---|---|---|---|
| *Productivity* | 100 | 97.0 | 94.5 | 92.6 |

In part this could be because the plant and machinery is getting older:

| | | | | |
|---|---|---|---|---|
| *Depreciation to date/cost* | 36.0% | 48.8% | 59.04% | 57.79% |

*Note:* Because of the depreciation method chosen this is not a direct indication of age.

*Management* should be aware of all these ratios and many others.

| | | | | |
|---|---|---|---|---|
| Depreciation charge for year on plant and machinery as a percentage of cost | 16.0% | 12.8% | 10.24% | 10.55% |

which suggests either (a) use of the reducing balance method or (b) a growing percentage of plant already fully written off. Study of the figures shows the company uses the reducing balance method on plant and machinery (20 per cent).

| | | | | |
|---|---|---|---|---|
| *Employee remuneration as a percentage of sales* | 15.0% | 15.4% | 15.8% | 15.7% |

a reflection of falling productivity, and lack of new investment in plant and machinery.

Despite this (as already shown), sales increased:

| | | | | |
|---|---|---|---|---|
| *Sales* (£000) | 220,000 | 240,000 | 200,000 | 280,000 |
| Growth | | + 9.09% | + 8.33% | + 7.69% |
| Index | 100 | 109.1 | 118.2 | 127.3 |

They are slowing down in percentage terms but still growing.

In two of the three years profits rose faster than sales:

| | | | | |
|---|---|---|---|---|
| *Profit before tax* (£000) | 28,000 | 32,600 | 32,360 | 38,450 |
| Growth | | + 16.43% | − 0.74% | + 18.82% |
| Index | 100 | 116.4 | 115.6 | 137.3 |

and finished 37.3 per cent up on sales only 27.3 per cent up on year 1.

This suggests a P/S ratio:

| | | | | |
|---|---|---|---|---|
| *Profit before tax/sales* | 12.73% | 13.58% | 12.45% | 13.73% |

which would not be at all bad, but dividends received have nothing to do with profit margin, and it might be better to remove also the profit on the sale of plant:

| | | | | |
|---|---|---|---|---|
| Profit before tax excluding dividends received and profit on sale of plant/sales | 11.82% | 11.83% | 10.29% | 8.02% |

a much less satisfactory performance.

What about the return on trading assets employed?

| | | | | |
|---|---|---|---|---|
| Profit after tax (£000) | 14,400 | 17,140 | 17,300 | 24,850 |
| *less:* Dividends received after tax (£000) | 1,400 | 2,940 | 3,920 | 5,600 |
| Profit on sale of plant (which does not appear from the question to have attracted tax. Tax seems to be 50% of profit excluding dividends and excluding the profit on sale) | | | | 8,000 |
| Profit after tax attributable to trading (A) | 13,000 | 14,200 | 13,380 | 11,250 |
| Capital employed (excluding investment) (B) | 130,000 | 112,740 | 105,640 | 92,490 |
| *Return on (closing) trading capital employed* | 10.0% | 12.6% | 12.7% | 12.2% |

which looks not unsatisfactory until one notes the falling capital employed.

Sales/capital employed is rising:

| | | | | |
|---|---|---|---|---|
| *Sales/capital employed* | 1.69 | 2.13 | 2.46 | 3.03 |

This is a good sign; unless over-trading is present.

Over-trading may be due to many factors. One possibility is the diverting of funds outside the business. What is happening here can be seen from this summary:

| | | | | |
|---|---|---|---|---|
| Retentions (£000) | 2,400 | 2,740 | 2,900 | 6,850 |
| Depreciation (£000) | 18,000 | 14,800 | 12,240 | 12,554 |
| Net cash flow (£000) | 20,400 | 17,540 | 15,140 | 19,404 |
| Increase in investment (£000) | ? | (20,000) | (10,000) | (20,000) |
| Investment in fixed assets* | ? | — | — | (11,808) |
| Change in net current assets | ? | (2,460) | 5,140 | (12,404) |

* £42,214 – (£40,960 – £10,554) = £11,808.

Recognising that £8,000,000 of the net cash flow in year 4 represents the profit on sale; net cash flow fell year after year.

In two of the three years we know about, net current assets fell despite increased turnover. They fell because of the massive increases in investment.

Although profitable, the investment is not as profitable as the remaining activities:

| | | | | |
|---|---|---|---|---|
| *Income from investment (after tax) as a percentage of cost of investment* | 7.0% | 7.35% | 7.84% | 10.01% |

and it is taking its toll of liquidity as has already been shown.

What is a little surprising in view of the strained liquidity is:

| | | | | |
|---|---|---|---|---|
| *Stocks/sales* | 21.9% | 23.3% | 25.2% | 26.3% |

which suggests lack of control, or more difficult trading conditions.

Collection period, too, has deteriorated:

| | | | | |
|---|---|---|---|---|
| *Collection period* (days) | 60.8 | 68.1 | 75.6 | 82.0 |

This could reflect weaker accounting, invoicing, collection or credit control; or the fact that customers were finding it more difficult to sell the goods, and hence to pay for them—as is often found in the later stages of over-trading.

On the assumption that the gross profit is constant (or nearly so) trade creditors ought to bear a fairly consistent relationship to sales. But they do not:

| | | | | |
|---|---|---|---|---|
| *Trade creditors/sales* | 13.0% | 16.1% | 19.0% | 23.7% |

This suggests creditors are being kept waiting—and could become restive.

It is perhaps a little early to worry about the need to replace the leasehold property, but the company has only 5 years lease left, and looks as though it will have to find, say, £20,000 in five years' time—which may not be easy.

What is most depressing is the lack of investment in the business itself.

## 12 INFLATION ACCOUNTING

### 111 Monetary and non-monetary items

(a) Monetary items are those which always retain the same money value but whose real value fluctuates according to the fluctuations in the value of the money in which they are expressed.

Non-monetary items tend to retain the same real value while their money value fluctuates as the value of money fluctuates. Non-monetary assets are also subject to other factors which cause their value to change, and the rate at which different non-monetary assets change in value will tend to vary.

In all systems of inflation accounting, monetary assets and liabilities appear in the balance sheet without adjustment at their money value on the balance sheet date.

Non-monetary items, on the other hand, are included at a figure which either attempts to reflect their real value (CCA) or at a figure which is their cost adjusted for movement in the Retail Price Index (CPP). The CPP method is also an attempt to express the asset at its real value, though the measure of real value is less precise in CPP because there are in practice wide variations in the rates at which different assets are affected by inflation.

Although monetary assets appear unchanged in the balance sheet, it is recognised that any gain or loss in value of net monetary assets held during the year must be calculated and included in the inflation-adjusted accounts.

(b) Treatment in inflation accounting

| *Item* | *CPP* | *CCA* |
|---|---|---|
| Stock in trade (opening and closing) Non-monetary | In the profit and loss account, both opening and closing stock are converted according to the movement in RPI between the average date of acquisition and the balance sheet date. In the balance sheet, closing stock is adjusted as for the profit and loss account. | In the profit and loss account, the actual figures of opening and closing stock remain unchanged, but a *cost of sales adjustment* is calculated comparing the historical cost gross profit with what the gross profit would have been if both opening and closing stock were revalued at the value to the business when they were consumed. For practical purposes this is frequently done by converting both stock figures to the average price during the trading period. In the balance sheet stock should appear at its value to the business at that date. |
| Debentures Monetary | No change from historical cost accounts. | No change from historical cost accounts. |
| Depreciation Non-monetary | Recalculated on the basis of the revised value placed upon the asset concerned (i.e. after applying the movement in the RPI to that asset). | Recalculated on the basis of the revised value placed upon the asset at the end of the year. (It is recognised that basing depreciation on the average value of the assets during the period would be technically superior, but as a matter of convenience the closing value is preferred.) |

## 112 Nimbus Ltd

Current Cost Balance Sheet 30th June 19X8

| | £ | £ |
|---|---|---|
| Fixed assets | | 987,500 |
| *less:* Depreciation (*see* working 2) | | 592,500 |
| | | 395,000 |
| Net current assets | | |
| Stock | 245,000 | |
| Debtors | 160,000 | |
| Cash | 120,000 | |
| | 525,000 | |
| *less:* Creditors | 80,000 | |
| | | 445,000 |
| | | 840,000 |
| Financed by: | | £ |
| Ordinary shares | | 100,000 |
| Current cost reserve (*see* working 1) | | 238,465 |
| Reserves | | 221,535 |
| 10% loan stock | | 280,000 |
| | | 840,000 |

Current Cost Profit and Loss Account
year ended 30th June 19X8

| | £ | £ |
|---|---|---|
| Turnover | | 1,300,000 |
| Profit before interest and taxation as in the historical cost accounts | | 123,000 |
| *less:* Current cost adjustments | | |
| Cost of sales (*see* working 4) | 35,000 | |
| Depreciation (*see* working 5) | 58,125 | |
| Monetary working capital (*see* working 6) | 7,760 | |
| | | 100,885 |
| Current cost operating profit | | 22,115 |
| Gearing (*see* working 7) | 27,420 | |
| Interest | 28,000 | |
| | | (580) |
| Current cost profit attributable to shareholders | | 21,535 |

## Workings

(1) Current Cost Reserve (CCR)

| | £ | £ |
|---|---|---|
| As at 30th June 19X7: | | |
| Fixed assets | 812,500 | |
| *less:* Depreciation 45% | 365,625 | |
| | 446,875 | |
| *less:* HC value | 330,000 | 116,875 |
| Stock £150,000 × $\frac{126}{115}$ | 164,300 | |
| *less:* HC value | 150,000 | 14,300 |
| Balance at 30th June 19X7 | | 131,175 |
| Revaluation of fixed assets (per working 2) | | 38,125 |
| Revaluation of stock (per working 3) | | (4,300) |
| Balance after asset revaluations | | 165,000 |
| Cost of sales adjustment (per working 4) | | 35,000 |
| Depreciation adjustment (per working 5) | | 58,125 |
| Monetary working capital adjustment (per working 6) | | 7,760 |
| | | 265,885 |
| Gearing adjustment (per working 7) | | (27,420) |
| Balance per CC balance sheet | | 238,465 |

(2) Fixed assets

| | £ |
|---|---|
| Value 30th June 19X8 | 987,500 |
| *less:* Depreciation 60% | 592,500 |
| Net current replacement price | 395,000 |
| *less:* HC value | 240,000 |
| Net increase in value | 155,000 |
| Current cost reserve for fixed assets at 30th June 19X7 | 116,875 |
| Credit to CCR | 38,125 |

(3) Stock

| | £ |
|---|---|
| £235,000 × $\frac{147}{141}$ | 245,000 |
| *less:* HC value | 235,000 |
| | 10,000 |
| CCR for stock at 30th June 19X7 | 14,300 |
| Debit to CCR | (4,300) |

## Workings

(4) Cost of Sales Adjustment

| | £ | £ |
|---|---|---|
| Opening stock adjusted to average cost: | | |
| $£150,000 \times \frac{138}{115}$ | 180,000 | |
| *less:* HC value of opening stock | 150,000 | 30,000 |
| Closing stock adjusted to average cost: | | |
| $£235,000 \times \frac{138}{141}$ | 230,000 | |
| *less:* HC value of closing stock | 235,000 | 5,000 |
| Transfer to CCR | | 35,000 |

(5) Depreciation (based on closing value)

| | £ |
|---|---|
| 15% × £987,500 | 148,125 |
| *less:* Per HC accounts | 90,000 |
| | 58,125 |

(6) Monetary Working Capital (MWC)

| | £ | £ |
|---|---|---|
| Opening MWC | | |
| Trade debtors | 120,000 | |
| Trade creditors | 90,000 | 30,000 |
| Closing MWC | | |
| Trade debtors | 160,000 | |
| Trade creditors | 80,000 | 80,000 |
| Increase during year | | 50,000 |
| $£30,000 \times \frac{138}{126}$ | | 32,860 |
| $£80,000 \times \frac{138}{147}$ | | 75,100 |
| Increase during year as adjusted | | 42,240 |
| MWCA £50,000 minus £42,240: | | 7,760 |

## Workings

(7) Gearing

| | Opening £ | Average £ | Closing £ |
|---|---|---|---|
| (a) Average net borrowings | | | |
| Loan stock | 280,000 | | 280,000 |
| *less:* Cash | 70,000 | | 120,000 |
| | 210,000 | 185,000 | 160,000 |
| (b) Average shareholders' interest (CCA) | | | |
| Share capital | 100,000 | | 100,000 |
| Reserves (per HC accounts) | 200,000 | | 295,000 |
| CCR (for assets revaluation only, per working 1) | *131,175 | | *165,000 |
| | 431,175 | 495,587 | 560,000 |
| | | 680,587 | |

* In calculating the average shareholders' interest in CCA terms, the adjustments between profit and loss account and CMR (COSA, depreciation MWCA and gearing) can be ignored as they do not affect the total.

Gearing adjustment:

$$\frac{185{,}000}{680{,}587} \times £100{,}885 \qquad £27{,}420$$

## 113 Current cost accounting adjustments

(a) *Cost of sales adjustment (COSA)*
The purpose of making the COSA is to charge against revenue the *value to the business* of stock at the time of its consumption rather than the *historical cost* of that stock.

In times of inflation the COSA will be a deduction from the historical cost (HC) profit, made with the object of eliminating from reported profit the gain attributable to inflation.

It is possible to calculate the COSA by reference to individual items bought and sold, but in most cases an averaging method based on a suitable index will be used. The idea will be to convert all items in the trading account to their equivalent values on the assumption that all transactions took place at the average price level ruling during the period. Unless there are substantial seasonal variations in the rate of purchasing and selling, purchases and sales will already appear at a value closely approximating to the average value for the year, and the only items requiring adjustment are opening and closing stock.

The calculation of the COSA is accordingly the sum of (i) and (ii) below:

$$\text{(i)} \quad \left(\text{Opening stock} \times \frac{\text{Average index}}{\text{Index when opening stock acquired}}\right) - \text{Opening stock}$$

$$\text{(ii) Closing stock} - \left(\text{Closing stock} \times \frac{\text{Average index}}{\text{Index when closing stock acquired}}\right)$$

(b) *Depreciation adjustment*
The depreciation adjustment is made so as to charge against profits a depreciation charge appropriate to the value to the business of the assets in question rather than their historical cost.

The depreciation adjustment may be made by reference to the value at the balance sheet date, though strictly speaking it should be done by reference to the *average* value of the asset during the year.

The value of the asset to be depreciated will be arrived at by the use of specific indices or by revaluation. If indices are used, the CCA depreciation charge will be calculated by taking the appropriate percentage of the gross current replacement price. The depreciation adjustment will be the difference between the CCA depreciation calculated in this way and the HC depreciation already charged.

If the asset is revalued, depreciation will be calculated by reference to that revaluation and the estimated remaining useful life of the asset. The depreciation adjustment will again be the difference between this CCA depreciation and the HC depreciation already charged.

(c) *Monetary working capital adjustment (MWCA)*
The MWCA reflects the amount of additional (or reduced) finance needed for monetary working capital for the period as a result of changes in prices.

The MWCA is normally confined to two items, *trade* debtors and *trade* creditors, though cash at bank, cash in hand and overdrafts may sometimes be included, especially if the nature of the trade is such that substantial amounts of, say, cash in tills is needed to carry it on. The MWCA may be calculated separately for trade debtors and for trade creditors, or alternatively a single calculation may be made for the net of the two items.

The MWCA for debtors charges against HC profits a sum to reflect the loss suffered when money is owed to a business during a period of inflation, while the MWCA for creditors adds to HC profit a figure to reflect the gain made because the effect of inflation on the trading of the period is partly borne by creditors.

The normal method of calculation will be:

(i) Calculate opening and closing monetary working capital figures (MWC) (trade debtors less trade creditors).

(ii) Subtract opening MWC from closing MWC.

(iii) Restate opening MWC and closing MWC in terms of average index for the period:

$$\text{Opening MWC} \times \frac{\text{Average index}}{\text{Index on first day of period}}$$

$$\text{Closing MWC} \times \frac{\text{Average index}}{\text{Index on last day of period}}$$

(iv) Subtract restated opening MWC from restated closing MWC.

(v) MWCA is then the net movement on MWC ((ii) above) plus or minus the difference between the restated MWCs in (iv) above.

(d) *Gearing adjustment*
Most businesses are financed to a greater or lesser extent by borrowings. As such borrowings are fixed in monetary amount, a gain will arise in a period of inflation and this gain will accrue to the equity shareholders. The gearing adjustment proposed by SSAP 16 is a way of calculating the gain so arising, which will partly offset the interest cost of the borrowings.

The procedure for calculating the gearing adjustment is:

(i) Ascertain average net borrowing during the period:
This will consist of debentures and loans, plus current monetary liabilities (other than trade creditors brought into the MWCA and proposed dividends brought into (ii) below), minus monetary assets (other than trade debtors or other items brought into the MWCA). A simple average of opening and closing figures will normally suffice, unless substantial movements during the year necessitate the use of a weighted average method.
If there are no net borrowings no adjustment is made.
If there are net borrowings, proceed to (ii) below.

(ii) Ascertain average shareholders' interest during the year:
This will be the average of the opening and closing figures for ordinary and preference share capital, reserves and proposed dividends as shown in the CCA accounts.

(iii) Calculate the gearing ratio. This is:

$$\frac{\text{Average net borrowings (i)}}{\text{Average net borrowings (i)} + \text{Average shareholders' interest (ii)}}$$

(iv) Multiply the current cost adjustments made in converting HC profit to CCA profit by the gearing ratio. This is the gearing adjustment.

## 13 CONSOLIDATION OF FOREIGN SUBSIDIARIES

### 114 Rostov Limited

(a) Consolidated Accounts Using Temporal Method
(showing relevant additions—*see* Working 2)

Consolidated Profit and Loss Account
year ended 31st December 19X1

| | £ | £ |
|---|---|---|
| Operating profit (£54,000 + £3,223 + £1,859) | | 59,082 |
| *less:* Taxation (£21,000 + £1,000) | | 22,000 |
| Retained profit for the year | | 37,082 |
| *add:* Retained profits brought forward (Rostov only) | | 152,000 |
| Retained profits | | 189,082 |

Consolidated Balance Sheet on 31st December 19X1

| | | | £ | £ |
|---|---|---|---|---|
| Share capital and reserves | | | | |
| Share capital | | | | 200,000 |
| Retained profits | | | | 189,082 |
| | | | | 389,082 |
| Fixed assets | | | | |
| Premises: | At cost | (£300,000 + £31,111) | 331,111 | |
| | *less:* Depreciation | ( £40,000 + £444) | 40,444 | 290,667 |
| Machinery: | At cost | (£180,000 + £11,111) | 191,111 | |
| | *less:* Depreciation | ( £60,000 + £1,333) | 61,333 | 129,778 |
| | | | | 420,445 |
| Goodwill on consolidation | | (*see* Working 1) | | 25,000 |
| Net current assets | | (£150,000 + £7,273) | | 157,273 |
| | | | | 602,718 |
| *less:* Long-term liabilities | | (£200,000 + £13,636) | | 213,636 |
| | | | | 389,082 |

(b) Consolidated Accounts Using Closing-Rate Method (showing relevant additions—*see* Working 3)

Consolidated Profit and Loss Account
year ended 31st December 19X1

| | | £ | £ |
|---|---|---|---|
| Operating profit | (£54,000 + £3,400) | | 57,400 |
| *less:* Taxation | (£21,000 + £1,000) | | 22,000 |
| Retained profit for year | | | 35,400 |

Consolidated balance sheet on 31st December 19X1

| | £ | £ |
|---|---|---|
| Share capital reserves | | |
| Share capital | | 200,000 |
| Reserves: | | |
| Retained profits at 1st January 19X1 (Rostov Limited only) | 152,000 | |
| Retained profit for 19X1 | 35,400 | |
| Loss on exchange | (5,672) | 181,728 |
| | | 381,728 |

*continued*

*continued*

| | | | £ | £ |
|---|---|---|---|---|
| Fixed assets | | | | |
| Premises: | At cost | (£300,000 + £25,455) | 325,455 | |
| | *less:* Depreciation | ( £40,000 + £364) | 40,364 | 285,091 |
| Machinery: | At cost | (£180,000 + £9,091) | 189,091 | |
| | *less:* Depreciation | ( £60,000 + £1,091) | 61,091 | 128,000 |
| | | | | 413,091 |
| Goodwill on consolidation | | (*see* Working 1) | | 25,000 |
| Net current assets | | (£150,000 + £7,273) | | 157,273 |
| | | | | 595,364 |
| *less:* Long-term liabilities | | (£200,000 + £13,636) | | 213,636 |
| | | | | 381,728 |

## Workings

(1) Calculation of goodwill on consolidation on 1st January 19X1

| | | £ |
|---|---|---|
| Equity interest in Oublier SA: | Fr270,000 | |
| Sterling equivalent | 270,000 ÷ 9 | 30,000 |
| Cost of investment | | 55,000 |
| Goodwill on consolidation | | 25,000 |

(2) Translation of accounts using temporal method

| | Fr000 | Rate | £ |
|---|---|---|---|
| Profit and loss account: | | | |
| Operating profit before depreciation | 50 | 10 | 5,000 |
| *less:* Depreciation | 16 | 9 | 1,777 |
| | 34 | | 3,223 |
| *less:* Taxation | 10 | 10 | 1,000 |
| Retained profit for the year | 24 | | 2,223 |
| Balance sheet: | | | |
| Share capital | 100 | | |
| Revaluation reserve at 1st January 19X1 | 40 | | |
| Retained profits at 1st January 19X1 | 130 | | |
| | 270 | 9 | 30,000 |
| Retained profit for current year | 24 | As above | 2,223 |
| Balance: Difference on exchange to be treated as ordinary profit | — | — | 1,859 |
| | 294 | | 34,082 |

*continued*

*continued*

| | | Fr000 | Rate | £ |
|---|---|---|---|---|
| Premises: | At cost | 280 | 9 | 31,111 |
| | *less:* Depreciation | 4 | 9 | 444 |
| | | 276 | | 30,667 |
| Machinery: | At cost | 100 | 9 | 11,111 |
| | *less:* Depreciation | 12 | 9 | 1,333 |
| | | 88 | | 9,778 |
| | | 364 | | 40,445 |
| Net current assets | | 80 | 11 | 7,273 |
| | | 444 | | 47,718 |
| *less:* Long-term liabilities | | 150 | 11 | 13,636 |
| | | 294 | | 34,082 |

(3) Translation of accounts using closing-rate method

| | Fr000 | Rate | £ |
|---|---|---|---|
| Profit and loss account: | | | |
| Operating profit before depreciation | 50 | 10 | 5,000 |
| *less:* Depreciation | 16 | 10 | 1,600 |
| | 34 | | 3,400 |
| *less:* Taxation | 10 | 10 | 1,000 |
| | 24 | | 2,400 |
| Balance sheet: | | | |
| Share capital | 100 | | |
| Revaluation reserve on 1st January 19X1 | 40 | | |
| Retained profits on 1st January 19X1 | 130 | | |
| | 270 | 9* | 30,000 |
| Retained profits for current year | 24 | As above | 2,400 |
| Balance: Difference on exchange to be treated as movement on reserves | — | — | (5,672) |
| | 294 | | 26,728 |

| | | Fr000 | Rate | £ |
|---|---|---|---|---|
| Fixed assets: | | | | |
| Premises: | At cost | 280 | 11 | 25,455 |
| | *less:* Depreciation | 4 | 11 | 364 |
| | | 276 | | 25,091 |
| Machinery: | At cost | 100 | 11 | 9,091 |
| | *less:* Depreciation | 12 | 11 | 1,091 |
| | | 88 | | 8,000 |
| | *carried forward* | 364 | | 33,091 |

| | | Fr000 | Rate | £ |
|---|---|---|---|---|
| | *brought forward* | 364 | | 33,091 |
| Net current assets | | 80 | 11 | 7,273 |
| | | 444 | | 40,364 |
| *less:* Long-term liabilities | | 150 | 11 | 13,636 |
| | | 294 | | 26,728 |

* If a rate other than that ruling at the date of acquisition is used here, the figure for goodwill on consolidation will differ from that determined in Working 1 above. Any such difference is, of course, merely due to the change in the exchange rate and, by adopting the treatment used above, this difference is retained within the balancing figure here.

(4) Analysis of difference on exchange

The loss on exchange which emerges as a balancing figure in Working 3 may be analysed as follows:

| | £ |
|---|---|
| Opening net investment: | |
| 270,000 francs at 9 francs to £1 | 30,000 |
| Profit for year per profit and loss account: | |
| 24,000 francs at 10 francs to £1 | 2,400 |
| | 32,400 |
| Closing net investment: | |
| 294,000 francs at 11 francs to £1 | 26,728 |
| Loss on exchange | (5,672) |

Thus the loss is due partly to the translation of the opening net investment at a different rate at the year end from that applied at the beginning of the year and partly to the use of one rate to translate the profit and loss account and another rate to translate the closing balance sheet. Exposure Draft 27 requires that such differences are treated as a movement on reserves.

## 115 Zhdanov Limited

(a) Where a UK company raises a foreign loan, that is a loan denominated in a foreign currency, that loan will be translated at the closing rate of exchange for inclusion in the company's balance sheet. Where the rate of exchange ruling at the end of a year differs from that ruling at the beginning of a year, such a treatment will give rise to a difference on exchange. Except in the circumstances discussed below, such a difference will be dealt with as part of the company's "ordinary" profit for the year. (ED 27, paragraphs 48 and 49.)

Where the proceeds of the foreign loan are used to finance equity investments in a foreign subsidiary or associated company, ED 27 *permits* differences on the loans to be offset by differences arising on the retranslation of the opening net assets relating to the foreign equity investment. This is only permissible provided that three conditions are satisfied:

(i) The equity investment is in the same currency as the loan.
(ii) The closing rate method is applicable to the subsidiary or associated company.
(iii) The accounting treatment is applied consistently from period to period. (ED 27, para. 57.)

(b) Translation of accounts of Vairon SA

Summarised Profit and Loss Account
year ended 31st December 19X5

| | Francs | Rate | £ |
|---|---|---|---|
| Operating profit | 160,000 | 9.3 | 17,204 |
| *less:* Taxation | 40,000 | 9.3 | 4,301 |
| Retained profit for year | 120,000 | | 12,903 |

Summarised Balance Sheet
on 31st December 19X5

| | Francs | Rate | £ |
|---|---|---|---|
| Share capital | 1,000,000 | | |
| Reserves: | | | |
| Pre-acquisition | 400,000 | | |
| | 1,400,000 | 10.0 | 140,000 |
| Post-acquisition: | | | |
| On 1st January 19X5 | 90,000 | Balance | 16,842 |
| | 1,490,000 | 9.5 | 156,842 |
| Current year | 120,000 | As above | 12,903 |
| | 1,610,000 | | 169,745 |
| Difference on exchange | — | Balance | 9,144 |
| | 1,610,000 | | 178,889 |
| Fixed assets: At cost *less* depreciation | 890,000 | 9.0 | 98,889 |
| Net current assets | 920,000 | 9.0 | 102,222 |
| | 1,810,000 | | 201,111 |
| *less:* Long-term loans | 200,000 | 9.0 | 22,222 |
| | 1,610,000 | | 178,889 |

(c) Summarised Consolidated Accounts for 19X5
(showing relevant additions)

Summarised Consolidated Profit and Loss Account
year ended 31st December 19X5

| | £ | £ |
|---|---|---|
| Operating profit: | | |
| Zhdanov | 270,300 | |
| *less:* Exchange loss (*see* Working 3) | 16,304 | |
| | 253,996 | |
| Vairon (Part (b)) | 17,204 | |
| | | 271,200 |
| *less:* Taxation (£130,100 + £4,301) | | 134,401 |
| | | 136,799 |
| *less:* Dividends | | 75,000 |
| Retained profit for the year | | 61,799 |

Summarised Consolidated Balance Sheet on 31st December 19X5

| | £ |
|---|---|
| Share capital | 500,000 |
| Reserves (*see* note below) | 604,737 |
| | 1,104,737 |
| Long-term loans (*see* Working 4) | 558,333 |
| | 1,663,070 |
| Fixed assets: At cost *less* depreciation (£730,300 + £98,889) | 829,189 |
| Goodwill on consolidation: At cost (£200,000 − £140,000) | 60,000 |
| Net current assets (£671,659 + £102,222) | 773,881 |
| | 1,663,070 |

Movement on Reserves
year ended 31st December 19X5

| | £ |
|---|---|
| Opening balance (£522,800 + £16,842) | 539,642 |
| Retained profit for the year | 61,799 |
| Exchange differences (*see* Working 3) | 3,296 |
| Closing balance | 604,737 |

**Workings**

(1) Retranslation of foreign loans at closing rate:

| | £ | £ |
|---|---|---|
| German loan | | |
| (£500,000 ÷ 4.0) | 125,000 | |
| *less:* Amount on 31st December 19X4 | 108,696 | |
| | | 16,304 |
| French loan | | |
| (£1,000,000 ÷ 9.00) | 111,111 | |
| *less:* Amount on 31st December 19X4 | 105,263 | |
| | | 5,848 |
| Loss on exchange | | 22,152 |

(2) Analysis of difference on exchange of Vairon SA:
The exchange gain of £9,144 which emerges in the answer to part (b) may be analysed as follows:

| | £ | £ |
|---|---|---|
| On opening net assets: | | |
| Fr1,490,000 at 9.5 to £1 | 156,842 | |
| at 9.0 to £1 | 165,556 | |
| | | 8,714 |
| On profit for year: | | |
| Fr120,000 at 9.3 to £1 | 12,903 | |
| at 9.0 to £1 | 13,333 | |
| | | 430 |
| Gain | | 9,144 |

(3) Treatment of above exchange differences:

| | £ |
|---|---|
| Gain on retranslation of opening net assets of Vairon (*see* Working 2) | 8,714 |
| *less:* Exchange loss on French loan (*see* Working 1) | 5,848 |
| | 2,866 |

| Thus | £ |
|---|---|
| *To reserves* | |
| Gain on retranslation of opening net assets *less* loss on foreign loan denominated in same currency | 2,866 |
| Gain as a result of using different exchange rate in profit and loss account and balance sheet | 430 |
| | 3,296 |
| *To profit and loss account* | |
| Loss on German loan | 16,304 |

(4) Long-term loans:

| | £ |
|---|---|
| Zhdanov Limited | |
| German loan (*see* Working 1) | 125,000 |
| French loan (*see* Working 1) | 111,111 |
| Other loans: Per balance sheet | 300,000 |
| | 536,111 |
| Vairon SA: Per answer to part (b) | 22,222 |
| | 558,333 |

APPENDIX 4

# Glossary of Accounting and Financial Terms

*Note: The chapter numbers indicated in parentheses show where a full treatment is given in the text.*

**Accounting bases.** The methods of applying the fundamental accounting principles. (Chapter 2)

**Accounting policies.** The accounting bases adopted by a company for its specific use. (Chapter 2)

**Acquisition or absorption.** One company sells all or most of its assets to another company, receiving in return cash, debentures or shares. (Chapter 5)

**Actuarial method.** A method of computing hire purchase interest based on a reducing balance which is outstanding. (Chapter 10)

**Adjusting event.** A post balance sheet event which provides additional evidence of the conditions existing at the balance sheet date. (Chapter 2)

**Advance corporation tax.** Corporation tax payable on distributions as an advance against the mainstream corporation tax liability. (Chapter 7)

**Amalgamation or merger.** Two or more companies sell their assets to a new company formed for the purpose of combining the operations of the two or more firms. (Chapter 5)

**Applied research.** An original investigation to gain new technical knowledge of use in a specific practical application. (Chapter 2)

**Associated company.** A company over which another company exercises significant influence. (Chapter 7)

**Capital based grant.** A grant made in relation to various types of capital expenditure. (Chapter 2)

**Capital reduction.** A way of writing down the share capital of a company in an attempt to put it on a better footing. (Chapter 6)

**Closing-rate method.** The method of translating foreign currencies by translating the whole profit and loss account and balance sheet to the reporting currency. (Chapter 7)

**Consolidated accounts.** The accounts of a group of companies including net assets and underlying earnings. (Chapter 7)

**Contingency.** A condition which exists at the balance sheet date, where the outcome will be confirmed only on the occurrence or non-occurrence of one or more uncertain future events. (Chapter 2)

**Cum dividend.** Where a share is sold or purchased and the right to the next dividend belongs to the new owner. (Chapter 2)

**Development.** The use of technical knowledge to produce new products prior to the commencement of commercial production. (Chapter 2)

**Exceptional item.** An item within the normal course of business of a company, but due to its materiality it requires separate disclosure. (Chapter 2)

**Ex dividend.** Where a share is sold or purchased and the right to the next dividend belongs to the old owner. (Chapter 2)

**Exposure Draft.** A discussion paper issued to promote debate on a contentious issue with the overall aim of producing consensus in the form of a Statement of Standard Accounting Practice. (Chapter 2)

**External reconstructions.** The formation of a new company to take over the assets and liabilities of a company in difficulty. (Chapter 6)

**Extraordinary item.** An item outside the normal business of a company; it is material and not likely to recur. (Chapter 2)

**Finance lease.** A lease that transfers substantially all the risks and rewards of ownership of an asset to the lessee. (Chapter 2)

**Fundamental accounting concepts.** The four main assumptions made by accountants in preparing financial accounts. These include "going concern", "accruals", "consistency" and "prudence". (Chapter 2)

**Fungible assets.** Assets where the individual items comprising an asset are identical and interchangeable. (Chapter 1)

**Goodwill on consolidation.** The excess of the cost of a subsidiary over the value of the net assets acquired. (Chapter 7)

**Hire purchase interest suspense.** The amount of hire purchase interest outstanding that has not yet been written off to the profit and loss account. (Chapter 10)

**Holding company.** A company that exercises control over another company. (Chapter 7)

**Income and expenditure account.** The equivalent of a profit and loss account for a non-trading concern. (Chapter 9)

**Internal reconstructions.** A capital reduction where the debenture-holders and creditors accept a reduction. This is done often in exchange for ordinary shares. (Chapter 6)

**Investment property.** A property held for its investment potential. Any rental income being negotiated at arm's length. (Chapter 2)

**Long-term contracts.** A contract that extends from one accounting period to another. (Chapter 2)

**Modified accounts.** A small company need only file a balance sheet and certain notes at Companies House whereas a medium-sized company need only file a modified profit and loss account with its balance sheet and notes. (Chapter 1)

**Monetary working capital.** Includes trade debtors and trade creditors but excludes bank and cash balances and stock. (Chapter 12)

**Non-adjusting event.** A post balance sheet event which concerns conditions which did not exist at the balance sheet date. (Chapter 2)

**Prior-year adjustment.** A material adjustment applicable to previous years arising from either a change in accounting policy or a fundamental error being corrected. (Chapter 2)

**Purchased goodwill.** Goodwill which is established as a result of the purchase of a business accounted for as an acquisition. (Chapter 2)

**Pure research.** An original investigation undertaken to gain new technical knowledge. (Chapter 2)

**Receipts and payments account.** A summary of actual cash received and paid during a period. (Chapter 9)

**Related company.** A company in which 20 per cent or more of the equity share capital is held on a long-term basis and with a view to influencing its activities. (Chapter 1)

**Revenue based grant.** A grant made by reference to a specified category of revenue expenditure. (Chapter 2)

**Royalty.** The charge made by the owner of a privilege or monopoly when letting another firm have use of its rights. (Chapter 10)

**Short-term timing difference.** Difference between the use of payments and receipts basis for taxation and the accruals basis for accounts normally reversing in the next accounting period. (Chapter 6)

**Subsidiary company.** A company that is controlled by another company. (Chapter 7)

**Sum of digits method.** A method of computing hire purchase interest by apportioning interest in approximate proportions to the amount outstanding at any time. (Chapter 10)

**Temporal method.** The method of translating the transactions for the year to the reporting currency. (Chapter 7)

**Translation.** The process by which financial data denominated in one currency are expressed in terms of another currency. (Chapter 2)

# Index